An Inventory of the
Historical Monuments in the

COUNTY OF
NORTHAMPTON

A group of Anglo-Saxon brooches from Newnham, now in Northampton Museum

ROYAL COMMISSION ON HISTORICAL MONUMENTS
ENGLAND

An Inventory of the
Historical Monuments in the

COUNTY OF
NORTHAMPTON

Volume III
Archaeological Sites
in North-West
Northamptonshire

LONDON · HER MAJESTY'S STATIONERY OFFICE

R   829633   5101

936.255

ISBN 0 11 700900 8* (Red binding)

ISBN 0 11 700901 6* (Grey binding)

TABLE OF CONTENTS

LIST OF ILLUSTRATIONS

(The prefixed numerals in brackets refer to the monument numbers in the text)

FOREWORD

This Inventory lists the archaeological sites in the north-west of Northamptonshire and is the third in a series of five volumes covering the whole of the county. Some of the 588 monuments described here are certainly of national importance and many are recorded for the first time.

Our staff have examined the archaeological sites in the field and have also drawn widely on published sources. The Commission is indebted, however, to local historians and archaeologists who have contributed much valuable new information. Many of the monuments listed are under serious threat of damage or total destruction and it is hoped that this Inventory may be a useful guide to planners and archaeologists who wish to establish the relative importance of sites, with a view to excavation or conservation.

ADEANE
Chairman

COMMISSIONERS

The Right Honourable the Lord Adeane, P.C., G.C.B., G.C.V.O.
Her Majesty's Lieutenant of Northamptonshire (*ex officio*)
Henry Clifford Darby, Esq., O.B.E.
Sheppard Sunderland Frere, Esq., C.B.E.
Richard John Copland Atkinson, Esq., C.B.E.
George Zarnecki, Esq., C.B.E.
John Kenneth Sinclair St Joseph, Esq., O.B.E.
Paul Ashbee, Esq.
Arthur Richard Dufty, Esq., C.B.E.
Mark Girouard, Esq.
Christopher Nugent Lawrence Brooke, Esq.
Andrew Colin Renfrew, Esq.
Mrs. Irene Joan Thirsk
Maurice Warwick Beresford, Esq.
Robert Angus Buchanan, Esq.
Albert Lionel Frederick Rivet, Esq.

Secretary
Robert William McDowall, Esq., C.B.E.

ROYAL COMMISSION ON THE ANCIENT AND HISTORICAL MONUMENTS AND CONSTRUCTIONS OF ENGLAND

REPORT to the Queen's Most Excellent Majesty

MAY IT PLEASE YOUR MAJESTY

We, the undersigned Commissioners, appointed to make an Inventory of the Ancient and Historical Monuments and Constructions connected with or illustrative of the contemporary culture, civilisation and conditions of the people of England from the earliest times to the year 1714, and such further Monuments and Constructions subsequent to that year as may seem in our discretion to be worthy of mention therein, and to specify those which seem most worthy of preservation, do humbly submit to your Majesty the following Report, being the thirty-eighth Report on the work of the Commission since its first appointment.

2. With regret we have to record the retirement from the Commission upon expiry of term of office of Professor William Francis Grimes, Commander of the Order of the British Empire, Fellow of the Society of Antiquaries, Doctor Arnold Joseph Taylor, Commander of the Order of the British Empire, Fellow of the British Academy, Fellow of the Society of Antiquaries, and Doctor Harold McCarter Taylor, Commander of the Order of the British Empire, Fellow of the Society of Antiquaries.

3. We thank Your Majesty for the appointment to the Commission of Professor Maurice Warwick Beresford, Doctor Robert Angus Buchanan, and Professor Albert Lionel Frederick Rivet, Fellow of the Society of Antiquaries, and for the reappointment of Professor George Zarnecki, Commander of the Order of the British Empire, Fellow of the British Academy, Fellow of the Society of Antiquaries.

4. We have pleasure in reporting the completion of our recording of archaeological sites in the north-west part of the County of Northampton, an area comprising sixty-nine parishes containing 588 monuments.

5. Following our usual practice we have prepared an illustrated Inventory of the earthworks in north-west Northamptonshire, which will be issued as a non-Parliamentary publication entitled *Northamptonshire* III. As in recent Inventories, the Commissioners have adopted the terminal date of 1850 for the monuments included in the Inventory.

6. The method of presentation of material has in general followed that adopted in the previous Inventories.

7. The descriptions of the more important monuments have been submitted to specialist authorities. We are satisfied that no significant monument which survived until 1976 has been omitted.

8. Our special thanks are due to owners and occupiers who have allowed access by our staff to the monuments in their charge. We are indebted to the Directors and Curators of many Institutions for their ready assistance to us, and particularly to Mr. P. I. King, the Northamptonshire County

Archivist. We have to record our indebtedness to the Director-General of the Ordnance Survey for access to his archaeological records, and for valuable work carried out by the field surveyors of his Department. We wish to record our gratitude to Professor J. K. S. St Joseph, Director in Aerial Photography in the University of Cambridge, for permission to use a large number of air photographs, and to Mr. J. Pickering for supplying other air photographs. We further wish to express our thanks to those persons who have given help to our executive staff during the field investigation; their co-operation is greatly appreciated. They include Mr. W. N. Terry and Mr. W. G. Moore (respectively Curator and Keeper of Archaeology, Northampton Central Museum and Art Gallery). Particular thanks are due to Mr. A. E. Brown (Department of Adult Education, Leicester University) and to Mr. D. N. Hall, who have generously made available much of their unpublished material on this part of Northamptonshire.

9. As a result of the limitations imposed on us by the continuing need for economy, only two members of our staff have been available to carry out work in the field.

10. We humbly recommend to Your Majesty's notice the following monuments in north-west Northamptonshire as being specially worthy of preservation:

Roman, prehistoric and undated monuments:

BRAMPTON, CHAPEL
(1)–(10) Brampton Complex

BRAMPTON, CHURCH
(1)–(10) Brampton Complex

DAVENTRY
(1)–(21) Borough Hill Complex
(35) Burnt Walls Enclosure

FARTHINGSTONE
(3) Enclosure

HARLESTONE
(1) East Harlestone Complex

NORTON
(4) Roman Town of Bannaventa

STOWE-NINE-CHURCHES
(13) Linear Banks and Ditches

Medieval and later earthworks

BARBY
(1) Deserted Village of Onley
(2) Manor House Site

BRAUNSTON
(1) Deserted Village of Braunstonbury

CANONS ASHBY
(1) Deserted Village of Canons Ashby
(2) Site of Augustinian Priory and of 16th-century House and Gardens
(3) Mound
(4) Fishponds
(5) Garden Remains

CATESBY
(4) Site of Priory, House and Garden Remains

CHARWELTON
(1) Deserted Village of Church Charwelton
(2) Ponds

CLIPSTON
(6) Deserted Village of Nobold
(7) Settlement Remains

COTTESBROOKE
(4) Site of Monastic Grange

EVERDON
(3) Deserted Village of Snorscomb

FARTHINGSTONE
(4) Motte and Baileys

FLORE
  (4) Deserted Village of Glassthorpe

HOLDENBY
  (4) Garden Remains

SIBBERTOFT
  (8) Motte and Bailey

STANFORD
  (4) Deserted Village of Stanford

SULBY
  (2) Site of Sulby Abbey
  (3) Deserted Village of Sulby

WATFORD
  (4) Settlement Remains

WINWICK
  (1) Settlement Remains

11. In compiling the foregoing list, our criteria have been the archaeological or historical importance and rarity, not only in the national but in the local field, and the degree of loss to the nation that would result from destruction. The list is based on academic considerations and does not take into account the problems of preservation.

However, destruction of field monuments continues to be rapid and widespread, and the increasing rarity of these monuments makes it desirable that as many as possible of those listed in the Inventory should be preserved. Also, the extent and impressiveness of surface remains are not the only indications of archaeological importance; their significance can often only be appreciated after excavation. Destruction should therefore not be permitted before archaeological investigation has taken place.

12. We desire to express our acknowledgement of the good work accomplished by our executive staff in the production of this volume. The fieldwork and preparation of the Inventory has been carried out by Mr. C. C. Taylor and Mrs. F. M. Brown. It has been edited by Mr. S. D. T. Spittle.

The illustrations have been drawn by Mr. R. E. Beeton and Mr. P. N. Hammond; Messrs. W. C. Light and R. Parsons have been responsible for the ground photography, Mr. J. Hampton for much of the aerial photography. Mr. H. Marsden has carried out specialized photographic work.

13. We desire to add that our Secretary and General Editor, Mr. R. W. McDowall, has afforded us constant assistance.

14. The next Inventory in the Northamptonshire series will record earthworks in the south-western part of that county.

Signed:

Adeane (*Chairman*)
John Chandos-Pole
H. C. Darby
S. S. Frere
R. J. C. Atkinson
G. Zarnecki
J. K. S. St Joseph
Paul Ashbee
A. R. Dufty

Mark Girouard
C. N. L. Brooke
Colin Renfrew
Joan Thirsk
M. W. Beresford
R. A. Buchanan
A. L. F. Rivet

R. W. McDowall (*Secretary*)

LIST OF PARISHES IN THE INVENTORY

1 ALTHORP
2 ARTHINGWORTH
3 ASHBY ST. LEDGERS
4 BADBY
5 BARBY
6 BOUGHTON
7 BRAMPTON, CHAPEL
8 BRAMPTON, CHURCH
9 BRAUNSTON
10 BRINGTON
11 BRIXWORTH
12 BROCKHALL
13 BYFIELD
14 CANONS ASHBY
15 CATESBY
16 CHARWELTON
17 CLAY COTON
18 CLIPSTON
19 COLD ASHBY
20 COTTESBROOKE
21 CREATON
22 CRICK
23 DAVENTRY
24 DODFORD
25 DRAUGHTON
26 ELKINGTON
27 EVERDON
28 FARNDON, EAST
29 FARTHINGSTONE
30 FAWSLEY
31 FLORE
32 GUILSBOROUGH
33 HADDON, EAST
34 HADDON, WEST
35 HARLESTONE

36 HASELBECH
37 HELLIDON
38 HOLDENBY
39 HOLLOWELL
40 KELMARSH
41 KILSBY
42 LAMPORT
43 LILBOURNE
44 LONG BUCKBY
45 MAIDWELL
46 MARSTON TRUSSELL
47 NASEBY
48 NEWNHAM
49 NORTON
50 OXENDON, GREAT
51 PITSFORD
52 PRESTON CAPES
53 RAVENSTHORPE
54 SCALDWELL
55 SIBBERTOFT
56 SPRATTON
57 STANFORD-ON-AVON
58 STAVERTON
59 STOWE-NINE-CHURCHES
60 SULBY
61 THORNBY
62 WATFORD
63 WEEDON BEC
64 WELFORD
65 WELTON
66 WHILTON
67 WINWICK
68 WOODFORD-CUM-MEMBRIS
69 YELVERTOFT

The parish boundaries, shown in red on the map in the pocket at the end of the volume, were those in effect when the Inventory was compiled.

ABBREVIATIONS AND SHORTENED TITLES
OF WORKS OF REFERENCE

Ant. J.	*Antiquaries Journal.*
Arch. J.	*Archaeological Journal.*
Ass. Arch. Soc. Reps.	*Reports and Papers of the Associated Archaeological Societies.*
Baker	G. Baker, *History and Antiquities of Northamptonshire*, I (1822–30), II (1836–41).
BAR	*British Archaeological Reports.*
BM	British Museum.
BNFAS	*Bulletin of the Northamptonshire Federation of Archaeological Societies.*
Bridges	J. Bridges, *History and Antiquities of Northamptonshire*, (1791).
Brit. Num. J.	*British Numismatic Journal.*
Cal. Chart.	*Calendar of Charter Rolls.*
Cal. Close	*Calendar of Close Rolls.*
Cal. Inq. Misc.	*Calendar of Miscellaneous Inquisitions.*
Cal. IPM	*Calendar of Inquisitions Post Mortem.*
Cal. Pat.	*Calendar of Patent Rolls.*
CBA	Council for British Archaeology.
CUAP	Cambridge University Air Photographs.
Current Arch.	*Current Archaeology.*
DMVRG	Deserted Medieval Village Research Group.
DOE	Department of the Environment.
FSL	Fairey Surveys Limited.
Gent's Mag.	*Gentleman's Magazine.*
JBAA	*Journal of the British Archaeological Association.*
J. Northants. Mus and Art. Gall.	*Journal of the Northampton Museum and Art Gallery.*
J. Northants. Natur. Hist. Soc. and FC	*Journal of the Northamptonshire Natural History Society and Field Club.*
JRS	*Journal of Roman Studies.*
Meaney	A. Meaney, *Gazetteer of Early Anglo-Saxon Burial Sites*, (1964).
Med. Arch.	*Medieval Archaeology.*
Morton	J. Morton, *Natural History of Northamptonshire*, (1712).
NM	Northampton Museum.
NMR	National Monuments Record.
Northants. Ant. Soc. Rep.	Northamptonshire Antiquarian Society Reports and Papers.
Northants. N. and Q.	*Northamptonshire Notes and Queries.*
Northants. P. and P.	*Northamptonshire Past and Present.*
NRO	Northamptonshire Record Office.
Num. Chron.	*Numismatic Chronicle.*
OS	Ordnance Survey.
PN Northants.	J. E. B. Gover, A. Mawer and F. M. Stenton, *The Place-Names of Northamptonshire*, (1933).
Post-med. Arch.	*Post-medieval Archaeology.*
PPS	*Proceedings of the Prehistoric Society.*
PRO	Public Record Office.
PSA	*Proceedings of the Society of Antiquaries of London.*
RAF VAP	Royal Air Force Vertical Air Photographs.
RCHM	Royal Commission on Historical Monuments
Trans. Leics. Arch. Soc.	*Transactions of the Leicestershire Archaeological Society.*
VCH	Victoria History of the Counties of England.
Whellan	F. Whellan, *History, Topography and Directory of Northamptonshire*, (1874).

INTRODUCTION

This Inventory of the earthworks of Northamptonshire covers parishes in the north-western part of the county. In it the policy regarding content and scope largely follows that of the earlier Inventories.

Apart from Roman roads (Appendix), the monuments are listed in the following order, under the names of the Civil Parishes in which they lie:

(1) Prehistoric and Roman Monuments.

(2) Medieval and Later Earthworks.

(3) Undated Earthworks, etc.

Each parish entry has a short introductory note, summarizing the physical topography, major monuments and history.

National Grid references are given for all monuments; a map of the whole area is in the pocket inside the back cover. A superior letter before a monument number refers to the sheet number in the OS 1:10000 map series, as listed at the head of the parish.

The entries in the Inventory are necessarily much condensed and where a site has been adequately described elsewhere few details are given and the reader is directed to the relevant publication.

Many of the plans included in the text have been prepared from air-photographic evidence. Every attempt has been made to avoid inaccuracy, but a number of drawings showing crop or soil-marks have been plotted from oblique air photographs only and therefore the locations shown may in some cases differ slightly from the actual, although general comparative sizes are correct. Furthermore, crop and soil conditions prevailing when the air photographs were taken have sometimes made interpretation difficult. Only those features considered as being archaeologically significant have been included in the illustrations. No attempt has been made to show the correct widths of ditches. Pit alignments and other arrangements of pits are shown conventionally; the precise number of pits, and variations in their size and shape, have not been reproduced.

The present locations of finds are, if known, indicated in the Inventory. Chance finds which are unrelated to monuments have not been included in the Inventory except when their importance warrants it or when it is likely that one of the monuments described in the Inventory was their provenance.

Roman roads in the area are described together in an Appendix, and are identified by the numbers given to them by I. D. Margary in *Roman Roads in Britain*, I (1955).

All earthworks listed in the Inventory have been inspected by our Investigator, and those which are of major importance, or have proved difficult of analysis, have been re-examined on a number of occasions. Some monuments have been destroyed since their investigation, but these have been included in the Inventory. All of the recording was carried out in 1976–7 and alterations to the monuments occurring since 1977 have not been described.

Work of this nature can seldom escape the inclusion of some errors, but it is believed that those in this survey are neither numerous nor serious. Any corrections may be sent to the Secretary with a view to their inclusion in the final Northamptonshire Inventory.

The present rate both of destruction and discovery of monuments renders it unlikely that any inventory will be definitive, particularly with regard to prehistoric and Roman remains. Archaeological sites are constantly being discovered and it is hoped that a record of material found subsequently to this publication will be incorporated in the appendix to a later Inventory.

SECTIONAL PREFACE

TOPOGRAPHY AND GEOLOGY

The part of Northamptonshire described in this volume covers an area of some 600 square kilometres, bounded on the N. by Leicestershire and on the W. by Warwickshire. Topographically the region consists of scarp and dip-slope features based on rocks of the Jurassic period but it has been so dissected by later streams that the general impression is of rolling countryside with little visible indication of the underlying structure. Most of the area is on clays of the Lower, Middle and Upper Lias, but Northampton Sand covers the higher watersheds in the N. and N.W., caps many isolated rounded hills in the S.W. and W. and forms broad open stretches of land N.W. of Northampton around Harlestone, Church and Chapel Brampton and Boughton. Large parts are overlaid by glacial deposits including sands, gravels and clays. Except in the extreme N., N.W., W. and S. the main drainage is S.E. down the Jurassic dip-slope where a series of small streams flow towards the River Nene. In the N. a group of shorter streams flow N. to join the River Welland which rises near Sibbertoft, and in the W. and N.W. streams flow into the River Avon, which also rises in the area, near Naseby. The extreme S. is drained by the headwaters of the River Tove and the River Cherwell. None of these streams is edged by gravel deposits of any extent and most flow in broad valleys cut directly into the underlying rocks.

Apart from one or two small timbered areas such as Badby Wood, there is no woodland in the region, though the many trees in the hedges give the landscape a wooded appearance. Rivers, streams and springs everywhere provide copious water supplies; building-stone of high quality comes from the beds of limestone.

Present-day settlement is evenly spread over the whole area. In the E. most of the villages lie on Northampton Sand. Many of these are on hilltops or ridges, for example Cold Ashby, Thornby, Creaton and Spratton, as well as Draughton, Lamport, Brixworth and Pitsford. Others, for example the Bramptons and Harlestone, are on lower, flatter areas of the same formation. Further W. the villages have more varied situations. Places such as Crick and Barby are on dry patches of low-lying glacial gravel; Preston Capes, Staverton and Farthingstone are on high ground, Newnham and Badby on low clay hills and Clay Coton on alluvium in a valley bottom. In the N., the villages of Naseby, Clipston and Sibbertoft are on high land largely covered by Boulder Clay.

Daventry is the only urban area, and even this was still a small market town until recent expansion took place. Long Buckby was a medieval market centre but never became much more than a large village.

Apart from extensive workings around Brixworth, the part of Northamptonshire here under review has suffered less from ironstone-mining than the area further E. Devastation caused elsewhere, for instance in the Nene valley, by gravel-working is absent here because of the lack of gravel deposits. The region is almost entirely agricultural and, as a result of a farming economy more mixed than in east and central Northamptonshire, permanent grassland is more common. An important consequence of this is that earthworks of a variety of periods survive to a greater degree here than elsewhere.

PREHISTORIC AND ROMAN SETTLEMENTS (Figs. 1–10)
Compared with the east and central parts of Northamptonshire, the area covered by this Inventory is poor in known remains of the prehistoric and Roman periods; moreover the distribution of the material is too uneven and unsatisfactory for any spatial analysis. The quantity of new sites coming to light as a result of increased local fieldwork is such that the distribution maps here presented will require continual revision.

The material from this region is no less difficult to interpret than that in the areas previously described, and for the same reasons (RCHM *Northants.*, I (1975), p. xxiv; II (1979), p. xxx. Indeed the difficulty in north-west Northamptonshire has been made the greater in some respects by the concentration of detailed fieldwork on specific periods in a few small areas. For example, the discovery of prehistoric flint-working sites in Brixworth (1–11) and of the Mesolithic site in Elkington (1) in the N. of the area adds little to our knowledge of prehistoric occupation patterns, whereas the implications would be great if similar discoveries were to be made throughout the county. The amount of work still needing to be carried out is considerable, but the evidence drawn together here and in the two previous Commission volumes on Northamptonshire implies a very much denser exploitation by man of almost every part of the landscape than used to be thought possible. It appears that the constraints of the natural environment such as heavy soils and dense woodland were more easily overcome than had previously been assumed, or were operating in a way as yet unknown to us.

In some respects the material in the Inventory is unsatisfactory, derived as it is from diverse sources over a long period of time and to very varied standards. Little is closely dated, or even recorded in an acceptable way. The relative ease with which material is recognised in field-walking may also lead to conclusions about the pattern of past settlement which may be false. For example, most of the flint-working sites listed lie on the Northampton Sand deposits, where it is easier to find them (e.g. Brixworth (1–11), Chapel Brampton (1–4, 6, 9) and Church Brampton (2–4, 9)), yet they have occasionally been recognised on heavier soils, such as Boulder Clay, for example at Chapel Brampton (11). Similarly, though most Iron Age and Roman settlements have been found on the lighter soils there are considerable numbers known on the Lias Clay deposits (Marston Trussell (1, 2), Cottesbrooke (1–3), Creaton (5–8) and Elkington (2, 5)). The evidence from air photographs too may be misleading. The light soils, especially the Northampton Sand and the glacial gravels, have revealed many remarkable complexes of cropmarks (e.g. Church Brampton (2, 8–11), Chapel Brampton (1–9) and Harlestone (1–5)) as well as individual enclosures and other features. On the much more extensive claylands, however, cropmarks are either very rare or, where recognised, are unclear and difficult to interpret. Yet such sites do occur (Kelmarsh (1, 2), Naseby (1)) and should not be ignored even though they are much less impressive than elsewhere. In addition, other sites may not be visible from the air at all.

An additional problem concerning soilmarks and cropmarks is that of distinguishing post-Roman sites from prehistoric or Roman ones. The growing evidence for a dispersed pattern of early Saxon settlement (see Saxon Remains) suggests that some sites known only from air photographs may be of this later period. Finds on the ground from one group of cropmarks at Chapel Brampton (2) indicate early Saxon occupation there, and although excavation might add to this picture, the possibility that some sites hitherto assumed to be prehistoric or Roman are in fact of Saxon date must be taken into consideration.

Few sites in the area have been excavated and not all of these have been fully published. Little can be usefully said, therefore, about the chronology, date, relationships, economy or social significance of most of them.

PREHISTORIC REMAINS

Of the prehistoric sites at present known within the area, few are datable since the fragile pottery of pre-Roman times is easily destroyed by later activity and cannot readily be found on the ground surface. A large number of the settlement sites shown clearly on air photographs as soilmarks or cropmarks but which have not produced Roman pottery are perhaps of prehistoric date. This is not certain, however, and no accurate dating evidence is obtainable without excavation; few cropmarks have any diagnostic features which enable them to be dated. Surviving earthworks of prehistoric times are extremely rare. The most notable is the vast hill fort of Borough Hill (Daventry (3)) and even this has suffered greatly over the last two centuries. The same is true of other sites which have been almost completely obliterated by modern cultivation, though they remained intact for centuries owing to their position on land which in medieval times was marginal. The enclosure at Farthingstone (3) is a good example of this.

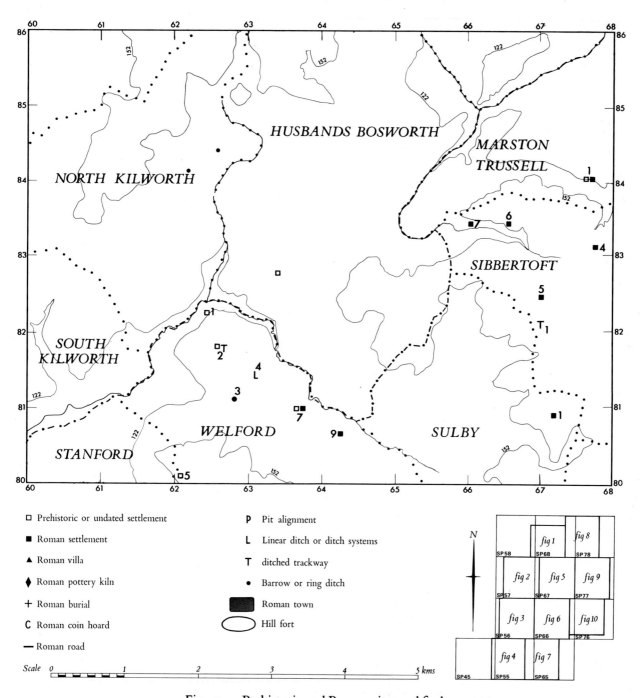

Fig. 1   Prehistoric and Roman sites and finds

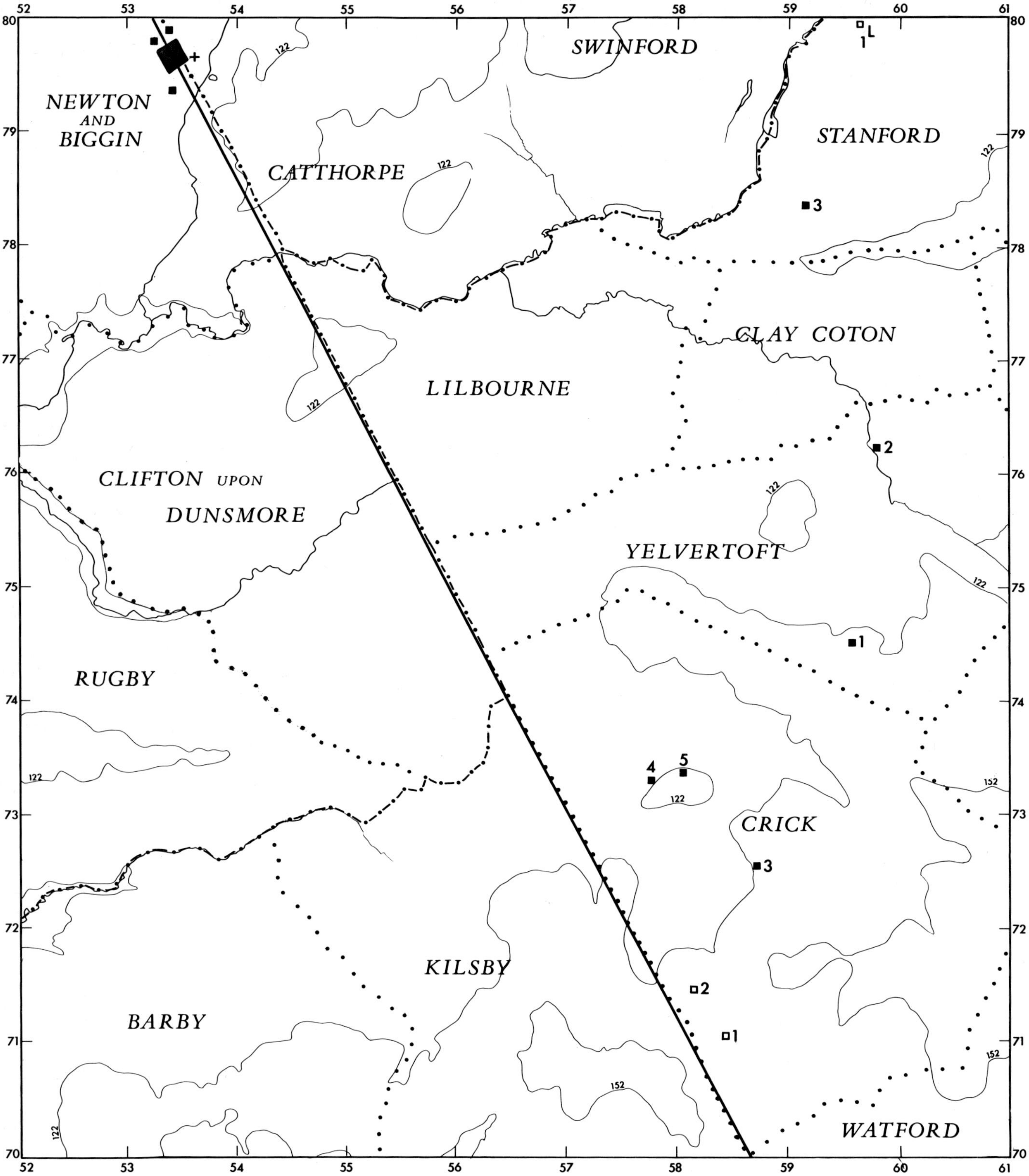

Fig. 2   Prehistoric and Roman sites and finds (for key see fig. 1)

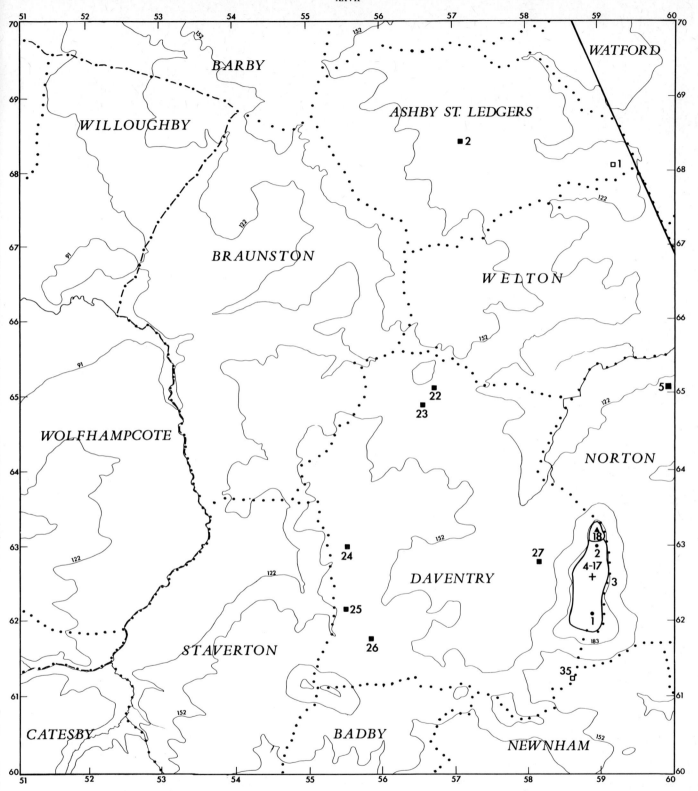

Fig. 3   Prehistoric and Roman sites and finds (for key see fig. 1)

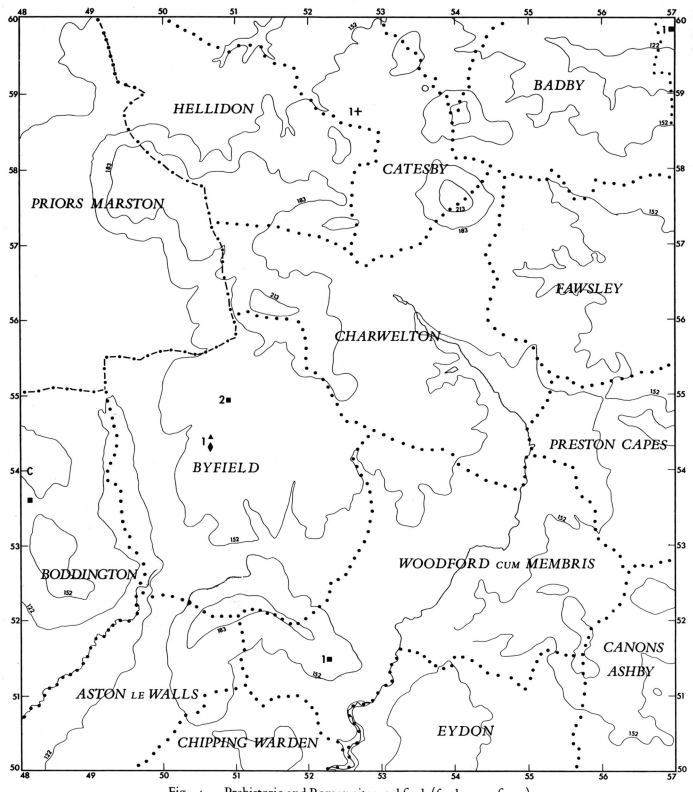

Fig. 4   Prehistoric and Roman sites and finds (for key see fig. 1)

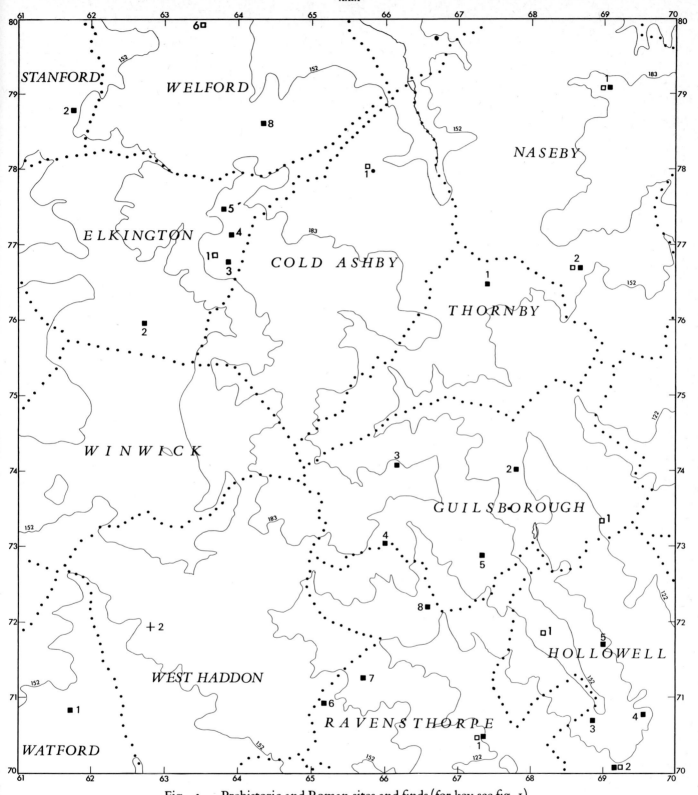

Fig. 5   Prehistoric and Roman sites and finds (for key see fig. 1)

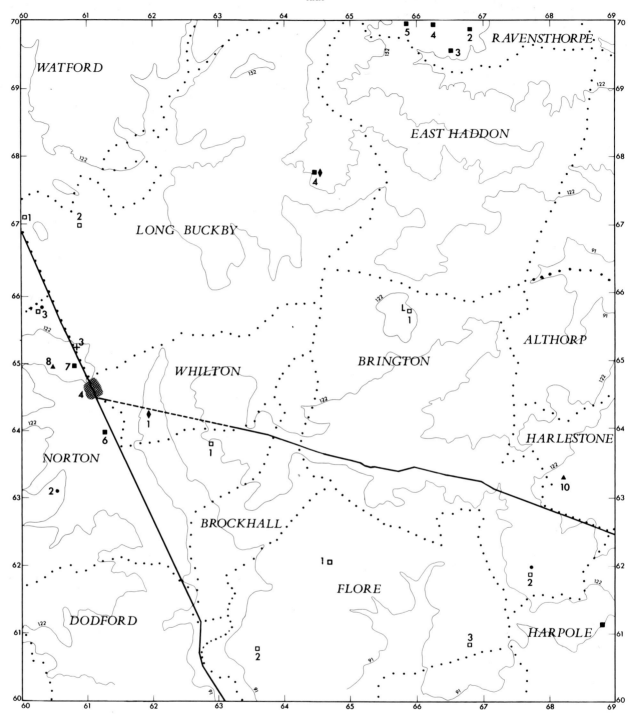

Fig. 6   Prehistoric and Roman sites and finds (for key see fig. 1)

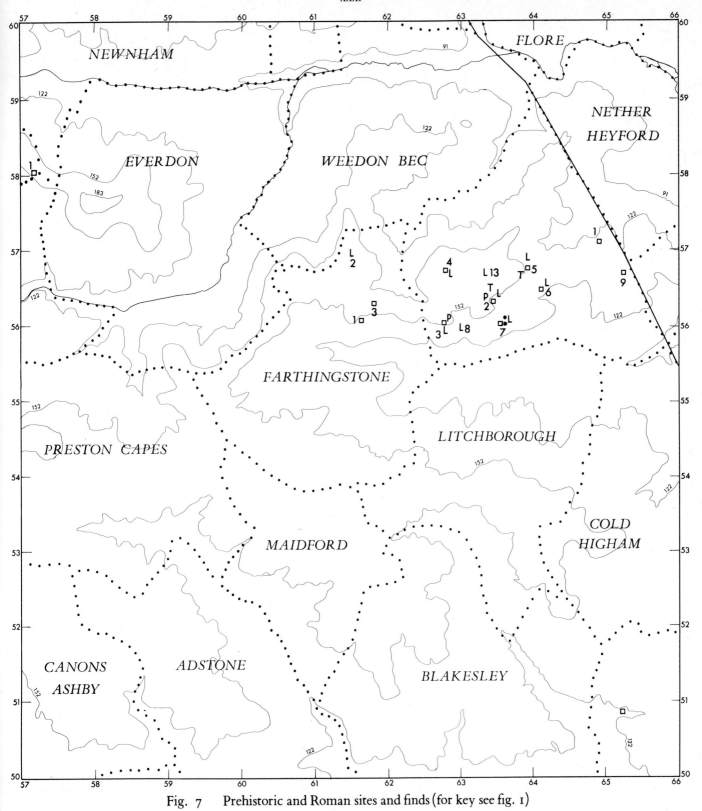

Fig. 7   Prehistoric and Roman sites and finds (for key see fig. 1)

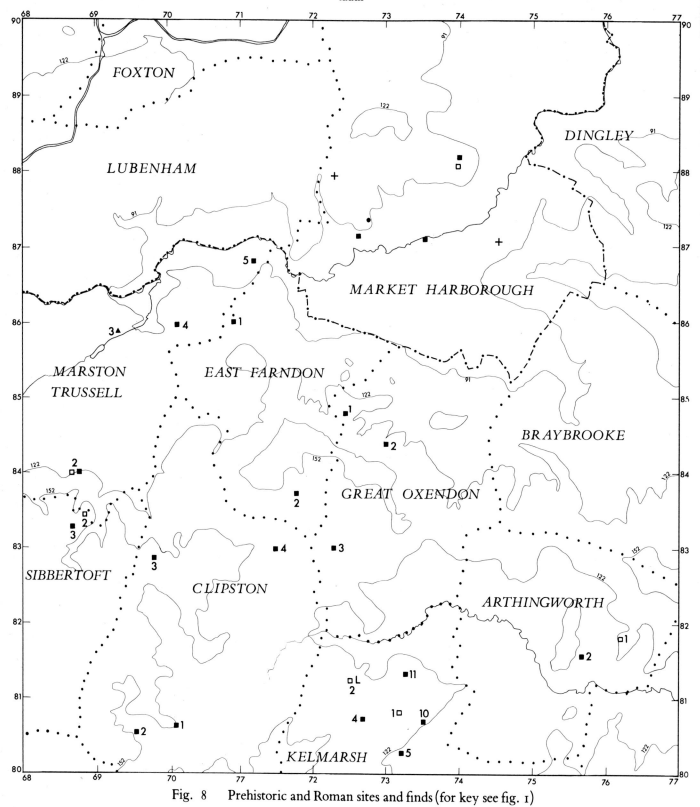

Fig. 8   Prehistoric and Roman sites and finds (for key see fig. 1)

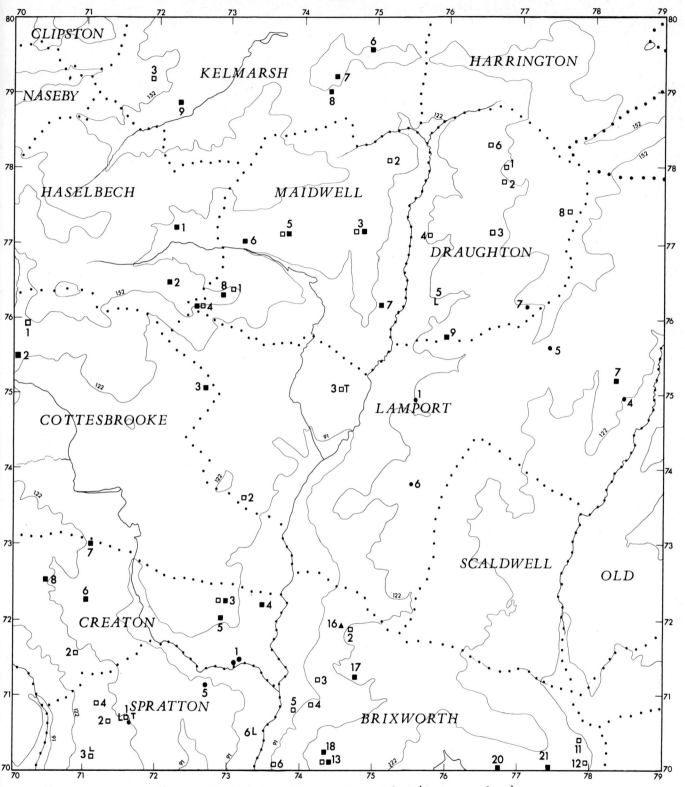

Fig. 9   Prehistoric and Roman sites and finds (for key see fig. 1)

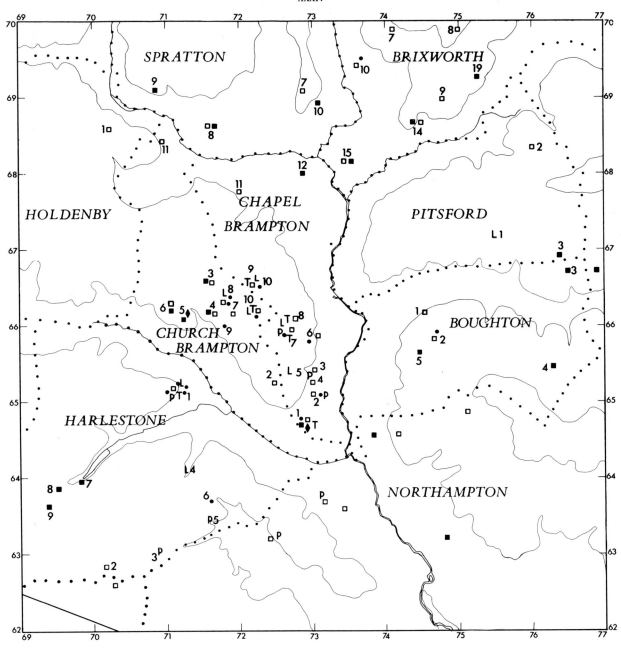

Fig. 10   Prehistoric and Roman sites and finds (for key see fig. 1)

Palaeolithic Period
Only three Palaeolithic axes are known in the area, one from Badby (p. 7) and two from Borough Hill, Daventry (p. 63). This lack of Palaeolithic material is probably related to the absence of gravel deposits.

Mesolithic Period
Until very recently little Mesolithic material had been noted in this part of Northamptonshire. Cores, said to be of Mesolithic type, are recorded from Pitsford (p. 161), Draughton (p. 75), Brockhall (p. 32)

and Creaton (p. 58); an axe is listed from Flore (p. 91). However, fieldwork over the last few years has produced a small number of identifiable Mesolithic or later sites in the S. of the area, as at Brixworth (5, 8, 15). The recent discovery of a large occupation area at Elkington (1) is especially notable, for its existence casts doubt on earlier theories that Mesolithic occupation in the English Midlands was extremely limited.

Neolithic Period
Little material of definite Neolithic date is recorded from north-west Northamptonshire. Flint axes are listed from Badby (p. 8), Brixworth (p. 27), Boughton (p. 14), Daventry (p. 63), Everdon (p. 80), Farthingstone (p. 86), Flore (p. 91) and Guilsborough (p. 95), as well as a hoard of six axes from Church Brampton (1). The numerous waste flakes, and more particularly the large flint-working sites at Brixworth (4–7, 9, 11, 15), Church Brampton (3), Chapel Brampton (2–4), Draughton (1–3) and Spratton (8), may indicate a widespread Neolithic occupation of the area, although detailed analysis of the material is needed before this can be confirmed. An unusual oval enclosure (Stowe-Nine-Churches (1)) and a long mound at Pitsford (4) have both been interpreted as long barrows, but there is no proof in either case. Many of the undated cropmark sites may be Neolithic settlements; there is extensive evidence of Neolithic and Bronze Age flint-working at a number of such sites, for example at Chapel Brampton (1–3).

The Bronze Age
A few stray finds, including spearheads from Canons Ashby (p. 35) and East Farndon (p. 82), palstaves from Arthingworth (p. 3), Daventry (p. 63, 67) and Everdon (p. 80), axes from Daventry (p. 63), a dagger from Marston Trussell (p. 138) and a late Bronze Age sword from Brixworth (p. 28), are listed in the Inventory. Apart from a possible settlement at Church Brampton (7), and flint-working sites noted above under the Neolithic period which may also be of Bronze Age date, no occupation site certainly of this period is known.

Several burials are recorded but only the cemetery at Chapel Brampton (10) has been properly excavated and this remains unpublished. A Beaker burial is listed from Norton (2) and three Beakers, all found during ironstone-mining, are known to have come from Brixworth (p. 28). A group of Collared Urns also came from ironstone-workings in Brixworth (p. 28).

Several possible or definite round barrows still survive, including a certainly identified one on Borough Hill, Daventry (2), with a probable one near by (Daventry (1)), now destroyed. Another certain barrow is at Boughton (2); this produced a sherd of Neolithic or Bronze Age type. Other mounds (Draughton (7) and Lamport (4–6)) may not be barrows. However, there are large numbers of ring ditches recorded in the Inventory, almost all of which are visible only from the air. Some of these, especially those located within areas of settlement, may prove to be hut-sites, e.g. Church Brampton (8), but others, as at Chapel Brampton (7), are almost certainly burial sites. No large barrow groups or cemeteries are known. Groups of ring ditches, usually visible as three conjoined circles with other single circles near by have been noted at Brixworth (p. 28), Brockhall (p. 32), Boughton (p. 14) and Harlestone (p. 97); these have been identified as the sites of Second World War anti-aircraft or searchlight batteries.

As with earlier periods, the records, however inadequate, suggest an intensive occupation of all parts of north-west Northamptonshire during the Bronze Age, although very little can be said in detail about the period.

The Iron Age
No more than 20 Iron Age settlements are listed in this Inventory. This paucity of sites, compared with the hundred or more recorded in central Northamptonshire (RCHM Northants., II (1979), xlii),

can only reflect the lack of detailed fieldwork in the area and many more must remain to be discovered. It is of interest that of the 15 small settlements four are on the Lias Clay and occur in parishes where fieldwork has not been carried out on a large scale (Marston Trussell (1, 2), Holdenby (1) and Cottesbrooke (1)). Nothing is known of these small settlements other than the scatters of pottery, except for one at Draughton (8) which was excavated during the Second War. This site is of considerable importance as it is still the only completely excavated example of what was probably the typical Iron Age farmstead in the county. It was a small defended settlement bounded by a single bank and ditch, enclosing three huts. Another Iron Age settlement of special interest is that at Farthingstone (3). This was a rare survival of a rectangular enclosure bounded by banks and ditches; its almost total destruction by modern ploughing is a considerable loss to the understanding of the Iron Age, but excavation might still recover some information. Many of the undated cropmarks may include other Iron Age sites.

The most important Iron Age monument is the great hill fort on Borough Hill (Daventry (3)). There is considerable evidence for occupation there from early prehistoric times through to the Saxon period, and the defences, assumed to be of the Iron Age, make the fort one of the largest in Britain with at least two stages of development. Here again the earthworks have been devastated by ploughing, by the construction of the BBC radio station and by other activities which over the last two centuries have greatly decreased its archaeological potential. It is imperative that this site be excavated before further damage or destruction occurs. The other supposed hill fort in the area, on Arbury Hill (Badby (2)), though documented as a fortified site as early as the Saxon period, is probably not man-made; what appear to be ramparts seem to be natural features.

A few pit alignments are listed in the Inventory, at Stowe-Nine-Churches (2, 3), Chapel Brampton (7) and Harlestone (1, 3, 5); no proof of date has been found but there is little reason to doubt that they belong to the later part of the Iron Age. As in the previous Northamptonshire Inventories there is no evidence for Iron Age or indeed earlier fields. Air photographs again show very large enclosures and lengths of linear ditches, but these are all undated and the pattern they form is obviously too incomplete for any exact interpretation to be possible. The only likely field system clearly of pre-medieval origin is at Church Brampton (10), where blocks of parallel linear features, perhaps recut many times, may be the boundaries of long rectangular fields. Other features which are also perhaps of late prehistoric date include the triple ditch system at Harlestone (4), visible as a cropmark, and the similar one at Stowe-Nine-Churches (13) which survives in part as an earthwork.

ROMAN REMAINS

In comparison with finds of earlier periods the amount of Roman material which has been discovered in north-west Northamptonshire is large. This is mainly due to the fact that Roman material has been and is more easily recognised both by the field archaeologist and by the layman; as a result it is difficult to draw a true comparison between the density of late prehistoric and of Roman settlement. Nearly 120 distinct settlements or probable settlements are listed as well as a number of isolated burials. This is considerably less than in the areas covered by the previous Inventories.

The evidence for Roman occupation is widespread but its pattern means very little in real terms. The densest distribution is in the S.E. corner of the area, in Church Brampton (3–6, 8), Chapel Brampton (1, 12), Brixworth (13–21), Spratton (8–10), Hollowell (2–5), Harlestone (7–10), Guilsborough (2–5), Cottesbrooke (2, 3), Boughton (4, 5) and Scaldwell (1). The finds are often the result of the combination of large-scale ironstone-mining in the area, which revealed a number of sites, and the fact that all these parishes have been subjected to intensive fieldwork by local archaeologists. The scattered distribution recorded in the N.E. of the area is mainly the result of random, localized fieldwork. The sites at Daventry (22–27) are known only through such activity, but those to the E., in Norton (5–8), may be an accurate reflection of a concentration of settlement around the town of Bannaventa (Norton (4)). Elsewhere some of the isolated Roman sites were chance discoveries, for example the Roman burial found at Catesby (1) during the construction of a railway tunnel.

Large tracts of land in the S. and W. of the area are at present devoid of known Roman settlements, but thorough field examination would probably result in the discovery of settlements of the period. However, permanent pasture, of which there is a considerable amount, would limit the detection of surface finds. The small, presumably rural, settlements have not been excavated and little can be said about them. The existence of scatters of stone-rubble at some indicates that there may have been stone buildings, but most are known only from pottery picked up on the surface. From this evidence all seem to have been very small, the majority under 1 hectare in area, but this may be misleading as extensive cropmarks are sometimes associated with only minimal concentrations of pottery and other material (e.g. Kelmarsh (6) and (9)). No fields have been identified at any of these sites.

There are several villas and other major buildings. The best understood, on Borough Hill (Daventry (18)), has been excavated twice. This villa, in its relationship both to the hill fort within which it stands and to the Roman town of Bannaventa (Norton (4)) a little to the E., is of considerable interest. The villa at Brixworth (16) has also been excavated but until the work is published it is impossible to be sure whether it will help to illustrate the problem of the undoubted continuity of settlement in that parish. The building at Harlestone (10) was dug into in the 1920s, but little could be made of the results; similarly, the plan made of a structure found in the 19th century at Byfield (1) clearly indicates a villa of considerable size, but nothing else is known about it. The rather vague cropmarks at Norton (8) also imply the existence of a villa.

The major Roman monument in the Inventory is the town of Bannaventa (Norton (4)). Although its general location had been known for over a century, it was not accurately identified until 1970, from air photographs. The town exhibits a number of unusual features, including a basic plan with oddly rounded corners, as well as a peculiar layout, askew to the main road which passes through it. Very little information is available concerning structures within the town but there is evidence of extra-mural occupation and a burial ground.

Other burials of the Roman period are noted at Catesby (1), Long Buckby (3) and West Haddon (2), but by far the most important are the Roman barrows on Borough Hill (Daventry (4–17)). At least 14 were excavated in 1823, and 18 are said once to have existed. They have all now been destroyed but some of the finds survive and constitute an important collection.

The only industrial monuments of any note are pottery kilns, but none of those listed has been excavated and all the records are unsatisfactory. Those at Scaldwell (1) have been destroyed, and the single kiln revealed at Byfield (1) is also unlikely to have survived. However evidence of kilns at Chapel Brampton (1) and Church Brampton (5) should encourage future work in that area.

SAXON REMAINS
The remains of this period fall into two distinct groups, burial sites and settlements. The Pagan Saxon cemeteries and other burials have been treated summarily in the Inventory since most of the ascertainable details have already been published elsewhere. A complete reassessment of Pagan Saxon burial sites is needed before any firm chronological framework can emerge. When this is accomplished the location of some of these burials may well be seen to be significant in relation to Roman sites. For example, those at Norton (9) and Welton (1) lie close to the town of Bannaventa (Norton (4)); on Borough Hill (Daventry (20)), and at Brixworth (24) the burials were actually within the ruins of villas.

Although there seems to be some general correlation between Pagan Saxon cemeteries and preceding Roman settlements, there is no real connection between the cemeteries and the subsequent medieval settlement pattern, apart from the unsatisfactorily recorded single burial at Clipston (5). As noted in the first two Inventories of the county (RCHM *Northants.*, I (1975), p. xxxvii; II (1979), p. xlvii), the growing evidence for sub-Roman or early Saxon settlements may throw new light on these relationships. In the present Inventory a considerable number of these assumed early Saxon settlements are listed, though their known distribution is fortuitous, being the result of very localized fieldwork. Eight such sites are recorded from Brixworth (24–32) and two from Spratton (11, 12), the next parish to the N.; three sites have been found at Welford (10–12), and single ones at Chapel Brampton (2), East Farndon (3) and Harlestone (11). Five are known from Maidwell (9–13). Much more work remains to be carried out, however, before the significance of this material can be assessed. It may possibly indicate that the early Saxon pattern of settlement was more akin to the Roman and late prehistoric one and that the typical medieval nucleated village evolved only in the late Saxon period or later.

MEDIEVAL AND LATER SETTLEMENT (Figs. 11–13. For ease of reference, small-scale plans of some villages have been grouped together in the Sectional Preface; large-scale plans of the earthworks in these villages appear in the Inventory).

The Domesday Survey, the earliest definitive account of medieval settlement, appears to show a regular pattern of nucleated villages 2 km.–4 km. apart over the whole area. This may be a true picture for most of the area but there are some indications that it may not be so everywhere. For example the now deserted village of Faxton (Lamport (15)) is recorded as a normal settlement in Domesday Book and has an apparently earlier, Scandinavian, name, but extensive excavations, as well as fieldwork after total destruction, have failed to discover any evidence, apart from some Roman pottery, of occupation on the site before the 12th century. This contradiction between the documentary and place-name evidence and the archaeological material cannot at present be explained.

Most nucleated medieval villages lay within an area of land which has survived to the present time as an ecclesiastical parish, but which must have originated as an agricultural entity or as a unit of land tenure. A few modern parishes represent the territory of a single village and its agricultural land, as at Whilton, Canons Ashby and Staverton, but in the majority a more complex situation can be detected. In such parishes there are other medieval settlements, in addition to the main village, which also appear to have had their own land units, agriculturally and often tenurially separate from the land of the main village. The boundaries of these earlier land units can sometimes be ascertained from Saxon and medieval charters or from later maps, as well as from the pattern of the ridge-and-furrow. In the past such places have usually been regarded as secondary or 'daughter' settlements of the main or 'mother' village. However a close examination of many parishes in north-west Northamptonshire shows that the true situation is less simple. In some places the theory of primary and secondary settlement holds good, as at Thornby (2) where the small settlement of Chilcote, from its position, name, history and extant earthworks, seems certainly to be a secondary settlement. The same can be said about the deserted village of Newbold in Catesby (6), the lost village of Thrupp in Norton (10) and perhaps the shrunken hamlet of Little Preston in Preston Capes (2). However the situation is more complicated elsewhere, as at Marston Trussell (8) and (9). There, although the deserted settlements of Hothorpe and Thorpe Lubenham seem at first sight to be secondary to Marston itself, both were in fact once linked at least ecclesiastically to villages across the R. Welland in Leicestershire. Similarly the deserted village of Little Oxendon, the name of which suggests a direct link with Great Oxendon in which parish it now lies, was linked as a parochial chapelry to

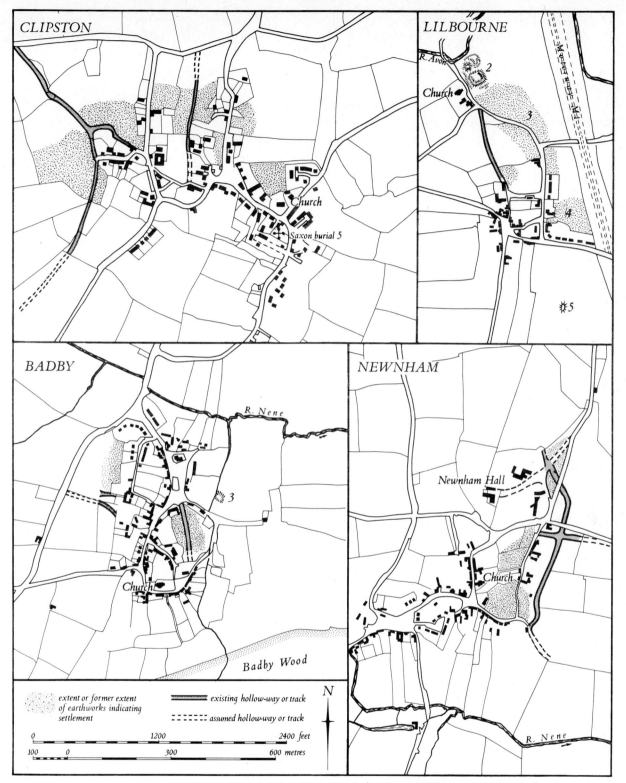

Fig. 11   BADBY, CLIPSTON, LILBOURNE AND NEWNHAM   Village plans

Great Bowden, also in Leicestershire. Again, the deserted village of Little Creaton is now in Creaton parish (10) and would seem to be secondary to Great Creaton, but its present position is the result of modern changes; before the 19th century it lay in Spratton parish to the S.

In other parishes the pattern is still more obscure. The abandoned village of Glassthorpe in Flore (4) appears to be a good example of a secondary settlement and yet part of its land unit, apparently even in medieval times, extended beyond Flore parish and into the adjacent parish of Brington. Similarly at Watford, the parish in medieval times contained not only the now deserted village of Silsworth (Watford (3)) but also part of the land and half the actual settlement of Murcott; the remainder of Murcott lay in Long Buckby parish (5). The situation at Barby is more difficult to explain. The parish is made up of the lands of Barby village (3) and of the abandoned village of Onley (Barby (1)). The latter may be a secondary settlement of Barby, but a third settlement and its land unit, Barby Nortoft, lay in Kilsby parish to the E. Certainly the situation at Norton, where the lost village of Muscott (Norton (11)) lies within a long narrow projection of the parish to the E. of Watling Street, suggests that Muscott was once a primary settlement with its own land unit and that it was joined to Norton for ecclesiastical purposes only at a relatively late date. The same is probably true of the settlements of Hinton, Woodford and West Farndon in Woodford-cum-Membris (2) and Snorscomb in Everdon (3). Elsewhere the names and shapes of parishes indicate that they were once single units which became divided administratively and ecclesiastically with the growth of secondary settlements. The relationship between Clay Coton (2) and Lilbourne (3) would seem to be an example of this. On the other hand, though the names, shape of the parishes and the admittedly late evidence for intercommoning at Badby and Newnham parishes might suggest the same process, the complex morphology of Newnham (2) and the possibility of a change of name, poses considerable problems of interpretation.

The inherent difficulties in this type of study are nowhere better demonstrated than in the Guilsborough area (Fig. 14). The settlement of Coton and its lands are now in Ravensthorpe (9) but were once in Guilsborough parish. The modern parish of Guilsborough is made up of two land units, each with its own settlement, Guilsborough and Nortoft. To the S. the present parish of Hollowell is also the result of the ecclesiastical unification of Hollowell and Teeton and their respective land units, but as Hollowell was once dependant on Guilsborough, there is some connection between these two also. In effect there seem to be not simply three parishes each made up of two separate settlements and their land, but one large area now covered by Ravensthorpe, Hollowell and Guilsborough parishes, which was perhaps at some time a tenurial or administrative unit made up of at least six distinct settlements and their land. If this supposition is correct then the original unified area must be of considerable antiquity, for the boundary between the medieval hundreds of Guilsborough and Nobottle Grove cuts across it. The possible significance of the borough element in the name Guilsborough and the existence of an important Roman site (5), now destroyed, in the village must also be taken into account.

In many other parishes which contain more than one medieval settlement there is no clear evidence that each of the latter ever had a separate land unit. In some cases, as at Clipston where there is an existing village of Clipston (7) and the deserted village of Nobold (Clipston (6)), lack of documentation makes it impossible to trace the boundaries of units that undoubtedly once existed. Other possible examples of this are at Charwelton (1) and (3), Stanford (4) and (6) and Catesby (2) and (3). Elsewhere it appears that there are genuinely secondary settlements which, because they were always small, never acquired their own land units, for example Cotton End in Long Buckby (7). In places such as Stowe-Nine-Churches, however, where both settlements in the parish are of equal size and status and yet seem to have been associated with a single agricultural unit, there is no clear explanation.

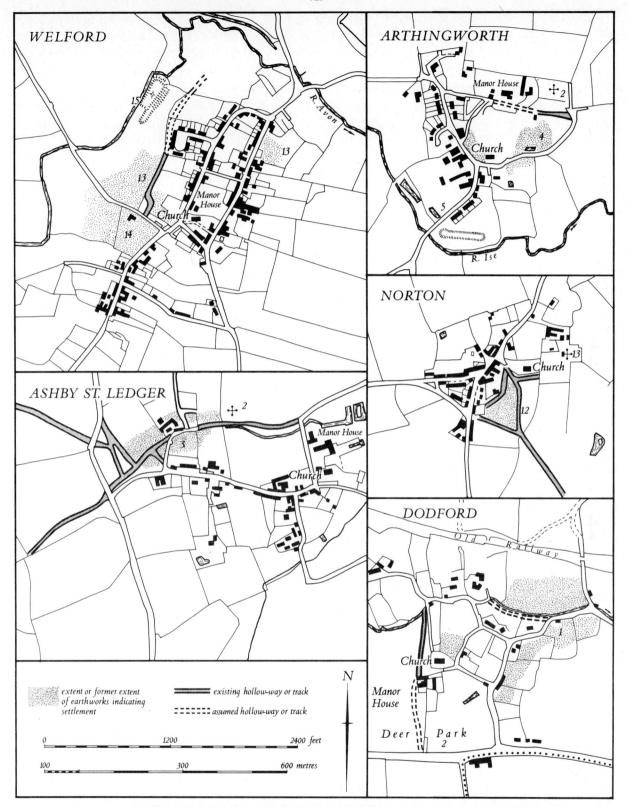

Fig. 12 ARTHINGWORTH, ASHBY ST. LEDGERS, DODFORD, NORTON and WELFORD Village plans

Another type of medieval settlement in the region is the polyfocal village; this has always had a single land unit but is the result of the merging of two or more discrete centres into one single settlement (*Med. Arch.*, 21 (1977), 189). In the area under review, Byfield and Hellidon are examples without any surviving earthworks and thus are not described in the Inventory. Others which are listed include Naseby (3), where the settlements of Nutcote and Naseby lie side by side, Cottesbrooke (5), where there are still two distinct parts to the village, and Holdenby (3), where there were certainly two centres although later activity has destroyed any evidence as to how close they were. The large deserted village of Kelmarsh (14) may be the result of growth from three centres, and Fawsley (1) is also made up of two parts. The origins of such villages are not understood. Newnham (2), which has at least three and perhaps more focal points, can be explained in a number of ways; the two centres at Sibbertoft (9) may be merely the result of planned extensions of the earlier settlement (Fig. 13). Despite the evidence from field analysis, documentary research and archaeology the origins of the medieval village in this area are still little understood.

Villages, once established, were subject to changes throughout the medieval and post-medieval periods; some grew larger while others declined or were abandoned completely, and many underwent changes of location. The Inventory describes a large number of monuments that have resulted from these processes. Although detailed topographical analysis can indicate the process in certain places, continuous growth or expansion by its very nature has no earthwork remains and is therefore not dealt with in the Inventory. One example is Scaldwell which seems to have resulted from gradual expansion from its central green.

Other circumstances have left visible archaeological features, usually in the form of earthworks. Some villages have been almost completely abandoned but there are many more which have undergone contraction or movement. The reasons for the desertion, shrinkage or movement of the majority of villages in the area are often obscure, partly because changes took place over many centuries as the outcome of complex events, local and national, social and economic, and rarely as the sudden result of one specific cause. The lack of surviving documentation giving information as to the size and population of these places or indicating any other history apart from the manorial descent, also makes it very difficult to isolate either general or specific conditions that caused changes in individual villages or in the overall pattern of settlement in the medieval and later periods. There is an inevitable tendency to pick out the more obvious potential reasons for change or decline but these produce an oversimplified view of the history of medieval settlement. Faxton (Lamport (15)) illustrates the potential weakness of generalizations based on a lack of firm evidence. This village has had large-scale excavation carried out on it, and there is also a wealth of post-medieval documentation. Without this evidence a simple but totally erroneous interpretation could be made of the decline and abandonment of Faxton. Unsatisfactory as the evidence is, it shows a complex picture of continuous change and movement as well as decline, spread over a period of 600 years, but with no obvious explanation for the processes involved.

The date and causes of desertion of the numerous abandoned villages described in the Inventory can be ascertained at only a very few, and even then the facts are probably more complicated than the existing evidence can reveal. It remains generally true that most of the villages that were eventually deserted were those which were always small and weak, but there are some which do not fit this description. Chilcote in Thornby (2) had a recorded population of two and Glassthorpe in Flore (4) of five in Domesday Book; these were obvious candidates for eventual desertion. Canons Ashby (1), however, which had a recorded population of 16 in 1086 and of 82 people over the age of 14 in 1377, and also Sulby (3) which had 89 people over the age of 14 in 1377, seem to be villages which, in spite of considerable prosperity, could still be removed by their monastic lords. On the other hand even the smallest of places might survive. Hothorpe in Marston Trussell (9) had only one person listed under it in Domesday Book. It grew larger so that 57 people over the age of 14 were living there in 1377 and,

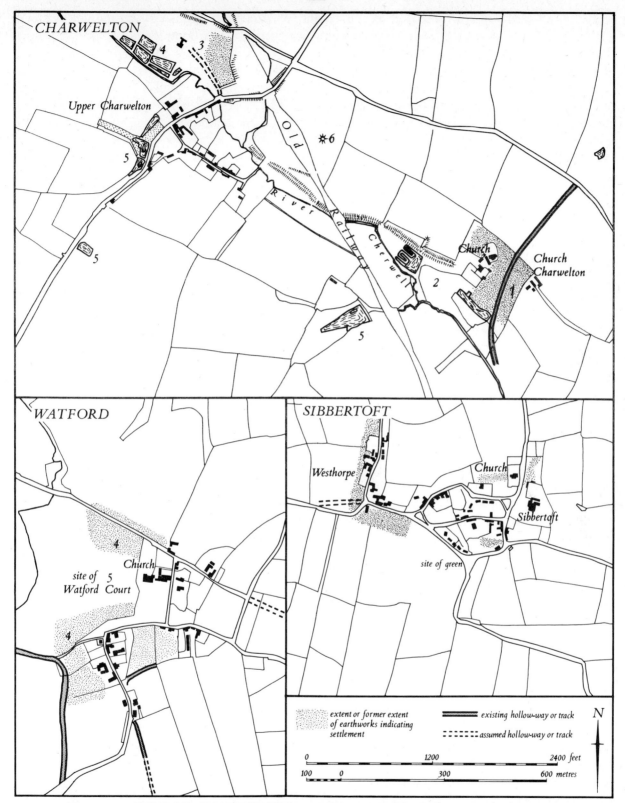

Fig. 13 CHURCH CHARWELTON, UPPER CHARWELTON, SIBBERTOFT and WATFORD Village plans

despite some clearly visible desertion or movement, it lasted until the 19th century when it was finally removed by emparking. Again the recoverable picture is one of considerable fluctuation for no clearly defined reason.

Many of the villages which still survive may be classified as true shrunken settlements with earthworks which appear to be the result of a reduction of population. Some of these show that part of the contraction took place in post-medieval times. The earthworks at Naseby (3) are especially interesting because sites of houses still standing in 1630 can be identified exactly. Even so, shrinkage at Naseby was taking place before 1630 and a long slow process is indicated, as it is more clearly at Faxton (Lamport (15)). Again, at Haselbech (3) some desertion was apparently the result of late 16th-century enclosure, but some may be earlier, and much was a consequence of 18th-century emparking. Some shrinkage is of very late date, as at Clay Coton (2) and Coton in Ravensthorpe (9), both of which have evidence of 19th-century contraction, although earthworks at both indicate earlier decline. Elsewhere the date of decline is largely unknown, for example at Little Preston in Preston Capes (2), Stanford (4) and Brockhall (1). Earthworks that reveal shrinkage can also provide evidence of earlier expansion. At Little Preston the fact that the abandoned gardens of former houses have cut through a dated deer park boundary implies that this part of the village did not exist when the deer park was created in 1227, nor, presumably, for some time afterwards. At Canons Ashby (1) too the evidence on the ground shows that the N. part of the village, now deserted, was laid out over former arable land. The same feature is detectable at Muscott in Norton (11).

In other villages, where there is no documentary evidence of a reduction in population, the surviving earthworks can indicate movement rather than shrinkage, though the two may sometimes have been combined. At Pitsford (7) the evidence is fragmentary, but at Yelvertoft (4) there is a strong possibility that the original village was situated in a low-lying valley and then moved W., encroaching upon its own fields. The best example of this is at Lilbourne (3) where two stages of apparent movement are detectable. The original village seems to have lain around the now isolated castle and church. It then moved S. into a new position with houses and crofts fitted into existing blocks of ridge-and-furrow. Finally it moved S. again to the hilltop where it still remains. The same process is traceable at Winwick, though the situation is here complicated by shrinkage as well. The evidence on the ground implies a movement of the village upstream along the valley, with the result that the abandoned part, including a manor house site, was ploughed over and incorporated into the village fields. Occasionally such movement appears to be the result of deliberate planning. At Long Buckby (6) the earthworks, now largely destroyed, together with the existing layout of the village indicate that the 11th-century village lay to the N.W. of the present one and that the new village was created around the market place, perhaps in 1280 when it received a market grant. At Sibbertoft the hamlet of Westhorpe, laid out in neat rectangular form, may have been consciously planned as an addition to the earlier village to the E. Likewise at Clipston (7) one part of at least three stages of development seems to have been a planned extension consisting of three parallel streets and a green added to the original village; a later unplanned growth occurred further W. At Welford (13) there is evidence that the whole village is planned. Although the existing settlement could be interpreted as a village along a simple N.–S. road with a back lane to the W., the location of the church and the manor house on that lane, and the earthwork evidence for a third street parallel to the existing ones to the W., make the idea of a completely planned settlement seem probable. The layout of Flore (5) suggests the same process.

In some of the completely deserted villages also there is evidence to suggest that they were laid out on a deliberate plan. The clearest is at Braunstonbury (Braunston (1)); the form of the surviving earthworks suggests a rectangular plan with 'greens' in two of the corners and the moated manor house in a third, and there are slight indications of an internal layout of straight property boundaries. The latter have clearly been distorted by later activity but can just be recognised. The name

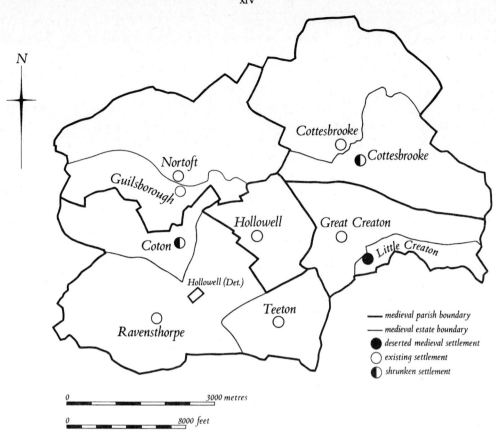

Fig. 14   COTTESBROOKE, CREATON, GUILSBOROUGH, HOLLOWELL and RAVENSTHORPE
Medieval settlements and estates

Braunstonbury, and the location of the village very close to the existing village of Braunston, might be taken as additional evidence for a late, planned origin. The deserted village of Braunston Cleves in the same parish (Braunston (3)) may also be planned. It is oddly arranged on one side of a single street and there is no evidence that any part of it lay on the other side. In addition, the diversion of the existing stream around the ends of the village closes could be the result of co-operative work in the layout of the settlement. Muscott (Norton (11)) also has an unusually regular plan, with a central axial hollow-way and a rectangular street system bounding the village; Glassthorpe (Flore (4)), though much altered by later activity, shows the same features. These may all have been planned settlements, as may the deserted village of Newbold in Catesby (6), now destroyed but clearly visible on air photographs. It is possible that in such apparently planned villages the earthworks reveal a widespread process, the traces of which have elsewhere been destroyed by late medieval and post-medieval occupation and change.

Even where the morphology of existing villages seems to be readily explicable the discovery and recording of associated earthworks can alter the interpretation. Several settlements in this part of Northamptonshire have in the past been described as 'loop' villages and have been regarded as the result of expansion in woodland areas where unused land was readily available. At two of these, Badby (4) and Crick (7), the earthworks in fact indicate a history far more complex. Even superficially simple villages may have considerable earthworks around them which cast doubt on the obvious interpretation of their history. Little Everdon (Everdon (2)) is one such settlement; it now survives only as a single street but in the surrounding fields are hollow-ways lined with former house-sites indicating a more complicated development.

The area also contains villages which have been greatly altered by 18th and 19th-century emparking. At Norton (12) the village was moved sideways in the 19th century as the park of Norton Hall was extended, and at Marston Trussell some of the buildings on one side of the main street were removed to provide a view for the new hall; at Hothorpe the entire village was cleared away in the early 19th century. At Cottesbrooke (5), though the earthworks described in the Inventory elucidate an earlier phase of the village's history, there is good cartographic evidence for two quite separate alterations to the S. part of the village in the 18th and 19th centuries, connected with the changes to Cottesbrooke Park. The enlargement of the park of Watford Court (Watford (5)) led to two distinct stages of change in one part of the village. In the 18th century some of the houses lost their gardens to the new park and a century later the houses themselves were removed as the park was enlarged again. Perhaps the most important example of the alteration of villages due to emparking is at Holdenby (3), not the least because of its early date. The great garden layout, implemented by Sir Christopher Hatton in the late 16th century to go with his new house, involved the replacement of one part of the village by a neatly planned estate village and probably the complete removal of the other part. This is one of the earliest known examples of a village being removed to make a park.

Some of the village earthworks recorded in the Inventory, although of considerable extent, defy interpretation and can only be said to indicate changes over a long period. Those at Lamport (8) and at Nobottle (Brington (3)) fall into this category. More interesting were the earthworks at Dodford (1), now destroyed, which must have been the result of a sequence of changes over several centuries. The continuing destruction of such sites as existing villages are enlarged or filled in by modern housing development is a serious problem, and their removal without excavation means that much of the archaeology of these places may soon be impossible to recover.

A most important aspect of the work on earthwork remains of medieval villages in this area relates to the period after abandonment. It has been recognised that many deserted villages (e.g. Nobold in Clipston (6), Glassthorpe in Flore (4), Onley in Barby (1), Sulby (3), Little Oxendon in Great Oxendon (9), Upper Catesby in Catesby (2) and Hothorpe and Thorpe Lubenham in Marston Trussell (9) and (8)), have later been completely or largely ploughed in ridge-and-furrow. Some of this ploughing, as over parts of Onley and Upper Catesby, is almost certainly of late date, perhaps late 18th or 19th century, but in most cases it is likely to be earlier. The details are discussed below under cultivation remains.

MEDIEVAL EARTHWORKS
Settlement Remains
Thirty-three deserted villages are recorded in the Inventory: Althorp (1), Barby Nortoft (Kilsby (2)), Boughton Green (Boughton (7)), Braunstonbury and Braunston Cleves (Braunston (1) and (3)), Canons Ashby (1), Calme in Clipston (p. 49), Church Charwelton (Charwelton (1)), Chilcote (Thornby (2)), Downtown (Stanford (6)), Elkington (6), Fawsley (1), Faxton (Lamport (15)), Glassthorpe (Flore (4)), Holdenby (3), Hothorpe (Marston Trussell (9)), Kelmarsh (14), Little Creaton (Creaton (10)), Little Oxendon (Great Oxendon (9)), Lower and Upper Catesby (Catesby (2) and (3)), Muscott (Norton (11)), Newbold (Catesby (6)), Nobold (Clipston (6)), Onley (Barby (1)), Shenley (Yelvertoft (3)), Silsworth (Watford (3)), Snorscomb (Everdon (3)), Stanford (4), Sulby (3), Thorpe Lubenham (Marston Trussell (8)), Thrupp (Norton (10)), and an un-named settlement in Watford (2).

Visible traces of some deserted villages were removed centuries ago. Calme in Clipston is hardly recorded after 1086 and its site has not been located. Boughton Green, if indeed it was a separate settlement, was largely destroyed in antiquity. The remains of one of the parts of the village at

Fawsley were levelled in the 18th century during emparking, and Thrupp was ploughed up apparently before the 19th century. The two separate parts of Holdenby were destroyed as early as the late 16th century; a new village was laid out on top of one of them and a garden on the other.

The sites of other deserted villages were also severely damaged or altered many years ago. Part of Lower Catesby was destroyed to make medieval monastic ponds (Catesby (4)), a section of Braunston Cleves was damaged by drainage works in the 19th century and a large piece of Kelmarsh seems to have been ploughed out during the 18th-century emparking. Another process, already noted and historically of more interest, has altered a number of sites, namely the late or post-medieval ploughing which has made the interpretation of surviving earthworks very difficult.

It is in recent years, however, that the greatest destruction has occurred. Lower Catesby has been almost completely levelled by modern ploughing, as have Silsworth, Elkington and Upper Catesby. The sites of Newbold in Catesby, Downtown and Faxton have all been totally destroyed since 1944 and small areas of Muscott and Church Charwelton have suffered a similar fate. Despite this destruction some of the most interesting deserted villages of Midland England still survive intact in the area under review, and a number of important features are recognisable. Most deserted villages, at least towards the end of their lives, lay either along important through roads or around complicated street systems, all now reduced to hollow-ways. At Braunston Cleves the single main street is still well preserved; a similar main hollow-way at Church Charwelton is blocked by a later fishpond at its S.W. end. Main hollow-ways blocked by later ridge-and-furrow exist at Onley and Sulby and there are also good examples of hollowed main streets at Little Oxendon and Nobold in Clipston. At Upper Catesby part of the through road still survives but the late 19th-century estate hamlet has been laid across one section. At Braunstonbury, Muscott and Glassthorpe more complex arrangements of streets and lanes are visible, perhaps as the result of conscious planning (see p. xliv). In some villages only the back lane survives as a hollow-way, as at Canons Ashby and Hothorpe. Many existing roads still follow the main medieval street, for example at Canons Ashby, Little Creaton and Kelmarsh. At a few places the unusual origin of medieval streets is still apparent. At Onley one of the streets followed the original course of a stream which even in medieval times was also the overflow channel from the manorial fishponds, and at Glassthorpe at least one of the abandoned hollow-ways seems once to have been a stream. Likewise the hollow-way at Snorscomb could not have been used as a through route unless the deeply cut stream which it meets at its N. end was also part of the road system of the area.

Well-preserved house-sites are comparatively rare. In villages with later ridge-and-furrow ploughing, only slight depressions or low rounded platforms indicate the sites of former buildings. Even where such destruction has not occurred the assumed wooden structures have left no clear surface trace. Earthworks of this form survive at Kelmarsh, Little Oxendon, Nobold in Clipston, Muscott and Braunstonbury. The best house-sites are seen at Snorscomb where the footings of what appear to be stone-built rectangular structures survive up to a height of 0.5 m.

As noted in a previous volume (RCHM *Northants.*, II (1979), liv), house-sites in villages that were removed for emparking at a late date hardly ever survive, presumably because they were deliberately destroyed rather than being left to gradual decay as in villages abandoned earlier. The former is well exhibited at Hothorpe.

All the deserted villages have embanked, ditched or scarped closes or paddocks around them. Closes lying along streets and with remains of buildings within them are probably the original gardens or crofts, but the exact function of these is not always clear. Others were probably small enclosed fields, now reduced to earthworks because of changing land use, and should not be regarded as evidence of large settlements now depopulated.

Sites comprising earthworks of moved or shrunken villages are more common than deserted villages in this area. Over 40 such places are recorded in the Inventory but these are only the major ones and those of special interest. Every village has at least one or two places where houses formerly stood, many of which may have been abandoned in relatively recent times. Some are extremely well preserved and often cover large areas. The one at Clipston (7) consists of a number of abandoned streets or lanes as well as good house-sites, closes and paddocks. At Lilbourne (3) the earlier furlongs into which the houses and gardens were fitted still survive. Other examples are at Little Everdon (Everdon (2)), Naseby (3) and Watford (4).

Embanked paddocks or closes lying behind surviving buildings are another type of settlement feature associated with existing villages. They do not imply shrinkage, only a change in land use or ownership. Such remains have been noted at Drayton (Daventry (31)), Cottesbrooke (5) and Barby (3).

Major areas of earthworks such as those at Dodford (1) and Long Buckby (6) have been totally destroyed within recent years, and many others, as at Cold Ashby (3), Draughton (10) and Marston Trussell (6), have been severely damaged. In other places, largely as a result of special circumstances, the survival of the earthworks is notable (e.g. Little Everdon (Everdon (2)).

The present process of expansion and infill in the majority of rural villages means inevitably that more of these monuments will be destroyed in the near future. In many places there are areas which need to be excavated before such destruction occurs. At Crick for example it would be of considerable interest to know if the earthworks represent an early part of the settlement or a later addition to it, and at Newnham (2) and Watford (4) the considerable problems surrounding the origins and development of the villages might be at least partly explained by excavation of the remaining earthworks. The assumed two-stage movement at Lilbourne (3) could be proved or refuted by relatively small-scale archaeological work.

Moated Sites

Fewer than ten moated sites are listed in the Inventory. Of these the earthworks at Thornby (3) may not be a moat and those at Thrupp (Norton (10)) and Faxton (Lamport (16)) have been partly destroyed, so their original form is unknown. The rest are all typical medieval moated sites and little new general information has been gained from their examination. All are small and appear to have consisted of a single moated enclosure except at Marston Trussell (7) and Barby (2) where outer enclosures can be traced. None of the sites is truly defensive, the ditches being neither wide nor deep. Indeed, at Arthingworth (4) and Winwick (1) the moats were dominated by adjacent rising ground. Except for the one at Badby (3), which was fed by a small stream, all seem to have been filled by springs or intermittent seepage; all appear to have been sites of medieval manor-houses. The Badby site was fully excavated before its total destruction and an interesting sequence emerged of buildings associated with a monastic grange of Evesham Abbey from the early 13th to the 16th century.

The moated site at Braunstonbury (Braunston (1)) may have been built as part of the original village for its lies neatly in the N.W. corner of the rectangular village earthworks. The moat at Winwick (1) was, with the adjacent village remains, ploughed over with later ridge-and-furrow.

Manor House Sites

Apart from the moated sites already noted and some of the smaller castles listed below there are 12 other places which appear to have been the sites of unmoated medieval manor houses. Some, such as that at Hanging Houghton (Lamport (13)), were not abandoned until well into the post-medieval period and have garden remains associated with them (see p. liv). Others may have been deserted earlier. Most are unimpressive earthworks of little intelligible plan, e.g. Catesby (5) and Hellidon (1), and others retain only the remains of former paddocks and closes, the house-sites themselves having been destroyed or built over, e.g. Welford (14). Of some interest is the manor house site at Holdenby

(3) which was turned into a formal garden in the 1580s. The best preserved, with its external boundary bank and building platforms still intact, is in the deserted village of Little Oxendon (Great Oxendon (9)); it lies along the edge of the former main street.

Castles

A number of motte and bailey castles are recorded in the Inventory. The finest is perhaps Lilbourne Castle (2) where two stages of development can be recognised; the original motte with its small bailey appears to have had a massive second bailey added to it on the uphill side. At Lilbourne there is a second motte (1), in an isolated position on a hill to the W. of the village; it is rare to find two mottes so close together. The motte at Farthingstone (4) is unusual in having three baileys, but at least one of these may be a much earlier, perhaps prehistoric, fortification. Another finely preserved motte and bailey at Sibbertoft (8), like those at Farthingstone and on the ridge-top at Lilbourne, lies remote from any known medieval settlement.

The purpose of these isolated mottes cannot be ascertained. All are in strong defensive positions, but none has great strategic importance. They contrast strongly with other mottes at Lilbourne (2) and at Preston Capes (1) which seem to control roads or river crossings as well as protecting adjacent settlements. Two other earthworks are possibly mottes, though this is uncertain. The mound at Little Preston (Preston Capes (3)) is damaged but seems to have been surrounded by a deep defensive ditch. It is in a strong tactical position but may be only a manor-house site. The so-called castle at Barby (2) is also well sited and strongly defended but can hardly be described as a true motte.

The ring and bailey at Long Buckby (8) is of interest for a number of reasons. Its position indicates that it protected not the present village but an earlier one on a different site. It is unusual in that it has a ring-work instead of the normal motte, and there is a possibility that it once had two baileys. In addition a small excavation has suggested late Saxon occupation on the site pre-dating the construction of the castle.

Of all the mottes in this area only the one at Preston Capes (1) can be dated; a document makes it clear that a castle was in existence by 1090.

Monastic Sites

Six monuments directly associated with religious houses are recorded in the Inventory. Two of them, the now destroyed moated site at Badby (3) and the finely preserved one at Cottesbrooke (4), are merely outlying grange farms of major houses. The only earthwork remains of Daventry Priory are the fishponds (Daventry (30)). Some fragmentary earthworks survive of the priory at Canons Ashby (2), but the best-preserved earthworks on the site appear to be the remains of a post-Dissolution garden and are probably not of monastic date as hitherto supposed. There is great potential for future excavation, however, including the greater part of the priory church. The small priory at Catesby (4) has left few surface remains, again because a large house and its gardens were later constructed on the site. These gardens, now reduced to earthworks, include a feature sometimes described as a moat and other remains which have been attributed to the priory but in fact only a group of ponds, some of which were altered in post-medieval times, are definitely associated with the priory. The most important monastic site is that of Sulby Abbey (Sulby (2)). The history of this house is well documented and the earthworks of the church and conventual buildings as well as fishponds, rabbit warrens, a mill site, paddocks and tracks are almost completely preserved in permanent pasture.

Deer Parks

A small number of deer parks have been identified in the area. The best example is at Badby (6); this is well documented, and its boundaries are almost completely preserved. The deer park at Little

1

Preston (Preston Capes (4)) is less complete but is of special interest because the abandoned remains of the hamlet of Little Preston overlie one section of the park pale. The deer park at Holdenby (5) was a very late one, created in the 1580s by Sir Christopher Hatton as part of the large-scale reorganization of the parish at that time. The Badby park has no ridge-and-furrow in it. At Preston Capes there is no indication as to whether surviving furlongs pre-date or post-date the park but at Holdenby the park was laid out across the former common fields of the parish and there is extensive ridge-and-furrow within it.

Fishponds

In north-west Northamptonshire there are many fishponds, dating mainly from the medieval period. Not all have been described in the Inventory in detail and several which may be medieval in origin but have been radically altered in recent times have been omitted. The ponds which have been recorded can be assigned to four of the types described in detail in an earlier volume, A, B, C, F; no examples of types D, E, or G have been recognised (RCHM *Northants.*, II (1979), p. lvii).

Type A. These ponds are formed by the construction of a simple earthen dam across a steep-sided valley. Examples are to be seen at Canons Ashby (4), though later alterations have taken place, at Catesby (4) where the ponds appear to be monastic in origin, at Creaton (10), Elkington (6) and Little Oxendon (Great Oxendon (9)), all within deserted villages, and at Sulby Abbey (Sulby (2)) where the main fishpond is of this type. A late example at Holdenby (3) was constructed in the 1580s.

Type B. Ponds in this category are formed by the construction of a dam as in Type A but in addition large quantities of material are removed to make them deep and flat-bottomed. They are characterised by steep artificial scarps along their sides where the valley slopes have been steepened or cut away. This type is well demonstrated at the deserted village of Braunstonbury (Braunston (2)), at Daventry (30) where the ponds belonged to Daventry Priory, at Lamport (9) and at Welford (15).

Type C. These ponds are set on valley sides and have dams on one of the long sides formed by spoil cut out of the hillside. This type was filled either by being built on a spring-line as at Dodford (2) or by means of an inlet channel carrying water to the pond from higher up the valley (Maidwell (15)).

Type F. These are small rectangular ponds, usually in groups. They were commonly called stews and were probably used for intensive fish-breeding. The best of these are at Sulby Abbey (Sulby (2)).

One of the most interesting aspects of many medieval fishponds is the great skill in large-scale hydraulic engineering which they reveal. Even some of the smaller fishponds show this, as at Maidwell (15) where water from a very large pond passed along a carefully graded high-level leat into another smaller pond set on the valley side. Other examples may be seen at Welford (15) where an inlet channel brought water from an adjacent stream to a large fishpond, and surplus water was carried round the pond in another channel and returned to the stream. The most complicated systems are those at Charwelton (2) and Sulby (2). At Charwelton at least two stages of development are visible, one of which appears to be later than the abandonment of Church Charwelton village (Charwelton (1)). At one stage water taken from the River Cherwell passed through a series of ponds and returned to the river. The later stage involved the construction of a leat some 500 m. long to carry water to another group of ponds at a higher level than the earlier ones. At Sulby (2) the monastic ponds represent a major feat of engineering. The River Avon appears to have been diverted along the valley side, passing at one point through a deep cutting, to feed a series of fish stews and probably also a watermill. Other ponds were set above the diverted river on a spring-line and a large dammed pond in the old river valley was also connected to the system.

The existence of islands in fishponds noted in the second Inventory (RCHM *Northants.*, II (1979), p. lix), has again been recognised. One of the ponds at Preston Capes (5) has a narrow elongated island within it, which certainly remained well above water level when the pond was full; the rectangular island in the pond at Welford (15) is similar. On the other hand the roughly circular islands at Maidwell (14) are only a few centimetres high and must have always been well below the water.

Watermills

In north-west Northamptonshire watermills have always been common; more than a hundred are documented for the region. Many survive as standing structures and are not included in this Inventory. Only those watermills which appear to have been abandoned at an early date or where the remaining earthworks are of exceptional interest have been described. These include the remains at Murcott (Long Buckby (5)), Little Oxendon (Great Oxendon (9)), Sulby Abbey (Sulby (2)) and Yelvertoft (4).

Windmills

As with watermills there are numerous documented windmills in the area and many are still marked on 19th-century Ordnance Survey, Tithe and Enclosure Maps. The inclusion of the mounds, which often remain after demolition, has been selective in the Inventory. Almost all are simple mounds with or without surrounding ditches, and the finest are those of an early date. There are good examples at Canons Ashby (6) Preston Capes (8), Thornby (4), Great Oxendon (8) and Charwelton (6).

CULTIVATION REMAINS
Ridge-and-furrow in Open Fields

In spite of modern arable farming, large areas of ridge-and-furrow remain intact, and air photographs often reveal the pattern of furlongs where it can no longer be seen on the ground. There is no doubt that in the medieval period some form of ridge-and-furrow cultivation existed throughout the area, in every land-unit associated with a major settlement. In the parish of Flore, for example, both Flore itself and the now deserted village of Glassthorpe (4) each had its own field system.

As in the two previous Inventories, examination of ridge-and-furrow on the ground or on air photographs has shown that at various times cultivation was more widespread than the surviving maps indicate. In many places the whole of the land-unit of each village appears to have been cultivated in ridge-and-furrow at some date except for small areas of meadow along streams (e.g. Naseby (5) and Welton (5)). At least one medieval deer park (Preston Capes (4)) has ridge-and-furrow within its boundaries, although the date of cultivation is unknown. Elsewhere areas which immediately before enclosure in the 18th or 19th century were permanent pasture or the waste limits of a group of parishes, have extensive areas of ridge-and-furrow. At Long Buckby (9), land in the E. of the parish known as North Heath Common and Thorney Heath Common in 1765 is almost completely covered with ridge-and-furrow; at Newnham (5) Langhill Common and Burnt Walls Common, so named in 1765, have ridge-and-furrow over them. In other places, however, there were large areas which were either always waste or cultivated by methods other than ridge-and-furrow. This is particularly true of parishes in the S.W. of the area where much land is on extremely steep slopes which were impossible to cultivate, as in Staverton (3) and Barby (4). Near Little Preston (Preston Capes (2)) the hillside, though not abnormally steep, has never been cultivated, apparently because of the unstable nature of the underlying clay which has collapsed in a series of landslips. Elsewhere there seem to be areas which have never been ploughed, simply because other land was available. The N. side of Fawsley parish illustrates this well, for there is a large area on a gentle slope with no trace of cultivation of any date. In a few places, for example at Barby (4), there are small pieces of land which seem to have been brought into cultivation as hedged fields; no ridge-and-furrow exists within them.

Very few maps survive to show the layout of the former common fields and only one, of Brixworth (1688), depicts the individual strips. Nevertheless there is no reason to doubt the accepted view that the surviving ridge-and-furrow usually represents individual strips, lands or selions made up of groups of ridges but with no physical demarcation.

Enclosure of the common fields was carried out over a long period. Some small-scale enclosure undoubtedly took place in medieval times, perhaps as early as the 14th or 15th century in some places where the date of enclosure is unrecorded. These villages include Onley (Barby (4)), Braunstonbury (Braunston (7)), Cold Ashby (4), Little Creaton (Creaton (11)), Kelmarsh (18), Little Preston (Preston Capes (10)), Coton (Ravensthorpe (10)), Draughton (14) and Hanging Houghton (Lamport (19)). Most of these settlements are either completely deserted or very small. Evidence of early enclosure on a limited scale is also recorded at Chapel Brampton (14) where it took place before 1584. In addition 15th-century enclosure probably occurred at Sulby (5), Althorp (3), Catesby (8), Newbold (Catesby (8)), Glassthorpe (Flore (6)) and Muscott (Norton (16)). The enclosure of Thrupp (Norton (16)) is firmly dated to 1489. All these villages are also now deserted.

Enclosure is known to have taken place in the 16th century at the following places: Canons Ashby (7), 1539–47; Haselbech (4), 1599; Holdenby (7), 1584–7; Teeton (Hollowell (7)), 1590. Other parishes probably enclosed in the 16th century are Fawsley (8), Elkington (7), Snorscomb (Everdon (6)) and Stanford (7), though all of these could be earlier. Once more, deserted or shrunken villages predominate in this list.

During the 17th century there was a gradual but steady process of enclosure. Part of East Haddon (3) was enclosed between 1598 and 1607, Cottesbrook (7) in the early 17th century, Brockhall (2) in about 1619, Dodford (3) in 1623, Sibbertoft (3) in 1650, Preston Capes (10) in 1659, Clay Coton (3) in 1663, part of Watford (6) in 1664, Lilbourne (6) in 1680, Stowe-Nine-Churches (12) in the late 17th century and Maidwell (16) in the late 17th or early 18th century. All these enclosures were carried out by agreement between major landowners and though some of the villages were large, e.g. Lilbourne and Preston Capes, others, e.g. Clay Coton and Watford, were much reduced in size by then. The first half of the 18th century saw little enclosure and it was not until the 1740s that the movement towards parliamentary enclosure began. In that decade both Brington (5) and Faxton (Lamport (19)) were enclosed. Thereafter parliamentary enclosure became common.

In the 1750s seven parishes were enclosed, Drayton (Daventry (34)), Farthingstone (6), Norton (16), Welton (5), Pitsford (8) and Hinton and Woodford (Woodford-cum-Membris (3)), followed by eleven parishes in the 1760s, West Farndon (Woodford-cum-Membris (3)), Everdon (6), Ashby St. Ledgers (7), Guilsborough (8), Spratton (15), West Haddon (3), Newnham (5), Harlestone (13), Long Buckby (9), Arthingworth (6) and Great Oxendon (10).

The 1780s were the years of the greatest number of formal Enclosure Acts; eighteen villages lost their common fields, Watford (6), Murcott (Watford (6)), East Haddon (3), Hellidon (2), Staverton (3), Scaldwell (3), Yelvertoft (5), Braunston (7), Clipston (8), Crick (10), Welford (17), Weedon Bec (3), Kilsby (5), Barby (4), Byfield (5), Flore (6), Whilton (3) and Badby (8). The process then slowed down and between 1780 and 1802 only six parishes or parts of parishes were enclosed, Brixworth (42), East Farndon (7), Creaton (11), Lamport (19), Ravensthorpe (10) and Daventry (34). The enclosure of Marston Trussell (10) in 1813 and Naseby (5) in 1820 saw the end of the process in the area.

Analysis of the ridge-and-furrow associated with the common fields in this area has not led to any new conclusions (RCHM *Northants.*, II (1979), p. lxi). The relationship between the natural configuration of the ground and the arrangement both of the shape of the furlongs and of the direction of the ridges sometimes causes striking patterns, but no new information on the origins and evolution of the fields has come to light. Such new evidence as has been recorded tends to show how little understood are the agricultural techniques used to produce ridge-and-furrow. Many minor details still defy explanation; for example in the N.W. of the area, especially in Kilsby (5), there are extensive areas of ridge-and-furrow of normal form but with a low narrow ridge set in each furrow between the main ridges (Fig. 88). One possible explanation is that it represents an attempt to increase the amount of grassland available. In Brixworth and in Wollaston in the S.E. of the county 17th-century documentary evidence shows that farmers were advised to leave grass strips between ridges so that tethered animals could graze on them (D. N. Hall, *Wollaston* (1977), 150), but whether this explains the large areas of ridge-and-furrow of this unusual form is not certain. Another detail difficult to interpret is the occurrence of high, rectangular mounds at the ends of ridges. Small rounded mounds on the ends of ridges are common throughout the English Midlands and have been explained as the spoil from the cleaning out of adjacent furrows for drainage or accumulated material removed from plough shares, the deposited spoil being reploughed to reduce the mounds. However the rectangular mounds at Brington (5) are so large and neat that it is difficult to see how they could have been either formed or ploughed over.

The detailed examination of ridge-and-furrow has continued to reveal not only the complexity of the agricultural techniques used but also their flexibility. A minor example at Watford (6) (Plate 21) shows this well. A later track cuts across a block of ridge-and-furrow, and mounds have subsequently been formed at the ends of the ridges on either side of the track. Sets of double and even triple mounds on the ends of furlongs in the same area are puzzling and not understood. Double headlands perhaps indicating a shortening of furlongs occur at Crick (10), where there is also evidence of the overploughing of apparently early quarry pits with ridge-and-furrow. Similar overploughed quarry pits have been noted at Great Oxendon (10). Also unusual are the circular areas of flattened ridge-and-furrow which occur at Brixworth (42). These can be identified as the places where ricks were shown on a 17th-century map of the parish. The parish was not enclosed until 1780 and the rick-stands were perhaps a permanent feature of the field system.

Ridge-and-furrow in 'Old Enclosures'

As in previous Inventories, ridge-and-furrow has been noted in many fields described on 19th-century or earlier maps as 'old enclosures'. Perhaps the most interesting aspect of ridge-and-furrow of this type is its occurrence over the remains of abandoned settlements. At the deserted villages of Nobold (Clipston (6)), Glassthorpe (Flore (4)), Onley (Barby (1)), Sulby (3), Little Oxendon (Great Oxendon (9)), Upper Catesby (Catesby (2)), Hothorpe and Thorpe Lubenham (Marston Trussell (9) and (8)) and at some shrunken or moved villages such as Winwick (1) the whole area or large parts of the earthworks have been overploughed with ridge-and-furrow. Unfortunately it is difficult to assign this ploughing to a particular date, but it appears to be of two different types, probably of different periods. Fine narrow-rig ploughing 2 m.–3 m. wide of a type usually dated to the late 18th or early 19th century lies over part of the deserted village of Onley (Barby (1)). This is very different from the ridges 5 m.–7 m. wide over most of the settlement sites. An example of the difficulty of dating this ridge-and-furrow may be seen at Glassthorpe (Flore (4)). The site is largely overploughed in broad ridge-and-furrow, but is now under pasture and has been so, according to local knowledge, for at least a century. It was certainly pasture in the mid 19th century according to the Tithe Map and also in 1758 from other cartographic evidence. In the early 18th century Bridges implied that it was a sheep-walk and sheep were grazed there in considerable numbers in the mid 16th century. The date of the final desertion of the village is not known with certainty but it appears to have been after the late 14th century. Thus the most likely periods for the ploughing to have taken place at Glassthorpe were either the 15th or the 17th century. However it is unlikely on general economic grounds to have been in the 15th century when the abandonment of arable land was common, and a 17th-century date is therefore more probable. Support for this is forthcoming from Sulby where the abandonment of the village for sheep certainly occurred between 1377 and 1428 and where sheep remained important until after the mid 16th century.

The 17th century might well be the period when this ploughing was done and a possible explanation is that pasture was broken up either for a rotation system of long leys or for the production of specialized crops such as woad or flax. Apart from these possibilities, this interesting if minor aspect of agricultural history is undated and unexplained.

Narrow Ridge-and-furrow

This part of Northamptonshire has cultivation remains of a type not seen in the areas previously described. Narrow ridge-and-furrow usually known as narrow-rig has been recognised. It is thought to be relatively recent, probably of late 18th or early 19th-century date. At Onley (Barby (1)) narrow-rig lies over part of the deserted village and from its appearance would seem to be comparatively recent. At Lamport (19) it clearly overlies medieval ploughing for the earlier headlands are still visible on the ground. Narrow ridge-and-furrow also exists at Crick (10), and at Sulby (2) where the whole of the former monastic fishpond is covered by such cultivation remains.

POST-MEDIEVAL EARTHWORKS
Fortifications

The Battle of Naseby of 1645 has prompted traditions concerning 17th-century fortifications in the N. part of the area under review. However nothing has been discovered that can be assigned to the battle or to events leading up to it, apart from the grave recorded at Sulby (4). A site at Kelmarsh (16) was excavated and published as a Civil War sconce but is much more likely to have been a medieval fishpond. The only certain post-medieval fortification is the unusual redoubt at Weedon Bec (2) which was probably built in the early 19th century, perhaps as a training exercise by troops stationed at Weedon Barracks.

Garden Remains

The remains of gardens, often elaborate, associated with great houses have continued to be discovered. Those listed in the Inventory cover a variety of garden designs from the mid 16th to the 18th century. The earliest is that at Canons Ashby (2) which though usually said to be of monastic origin appears to be immediately post-Dissolution in date. The site has been largely destroyed but enough remains for the general outline to be reconstructed. The next in date are probably the gardens at Holdenby (4), among the finest in the county, laid out by Sir Christopher Hatton in the 1580s. The great terraces and ponds and even some of the flower-beds are well preserved. An extension to the original garden, perhaps of the early 17th century, includes an elaborate series of sloping terraces, forming a zigzag path. The gardens at Catesby (4), which consist of impressive terraces and ponds, are also likely to be early 17th century, and at Arthingworth (4), Fawsley (1), Lamport (12) and Hanging Houghton (Lamport (13)) are other definite or assumed 17th-century remains. The garden at Cottesbrooke (6) was of very different character and apparently of the early 18th century. The original layout at Watford (5) is also of the 18th century, though considerable later alterations have taken place there. Other earthworks connected with gardens or emparking have been noted at Althorp (2), Canons Ashby (5), Draughton (11) and Haselbech (3).

Undated Earthworks

Without excavation the purpose and date of a number of monuments in the Inventory must remain speculative. The most important of these is the earthwork known as Burnt Walls (Daventry (35)). This site has an obvious defensive function and may be pre-medieval, but its unusual form and position prevent any precise date being given to it. The enclosures on Borough Hill (Daventry (3) and

Norton (17)) are also of unknown purpose, and their almost total destruction makes any future understanding of them unlikely.

Miscellaneous Earthworks

As in previous volumes earthworks resulting from medieval and later woodland management and 19th-century ironstone tramways have been omitted from the Inventory for the reasons stated (RCHM *Northants.*, II (1979), p. lxv). Such remains would well repay detailed study for they illustrate two important aspects of Northamptonshire's history. Earthworks associated with the canals and early railways of the county have also been omitted.

TOTAL LANDSCAPES

The Inventory is, by definition, a detailed list of individual monuments. Many are of considerable historical or archaeological interest, even when viewed in isolation, but all are part of the history of a slowly evolving landscape and should always be regarded as such. It is often difficult to appreciate relationships between individual sites, whether contemporary or of different date. In the area covered by the present Inventory, however, two parishes stand out as excellent examples of the total historic landscape. The first is Holdenby, which is remarkable in that its medieval pattern, with two villages, was entirely reorganized in the space of a decade by Sir Christopher Hatton in the 1580s. The villages were removed and replaced by a single village, the fields enclosed, a deer park constructed and an elaborate garden laid out around the new house. Though many of the surviving remains have been damaged the parish is a clear example of a complete and dated change of landscape. At Fawsley, on the other hand, most of the parish has been preserved by the 18th-century park so that earlier landscapes including two medieval villages and their fields, areas of pasture and waste as well as part of a deer park and other medieval and post-medieval features have survived. These historic landscapes are particularly worthy of conservation.

AN INVENTORY OF
THE ARCHAEOLOGICAL MONUMENTS
IN NORTH-WEST NORTHAMPTONSHIRE
Arranged alphabetically by Parishes

1 ALTHORP

(OS 1:10000 ^a SP 66 NE, ^b SP 66 SE)

The small parish, covering only 330 hectares, lies mainly on Jurassic Clay between 85 m. and 125 m. above OD but the higher S.E. corner is on Northampton Sand and part of the W. is overlaid by glacial sands and gravels. In medieval times Althorp was part of Brington parish and the greater part of the present parish is occupied by the landscaped park of Althorp House, the home of the Spencer family since the early 16th century. The probable site of the medieval village of Althorp (1) has been suggested and other features of interest are the extensive earthworks associated with the various stages of landscaping the park (2).

MEDIEVAL AND LATER

^b(1) DESERTED VILLAGE OF ALTHORP (SP 678648; Fig. 15), probably lay on the S.W. side of the park immediately E. of West Lodge, on Jurassic Clay and Northampton Sand, on land sloping N. between 120 m. and 100 m. above OD. These remains cannot be positively identified as the site of Althorp but it seems likely that they are.

The village is first noted in Domesday Book with a recorded population of ten (VCH *Northants.*, I (1902), 323, 337). Twenty people paid the Lay subsidy of 1301 (PRO, E179/155/31) and 21 people that of 1327 (M. W. Beresford, *The Lost Villages of England* (1954), 369). Fifty people over the age of 14 paid the Poll Tax in 1377 (PRO, E179/155/28). In the 15th century the manor was held by the Catesby family who probably cleared the village for in 1505 no tenants appear to have lived there. In 1508 the parish was sold to John Spencer of Wormleighton, Warwickshire, and by 1577 most of the land was divided into four great sheep pastures (K. J. Allison *et al.*, *The Deserted Villages of Northants.* (1966), 34).

The surviving earthworks have been damaged by later activities, but the main feature is a very broad hollow-way some 1.5 m. deep which runs up the hillside. As it reaches the hilltop it becomes a wide terrace-way which can be traced in a broad curve as far as the edge of the park. On the S. side of the hollow-way, near its N.W. end, are several platforms bounded by scarps, perhaps the sites of former buildings, with ridge-and-furrow beyond. To the N.E. of the hollow-way are some very slight features forming no coherent pattern but which may also be sites of buildings. A later avenue has been planted along the line of the hollow-way and some of the trees have been set in large mounds (RAF VAP CPE/UK/1994, 4368–9).

^{ab}(2) GARDEN REMAINS (centred SP 681651), lie around Althorp House, in the park. Although the Spencers acquired the estate in 1508 the first house was probably not built there until later in the 16th century. Little is known about this house and nothing about its surroundings. In the 1660s Robert Spencer, 2nd Earl of Sunderland, remodelled the house and employed the celebrated Le Notre to lay out the park and gardens. This work was drawn by Kip (*Britannia Illustrata* (1709)) who showed the house with a broad rectangular courtyard on the main S. front. To the E., terraces led down into a formal walled garden divided into rectangles planted with flower-beds and lawns. Beyond the house to the N. and S. tree-lined avenues extended to the limits of the park; elsewhere there were plantations and radiating avenues. Alterations were probably made to the park in the 1730s, in the early 19th century and in the 1860s; at some time the enclosed gardens and the rigidly formal plantations were removed and a more informal landscape was created. A number of date-stones between 1567 and 1901 commemorating tree planting exist in the park. The estate papers, if they become accessible, may show further details. Some earthworks associated with either the 17th century or the later work survive in the park though no trace of the formal walled gardens or terraces exists. For example S. of the house, parallel to and S.W. of the existing avenue (SP 682649), there is a large scarp 2.5 m. high and almost 200 m. long. This has been created by cutting away the lower slopes of the hillside in order to procure an open view from the house. Within the same avenue the medieval ridge-and-furrow has been carefully flattened and a raised walk or carriage-way, 6 m. wide and 0.25 m. high, has been laid out down the centre. In two wide rectangular areas to the S.W. and N.W. of the house (SP 678650 and 681653) the pre-existing ridge-and-furrow has also been removed though the latter survives over much of the rest of the park. Just S.W. of the stables (SP 681649) there is a semi-circular feature 40 m. across and 2 m. deep, cut back into the hillside (RAF VAP CPE/UK/1994, 4368–9).

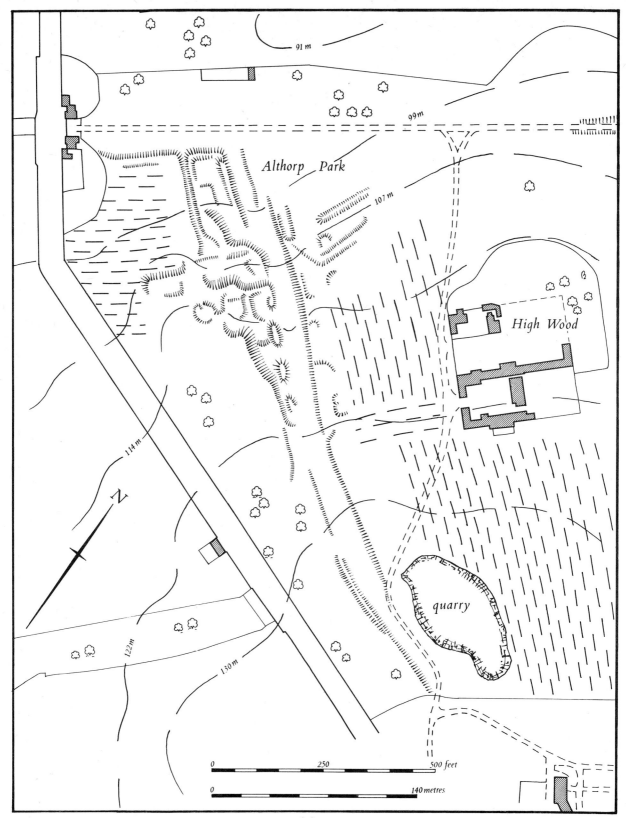

Fig. 15   ALTHORP   (1) Deserted village of Althorp

(3) CULTIVATION REMAINS. The enclosure of the common fields of Althorp took place at an unknown date, but presumably in the 15th century when the village (1) was finally removed. Ridge-and-furrow of these fields remains on the ground or can be traced on air photographs over much of the parish, arranged in interlocked furlongs, many of reversed-S form. It is particularly well preserved in Althorp Park where there are extensive areas of almost complete ridge-and-furrow (RAF VAP CPE/UK/1994, 2254–7, 4367–70).

2 ARTHINGWORTH

(OS 1:10000 ᵃ SP 78 SW, ᵇ SP 78 SE)

The parish, covering some 700 hectares, lies across the upper reaches of the R. Ise here flowing E. between 150 m. and 105 m. above OD. Most of the land is on Upper Lias Clay though this is overlaid by Boulder Clay along the N. boundary and there are small patches of glacial sands and gravels elsewhere. To the W. of the village the river flows across extensive areas of gravel. Little of archaeological note is recorded from the parish though the settlement remains (4) suggest that a major change in the village plan has occurred.

PREHISTORIC AND ROMAN

A bronze palstave (NM; Plate 22) and a Roman silver coin of Julia Domna were both found in the parish before 1904 (T. J. George, *Arch. Survey of Northants.* (1904), 10).

ᵇ(1) ENCLOSURE AND DITCHES (SP 762818), N.E. of the village on clay at 120 m. above OD. Air photographs (not seen by RCHM) are said to show cropmarks of a rectangular enclosure and ditches. A fragment of a quern, thought to be medieval, has been found nearby (at SP 762817; *BNFAS*, 5 (1971), 42, 44).

ᵇ(2) ROMAN SETTLEMENT (SP 756816; Fig. 12), immediately E. of Arthingworth manor house, on glacial sands and gravels at 120 m. above OD. In the gardens below the house large quantities of Roman pottery, mainly of 2nd and 3rd-century Nene Valley types, have been found.

MEDIEVAL AND LATER

ᵇ(3) ENCLOSURES (SP 755819), immediately N. of the village, on limestone at 125 m. above OD. Two rectangular enclosures are said to have been noted here in 1968. Pottery of the 12th and 13th centuries, part of a medieval hone and two flint scrapers were later found on the site (*BNFAS*, 4 (1970), 15). However, on air photographs taken in 1947 (RAF VAP CPE/UK/2109, 3286–7) the area is shown covered with ridge-and-furrow.

ᵇ(4) SETTLEMENT REMAINS, MOAT AND (?) GARDEN REMAINS (centred SP 756815; Figs. 12 and 16), lie of a S.E.-facing slope E. and N.E. of the church and S.E. of the manor house on Boulder Clay, glacial sand and Upper Lias Clay, between 122 m. and 110 m. above OD.

Apart from the *Moat* ('a' on plan) it is not entirely clear what the surviving earthworks represent. Although the main area ('b' on plan) N. of the moat appears to be the site of a garden, it is possible that some of the extant earthworks represent former medieval settlement. These are perhaps the result of movement rather than shrinkage as there is no indication in the surviving records of a marked drop in population of the village at any time. Domesday Book (VCH *Northants.*, I (1902), 306, 318, 322) gives a total recorded population of 20. By the early 18th century there were 45 families in the village (J. Bridges, *Hist. of Northants.*, II (1791), 2). In 1801, 207 people lived in the parish. The indeterminate earthworks S. of the moat ('c' on plan) may be the remains of former houses, and the uneven ground between Home Farm and the Church on the N.E. side of Main Street may mark the position of other structures. To the N.E. of the moat and E. of the manor house a hollow-way ('d' on plan) up to 2.5 m. deep extends down the hillside. It is blocked at the W. end, perhaps indicating its re-use as a quarry, but appears once to have run on further W. Its alignment is continued to the W. of the manor house by a lane which meets the end of Main Street; it may have been an original through-road of the village.

The *Moat* ('a' on plan) is damaged but consists of a broad ditch, up to 2 m. deep on the W. but only 1 m. deep on the N. and E., surrounding a square level island. The S. side is occupied by a modern pond. The site is probably that of the medieval manor house of Arthingworth. Immediately to the N. ('b' on plan) is a series of low scarps and banks, nowhere above 0.5 m. high, forming a rigidly rectangular layout; former N. and W. extensions have been destroyed by later activity. The purpose of the site is unknown but it may be the remains of a formal garden of the late 16th or 17th century associated with the manor house. If this interpretation is correct the remains may represent the work of the Catesby family who held Arthingworth from the late 15th century until the late 16th century, or, more probably, of their successors the Stanhopes or Langhams (Bridges, op. cit., 2–3; RAF VAP CPE/UK/2109, 3286–7).

ᵇ(5) FISHPONDS (SP 752812 and 753811; Fig. 16), lie S. and S.W. of the village on either side of the Kelmarsh Road, along the R. Ise on Upper Lias Clay at 105 m. above OD. There are three ponds N. of the river and parallel with it. The westernmost is roughly rectangular, cut back into the rising ground to the N.E. with an outer retaining bank 1.5 m. high between it and the river. To the S.E. is a smaller but similar pond of which the outer bank is up to 1.75 m. high. Further S.E. again is a long narrow pond, now dry and only 0.5 m. deep, with a rounded W. end and a low bank along the S. side and on the W. To the N.W. are several low banks and scarps of unknown date and

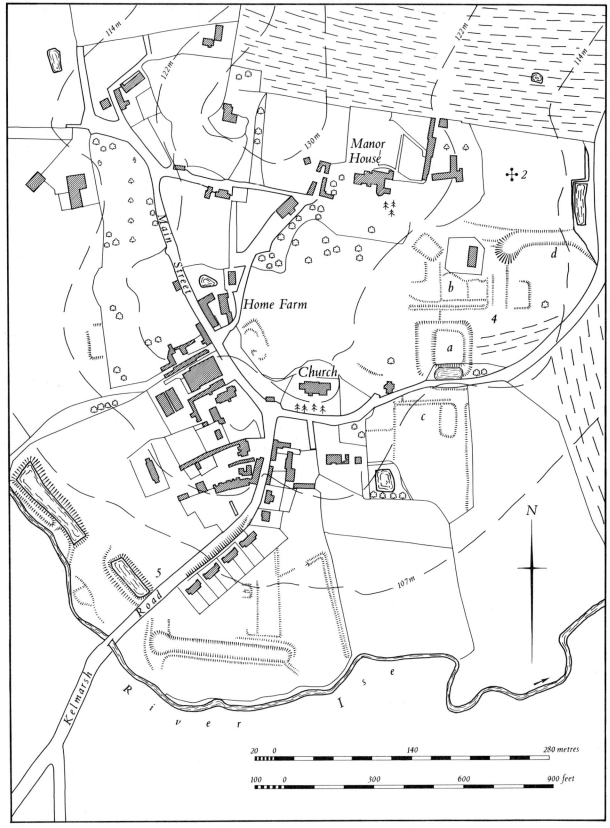

Fig. 16 ARTHINGWORTH (2) Roman settlement, (4) Medieval settlement remains, moat and garden remains, (5) Fishponds

purpose. This area was known as Townsend Close in 1851 (NRO, Tithe Map). Two of the ponds have outlet channels, but no inlet channels are visible and all three were presumably filled by seepage (RAF VAP CPE/UK/2109, 3286).

(6) CULTIVATION REMAINS. The common fields of the parish were enclosed by an Act of Parliament of 1767, though no Enclosure Map survives. Very little ridge-and-furrow of these fields exists on the ground as most of the parish is under permanent arable but the little that can be traced appears to be arranged in rectangular furlongs of reversed-S or C form arranged so that the ridges run across the contours. Though little ridge-and-furrow remains a number of former headlands between furlongs can be traced as low ridges up to 20 m. across and 0.25 m. high (e.g. SP 756817). Complete cover of vertical air photographs has not been available to the Commission (RAF VAP 106G/UK/636, 3123–7; CPE/UK/2109, 3286–9).

3   ASHBY ST. LEDGERS

(OS 1:10000 SP 56 NE)

The parish lies W. of Watling Street (A5) which forms a short part of its E. boundary; it occupies some 854 hectares of land lying across the valleys of three small E.-flowing streams between 130 m. and 175 m. above OD. Almost the whole area is covered by glacial deposits, including much sand and gravel, and only in the N.E. corner is the underlying Jurassic Clay exposed. The village lies across the central stream. The settlement remains (2) which lie to the W. of the village are so extensive as to suggest that at least in later medieval times its location and shape were fundamentally different.

PREHISTORIC AND ROMAN

A Roman silver coin of Faustina was found 'in Legers-Ashby Field' sometime before 1712 (J. Morton, *Nat. Hist. of Northants.* (1712), 532).

(1) ENCLOSURE (SP 592681), in the E. of the parish, on glacial sands and gravels at 133 m. above OD. Air photographs (not seen by RCHM) are said to show a small enclosure and a 'field' (*Northants. Archaeol.*, 12 (1977), 228).

(2) ROMAN SETTLEMENT (SP 570684; Fig. 17), on the N. side of the village above a small E.-flowing stream, on glacial gravel at 132 m. above OD. A quantity of pottery, mainly thin grey ware probably of 2nd or 3rd-century date but also including some earlier material and pieces of tile, has been found.

MEDIEVAL AND LATER

(3) SETTLEMENT REMAINS (centred, SP 567683; Figs. 12 and 17), formerly part of Ashby St. Ledgers, lie on both sides of a small E.-flowing stream at the W. end of the

village around Reynold's Farm, on glacial sands and clays between 132 m. and 145 m. above OD.

Ashby is first documented in Domesday Book with a recorded population of 24 (VCH *Northants.*, I (1902), 330). In 1377, 81 people paid the Poll Tax (PRO, E179/155/28), in 1673, 52 people are listed in the Hearth Tax Returns (PRO, E179/254/14) and in the early 18th century Bridges (*Hist. of Northants.*, II (1791), 14) said there were 50 houses in the village. By 1801 there were 232 inhabitants of the parish. These admittedly inadequate figures do not indicate any marked fall in the population of the village at any time and the remaining earthworks may thus be the result of movement rather than shrinkage. Evidently the village had in the past a layout very different from its present one, but the date at which the change took place is not known. By the 18th century it was already forgotten for Stukeley recorded that 'At Legers Ashby ... has been another old town, as they say, destroyed by the Danes; there are great ditches, causeways and marks of streets' (W. Stukeley, *Itinerarium Curiosum*, I (1776), 113). However part of the abandoned area was occupied or at least in use in the early 19th century (1st ed. OS 1 in. map (1834)). Some of the earthworks have been interpreted as the site of a manor house (Whellan, *Dir.*, 381), but this is uncertain.

The main though not the most obvious feature of the site is an old street, now a hollow-way extending from the main Kilsby-Daventry road on the W. to the sharp bend in the Ashby-Crick road, N. of the church, on the E. ('a'–'b' on plan). It coincides with the existing stream and, apart from a short length on the S. side of Reynold's Farm which is still in use, is now nothing more than a steep-sided wide stream bed. In the early 19th century, however, it was still a through road (1st ed. OS 1 in. map (1834)). On either side of this hollow-way are other features connected with it. At the W. end, two roughly parallel hollow-ways extend N. from it then join and fork again. One runs N.W. and, after crossing the Kilsby-Daventry road, can be traced as a broad access-way through the adjacent ridge-and-furrow heading towards Barby. The other runs N. and meets the existing road to Kilsby. Between the two roads is a disturbed area of ground in which stands a low circular mound with a slight depression within it, perhaps the site of a dove-cot ('c' on plan).

To the E., between the E. hollow-way and Reynold's Farm, are at least three rectangular closes ('d' on plan), separated by low banks and ditches and bounded on the N. by a well-marked bank and outer ditch beyond which is ridge-and-furrow. The interior of these closes is much disturbed by later gravel pits, but traces of former buildings exist at their S. ends, and massive stone-rubble foundations are exposed in the side of the stream and hollow-way. In addition, pottery, mainly post-medieval but including some of the 14th and 15th centuries, has been found here. To the S. of the stream and S.W. of Reynold's Farm are other earthworks ('e' on plan); these are more indeterminate but enough remains to indicate that

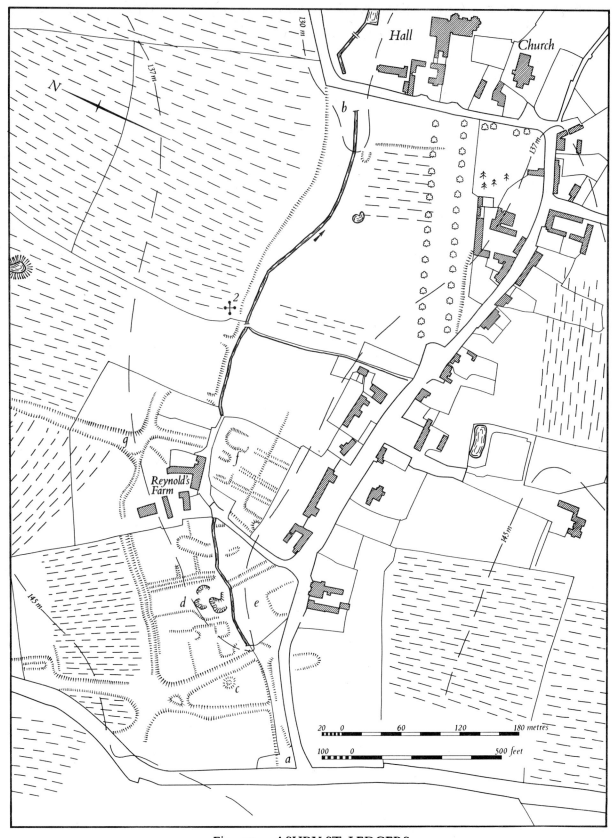

Fig. 17 ASHBY ST. LEDGERS

(2) Roman settlement,   (3) Medieval settlement remains,   (7) Cultivation remains

buildings also once stood here. Further E., immediately S. of the farm and E. of the present road to it, is another field containing earthworks of a series of closes with house-sites at their N. ends ('f' on plan). In the early 19th century there were still some buildings at the W. end of this field along the road to the farm (1st ed. OS 1 in. map (1834)). Immediately N.E. and E. of Reynold's Farm another hollow-way ('g' on plan) extends N. from the stream between ridge-and-furrow, and other ditches lie to the E. and W. of it.

These earthworks, together with the existing part of the village, suggest that, in the late medieval period at least, the village was Y-shaped in plan with a number of small roads extending from it in various directions (RAF VAP CPE/UK/1994, 2352–4; RAF VAP 2F22 543/RAF/2337, 0381–2; CUAP, AGY 87).

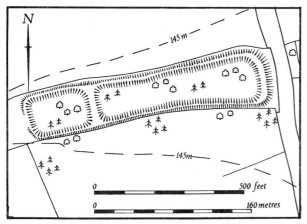

Fig. 18   ASHBY ST. LEDGERS
            (4) Fishponds

(4) FISHPONDS (SP 563691; Fig. 18), occupy the bottom of a small E.-draining valley cut into Boulder Clay, N.W. of the village, at about 145 m. above OD. They consist of two adjoining rectangular embanked ponds up to 2 m. deep and now dry but shown on the 1st ed. OS 1 in. map of 1834 as full of water. On the Tithe Map of 1850 (NRO) the easternmost pond is shown still full of water but as the map does not extend further W. the other pond is not marked.

(5) SITE OF MEDIEVAL BUILDING (?) (SP 564671), on Bragborough Hill in the extreme S. of the parish on Marlstone at 167 m. above OD. Fourteenth-century pottery, both glazed and unglazed, and tile were found during ploughing in 1966 (BNFAS, 3 (1969), 1).

(6) WINDMILL MOUND (SP 57056701), on the S. boundary of the parish, immediately W. of the minor road out of the village. It lay on Marlstone Rock at 165 m. above OD. Although now totally destroyed by ploughing, in 1969 it still consisted of a low, circular, grass-covered mound 0.8 m. high and 15 m. in diam. There was no trace of an outer ditch (OS Record Cards). On the Tithe Map of 1850 (NRO) a windmill is depicted on the site (RAF VAP CPE/UK/1994, 2352–3).

(7) CULTIVATION REMAINS. The common fields of the parish were enclosed by Act of Parliament of 1764 (NRO, Enclosure Map). Ridge-and-furrow of these fields survives on the ground or can be traced on air photographs over almost all of the parish, arranged mainly in interlocked furlongs except along the valley sides where end-on furlongs at right-angles to the contours predominate. Exceptionally well-preserved blocks exist S. and W. of the village (at SP 573675 and 564608). In the latter area broad access-ways extending down the valley sides through the ridge-and-furrow and into the village still remain (see (2); Fig. 17; RAF VAP CPE/UK/1994, 1479–82, 2349–54; 2F22 543/RAF/2337, 0378–84).

4   BADBY

(OS 1:10000 [a] SP 55 NW, [b] SP 55 NE, [c] SP 56 SW, [d] SP 56 SE)

The almost rectangular parish of some 980 hectares is roughly bisected by the upper reaches of the E.-flowing R. Nene. In the extreme N. are three isolated hills, two capped with Northampton Sand rising to well over 180 m. above OD and the centre one overlaid by glacial gravel rising to 165 m. above OD. From there the land slopes gently across Lias Clays to the R. Nene, here flowing at about 120 m. above OD; beyond the river it rises more steeply, still on clay, to a maximum height of just over 180 m. on Badby Down, an E.–W. ridge capped with Northampton Sand. In the extreme S.E. of the parish is another isolated hill known as Arbury Hill which is of strangely rectangular form and has traditionally been said to be the site of an Iron Age hill fort (2); however this is in some doubt as the assumed defences appear to be natural features. The village of Badby lies S. of the Nene on a low rounded clay hill. Its plan is complex and not fully understood (4). Much of the S. part of the parish is occupied by Badby Wood, the site of a medieval deer park (6); its boundary pale is one of the best preserved in the county. A number of minor earthworks on the periphery of the parish have been recorded in detail elsewhere and are not listed below (Northants. Archaeol., 12 (1977), 155–76).

PREHISTORIC AND ROMAN

A Palaeolithic hand-axe has been found in the parish (OS Record Cards; PPS, 29 (1963), 383). A scatter of Roman pottery has been found N. of the village (SP 559598; Northants. Archaeol., 12 (1977), 211).

[b](1) FLINT-WORKING SITE (SP 573580), just outside the S.E. corner of Badby Wood, on Northampton Sand at 165 m. above OD. A large quantity of worked flints and

waste flakes has been found here (local inf.).

a(2) SUPPOSED HILL FORT (SP 541587; Fig. 19), covers some 4 hectares on the summit of Arbury Hill, a flat-topped, steep-sided knoll of Northampton Sand at 217 m. above OD. The site has for a long time been regarded as fortified and indeed was first described as such in an Anglo-Saxon Charter of 944 (BCS 792). There the site is called the 'ealden burh æt Baddanbyrig' and the charter describes the Badby boundary as running along the *dic* to the west of the *burh*. The present name of the site seems relatively modern for it does not appear in the records until 1712 (PN *Northants.*, 13). In 1830 the site was described by G. Baker (*Hist. of Northants.*, I, 258) as having a very high rampart and 'encompassed, except at the entrance on the E. side, by a wide single trench which has been 20 ft. deep, though farming has reduced the bank'. However in 1906 (VCH *Northants.*, II, 401–2) though the scarps on the S. and W. sides were recognised they were not accepted either as of a defensive nature or as of ancient origin. Later investigators also rejected the antiquity of the site and suggested that the banks were caused by soil-creep and that the ditches on the N. and W. were modern drains (*J. Northants. Natur. Hist. Soc. and FC*, 24 (1928), 188). The site has been rejected as an antiquity by the OS and was not accepted for inclusion on the Map of Southern Britain in the Iron Age. It is not now possible to determine whether there was a hill fort here as ploughing of the summit and slopes over a long period has removed most of the evidence, but the features which had the appearance of ramparts were probably natural.

The flat summit is edged by a rounded and much degraded scarp, except in the N.E. corner where a natural gulley gives the appearance of an entrance. Below this upper scarp there is a wide sloping terrace below which the ground falls steeply and this is almost certainly the feature thought of as a ditch. It appears in fact to be the junction between the Northampton Sand and the underlying Upper Lias Clay and to be formed partly from the erosion of the sandstone but also partly as a result of the geomorphological process known as cambering and valley bulging (*Q. J. Geol. Soc. London*, 100 (1944), 1–44). On the E. of each side of the so-called entrance are large irregular mounds, which produce a ditched effect. These are almost certainly the result of landslips from the main scarp, and indeed the origin of the S. mound is visible as a deep indentation in the scarp face above it. Other landslips exist on the hillside, especially N. of the N.E. corner.

No finds have been made on Arbury Hill except for a fragment of a flaked and polished Neolithic flint axe, said to have been found there before 1893 (NM Records; RAF VAP CPE/UK/1994, 1158–9, 1277–8).

MEDIEVAL AND LATER

For Saxon cemetery, sometimes said to be at Badby, see Newnham (2).

b(3) SITE OF MOATED MONASTIC GRANGE OR MANOR HOUSE (SP 562591; Fig. 20), now completely destroyed, lay on the S. side of the R. Nene, N.E. of the village, on low-lying marshy ground at 107 m. above OD. The manor of Badby belonged to the Abbey of Evesham from before the Norman Conquest until the Dissolution.

The site consisted of a small rectangular area of just under 0.5 hectares, bounded by a shallow ditch except on the W. side where there was a small N.-flowing stream. It was fully excavated in 1967–9 and three major periods of construction were identified. In period I (early to mid 13th century) the moat was constructed and a series of stone buildings erected within it, consisting of a stone hall and various detached domestic buildings. A chapel and a chamber were later added, at opposite ends of the hall. In period II (14th century) bakehouses and other structures were built, the hall was altered, the chapel extended and a stable-wing added. In period III (15th to 16th century) most of the buildings except the chapel were demolished and replaced by a group of structures round a courtyard. The moat was enlarged at the same time (G. Baker, *Hist. of Northants.*, I 1822–30), 256; BNFAS, 2 (1967), 21; 3 (1969), 19; 4 (1970), 15; *Med. Arch.*, 12 (1968), 190; 13 (1969), 270; 14 (1970), 191).

To the E. were other earthworks now also destroyed by ploughing (RAF VAP CPE/UK/1994, 1275–6). These included a large embanked paddock N.E. of the moat (at SP563591) and, to the E., a long pond with an embanked N. side orientated E.–W., possibly a mill pond or a fishpond (SP 563590). There were also hollow-ways or tracks crossing the area from the village to the river. On the Enclosure Map of Badby (NRO, 1779) what appear to be the N. and E. sides of a very large moated site with an entrance through the middle of the E. side are shown a little to the N. of the excavated moat. At that time the whole area was known as Court Yard.

b(4) SETTLEMENT REMAINS (centred SP 560589; Figs. 11 and 20), formerly part of Badby village, lie around and between the existing houses, on Middle Lias Clay between 120 m. and 137 m. above OD. They add to the complexity of the village plan which is in any case difficult to interpret.

The S. part of Badby consists of a loop road set on land sloping down to the N. The church with a small triangular green on the E. occupies the highest point, and the loop is divided into two unequal parts by a further lane running N.W. from the green. Outside the loop, on the N.W., is another small green. The N. part of the village, beyond the loop, is built round a large roughly rectangular green. This plan has been explained as a characteristic type of settlement in a forest environment, with the freedom to develop loops and greens unconfined by the limits of the common fields (M. W. Beresford and J. K. S. St Joseph, *Medieval England: An Aerial Survey* (1958), 129). However it seems that the true explanation is more complex, for example the large rectangular green to the N. of the loop with a back lane on the W. might be interpreted as a

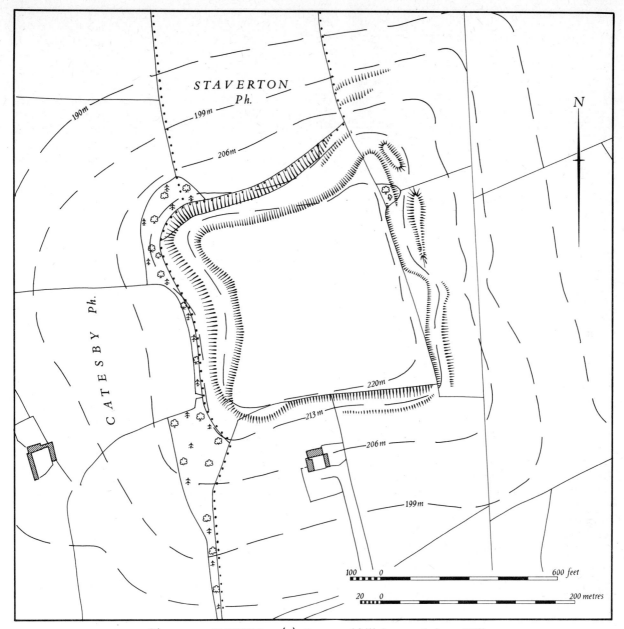

Fig. 19   BADBY   (2) Supposed hill fort on Arbury Hill

deliberately planned extension to the original village (see also Newnham (2)). In addition, on the Enclosure Map of Badby (NRO, 1779) other lanes are shown which have now fallen out of use, especially on the S.W. side of the village.

The earthworks associated with the village fall into two groups. To the N.E. of the church, within the N.E. half of the area contained by the loop road ('a' on plan), was another street which survived until recently as a broad hollow-way dividing this larger part of the area within the loop into two. On the E. side of this hollow-way,

extending from it down the slope, were at least five or six rectangular closes bounded by banks, scarps or ditches. The area has now been built over and all the earthworks destroyed, but a large quantity of medieval pottery has been discovered in the vicinity. It consists of 13th and 14th-century types and included unglazed Potterspury and Coventry wares, part of a Lyveden ware jug and most of an onion-shaped jar of orange fabric with a green glaze and was found in association with a large area of stone flags (*Northants. Archaeol.*, 9 (1974), 103). The hollow-way itself was marked by a band of gravel (local inf.). No building

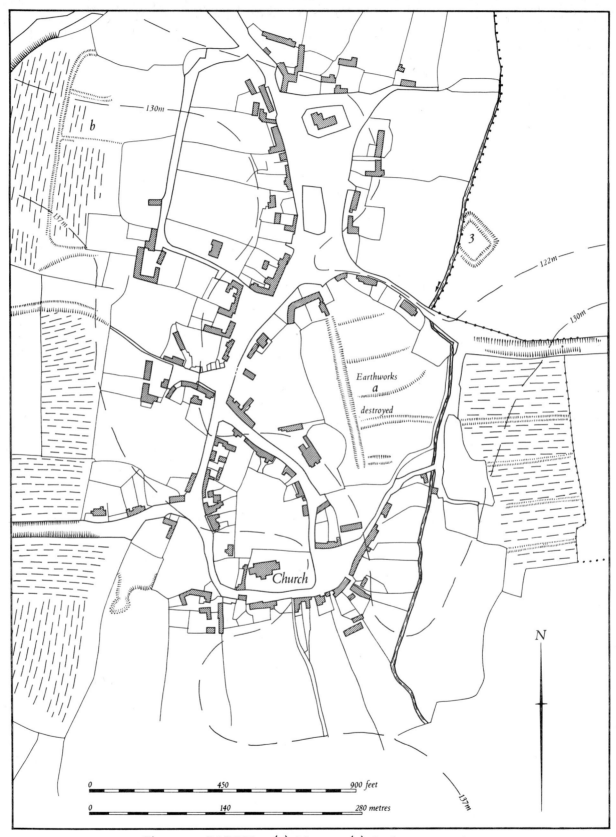

Fig. 20   BADBY   (3) Moat,   (4) Settlement remains

existed here in 1779 (NRO, Enclosure Map) but some of the close boundaries E. of the hollow-way still had hedges on them and the N. part of the hollow-way itself was a long narrow close. Further N.W., at the N.W. end of the back lane, are three embanked closes ('b' on plan) behind existing houses. In the N. of the village, on the W. side of the large rectangular green (SP 559591) late Saxon and 12th-century pottery has been recovered from gardens (local inf.; RAF VAP CPE/UK/1994, 1275–6).

b(5) HOLLOW-WAY (SP 55895782–55955801; Fig. 21), on Badby Down, along the southern parish boundary with Fawsley, cutting through the flat-topped summit of the E.–W. Northampton Sand ridge at 180 m. above OD.

The hollow-way is referred to in an Anglo-Saxon Charter of 944 (BCS 972) giving the boundary of 30 hides of land at Badby, Dodford and Everdon and is there described as the road from Fawsley to Badby. It consists of a narrow hollow-way almost 200 m. long and 1.5 m. deep. At the S. end it fades out and becomes a modern track leading down towards Fawsley Hall; at the N. end it cuts through the steep natural scarp above the edge of Badby Wood and is then blocked by a low scarp which is a remnant of the pale of the deer park (6). No trace of the hollow-way exists below the park pale as the area is a spring head and there is much marshy ground. It probably ran N. across the E. part of Badby Wood and entered the village near the church on or near the present footpath (at SP 560586) which is also deeply hollowed.

b(6) DEER PARK (centred SP 565582; Fig. 21), occupies 80 hectares to the S.E. of the village, in the area now largely covered by Badby Wood. It lies on land sloping down steeply to the N. and N.E., mainly on Upper Lias Clay between 180 m. and 145 m. above OD. The park was created in 1245–6 when the Abbey of Evesham which held the manor obtained permission from the Crown to enclose Badby Wood for a park (J. Bridges, *Hist. of Northants.*, I (1791), 20) but its later history is unknown.

Remains of the park pale survive round almost the whole circuit of the park and are among the best preserved in the county. Along the lower N. side of Badby Wood (SP 559583–569586) the pale is an almost continuous bank 6 m.–7 m. wide and up to 1.75 m. high above the interior of the wood but only 0.25 m. above the higher land of the surrounding fields. It turns S. along the E. edge of the wood where it also marks the parish boundary with Newnham. At the S.E. corner of the wood (SP 572581) the pale, following the Fawsley–Badby parish boundary, leaves the wood and runs down the slope into Fawsley Park where the bank is very low and indistinct but can just be traced to a point N. of the Dower House in Fawsley Park (SP 570578). It then swings N.W. and becomes larger until, at the point where it meets the wood again (at SP 563578), it is 7 m. wide and 1.5 m. high. For some 200 m. beyond that the bank has been almost completely destroyed by ploughing which here runs to the edge of the woods. Just

W. of an old sand pit the bank reappears and runs diagonally across a massive natural scarp 4 m. high which is the junction between the Northampton Sand to the S. and the Lias Clay to the N. Here the pale is 2 m. high and 7 m. wide. It reaches the bottom of the natural scarp and, turning N.W., runs along its foot. A little further on (at SP 55955801) it blocks the hollow-way (5) which clearly predates the pale, though here the latter is reduced to a low scarp. Beyond, the pale continues around the edge of the wood, still below the natural scarp which increases to a maximum height of 6 m. The pale here is about 1 m. high and 8 m. wide and continues in this form until it reaches the N.E. corner of the wood.

Badby Wood is very uneven and overgrown, but there are traces of a number of low banks and scarps within it. These may be the remains of the boundaries of coppicing enclosures (RAF VAP CPE/UK/1994, 1274–6; *Northants. Archaeol.*, 12 (1977), 155–76).

b(7) TERRACED WAY (SP 552586), W. of Badby village on the E. side of a deep narrow valley draining N. Air photographs (RAF VAP CPE/UK/1994, 1276–7) show what appear to be several strip lynchets, but on the ground a shallow terraced trackway can be seen, curving along the edge of the valley. It was probably an old line of the road from Catesby into Badby village.

(8) CULTIVATION REMAINS. The common fields of the parish were enclosed by an Act of Parliament of 1779 (NRO, Enclosure Map), though areas of old enclosures already existed then. Ridge-and-furrow of these fields exists on the ground or can be traced on air photographs over a large part of the parish, but certain areas are completely devoid of any remains, presumably as a result of modern cultivation. Where it survives it is almost all in rectangular interlocked furlongs, often with reversed-S curves and carefully arranged so that it runs at right-angles to the contours.

Immediately E. of Badby village on a steep W.–facing slope (SP 562588; Fig. 20) there is a remarkably well-preserved furlong of ridge-and-furrow with dividing ditches between the blocks of ridges. The Enclosure Map of 1779 (NRO) shows that immediately before then most of the eastern part of the parish, as well as a small area W. of the village called Bare Hill Ground and another place near Fox Hill in the N.E. of the parish, was already divided into hedged fields (RAF VAP CPE/UK/1994, 1158–63, 1274–8).

UNDATED

d(9) MOUND (SP 56086009), possibly a windmill mound, lies immediately W. of the Daventry–Banbury road, N. of the village on the N. side of the Nene valley, on clay at 155 m. above OD. It was recorded as a 'tumulus' in 1923 (W. Edgar, *Borough Hill*, (1923), 38) and was marked as such on OS maps from 1923 to 1950. A more recent record suggests that the mound was one of a former group of

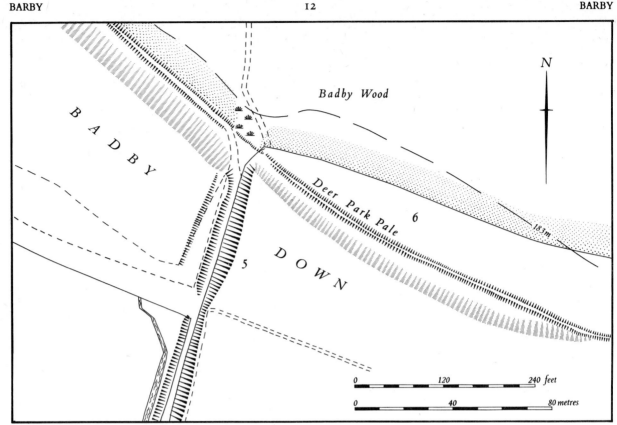

Fig. 21   BADBY   (5) Hollow-way,   (6) Deer park

barrows, but no evidence for this theory exists (Pevsner, *Northamptonshire*, (1961), 91).

The mound is now ploughed over and only survives as a gentle rise 23 m. in diam. and 0.25 m. high (OS Record Cards).

5   BARBY

(OS 1:10000 [a] SP 57 SW, [b] SP 57 SE, [c] SP 56 NW, [d] SP 56 NE)

The large parish, of some 1400 hectares, is roughly triangular and projects W. into Warwickshire. It formerly included the hamlet and land of Barby Nortoft, a detached area covering about 80 hectares now in Kilsby parish (Kilsby (2)). The E. part of the parish which contains the village of Barby is mainly undulating land between 120 m. and 175 m. above OD, on Middle Lias silts and Marlstone, capped with glacial clays and gravels in the S.E. To the W., N.W. and S.W. the land slopes steeply down to an almost level area floored by Lower Lias Clay at about 90 m. above OD. Most of the flat W. part of the parish was, in medieval times, the land of the village of Onley (1), now deserted (Fig. 87). Its well-preserved remains are of special interest because the whole village appears to have been ploughed after its abandonment. The only other monument of note

is Barby Castle (2), a small fortified manor house site just N. of the village.

MEDIEVAL AND LATER

[a](1) DESERTED VILLAGE OF ONLEY (SP 511707; Figs. 22 and 87; Plate 9), in the N.W. of the parish, on Lias Clay at 88 m. above OD. It lies in the centre of a roughly triangular area and on two maps of Barby (NRO, Enclosure Map, 1779 and Parish Map, 1840) it is clear that this area was formerly the lands of the village of Onley (Fig. 87).

The village of Onley is not mentioned in documents until 1272 (PRO, C133/2) and is presumably included under Barby in all the national taxation records. In 1272 it is recorded that one George de Cantelupe held Onley, together with the manor of Barby. At Onley were '13 virgates in villeinage, value 9s. per annum'. In 1345 there is a reference to 'tenements in Onle' perhaps implying that the village still existed. Thereafter there is no indication of its status until the early 18th century when it was described as 'a hamlet of seven shepherds houses' (J. Bridges, *Hist. of Northants.*, I (1791), 24). By 1841, nineteen people lived in the area, all in the five scattered farms which still exist (K. J. Allison *et al.*, *The Deserted Villages of Northants.* (1966), 44).

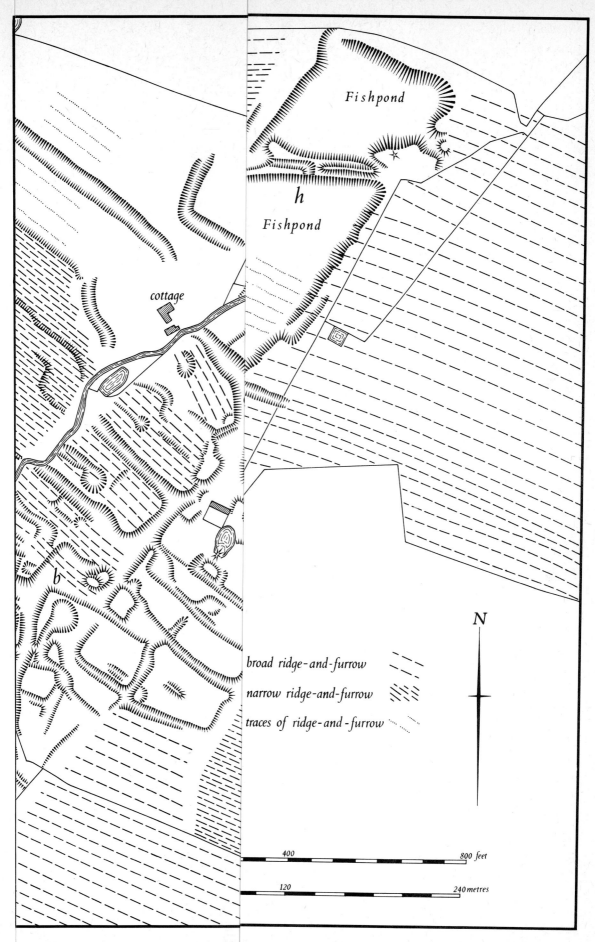

Fishpond

h

Fishpond

b

cottage

broad ridge-and-furrow

narrow ridge-and-furrow

traces of ridge-and-furrow

N

| 400 | | 800 feet |

| 120 | | 240 metres |

Fig. 22   BA

The remains of the village cover some 28 hectares and are well preserved. Some difficulty in interpretation results from the fact that most of the site has been over-ploughed in narrow ridge-and-furrow which has smoothed and flattened the village earthworks. This fact alone would make the site of unusual interest, and a number of other features combine to make it one of the most important in the county despite the unfortunate lack of documentation.

The remains lie on either side of a small S.W.-flowing stream, the N.E. part of which is now in a culvert and visible only in wet weather. The site can be divided into four parts the best preserved of which is on the S. and consists of a series of rectangular scarped closes lying on each side of a hollow-way or main street. The latter ('a'–'b'–'c' on plan) is of irregular form and, in one place ('b'), is almost totally obliterated by later narrow-rig which lies over it. At the N. end it curves N.W. to meet the stream. From this hollow-way another runs E. ('d') and a third runs W. (from 'b') to the stream. Further N. two short hollow-ways or lanes also extend N.W. of the stream. On the N.W. side of the main hollow-way are at least six long embanked closes, presumably former crofts and tofts, but all are over-ploughed by later ridge-and-furrow and any house-sites that may have existed have been destroyed. To the S.E. of the hollow-way is a further series of long closes. These do not appear to have been ploughed but no definite building platforms are visible. Further S.E. narrow-rig covers the area, but traces of a long low scarp there ('e' on plan) suggest that there may have been closes.

To the N. of one of the lesser hollow-ways ('d' on plan) and N.E. of the end of the main one ('c') is another series of closes, most of which have faint traces of later ploughing within them, but which form no coherent plan. These closes are bounded on the N. by a hollow-way ('f' on plan) which is the largest feature of the whole site, being as much as 2.5 m. deep in places. Though the hollow-way has certainly been used as a street it is in fact also the line of the original stream and must have been used as a watercourse when the village was occupied, as the water from the fishponds to the E. must have run along it.

Immediately N. of this hollow-way is a long rectangular area ('g' on plan) bounded on the N. by a narrow ditch beyond which is an area of narrow-rig ploughing. This area has been completely ploughed over at some time, but slight banks and scarps indicate that it was formerly divided into closes of various sizes. To the W. are two *Fishponds* of irregular shape ('h' on plan), separated by a mutilated bank or dam only 1 m. high at the W. but 2 m. high at the E. The ponds are cut into the adjacent ground and the scarps along their E. sides are up to 2 m. high. The southernmost has traces of later ploughing within it and the adjacent medieval ridge-and-furrow to the E. appears to overlie its E. edge.

On the N.W. of the stream ('i' on plan) is a large area of land covered with narrow-rig ploughing and bounded on

the N.W. by a broad ditch or hollow-way, beyond which is normal medieval ridge-and-furrow. Within this area, and almost totally destroyed by the later ploughing, are traces of long narrow closes edged by low scarps. These closes appear to be more regular than those elsewhere on the site and might be regarded as a late addition to the village. On the other hand the subsequent ploughing may have altered their original form and made them look more regular than they were.

The ruinous cottage N.W. of the stream though mainly of 19th-century date contains some late 18th-century features and may be a rebuilding of one of the shepherds' cottages recorded in the early 18th century. A few sherds of 14th-century pottery have been found along the bed of the stream (CUAP, SB2–4, NT32, 33, AWQ45, 48).

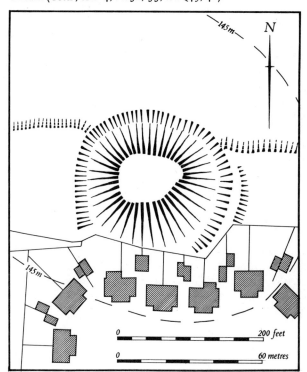

Fig. 23　　BARBY　　(2) Site of manor house

a(2) SITE OF MANOR HOUSE (SP 543707; Fig. 23), known as Barby Castle, lies on a prominent rounded hill of clay at 145 m. above OD, dominating the village centre. It is presumably the site of an early manor house which had some form of defence. The field in which it stands was known as Hall Close in the early 19th century (G. Baker, *Hist. of Northants.*, I (1822–30), 264).

The site consists of an oval flat-topped mound only 1 m.–1.5 m. above the surrounding hillside, bounded by a broad flat-bottomed ditch 1 m. deep. There are slight traces of an outer bank on the S.E. side but modern housing development has encroached upon the ditch on the S. and has destroyed a section of this outer bank which is visible on air photographs. From the E. and W. sides of the site broad scarps up to 1 m. high extend in both directions. These are the boundaries of old enclosures, some still with traces of ridge-and-furrow within them. To the S. of the site, in an area now covered by modern housing, air photographs show a hollow-way which presumably once linked the manor house to the village (see (3); RAF VAP CPE/UK/1994, 1353–4, 1482–3; CUAP, ACA74, 75).

a(3) SETTLEMENT REMAINS (centred SP 543705), formerly part of Barby village, lay immediately S. of the site of the manor house (2) and N. of Ware Road. The area has been completely built over, but air photographs taken before destruction (RAF VAP CPE/UK/1994, 1482–3; CUAP, ACA75) show a number of rectangular embanked closes along Ware Road, with a hollow-way between them linking the road with the manor house site. A quantity of medieval pottery, mainly of the 13th century, has been found in the garden of a house (local inf.). The area was already devoid of building by 1779 (NRO, Enclosure Map). These remains, together with the Enclosure Map, go a long way towards explaining the morphology of the village of Barby. The present plan suggests that it originated as one of the so-called 'double-looped' villages. However, as the map clearly shows, the village was formerly arranged around a very large rectangular green with a fortified manor house (2) on the N. and the church in the S.E. corner. From the E. side of the green three lanes extended E. to meet a back lane. The green had already been partly encroached upon before 1779, but at Enclosure the remainder was divided into small fields some of which were later built over.

Elsewhere in the village various closes bounded by low banks and scarps still remain. These appear to be former paddocks now incorporated into the adjacent fields (e.g. in the N.E. corner of the village at SP 547706 and 546704). More existed S. of the church (at SP 544701) but these have also been destroyed by modern housing (RAF VAP CPE/UK/1994, 1482–3).

(4) CULTIVATION REMAINS. The common fields of the village of Barby were enclosed by an Act of Parliament of 1778 (NRO, Enclosure Map, 1779). Immediately before that date there were three large open fields surrounding the village, Wood Field to the W., Brackleydale Field to the E., and Nether Field to the N. There was a small area of old enclosures lying W. of the village at the N. end of Wood Field (centred SP 533705) with an outlying farmstead, now destroyed, at its S. end.

Ridge-and-furrow of these common fields exists on the ground or can be traced on air photographs over almost the entire area. It is arranged in end-on and interlocked furlongs, many of reversed-S form, except in the S.E. of the parish where, on the steep slopes of Barby Hill, it radiates outwards around the spur. No ridge-and-furrow is visible in the area of the old enclosures W. of the village.

The date of the enclosure of the common fields of Onley is unknown. Ridge-and-furrow of these fields exists on the ground or can be traced on air photographs around the site of the deserted village (1) and in the N. and W. parts of the land attributable to the latter. It is arranged mainly in interlocked furlongs and is still exceptionally well preserved over wide areas. The site of the village of Onley is largely covered by narrow ridge-and-furrow (Fig. 22 and Plate 9) probably of late 18th or early 19th-century date (RAF VAP CPE/UK/1994, 1352–5, 1481–6; 106 G/UK/636, 4433–40).

6 BOUGHTON

(OS 1: 10000 a SP 76 NW, b SP 76 NE, c SP 76 SW, d SP 76 SE)

The present parish only covers about 500 hectares having lost some land in the S. to Northampton. It consists of a roughly rectangular area mainly on Northampton Sand between 85 m. and 115 m. above OD, except along the streams which form the boundary on the W. and N. where the underlying Upper Lias Clay is exposed and in the extreme S.W. where on ground rising to just over 120 m. there are areas of limestone.

Some prehistoric and Roman material is recorded from the parish but much has probably been lost as a result of ironstone quarrying in the N.W.

Though Boughton itself appears always to have been a centre of settlement in medieval and later times the existence of the now deserted Boughton Green (7), with the parish church and evidence of a medieval fair there, indicates either a second or even an earlier centre of medieval settlement.

PREHISTORIC AND ROMAN

A Neolithic axe of whitish flint was found in the parish before 1904 (NM). Worked flints, including arrowheads, have also been discovered (e.g. SP 764655; BNFAS, 5 (1971), 35). A leaf-shaped arrowhead came from SP 75276569 (OS Record Cards) and a barbed-and-tanged example from SP 75086480 (BNFAS, 4 (1970), 2). Two quernstones, upper and lower, of local stone and probably of Iron Age date, were found during ironstone-working near SP 739668. The area is now reclaimed and ploughed (OS Record Cards). A feature recorded as a ring ditch (SP 74656520; BNFAS, 6 (1971), 3) is part of a Second World War anti-aircraft battery.

a(1) ENCLOSURE (?) (SP 745662), N.E. of Boughton Grange on Northampton Sand at 93 m. above OD. Air photographs (not seen by RCHM) are said to show the cropmarks of an enclosure but it may simply be the result of frost fracture (BNFAS, 5 (1971), 39).

a(2) BARROW, PITS AND DITCHES (centred SP 74756585), E. and S.E. of Boughton Grange on Northampton Sand at 106 m. above OD. The mound, which stands on the N. edge of the field, is tree covered, and an attempted excavation shortly before 1968 was not completed because of the roots. The mound is 2.2 m. high and 15 m. in diam. and no ditch is visible. Two pits or ditches were found in

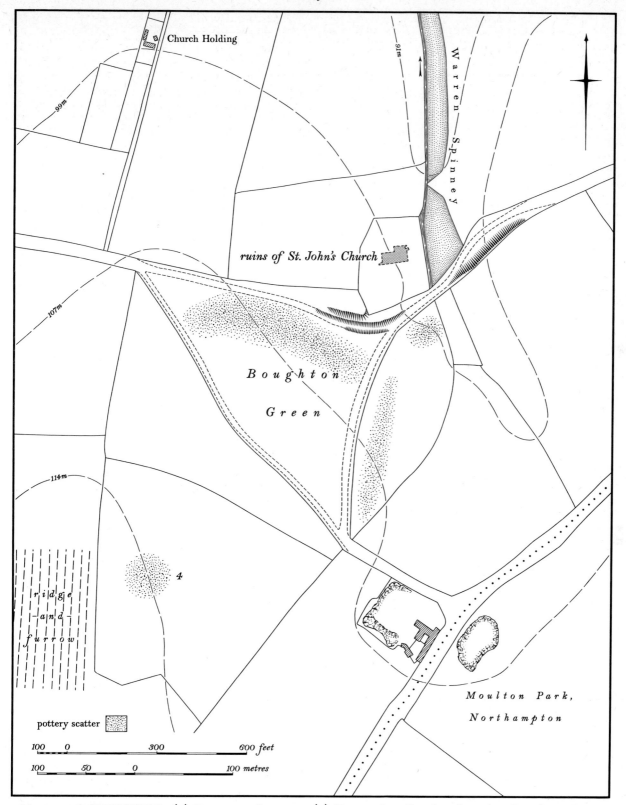

Fig. 24 BOUGHTON (4) Roman settlement, (7) Deserted medieval settlement at Boughton Green

the face of the ironstone quarry in the same field in 1973. From one of these came a sherd of a Neolithic or Bronze Age vessel with a pronounced shoulder-ridge and finger-nail decoration on the collar (SP 74746569). Several worked flints have been found in the same field (OS Record Cards; *Northants. Archaeol.*, 9 (1974), 83; air photographs in NMR).

[b](3) ROMAN SETTLEMENT (?) (SP 765667), in the extreme N.E. of the parish on Northampton Sand at 100 m. above OD. Several sherds of Roman coarse wares were found on spoil heaps at a disused quarry (*BNFAS*, 5 (1971), 22, described as from Moulton). Air photographs (in NMR) show some very indistinct cropmarks in the general area. These include part of an irregular enclosure intersected by linear ditches, as well as other possible ditches or enclosures, all covering six hectares.

[b](4) ROMAN SETTLEMENT (?) (centred SP 763655; Fig. 24), lies in and around the deserted medieval settlement of Boughton Green (7), on Northampton Sand at 105 m. above OD. Roman pottery, found in 1969, is recorded from immediately S. of the green (SP 762653; *BNFAS*, 4 (1970), 16). More, including Nene Valley type wares, was discovered on the green itself in 1976 (RCHM) and a coin of Faustina was found in 1977 (NM Records).

[a](5) ROMAN SETTLEMENT AND WELL (SP 745657), S. of Boughton Grange, on Northampton Sand at 105 m. above OD. A well, Roman pottery and 'leather' are said to have been discovered in this area in 1936 (OS Record Cards). The site has been quarried away.

MEDIEVAL AND LATER

[b](6) SAXON BURIAL (around SP 753658), within the village, on Northampton Sand at 100 m. above OD. An inhumation burial was found in Boughton in 1917 but there is no detailed information about the find (OS Record Cards; Meaney, *Gazetteer*, 187).

[b](7) DESERTED SETTLEMENT OF BOUGHTON GREEN (SP 763655; Fig. 24), lies 800 m. E. of the present village on the W. side of a small valley on Northampton Sand between 98 m. and 108 m. above OD. The triangular green and the isolated church of St. John the Baptist suggest that there was a settlement here, but its history is ill documented. The site was deserted by the early 16th century, for then it was said that the parish church of St. John the Baptist was 'distant iii pts of a myle from ye towne or any house' (Whellan, *Dir.*, 227). In the early 18th century Bridges (*Hist. of Northants.*, I (1791), 411) described the church, then in ruins. The site was still completely deserted in the early 19th century (OS 1st ed. 1 in. map (1834)). A well-known medieval fair was held on the green from the middle of the 14th century onwards (VCH *Northants.*, IV (1937), 77).

The site consists of the former triangular green, covering about 3 hectares, now under permanent arable.

No buildings remain except in the N.E. corner where the ruined church stands in its walled churchyard. All the land to the E., W. and S. of the green is now arable, but that to the N. is pasture. Along the E. of the green a scatter of stone and pottery of 12th to 18th-century date has been noted recently, and from the S. further unspecified medieval pottery is recorded (SP 762653; *BNFAS*, 4 (1970), 16). On the green itself four 17th-century coins and a Nuremburg token, large quantities of medieval and post-medieval pottery, post-medieval glass and clay pipes have been found as well as Roman material (see (4) above; *BNFAS*, 5 (1971), 35). Before it was ploughed the green is said to have had an 'undulating surface caused partly by extensive quarrying' (VCH, op. cit.) and also to have had a turf-cut maze on it (8).

[b](8) MAZE (around SP 763655), lay somewhere on Boughton Green (7) but has been destroyed. It was a turf-cut maze known as the Shepherds Race, Maze or Labyrinth, and was already said to be neglected in 1849 though apparently still discernible in 1946 (Wetton, *Guide to Northampton*, (1849), 96; G. E. Stephenson, *Guide to Boughton* (c. 1946); *Ass. Arch. Soc. Reps.*, 4 (1857–8), 260; W. H. Matthews, *Mazes and Labyrinths* (1922), 75–6).

[b](9) MEDIEVAL POTTERY (SP 757663), E. of Butchers Spinney on Northampton Sand at 80 m. above OD. Sherds of early medieval pottery including St. Neots ware were found during field-walking in 1970 (*BNFAS*, 5 (1971), 30).

[b](10) MEDIEVAL POTTERY (SP 759659), E. of the village on Northampton Sand at 100 m. above OD. Medieval pottery was found during field-walking in 1969 (*BNFAS*, 4 (1970), 16).

(11) CULTIVATION REMAINS. The common fields of the parish were enclosed by Act of Parliament of 1756 (VCH *Northants.*, IV (1937), 77). Very little ridge-and-furrow survives on the ground or can be traced on air photographs, probably because of the light sandy soils combined with modern cultivation. A curving block of reversed-S ridge-and-furrow is visible S.E. of the village (SP 754654) and another to the S.W. (SP 749655; RAF VAP CPE/UK/1994, 2244–50, 4248–55).

7 BRAMPTON, CHAPEL

(OS 1:10000 [a] SP 76 NW, [b] SP 76 SW)

The modern parish, covering just over 500 hectares, lies W. of the Pitsford Brook which forms the W. boundary. From the brook where a narrow band of Upper Lias Clay is exposed the land rises gently to a maximum height of 122 m. above OD. Most of the S. part of the parish is on Northampton Sand but in the extreme N.W. this is overlaid by glacial deposits. The parish, together with Church Brampton to the W., is remarkable for the large

areas of prehistoric and Roman sites visible from the air
(1–10). Except for a number of important finds made on
the ground almost nothing is known about these
cropmarks apart from their approximate extent. The
parish, as its name implies, was in medieval times a
chapelry of Church Brampton, but the site of the chapel
remains unknown.

PREHISTORIC AND ROMAN

A large flat stone implement, probably of foreign origin,
was found in the parish before 1949 (NM). In addition to
the flint-working sites listed below small numbers of
worked flints have been found at SP 730672 (*BNFAS*, 2
(1967), 5).

BRAMPTON COMPLEX (Chapel Brampton (1–10) and
Church Brampton (1–10); Figs. 25 and 26), occupies the
greater part of both parishes. Between and to the N. and S.
of the two villages there is an almost continuous expanse of
cropmarks, covering at least 175 hectares, on
Northampton Sand, between 80 m. and 120 m. above OD.
From within the area of cropmarks and from the
surrounding fields have come objects of Neolithic, Bronze
Age, Iron Age, Roman and Saxon date; this lends support
to the assumption that the cropmarks themselves represent
occupation over a very long period. Although the complex
must be viewed as a whole, individual sites and finds are
listed under the parish in which they lie.

b(1) PREHISTORIC AND ROMAN SETTLEMENTS AND ROMAN
KILNS (centred SP 729647; Fig. 25), in the extreme S. of the
parish, on Northampton Sand between 75 m. and 87 m.
above OD. Air photographs (in NMR; CUAP, ZFI9, 20,
ZU77, ADP4, AXFI2, 13, BYN69–70) show cropmarks
covering some 8 hectares. These include at least 14 ring
ditches or hut-circles, three double-ditched enclosures, a
ditched trackway and numerous linear features. There are
also several rectangular enclosures. At the N. end of the site
a pit alignment runs N. and may be a continuation of that
visible to the N. (2).

A large quantity of worked flints has been found on the
ground, including waste flakes, cores and scrapers
described as being of Neolithic and Bronze Age type, as
well as part of a polished stone axe and three flakes, all of
Group VI (NM Records). Iron Age pottery and the upper
part of a rotary quern have also been found (SP 729646),
apparently within or close to a ditched enclosure (*BNFAS*,
2 (1967), 5; NM; inf. W. R. G. Moore). A scatter of
Roman pottery and burnt clay with grass impressions,
probably the site of a Roman kiln, was found on the E. edge
of the area in 1966 (*BNFAS*, 2 (1967), 9, wrongly located
in Church Brampton parish; inf. W. R. G. Moore).

a(2) SETTLEMENT AND PIT ALIGNMENT (SP 730651;
Fig. 25), 300 m. N. of (1), on Northampton Sand at 85 m.
above OD. Air photographs (in NMR; CUAP, ZV21, ADP2)
show a small group of interlocked rectangular enclosures
with a number of ring ditches or hut-circles within them,

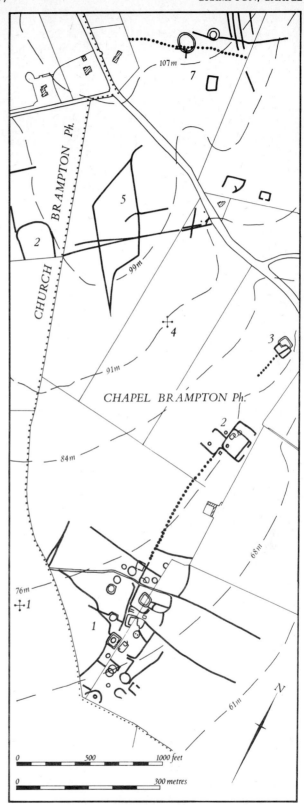

Fig. 25   BRAMPTON, CHAPEL   (1–3, 5, 7)
and BRAMPTON, CHURCH   (1, 2)
Brampton Complex

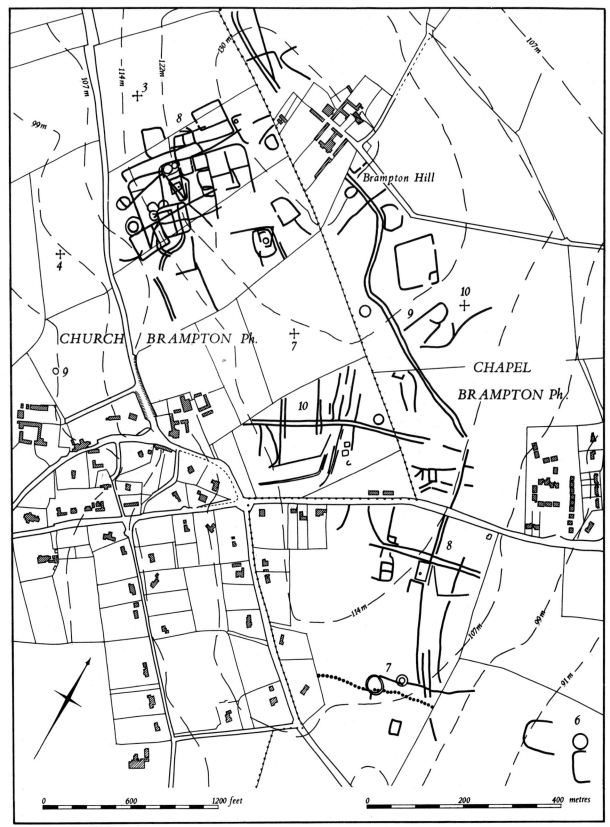

Fig. 26   BRAMPTON, CHAPEL   (6–10) and BRAMPTON, CHURCH
(3–10) Brampton Complex

and some small rectangular features. Several early Saxon sherds have been discovered (inf. W. R. G. Moore), and worked flints of Neolithic and Bronze Age type have been found over the site and in the surrounding area. These are listed below (4) (*BNFAS*, 2 (1967), 32).

ab(3) SETTLEMENT (SP 730654; Fig. 25), S. of Brampton Grange, on Northampton Sand at 85 m. above OD. Air photographs (in NMR; CUAP, ZV21) show rather indistinctly a group of small interlocked enclosures with a short length of pit alignment running S.W. from them. Worked flints of Neolithic and Bronze Age type from the site and the surrounding area are listed below (4) (inf. W. R. G. Moore).

a(4) FLINT-WORKING SITES (centred SP 730652), cover an area of some 26 hectares S. and S.W. of Brampton Grange on Northampton Sand between 70 m. and 100 m. above OD. Some of these may be associated with cropmarks (2) and (3) described above. Over 2000 flints, mainly of Neolithic and Bronze Age type, including waste flakes, scrapers and cores, have been found. The general locations are SP 732654, 729652, 727651 and 727652. To the S.S.E. of Brampton Grange (SP 732652) a large area of mainly Mesolithic flints has been discovered (inf. W. R. G. Moore; OS Record Cards; *BNFAS*, 2 (1967), 5).

a(5) LINEAR DITCHES (SP 726654; Fig. 25), lie close to the parish boundary with Church Brampton, on Northampton Sand at 100 m. above OD. Air photographs (in NMR) show a group of linear ditches, but one is a modern pipeline and another an old hedge (not shown on plan). The earlier ditches form no coherent pattern but may be associated with other features immediately to the S.W. (Church Brampton (2)).

a(6) RING DITCH AND ENCLOSURES (SP 730658; Fig. 26), N. of Brampton Grange, on Northampton Sand at 95 m. above OD. Air photographs (in NMR) show one large circular feature, perhaps a ring ditch, with two incomplete rectangular enclosures to the W. and S.E. Worked flints, including scrapers and cores, have been found a little to the S.W. (*BNFAS*, 2 (1967), 5; 5 (1971), 39; 6 (1971), 5–7).

a(7) RING DITCHES, ENCLOSURES AND PIT ALIGNMENT (SP 726658; Figs. 25 and 26), W. of (6), on Northampton Sand at 105 m. above OD. Air photographs (in NMR) show a pit alignment running W.–E. and traceable for 250 m. It cuts an oval double-ditched enclosure which is also intersected by a small L-shaped length of ditch. To the S. is a rectangular enclosure, and to the N. a double ring ditch which has linear ditches running E. and W. from it. The E. linear ditch appears to intersect several other features including a ditched trackway running S.E. from (8) (*BNFAS*, 2 (1967), 5, 32; 4 (1970), 31).

a(8) DITCHED TRACKWAY AND ENCLOSURES (SP 725660; Fig. 26), S.W. of Chapel Brampton village, on Northampton Sand at 110 m. above OD. Air photographs

(in NMR) show somewhat indistinctly a ditched trackway running E.S.E.–W.N.W. Another trackway possibly continuing from the S. (7) runs N. apparently to meet two other trackways (Chapel Brampton (9) and Church Brampton (10)), just W. of Chapel Brampton village. This trackway is intersected at right-angles by several roughly parallel linear ditches and there are various enclosures and other linear features linked to the trackway or visible in the surrounding area.

a(9) DITCHED TRACKWAY, ENCLOSURES, LINEAR DITCHES AND FLINT-WORKING SITES (centred SP 722665; Fig. 26), W. and N.W. of Chapel Brampton village, on Northampton Sand between 110 m. and 120 m. above OD. Air photographs (in NMR; CUAP, ZW38) show a sinuous ditched trackway traceable for more than 500 m. S.E. from Brampton Hill to a point just W. of the village. Here, though little is visible on air photographs, it seems to have met two other trackways approaching the site from the S. (8) and from the W. (Church Brampton (10)). Some short ditches and a small rectangular enclosure are visible to the S.W. of the assumed junction and other indeterminate ditches to the N. To the N.W. (SP 722665) there is a large, well-marked rectangular enclosure with rounded corners and entrances in the S.E. and N.E. sides; it has a small internal enclosure in its E. corner. Linear ditches run to the S.E. Further N.W., on both sides of the trackway, are further traces of rectangular and irregular enclosures. The trackway can be traced to the W. of Brampton Hill (at SP 717667) where a short length of it, intersected by a linear feature, is visible on air photographs. This trackway was cut obliquely by a pipe-line trench in 1970 (at SP 72226644). The ditches were said to be 3 m.–4 m. wide at the top and almost 2 m. deep. No dating evidence or metalling was discovered between the ditches (*BNFAS*, 5 (1971), 2). Worked flints, including cores and scrapers, have been found over the area around the large enclosure (*BNFAS*, 2 (1967), 5; 4 (1970), 31; inf. W. R. G. Moore).

a(10) BRONZE AGE CEMETERY (SP 72276645; Fig. 26), immediately S.E. of a large enclosure (9), on Northampton Sand at 112 m. above OD. The site was completely excavated in 1970–1 and proved to be a middle Bronze Age cemetery with some 25 cremations. About half of these were in bucket urns, one of which was in a rectangular cist of sandstone slabs and contained a bead and a plain bronze bracelet. Two radiocarbon dates were obtained from the material, one of 1114 bc ± 120 from a cremation pit and one of 1296 bc ± 100 from another, charcoal-filled pit (DOE *Arch. Excavations 1971*, (1972), 52; *BNFAS*, 5 (1971), 1; *Northants. Archaeol.*, 8 (1973), 3).

a(11) FLINT-WORKING SITE (centred SP 720677), N.E. of Sanders Covert, on Boulder Clay between 90 m. and 100 m. above OD. Worked flints, including one leaf-shaped and one barbed-and-tanged arrowhead, have been found over an area of about 4 hectares (*BNFAS*, 2 (1967),

5; inf. W. R. G. Moore). Air photographs (in NMR) show the rather indistinct cropmarks of a rectangular enclosure covering 0.5 hectares in the centre of the area. At least one linear ditch runs N.E.–S.W. across the S.E. side of the site.

[a](12) ROMAN SETTLEMENT (?) (SP 729680), in the extreme N.E. of the parish, on gravel at 75 m. above OD. Roman pottery and a few worked flints have been discovered on the ground and cropmarks of enclosures are said to have been seen from the air (*BNFAS*, 2 (1967), 9).

MEDIEVAL AND LATER

For early Saxon pottery, see (2).

[a](13) SETTLEMENT REMAINS AND HOLLOW-WAY (SP 731663), lie immediately E. of Chapel Brampton village, on land sloping down to a small S.– flowing stream, on Northampton Sand at 75 m. above OD. The earthworks lie within the former park of the now demolished Chapel Brampton Hall. The main feature is a hollow-way 10 m.–12 m. wide, as much as 1.5 m. deep below the land to the N. but only 0.5 m. deep below that to the S. It runs down the hillside to the stream and marks the line of the original street which ran to Pitsford from the cross-roads at the S. end of the village. This existed in 1584 (Map in NRO; Plate 15) but was probably closed when the park was made. It was still in use in the early 19th century as the only road across the valley to Pitsford (OS 1st ed. 1 in. map, (1834)). Along the present Pitsford road, to the S. of the hollow-way, is a series of embanked enclosures and platforms the S. ends of which are cut by the road. These may be the sites of former buildings and closes though no buildings are shown here on the map of the parish of 1584.

(14) CULTIVATION REMAINS. The common fields of the parish were enclosed by agreement in 1662 (NRO). A map of 1584 (NRO; Plate 15) shows three fields, Middle, Nether and Rie, as well as areas of old enclosures. Ridge-and-furrow of these fields exists on the ground or can be traced on air photographs only in the N. and E. of the parish, largely on the heavier soils. It is rare or completely absent on the lighter Northampton Sand in the S. of the parish. In the extreme N.W. of the parish, in the former Middle Field, the pattern of the ridge-and-furrow is almost completely recoverable, comprising mainly rectangular interlocked furlongs, many of reversed-S form. These, in sharp contrast to the layout on the more broken country to the W., are not always laid out at right-angles to the slope; this applies in particular to some furlongs close to the N. and W. boundaries (e.g. SP 720680 and 732672), where the ridges run parallel to the streams. However around the low isolated Hoe Hill in the N. of the parish (SP 725678), at the extreme N. end of Nether Field, the ridges radiate outwards from the summit. To the S.E. of the village (SP 733660) only one small area of ridge-and-furrow is traceable in the former Rie Field (RAF VAP CPE/UK/1994, 2250–1, 2369–70, 4253–7, 4732–6).

8 BRAMPTON, CHURCH

(OS 1:10000 [a] SP 76 NW, [b] SP 76 SW)

The long narrow parish occupies some 460 hectares of land, between 70 m. and 125 m. above OD, most of which slopes S.W. to a small stream on the S.W. and S. boundaries. It is mainly on Northampton Sand, except in the N. where the sand is overlaid by heavier glacial deposits and along the stream where down-cutting has exposed the underlying Upper Lias Clay. The parish once formed a single unit with Chapel Brampton, formerly a parochial chapelry of Church Brampton. The parish is remarkable for the extensive prehistoric and Roman sites (1–11) which are mainly visible as cropmarks.

PREHISTORIC AND ROMAN

For a general note on the prehistoric and Roman material in this parish, see Chapel Brampton.

Worked flints have been found at a number of places in the parish in addition to the sites listed below. From S.W. of the village (SP 718653) six flakes and two possible blades are recorded, and from S. of the village (SP 721652) two scrapers, worked flints and blades. To the W. of the village (SP 714664, 714674, 714676 and 721663) other tools and flakes have been discovered (*BNFAS*, 5 (1971), 2; 7 (1972), 2; NM Records).

[b](1) HOARD OF NEOLITHIC AXES (SP 72716461; Fig. 25), in the extreme S.E. of the parish, on Northampton Sand at 85 m. above OD. In about 1962 a hoard of six polished flint axes was found on this site. Only two survive (NM).

[a](2) ENCLOSURES (?) (SP 724653; Fig. 25), S. of the village, on Northampton Sand at 100 m. above OD. Air photographs (in NMR) show two incomplete rectangular enclosures which may be connected with the linear features to the E. (Chapel Brampton (5)). Worked flints including two barbed-and-tanged arrowheads have been found on the site (*BNFAS*, 2 (1967), 32; 7 (1972), 2; OS Record Cards).

[a](3) WORKED FLINTS AND ROMAN SETTLEMENT (?) (SP 716666; Fig. 26), W. of Brampton Hill, on Northampton Sand at 112 m. above OD. Worked flints classified as Neolithic, including scrapers, and some Roman pottery are recorded from this area (*BNFAS*, 7 (1972), 2).

[a](4) WORKED FLINTS AND ROMAN SETTLEMENT (?) (SP 716662; Fig. 26), 300 m. S. of (3), on Northampton Sand at 100 m. above OD. A few worked flints and Roman pottery have been noted here (*BNFAS*, 2 (1967), 9).

[a](5) ROMAN SETTLEMENT AND KILNS (SP 713661), 300 m. S.W. of (4), on Northampton Sand at 96 m. above OD. A scatter of 3rd to 4th-century pottery, including Oxfordshire mortarium sherds, and fragments of kiln bars and a clay dome were found here in 1973 (NM; *Northants. Archaeol.*, 9 (1974), 88). A small sub-rectangular enclosure,

covering only 0.25 hectares, is visible on air photographs (in NMR) in the centre of the site.

a(6) IRON AGE AND ROMAN SETTLEMENT (?) (SP 711662), 200 m. N.W. of (5), on Northampton Sand at 98 m. above OD. Iron Age and Roman sherds associated with a scatter of pebbles were discovered in the area in 1966 (BNFAS, 2 (1967), 9, published grid reference incorrect; inf. W. R. G. Moore).

a(7) PREHISTORIC SITE (?) (SP 71926622; Fig. 26), N. of the village, on Northampton Sand at 110 m. above OD. In 1970 a pipeline trench cut through a single post-hole, 1 m. deep at this point, which contained a single sherd of prehistoric pottery. Another sherd was found nearby (BNFAS, 5 (1971), 2).

a(8) ENCLOSURES, RING DITCHES AND LINEAR DITCHES (centred SP 717664; Fig. 26), N. of the village, on Northampton Sand between 105 m. and 120 m. above OD. Air photographs (in NMR; CUAP, ZW32–5) show cropmarks of great complexity, covering some 10 hectares. They include a multitude of conjoined and intersecting sub-rectangular enclosures and linear ditches some of which may be trackways. There is a double ring ditch (at SP 71706633) on the S.W. edge of the complex, and other ring ditches within enclosures lie to the N. (SP 71956643 and 71716646). Within the area (SP 717664) worked flints, said to be of Bronze Age type, and Roman pottery of the 2nd to 4th centuries have been discovered (BNFAS, 4 (1970), 31; 5 (1971), 2; 6 (1971), 5–7).

a(9) RING DITCH (?) (SP 71816599; Fig. 26), N. of Manor Farm, on Northampton Sand at 95 m. above OD. Air photographs (in NMR) show, rather indistinctly, a circular feature 12 m. in diam. (BNFAS, 5 (1971), 41).

a(10) DITCHED TRACKWAY, ENCLOSURES, RING DITCH AND LINEAR FEATURES (centred SP 723662; Fig. 26), immediately N.E. of the village, on Northampton Sand at 110 m. above OD. Air photographs (in NMR) show a ditched trackway running S.W.–N.E. which can be traced across the parish boundary into Chapel Brampton where it may have joined two other trackways (Chapel Brampton (8) and (9)). Two small rectangular enclosures are also visible (SP 72306615) as well as a ring ditch 20 m. in diam. (SP 72336623). All these cropmarks are crossed by a series of linear features running N.N.W.–S.S.E. These are difficult to interpret since some appear as broad bands up to 20 m. wide whereas others are certainly narrow ditches set close together. Their purpose is unknown but they may indicate a field system the boundaries of which have been re-cut on a number of occasions.

a(11) ENCLOSURES (?) (SP 709684), in the N. of the parish, on Northampton Sand at 97 m. above OD. Air photographs (not seen by RCHM) are said to show cropmarks of two conjoined sub-rectangular enclosures (BNFAS, 7 (1972), 55).

MEDIEVAL AND LATER

a(12) SETTLEMENT REMAINS (SP 717657; Plate 15), formerly part of Church Brampton, lie immediately W., S.W. and N. of the church and S. of Manor Farm, along the W. side of the main village street. The remains consist of a row of raised platforms and grassed-over rubble foundations, presumably once the sites of buildings along the road. In 1584 (Map in NRO; Plate 15) the area was occupied by five buildings, four of which appear to have been houses. By the early 19th century the area was devoid of buildings (1st ed. OS 1 in. map (1834)).

(13) CULTIVATION REMAINS (Plate 15). The common fields of the parish were enclosed by agreement in 1662 (NRO). On a map of 1584 (NRO; Plate 15) four fields are shown, lying around and N.W. of the village, Rie Field, West Field, Middle Field and Furr Field; these by that date already had small blocks of old enclosures within them. Ridge-and-furrow of these fields exists on the ground or can be traced on air photographs only in the N. of the parish on the heavier glacial deposits, in the area of the former Middle and Furr Fields. There three separate areas of rectangular or curved interlocked furlongs are visible (e.g. centred SP 709665, 713673 and 708678). In 1584 all the S. half of the parish was heathland, but a small area of very slight, low ridge-and-furrow remains (SP 728643), indicating that at some time this land was under cultivation. More ridge-and-furrow exists further W. in the extreme S.W. of the parish, along the side of a small stream (SP 734643). This was meadowland in the late 16th century, but again the remains indicate cultivation here in the past (CBA Group 9, Newsletter, 6 (1976), 28; RAF VAP CPE/UK/1994, 2368–70, 2250–52, 4254–58, 4371–74).

9 BRAUNSTON

(OS 1:10000 a SP 56 NW, b SP 56 NE, c SP 56 SW, d SP 56 SE)

The parish is roughly lozenge-shaped and occupies 1260 hectares of land immediately N.W. of Daventry and adjoining Warwickshire. The highest part is along the N.E. edge where a broad band of Marlstone Rock outcrops at between 150 m. and 165 m. above OD. To the S.W. the land falls steeply across a scarp of Middle Lias clays and silts to an almost level area of Lower Lias Clay at around 120 m. above OD cut into by two E.-flowing streams. This clayland slopes down to a wide area of gravel which edges the R. Leam, the W. boundary of the parish. The village of Braunston is of linear form, running along the gravel-capped top of the clay ridge between the two streams. Below it, on the river gravel, is the deserted village of Braunstonbury (1). Its history is largely unknown but the close proximity of the site to Braunston is unusual and the earthworks suggest that it may have originated as a deliberately planned settlement. The interest of the site is further enhanced by the existence of the adjacent deserted village of Wolfhampcote to the W., in Warwickshire. In the N. of the parish, in a small valley in the Middle Lias scarp, is another deserted village known as Braunston Cleves or Fawcliff (3). The history of this settlement is also unknown.

MEDIEVAL AND LATER

ᵃ(1) DESERTED VILLAGE OF BRAUNSTONBURY (SP 533656; Figs. 27 and 28; Plate 8), lies immediately S.W. of Braunston village on almost level gravels at about 90 m. above OD. To the W., across the county boundary with Warwickshire here formed by the R. Leam, is the deserted village of Wolfhampcote.

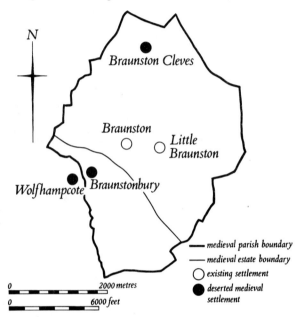

Fig. 27   BRAUNSTON   Medieval settlements
and estates

The history of the site is almost unknown, probably because it was regarded as part of Braunston village and was thus never listed separately in the national taxation records. The existence of two other settlements, Little Braunston, now part of the existing village, and the now deserted Braunston Cleves (3), further complicates the picture. Braunstonbury is thus presumably included within one of the two entries for Braunston in Domesday Book and is perhaps part of the three and a half hide manor of Walter de Aincurt with a recorded population of 17 (VCH Northants., I (1902), 308, 340). Soon after the conquest this manor appears to have passed to William Trusbott and was then divided between his three surviving daughters. One daughter, Hilary de Bulliers, gave her part to the Abbey of Lilleshall in Shropshire and this appears to have included at least part of Braunstonbury (Whellan, Dir., 386; J. Bridges, Hist. of Northants., I (1791), 26). The manor held by

Lilleshall Abbey was still tenanted in 1421 when the demesne was leased. At the Dissolution this land was sold to the Earl of Rutland who appears to have had other property there already. Other land in the village or in its fields was held by the Priory of Newstead, Stamford (LPFD 15, no. 612, f 15). By the early 18th century Bridges (Hist. of Northants., I (1791), 26) wrote that 'in Bery-field ... is a place moated around with appearance of a ruined building. The foundations of walls have frequently been discovered and near it is a field, bearing the name of the Chapel field ...'. An Estate Map of 1785 (NRO) shows the area devoid of buildings and called Church Field, though on the Tithe Map of 1842 (NRO) it is described as Chapel Field. The 1785 map also shows the undoubted medieval boundaries of the land of Braunstonbury (Fig. 27; M. W. Beresford and J. K. S. St Joseph, Medieval England: an Aerial Survey (1958), 19–20; K. J. Allison et al., The Deserted Villages of Northants. (1966), 36).

The remains lie within an almost square area bounded on the N. by a shallow valley occupied by the manorial fishpond (2), on the W. by a bank 1 m.–2 m. high, on the S. by a low bank and scarp and on the E. by the remains of a bank, partly over-ploughed by the adjacent ridge-and-furrow. In the N.W. corner a hollow-way which presumably once led from Braunston village (see (4) below) enters the site and widens to form a roughly triangular 'green' ('a' on plan). From the S. end of this green the hollow-way continues along the E. edge of the site and, though partly blocked by a later bank, widens again to form another 'green' ('b' on plan). It then continues to the S.E. corner of the site where it has been destroyed by a railway embankment. Beyond the railway to the S. its continuation is visible as a broad space between the adjacent furlongs of ridge-and-furrow.

The N.W. corner of the site is occupied by a small homestead Moat ('c' on plan) consisting of a ditch up to 2.5 m. deep surrounding a sub-rectangular island; it is probably the site of a medieval manor house. The rest of the village survives as extensive earthworks. Some cannot be explained but certain features are clear. There are at least five small house-sites, some with traces of stone walls, set within or at the ends of embanked or scarped closes ('d'–'h' on plan). Near the centre of the site ('i' on plan) is the outline of a two-roomed building set on the W. side of a close with another very large structure on the S. side and this may be a courtyard farm. A large depression to the S. ('j' on plan) may be a crew-yard where cattle were penned. Apart from the hollow-way on the E. there is no clear evidence for a street system, nor any indication of how the village was linked to Wolfhampcote to the W. It is just possible to detect at least two almost continuous banks or scarps crossing the site from E. to W., almost parallel with the N. and S. edges of this village.

This roughly rectangular plan, though it has clearly been distorted by later activity, and the neat placing of 'greens' on the E. side and of the manor house in the N.W. corner,

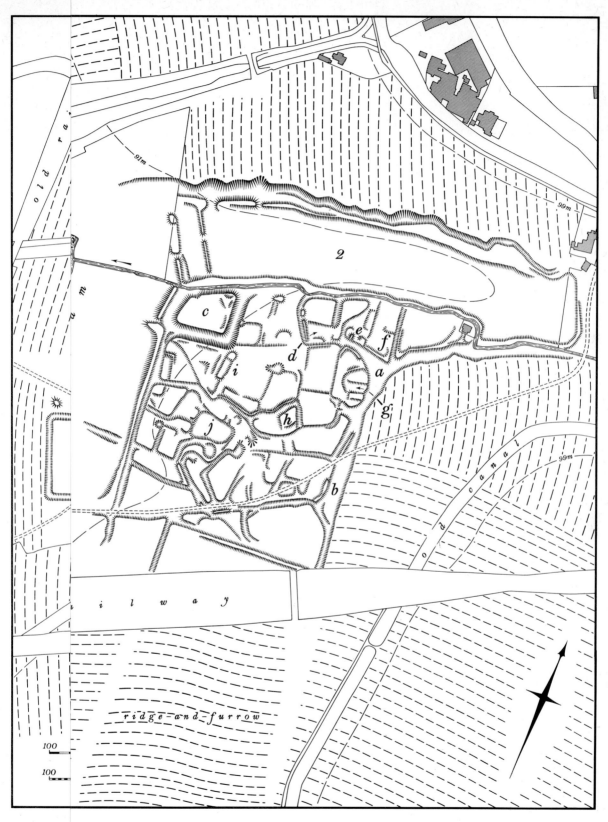

2

c

d

i

e f

a

g

h

j

b

old rai

m

99m

99m

old canal

r a i l w a y

ridge-and-furrow

100

100

astonbury,   (2) Fishpond

suggest that the whole village may have been deliberately laid out. The name too, with the use of the word *burh* apparently in its manorial sense (PN *Northants.*, 15), may indicate a planned manorial settlement rather than an organically evolved village. A large quantity of medieval pottery, all of the 13th and 14th centuries, has been found along the edge of the stream on the N. side of the area.

Wolfhampcote to the W. consists of a main E.–W. hollow-way, now blocked at its W. end by the present Wolfhampcote Hall. On either side of the hollow-way lie embanked or scarped closes, some containing possible house-sites and some with side lanes, now narrow hollow-ways, between them. In the S.E. corner is a large circular moat, presumably the manor house site, with the now isolated church beyond. A large depression to the E. of the manor is perhaps the manorial crew-yard, and E. again two parallel banks which must once have enclosed water may have been part of a mill. There is no trace of any extension of the main through hollow-way across the river to Braunstonbury. The final desertion of Wolfhampcote seems to have occurred in the early 16th century. In 1501 the common fields were enclosed and in 1517 the village was described as ruined (*Trans. Birmingham Archaeol. Soc.*, 66 (1945–6), 98–9). Limited excavation in 1955 revealed occupation from the 12th to the 15th centuries (DMVRG, *3rd Annual Rep.*, (1955), 12–13; RAF VAP CPE/UK/1994, 4352–3; CUAP, AGV 20, AHG 29, LT19–20, XT 50–3).

^a(2) FISHPOND (SP 532657; Fig. 28; Plate 8), lies immediately N. of the deserted village of Braunstonbury (1) and occupies the broad flat-bottomed valley of a small tributary stream of the R. Leam.

The remains consist of a flat rectangular area bounded by a scarp only 0.25 m.–0.5 m. high with two very low dams, again under 0.5 m. high, at the W. end. Unless there has been considerable levelling or silting in the post-medieval period the original pond could not have been more than 0.25 m. deep. Along the N. side of the pond, just below a steep natural scarp, is a shallow channel which presumably carried surplus water round the outside of the pond; its E. end has been destroyed by the modern sewage works and it is not clear how the leat ended. On both the 1785 Estate Map and the 1842 Tithe Map (NRO) the area is called Fish Wier. It is almost certainly the place described as 'a meadow called Fiswere' at Braunstonbury in 1305 (*Cal. IPM* IV, no. 298; RAF VAP CPE/UK/1994, 4352–3; CUAP, AGV 20, AHG 29).

^a(3) DESERTED VILLAGE OF BRAUNSTON CLEVES OR FAWCLIFF (SP 544682; Figs. 27 and 29), lies in the N. of the parish on the steep S.W. side of Cleve Hill, on Jurassic Clay between 125 m. and 150 m. above OD. Its history is largely unknown (see (1) above) but it can perhaps be identified as the part of the 11th-century manor of Braunston belonging to William Trusbott which was divided between his three daughters. One third passed to Agatha Meinfelin who, dying without issue, bequeathed

her possessions to Delapré Abbey in Northampton and to the Priory of Newstead near Stamford. A charter of Edward III confirming the possessions of Delapré Abbey mentions a place called Fawcliff in Braunston and this seems to have been the original name of the village (PN *Northants.*, 15). Nothing is known of the date of its desertion and certainly by the early 18th century Bridges (*Hist. of Northants.*, I (1791), 26) could say that it had been 'destroyed some ages since'. Sometime before 1828, drainage work on the site resulted in the discovery of 'extensive foundations' (T. Deacon, *Hist. of Willoughby* (1828), 9).

The remains of the village lie around the head of a small valley just below a spring, and are confined solely to the W. side of a broad hollow-way which bifurcates at its N. end (cf., the deserted village of Mallows Cotton, RCHM *Northants.*, I (1975), Raunds (19)). A series of slight depressions or platforms close to the hollow-way may be house-sites and there are fragments of closes bounded by low scarps and banks, extending W., two of which end on the edge of a stream. Below the stream and at the S. end of the site are other ditched enclosures and ditches along some of which the diverted stream flows. Several of these appear to be relatively modern and indeed had hedges beside them until recent years. They may be connected with the drainage work recorded in 1828 (M. W. Beresford, *The Lost Villages of England* (1954), 367; RAF VAP CPE/UK/1994, 2349–50).

^a(4) HOLLOW-WAY (SP 536660), immediately S.W. of the manor house, at the W. end of Braunston village, on a very steeply sloping hillside of clay between 100 m. and 115 m. above OD. It is slightly curved and up to 2 m. deep and appears to be an earlier line of the main street leading from the village to Braunstonbury (1) before the existing L-shaped road to the N. was laid out. The latter had been constructed before 1785 (Map in NRO); at that date the area containing the hollow-way was called Home Close and was part of the grounds of the manor house (RAF VAP CPE/UK/1994, 4352–3).

^a(5) WINDMILL MOUND (SP 54116527), S. of Braunston village on the S. side of the old Daventry Road on the summit of a N.W.-facing spur at 135 m. above OD. The low mound, which is 15 m. in diam., 0.5 m. high and surrounded by a ditch 0.25 m. deep, is almost certainly the site of a former windmill for in 1785 (Map in NRO) the small field in which it lay was known as Windmill Close though no windmill existed there at that time. It is probably the site of the manorial mill of the deserted village of Braunstonbury (1) in whose land it lies (RAF VAP CPE/UK/1994, 4276–7).

^b(6) WINDMILL MOUND (SP 552659), on the summit of a rounded hill, on Boulder Clay at 134 m. above OD. On a map of 1830 (NRO, Braunston Charity Lands) a smock-mill is depicted on this site and a mill is also shown on the 1st ed. OS 1 in. map of 1834. On the ground only a very

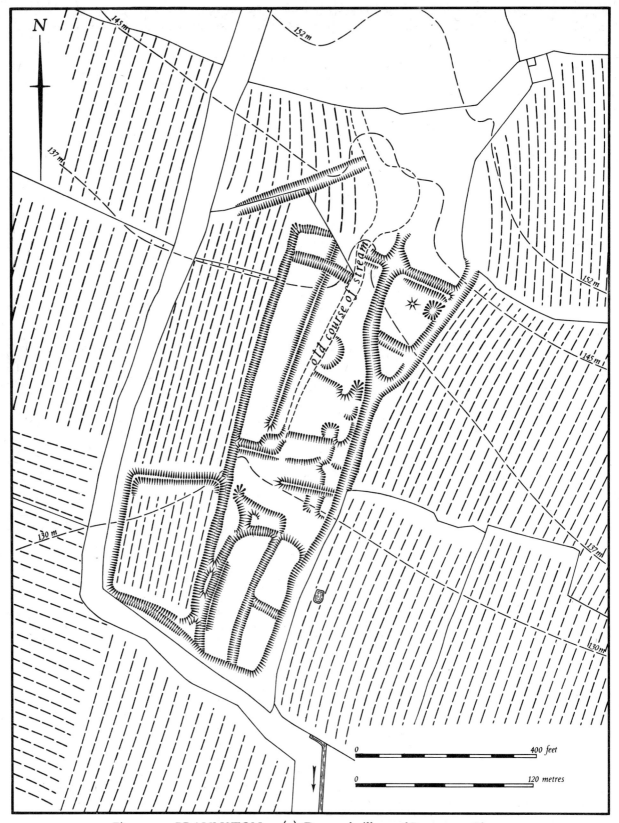

N

145 m

152 m

137 m

Old course of stream

152 m

145 m

130 m

137 m

130 m

0   400 *feet*

0   120 *metres*

Fig. 29   BRAUNSTON   (3) Deserted village of Braunston Cleves

low ploughed-out mound some 10 m. across is visible and on air photographs (RAF VAP CPE/UK/1994, 4355–6) a slight circular soil mark can be seen.

(7) CULTIVATION REMAINS. The common fields of the villages of Braunston and Little Braunston were enclosed by Act of Parliament in 1776, but in the absence of an Enclosure Map no details of their layout are known. As the land attributable to the now deserted village of Braunston Cleves (3) is unknown it is not possible to say whether the latter ever had separate common fields. Ridge-and-furrow exists on the ground or can be traced on air photographs over almost all of the areas of the parish cultivated by the inhabitants of Braunston, Little Braunston and Braunston Cleves. It consists of end-on or interlocked furlongs, many of reversed-S form, and over the small rounded hills and spurs as well as on the steep-sided valleys much of it runs directly down the slopes or radiates outwards from the higher ground. It is exceptionally well preserved in many places, for example W. of the village (SP 530663) where it consists of rounded ridges with subsidiary low ridges between them occupying the usual position of the furrows (see Sectional Preface and Kilsby (5)).

The date of enclosure of the common fields of the deserted village of Braunstonbury (1) is not known, but the process presumably took place when the village was finally abandoned. Ridge-and-furrow of this village exists on the ground or can be traced on air photographs over almost the entire area of land attributable to Braunstonbury (Fig. 27). It is mainly arranged in large interlocked curving furlongs and is particularly well preserved in the extensive pasture around the site of the village (Fig. 28; RAF VAP CPE/UK/1994, 2273–4, 2349–53, 4275–80, 4352–7).

10   BRINGTON

(OS 1:10000 [a] SP 66 NW, [b] SP 66 NE, [c] SP 66 SW, [d] SP 66 SE)

The parish, covering just over 1250 hectares, is roughly rectangular with a large projection in the S.E. Most of it is an undulating plateau between 120 m. and 130 m. above OD, mainly on glacial sands and gravels, with the underlying Jurassic Clay exposed in the N. and E.

The medieval parish included the now deserted settlement of Althorp (Althorp (1)) and its land, now a separate parish, as well as three other settlements, Great Brington, Little Brington and Nobottle (4). The land of Nobottle was presumably the present S.E. projection of the parish. Part of the land of the deserted village of Glassthorpe (Flore (4)) also lay within this parish (Fig. 73).

PREHISTORIC AND ROMAN

[b](1) ENCLOSURE (?) AND DITCHES (SP 659657), in the N. of the parish, on Northampton Sand at 120 m. above OD.

Air photographs taken in 1970 (not seen by RCHM) are said to show two lengths of curving ditch possibly with a small sub-rectangular enclosure to the S.W. (BNFAS, 6 (1971), 5).

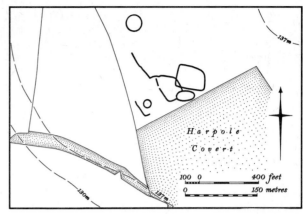

Fig. 30   BRINGTON   (2) Cropmarks

[d](2) ENCLOSURES AND RING DITCHES (?) (centred SP 67756185; Fig. 30), in the S. of the parish immediately N. of Harpole Covert, on Northampton Sand at 137 m. above OD. Air photographs show, very indistinctly, at least three conjoined sub-rectangular enclosures and other lengths of ditch which may be parts of further enclosures. There is a small ring ditch in the S.W. of the area (SP 67716182). A larger ring ditch, 15 m. in diam., shows as a parch-mark (SP 67686198; BNFAS, 5 (1971), 41).

For Roman Road 17, see Appendix.

MEDIEVAL AND LATER

[d](3) SETTLEMENT REMAINS AND HOLLOW-WAYS (SP 671632), formerly part of the hamlet of Nobottle, lie around and N. of Townsend Farm at the head of a S.-draining valley on Northampton Sand and Boulder Clay between 110 m. and 135 m. above OD. The settlement gave its name to the Hundred of Nobottle Grove. The meeting place of the Hundred was therefore presumably near it and indeed it has been plausibly suggested that the field 'Harrow Hill' which lies just N.W. of the hamlet on the summit of a ridge (SP 669633) is the site of the Hundred meeting place (PN Northants., 78, 280; BNFAS, 5 (1971), 44).

Little is known of the history of Nobottle but its name, 'new building', indicates that it may be a relatively late settlement in the area (PN Northants., 80). It is first noted in 1086 when Domesday Book lists it with a recorded population of nine (VCH Northants., I (1902), 337). Thereafter nothing is known of its size until 1673 when eleven people paid the Hearth Tax (PRO, E179/254/14). Bridges (Hist. of Northants., I (1791), 472), writing in about 1720, said there were twelve houses there. Today the hamlet is much the same size, though its houses are somewhat scattered.

The earthworks fall into two parts. The more extensive are perhaps the remains of former settlement in Nobottle itself and include a large sub-rectangular enclosure on the N. side of the hamlet (SP 671632), bounded on the N. and W. by a bank and inner ditch and on the S. by a low scarp. The latter has been said to be connected with the Roman road which crosses the area at this point but this is unlikely (see Appendix). The enclosure is divided internally into four closes bounded by shallow ditches. To the S., along both sides of the track leading S. to Glassthorpe and Flore (SP 672630), are other more indeterminate earthworks, mainly rectangular closes bounded by low banks and shallow ditches, some of which have later ridge-and-furrow within them. All may be sites of former houses and crofts.

The other earthworks are hollow-ways which may be connected, at least in part, with the existence of the Hundred meeting place here. In the centre of the hamlet, at the point where the Glassthorpe track meets the main road between Whilton and Northampton, a broad hollow-way runs N. across a pasture field, continuing the line of the track and forming the E. boundary of the large enclosure noted above. This hollow-way turns and climbs the hill in a broad curve (SP 672632) and at this point there are several deeply cut hollows up to 1.5 m. deep. It is possible that the line of these hollow-ways was determined by early enclosures here, for the S. side of the hollow-way is bounded by a low bank 0.5 m. high. The hollow-ways run into the modern road to Harlestone, just below the assumed site of the Hundred meeting place (Air photographs in NMR).

d(4) SETTLEMENT REMAINS (centred SP 661636), formerly part of Little Brington, survive in two places in the present village. On the S. side of the main E.–W. street (SP 661637) are two empty plots with traces of abandoned buildings within them. These were both devoid of houses in 1840 (NRO, Tithe Map). At the S.W. end of the village, behind the existing houses (SP 659635), a small close still retains its original W. side, with a modern hedge outside it. A bank 1.25 m. high is visible.

(5) CULTIVATION REMAINS. The common fields of Great and Little Brington were enclosed by an Act of Parliament of 1742. Ridge-and-furrow of these fields exists on the ground or can be traced on air photographs over large areas of the parish, arranged in end-on and interlocked furlongs. A particularly well preserved block of it, cut into by later quarrying, exists in pasture S.W. of Great Brington (SP 662645). In the same area is a reversed-S furlong (SP 664646), orientated N.–S., which has remarkably high terminations at the S. ends of the ridges. These are large sub-rectangular mounds, up to 1.25 m. high, which would seem to have prevented a plough from turning. Their function and method of formation are not clear.

The date of the enclosure of the common fields of Nobottle is unknown, but was before 1840 (NRO, Tithe Map). Ridge-and-furrow of these fields exists on the ground or can be traced on air photographs over much of the land attributable to Nobottle. It is arranged in end-on and interlocked furlongs and, S. of Nobottle itself, is well preserved in pasture, laid out around a number of small spurs.

The small area of land in the S. of the parish (centred SP 667630) which was part of the territory of the deserted village of Glassthorpe (Flore (4)) also has ridge-and-furrow within it. Three furlongs immediately S. and S.W. of Grange Farm (SP 669628) run across both the modern and the medieval parish boundary lines, which do not quite coincide (NRO, Tithe Maps of Glassthorpe, 1850, and Brington, 1840; RAF VAP CPE/UK/1994, 1261–3, 2361–3, 2256–62, 3349–55, 4260–5, 4364–8).

UNDATED

d(6) MOUND (SP 65256348), lies on the N. side of the road to Whilton on glacial gravel at 130 m. above OD. It is 7 m. in diam. and 0.5 m. high and lies across the assumed line of the Roman Road 17; the present road is diverted around it. It stands on the end of a block of ridge-and-furrow orientated N.–S. and is probably medieval or later though this is not certain (BNFAS, 5 (1971), 1).

11 BRIXWORTH

(OS 1: 10000 a SP 77 SW, b SP 77 SE, c SP 76 NW, d SP 76 NE)

The parish is roughly triangular and occupies some 1270 hectares between the S.W.-flowing Pitsford Brook and a S.-flowing stream which meet in the S.W. corner of the parish. The village of Brixworth stands at the highest point, on a broad almost level plateau between 120 m. and 130 m. above OD. Northampton Sand covers most of the centre of the parish, but in the E. of the village it is overlaid by Boulder Clay; on the lower slopes, down-cutting of the main streams and their tributaries has exposed wide areas of Upper Lias Clay. The parish is notable for the wealth of sites and finds of all periods. Their discovery is due, at least in part, to extensive ironstone-mining in the late 19th and early 20th centuries, but even more to intensive modern fieldwork and excavation carried out in an attempt to understand the background of the unique Saxon church at Brixworth. The history and architectural development of the church is beyond the scope of this volume but the discoveries described below help to provide a context (Fig. 31). There is evidence of extensive Roman settlement (13–21) in the parish, probably on or near the hill on which the church now stands, and this appears to have been superseded by a rather dispersed pattern of early Saxon occupation sites (24–32), with which two known cemeteries (22, 23), and perhaps others, may have been

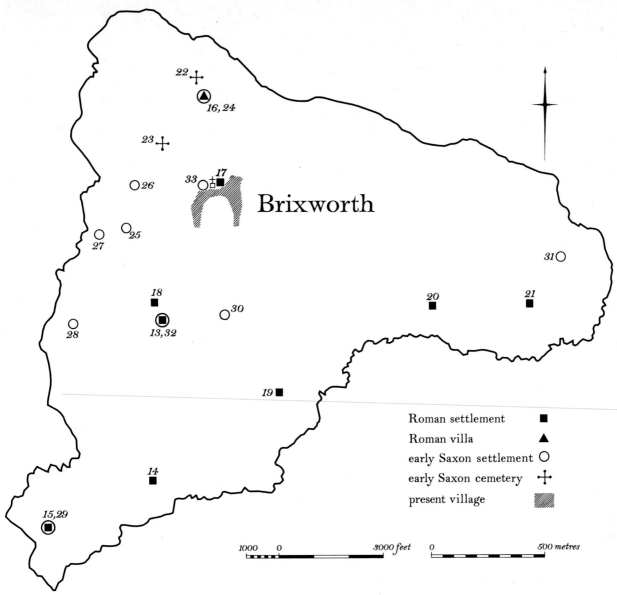

Roman settlement ■
Roman villa ▲
early Saxon settlement ○
early Saxon cemetery ✝
present village ▨

Fig. 31 BRIXWORTH (13–32) Roman and early Saxon settlements and burials

associated. Excavations in and around the churchyard (33, 34) suggest that a monastic establishment was in existence by about 700 A.D. This supports the documentary evidence which may imply that the original monastic church was founded in 666–9 A.D. by St. Wilfred. The same excavations also seems to show that in the late Saxon period at least part of the monastic precinct was converted to secular use.

PREHISTORIC AND ROMAN

In addition to the flint-working sites (1–11) listed below, numerous flint tools have been discovered in the parish including many arrowheads and a flint axe said to have come from near Hill Farm (SP 747690). Small quantities of flints have been noted at SP 738704, 743706 and 748685 (inf. D. N. Hall). At least four polished stone axes are known to have come from the parish, two of Group VI, one of Group XX and one of Greywacke (T. J. George, *Arch. Survey of Northants.* (1904), 11; NM Records). Prehistoric pottery from Brixworth includes three beakers, all discovered before 1918, probably during ironstone-mining. One is handled (D. L. Clarke, *Beaker Pottery of Great Britain and Ireland* (1970), 490, SH3 (B); *Northants. N. and Q.*, 5 (1892), 80; OS Record Cards; NM), one is biconical with an everted rim and three zones of horizontal lines (Clarke, op. cit., W/MR; NM) and the third is a tall beaker (Clarke, op. cit., S2 (E); NM). There are also three or four Bronze Age urns from the parish, including two Primary Series Collared Urns (*PPS*, 27 (1961), 296, Nos. 109 and 110; Abercromby, *Bronze Age Pottery, II* (1912), Figs. 67 and 95; NM). A late Bronze Age leaf-shaped sword is also known (VCH *Northants.*, I (1902), 143; *J. Northants. Mus. and Art Gall.*, 6 (1969), 4; *Beds. Arch. J.*, 10 (1975), 17; *Arch. J.*, 125 (1968), 1–45; Burgess, Class IIc; NM). An iron bar which had been described as an Iron Age currency bar is now thought to be an agricultural implement of unknown date (OS Record Cards; T. J. George, *Arch. Survey of Northants.* (1904), 11; *PPS*, 33 (1967), 334).

A number of barrows or ring ditches have been recorded at various times. On a map of Bannaventa and its environs (*Archaeologia*, 35 (1853), 395, Pl. XVI) three 'tumuli' are marked in Brixworth village (two at SP 748706, and the other at SP 749712). The areas involved are now built over, but the sites are unlikely to have been barrows. More recently an air photograph (CUAP, ABD92) has revealed the cropmarks of three joined ring ditches with others some 45 m. to the E. (SP 771706). These are known to be the remains of a Second World War anti-aircraft battery (see also Brockhall and Harlestone).

A hoard of about 30 Roman silver coins was found somewhere in the parish in about 1885 (T. J. George, *Arch. Survey of Northants* (1904), 11); other coins, of Pius, Carausius and others, also found in the 19th century, may have come from the site of the villa (16) (VCH *Northants.*, I (1902), 194). Another hoard, of 24 coins from Vespasian to Crispina, was found in 1892 (*Num. Chron.*, 5 (1945), 164). Roman pottery is also said to have been found in the parish around 1900, during ironstone-quarrying (T. J. George, *ibid.*). A Roman well mentioned by T. J. George (*ibid.*) cannot be located.

In Brixworth church there is a piece of decorated stone cornice, probably 3rd-century in date and presumably from a monumental structure. It was apparently found in 1958 during excavations in the church. Whether it was originally part of a building on the site or was brought from elsewhere is not known (*Northants. Archaeol.*, 13 (1978), 82).

(1) FLINT-WORKING SITE (unlocated), said to be somewhere E. of the main A508 road, S. of the village, probably on Northampton Sand. A large number of flint tools, waste flakes and cores is recorded (NM Records).

^a(2) FLINT-WORKING SITE (SP 746719). Worked flints, including leaf-shaped and barbed-and-tanged arrowheads, scrapers and blades as well as cores, were found during excavation on the Roman villa (16) (*J. Northants. Mus. and Art Gall.*, 8 (1970), 5). More flints have since been noted, in the area to the N., extending E. to the Saxon site (22) (inf. D. N. Hall).

^a(3) FLINT-WORKING SITE (SP 742712), W. of the village on Northampton Sand at 107 m. above OD. Worked flints of Bronze Age type are recorded, including ten flint arrowheads of various forms, 99 scrapers, 600 waste flakes and nearly 60 cores (inf. D. N. Hall; for Saxon finds from this area, see (25) below).

^a(4) PREHISTORIC SETTLEMENT (?) (SP 741708), W. of the village, on Northampton Sand at 105 m. above OD. Worked flints of Neolithic and Bronze Age type, late Bronze Age pottery and part of a saddle quern have been found. The flints included 5 arrowheads, 61 scrapers, 188 waste flakes and over 40 cores (inf. D. N. Hall; for Saxon finds from this site, see (26) below).

^a(5) FLINT-WORKING SITE (SP 738707), W. of the village, on Upper Lias Clay at 90 m. above OD. Worked flints said to be of Mesolithic, Neolithic and Bronze Age type have been found. They included nearly 60 scrapers, 316 waste flakes and 43 cores (inf. D. N. Hall; for Saxon finds from this site, see (27) below).

^{ac}(6) FLINT-WORKING SITE (SP 735701), in the W. of the parish, on Northampton Sand at 91 m. above OD. A quantity of worked flints, described as being of early Neolithic type, have been found (inf. D. N. Hall; for Saxon finds from this site, see (28) below).

^c(7) FLINT-WORKING SITE (SP 741699), S.W. of the village, on Northampton Sand at 120 m. above OD. Worked flints, said to be of Neolithic type, have been found. Bronze Age flints are recorded near by (SP 739698). These two groups included over 50 arrowheads, over 1100 scrapers, over 7500 waste flakes and nearly 1400 cores. Two saddle querns were also discovered (inf. D. N. Hall).

^{cd}(8) FLINT-WORKING SITE (SP 750699), S. of the village, on Northampton Sand at 125 m. above OD. Worked flints described as being of Mesolithic and Bronze Age type have been discovered. These included two arrowheads, 31 scrapers, nearly 100 waste flakes and 29 cores (inf. D. N. Hall; for Saxon finds from this site, see (30) below).

^c(9) FLINT-WORKING SITE (SP 748690), in the S.E. of the parish, E. of Hill Farm, on Northampton Sand at 110 m. above OD. A number of worked flints, apparently of late Neolithic or early Bronze Age type, have been found here in two places. Cropmarks of unspecified form are also recorded. The flaked flint axe noted above may have come from this site (inf. D. N. Hall).

^c(10) RING DITCH AND FLINT-WORKING SITE (SP 736694), in the W. of the parish, on Upper Lias Clay at 80 m. above OD. Cropmarks of a ring ditch are said to have been seen, and on the ground a number of worked flints, described as of Bronze Age type, have been found. The flints included 66 scrapers, nearly 80 cores and over 300 waste flakes (inf. D. N. Hall).

^b(11) PREHISTORIC SETTLEMENT (SP 778704), in the E. of the parish, on Upper Lias Clay at 90 m. above OD.

Worked flints, described as Neolithic and Bronze Age in type, and sherds of late Bronze Age pottery have been found. The flints included 34 arrowheads of various forms, over 250 scrapers, some 2000 waste flakes and 400 cores (inf. D. N. Hall; for Saxon finds from the site, see (31) below).

b(12) IRON AGE SETTLEMENT (?) (SP 779702), in the extreme E. of the parish, on Northampton Sand at 100 m. above OD. Some badly abraded sherds, probably of early Iron Age date, have been found (*BNFAS*, 3 (1969), 1).

a(13) IRON AGE AND ROMAN SETTLEMENT (SP 743701; Fig. 31), immediately S.W. of the village, on Northampton Sand at 125 m. above OD. A trial trench revealed sherds of late Iron Age and Roman pottery, but the soil has been restored after quarrying (*Northants. Archaeol.*, 8 (1973), 5–6). In addition large quantities of worked flints have been noted in the surrounding area (inf. D. N. Hall; for Saxon finds from the same site, see (32) below).

c(14) IRON AGE AND ROMAN SETTLEMENT (?) (SP 743687; Fig. 31), S.W. of Hill Farm, on Northampton Sand at 95 m. above OD. Iron Age and Roman sherds have been found here and cropmarks are said to have been seen some 100 m. to the N. (inf. D. N. Hall).

c(15) PREHISTORIC AND ROMAN SETTLEMENT (SP 734682; Fig. 31), in the extreme S.W. of the parish, on Northampton Sand at 85 m. above OD. Worked flints of Mesolithic, Neolithic and Bronze Age type have been found, as well as Roman pottery. The flints include 100 scrapers, 3 fragments of flint axes, 219 cores and nearly 1000 waste flakes (inf. D. N. Hall; for Saxon finds from this site, see (29) below).

a(16) ROMAN VILLA (SP 746719; Fig. 31), lies N.W. of the church, on Northampton Sand at 120 m. above OD. Excavations between 1965 and 1970 revealed the remains of a large building of several periods but, although the pottery from the site has been published in detail, only a brief summary of the structure exists. Five periods of occupation were recovered. The earliest is represented by ditches and a circular hut some 6 m. in diam., all dating from before 70 A.D., which was replaced by a small five-roomed rectangular masonry structure, orientated N.–S. with a timber colonnade on the W. and some painted walls. It was dated to between 70 A.D. and 100 A.D. In the late 2nd or early 3rd century the N. end of the range was reconstructed and a detached outbuilding was erected to the S. The latter remained in use until the end of the 3rd century and at one time was used for the manufacture of bronze implements. In the late 3rd or early 4th century the villa was doubled in size by the addition of another room to the N., a corridor to the E. and a large bath suite to the S. Two infant-burials were found below the floor of one of the rooms in the bath suite. The later history of the site is not clear, as a result of extensive robbing and deep ploughing, but surface finds indicate occupation lasting well into the 4th and perhaps into the 5th century. The villa may have been partly occupied in the early Saxon period (see (24) below; *J. Northants. Mus. and Art Gall.*, 1 (1967), 5–27; 8 (1970), 3–97; *JRS*, 56 (1966), 207; *BNFAS*, 2 (1967), 7–8; CBA Group 9, *Newsletter*, 2 (1972), 9; for prehistoric finds, see p. 27 and (2) above).

a(17) ROMAN SETTLEMENT (?) (SP 74727122; Fig. 31), perhaps under Brixworth church. In 1971 a small excavation in the N.W. angle between the tower and the nave led to the discovery of a few stratified Roman sherds, a piece of roof tile and a pit or ditch which was also probably Roman. Medieval pottery and coins were found in the same area (inf. D. N. Hall; *Med. Arch.*, 16 (1972), 158; *BNFAS*, 7 (1972), 39; *Northants. Archaeol.*, 8 (1973), 18; CBA Group 9, *Newsletter*, 3 (1973), 20).

a(18) ROMAN SETTLEMENT (?) (SP 743703; Fig. 31), S.W. of the village, on Northampton Sand at 125 m. above OD. A quantity of Roman pottery and a single Saxon sherd were found in soil dug from a trench in 1975 (*Northants. Archaeol.*, 11 (1976), 186).

d(19) ROMAN SETTLEMENT (?) (SP 753693; Fig. 31), on the edge of Pitsford Reservoir, in the E. of the parish, on Northampton Sand at 92 m. above OD. Roman pottery and a quern have been found (inf. D. N. Hall).

d(20) ROMAN SETTLEMENT (?) (SP 767700; Fig. 31), S.W. of Grange Farm on Upper Lias Clay at 90 m. above OD. Roman pottery and worked flints have been found (*Northants. Archaeol.*, 9 (1974), 86).

d(21) ROMAN SETTLEMENT (SP 774700; Fig. 31), in the E. of the parish, immediately W. of the Lower Brixworth Lodge, on Northampton Sand at 103 m. above OD. Quantities of Roman pottery and a well were discovered during ironstone-mining in 1960 (CBA Group 9, *Newsletter*, 3 (1973), 32; inf. D. N. Hall).

MEDIEVAL AND LATER

Saxon finds, except for those from the cemeteries and possible settlements listed below (24–32), include three pennies of Edward the Elder and a penny of Aethelred, the latter from the churchyard (T. J. George, *Arch. Survey of Northants.* (1904), 11). A silver penny of Cuthred and a silver-plated iron pin with an ornamental head once said to have been found in the churchyard came in fact from ironstone quarries in about 1887. A penny of Aethelward and two bronze pins are also recorded from 'near Brixworth' (*The Antiquary*, 30 (1894), 104; *PSA*, 29 (1916–17), 59–60). Two rotary querns, said to be Saxon or medieval, are recorded from Silver Street (SP 750712), as well as a 'deposit' of medieval pottery in Church Street (SP 747711), more medieval pottery immediately to the S. and some 13th to 14th-century rubbish pits in Hall Park (SP 748710; local inf.).

(22, 23) SAXON CEMETERIES (Fig. 31). The sites of two cemeteries, described below, are known with certainty and were found during ironstone-mining before 1904. A third has been given various suggested locations in the S.W. of the parish. There is a large collection of Saxon objects in NM which may be either from these cemeteries or from other unlocated ones, all apparently discovered during ironstone-quarrying in the late 19th or early 20th century. They include parts of a large square-headed brooch, three cruciform brooches, eight small-long brooches, three necklaces of amber and glass, a buckle, a horse bit, knives and 26 spearheads, as well as a rough hand-made pot and other fragments of decorated pottery (Meaney, *Gazetteer* (1964), 187–8; T. J. George, *Arch. Survey of Northants.* (1904), 11; *JBAA*, 4 (1849), 142; J. N. L. Myres, *Anglo-Saxon Pottery and the Settlement of England* (1969), Fig. 25, No. 789; *BAR*, 7 (1974), 38; *Ant. J.*, 19 (1939), 325–6; *BNFAS*, 7 (1972), 39; *J. Northants. Mus. and Art Gall.*, 10 (1974), 20–37).

[a](22) SAXON CEMETERY (SP 747720; Fig. 31), 800 m. N. of the church, on Northampton Sand at 120 m. above OD. Inhumation and cremation burials were discovered, accompanied by urns, spearheads, shield bosses, knives etc. Early Saxon pottery has subsequently been found in the area to the S. (inf. D. N. Hall).

[a](23) SAXON CEMETERY (SP 744715; Fig. 31), 400 m. N.W. of the church in a situation similar to (22). Inhumation and cremation burials are recorded, together with urns, spearheads and knives.

[a](24) SAXON BUILDING AND BURIAL (SP 746719; Fig. 31), found during the excavation of the Roman villa (16) between 1965 and 1970. Ten post-holes, arranged in two parallel rows of five 1.2 m. apart across one of the rooms in the villa, were dated to the early Saxon period and were thought to be for a structure erected within the already ruined villa. An inhumation burial, under a rough cairn made from stone from the collapsed Roman building, was also found. No grave goods were noted. Saxon pottery has been discovered in the surrounding area (*J. Northants. Mus. and Art Gall.*, 8 (1970), 5; *Med. Arch.*, 17 (1973), 147).

[a](25) SAXON SETTLEMENT (?) (SP 742712; Fig. 31), found with a flint-working site (3). Early Saxon pottery has been noted (inf. D. N. Hall).

[a](26) SAXON SETTLEMENT (?) (SP 741708; Fig. 31), found with a prehistoric settlement (4). Early Saxon pottery has been discovered (inf. D. N. Hall).

[a](27) SAXON SETTLEMENT (?) (SP 738707; Fig. 31), found with a flint-working site (5). Early Saxon pottery has been discovered (inf. D. N. Hall).

[ac](28) SAXON SETTLEMENT (?) (SP 735701; Fig. 31), found with a flint-working site (6). Two separate areas of early Saxon pottery have been found in this vicinity (inf. D. N. Hall).

[c](29) SAXON SETTLEMENT (?) (SP 734682; Fig. 31), found with a prehistoric and Roman site (15) in the S.W. of the parish. Early Saxon pottery has been discovered (inf. D. N. Hall).

[cd](30) SAXON SETTLEMENT (?) (SP 750699; Fig. 31), found at a flint-working site (8). Early Saxon pottery is recorded (inf. D. N. Hall).

[b](31) SAXON SETTLEMENT (?) (SP 778704; Fig. 31), found with a prehistoric site (11). Early Saxon pottery is recorded (inf. D. N. Hall).

[a](32) SAXON SETTLEMENT (?) (SP 743701; Fig. 31), found with Iron Age and Roman material (13). Early Saxon sherds have been noted (*Northants. Archaeol.*, 8 (1973), 5–6).

[a](33) MONASTIC CEMETERY AND MEDIEVAL SETTLEMENT (SP 74647121; Fig. 31), in the vicarage garden, immediately E. of Brixworth church, on Northampton Sand at 120 m. above OD. Various excavations in the area have revealed burials. Two skeletons, described as lying in a crouched position, were found in 1939, and in 1949 a small excavation uncovered four or five skeletons in at least two distinct layers. In 1972 further work was undertaken and part of the monastic precinct of the Saxon church, including a section of its boundary and part of the cemetery within, was discovered. The precinct boundary was a large ditch, running N.–S., V-shaped in section, 3.4 m. wide at the top and 2 m. deep. A radiocarbon date of 710 ad ± 80 was obtained from the organic material in the primary silt. The later fill of the ditch contained Saxo-Norman pottery including Stamford and Northampton wares. Inside the boundary 11 inhumations were excavated, all orientated E.–W., with no evidence of coffins or grave goods. Radio-carbon dates 840 ad ± 70 and 780 ad ± 80 were obtained from two of the burials and all must have been earlier than 12th-century features which had cut into them. The latter indicated that in the post-Conquest period the area was in secular use, and this continued until the 15th century when the area was abandoned. The remains included evidence of stone and timber buildings and walls, as well as rubbish pits (*Med. Arch.*, 17 (1973), 147; 19 (1975), 225; *Northants. Archaeol.*, 10 (1975), 164; *JBAA*, 130 (1977), 52–122).

[a](34) LATE SAXON BURIALS AND MEDIEVAL BUILDING (SP 747712), immediately S. of the church, just beyond the churchyard boundary. An excavation in 1972 revealed three late Saxon burials, orientated E.–W., without grave goods, and four possible contemporary pits containing domestic refuse and sherds of St. Neots ware. Subsequently, perhaps in the 11th or 12th century, a wall was built across the site and this was replaced in the 13th century by a large building 10 m. by 5 m., divided into four rooms. Other buildings were added later; the whole site was levelled in the early 18th century (*Northants. Archaeol.*, 8 (1973), 18).

[a](35) MEDIEVAL BUILDING (SP 74657116), at the former

site of Fox's Farm, in Church Street, on Northampton Sand at 120 m. above OD. Excavations in 1972 revealed post-holes and beam-slots associated with fine shelly pottery, probably of 12th to 13th-century date (*Northants. Archaeol.*, 8 (1973), 19–20).

a(36) MALT-DRYING KILN (SP 747711), found in the churchyard during excavations before 1970. The kiln was aligned N.–S. with the flue on the S. side, and was built from sandstone blocks with a floor of limestone slabs, discoloured by burning. Its date is not known but it may be associated with the 13th-century building to the N. (34) (*Med. Arch.*, 14 (1970), 207).

a(37) POST-MEDIEVAL FARMHOUSE (SP 74657113), immediately S. of (35), and also at the site of Fox's Farm. The foundations of the 17th-century farmhouse and outbuildings were recovered, and two wells. Much of the excavated area had been quarried, apparently between the 14th and 17th centuries, and the fill contained pottery from early Saxon times onwards (*Northants. Archaeol.*, 8 (1973), 20).

a(38) SITE OF CHANTRY CHAPEL (?) (SP 74797115), in the centre of the village, on Northampton San at 120 m. above OD. Foundations, thought to be of a medieval chantry chapel, are said to have been discovered here in 1945. The site is under grass and no remains are visible (OS Record Cards).

a(39) MANOR HOUSE SITE (SP 738705), lies S.W. of the village, near the W. boundary of the parish and S. of the Spratton road, on the side of a deep, narrow valley, on Upper Lias Clay at 90 m. above OD. The earthworks are the site of Wolfage Manor which, though not mentioned by name until 1509, was probably the main manor of Brixworth in the medieval period (VCH *Northants.*, IV (1937), 151–2). Nothing is known of the history of the site until 1668, but a map of that date (NRO) shows a building called Wolfage Manor, set in a large rectangular area called a park. The remains include a number of well-marked building platforms and embanked enclosures, set on a spur projecting from the valley side. Below in the valley bottom is a mutilated dam, possibly for a fishpond, as well as other more indeterminate earthworks. The site was completely abandoned by 1846 (NRO, Map of Brixworth).

a(40) SITE OF WATERMILL (SP 746709), at the junction of Church Street and Newland, on the W. side of the village, in the valley of a small W.-flowing stream, on Upper Lias Clay at 103 m. above OD. In 1970 two parallel walls, apparently the wheel-pit of a watermill, were discovered about 2.5 m. below the modern road surface and large deposits of silt upstream, on the E. side of the road, indicated a former mill pond (*BNFAS*, 5 (1971), 38). The site of the pond is now built over. This mill and another further downstream (41) may be those recorded under Brixworth in Domesday Book as being held by the King (VCH *Northants.*, I (1902), 306). A watermill is listed as

being part of the manor in 1315, and there are other records of a 'Kyngsmulne' and 'Kingsmilne' in the 13th century and early 14th century (VCH *Northants.*, IV (1937), 152). Immediately E. of the site is a large pond, bounded on the E. by a massive dam up to 4 m. high. This is an ornamental feature connected with Brixworth Hall.

a(41) SITE OF WATERMILL (SP 743709), lies W. of (40), further downstream but in a similar position, at 92 m. above OD. The remains consist of a small rectangular embanked pond, set 2 m. above the stream and linked to it by an approach leat from the W. It may be one of the mills referred to in various medieval documents (see (40) above; *BNFAS*, 5 (1971), 38).

(42) CULTIVATION REMAINS. The common fields of the parish were enclosed by an Act of Parliament of 1780. On a map of 1688 (NRO) the names of these fields and the individual furlongs are shown, though not the strips. At that time there were three large fields, Shotnell Field N. and N.E. of the village, Whaddon Field S.W. and W. of the village, and Demwell Field S. and S.E. of the village. There were some old enclosures in the extreme N.W. of the parish. Ridge-and-furrow of these fields survives on the ground or is visible on air photographs over much of the parish though extensive ironstone-quarrying has removed all trace over wide areas in the N. and to a lesser extent elsewhere. The Pitsford Reservoir which now covers a large part of the southern edge of the parish has drowned much ridge-and-furrow though this can be seen on early air photographs. Where it survives the ridge-and-furrow is arranged in interlocked and end-on furlongs, some up to 300 m., a considerable length, arranged to ensure that, where possible, the ridges run across the contours.

In several places (e.g. SP 770702) there are rectangular areas 20 m. by 30 m. where the underlying ridges have been almost obliterated. These have been identified as sites of 'rick-places' marked on the 1688 map and are presumably places where stacks were regularly built within the open fields (CBA Group 9, *Newsletter*, 3 (1973), 32; RAF VAP CPE/UK/1994, 1377–9, 2371–5, 4375–9).

UNDATED

a(43) EARTHWORKS (about SP 747712 and 748712). Bridges (*Hist. of Northants.*, II (1791), 80), writing in about 1720, recorded that there were 'vestiges of old trenches' N. of Brixworth church and, to the E. of it, some 'butts or hillocks'. No trace of these now remains as the area has been worked for ironstone.

12 BROCKHALL

(OS 1:10000 a SP 66 SW, b SP 66 NW)

The parish occupies only 300 hectares and lies on the E. side of Watling Street which forms the whole of the W. boundary; the S. boundary is determined by the Whilton

Brook. Another Roman Road, 17, crosses the parish, running E.–W., but does not ever seem to have formed part of its boundary. The parish is roughly rectangular except for an oval projection from the N.E. corner, an area known as Roughmoor. The latter is contiguous with Whilton, with the former land of Muscott (Norton (11)) and with Brington; its name, shape and position suggest that it was once an area of common waste (see (2)).

The E.-sloping land in the W. of the parish, between 120 m. and 90 m. above OD, is covered by glacial sands and gravels, and E. of this a wide band of alluvium occupies the valley floor. From there the land rises again to the E., across Lias clays and Marlstone. The higher ground, over 125 m. above OD, is overlaid by Boulder Clay; glacial deposits also cover most of the area of Roughmoor. The settlement remains of Brockhall village (1) constitute the main monument in the parish.

PREHISTORIC AND ROMAN

A polished axe of mottled green stone, found in 1959, is in Daventry School. A Mesolithic core is recorded from the parish (NM Records). Roman coins have also been found, perhaps near Watling Street, for in the 19th century Baker said that 'Roman coins are still occasionally found at Brockhole' (*Hist. of Northants.*, I (1822–30), 119).

On air photographs (CUAP, AWO48, 50, and in NMR) a circular feature 15 m. in diam. with an entrance on the W. is visible with, to the W., a group of three more circles arranged in a clover-leaf pattern. These have been described as ring ditches but are more likely to be the remains of a Second World War anti-aircraft battery (SP 628614; see also Brixworth and Harlestone).

For Roman Roads 1f, Watling Street, and 17, see Appendix.

MEDIEVAL AND LATER

[a](1) SETTLEMENT REMAINS (SP 634625 and 632629; Fig. 32), formerly part of Brockhall, lie at each end of the existing hamlet on Marlstone Rock at about 110 m. above OD. The village has been included in the county list of deserted villages (K. J. Allison *et al.*, *The Deserted Villages of Northants.* (1966), 36) but in fact it appears to be much the same size today as it always has been and the remains indicate little more than minor shrinkage.

Brockhall is first mentioned in Domesday Book, and is described with Muscott (Norton (11)) which lies only 1 km. to the N.W., the two having a recorded population of six (VCH *Northants.*, I (1902), 325). In the 1301 Lay Subsidy it is again listed with Muscott, with a total of 48 tax-payers (PRO, E179/155/31), but this figure probably refers mainly to Muscott, for there is no evidence that Brockhall was ever large whereas earthworks at Muscott suggest that this was once a substantial village. Brockhall is separately mentioned in the *Nomina Villarum* of 1316, and in 1334 it paid 53s. 6½d. for the Lay Subsidy (PRO,

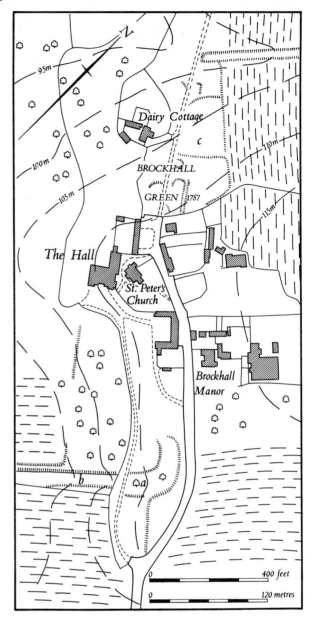

Fig. 32   BROCKHALL   (1)
Settlement remains

E179/155/3). By 1377 only five people over the age of 14 paid the Poll Tax in Brockhall and Muscott (PRO, E179/155/27) but most if not all of these must have lived in Brockhall as Muscott had probably been abandoned by then. In 1524 when the two places were again combined for the Taxation of the Laity only nine people were recorded (PRO, E179/155/134) most of whom presumably lived at Brockhall. The Hearth Tax Returns of 1674 list 17 houses for Brockhall and Muscott (PRO, E179/254/14) but as, by 1720, Bridges noted that there were 12 houses at Brockhall and three at Muscott the 1674 figure must again refer mainly to Brockhall (*Hist. of Northants.*, I(1791), 483). The earliest map of the parish to show any part of the village is dated 1787 (NRO) but this only covers the area N.W. of the main N.–S. road. It shows that the road did not make a marked bend at the S. end of the park as it does today, but ran on a little further to meet another road climbing the hillside from Dodford. It then swung N.E. onto the line of the existing road immediately W. of Brockhall Manor. The old road is still visible in the shrubbery near the park entrance as a fragmentary hollow-way 1.5 m. deep ('a' on plan) and the road to the S.W. survives as a massive ditch some 2 m. deep running down the hillside ('b' on plan).

The existing Brockhall Hall was built soon after 1625 when the Thornton family acquired the manor. The 1787 map shows the hall much as it is today but with two ranges of buildings extending S.W. from it to form an enclosed courtyard. These buildings are traditionally said to have been part of the village, but the plan shows clearly that they were outbuildings of the hall and this is confirmed by an engraving of the house of *c.* 1800 (BM). The same map shows that the area N.E. of the church and N. of the through-road was then called Brockhall Green.

A slightly later map, of 1793 (NRO), depicts only a small part of the village E. of the church. It shows that Dairy Cottage did not exist at that time, but that the cottages E. of the church were there. It also shows that three embanked closes further N.E. along the road ('c' on plan) were already devoid of buildings though they are obviously the sites of at least three former houses and gardens. Two other maps, an Estate Plan of 1821 and the Tithe Map of 1839 (both in NRO), show the village as it is today with the buildings around the courtyard of the hall demolished and the present road system in being.

The written sources and the map evidence thus suggest that Brockhall was always a small village laid out along a single street, but had perhaps suffered some shrinkage at its N. end by the late 18th century. The building of the hall in the early 17th century may have led to the removal of earlier buildings S.E. of the church but there is no direct evidence for this; the alterations to the park between 1787 and 1821 led to the abandonment and alteration of the roads at the S.E. end of the village.

(2) CULTIVATION REMAINS. The common fields of the parish were enclosed by private agreement in 1619–20. The earliest map of the parish, dated 1614 (NRO), only covers the land immediately E. of Watling Street but shows that this area was already partly in old enclosures at that date. This suggests that some enclosure had taken place before 1620. Ridge-and-furrow can be traced on the ground or on air photographs throughout the greater part of the parish; in the centre and E. the pattern is virtually complete. It is laid out in end-on and interlocking furlongs carefully adapted to the direction of the often rather steep slopes. It is noteworthy that ridge-and-furrow exists in the part of the parish projecting to the N. and known as Roughmoor or sometimes as Ringmere, which was probably an area of common waste. There are extremely well-preserved areas of ridge-and-furrow S.E. of the village (SP 365623) and to the N. on either side of a broad valley (SP 633630; RAF VAP CPE/UK/1994, 3254–6, 2260–3, 4264–6, 4363–5).

13   BYFIELD

(OS 1 : 10000 [a] SP 45 NE, [b] SP 45 SE, [c] SP 55 NW, [d] SP 55 SW)

The roughly rectangular parish of 1230 hectares lies across the valleys of four small S.-flowing tributary streams of the R. Cherwell. The N. part is mainly on Upper Lias Clay at 165 m.–200 m. above OD. To the S., between the streams, large areas of Marlstone Rock are exposed with Lower and Middle Lias Clay in the valley bottom between 120 m. and 150 m. above OD. Immediately S. of the village the land rises steeply across a broken scarp of Upper Lias Clay to a maximum height of just over 180 m. above OD. Two Roman sites (1) and (2) have recently been discovered in the parish; one (1) appears to be the site of a villa or major building, with at least one kiln, recorded in the 19th century but never published.

The village of Byfield consists of three separate parts, Church End, High Street and Westhorp, each based on a N.–S. street running along a ridge. This is best depicted on the Enclosure Map of 1779 (NRO) before modern development obscured the pattern.

PREHISTORIC AND ROMAN

A flint scraper was found in 1970 (SP 505526; NM; *BNFAS*, 5 (1971), 1). A small quantity of Roman pottery and a metal dagger scabbard have been discovered in the N.E. (SP 521546) and other Roman sherds in the E. (SP 526531). A complete 4th-century pot was found in an ironstone-quarry N. of the village in 1960 (SP 519542) and a puddingstone quern further to the S. (SP 518538; OS Record Cards).

[d](1) ROMAN VILLA AND KILN (centred SP 506545; Fig. 33), N.E. of Pitwell Farm on Northampton Sand at 177 m. above OD. Roman pottery, including grey and colour-coated wares and a mortarium sherd, associated with patches of burnt earth, stones and roof tiles, has been found in recent years E. of the farm (SP 506543; *BNFAS*, 5 (1971), 44; NM). Earlier unpublished discoveries, in the mid 19th century, show that this is probably the site of a villa with at least one outbuilding and a pottery kiln.

In the Dryden Collection (Central Library, Northampton) are notes made by Sir Henry Dryden on two separate discoveries in the area. He gives a plan of a building which was uncovered in 1851 in a field 'of Mr. Fairbrother joining the Byfield–Marston road, a short distance south west of Iron Cross'. This would be perhaps

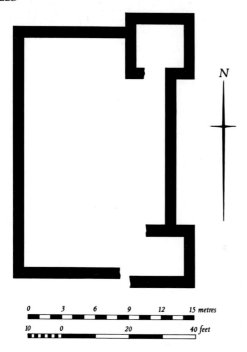

N

0   3   6   9   12   15 metres

10   0   20   40 feet

Fig. 33   BYFIELD   (1) Roman villa

about SP 506546. The plan shows the external walls of a large rectangular stone building, orientated N.–S. with almost square compartments projecting at the N.E. and S.E. corners. The walls were said to be of 'red stone' and up to 1 m. thick. No dating evidence is given on the plan though the building is described as 'Roman Remains'. The plan is obviously incomplete but suggests a corridor villa with projecting wings.

A later plan and note recorded further features discovered in 1863 in the same area and these can be more accurately located (probably at SP 50635449). They comprised a piece of walling, L-shaped in plan with arms about 3 m. long and with another piece of wall in the angle. This was associated with ashes, charcoal and 'grey pottery'. A 'mill stone or quern' was also found about 30 m. to the N.W. and an iron knife 60 m. to the N. Just N. of the wall the remains of a circular stone-lined kiln, containing pottery and ashes and with a stoke-hole on the S. side, were discovered.

^d(2) ROMAN SETTLEMENT (SP 508549), in the N. of the parish, 700 m. N.E. of (1), and in a similar position. A scatter of Roman pottery, mostly grey ware but also some samian and colour-coated ware, pieces of tiles and a patch of burnt stones, have been discovered (*BNFAS*, 5 (1971), 44; NM).

MEDIEVAL AND LATER

^d(3) SETTLEMENT REMAINS (SP 518532), formerly part of Byfield village, lay along the E. side of the road between the manor house and Church End, on a steep W.-facing slope at 145 m. above OD. Air photographs (RAF VAP CPE/UK/1994, 4155–6) show what may have been a series of shallow ditches bounding closes between the road and the adjacent ridge-and-furrow to the E. but the remains have been entirely destroyed by modern cultivation. The site was already devoid of building in 1779 (NRO, Enclosure Map).

^d(4) WINDMILL MOUND (SP 515523), S. of the village on Northampton Sand at 172 m. above OD. A low mound, and a circular soil-mark visible on air photographs, represent the site of a windmill which stood here in 1779 (NRO, Enclosure Map) and which remained until the mid 19th century (1st ed. OS 1 in. map (1834); RAF VAP CPE/UK/1994, 4155–6).

(5) CULTIVATION REMAINS. The common fields of the parish were enclosed by an Act of Parliament of 1778 (NRO, Enclosure Map, 1779). Ridge-and-furrow of these fields remains on the ground or can be traced on air photographs over most of the parish except where extensive ironstone-quarrying has removed all trace. It is mainly arranged in rectangular end-on or interlocked furlongs, often of reversed-S form, except in the S. of the parish (around SP 518524) and in the E. (around SP 528536) where the curving hillsides produce a radiating pattern of furlongs (RAF VAP CPE/UK/1994, 2148–53, 3142–7, 4102–7, 4153–7).

14   CANONS ASHBY

(OS 1:10000 ^a SP 55 SE, ^b SP 54 NE)

The parish occupies some 750 hectares and is bounded on the E. and S. sides by a small tributary which runs W. to the R. Cherwell. It is on land sloping gently S. between 180 m. and 130 m. above OD, and is covered by Boulder Clay, except round the church and the site of the former village which stand on a narrow outcrop of Northampton Sand, and in the N.W. of the parish where the down-cutting of another stream has exposed the underlying Upper Lias Clay. The village of Canons Ashby (1), now almost deserted, is of considerable interest, both because it appears to have been a large and prosperous place until its apparently deliberate abandonment and because its earlier expansion seems to have been achieved at the expense of former arable land. Of the monastic foundation that gives its name to the village little survives apart from the church; the earthworks close by, although usually interpreted as of monastic origin, are probably in part post-medieval gardens (2).

PREHISTORIC

In 1873 a jade axe was exhibited at the Society of Antiquaries. It was said 'to have been found in a British station, near Ashby about thirty-five or forty years ago', but in fact came from King's Sutton parish (*PPS*, 29 (1963), 163).

A late Bronze Age spearhead, also said to have been found in the parish in the 19th century, was exhibited at the same time. Part of the ashwood shaft still remained in the socket (*PSA*, 5 (1873), 442; OS Record Cards).

MEDIEVAL AND LATER

^a(1) DESERTED VILLAGE OF CANONS ASHBY (SP 576507; Fig. 34; Plate 20), lies immediately N. of Canons Ashby House, on Northampton Sand at 157 m. above OD. The village was first mentioned in Domesday Book (VCH *Northants.*, I (1902), 341, 372) with a recorded population of 16. In about 1150 the Augustinian priory (2) was founded; it apparently lay at the S. end of the village, but it later acquired most of the parish. In 1301, 18 taxpayers paid the Lay Subsidy (PRO, E179/155/31) and the village is mentioned in the 1316 *Nomina Villarum*. There were 41 houses in 1343 (M. W. Beresford, *The Lost Villages of England* (1954), 366); in 1377 82 people over the age of 14 paid the Poll Tax (PRO, E179/155/27–9). However, in 1489 the prior of Canons Ashby enclosed 100 acres of land, converting it to pasture and destroying three houses at the same time, and in 1492 he evicted 24 people. By 1524 only 21 taxpayers were listed (PRO, E179/155/122–64) and by 1535 only nine tenants paid rent to the priory. On the dissolution of the priory in 1537 the manor passed to Sir Francis Bryan and a year later to Sir John Cope who, by 1547, had 2000 sheep in the parish. The Hearth Tax Returns of 1674 list five people paying tax (PRO, E179/254/14) and Bridges, writing around 1720, said that there were three farm-houses and two or three lodges in the village (*Hist. of Northants.*, I (1791), 223); he also recorded the tradition that the village 'was formerly very considerable'. By 1801 the population of the parish was 40 (K. J. Allison *et. al.*, *The Deserted Villages of Northants.* (1966), 35).

The surviving earthworks are in good condition. They not only confirm the evidence of the 1377 Poll Tax Returns, indicating that the village was then a large one, but also suggest that the increase in size between 1301 and 1377 may have resulted in the expansion of the village northwards across former arable land.

The original main street appears to have been approximately on the line of the present road which runs N.W. past Canons Ashby House. Traces of a hollow-way still remains on the E. side of this road, and then W. of the road, running N.W. across the park towards the mound (3). There are no indications of former buildings to the W. of the hollow-way, but the area may have been levelled for landscaping. To the E. of the hollow-way there is a series of embanked paddocks or closes, some with possible building platforms at their W. ends; the E. ends of the closes terminate against a shallow hollow-way or back lane running N.W.–S.E. To the S.E., along the Adstone

road, other closes remain.

At the N. end of the site, and separated from the rest by a later quarry pit probably dug through a hollow-way, are more closes with house-sites at their W. ends. Here, however, between the W. ends of the closes and the back lane to the E., are three blocks of very short and degraded ridge-and-furrow. The southernmost ridges are too short ever to have been ploughed after the closes were created and the W. ends are all cut through by the close boundaries. This indicates that the ridge-and-furrow originally extended further W. and that the closes and house-sites have been laid out on it. A few sherds of medieval pottery, all of 13th or 14th-century date, have been found on the site, mainly in the areas formerly occupied by buildings.

In addition to the hollow-ways in and around the deserted village various others survive or are visible on air photographs. For example S.W. of the gardens of Canons Ashby House and parallel to the existing road to Eydon (SP 574504) a broad hollow-way extends down the hillside towards the fishponds (4). Another, at the extreme N. of the site, appears to run on E. of the present road and then meet it. From such evidence it is possible to make a tentative reconstruction of the late medieval road system of the area (RAF VAP CPE/UK/1994, 4096–7; CUAP, BEN25).

^a(2) SITE OF AUGUSTINIAN PRIORY AND OF 16TH-CENTURY HOUSE AND (?) GARDENS (SP 577505; Fig. 34; Plate 23), lies around the parish church which still retains a large part of the fabric of the original priory church.

The priory, dedicated to the Blessed Virgin, was founded in 1147–51, probably for 13 canons, and was dissolved in 1536. A church, land, houses, crofts, a fishpond and a horse-mill were among the gifts at its foundation (D. M. Knowles and R. N. Hadcock, *Medieval Religious Houses* (1957), 132; VCH *Northants.*, II (1906), 130). After the Dissolution Sir John Cope acquired the site and built a house, apparently to the S. of the church and partly out of the monastic buildings. This was superseded by the present house after the estate had passed to Cope's brother-in-law, John Dryden, in 1551.

The church now consists of two bays of the nave and part of the north aisle of the priory church; excavations carried out in 1828 by Sir Henry Dryden to the E. and S. of the present building revealed parts of the rest of the nave and north aisle as well as of the chancel. There was no south aisle; the cloister was directly attached to the S. side of the nave and was surrounded by the usual conventual buildings, including a large chapter house (G. Baker, *Hist. of Northants.*, II (1836–41), 7–15; copies of conjectural plans in NMR).

In 1970 excavations were carried out in the S.W. corner of the cloister on behalf of the DOE. As this was done in order to ascertain possible damage to the medieval layers by proposed buildings it was mainly restricted to the upper levels and little of medieval date was recorded. Only the S.W. corner of the cloister was revealed, above which was a late 16th-century floor. The excavator concluded that the medieval building was the vaulted undercroft of the monastic refectory which had been incorporated into a 16th-century building on the site. The latter was demolished in the 18th century. It is probable that this structure was part of the house built by Sir John Cope in the mid 16th century. Large quantities of medieval floor tiles (NM; Plate 23) were recovered as well as fragments of a late 16th or early 17th-century Venetian glass goblet (*BNFAS*, 4 (1970), 16; *Med. Arch.*, 14 (1970), 169; *Northants. Archaeol.*, 9 (1974), 57–67).

The surviving earthworks fall into three groups. Immediately E. of the church, within the graveyard, are several low scarps up to 1 m. high which may be, in part, the foundations of the medieval church.

To the S.E. is a large trapezoidal area occupying most of a shallow valley and formerly bounded, except on the N.W. side, by a broad flat-topped bank or terrace 1 m.–1.5 m. high with a slight inner ditch. The S. and S.W. sides have recently been destroyed and little trace remains. Within this enclosure, along its E. side, were three irregular ponds, now reduced to one large marshy area in the valley bottom (The plan shows these features and the destroyed bank as on the OS 25 inch map, Northants. LV.2, 1900 ed.). In the N.W. corner of this area and projecting into it there was formerly an L-shaped pond, with a large outer bank which retained the water. This is usually described as a moat. It, too, has recently been altered and partly filled in. In the centre of the area and immediately N. of the northernmost pond is a circular mound only 0.5 m. high.

This embanked area and the 'moat' have previously been ascribed to the priory and are traditionally called 'The Canons Walk' or 'The Vineyard'. However there is no direct evidence for this assumption and indeed one feature may indicate the earthworks are of a different period. Air photographs show that before the recent destruction the bank along the S.W. side of the area overlay ridge-and-furrow (CUAP, BEN25; RAF VAP CPE/UK/1994, 4096–7). Unless this ridge-and-furrow is of a very early date the overlying bank or terrace-walk is of the late or post-medieval period. Therefore these earthworks are the remains either of part of the monastic gardens or of a mid 16th-century garden to the S. and S.E. of Sir John Cope's house. The form of the earthworks would agree with either hypothesis, though the latter is more likely.

In the two modern paddocks N. and W. of the church are other earthworks. Most are indeterminate scarps and hollows of unknown purpose and date, but a long rectangular depression N.E. of the church may be a former *fishpond*. In the same area is the 'Monks Well' which consists of an 18th or 19th-century stone structure above a spring; in the 19th century numerous lengths of lead and wooden pipe were discovered which may have been part of the monastic water supply.

a(3) MOUND (SP 57505091; Fig. 34; Plate 21), lies N.W. of Canons Ashby House on clay at 158 m. above OD. It has previously been described as a barrow (1st ed. 1 in. OS map (1834)) or as a motte (Pevsner, *Northamptonshire* (1961), 135). From its present form it is more likely to have been part of post-medieval landscaping of the park, particularly as it is in line with the N.W. elevation of Canons Ashby House. However even by the early 18th century its original purpose was forgotten for Bridges (*Hist. of Northants.*, I (1791), 223) described it as 'anciently a fortification', and said that 'Cannon-balls have frequently been dug up there and the place still retains the name of Castle-hill'. It is possible that there was an earlier mound here, which was later landscaped to its present form.

The mound is polygonal, with several straight lengths around its circumference. It is up to 3 m. high, with an uneven summit and an inner bank on the N.E. side. Traces of a shallow ditch surround it except on the E. To the S. and N. are broad hollow-ways leading into the former village (1) (CUAP, BEN25).

a(4) FISHPONDS (centred SP 569507), in the valley of the small stream to the W. of the village, on clay and alluvium at about 150 m. above OD. There are four ponds each covering some 3 hectares, and each formed by the construction of a simple dam across the valley. The dams are earthen, up to 2 m. high, with the exception of the southernmost one, close to the Eydon road (at SP 57405034), which is a large structure with a dressed stone rear revetment probably of 18th or 19th-century date.

A small wood 200 m. in length separates the ponds into two pairs; there are no indications that there was ever a fifth, linking pond occupying this area. The two lower, southernmost ponds are still water-filled but the other pair are now marshy depressions within a plantation. It is not clear whether the two pairs of ponds are contemporary. As they now appear they may all have been ornamental, part of a landscaped park around Canons Ashby House. Alternatively they could all have originated as medieval fishponds two of which have been modified and maintained as landscape features. The lowest pond certainly appears to have existed and to have extended to more than its present area during the period when the field to the E. was being ploughed in ridge-and-furrow; the ridges end several metres from the pond, except at one point where treading by cattle has destroyed the edge of the pond and cut into the ridges. This suggests that this pond at least was in existence by the 16th century (see (7)). However, in the early 19th century it is depicted as having a different shape (1st ed. 1 in. OS Map (1834)). It was then more rectangular with a small projection at its S.E. corner, giving a formal appearance reminiscent of a 17th-century ornamental lake. At the same time a building below this lake was termed a mill.

a(5) GARDEN REMAINS (SP 576506; Fig. 34), lie immediately S.W. of Canons Ashby House, on Upper Lias

Clay, between 150 m. and 155 m. above OD. These gardens were laid out between 1708 and 1710, in what was for that period a relatively old-fashioned design, by Edward Dryden who also altered the house. It is now partly overgrown and abandoned but the main outlines can be recovered. The main part was a long rectangular area extending down the slope from the S.W. side of the house, bounded by high walls. It was divided into four compartments, separated by low scarps all 1 m.–2 m. high, with a long axial path down the centre. The upper two compartments were originally gravelled parterres and the lower two were used for vegetables and fruit. To the N.E. of the upper two compartments there is now a large level area, also bounded by walls, which was formerly divided into two unequal parts, one probably a bowling green, the other with two small ponds in it. On the N.W. side of the house is another walled area known as the Green Court. This was originally planted with clipped yew trees. The surviving gate piers are decorated with carved demi-lions holding spheres, the crest of the Drydens, large urns, suits of armour and pinnacles (*Country Life*, Feb.–March, 1921; C. Hussey, *English Gardens and Landscapes, 1700–1750* (1967), 18).

[a](6) WINDMILL MOUND (SP 56935033), immediately N. of the road to Eydon, on Boulder Clay at 150 m. above OD. The mound is some 20 m. in diam.; there is no indication of a ditch. Although it has been ploughed it still remains about 1 m. high.

(7) CULTIVATION REMAINS (Fig. 34). The enclosure of the common fields of the parish probably took place between 1539 and 1547 although the exact date is not known. In 1539 it is recorded that the whole of the former arable

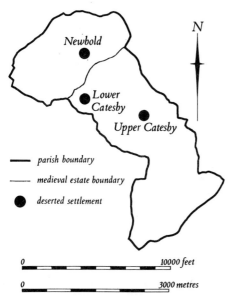

Fig. 35   CATESBY   Medieval settlements and estates

demesne land of the priory, comprising some 341 acres, lay in the common fields (PRO, E315/399/f126) but by 1547 Sir John Cope was running 2000 sheep on the land of the parish (see (1)).

Ridge-and-furrow of these fields remains on the ground or can be seen on air photographs over most of the parish arranged mainly in interlocked furlongs often of reversed-S form. It is particularly well preserved in Canons Ashby Park (SP 574505) and N. and E. of the deserted village (1) (at SP 575512 and 578507). In the N. part of the former village a block of short ridge-and-furrow has been cut into by later closes, suggesting that the village has expanded over arable land.

In addition a number of former lanes, now reduced to hollow-ways, are visible either on the ground or on air photographs. As a result a large part of the medieval landscape of the parish can be reconstructed (RAF VAP CPE/UK/1994, 4094–9, 2090–5, 4160–4).

15   CATESBY

(OS 1:10000 [a] SP 56 SW, [b] SP 55 NW)

The long narrow parish, covering some 825 hectares, lies on either side of the R. Leam which flows across the N.W. part. From the higher S.W. end of the parish where Northampton Sand outcrops on the isolated Arbury Hill and Sharmans Hill at 210 m. above OD, the land slopes gently N.W. on Upper Lias Clay and Middle Lias Marlstone Rock and then more steeply down an indented scarp face of silts and limestone to the R. Leam, here flowing N.E. in a broad valley of Lower Lias Clay at 122 m. above OD. Beyond the river, to the N.W., is a broad area of undulating clayland between 130 m. and 145 m. above OD, which was the land associated with the now deserted village of Newbold (6). The rest of the parish was divided between two other now largely deserted villages, Upper and Lower Catesby (2) and (3). The history of the three villages is obscure and the remains of each have been either totally or partly destroyed. The 17th-century garden remains (4) on the site of an earlier Cistercian priory are of considerable interest.

ROMAN

Roman coins, including some of Faustina and Maximianus, are said to have been found in Catesby Park (around SP 516595) before 1720 (J. Bridges, *Hist. of Northants.*, I (1791), 36; OS Record Cards).

[b](1) ROMAN BURIAL (SP 52715885), S. of Upper Catesby on clay at 175 m. above OD. A Roman cinerary urn was found in 1895 during the sinking of an air shaft in Catesby Tunnel (OS Record Cards).

MEDIEVAL AND LATER

b(2) DESERTED VILLAGE OF UPPER CATESBY (SP 528594; Figs. 35 and 36), stands near the W. end of a prominent W.-facing spur of limestone at 167 m. above OD. A village of Catesby was first mentioned in 1086 when Domesday Book listed it as a four-hide estate with a recorded population of 25, including a priest (VCH *Northants.*, I (1902), 338). However this entry certainly included the village of Lower Catesby (3) and probably yet another village in the parish, Newbold (6), both now deserted. About 1175 Robert de Esseby, grandson of Sasfrid who held the manor of Catesby under William Peveral in 1086, founded a house of Cistercian nuns at Lower Catesby (4). This priory was granted the church of Catesby, the chapel of Hellidon and lands, tenements and mills in the parish. It later received a number of other grants of land in Catesby from the Esseby family. In 1301 thirteen taxpayers are listed for Catesby and Newbold (PRO, E179/155/31); 172 people paid the Poll Tax in 1377 and 126 in 1379 (M. W. Beresford, *The Lost Villages of England* (1954), 366). In the early 15th century land in the parish had certainly reverted to pasture for 'untilled Grounds in Catesby and Newbold, let to Divers tenants' are recorded. In addition the priory was running sheep on its land for in the same period accounts record large sums of money received by the priory for wool (J. M. Steane, *The Northants. Landscape* (1974), 174). In 1491 the prioress of Catesby destroyed 14 houses at 'Catesby', evicting 60 people, and enclosed land and converted it to pasture (M. W. Beresford, op.cit.). However it is not certain that this destruction and enclosure was at either Upper or Lower Catesby; it may have been at Newbold. In 1517–18 sixty people were said to have been evicted from Catesby (J. M. Steane, op. cit.). The priory was dissolved in 1536 and the parish church destroyed though part of it survived in a ruinous state for some years. Five houses are said to have existed at this time in 'Catesby'. In 1537 the site of the nunnery and its lands was sold to John Onley and either he or his descendants built a large house out of the priory, attached to which was a set of elaborate gardens (4). In 1801 there were 95 people living in the parish (J. Bridges, *Hist. of Northants.*, I (1791), 32; Whellan, *Dir*, 390–3; K. J. Allison, *et al.*, *The Deserted Villages of Northants.* (1966), 37).

The documented history noted above conceals a complex picture of settlement which some post-medieval documentation and the earthwork remains partly reveal. There appear to have been two villages, one at Upper Catesby where the medieval parish church stood, the other at Lower Catesby, both presumably listed under the one entry for Domesday Book together with Newbold. The priory was apparently sited just outside the village of Lower Catesby and it was perhaps part of this village which was destroyed in 1495. Upper Catesby, recorded as Overcatsby in 1389 (PN *Northants.*, 16), may also have been partly deserted, but the five houses still remaining at 'Catesby' in

1536 were probably here. Certainly by about 1720 Bridges (op. cit.) noted that there were still 'eight houses with about five and twenty inhabitants' at Upper Catesby, and on Eyre's *Map of Northants.* (1791) seven buildings are depicted. In the early 19th century there were at least six buildings on the site (1st ed. OS 1 in. map, (1834)). These must have been removed; the present six pairs of semi-detached cottages were erected between 1863 and 1901 on a new alignment.

The remains of Upper Catesby fall into two parts. Immediately S.E. of the existing houses, and now entirely destroyed by modern cultivation, was a series of embanked closes, separated from the adjacent ridge-and-furrow to the S. by a low bank and ditch and with traces of buildings at the N. ends where the existing lane to Badby seems to have been the main street. The closes at the W. end were cut by a later quarry.

To the N. and W. of the existing houses the earthworks of the former village still remain. The most marked feature is a hollow-way up to 1 m. deep which runs N.W. from the garden of the northernmost house to the crest of the spur. Here its depth increases to 2.5 m. as it runs down the hillside. It can be traced as a continuous feature for about 1 km. until it becomes the main street of the deserted village of Lower Catesby (3). To the E. it presumably continued along the line of the present houses to meet the Badby lane. To the S. of the hollow-way and W. of the existing houses are some indeterminate low scarps, and a rectangular paddock which was the graveyard and the site of the parish church. To the N. of the hollow-way and the modern houses are the fragmentary remains of further closes and some possible house-sites. However, apart from a section in the centre where a later quarry-pit has been dug, all the remains have been overploughed in a narrow ridge-and-furrow only 5 m. wide. The ridges are very slight and probably only represent a short period of ploughing (RAF VAP CPE/UK/1994, 1279–80; CUAP, SA66).

b(3) DESERTED VILLAGE OF LOWER CATESBY (SP 515597; Figs. 35 and 37), lies N. of Catesby Church at 122 m. above OD, on the N. side of a shallow valley, opposite the sites of the priory and of the later gardens (4). The history, size and date of desertion of this village is not known with certainty, owing to the fact that most of the documentary evidence includes not only Upper Catesby (2) but also Newbold (6), both now also depopulated. The documentary record as it is known is summarised under Upper Catesby.

About half the remaining earthworks of the village were destroyed in 1975 immediately before the Commission first visited the site but enough remains on the ground or can be seen on air photographs for the general layout to be recovered. The main feature was a broad hollow-way up to 1 m. deep running E.–W. along the valley side. At its W. end it curved N.W. into the valley of the R. Leam and faded out. To the E. it can be traced for about 1 km. until it

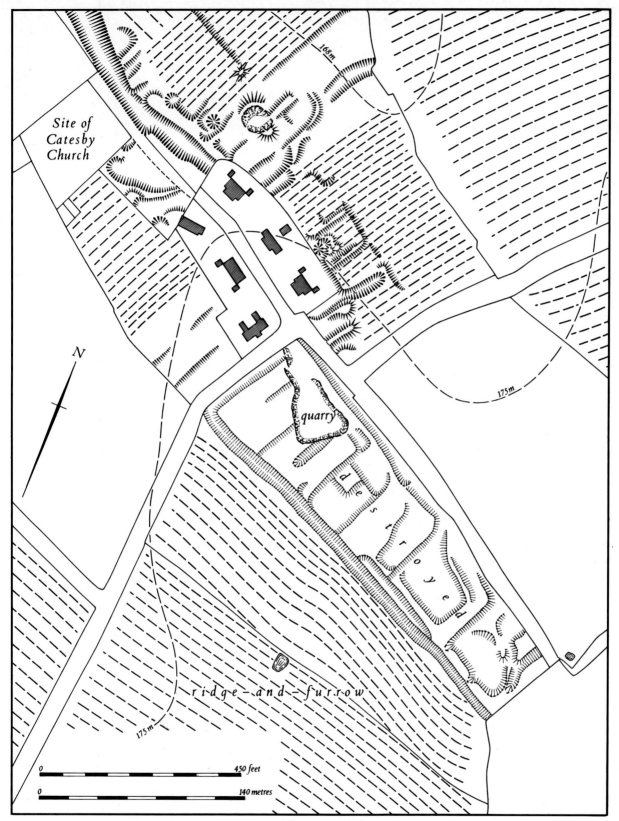

Site of
Catesby
Church

N

quarry

destroyed

175 m

168 m

175 m

r i d g e - a n d - f u r r o w

| 0 | | | | 450 feet |
| 0 | | | | 140 metres |

Fig. 36   CATESBY   (2) Deserted village of Upper Catesby

becomes the main street of Upper Catesby (2). Large sections of this hollow-way between the two villages have been destroyed by ploughing, but a great deal of stone rubble was noted along its line (around SP 522597; local inf.). On the N. side of the hollow-way, at Lower Catesby, were rectangular closes or paddocks bounded by low scarps or ditches. The part to the E., which was the best preserved, has now been destroyed, but some possible building platforms exist in the part which survives. To the S. of the hollow-way there are several scarps and ditches extending down the hillside and these may also be the remains of closes along the former main street; their S. ends have all been destroyed or cut across by a later line of ponds in the valley bottom. These ponds probably date from the medieval period and were perhaps originally the fishponds of Catesby Priory. This would suggest that at least part of the village had been abandoned or removed at an early date (RAF VAP CPE/UK/1994, 1279–80; CUAP, AHG39, 41).

b(4) SITE OF CISTERCIAN PRIORY AND OF POST-MEDIEVAL HOUSE AND GARDEN (SP515595; Fig. 37), lie around the existing church at Lower Catesby at 122 m. above OD. The R. Leam forms the S. and W. boundary of the site.

The N. part of the area was occupied by the former village of Lower Catesby (3) but in 1175 Robert de Esseby, who held the manor, founded a house of Cistercian nuns there. This was originally endowed with the church of Catesby, the chapel of Hellidon and apparently with at least part of the villages of Upper and Lower Catesby (2) and (3) and Newbold (6). Little of its earlier history is known, but in 1229 the King granted wood from the Forest of Silverstone for the building of the priory church (VCH Northants., II (1906), 121–5).

The priory was dissolved in 1536 and the following year the site and its lands were sold to John Onley, whose family held it until the early 17th century when it passed to the Parkhursts. At least part of the priory buildings were turned into a mansion house for the Onleys who presumably demolished the rest and, either then or perhaps later in the 17th century, laid out an elaborate garden around and to the E. of the house. An engraving of the house in about 1720 (J. Bridges, Hist. of Northants., I (1791), 32) and drawings of the house made in 1844 (in the present Catesby House) suggest that the 16th-century house was arranged around a central courtyard, perhaps the original cloister, but that the main W. front was rebuilt around 1700, probably by the Parkhursts, with a symmetrical elevation and projecting wings. A late 18th-century map (Eyre, Map of Northants. (1791)) shows a rigidly formal garden E. of the house, with rectangular ponds and intersecting footpaths, but this may be partly conventionalized as the earthworks, apparently of earlier date, do not agree with the map. The house was finally demolished in 1863 and the materials used in the new Catesby House erected near Upper Catesby. The church

was rebuilt at the same time.

It is difficult to ascertain exactly which of the remaining earthworks belong to the priory and which to the later house and garden but the main outlines appear to be clear. The present church is probably on the site of the priory church and the conventual buildings would have been to the S. of it ('a' on plan). Maps of 18th and 19th-century date and surviving illustrations of the house, which seems to have incorporated at least part of the cloister range, lend support to this supposition. The large terrace ('a' on plan), which is still 2 m. high, and the indeterminate earthworks to the W. and N., are mainly the remains of the house and perhaps an outer terrace wall with, to the E., a series of earthworks which must be the 17th-century gardens. These consist of two retangular sunken basins 1.5 m. deep, with a raised terrace 1 m. high on the W. and a higher terrace 1.5 m. high on the E. ('b' on plan). Further E. again is a rectangular pond and beyond, E. of the track to Hellidon, a straight sunken way ('c' on plan).

On the S. side of the garden is the site of a large pond with a broad dam up to 2 m. high at its W. end ('d' on plan). This may have been part of the gardens but it could also have had earlier origins as a fishpond of the priory.

The W. edge of the site is bounded by a deep ditch with an outer bank which curves in an arc above the R. Leam ('e' on plan). Although this has previously been described as a moat, it is unlikely to have had any defensive purpose. It may have been the W. boundary of the 17th-century garden, for the main W. front of the house certainly faced it, but it is likely to be medieval in origin for it appears to have been used to carry water from the R. Leam around the spur into the next valley. It is up to 2 m. deep and the outer bank is faced with stone rubble. Its N. end has been damaged but the presence there of blocks of limestone and ashlar suggests that the channel may have been a leat leading water to a mill. If this explanation is correct, the ditch must certainly have been altered in later times, perhaps as a part of the 17th-century gardens.

On the N. side of the area, in the valley bottom below the existing cottages, are two sub-rectangular depressions each with traces of a low bank or dam only 1.25 m. high at its lower, W. end. These appear to be the remains of two ponds which, perhaps, were either fishponds of the priory or a source of additional water for the assumed mill, or both. Above them to the E. is a larger pond, still water-filled, which appears to be ornamental and part of the 17th-century garden though it may have had earlier origins. These ponds appear to cut through, and are thus later than, a series of low scarps which extend northwards and which are the close boundaries of the deserted village of Lower Catesby (3) which lies immediately to the N. (RAF VAP CPE/UK/1994, 1279–80; CUAP, AHG39–41).

b(5) EARTHWORKS (SP 521594; Fig. 38), S. of the road from Upper to Lower Catesby, at 105 m. above OD. The earthworks lie in a flat field, with a pond to the W., and

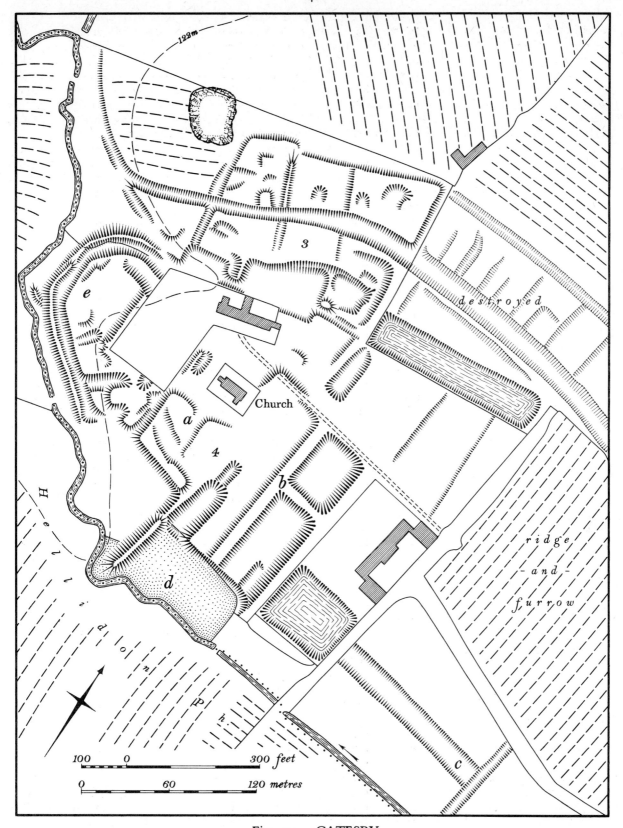

Church

destroyed

ridge

-and-

furrow

H e l l i d o n

e

3

a

4

b

d

P

h

c

100   0   300 *feet*

0   60   120 *metres*

122m

Fig. 37   CATESBY
(3) Deserted village of Lower Catesby,   (4) Site of priory and of house and gardens

consist of a roughly rectangular arrangement of banks and ditches. On the S. side is the recut channel of a small stream, now dry, up to 2 m. deep. This is joined at right-angles by a smaller, shallower channel. The N.E. angle thus formed is occupied by an L-shaped platform following the line of the two channels. This platform is level and varies in height above the uneven land-surface, so it is highest, some 0.5 m., in the S. and fades to the N. There is a small bank 0.25 m. high on top of the platform. To the N. are ill-defined ditches and scarps.

Neither the date nor the function of the earthworks is known; they may be the remains of a manor house or of a group of farm buildings. The field in which they stand is known as Court Close (RAF VAP CPE/UK/1994, 1279–80; CUAP, SA63).

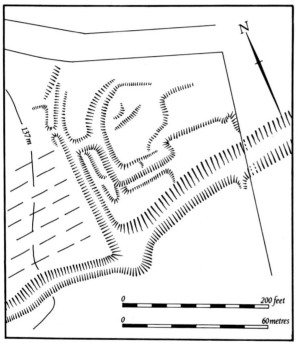

Fig. 38   CATESBY   (5) Earthworks

ᵃ(6) DESERTED VILLAGE OF NEWBOLD (SP 517606; Fig. 35; Plate 5), situated in the N.W. part of Catesby parish on a S.-facing slope above the R. Leam, on clay at 125 m. above OD. It lay on the E. edge of an area of some 280 hectares N.W. of the R. Leam; this land probably represents the original estate of Newbold. The village is not mentioned in Domesday Book, but it is almost certainly included there in the entry for Catesby (2, 3) which, with a recorded population of 25, seems abnormally large. It is first noted in documents in 1203 (PN Northants., 17) and its position and its name 'new building' suggest that it originated as a secondary settlement of Catesby. In 1301 it was listed together with Catesby with a total of 13 taxpayers (PRO, E179/155/31). Part of the village held by Catesby Priory was perhaps destroyed and its site converted to pasture in

1495 at the same time as the two Catesby villages (2) and (3). Indeed some of the 14 houses at Catesby which were removed in that year by the prioress of Catesby may have been at Newbold.

The expulsion of 60 people from Catesby, again by the priory, in 1491 may also refer to Newbold (M. W. Beresford, *Lost Villages of England* (1954), 366–8). Certainly by 1535 the priory held a 'Newboldefeld', indicating perhaps that it was already a sheep-walk by then (K. J. Allison *et al.*, *The Deserted Villages of Northants.* (1966), 43) and even at an earlier date, in the early 15th century, the priory received rents from the pasture of untilled ground in Catesby and Newbold let to tenants and this suggests that sheep were already important there (J. M. Steane, *The Northants. Landscape* (1974), 174). In the early 18th century Bridges (*Hist. of Northants.*, I (1791), 32) recorded that there were then only four houses with ten inhabitants at Newbold. These houses were almost certainly the present dispersed farmsteads.

Until 1966 the extremely fine earthworks of the village remained complete. They were then ploughed and completely destroyed but from air photographs taken before destruction it is possible to ascertain the main features of the site. Most of the village earthworks lay in a rectangular block orientated S.W.–N.E. and bounded by a bank and outer ditch on the S.E. and N.E. and by a hollow-way on the N.W. The interior of this area was divided into three main parts. The S.E. block consisted of a number of ditched and embanked closes, including one with ridge-and-furrow on it, all of which had the remains of former buildings at their N.E. ends fronting a broad hollow-way. The latter also formed the S.W. side of the central part of the village which was entirely occupied by a large number of closes. Some of these contained raised platforms of various sizes, all probably the sites of former buildings. On the N.W. side of this area was a very wide road or access-way, bounded by scarps and ditches, which extended S.E. beyond the village to the edge of the R. Leam. To the N.W. of that was the third part of the village, divided into two distinct areas. In the S.E. corner was a large embanked enclosure with traces of smaller sub-divisions in the form of low banks and scarps as well as building platforms, and to the N.W. was a block of ridge-and-furrow. Outside the village and immediately to the N.W. of it was a large sub-rectangular area edged by ridge-and-furrow which contained no major visible remains. Two hollow-ways, one from the W. and the other from the S.W. ran through ridge-and-furrow to enter this area on its W. side (J. K. S. St Joseph, *The Uses of Air Photography* (1966), pl. 64; J. M. Steane, *The Northants. Landscape* (1974), pl. 9; CUAP, AHG33–7, AWV21–3, SA69–74, SN81–2; CPE/UK/1994, 1281–2).

When the site was levelled and ploughed in 1967 areas of grey daub were noted on the former house-sites. Much 12th-century pottery was found together with a gilded buckle and the bowl of a pewter spoon. At the W. end of the village, foundations of a large stone building were recorded (*Med. Arch.*, 12 (1968), 203; DMVRG *15th Annual Rep.*, (1967), 4; 17 (1969), 7).

a(7) POND (SP 508604), lies immediately S. of Lower Farm, Newbold, at the head of a small S.-draining valley on clay at 140 m. above OD. It consists of a long rectangular depression orientated E.–W. and extending in a semicircle on the N. side with a circular island in the centre. To the N. are other low scarps, and the whole may be the remains of a small 17th or 18th-century garden associated with the farm (pond correctly shown on OS 1 : 25000 plan, SP 5060; RAF VAP CPE/UK/1994, 1281–2).

(8) CULTIVATION REMAINS. The date of the enclosure of the common fields of Upper and Lower Catesby is unknown. The prioress of Catesby is said to have enclosed 16 virgates (about 75 hectares) and converted it to pasture in 1496, but some of this may have been in the land of Newbold (6). Even in the early 15th century, the priory received rent from pasture in Catesby and Newbold (see (2) and (6)). However, when the priory was dissolved in 1539, although it possessed 250 acres of enclosed pasture at Catesby, of its 160 acres of arable land there, all but seven acres was in the common fields (PRO, E315/399/f 120).

Ridge-and-furrow of these fields exists on the ground or can be traced on air photographs over almost the entire area of land which is attributable to the villages of Catesby. It is all arranged in interlocked rectangular furlongs, some with reversed-S ridges, except to the S.E. of Upper Catesby (SP 535586) where there is an area of end-on furlongs on the slopes below Arbury Hill. Among the best preserved ridge-and-furrow is that immediately E. of Lower Catesby (SP 518596).

Other ridge-and-furrow of interest overlies part of the deserted village of Upper Catesby (2) (Fig. 36) and must post-date the abandonment of that part of the village. This ridge-and-furrow is narrow, only 5 m. wide, and is likely to be relatively recent. The fact that the ploughing has not obliterated the underlying village remains suggests that it was short-lived, and perhaps was only carried out once. In the same area, immediately S.E. of that part of the deserted village which has been destroyed, was a block of double reversed-S ridge-and-furrow (SP 531590), an example of the replough of two end-on furlongs into one, as quite commonly occurs.

The date of the enclosure of the common fields of Newbold (6) is also unknown, though they appear to have disappeared by 1535 and perhaps were partly enclosed in the 15th century (see above).

Ridge-and-furrow of these fields can be traced over the entire area of land that belonged to Newbold. It is arranged mainly in rectangular end-on and interlocked furlongs except around the isolated hill in the S.W. (SP 505602) where the ridges radiate outwards from the rounded summit (RAF VAP CPE/UK/1994, 1156–60, 1277–85).

16 CHARWELTON

(OS 1 : 10000 a SP 55 NW, b SP 55 NE, c SP 55 SW, d SP 55 SE)

The parish, covering some 940 hectares and of irregular shape, lies across the valley of the R. Cherwell. The river rises in the N.W. and flows S.E. in a broad open valley from 175 m. to 135 m. above OD. The undulating land beyond is almost entirely on Jurassic clays with small areas of glacial sands and gravels overlying these. In the extreme S., S.W. and N. of the parish the land rises to steep-sided, rounded hills of Northampton Sand, some over 210 m. above OD. Nothing of prehistoric or Roman date is known from the area and the main interest lies in the existence of the two villages, Church Charwelton (1), now deserted, and Upper Charwelton (3) (Fig. 13). Both seem to have suffered as a result of enclosure for sheep in the late 14th or early 15th century. The number of ponds in the parish (2), (4) and (5), apparently for both fish and wild fowl and probably of late medieval or post-medieval date, is also notable.

PREHISTORIC

There is said to have been a tumulus, destroyed in the early 19th century, at around SP 540563 (*Archaeologia*, 35 (1853), 394). The site is covered by ridge-and-furrow and there is no sign of a mound at this point. The reference may be a misplacement and misinterpretation of the mill mound (6). The same article (*Archaeologia*, ibid.) refers to an undated burial 20 m. to the N.W.

MEDIEVAL AND LATER

a(1) DESERTED VILLAGE OF CHURCH CHARWELTON (SP 544554; Figs. 13 and 39), on the N.E. side of the R. Cherwell on clay between 140 m. and 152 m. above OD. It was called Church Charwelton because the parish church, which still-stands, was located there and to distinguish it from the village of Upper or Over Charwelton (3) which lies 1200 m. up stream. The two villages are combined in most of the national taxation records so that it is almost impossible to ascertain the population of either at any one time.

In 1086 Charwelton was divided into four manors with a total recorded population of eleven (VCH *Northants.*, I (1902), 319, 324, 326 and 331). It is possible that one of these manors, belonging to Thorney Abbey and with a recorded population of two, was part or all of Upper Charwelton and therefore the maximum recorded population of Church Charwelton could be nine. The village was mentioned by name in the *Nomina Villarum* of 1316. In 1491 John Rous (T. Hearne (ed.), *Historia Regum Angliae* (1745), 122–3) recorded that Church Charwelton was in danger of depopulation and Bridges (*Hist. of Northants.*, I (1791), 36), writing in the early 18th century, also claimed that the village was 'in great measure depopulated at this time'. Bridges said that the village was

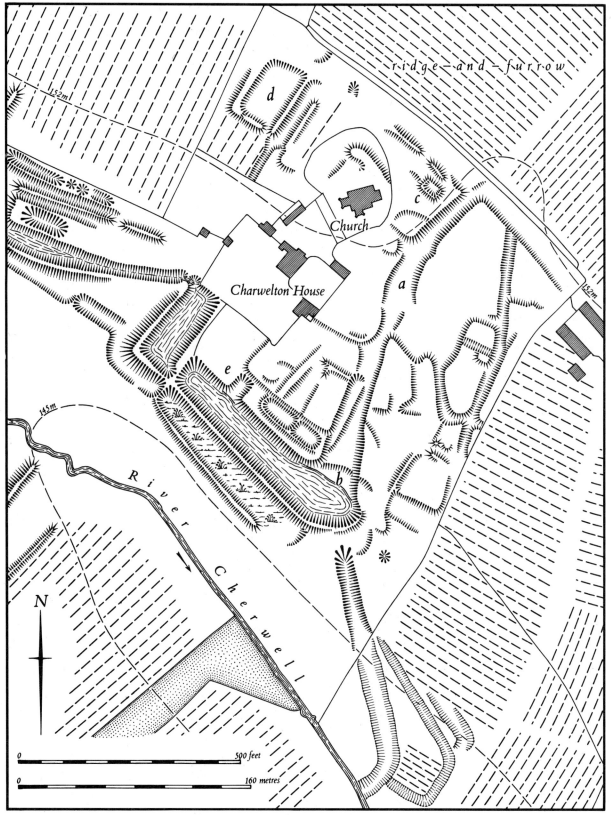

Fig. 39 CHARWELTON (1) Deserted village of Church Charwelton, (2) Ponds

deserted in the 15th century because of the civil war of the period, but in fact it is far more likely that enclosure for sheep led to its final abandonment. In 1417 Thomas Andrews, a merchant, acquired a small estate in the parish and later he or his son, another Thomas, leased most of the rest of the land held there by Thorney and Bittlesden Abbeys. By 1547 the third Thomas Andrews kept 1200 sheep in the parish, another 500 sheep were owned by the Knightley family of Fawsley and a further 300 by another freeholder (K. J. Allison et al., *The Deserted Villages of Northants.* (1966), 37). The whole site was certainly abandoned by 1847 (NRO, Tithe Map) when it was known as Home Close and belonged to the still-surviving Charwelton House.

The remains of the village lie S. and S.E. of the isolated church and Charwelton House and the main feature is a broad hollow-way ('a' on Fig. 39) only 0.5 m.–1 m. deep, which runs roughly N.–S. in a broad curve. As this nears the R. Cherwell it is cut by the most south-westerly of the fishponds (2) ('b' on Fig. 39), so this pond must post-date the abandonment of the village. Below the pond the hollow-way reappears and although its S.E. end has now been destroyed by ploughing it can be traced on air photographs further S.E. until it meets the river. On either side of the hollow-way are traces of former closes, all damaged by later activity and none complete. Only one definite house-site is visible, at the N. end of the hollow-way ('c' on Fig. 39). N.W. of the church ('d' on Fig. 39) is a small rectangular pond set back into the hillside and overlying ridge-and-furrow (RAF VAP CPE/UK/1994, 3147–8; CPE/UK/1926, 2059–60; CUAP, SA55–61, AHG47–8, AKV88–9, AWO41–5, AZV84–5).

a(2) PONDS (centred SP 541555; Figs. 39 and 40), lie in the valley of the R. Cherwell, immediately S.W. and N.W. of the deserted village of Church Charwelton (1), on clay at 145 m. above OD. There appear to be two distinct systems, with different functions and perhaps of different dates. The earliest is probably the pond close to the river ('a' on Fig. 40); this is a roughly triangular sunken area bounded by scarps or dams and occupied by a complex system of islands. The water to feed it entered at its N.W. end, diverted from the river along the short inlet channels, and then passed along an outlet channel which still survives in the S. corner, back into the river. The purpose of this pond and its islands is not known but it may have been for ducks or wild fowl, the islands providing an extensive refuge for nesting. Its date is unknown. On the Tithe Map of 1847 (NRO) it is described as a fishpond.

The other ponds form a more complex group. The water for them was taken from a small tributary of the R. Cherwell, 600 m. upstream, just S.W. of Upper Charwelton ('a' on Fig. 41). At this point a channel, 2 m. deep and embanked on its down-slope side, runs S.E. along the side of the valley. Beyond the point where it crosses the road to Church Charwelton the channel has been ploughed

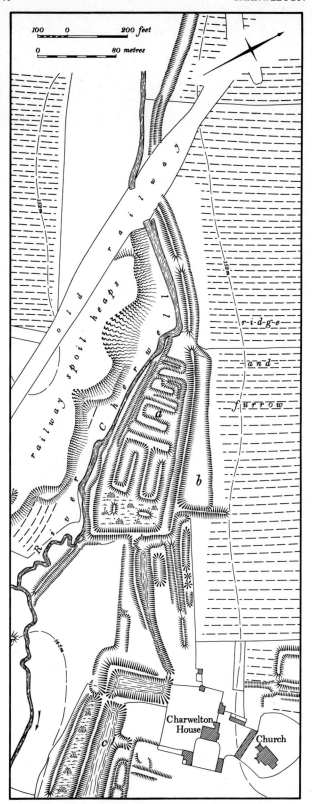

Fig. 40   CHARWELTON   (2) Ponds

over and now remains only as a broad hollow ('b' on Fig. 41) but near the railway it returns to its original form, and on the far side of the railway embankment it continues along the valley to the first of the ponds ('b' on Fig. 40). This first pond is a long trapezoidal feature with an embankment 2 m. high on its S.W. side, above the pond with the islands already described. From it the water seems to have passed S.E. into a long narrow sinuous channel leading to a narrow slightly curved pond. An outlet at the S.E. end of this led into a small rectangular pond and thence into two large parallel ponds separated by a massive embankment 2.5 m. high ('e' on Fig. 39 and 'c' on Fig. 40). The S.E. end of the lower of these two ponds has been destroyed. The upper pond cuts the hollow-way of the deserted village of Church Charwelton ('b' on Fig. 39) and is therefore of later date. The outfall channel may have been the S. end of the hollow-way which met the R. Cherwell further S.W. since no leat is visible. The purpose of these ponds is not known, though they are likely to have been for fish. They were presumably built after the desertion of Church Charwelton and therefore not earlier than the late 15th century; they must also be later than the pond with islands described above, which they respect. The long leat to the second set of ponds was apparently out of use by 1847 (NRO, Tithe Map) for only the extreme S.E. end is shown. At the same time the larger pond, shown full of water, was called Fish Pond.

[a](3) SETTLEMENT REMAINS (SP 535562; Figs. 13 and 41), lie immediately N. of the present village of Upper or Over Charwelton, between it and Charwelton Hall, on clay and glacial gravels at 160 m. above OD. As most national taxation records combine Upper Charwelton and the now deserted village of Church Charwelton (1) it is difficult to assess the size of the village at any period. It is recorded in Domesday Book of 1086, but its population at that date is impossible to ascertain. In 1491 John Rous wrote that the village had been completely depopulated (T. Hearne (ed.), *Historia Regum Angliae* (1745), 122–3) and Bridges (*Hist. of Northants.*, I (1791), 36) also said that it had suffered in the 15th century 'from the depredations of the soldiers and was in danger of being wholly destroyed', but whether the village was completely removed is not known. Presumably part of it was, probably as a result of enclosure for sheep in the 15th or early 16th centuries (see (1) above). By the late 17th century it had recovered, for the 1673 Hearth Tax Returns list 27 houses in the parish, most of which are unlikely to have been of medieval date (PRO, E179/254/14). On the Tithe Map of 1847 (NRO) the area of the remains was called Home Close.

The remains suggest that the village was once aligned on a N.W.–S.E. axis along the R. Cherwell and then either moved to or was resettled along the main Daventry-Banbury road which crosses the river at right-angles. The earthworks are in poor condition having been damaged by quarrying, and by the construction of Charwelton station

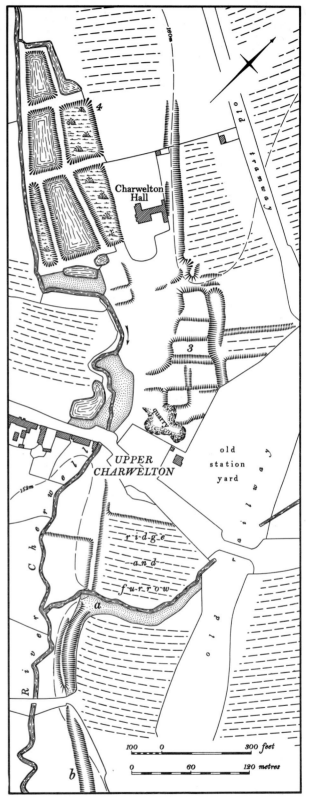

Fig. 41   CHARWELTON   (3) Settlement remains at Upper Charwelton,   (2, 4) Ponds

yard in 1896. They consist of a line of at least five embanked closes bounded on the N.E. by a massive scarp some 2 m. high. Their S.W. ends appear to have been cut away and they may have extended almost to the river (RAF VAP CPE/UK/1994, 3147–8; CUAP, AMS24–7, AZV78).

^a(4) FISHPONDS (SP 533562; Fig. 41), lie in the valley of the R. Cherwell immediately S.W. of Charwelton Hall, on clay at 155 m. above OD. They consist of six roughly rectangular ponds of various sizes fed by a narrow leat from the river. They are now overgrown and in poor condition but were presumably a set of medieval stews connected with Charwelton Hall. On the Tithe Map of 1847 (NRO) they are all described as fishponds.

^a(5) PONDS (SP 530555, 532558, 540553), S.W. of Upper Charwelton and W. of Church Charwelton, on clay at around 150 m. above OD, in small tributary valleys of the R. Cherwell. They vary in size but all are characterized by having small islands within them, probably for the protection of wildfowl. Their date is unknown. All are shown in their present form on the Tithe Map of 1847 (NRO) and called Fish Ponds. The same map also shows another similar pond, again with an island in it, in the S. part of the parish (SP 543542); this was destroyed by the railway (RAF VAP CPE/UK/1994, 3147–8).

^a(6) WINDMILL MOUND (SP 53845599), lies E. of Upper Charwelton on the summit of a low E.–W. ridge on clay at 158 m. above OD. It is circular, 20 m. in diam. and 1 m. high, with a ditch 0.25 m. deep crossed in two places by causeways. It is surrounded by ridge-and-furrow and the ridges on the N.E. and S.W. terminate short of it indicating that the mound could be contemporary with the ridge-and-furrow. However the general pattern of the ridge-and-furrow and, in particular, the neat alignment of it on either side of the mound may indicate that the latter was erected on existing plough ridges. The mound is not shown on the Tithe Map of 1847 (NRO; RAF VAP CPE/UK/1994, 3147–8; CUAP, AZV81).

^a(7) WINDMILL MOUND (SP 52555520), S.W. of the village, on Charwelton Hill, on Northampton Sand at 200 m. above OD. A low mound, now almost destroyed, marks the site of a windmill shown here on the Tithe Map of 1847 (NRO) when the area was known as Windmill Hill (RAF VAP CPE/UK/1994, 3146–7).

^c(8) WINDMILL MOUND (SP 545543), in the S.E. of the parish, S.W. of Hollingwood House, on the summit of a hill of Northampton Sand at 152 m. above OD. A low mound, almost ploughed flat, with a disturbed area around it, marks the site of a windmill shown on the Tithe Map of 1847. The area was then known as Windmill Ground (RAF VAP CPE/UK/1994, 2154–5).

(9) CULTIVATION REMAINS. The common fields of the parish were enclosed by agreement in 1531 (NRO, YZ 4523).

Ridge-and-furrow of these fields exists on the ground or can be traced on air photographs over most of the parish except in the extreme W., around and N.W. of Charwelton Hill Farm (SP 522555), but even here it is more likely that modern cultivation has removed all traces rather than that there was never any ridge-and-furrow. Along the valley of the R. Cherwell where it is still well preserved it is mainly arranged in end-on furlongs extending down the valley side. A similar pattern exists around the high land in the parish, especially in the N.E., around the S. and S.E. sides of Sharman's Hill (SP 542574) where the ridges radiate outwards. Elsewhere on the flatter ground interlocked rectangular furlongs are more common (RAF VAP CPE/UK/1994, 1155–60, 2152–6, 3145–9).

UNDATED

^a(10) BURIAL (SP 539565), marked as 'site of interment' on a map in *Archaeologia*, 35 (1854), 394. No other details are known.

17 CLAY COTON
(OS 1:10000 ^a SP 57 NE, ^b SP 67 NW)

The parish is one of the smallest in Northamptonshire, only a little over 400 hectares in area, and is almost rectangular. It occupies the E. part of valley of a W.-flowing tributary of the R. Avon so that the highest points are on the N., S. and E. boundaries of the parish where the land rises to 120 m. The wide, flat valley floor with its meandering stream is at about 100 m. above OD. In the N. an area of Lower Lias Clay is exposed but the greater part of the parish is covered by glacial deposits, particularly Boulder Clay, and by alluvium.

The village may be secondary to Lilbourne. This is suggested not only by the name Coton, but also by the shapes of the two parishes in relationship to each other (Fig. 42).

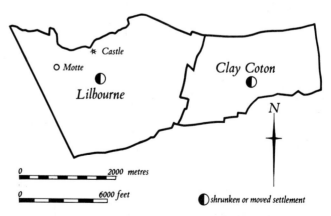

Fig. 42   CLAY COTON and LILBOURNE
Medieval settlements and estates

MEDIEVAL AND LATER

(1) MEDIEVAL COIN HOARD (unlocated), found near the village several years before 1865. A hoard of 435 15th-century groats, mostly of Edward IV but some as early as Henry IV and some as late as Henry VII, was discovered in a small earthenware pot with an olive-green glaze (*PSA*, 3 (1865), 77; *Num. Chron.*, New Series, 6 (1866), 136).

^a(2) SETTLEMENT REMAINS (SP 594770; Figs. 42 and 43), formerly part of Clay Coton, lie in and around the existing village on alluvium at 103 m. above OD. The village is not recorded by name until 1175 (PN *Northants.*, 66) but it is almost certainly included silently in Domesday Book in the entry for the adjacent village of Lilbourne. Its name, its position on low-lying ground in the valley of the small W.-flowing brook, and the relationship of its parish boundary to that of Lilbourne (Fig. 42) all suggests that the settlement may have been a secondary or daughter hamlet of Lilbourne and may always have been very small. There is no record of its size until 1523 when the village was taxed at 22s. 6d. (PRO, E179/155/161), the smallest amount paid in this part of Northamptonshire except by settlements already deserted, but 34 people paid the Hearth Tax in 1673 (PRO, E179/254/14), an unusually high figure indicating that the village had increased in size. In the early 18th century Bridges (*Hist. of Northants.*, I (1791), 548) said that

there were 25 houses in the village and in 1801, 116 people lived in the parish. On the Tithe Map of 1839 (NRO) some 15 buildings are marked, all possibly houses though some must have been sub-divided into separate tenements. Three of these houses have since been demolished.

The remains are very fragmentary, consisting of mutilated scarps, banks and ditches forming no coherent pattern but, though difficult to interpret, the earthworks and the limits of the surrounding ridge-and-furrow serve to indicate that there were once houses on both sides of the road leading N. from the church and possibly on the N. side of the road which formerly ran W. to Lilbourne. From the Tithe Map it appears that the village once had a large, roughly triangular green S. of the church and on both sides of the stream. This green had already been encroached upon by 1839 and is now almost destroyed (RAF VAP 106G/UK/636, 4164–66; air photographs in NMR).

(3) CULTIVATION REMAINS. The common fields of Clay Coton were enclosed by agreement in 1663 (NRO, s (G) 79). Ridge-and-furrow of these fields can be traced on the ground or from air photographs over almost the entire parish with the exception of about 30 hectares in the S.E. The greater part of the ridge-and-furrow is arranged in end-on furlongs, orientated N.–S. down the main valley sides (RAF VAP 106G/UK/636, 4162, 4473–9).

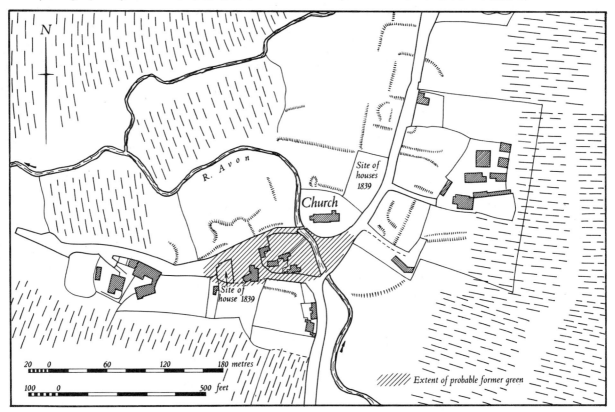

Fig. 43   CLAY COTON   (2) Settlement remains

18 CLIPSTON

(OS 1:10000 [a] SP 78 SW, [b] SP 77 NW, [c] SP 68 SE, [d] SP 67 NE)

The diamond-shaped parish occupies 1185 hectares, across the head-waters of the R. Ise and several small tributary streams. The latter have cut down into the Boulder Clay which covers the higher ground between 135 m. and 180 m. above OD, to reveal bands of Upper Lias Clay along the steep valley sides. As well as four recently discovered small Roman settlements the parish contains two important medieval monuments. The extensive settlement remains (7) which lie within and to the W. of Clipston itself indicate that the development of the village has been very complex. The deserted village of Nobold or Newbold (6) lies in the N.W. of the parish but the boundaries of its land cannot be ascertained.

Roman

[a](1) ROMAN SETTLEMENT (?) (SP 701806), lies S.W. of the village on gravel at 145 m. above OD. A small quantity of Roman pottery has been found here (*Northants. Archaeol.*, 11 (1976), 191).

[c](2) ROMAN SETTLEMENT (?) (SP 695805), lies W. of (1) on Boulder Clay at 150 m. above OD. A scatter of Roman pottery has been found in the area around an abandoned farm-house (*Northants. Archaeol.*, 11 (1976), 191).

[c](3) ROMAN SETTLEMENT (?) (SP 697828), lies N.W. of the village, on Boulder Clay, at 150 m. above OD. A scatter of Roman pottery has been discovered (*Northants. Archaeol.*, 12 (1977), 211).

[a](4) ROMAN SETTLEMENT (?) (SP 714830), lies N. of the village, on Boulder Clay, at 150 m. above OD. A scatter of Roman pottery is recorded here (*Northants. Archaeol.*, 12 (1977), 211).

Medieval and Later

The site of the deserted settlement of Calme, which is only known from Domesday Book where it is listed with a recorded population of five (VCH *Northants.*, I (1902), 318), has not been located (K. J. Allison *et al.*, *The Deserted Villages of Northants.* (1966), 36). The most likely position for it is in the extreme N. of the parish near Twantry Farm (SP 702840). A number of fields in this area have the name Comb (NRO, Field Name Map, 1932) but no remains have been found.

During the 19th century a skeleton, accompanied by a spear, an arrowhead or spear and a spur said to be of the 15th century, is recorded as being found in the parish (*Trans. Leics. Arch. Soc.*, 2 (1870), 354). It is possible that this refers to the Saxon burial (5).

[a](5) SAXON BURIAL (SP 714815), perhaps in the S.E. part of the village, on clay at 126 m. above OD. One skeleton was discovered in 1867, accompanied by a knife, a scramasax and part of a spearhead of Swanton's type C2 (M. J. Swanton, *The Spearheads of the Anglo-Saxon Settlements* (1973), 157; *BAR*, 7 (1972), 42; VCH *Northants.*, I (1902), 237; T. J. George, *Arch. Survey of Northants.* (1904), 12; Meaney, *Gazetteer*, 188; *J. Northants. Mus. and Art Gall.*, 6 (1969), 49).

[c](6) DESERTED VILLAGE OF NOBOLD (SP 695821; Fig. 44; Plate 10), lies on the E.-facing slope of a high N.-S. ridge in the extreme N.W. of the parish, against the Sibbertoft boundary, on Boulder Clay at 165 m. above OD. Little is known of the history of the village and its name is not recorded until 1284 when it had 35 virgates of land divided between three manors. The meaning of its name 'New Building', as well as the site of the village, suggests that it was a later secondary settlement of Clipston (PN *Northants.*, 111). Nobold is rarely named in the national taxation records and is presumably included with Clipston. It is mentioned by name in the *Nomina Villarum* of 1316, and in 1381 its three common fields are noted and tenants are recorded in the largest of the manors. By 1459 only two houses existed in this manor though nothing is known of the situation on the other two manors. The only certainty is that the village was totally deserted by the early 18th century and had been so for a long time. Bridges (*Hist. of Northants.*, II (1791), 23–4) gives a long description of the earthworks lying in a field known as Old Nobold Close. He recognized the central hollow-way of the main street and recorded the house-sites on both sides of it. He also noted that 'In one part is a plot of ground immemorially called the church-yard. ... Human skulls have been dug up here' (K. J. Allison *et al.*, *The Deserted Villages of Northants.* (1966), 43; J. M. Steane, *The Northants. Landscape* (1974), 160–2).

The remains are in good condition except that, like other deserted villages in the area, e.g. Onley (Barby (1)), Glassthorpe (Flore (4)) and Sulby (3), the site has been almost completely overploughed with ridge-and-furrow at some time after desertion. The main feature of the site is a broad hollow-way up to 1.5 m. deep which crosses the site from E.–W. but is blocked at its W. end partly by later ridge-and-furrow and partly by a relatively modern ditch. On both sides of this hollow-way are the remains of platforms set within small embanked or scarped yards. These are well preserved at the E. end of the hollow-way, on its N. side, but all those on the S. are very broken down by later ridge-and-furrow, and those on the N. side towards the W. end have been completely obliterated by the plough. Behind the sites of houses and yards there are traces of long closes, but again ploughing has almost entirely destroyed them.

One small area of earthworks at the W. end, beyond the blocking of the hollow-way, has no trace of ridge-and-furrow, but this too has been ploughed over, at a later date than the ridge-and-furrow, and thus the remaining earthworks are indistinct. In the S.E. corner of the site is a

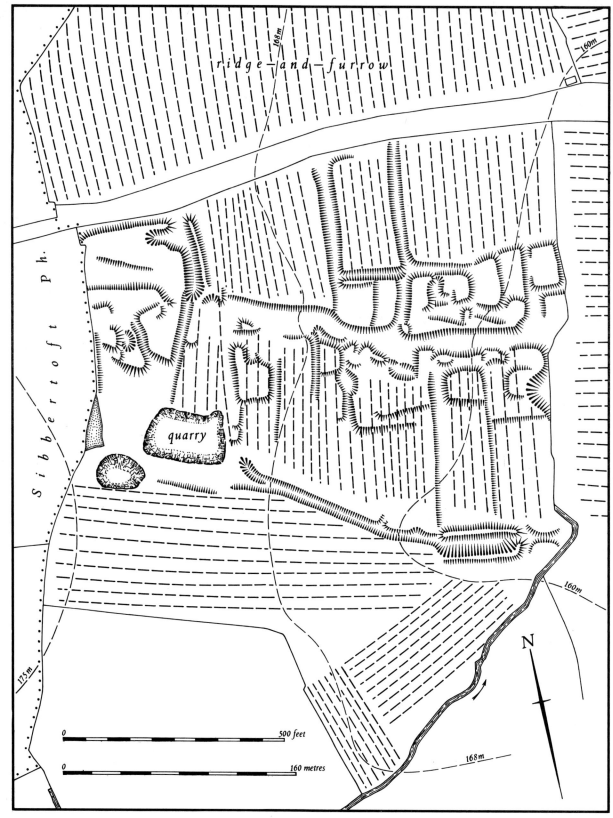

Fig. 44   CLIPSTON   (6) Deserted village of Nobold

small rectangular embanked pond which is approached from the W. by a narrow ditch (RAF VAP 106G/UK/636, 3182–3).

^a(7) SETTLEMENT REMAINS (centred SP 706818; Figs. 11 and 45), lie within and around the existing village between 130 m. and 150 m. above OD. The size of Clipston village at any one time is impossible to ascertain because the parish also included the now deserted village of Nobold (6) and both settlements were always recorded together. However the village was presumably always large for in Domesday Book there are four manors listed for Clipston, three of which have a combined recorded population of 41, though the fourth, part of the royal manor of Rothwell, has no separate population figures (VCH *Northants.*, I (1902), 306, 310, 318, 337). In 1377, 119 people over the age of 14, most of whom lived at Clipston, paid the Poll Tax (PRO, E179/155/28). In 1674, 48 householders paid the Hearth Tax, all of whom were probably from Clipston, Nobold by then having been abandoned; in addition two 'empty ruined town houses' and two empty cottages are recorded (PRO, E179/254/14). Bridges (*Hist. of Northants.*, II (1791), 17) said that 120 families lived at Clipston in the early 18th century. In 1801, 331 people lived in the parish.

The main significance of the settlement remains is that they indicate the complicated evolution of the village's morphology, and a tentative sequence can be inferred from the modern layout and the surviving earthworks. It is possible that the earliest part of the village was the area around High Street and Church Lane, centred on the church in which there is some evidence of a 12th-century structure. The Saxon burial (5) was perhaps found hereabouts.

The second stage of development may have been a planned extension in the N.W., comprising three parallel streets, with the village green in the S.E. corner. Two of these streets survive as Chapel Lane and Harborough Road, and the third which lies equidistant between them is a broad hollow-way up to 2.5 m. deep ('a'–'b' on plan). On both sides of this hollow-way, on the E. side of Chapel Lane ('c' on plan) and on both sides of Harborough Road ('d' and 'e' on plan) there are closes of former houses, bounded by shallow ditches or low banks and scarps.

Later expansion may have been in the area S.W. of Chapel Lane where there are extensive settlement remains apparently based on two hollow-ways. One of the latter extends from the bend in Pegs Lane ('f' on plan) and runs N.W. until it meets the other, which is longer and curves S.E. and then S.W. ('g'–'h' on plan). Pegs Lane itself may be part of this development. On both sides of these hollow-ways are many small closes, some with identifiable house-sites within them.

Elsewhere in the village are small areas of old embanked closes (not shown on plan) which do not appear to have been occupied by dwellings. One such area lies immediately N. of the church (SP 714817; RAF VAP CPE/UK/2109, 3291–5, 4293–5; CUAP, AHE83–4, BAP74).

(8) CULTIVATION REMAINS. The common fields of Clipston and Nobold were apparently enclosed by an Act of Parliament in 1776, but it is not clear whether all the land previously belonging to Nobold was affected. Some of the ridge-and-furrow of these fields has been destroyed but most of it survives or can be traced on air photographs, and much of it is of considerable size and well preserved. Such areas lie both around Clipston village and around the deserted village of Nobold and also in the S. part of the parish. The furlongs are often short and interlocked in response to the broken nature of the landscape, particularly W. and N. of the village, but there are also groups of end-on furlongs, for example S. of Nobold (SP 698817), N. of the Sibbertoft road (SP 750825) and S.E. of the village (SP 716810). The deserted village of Nobold has been completely overploughed with ridge-and-furrow, perhaps of post-medieval date (RAF VAP 106G/UK/636, 4130–33, 3128–33, 3182–86, 4460–3; CPE/UK/2109, 4293–8, 3291–9).

19   COLD ASHBY

(OS 1:10000 ^a SP 67 NW, ^b SP 67 NE, ^c SP 67 SW, ^d SP 67 SE)

The parish occupies a diamond-shaped area about 865 hectares in extent, on a watershed with radiating streams flowing generally N. towards the R. Avon and S. towards the R. Nene. The highest ground, W. of the village, rises to 206 m. above OD and is part of a large outcrop of Northampton Sand which makes up the central part of the parish. Upper Lias Clay is exposed by the down-cutting of the streams, and along the N.E. edge and in the S. are expanses of Boulder Clay. The only monument of interest in the parish is the group of earthworks (2) immediately N. of the village. These are bounded on the N. by an unusually wide hollow-way and may be either the remains of an abandoned part of the village or the site of a monastic grange of Sulby Abbey which is known to have existed in the parish.

PREHISTORIC

^b(1) RING DITCH AND ENCLOSURE (SP 65867803), S.W. of Portly Ford Bridge, in the N. of the parish, on gravel at 152 m. above OD. Air photographs (in NMR) show three sides of a small trapezoidal enclosure only 20 m. by 25 m., with a ring ditch 8 m. in diam. within it.

MEDIEVAL AND LATER

^b(2) HOLLOW-WAY AND SITE OF MONASTIC GRANGE (SP 656765; Fig. 46), lie in a large pasture field immediately N. of Main Street, on the N. side of the village, on Northampton Sand at 195 m. above OD. The main feature is a broad hollow-way, 10 m. wide and 0.5 m. deep. It runs from the existing track which leads S. to the village (at

52

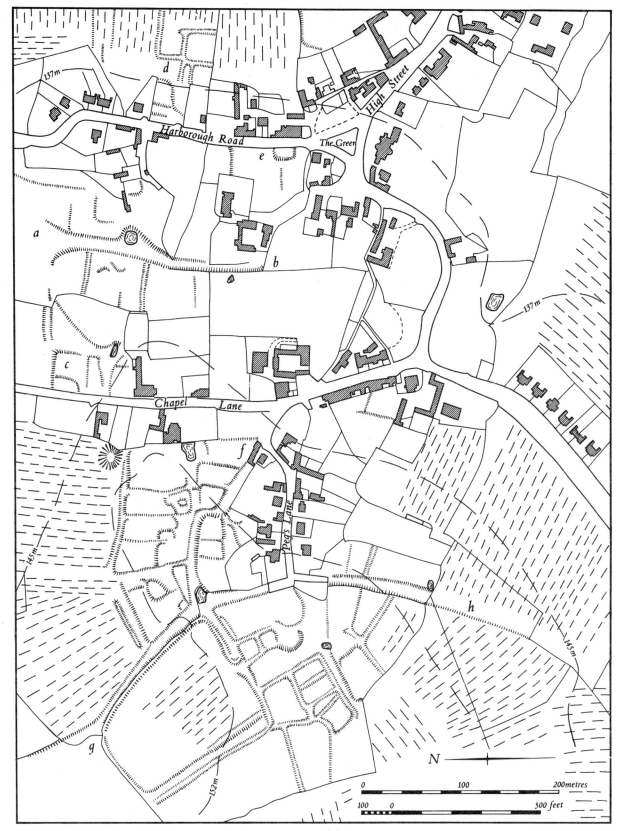

Fig. 45   CLIPSTON   (7) Settlement remains

sp 65537660), and curves around the marshy source of a N.-flowing brook to meet the road from Naseby (at sp 65757654). Here a N. branch continues as the modern road but the main hollow-way also continues in a mutilated form further E. across the next field until it is lost in the modern arable land. On the N. side of the hollow-way, near its junction with Naseby Road, a small subsidiary hollow-way only 5 m. across runs N.E. for a few metres before it reaches arable land. In the area to the S. of the hollow-way, between it and the present village, are five large rectangular closes bounded by low scarps and banks only 0.25 m. high. At the S. ends, and extending as far as the back gardens of the modern council houses which line Main Street, there is a group of small rectangular paddocks edged by low stone walls within which are several building platforms. Throughout much of the medieval period the main manor of Cold Ashby was held by Pipewell Abbey and the monastic farm was apparently of considerable size and importance. Bridges, writing in the early 18th century (*Hist. of Northants.*, I (1791), 550–1), said that at that time the building still stood 'in the fields'. The earthworks probably represent the site of this grange; the field is still known as Grange Field (RAF VAP CPE/UK/1994, 4175–6).

b(3) SETTLEMENT REMAINS (SP 656760; Fig. 47), formerly part of Cold Ashby, lie on the S. side of the village, S.E. of the church, on Northampton Sand, at 180 m. above OD. A group of long closes, bounded by low banks and shallow ditches, extend down the hillside towards a small stream. At their upper, N. ends are rectangular raised platforms, presumably the sites of former houses which lay along an

Fig. 47 COLD ASHBY
(3) Settlement remains

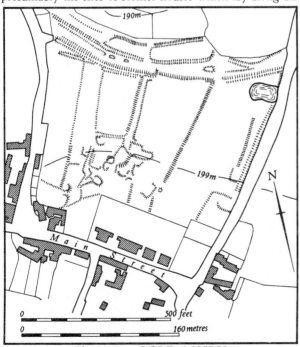

Fig. 46 COLD ASHBY
(2) Hollow-way and site of monastic grange

old road running S.E. from the village and roughly parallel to the present Thornby Road to the N.E. Further N.W., in the angle between Church Lane and West Haddon Road (SP 653763), are further earthworks of houses and closes (not shown on plan). These remains indicate either that the village plan has been altered in the past or that there has been a fall in population at some time. In view of the evidence of surviving records the former suggestion is more likely. In 1086 Domesday Book gives a recorded population of 14 (VCH *Northants.*, I (1906), 320, 325, 339, 347). In 1377, 82 people over the age of 14 paid the Poll Tax (PRO, E179/155/28) and in 1673, 39 people paid Hearth Tax (PRO, E179/254/14).

(4) CULTIVATION REMAINS. The date of the enclosure of the common fields of Cold Ashby is not known. Ridge-and-furrow of these fields survives on the ground or can be traced on air photographs to the N. and N.E. of the village, mainly in end-on furlongs, although in the N. some furlongs were arranged obliquely to one another in response to the direction of the slope (RAF VAP CPE/UK/1994, 4465; 106G/UK/636, 4276–9, 3177–8).

20 COTTESBROOKE

(OS 1:10000 [a] SP 67 NE, [b] SP 67 SE, [c] SP 77 NW, [d] SP 77 SW)

The parish, covering some 1150 hectares, lies on either side of a small S.E.-flowing stream, between 210 m. and 150 m. above OD. It is almost entirely on Lias Clay except for the higher areas to the S.W. and N. which are overlaid by Boulder Clay. In spite of the relatively heavy soils two Roman sites (2) and (3) and an Iron Age site (1) have been found during recent fieldwork and others undoubtedly await discovery. Of the medieval and later earthworks in the parish the settlement remains (5), though not of great interest in themselves, add to the history of the village's topography. Cottesbrooke appears always to have been two separate settlements each with its own land unit and separate field system (Fig. 14; NRO, Map of 1628). The well-preserved moated site with its enclosures (4) is usually said to be a monastic cell, but is more likely to be a small grange of Sulby Abbey.

PREHISTORIC AND ROMAN

[c](1) IRON AGE SETTLEMENT (centred SP 703759), in the N.W. corner of the parish W. of Old Covert, on clay at 145 m. above OD. Iron Age sherds were found on a dark occupation surface (Northants. Archaeol., 9 (1974), 89; CBA Group 9, Newsletter, 4 (1974), 27).

[ac](2) ROMAN SETTLEMENT (SP 700755), S.W. of (2) at 120 m. above OD. A large area of Roman pottery, building stone and patches of dark soil has been discovered (Northants. Archaeol., 9 (1974), 89; CBA Group 9, Newsletter, 4 (1974), 27).

[c](3) ROMAN SETTLEMENT (?) (SP 727751), in the N.E. corner of the parish on clay at 100 m. above OD. Air photographs (RAF VAP CPE/UK/1994, 1460–1) show a rectangular enclosure 85 m. by 30 m., orientated N.E.–S.W. at right-angles to a small stream. It is overlaid by ridge-and-furrow. On the ground the enclosing bank still survives 0.25 m. high. Roman pottery, and some other sherds of unknown date but probably Roman, have been discovered but the earthworks themselves may not necessarily be of Roman origin (BNFAS, 6 (1971), 8; Northants. Archaeol., 9 (1974), 89).

MEDIEVAL AND LATER

[b](4) SITE OF MONASTIC GRANGE OR CELL (SP 690746; Fig. 48; Plate 4), lies in the N.W. corner of the parish, on Boulder Clay, on land sloping S.W. to a small stream at around 120 m. above OD. It has been said to be the site of a cell of Premonstratensian Canons, founded soon after 1155 and probably abandoned by 1291 (M. D. Knowles and R. N. Hadcock, Medieval Religious Houses in England and Wales (1953), 166; J. Bridges, Hist. of Northants., I (1791), 557). However there is no real evidence for a true cell ever having been there and the site is more likely to have been

merely a grange or farmstead of Sulby Abbey. The land, called Kalender or 'Kayland', was given to Sulby Abbey by one William de Buttivillar, apparently soon after the foundation of the abbey in 1155. No other details of its history are known.

The main feature of the earthworks is a small Moated Site ('a' on plan) consisting of a rectangular island surrounded by a ditch 2 m. deep on the S.E. and 1.75 m. deep on the N.E. and N.W. but only 1 m. deep on the S.W. A low irregular mound in the interior may be the remains of a building. To the N.W. of the moat is a small embanked close with no visible entrance with, possibly, a second large close extending to the stream on the S.W. To the S.E. of the moat is another close with a number of interior scarps, bounded on the S. by a broad shallow trackway leading towards a rectangular sunken area S. of the moat. To the S. of the trackway is a further small ditched and embanked enclosure. There is a small rectangular pond on the S.W. side of the site ('b' on plan) with a large bank or dam on its down-slope side. This appears to have been filled by seepage of water from the hillside. To the S.E. of the pond but not connected to it is a long ditch, embanked on its S.W. side, the S.E. end of which passes into a large sub-rectangular depression ('c' on plan); the latter has largely been destroyed by modern cultivation but it was probably a fishpond (Ass. Arch. Soc. Reps., 33 (1923), 131–3; RAF VAP 540/474, 3151–2; CUAP, AGU64–5, NR64).

[a](5) SETTLEMENT REMAINS (SP 709735; Figs. 14, 49 and 50; Plate 19), lie at the S.E. end of the village around and W. of the church, on Lias Clay at about 100 m. above OD. The interpretation of the earthworks is difficult, and involves the whole history of the village's development.

The main area of earthworks, immediately W. of the church ('a' on plan), appears at first sight to be the remains of closes belonging to houses which once lined the road to the N. where part of a possible hollow-way indeed survives. This area could be interpreted as part of an original single-street village, the N. and S.E. parts of which still remain. However at least one other explanation must be considered. On the earliest map of Cottesbrooke, dated 1628, and indeed on the Tithe Map of 1839 (both in NRO; Fig. 50; Plate 19) neither the existing road nor the assumed hollow-way is shown. Both plans depict a road which left the present one at the N.E. corner of the churchyard and ran N. towards the lake or stream as it was in 1628, and then turned W. to run along the valley. After some 200 m. it swung S.W. to meet the modern road again near the last houses at the N. end of the village. The whole area of surviving earthworks, with the land now N. of the present road and occupied by the lodges to Cottesbrooke Hall, was a single field in 1628, with a pond on its N. side and a dove-cot N. of the church on the site of the present ice-house mound. By 1839 this field had been sub-divided into closes and two of the boundary hedges shown on the Tithe Map are marked by low scarps on the ground today.

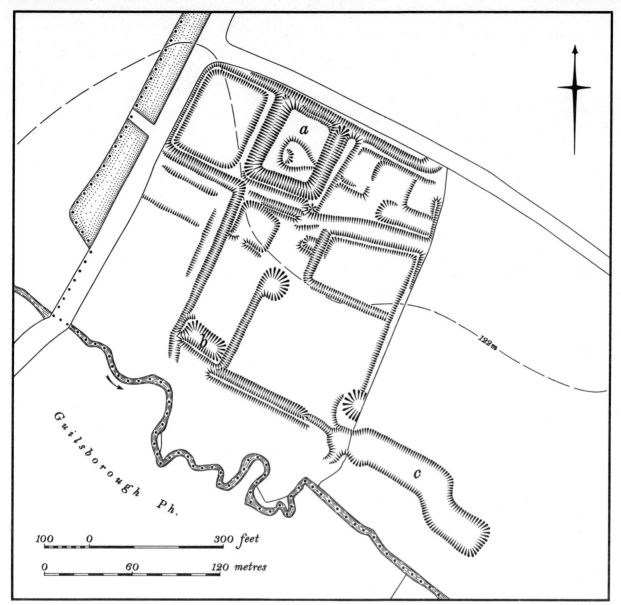

Fig. 48   COTTESBROOKE   (4) Site of monastic grange

The ponds still existed but the dove-cot had disappeared and had been replaced by two buildings nearby; another building stood to the N. of the pond. The general area was then known as Horse Close. On a later map (NRO, said to be of 1874 but in fact made before 1858) the area is shown as a single field called Horse Close, but without pond and buildings. In 1858 (map in NRO) the old road had been abandoned and the present road cut across the site.

It is thus possible that the surviving earthworks are no more than the remains of old paddocks and subsequent quarrying, all of which took place after 1628 and which had mostly been abandoned by 1839. If this is so then Cottesbrooke village was not originally of single-street type, but consisted of two separate settlements and is an example of a polyfocal village (*Med. Arch.*, 21 (1977), 189). Whether this double-focus settlement existed at an early date is not known. The manorial boundary apparent on the 1628 map may indicate the division between the estates of the two settlements (Fig. 14). On the ground little remains in the area of the features shown on the early map apart from the earthworks immediately W. of the church ('a' on plan). The original road near the stream does not survive, as the construction of later gardens and the hall drive and especially the dredging of material from the lake has removed all trace. One low scarp, probably the side of the pond on the N. side of Horse Close, exists.

56

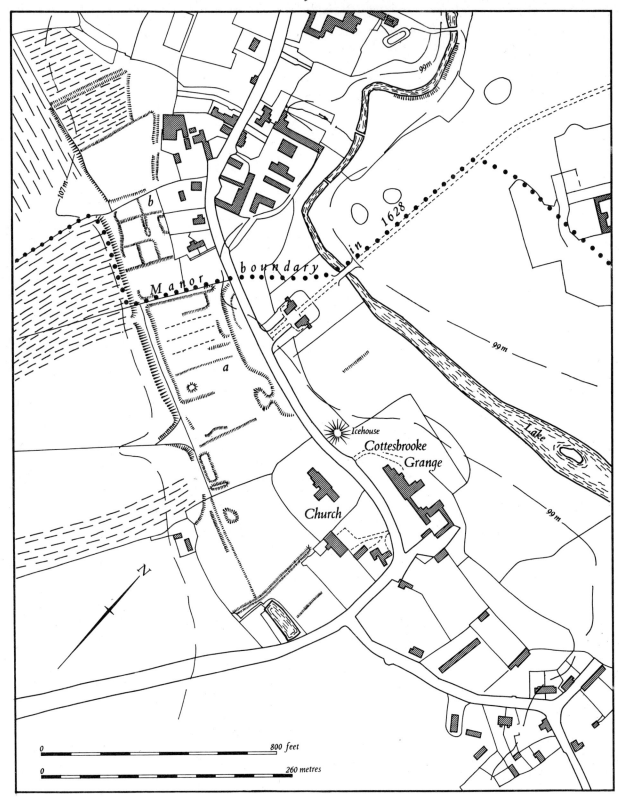

Fig. 49   COTTESBROOKE   (5) Settlement remains

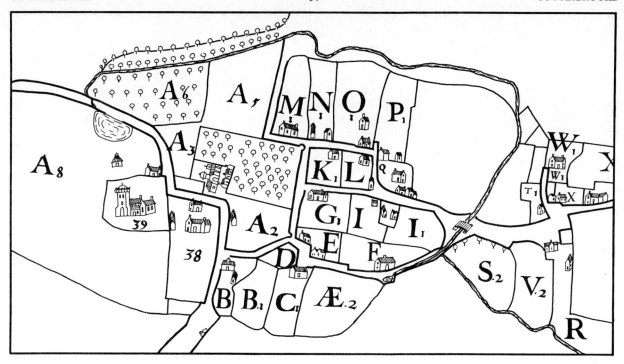

Fig. 50   COTTESBROOKE   (5) Plan of village in 1628 (from a map in NRO)

Immediately S.W. of the last houses in the N.W. part of the village ('b' on plan) are the remains of former closes and paddocks which presumably once belonged to houses there.

The E. part of the village underwent major changes in the 19th century but no earthworks bear witness to this. In 1628 the area was rather rectilinear in layout with a large number of houses scattered along its lanes. By 1839 this pattern had been much modified, partly by shrinkage but largely by the encroachment of the park from the N. Soon afterwards there were further alterations as the 1858 map shows and later in the 19th century most of the area was altered again and the kitchen gardens of the hall were laid out across it. At the extreme E. end of the village on both sides of the road, E. and S.E. of Home Farm (SP 717735), is a series of small rectangular enclosures bounded by low banks and scarps. These may represent another part of the village, but the area was already devoid of occupation by 1628 (CUAP, AZU16).

d(6) GARDEN REMAINS (SP 709741; Fig. 51), lie immediately N.W. of Cottesbrooke Hall on land sloping N.W. towards the stream, on Lias Clay at around 100 m. above OD. John Langham, a London merchant, bought Cottesbrooke in 1637. Between 1702 and 1712 his grandson Sir John Langham built the present hall on a new site well away from the village (Pevsner, *Northamptonshire* (1961), 160–1). The remains of the garden are of such a form that they must date from the early 18th century and are thus probably contemporary with the house. Later in

the 18th century the area around the hall was emparked and landscaped and the original gardens abandoned. This was carried out before or around 1770–80, the date of the bridge across the lake and the lodge gates (Pevsner, op. cit.).

The earthworks, though fragmentary, fall into three parts. The main section ('a' on plan), consisting of a long rectangular area, cut down into the sloping ground, and thus edged by two parallel scarps 1.5 m. high, is certainly the remains of the early 18th-century gardens. At the N.W. end, close to the stream, are the remains of a small pond which was clearly once much larger. To the S.E. the scarps turned and presumably opened out into a formal garden fronting the hall.

To the N.E. is a long bank ('b' on plan) up to 1 m. high with a flat top. It extends across the park from near the stream to a point N. of the hall, crossing and thus blocking an earlier hollow-way which can be traced to the S.E. and N.W.; its date and function are unknown. On the N. side of the bank, and within the bend of the hollow-way, is a large circular mound ('c' on plan) up to 4 m. high, much disturbed by later trees, which may be part of the original garden layout.

(7) CULTIVATION REMAINS. The date of the enclosure of the common fields within the parish is not known, though certainly the whole of the S.E. part (Fig. 50) was already divided into hedged fields by 1628 (Map in NRO) and the N.W. part by 1841 (NRO, Tithe Map; Plate 19). It is possible that the whole parish was enclosed by the early 17th century though there is no proof of this nor indeed of

whether there were two field systems attributable to the two apparently separate medieval settlements there (5). Ridge-and-furrow of these fields exists on the ground or can be traced on air photographs over much of the parish and is particularly well preserved within Cottesbrooke Park. It is arranged in mainly rectangular interlocked furlongs, many of reversed-S form. A number of access-ways between furlongs are visible, for example S.W. of the village (at SP 702732) and at the N.E. end of Cottesbrooke Park (SP 702742; RAF VAP CPE/UK/1994, 1373–7, 1459–65; 540/474, 3151–2).

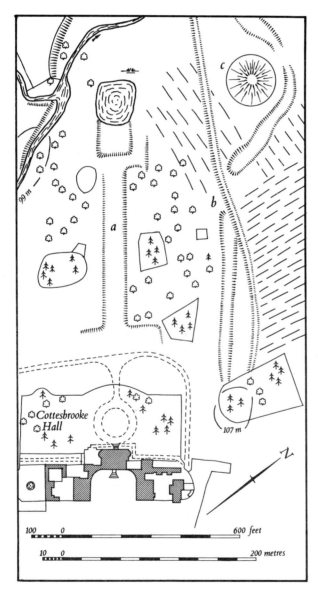

Fig. 51   COTTESBROOKE
(6) Garden remains

21   CREATON

(OS 1:10000 [a] SP 67 SE, [b] SP 77 SW)

The parish, covering about 450 hectares, is made up of the land of two medieval settlements (Fig. 14) but the actual boundary between them is not known with certainty. Most of the area was the land of Great Creaton, but a strip along the S. part belonged to the village of Little Creaton (10), now deserted, and was once part of Spratton parish. The parish lies mainly across the valley of a small S.E.-flowing brook cut into Upper Lias Clay between 140 m. and 80 m. above OD. In the S.W. the land rises steeply to a flat-topped ridge capped with Northampton Sand, and falls again into the clay valley of another small S.E.-flowing stream which forms the parish boundary there. Both Great and Little Creaton lie on the steep hillside above the main stream.

PREHISTORIC AND ROMAN

Part of a Mesolithic or later core is recorded from the parish (NM Records).

[b](1) RING DITCHES (SP 732713), in the S.E. of the parish and lying across the boundary with Spratton, on clay and Northampton Sand at 84 m. above OD. Air photographs taken in 1967 (not seen by RCHM) are said to show various cropmarks including two small ring ditches (OS Record Cards).

[b](2) IRON AGE SETTLEMENT (?) (SP 708715), S. of the village, on Northampton Sand, at 135 m. above OD. A scatter of Iron Age pottery has been found (*Northants. Archaeol.*, 12 (1977), 212).

[b](3) IRON AGE AND ROMAN SETTLEMENT (SP 728723), in the E. of the parish, on the summit of a ridge capped by Northampton Sand, at 115 m. above OD. A considerable amount of Iron Age and Roman pottery has been discovered (*Northants. Archaeol.*, 12 (1977), 212).

[b](4) ROMAN SETTLEMENT (?) (SP 734722), 600 m. E. of (3), on gravel at 85 m. above OD. Roman pottery has been noted (*Northants. Archaeol.*, 12 (1977), 212; for Saxon pottery from this site see (9)).

[b](5) ROMAN SETTLEMENT (?) (SP 729720), 300 m. S.E. of (3), on Upper Lias Clay at 95 m. above OD. A small scatter of Roman pottery is recorded (*Northants. Archaeol.*, 12 (1977), 212).

[b](6) ROMAN SETTLEMENT (?) (SP 710723), immediately N.E. of the village, on clay at 107 m. above OD. A scatter of Roman sherds has been noted (inf. A. E. Brown).

[b](7) ROMAN SETTLEMENT (?) (SP 711730), close to the N. boundary of the parish, on clay at 114 m. above OD. A quantity of Roman pottery is recorded from this site (inf. A. E. Brown).

b(8) ROMAN SETTLEMENT (?) (SP 705725), N. of the village, on clay at 122 m. above OD. Roman pottery has been found in this area (inf. A. E. Brown).

MEDIEVAL AND LATER

b(9) SAXON SETTLEMENT (?) (SP 734722), on the same site as the Roman settlement (4) above. Sherds of Saxon pottery have been discovered (*Northants. Archaeol.*, 12 (1977), 212).

b(10) DESERTED VILLAGE OF LITTLE CREATON (SP 712716; Figs. 14 and 52), lies on a steep N.E.-facing slope a little to the S.E. of Great Creaton village, on Upper Lias Clay between 100 m. and 130 m. above OD. Little is known of

its history because for most of its life it appears to have been included either with Spratton parish of which it was once part or with Great Creaton.

It is not mentioned by name in Domesday Book, but has been identified as the small manor of Creaton held by William de Cahagnes of the Count of Mortain, in which case it then had a recorded population of four (VCH *Northants.*, I (1902), 325). There is no further reference to its size until the early 18th century when Bridges noted eight surviving houses (*Hist. of Northants.*, I (1791), 564). However it is certain that by this time the village site itself was already deserted and that these houses included the present Creaton Grange Farm, Stone Cottage and Orchard Farm.

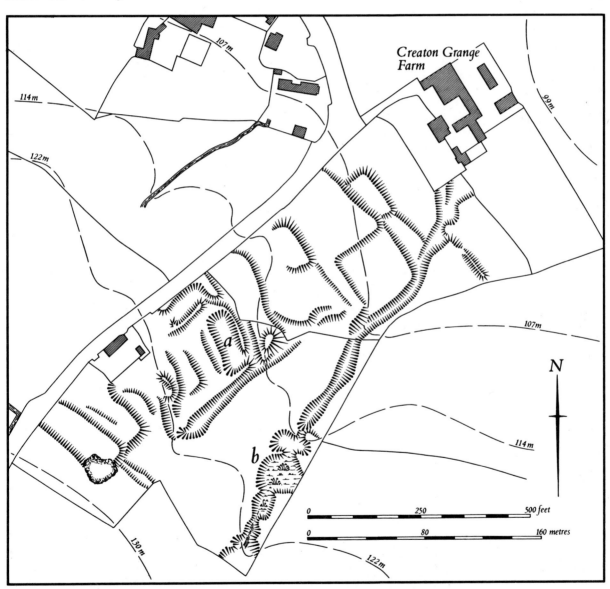

Fig. 52   CREATON   (10) Deserted village of Little Creaton

The remains of the village are in poor condition, and little can be deduced from them. They seem to consist of a series of long closes extending S.E. from the existing road, bounded by low scarps up to 0.5 m. high and some of them subdivided. In the centre ('a' on plan) is a large rectangular pond, and on the S.E. of the site is a long water-course, mainly natural, but which seems to have been dammed at its S.W. end to form two irregular ponds ('b' on plan; RAF VAP CPE/UK/1994, 1373–4).

(11) CULTIVATION REMAINS. The common fields of Great Creaton were enclosed by an Act of Parliament of 1782. Though no map seems to have survived, the Enclosure Award (Central Library, Northampton) indicates that there were four open fields in 1782. These were Upper Field in the N.W., Middle Field to the N. and N.E. of the village, West Field to the S.W., and Nether Field occupying the long E. projection of the parish. Ridge-and-furrow of these fields can be traced on air photographs over large areas, though little remains on the ground. Two end-on furlongs are partly preserved in the N.E. of the parish in Creaton Covert (SP 720725) and later artificial fox-earths have been inserted into the ridges. Further S.E. (SP 723722) the ends of another furlong are preserved in a narrow belt of scrub along a field boundary. Elsewhere air photographs show blocks of interlocked and end-on furlongs carefully adapted to the broken valley sides with their numerous spurs.

The date of the enclosure of the common fields of Little Creaton is unknown. Ridge-and-furrow of these fields exists on the ground S. and S.E. of the site of the deserted village (10) and elsewhere air photographs show traces of end-on and interlocked furlongs (RAF VAP CPE/UK/1994, 1372–7, 1462–5).

22   CRICK

(OS 1:10000 [a] SP 57 SE, [b] SP 67 SW)

The parish, covering nearly 1340 hectares, is E. of Watling Street which forms its W. boundary. It lies mainly on undulating clayland between 100 m. and 160 m. above OD, drained by a series of small streams flowing N.W. to the R. Avon. The settlement remains (7), which contribute much towards an understanding of the village's development, constitute the main monument in the parish.

PREHISTORIC AND ROMAN

A silver coin of Hadrian was found at Crick before 1712 (J. Morton, *Nat. Hist. of Northants.* (1712), 532).

[a](1) ENCLOSURE (SP 584710), in the S.W. of the parish on Boulder Clay at 144 m. above OD. Air photographs (not seen by RCHM) are said to show a small rectangular ditched enclosure (*Northants. Archaeol.*, 12 (1977), 229).

[a](2) IRON AGE SETTLEMENT (?) (SP 581714), S.W. of the village and immediately E. of the M1, on Middle Lias Clay at 135 m. above OD. Iron Age pottery, burnt stone and dark soil have been found here (CBA Group 9, *Newsletter*, 7 (1977), 29; *Northants. Archaeol.*, 11 (1976), 183).

[a](3) ROMAN SETTLEMENT (?) (SP 587725; Fig. 53), within Crick village, N.W. of the church, on glacial gravel at 130 m. above OD. Roman pottery is recorded from this area (CBA Group 9, *Newsletter*, 7 (1977), 29).

[a](4) ROMAN SETTLEMENT (?) (SP 577733), W. of the village, on the E. side of the M1, on glacial gravel at 120 m. above OD. Roman pottery and building stone have been found on the edge of the motorway cutting which probably destroyed the rest of the site (CBA Group 9, *Newsletter*, 7 (1977), 29; *Northants. Archaeol.*, 11 (1976), 191).

[a](5) ROMAN SETTLEMENT (?) (SP 581734), 500 m. E.N.E. of (4), on glacial gravel at 120 m. above OD. Roman pottery has been found in this area (CBA Group 9, *Newsletter*, 7 (1977), 29; *Northants. Archaeol.*, 11 (1976), 191).

For Roman Road 1f, Watling Street, see Appendix.

MEDIEVAL AND LATER

In the early part of the 18th century it was recorded that in 'a part of the Lordship called Portlow are several eminences which have the appearance of tumuli' (J. Bridges, *Hist. of Northants.*, I (1791), 558). No trace of these can now be seen.

[a](6) SAXON BURIALS (?) (SP 569732), in the Roman road, on the W. boundary of the parish, on alluvium at 106 m. above OD. When a section was cut across the road in 1947 a female skeleton, lying on its back and orientated E.–W., was discovered buried at the centre of the road. A second pit some 1.75 m. to the N. contained a small human skull, and the skeleton of a dog. There were no grave goods, except perhaps for two pieces of belemnite found close to the human skeleton (*Rugby School Magazine* (1948), 34–7). More recently another burial, said to be Saxon, was discovered during roadworks on the modern A5 a little to the N.E. and E. of the Roman road (SP 568734; CBA Group 9, *Newsletter*, 7 (1977), 29). Saxon cemeteries have been found on Watling Street a few miles to both N. and S. and these remains are perhaps of the same period (see Norton (9)).

[a](7) SETTLEMENT REMAINS (SP 589726; Fig. 53), formerly part of Crick village, lie immediately N.E. and E. of the church, on land sloping gently N.E., at about 133 m. above OD. The earthworks are not impressive, for they consist only of a series of long closes bounded either by low scarps or by modern hedge-banks. Most of these have ridge-and-furrow within them which, in some cases at least, is secondary. Two hollow-ways pass between them. A disturbed area at their S.W. ends shows no recognisable features.

The date of abandonment of these remains is unknown though it is possible that the 'wasting' of two halls, a cottage and a 'sheepscote' carried out in 1380 by one Andrew Gyldford who then 'had the keeping of the manor of Crick ... owing to the minority of the ... Earl (of Nottingham)' may relate to this area (*Cal Inq. Misc.* iv, 123).

The existence of the earthworks perhaps throws some light on the origins of the village's layout as it is now. The modern street plan of Crick consists of a peculiar arrangement of loops on either side of the present main E.–W. road. However if the earthworks noted here are interpreted as former house-sites and closes along an old N.W.–S.E. road approximately followed by the present footpath, then it can be postulated that the village originated along two roughly parallel streets running

S.E.–N.W. The westernmost of these was on the present High Street–Church Street alignment which possibly continued N.W. from the bend in the Yelvertoft road. The other street, to the E., would have been along Laud's Road and The Marsh, and across The Green then through the earthworks and around the E. end of Oak Lane and finally along Drayson Lane into the Yelvertoft Road (Air photographs in NMR).

^a(8) FISHPONDS (SP 591720), on the S. side of the village, S. of Boat Horse Lane on Middle Lias Clay at 140 m. above OD. Two rectangular depressions lying parallel to each other and 0.5 m. deep are probably medieval fishponds. There are traces of later ridge-and-furrow lying within them (CBA Group 9, *Newsletter*, 7 (1977), 29).

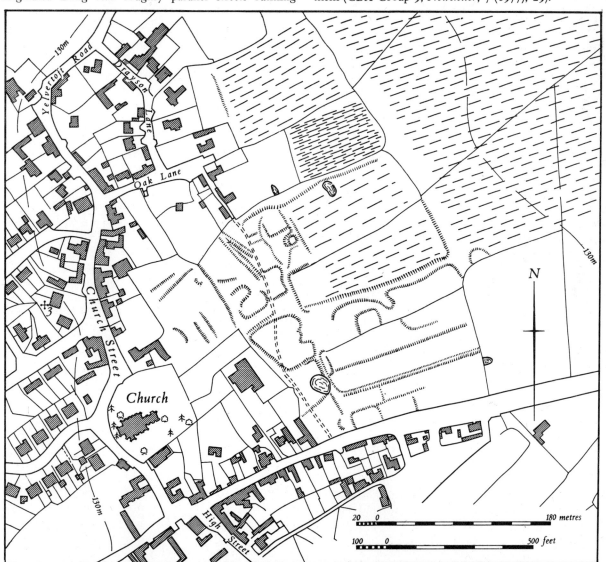

Fig. 53   CRICK   (3) Roman settlement,   (7) Medieval settlement remains

ᵃ(9) WINDMILL MOUND (SP 59157188), S. of the village, on Middle Lias Clay at 152 m. above OD. A low mound 1 m. high and 12 m. in diam. is the site of a windmill which still existed in the early 19th century (OS 1st ed. 1 in. map (1834); CBA Group 9, *Newsletter*, 7 (1977), 29).

(10) CULTIVATION REMAINS. The common fields of the parish were enclosed by an Act of Parliament of 1776. Ridge-and-furrow of these fields exists on the ground or can be traced on air photographs over most of the parish so that the original pattern is almost wholly recoverable. It is arranged mainly in rectangular interlocked furlongs though on the steep slopes, around Crack's Hill for example (SP 595735), it lies across the contours in a radiating pattern. The ridges are still exceptionally well preserved in many places, especially N. and S. of the village (e.g. at SP 590734 and 589715), and as a result a number of details which have been destroyed elsewhere are still visible. In a few places two end-on furlongs have been thrown together and ploughed as one. A particularly good example lies N.W. of the village (SP 584735) where two curving end-on furlongs have been joined up, thus producing a double bend in the ridges as they cross the original headland. Elsewhere hollow trackways through the fields still exist (e.g. SP 582715). Examples also occur of double headlands; the original headland has been abandoned, perhaps to provide extra pasture at some time, and the plough, turning 10 m.–15 m. short of this, has created a new headland. These occur S.W. and S.E. of the village (SP 582720 and 595715). Another feature of the ridge-and-furrow here is the existence of small shallow quarry pits, probably for gravel, which have been dug through the earlier ridge-and-furrow but have subsequently been reploughed in ridges (e.g. SP 584715; CBA Group 9, *Newsletter*, 6 (1976), 28; 7 (1977), 29; RAF VAP CPE/UK/1994, 1356–61, 1474–9, 1472–7; 106G/UK/636, 3440–1, 4441–4; 541/15, 4378–83).

23 DAVENTRY

(OS 1:10000 ᵃ SP 56 NE, ᵇ SP 56 SE)

The modern parish, covering about 1700 hectares, comprises the medieval parishes of Daventry and Drayton, the latter now a suburb of the town. Most of the area consists of undulating Jurassic clayland sloping generally N.E. between 210 m. and 110 m. above OD and drained by a series of small N.E.-flowing streams. In the N.W. of the parish the clays are overlaid by glacial clay, sands and gravel.

Along the E. side lies the great irregular flat-topped block of Borough Hill, rising to 200 m. above OD and capped by Northampton Sand. Its summit is ringed by a

hill fort (3) which is by far the largest in the county and one of the largest in England. Despite the fact that its defences, except on the N., are negligible, finds from the area indicated a long period of occupation through much of the prehistoric and Roman periods and later. It is likely that it was the immediate predecessor of the Roman town of Bannaventa (Norton (4)) which lies to the E. The other monument of note in the parish is the enclosure known as Burnt Walls (35), which lies to the S. of Borough Hill; not only is it of unusual form, but also of unknown date and function.

ᵇ(1)–(21) BOROUGH HILL COMPLEX (Fig. 54; Plate 1). Borough Hill is a large, roughly triangular hill covering more than 200 hectares in the E. part of Daventry parish. It is mainly of Lower Lias Clay, but is capped by Northampton Sand which gives it a rounded summit below which are steep clay-covered slopes. The highest point, almost 200 m. above OD, is near the S. end. The base of the whole hill is at about 145 m. above OD.

The site is one of the most important in the county, because of both the variety and the historical implications of the remains. Chance finds indicate occupation during much of the later prehistoric period, culminating in the great hill fort itself. The latter seems to be of two distinct phases, a large but slightly defended contour fort, succeeded by a massively protected but much smaller fort at the N. end of the hill. During the Roman period there seems to

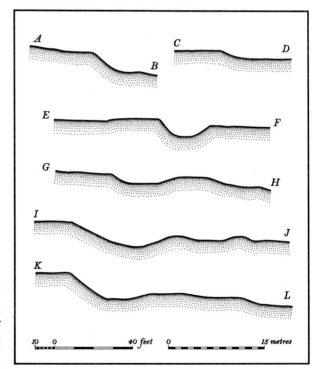

DAVENTRY   (3) Borough Hill
Profiles (see Fig. 54)

have been much occupation here and the known remains include a large villa and a number of burial mounds.

Two or perhaps three Saxon burials are recorded from the hill and, unusually, some Viking weapons. In the 10th century the hill fort is called a *burh* in a Saxon Charter (BCS 792; 944 AD) but elsewhere in the same charter it is also termed the *stod-fald* perhaps indicating that it was used for livestock at that time (PN *Northants.*, 10–12). For most of the medieval period the hill was apparently pasture for the township of Daventry. In 1645 at least part of the Royalist army encamped there immediately before the Battle of Naseby. By the early 18th century the hill was used as a race course, races being held annually up to 1741 and then infrequently until 1801. At that date the archaeological remains were probably still well preserved, but since then a continuous process of destruction and mutilation has affected the site.

After the enclosure of the parish in 1801 the hill was divided into fields and much of the summit was ploughed. A farm was then built on the N. end of it, large parts of the hill fort defences were damaged or destroyed, and the barrows ploughed over. In the 1930s the site became a large BBC transmitting station; destruction and disturbance, still continue. Recently a golf course has been made across the N. part of the hill, resulting in further damage. As a consequence of this modern activity archaeological knowledge is fragmentary. Two separate excavations in the 19th century, first by Baker in 1823 and then by Botfield in 1852, produced much valuable evidence though by modern standards the methods used were totally inadequate. Further work in the early 1920s also led to valuable discoveries.

The literature is extensive. The main sources are: J. Morton, *Nat. Hist. of Northants.* (1712), 519–20, 546–7; J. Bridges, *Hist. of Northants.*, I (1791), 42; G. Baker, *Hist. of Northants.*, I (1822–30), 339–47; *JBAA*, I (1846), 245; C. Roach Smith, *Coll. Antiq.*, I (1848), 113; *Archaeologia*, 35 (1853), 383–95; W. Edgar, *Borough Hill and its History* (1923). This latter work includes a collection of almost all the early commentaries on the area by Camden, Walpole, Brayley and Pennant.

Many of the finds from the hill are in NM and BM, but an important collection made by Edgar is situated in Daventry School (hereafter DS). This collection has been examined by A. E. Brown whose catalogue, including detailed descriptions and drawings, is deposited in NM and NMR.

The finds and the monuments on Borough Hill are here listed together for convenience.

PREHISTORIC AND ROMAN

At least two Palaeolithic implements have been discovered on the hill. One is a small twisted ovate of developed middle Acheulean type (NM: *PPS*, 29 (1963), 382–3; Edgar, op. cit., Plate 4). The other, a small pointed hand axe, was found in 1932 during the construction of the

BBC transmitting station and thus must have come from SP 588621 (DS).

In 1932 Edgar made a 'representative collection of flint implements' from within the hill fort. These include leaf-shaped and tanged arrowheads, circular and oval scrapers and notched flakes as well as cores and waste flakes (DS). Two Neolithic axes are also recorded (both in DS), one of chipped flint and the other, incomplete, of polished greenish-grey stone. The latter came from the foundation trenches of the BBC transmitting station (SP 588621).

Bronze Age discoveries include three looped palstaves. One was found before 1893 (lost; NM Records) and the two others (DS) are labelled 'from Borough Hill Camp'. Two socketed axes (DS) were found together in 1932 at the BBC transmitting station with the broken stone axe noted above, and part of a bronze sword-blade in the school's collection is also labelled 'from Borough Hill Camp'.

Further Bronze Age and Iron Age objects recorded as 'from Daventry' (see p. 67) may have come from the hill fort. Among other unlocated finds from the hill are two coins, of Gallienus and Julian, a 'metal kettle' and quantities of teeth and bones (letter dated 23 March 1865, in Dryden Collection, Central Library, Northampton).

(1) BARROW (SP 58896210; Fig. 54), E. of the BBC transmitting station on ground sloping gently E. at 195 m. above OD. In 1830 Baker (op. cit., 347) said that it was the most prominent 'tumulus' on Borough Hill. By 1932 Edgar (op. cit., 37) noted that it was 'visible but inconspicuous'. No trace now remains.

(2) BARROW (SP 58946306; Fig. 54), immediately S. of the northern fort on almost level ground at 190 m. above OD. It consists of a small roughly circular mound some 10 m. in diam. and 0.25 m. high, much mutilated, with no trace of a ditch. It was excavated by Baker in 1823 after it had already been ploughed (Baker, op. cit., 347). He discovered a primary cremation accompanied by fragments of a large urn 'ornamented below the rim with a zig-zag pattern', possibly a Collared Urn, as well as fragments of at least two or three other urns and a 'small part of a patera of light-red ware'. The latter may have been Roman and thus a secondary feature. Certainly a secondary inhumation with animal bones was also found. Baker records that two or three years before his work a broken jet amulet had been picked up on the surface of the barrow.

(3) HILL FORT (centred SP 588626; Fig. 54; Plate 1), known as Borough Hill Camp, can be assigned to two separate periods. At the N. end of the hill is a small roughly triangular fort bounded by a massive bank and ditch but the whole hill top is surrounded by a much smaller bank and ditch. The relationship between the two defence systems has never been clear and most authorities have assumed that the northern fort was earlier and that the contour fort was added later. However, as the present survey indicates, it is more likely that the outer contour fort was the earlier defence and that the main northern fort

was a later addition. This conclusion is the same as that reached by Edgar in 1923 (op. cit., 30–31). If this is so then the contour fort may be interpreted as a pre-Iron Age fortification of a type recently identified elsewhere. The late Bronze Age finds both definitely or possibly from the interior of the fort (see above) might support this idea.

The *Contour Fort* covers an area of some 54 hectares and was once probably bounded by a number of banks and ditches. However as a result of later destruction the original defences do not survive in their original state anywhere. In the S.W. these defences ('a' on plan) have been entirely flattened and no trace exists on the ground. Even in the early 19th century this section had probably almost disappeared, as a result of ploughing, though Baker's map of 1822 (Baker, op. cit., 343) showed the defences still existing. By 1923 Edgar (op. cit., Fig. 1; 29) noted that the 'old line of the defences can yet be seen under favourable circumstances'. Further N. the defences are still partly preserved for a distance of 400 m. ('a'–'b' on plan). Here, though the inner bank is reduced to little more than a scarp, the ditch is in good condition, being 1.25 m. deep with the counterscarp bank 1 m. high. Near the S. end of this section the ditch is blocked by two causeways of unknown, but perhaps recent, date. Neither of these was shown on Edgar's plan of 1923 (Edgar, op. cit., Fig. 1). A little to the N. of the causeways the line of the defence system is broken for a short distance at the head of a small spring. No earthworks existed here in 1923 according to Edgar though Baker in 1823 showed the line of defences unbroken at this point.

Beyond this the ditch and the counterscarp bank reappear and continue for some 210 m., after which only the downhill side of the counterscarp bank, a scarp 1 m. high, is visible ('b'–'c' on plan). For the next 150 m. no trace of the defences remains. Again Baker's map of 1823 showed the defences complete here, though Edgar's map indicated nothing.

At the edge of the golf course ('d' on plan) the outer side of the inner bank or rampart, now mutilated by a golf tee, is again visible, with, after a small break, the other face of the counterscarp bank below it. There is no indication of a ditch at this point. A little further N. these defences have been altered by the later defences of the northern fort, which at this point ('e' on plan) sweep N.W. and behind the contour fort's counterscarp bank.

From here to the N. corner of the hill ('e'–'f' on plan) all that remains of the earlier fort is a rounded bank, nowhere more than 1 m. high, which appears to be the counterscarp bank. The original ditch and inner bank or rampart have apparently been destroyed by the later ditch of the northern fort. These features are not shown on either Baker's or Edgar's maps.

At the N. end of the hill ('f' on plan) the counterscarp bank and indeed the defences of the northern fort are cut by a deeply hollowed trackway climbing the hill from the N.W.; it is not depicted on Baker's map of 1823 and Edgar

described it as modern in 1923. Beyond this hollow-way are two short lengths of scarp; another further downhill (not shown on plan) is modern. The former appear to be the outer faces of the rampart and of the counterscarp bank of the contour fort, but there is no trace of the intermediate ditch. From this point, for some 330 m. along the E. side of the hill ('f'–'g' on plan), nothing remains of the contour fort defences apart from the well-marked scarp 2 m. high following the existing hedge-line, which probably represents the position of the original rampart. A slight ledge or scarp (not shown on plan) to the E. below the hedge, along this section and further S., is not part of the fort but is a natural feature occuring at the junction between the Northampton Sand and the underlying Lias Clay.

In the S.E. corner of the golf course ('g' on plan) the main contour fort scarp is broken and after a short gap reappears inside the line of the modern hedge, still as a scarp 1 m.–2 m. high. Below it, on the hedge-line, are traces of a much smaller scarp surmounted in places by the hedge-bank. This is probably all that remains of the original counterscarp bank. By 1823 Baker indicated that the defences here were already in this condition, but just over a century earlier in 1712, Morton (op. cit., 520) said that they consisted of 'two deep trenches and three banks'.

Further S. again ('h' on plan) a later terrace-way or track cuts across both scarps and, a short distance beyond, the upper scarp fades out. For the next 160 m. ('h'–'i' on plan) only the lower scarp remains, up to 2 m. high. There is then a short gap where even this scarp has been destroyed, after which it reappears, only 0.5 m. high, for some 40 m. ('j' on plan). In 1712 Morton described the defences here as consisting of 'three trenches and four banks'. Today there is then another gap beyond which the scarp reappears and can be followed as far as the S.E. corner of the hill ('j'–'k' on plan). Along the N. part of this section the scarp is 2 m.–3 m. high, but further S., as it curves across the S.E. corner of the hill, it has been reduced by ploughing and other activities to little more than 0.25 m. high. In 1823 Baker described a similar situation but in 1712 Morton said that the defences comprised two ditches and three banks.

In the S.E. corner of the fort ('k' on plan) the defences reappear in a state somewhat near their original form, and run N.W. for 270 m. Here they consist of a low flat-topped rampart 0.25 m.–0.5 m. high above the interior, with a steep-sided ditch in front of it, cut 2.25 m. deep below the top of the rampart and 1.25 m. below the ground surface to the S. There is no trace of a counterscarp bank. However here also much modern destruction seems to have occurred for Morton in 1712 recorded two ditches and three banks, perhaps implying that there was at least another ditch with a bank on each side of it beyond the present ditch. The face of the surviving rampart is now in poor condition and has partly collapsed to reveal that it was constructed of Northampton Sand. Towards the W. end of this section the ditch disappears and the rampart fades out; beyond, all trace of the defences is lost. In 1971, during excavation for new radio masts and cables on this southern section (SP 588619), part of a ditch was exposed. This showed that the original ditch was dug to a depth of 3 m. and later recut after some silting. After more silting it seems to have been recut again to a depth of 2.25 m. with a much narrower profile. It was then abandoned. No finds were made (DOE *Arch. Excavations 1971*, (1972), 11–12). Similar evidence was noted in 1918 when a trial trench for ironstone was dug here. Then Edgar and T. J. George noted that the ditch was silted up at least 1.2 m.–1.5 m. (4 ft.–5 ft.) deep (Edgar, op. cit., 29).

Apart from the barrows (1, 2, 4–17) and the chance finds listed above little is recorded from the interior. Baker's map (op. cit., 343) shows a large roughly rectangular earthwork near the W. side, S. of the northern fort (centred at SP 588628). Baker (op. cit., 344) described it as having a slight bank inside a ditch. In its S.W. corner and S. side met the W. rampart of the contour fort, but the N. side, Baker claimed, passed through the defences and extended down the hill as a 'covered way'. By 1923 all but the N. corner of this enclosure had gone (Edgar, op. cit., 32) and this N. corner survives now only as a scarp 0.2 m. high; however, another scarp continues N.E. for some 45 m. before turning S.E. and fading out. Baker also marked what he called a 'small trench' crossing the S. part of the hill but no trace remains. It was almost certainly an old hollow-way.

During work for new radio masts in 1971 (DOE *Arch. Excavations 1971*, op. cit.) two features were noted immediately N. of the S. defences of the contour fort. One was a round-bottomed pit or ditch with no evidence of silting and no finds. The other was a pit, at least 1.25 m. deep and 1 m. wide, with vertical sides. It was perhaps originally a storage pit, but may later have been used in an iron-making process. One sherd, possibly of early Iron Age date, was found in it. Morton (op. cit., 521) records the discovery of 'Roman money' in a cut through the ramparts though exactly where is not specified.

The *Northern Fort* covers just under 5 hectares and consists of a roughly triangular area, bounded by a massive rampart, a ditch and a counterscarp bank on the E. and W. sides. On the S. side a rampart, ditch and counterscarp bank, possibly with an outer and later bank and ditch beyond, cut across the hill top. The W. side is the best preserved. Here the inner rampart is no more than a scarp falling into the main ditch, except at the N. end where slight traces of the inner side of the bank, only 0.25 m. high, remain. The ditch is steep-sided and flat-bottomed, cut 3 m. below the summit of the rampart and 1.5 m. below the counterscarp bank on the outside. The counterscarp bank is much damaged and in places is only a low scarp 1 m. high. Elsewhere it is a bank of similar height. At the extreme N. corner of the fort ('f' on plan) a later, deeply hollowed trackway has cut across the ditch and apparently continues within the fort ditch along the

N.E. side where it is 3 m. deep below the interior of the fort though no inner rampart is visible. Beyond the ditch the counterscarp bank still exists 1 m. high. After some 140 m. the latter fades out, the hollow-way ends and the inner side of the ditch turns W. to form an entrance-like feature before continuing S. in a mutilated form for another 40 m. This possible entrance is marked on Baker's map of 1823 as is the continuation of the scarp to the S. Baker also showed the counterscarp bank as still existing below it.

The S.E. corner of the fort and the E. part of its S. defences no longer exist. The earthworks were almost entirely destroyed by the farm built here in the early 19th century and now demolished. Some of the remaining scarps can be interpreted as the sites of farm buildings, and a deep pit to the W. is also to be connected with the farm. In 1823 the main rampart which had undoubtedly existed here had already gone, according to Baker's map, though what appears to be a broad ditch with another bank and ditch beyond it is depicted. To the W. again ('l' on plan) the S. defences are mainly intact and consist of an inner rampart, now reduced to a scarp, and a deep ditch, 4 m. below the rampart and 2 m. below the outer counterscarp bank, the latter here only 0.25 m. high. Below and some 10 m.–15 m. in front of the counterscarp bank is another bank 0.2 m. high with traces of an outer ditch up to 2 m. deep at its W. end. The position and appearance of this outer bank and ditch may indicated that it is a later addition to the defences on this side in order to strengthen the weakest side of the fort. At their E. ends this outer bank, the counterscarp bank and the main ditch all fade out, and the inner rampart curves inwards to form an ovoid flat-topped mound some 2 m. high. This suggests that before destruction there was some form of inturned entrance to the fort at this point. In 1823 Baker dug into the ovoid mound on the assumption that it was a barrow, as shown on his plan (Baker, op. cit., 343). In it he found 'part of a skeleton of a man, the tooth of a horse and several other bones', near the surface. Apart from the Roman Villa (18), the Saxon burials (19–21) and Viking finds (see below) no other discoveries are recorded from the interior of this northern fort (RAF VAP CPE/UK/1994, 2267–8).

(4)–(17) ROMAN BARROWS (SP 589626; Fig. 54), lay on the summit of the hill at 195 m. above OD. In the early 18th century, Morton (op. cit., 520) wrote that there were 18 'tumuli' in a N.–S. row, with small depressions in their summits. Baker (op. cit., 346–7) noted that some were dug into, without any recorded results, around 1800. By 1823 only 14 remained and all had been ploughed over. In that year Baker trenched all the main barrows. His map shows all the 14, 11 of which were in a roughly N.–S. line, with three more to the E. It is not possible to identify these exactly with his descriptions of the excavation though he appears to have numbered them from N. to S. No trace of them remains on the ground today.

(4) BARROW (SP 58916276), Baker's (1), at the N. end of

the group, described as very slight. Nothing was found in it and Baker doubted if it was a barrow.

(5) BARROW (SP 58916275), Baker's (2), immediately S. of (4), described as very slight. Nothing was found in it and again Baker doubted if it was a barrow.

(6) BARROW (SP 58916273), Baker's (3), immediately S. of (5). Baker discovered charcoal and bones and a cist with a covering stone.

(7) BARROW (SP 58916271), Baker's (4), immediately S. of (6). Baker found nothing.

(8) BARROW (SP 58916269), Baker's (5), immediately S. of (7), and in 1823 the 'most prominent' of the group with a diameter of 9.8 m. (32 ft) and nearly 1.5 m. (5 ft.) high. It covered an area of black earth and was probably constructed of stone but it had been dug into earlier.

(9) BARROW (SP 58916268), Baker's (6), immediately S. of (8). It was constructed of earth and covered four separate burials, all cremations contained in urns and three with other vessels near them. Baker described this as a 'family barrow'. All the pottery survives (in NM and DS).

(10) BARROW (SP 58916266), Baker's (7), immediately S. of (9). Baker described it as 'doubtful or had been previously examined'.

(11) BARROW ((?) SP 58916265), Baker's (8), probably immediately S. of (10), and one of the most 'conspicuous'. It consisted of a cairn of stones 0.6 m. (2 ft.) thick, below which was a layer of dark earth almost 0.3 m. (1 ft.) thick. This covered a circular area 1.2 m. (4 ft.) in diam. paved with small stones on which were spread burnt ashes and bones mixed with red earth and charcoal. At its E. end was a 'rude buckle of brass' as well as a considerable quantity of the same metal, much corroded.

(12) BARROW ((?) SP 58916263), Baker's (9), at least 1 m. (3 ft. 6 in.) high, covering a floor of burnt earth, charcoal, and bones, presenting 'the appearance rather of the spot where the body was burnt than of the actual place of interment'.

(13)–(15) BARROWS ((?) SP 58926264), Baker's (10), (11) and (12) probably lay to the E. of (11). All 'furnished traces of the rites of cremation, but nothing of particular detail'.

(16) BARROW ((?) SP 58916261), Baker's (13), probably immediately S. of (12), at least 0.6 m. (2 ft.) high. It contained a small urn covered with five 'rude stones of the neighbourhood'. On the E. side of the urn was a considerable amount of burnt earth and charcoal which Baker suggested was the 'place of cremation'. The urn survives (in NM).

(17) BARROW ((?) SP 58916260), Baker's (14), probably S. of (16), only 0.3 m. (1 ft.) high. Below the mound and dug about 1 m. (3 ft. 6 in.) into the original ground surface was a circular stoned-lined cist, 1 m. (3 ft. 6 in.) in diam. In it was a small urn, containing a cremation burial, associated with a small handled vessel and a samian dish. These three items survive (in NM). Near by were corroded nails and fragments of iron.

All the surviving pottery, eleven complete pots, can be assigned to individual barrows (*Northants. Archaeol.*, 12 (1977), 185–190; Edgar, op. cit., Plates 12 and 13). It all appears to be Roman, 2nd-century in date. In addition there is a small Roman bronze cooking pot of the 'Eastland' type (DS; *Jahrbuch des Romisch-Germanischen Zentralmuseum, Mainz*, 13 (1966), 67–164) which was not mentioned in Baker's account of the barrows but was included by Edgar (op. cit., Plate 12) in the pottery from the excavation.

(18) ROMAN VILLA (SP 58896320; Figs. 54 and 55), near the S.W. corner of the northern fort on a small knoll at 191 m. above OD. It was first excavated by Baker in 1823 (op. cit., 344–6) and then by Botfield in 1852 (*Archaeologia*, 35 (1853), 383–95).

Botfield re-excavated the area Baker had dug and then extended the work to reveal other parts of the building, but only a small part of the complete villa was exposed and little can be concluded from the plan made at the time (Fig. 55). The excavation uncovered a large range of rooms orientated N.–S., the S. part of which was a bath suite.

The building was constructed of sandstone rubble and there was ample evidence of tiled roofs. Many of the walls were decorated with painted plaster and a number of mosaic pavements, mostly in a very fragmentary condition, were discovered. One of the latter was virtually complete and was removed, but only a small fragment now survives (NM; Edgar, op. cit., Plate 1; C. Roach Smith, *Coll. Antiq.*, 1 (1848), 113). There was clear evidence that the building was not all of one date, and both Baker and Botfield noted that one of the rooms had been adapted to form a corridor. Botfield also claimed that the most northerly room appeared to be a later addition to the rest.

The numerous finds (Edgar, op. cit., Plates 15–20 and 27–34) included large quantities of pottery of early 2nd to 4th-century date. Some of this was of Nene valley type and there was also some samian ware. Among other objects either recorded or surviving were a marble moulding (NM; *Northants. Archaeol.*, 13 (1978), 85), miscellaneous ironwork such as an axe, keys, knives, buckles and part of a fibula, some pieces of bronze largely unidentifiable but including a razor and a bracelet (BM), tesserae, hypocaust tiles, flue and roof tiles, painted wall-plaster, a lead weight, a gaming object, two stone spindle whorls, part of a glass bottle, fragments of window glass, coal and pieces of antler. There are also at least 18 surviving coins (DS) mostly of late 3rd to mid 4th-century date.

Botfield's excavations also included the discovery of a stone-lined well immediately S.W. of the building, which contained, in its upper levels, a skeleton with bronze 'accoutrements' as well as an iron fibula and a hook. To the S. of the villa, at the rear of the S. rampart of the

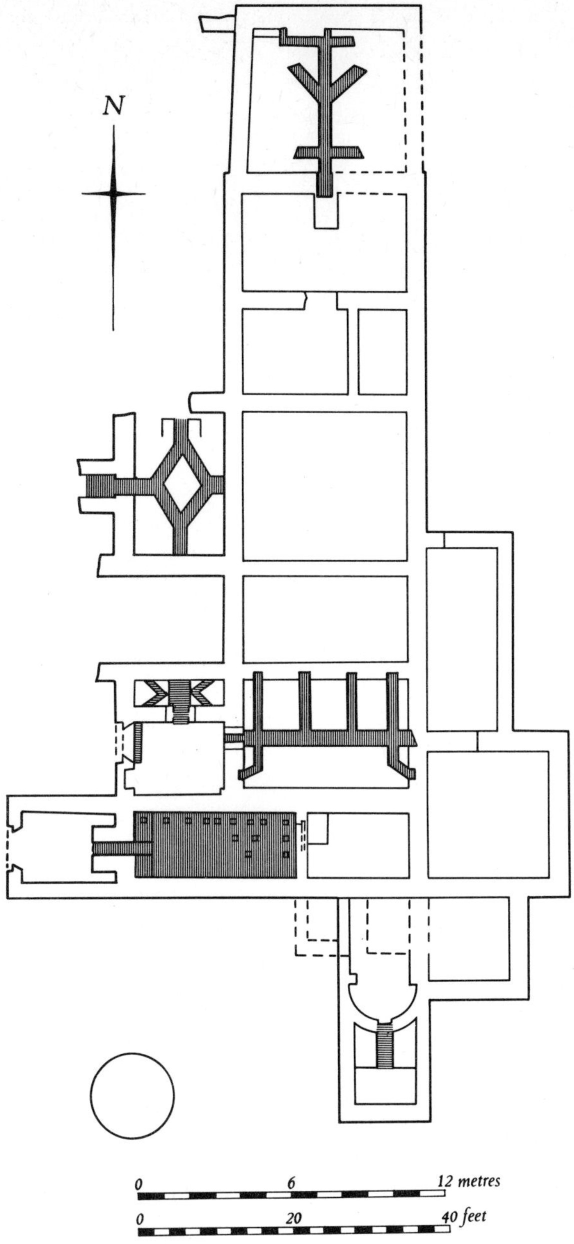

MEDIEVAL AND LATER

Two Viking battle-axes of Wheeler's type V1, dating from the later 10th or 11th century (Edgar, op. cit., Plate 8; *J. Northants. Natur. Hist. Soc. and FC*, 25 (1931–2), 177–8) and two spearheads (Edgar, op. cit., Plate 9) are all said to have been found during the cutting of a road on the N. side of Borough Hill around 1850. However it is possible that the spearheads are in fact those recorded as being associated with two of the Saxon burials listed below (20) and (21) and which cannot otherwise be traced.

(19) SAXON BURIAL (unlocated), said to be from one of the numerous barrows on Borough Hill which Baker excavated in 1823, although Baker himself does not mention any such finds (Edgar, op. cit., Plate 14; VCH *Northants.*, I (1902), 255). An inhumation burial, probably secondary in the barrow, was accompanied by a square-headed small-long brooch, a bronze buckle with a stylized dolphin's head on one plate, a bronze pin, a bronze boss, beads of glass, paste and amber, and two bronze Roman coins, both pierced for use as pendants and one certainly of the 4th century. It has been suggested that the burial is 5th-century (Meaney, *Gazetteer*, 186–7; *J. Northants. Mus. and Art Gall.*, 6 (1969), 44–6).

(20) SAXON BURIAL (SP 58896320), found in one of the rooms of the Roman villa (18) by Botfield (op. cit., 384) in 1852. A skeleton, lying N.–S. with a small spearhead at its side, was discovered within one of the rooms of the bath block. The spearhead may be one of those illustrated by Edgar (op. cit., Plate 8; now in DS) and said by him to have been found with the Viking axes noted above.

(21) SAXON BURIAL (?) (SP 58946335), found at the northern end of Borough Hill a few years before 1823. A skeleton of a man in a stone cist with a spearhead by his side was dug up (Baker, op. cit., 347).

UNDATED

Baker (op. cit., 344) said that lynchets 'and other peculiarities' existed on the W. side of Borough Hill. Apart from the ridge-and-furrow on the lower slopes in this area (34), the only features which survive are uneven scarps and banks (at SP585622). These are of purely natural origin, being land-slips of the underlying Lias Clay.

DAVENTRY PARISH (EXCLUDING BOROUGH HILL)

PREHISTORIC AND ROMAN

The following finds are recorded only as 'from Daventry' but some or all of them may have come from Borough Hill: two bronze palstaves (BM; VCH *Northants.*, I (1902), 143; NM; T. J. George, *Arch. Survey of Northants.* (1904), 13; Plate 22); a bronze Hallstatt boat-shaped brooch (DS) of Italian type, probably dating from the 6th or 7th century BC; an Iron Age gold coin, a

Fig. 55 DAVENTRY
(18) Roman villa (based on excavator's plan, 1852)

northern fort, Baker found a length of wall running roughly parallel to the rampart. Beyond was a deposit of burnt earth, charred wood, a knife and a socket of a spear, bones of horses, cows, sheep, deer and pigs and a large quantity of Roman pottery. The wall may have been the boundary of the villa complex with a rubbish dump outside it.

No trace of the villa remains on the ground and only a disturbed area marks its position.

For the Saxon burial from this site, see (20) below.

quarter stater of the North of Thames Group (Mack 271), said to be in NM but not recorded there (S. S. Frere (ed.), *Problems of the Iron Age in Southern Britain* (1958), 187).

The supposed long barrow, recorded by Baker (*Hist. of Northants*, I (1822–30), 340) at the E. end of Daventry Wood Hill (around SP 580610) was probably either part of the deer park pale (33) or part of the moated site of John Gaunt's Castle (32).

Edgar (*Borough Hill and its History* (1923), 38) said that a 'tumulus existed in Daventry until quite recently; its site is now occupied by the Council Schools' (SP 573626). As this location is very close to the old town centre the survival of a barrow here is unlikely.

Roman material, including 3rd-century pottery, horse bones and oyster shells, was found during road construction in 1968 S. of Drayton village (SP 565623). However it is probable that the material was brought from elsewhere when old quarries were filled in during the 19th century (*BNFAS*, 3 (1969), 1).

Baker recorded Roman bricks and tiles found on the 'opposite side of the road to Burnt Walls' (about SP 581611; Baker op. cit., 339). This material may have been medieval in date and connected with John of Gaunt's Castle (32) though several Roman coins are also said to have come from here (Whellan, *Dir.*, 398).

^a(22) ROMAN SETTLEMENT (?) (SP 566651), in the N. of the parish on Boulder Clay at 140 m. above OD. Roman pottery and worked flints have been found (*Northants. Archaeol.*, 8 (1973), 26).

^b(23) ROMAN SETTLEMENT (?) (SP 564649), S.W. of (22) on Boulder Clay at 145 m. above OD. Roman pottery and worked flints are recorded (*Northants. Archaeol.*, 8 (1973), 26).

^b(24) ROMAN SETTLEMENT (?) (SP 554630), in the W. of the parish on Middle Lias Clay at 160 m. above OD. Roman pottery and worked flints have been found here (*Northants. Archaeol.*, 8 (1973), 26).

^b(25) ROMAN SETTLEMENT (?) (SP 554622), 800 m. S. of (24) near the W. parish boundary, on Marlstone Rock at 155 m. above OD. Roman pottery and worked flints have been recorded at this site (*Northants. Archaeol.*, 9 (1974), 89).

^b(26) ROMAN SETTLEMENT (?) (SP 557618), in the S.W. part of the parish on Marlstone Rock at 165 m. above OD. Roman pottery and worked flints have been recorded (*Northants. Archaeol.*, 9 (1974), 89).

^b(27) ROMAN SETTLEMENT (?) (SP 58166280), E. of Daventry, at the foot of Borough Hill, on Upper Lias Clay at 145 m. above OD. Roman pottery, including Nene Valley wares, and floor and roof tiles were discovered here in 1965 (NM Records). Medieval pottery was also found on the site.

MEDIEVAL AND LATER

For medieval pottery at SP 58166280 see (27) above. Other medieval finds (in DS) include two glazed floor tiles from 'Rectory Park', an iron spur and a Nuremberg token.

^b(28) MEDIEVAL QUARRIES AND POST-MEDIEVAL PITS (SP 57486255), on the S. side of Daventry High Street. Development of the area in 1973 revealed a number of deep quarry-pits filled with loose stones and containing a few fragments of 14th-century Potterspury roof tile. Sherds of 13th and 14th-century pottery, a number of post-medieval pits and ditches, and walls of 19th-century property boundaries were also discovered (*Northants. Archaeol.*, 9 (1974), 104–5).

^b(29) MEDIEVAL BUILDING (?) (SP 57486255), lay immediately E. of Daventry church. During redevelopment in 1974 part of a stone wall cut into by later cellars was noted. A 13th-century pot of green-glazed ware was found near by (*Northants. Archaeol.*, 10 (1975), 166).

^b(30) FISHPONDS (centred SP 578623; Fig. 56), now entirely destroyed by building developments and playing fields, lay in the valley of a small N.E.-flowing stream immediately S.E. of the old town centre of Daventry on Middle Lias Clay at about 135 m. above OD. The only indication of their form comes from OS records and air photographs (RAF VAP CPE/UK/1994, 2269–70) on which Fig. 56 is based. Nothing is known of their history, but they are probably to be associated with the Cluniac Priory of Daventry. The priory was founded around 1090 at Preston Capes and moved to Daventry in 1107–8. It was situated immediately to the W. of Daventry church, at the E. end of the High Street (VCH *Northants.*, II (1906), 109–13).

The fishponds consisted of four roughly rectangular ponds cut down into the valley bottom and separated by dams. No dimensions are known except that one of the dams ('a' on plan) was 1.6 m. high and that the scarp along the S.W. side of the upper pond ('b' on plan) was 1 m. high. The original stream through the valley was diverted to pass along the S. and S.E. sides of the ponds.

^b(31) SETTLEMENT REMAINS (SP 566625), formerly part of the village of Drayton, lie immediately S. of the old village on a N.-facing slope on Middle Lias Clay at 150 m. above OD. A series of embanked closes extend S. from the existing houses and probably represent former gardens.

^b(32) MOATED SITE (SP 581612; Fig. 57), known as John of Gaunt's Castle, lay in the S.E. corner of the parish within the deer park (33) on almost flat ground at the base of a steep slope, on Upper Lias Clay at 15 m. above OD. It was probably a medieval moated hunting-lodge, but little is known of its history.

There are various records of Roman bricks and tiles having been found on the site; this may be a mis-

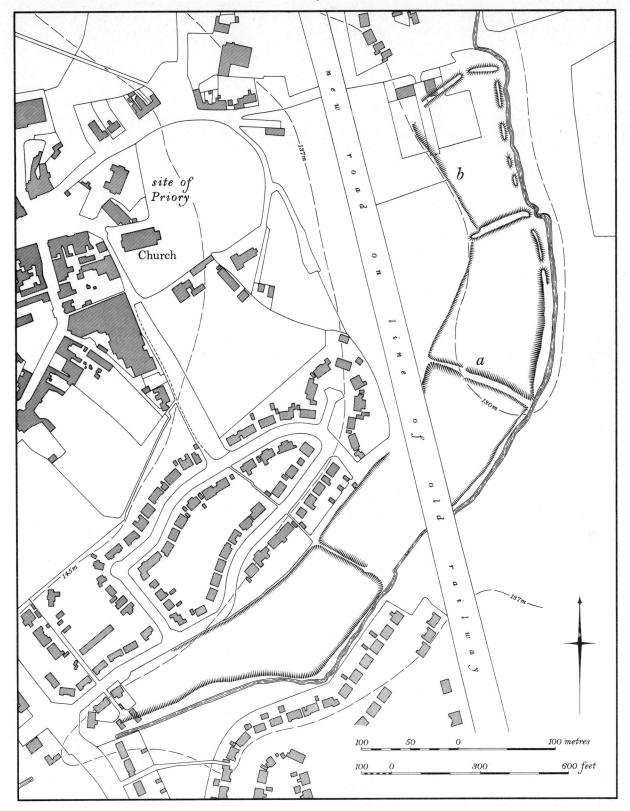

site of
Priory

Church

b

a

100   50   0   100 metres

100   0   300   600 feet

Fig. 56   DAVENTRY   (30) Fishponds

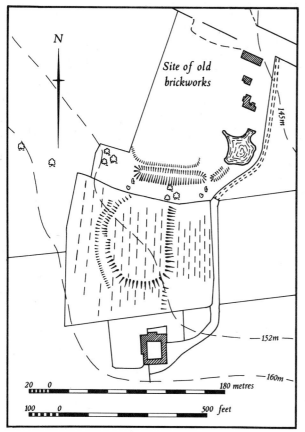

Fig. 57   DAVENTRY
(32) Moated site known as John of Gaunt's Castle

identification of medieval materials. In 1816 the wood which then covered the area was removed and a 'double ditch was disclosed within which, just below the surface, was the foundation wall, varying from 4 ft. to 5 ft. in thickness, of a rectangular building 40 yards long and intersected with three cross walls' (G. Baker, *Hist. of Northants.*, I (1822–30), 339).

The N. part of the site, including all but the S. side of the moat, was worked for clay for a brickyard from at least 1857 until 1904 and during this time massive foundation walls were exposed and then destroyed. A building, apparently the one described by Baker, is recorded and described as 'square' and occupying an area of about one third of an acre with 'three cross walls'. On the S.W. side the foundations of a detached round tower 8 m. in diam. were discovered and traces of another, similar one were noted on the E. side. Foundations of 'an entrance which had evidently been approached by a drawbridge' were found there apparently on the S.E. of the building (W. Edgar, *Borough Hill and its History* (1923), 49–51; *Northants. N. and Q.*, 5 (1921–3), 212–3). Recently the whole site has

been built over except for the S. side of the moat which remains as a long ditch 1.2 m. deep. In the field to the S. is a small roughly D-shaped enclosure, bounded by a low scarp 0.5 m. high, with traces of an outer ditch on its W. side; this enclosure has been completely overploughed in ridge-and-furrow. There are slight indications that there was once a further enclosure to the S. again. A medieval glazed roof tile, said to be from the site, survives (DS), but a stone mortar of the 14th or 15th-century date and found in about 1853 on the site is lost (*BNFAS*, 3 (1969), 1; *Northants. Archaeol.*, 8 (1973), 26; J. Morton, *Nat. Hist. of Northants.* (1712), 519).

b(33) DEER PARK (centred SP 580610), lies in the extreme S.E. of the parish, against the Newnham parish boundary. It occupies some 25 hectares of land on Upper Lias Clay, N.E. of Newnham Hill and mainly in a broad open combe facing N.E.

The park is first recorded in documents in 1284 when it belonged to Robert Fitz Walter (G. Baker, *Hist. of Northants.*, 1 (1822–30), 311). Bridges (*Hist. of Northants.*, I (1791), 43) said that it was 'formerly enclosed by a stone wall ... long demolished'. The area appears always to have been woodland and was known as Daventry Wood or The Wood (NRO, Enclosure Map, 1803) until 1816 when all the trees were removed (Baker, op. cit., 339). Within the park, near its N. side, stood John of Gaunt's Castle (32) with which it was presumably associated.

Very little remains of the park boundary although its outline is clearly defined by the parish boundary on the S. and E., by the A45 road on the N. and by a continuous hedge-line on the W. However what may have been its original boundary wall is recorded by Edgar (*Borough Hill and its History* (1923), 50–1); when discussing the finds from John of Gaunt's Castle, discovered during the 19th century clay-digging, he mentions the fact that a 'boundary wall was found near the highway'. No trace now exists along the N. side, as road-widening and modern buildings have destroyed any former remains. Along the W. side only a modern hedge bank is visible. However along the N. and W. sides, just inside the parish boundary, is a spread bank up to 5 m. wide but only 0.25 m. high. This may be the original boundary.

(34) CULTIVATION REMAINS. The common fields of the old parish of Daventry were enclosed by an Act of Parliament of 1802 (NRO, Enclosure Map, 1803; Pre-Enclosure Map, 1802). Immediately before that date there were three open fields lying to the N., E. and S. of the town, known as Bean, Barley and Wheat Field respectively.

Ridge-and-furrow of these fields survives on the ground or can be traced on air photographs taken before modern urban expansion destroyed it over large areas. It was arranged in end-on and interlocked furlongs, mainly laid out across the contours although near the foot of the N.W. corner of Borough Hill (SP 586633) are two end-on

furlongs of ridge-and-furrow which, unusually, lie
skewed across the contours on a steep slope. These lay in
Norton Road Furlong and Under Thrup Leys Furlong in
1802.

The common fields of the parish of Drayton were
enclosed by an Act of Parliament of 1752, but no map
apparently survives. Ridge-and-furrow of these fields
remains on the ground or can be traced on air photographs
over much of the area. It is best preserved in the N.W. of
the parish where almost the total pattern of furlongs is
recoverable in both end-on and interlocked blocks (RAF VAP
CPE/UK/1994, 2267–73, 4271–7, 4355–9).

UNDATED

b(35) ENCLOSURE (SP 585612; Fig. 58), known as Burnt
Walls, lies in the S.E. of the parish, immediately N. of the
A45 road, against the Newnham parish boundary in the
valley of a small E.-flowing brook. It is set on a low ridge
of Jurassic Clay at 136 m. above OD, between the main
stream and a small tributary stream on the S. The remains
consist of a roughly triangular enclosure bounded on the
S.W. by a bank 2 m. high, with an external ditch 2 m.
deep and a low counterscarp bank beyond. There is a
causeway across the ditch near the S. end which may be an
original entrance. At the S. corner the ditch and

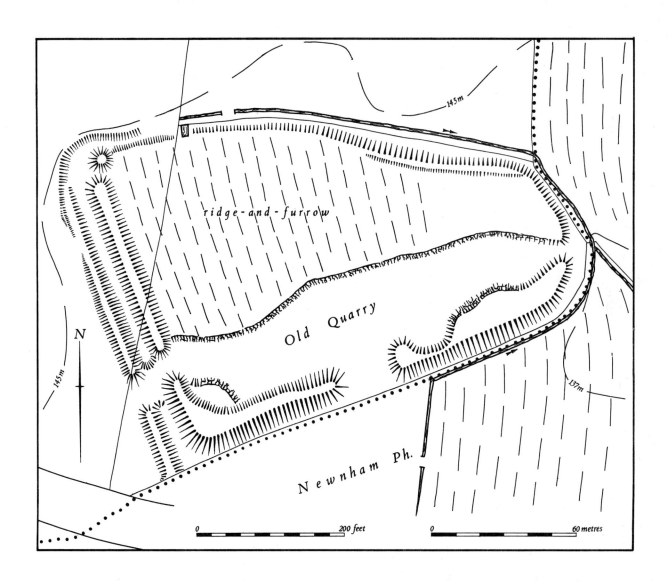

Fig. 58   DAVENTRY   (35) Enclosure known as Burnt Walls

counterscarp bank disappear and the main bank turns N.E. to follow the edge of the tributary stream. The bank here is between 1 m. and 2 m. high but badly mutilated, especially by quarrying on the inside. A gap which does not appear to be original lies in the centre of the S.E. side. At the N.E. corner the bank is mutilated and only a low scarp above the stream now remains along the N. side and N.E. corner. At this latter place there is a modern entrance gap. The S. half of the interior has been entirely quarried away; the N. half is covered by ridge-and-furrow.

The site has been a curiosity for centuries and no satisfactory explanation for either its date or function has been forthcoming. Morton (*Nat. Hist. of Northants.* (1712), 519) recorded that 'many Loads of Stones of ruined Walls and Foundations have been digg'd up' and this is repeated by many later writers. Baker (*Hist. of Northants.*, I (1822–30), 339) identified it with the site of Bannaventa, but noted that as it 'had been used before the inclosure as a kind of open quarry, further research would be fruitless'. Since that time dates ranging from the Iron Age to the medieval period have been suggested for this earthwork (OS Record Cards; VCH *Northants.*, II (1906), 399; W. Edgar, *Borough Hill and its History* (1923), 48–9). About 1899 some depressions within the interior were examined. 'Trenches were run through several of them, but nothing was found' (*Ann. Rep. Northants. Exploration Soc.*, (1900), 7). The site was described as early as 1255 as *Les Brendewalles* (PN *Northants.*, 19) which suggests that it not only existed at that time, but that its use was already forgotten (air photographs in NMR).

24   DODFORD

(OS 1 : 10000 ᵃ SP 56 SE, ᵇ SP 66 SW, ᶜ SP 65 NW)

The parish, of some 560 hectares, lies W. of Watling Street which forms much of the E. boundary, though a small area extends across the Roman road as far as an S.-flowing stream. Most of the parish lies astride the valley of an E.-flowing brook which, together with a number of small tributaries, has cut deeply into the underlying Middle Lias clays and silts between 120 m. and 80 m. above OD. To the N. and S. of the stream the land rises to more than 130 m. above OD and there are extensive spreads of glacial clays, sands and gravels. A small S. projection of the parish extends across a ridge into the valley of the R. Nene.

The major monument of the parish was the settlement remains (1). These have been almost entirely destroyed, and thus the main contribution to the understanding of the complex history of the village's structure has been lost.

PREHISTORIC AND ROMAN

Several Roman coins, some of Constantine and one of Tetricus, have been found in the parish, mostly along Watling Street which forms part of the E. boundary

(Morton, *Nat. Hist. of Northants.* (1712), 532; J. Bridges, *Hist. of Northants.*, I (1791), 50).

For Roman Road If, Watling Street, see Appendix.

MEDIEVAL AND LATER

A 14th-century coin, identified as a Burgundian imitation of an English quarter-noble of the type struck in Flanders for Philip the Bold was found in 1955 in the N. of the village (SP 61356085; BM; *Brit. Num. J.*, 28 (1955), 201).

ᵇ(1) SETTLEMENT REMAINS (centred SP 615606; Figs. 12, 59 and 60), formerly part of Dodford, lay in and around the existing village on the sides of a small E.-flowing stream and its tributaries, on glacial sands and gravels and Jurassic Clay between 90 m. and 120 m. above OD. Most of the earthworks have been ploughed out in recent years and the accompanying plan has been compiled, in great part, from air photographs taken before destruction.

The remains suggest either a large-scale depopulation at some time or, more likely, a considerable movement of the village over the centuries. However the surviving documents do not give any clue as to which of these alternatives is correct. Dodford is first mentioned in an Anglo-Saxon charter of 944 (BCS 792). It is recorded in Domesday Book as a manor of three hides belonging to the Count of Mortain, with a recorded population of 22 including a priest (VCH *Northants.*, I (1902), 326). Thereafter no certain indication of its size is ascertainable until 1673 when 39 people paid the Hearth Tax (PRO, E179/254/41). By the early 18th century there were 21 houses in the village (J. Bridges, *Hist. of Northants.*, I (1791), 50). In 1801 two hundred and five people lived in the parish. A map of 1742 (NRO; Fig. 60) shows the village exactly as it is today with the settlement remains already abandoned.

The surviving earthworks, together with those which have been destroyed, fall into four distinct groups. To the S. of the stream and E. of the main through street ('a' on plan) was a series of long rectangular paddocks bounded by shallow ditches. These have all been destroyed but stone-rubble and pottery, mainly of the 13th and 14th centuries, has been found at the W. and N. ends of some of them indicating that they were once tofts and crofts of the village. In 1742 many of these were still hedged closes.

To the N. of the stream ('b' on plan) and now also destroyed were some unusual rectangular tofts and crofts extending up the hillside. These too have scatters of stone and medieval pottery at their S. ends and must be the remains of former houses and gardens. The extremely regular plan of the earthworks implies an element of planning here.

Immediately N. of the church are other slight earthworks which may be former closes ('c' on plan) though little remains on the ground. Only to the W. of the

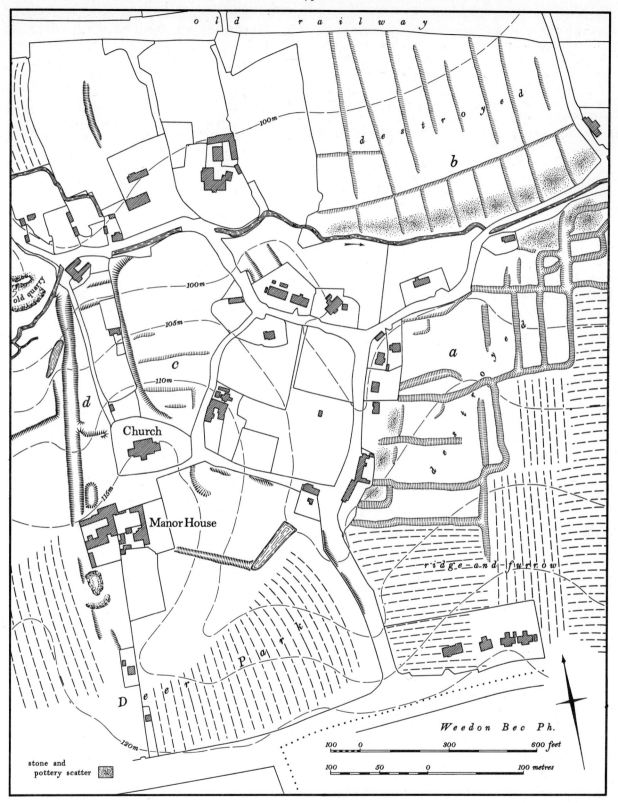

old railway

destroyed

100m

b

old quary

100m

105m

c

110m

d

a

destroyed

destroyed

Church

115m

Manor House

ridge-and-furrow

P a r k

D e e r

120m

stone and
pottery scatter

Weedon Bec Ph.

100   0   300   600 feet

100   50   0   100 metres

Fig. 59   DODFORD   (1) Settlement remains,   (2) Deer park

church and the N. of the manor house do earthworks survive ('d' on plan). Here a shallow hollow-way, which perhaps once extended S. to the present main Northampton-Daventry road, runs N. down the valley side to meet the E.–W. village street. Slight banks on either side may be former closes (RAF VAP CPE/UK/1994, 1269–70).

[b](2) DEER PARK (centred SP 613603; Figs. 59 and 60), lies immediately S. of the village, between it and the A45 road on glacial sands and gravels, between 100 m. and 120 m. above OD. Its exact extent is not known.

Bridges (*Hist. of Northants.*, I (1791), 50) records that 'there was formerly a park including 30 acres of wood ... but the ground hath long since been applied to other uses'. It was apparently enclosed by William de Keynes who acquired the manor of Dodford in 1222. By the 14th century it was said to be 50 acres in extent (*Cal. IPM* xii,

49–50). The location of the park is partly shown on the map of Dodford of 1742 (NRO); the latter gives the name Park to the large pasture field S. of the manor house. However as this field is relatively small the park must have extended further W. than the present field. The S. side of the park is formed by a precipitous slope with a small bank below it immediately N. of the main A45 road. Along the E. side of the park a low bank or scarp runs along the W. side of the road to Dodford village. No other convincing boundaries survive, though a very low bank extends W., N. of and roughly parallel to the A45 (SP 61056026) for some 200 m. The park may have occupied the land N. of this bank as far as the marshy area N.W. of the village. In the bottom of the valley, near the N.E. corner of the park (SP 61376032), is a rectangular pond embanked on its S.E. and N.E. sides (*Northants. P. and P.*, 5 (1975), 221).

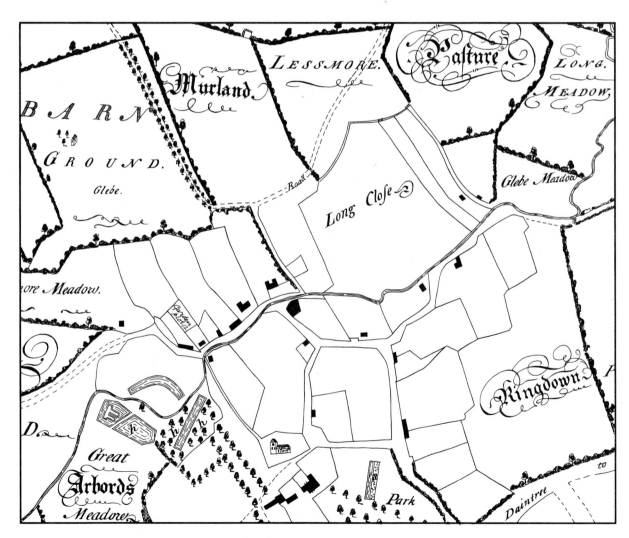

Fig. 60   DODFORD   (1, 2) Village and deer park in 1742 (from a map in NRO)

(3) CULTIVATION REMAINS. The common fields of Dodford were enclosed by private agreement in 1623 (NRO, Grant (Li) H5), though the earliest map of the parish is of 1742 (NRO). Ridge-and-furrow of these fields survives on the ground or can be traced on air photographs immediately N., E. and S. of the village. The furlongs to the S. are mainly orientated N.–S. as the land falls S. to the R. Nene but elsewhere they interlock, in response to the more broken terrain (RAF VAP CPE/UK/1994, 1166–8, 1268–71).

25   DRAUGHTON

(OS 1 : 10000 SP 77 NE)

Draughton is a small oval parish of 625 hectares, lying on the W. slopes of a flat-topped ridge and bounded on the W. by a S.-flowing stream. Most of the higher ground, over 150 m. above OD, is covered by Boulder Clay, but to the W. a number of small W.-flowing streams have produced a rolling landscape of spurs and valleys cut into Northampton Sand and Upper Lias Clay. Near the village, beds of the Lower Estuarine Series are exposed.

Of the small number of prehistoric and Roman sites in the parish the best known is the Iron Age settlement (8) which was excavated during the Second World War before it was destroyed by the airfield which occupies much of the eastern half of the parish.

PREHISTORIC AND ROMAN

Many worked flints have been discovered in the parish including two Mesolithic or later cores, at least four leaf-shaped arrowheads, and one barbed-and-tanged arrowhead (NM; OS Record Cards).

(1) FLINT-WORKING SITE (SP 768780), lies in the N.E. of the parish on Northampton Sand at 160 m. above OD. A large quantity of worked flints, said to be of late Neolithic or early Bronze Age type, have been found here (CBA Group 9, Newsletter, 7 (1977), 27).

(2) FLINT-WORKING SITE (SP 768778), lies 200 m. S. of (1) on Northampton Sand at 152 m. above OD. A quantity of worked flints said to be of late Neolithic or early Bronze Age type has been found here (CBA Group 9, Newsletter, 7 (1977), 27).

(3) FLINT-WORKING SITE (SP 766772), lies N.E. of the village, on Northampton Sand, at 146 m. above OD. A large quantity of worked flints, said to be of late Neolithic or early Bronze Age type, is recorded from the area (CBA Group 9, Newsletter, 7 (1977), 27).

(4) ENCLOSURE (SP 756771; Fig. 61), lies N.W. of the village, on Boulder Clay at 122 m. above OD. Air photographs (in NMR) show the cropmarks of a large rectangular enclosure divided into two parts. Traces of ditches are visible extending S. and S.E. from it.

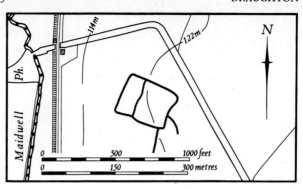

Fig. 61   DRAUGHTON   (4) Cropmarks

(5) DITCHES (SP 757763), in the S.W. of the parish, on Northampton Sand, at 120 m. above OD. Air photographs (in NMR) show indistinct cropmarks of some short linear ditches set at right angles to each other. These may be parts of overlapping enclosures, though this is uncertain. Further S.E. (at SP 758760) the same photographs show at least three linear ditches running N.W. and W. across the valley side.

(6) ENCLOSURES (SP 766783), lie in the N. of the parish, N.E. of Draughton Lodge, on Northampton Sand and clay at 145 m. above OD. Air photographs (not seen by RCHM) are said to show cropmarks of several irregular adjoining enclosures (BNFAS, 5 (1971), 42).

(7) BARROW (?) (SP 77197628), lies close to the S.E. boundary of the parish on Boulder Clay at 154 m. above OD. It was first recorded in 1962 as a ploughed-down grassy mound, 11 m. in diam. and 0.4 m. high, with no surrounding ditch, and was described as a probable bowl barrow. The site has since been ploughed and the mound further spread. No evidence of the function of the mound has been discovered (OS Record Cards).

(8) IRON AGE SETTLEMENT (SP 77787749), lies on the E. boundary of the parish, on Boulder Clay at 158 m. above OD. The site consisted of a circular area with a diam. of about 30 m. and a ditch. Excavation before destruction by the building of a wartime airfield revealed three hut-sites in the interior. The largest, with a diam. of 10 m., was defined by a continuous roof-water gully 0.9 m. deep from which an overflow gully led to the main external ditch. The two smaller huts, both about 6 m. in diam, were also surrounded by gullies, though these were not complete circles, and had short overflow gullies. Finds included pottery of early Iron Age type and a small amount of fine ware with curvilinear decoration similar to that from Hunsbury. A quantity of high-quality ironstone was thought to indicate that this was the settlement of a small group of iron-workers (S.S. Frere (ed.), Problems of the Iron Age in S. Britain (1955), 21–3; J. Northants. Natur. Hist. Soc. and FC, 31 (1949), 25–31; OS Record Cards).

(9) ROMAN SETTLEMENT (centred SP 76057573), extends across the S. boundary of the parish into Lamport, on Northampton Sand at 137 m. above OD. Large quantities of Roman pottery, mostly colour-coated and grey wares of 2nd to 4th-century date, were found in 1969 and near the centre of the area there was a scatter of sandstone. A coin of Hadrian was found in the same area in 1943 (*J. Northants. Natur. Hist. Soc. and FC*, 31 (1949), 35; *BNFAS*, 4 (1970), 8; NM).

MEDIEVAL AND LATER

(10) SETTLEMENT REMAINS (SP 761767; Fig. 62), formerly part of Draughton, lie around the village, on Northampton Sand between 130 m. and 138 m. above OD. The village stands on a high spur of sandstone orientated roughly S.W.–N.E. and consists of a group of houses and cottages

scattered along the main street. At the W. end roads run N. and S. to Maidwell and Lamport. The surviving earthworks, as well as those destroyed, suggest that at some time the village was much more orderly in its layout; it perhaps consisted of a single main street which continued W. of the rectory towards Maidwell, and had a neat arrangement of crofts on the S. extending to a back lane.

The surviving documents do not indicate any marked reduction in population, but this may be due to the lack of accurate figures before the late 14th century. Draughton is noted in Domesday Book where it is described as three separate manors but no population is recorded for two of them as these belonged to other larger holdings at Rothwell and Maidwell and the three sokemen listed under the third manor are thus of little importance in assessing the size of the village in 1086 (VCH *Northants.*, I (1902), 306, 349, 350). In 1377, 66 people over the age of 14 paid the Poll Tax

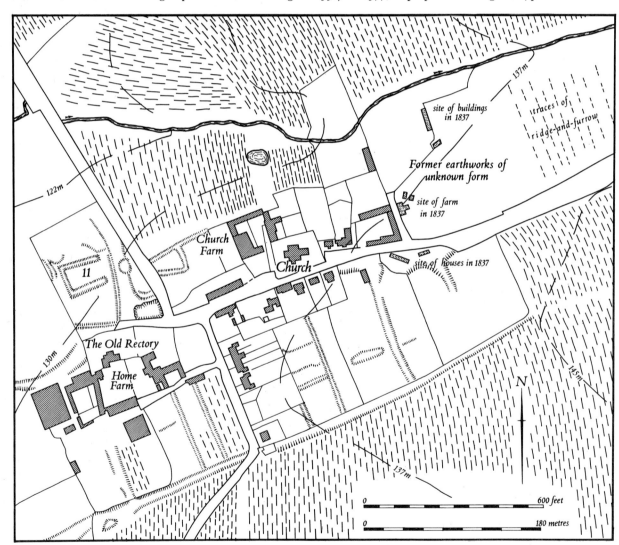

Fig. 62   DRAUGHTON   (10) Settlement remains,   (11) Site of manor house

(PRO, E179/155/28) and in 1674, 49 households paid the Hearth Tax (PRO, E179/254/14). Soon afterwards, in about 1720, Bridges (*Hist. of Northants.*, II (1791), 28) noted that there were about 40 houses here. By 1801, 179 people lived in the parish.

Apart from the manor house site (11), which is described separately, the remains fall into three groups. Behind the existing gardens on the S. side of the main street lie a series of low banks and shallow ditches. These, together with the existing property boundaries, are the remains of former crofts which extended S. to meet a narrow back lane, now a hollow-way, which divided the village from the adjacent ridge-and-furrow. Along the E. side of the Lamport Road modern houses have destroyed other assumed close boundaries. At the E. end of the street a large oval depression cut back into the hillside with a hollow-way to the S.E. is the site of two rows of cottages shown on the Tithe Map of 1837 (NRO). At the W. end of the village, S. of Home Farm, the closes continue; they have been damaged by modern farming but the back lane is still well preserved.

On the N. side of the main street little now remains. To the W. of Church Farm air photographs show part of a small ditched enclosure, now destroyed, and at the extreme E. end of the village there were other earthworks. These are not clear on any available air photographs and have now been entirely destroyed. In 1837 (NRO, Tithe Map) a farm is shown at the W. end of this area and other buildings to the N. (RAF VAP CPE/UK/1994, 2450-2; CUAP, BAP83, 84).

(11) MANOR HOUSE SITE (SP 759768; Fig. 62), lies N. of the Old Rectory at the W. end of Draughton village, on Northampton Sand at 127 m. above OD. The remains consist of a wide ditch only barely visible, on three sides of a sub-rectangular area, and were perhaps part of a formal garden. This narrow garden lies at the N. end of an open area which is bounded on the E. and S. by a low bank. Beyond the E. bank is a broad, shallow hollow-way, probably the predecessor of the present road to Maidwell. In 1837 the name given to this field was Nineveh (NRO, Tithe Map; RAF VAP CPE/UK/1994, 2451-3; CUAP, BAP83).

(12) DAM (SP 760762), lies S. of the village, within a steep-sided narrow valley draining S.W., on Upper Lias Clay at 115 m. above OD. The site may be that of a medieval mill or fishpond.

The remains consist of a dam, breached in the centre to allow the present stream through and thus consisting of two banks projecting into the valley bottom. These banks are 10 m. long overall and 1.5 m.-1.75 m. high, with flat tops 2 m. across. The N. bank is separated from the valley side above it by a narrow channel which extends S.W. to form a very large ditch up to 12 m. wide and 2.5 m. deep and embanked on its S. side. After a short distance the channel turns S. and fades out when it reaches the stream. Its purpose is not clear but it may have once been an over-flow channel from the pond behind the dam, though its level in relation to the dam is peculiar.

(13) POND (SP 757768), lies N.W. of Draughton village, in the valley of a small W.-flowing brook, on Upper Lias Clay at 114 m. above OD. Before damage by modern ploughing it consisted of a rectangular depression 40 m. by 25 m. with an outlet channel on the N.W. leading into the stream. It was fed by a smaller stream which flowed down the hillside from a spring to the S.E. Both the pond and the springhead have now been reduced to marshy depressions as a result of modern agricultural activities (RAF VAP CPE/UK/1994, 2451-2).

(14) CULTIVATION REMAINS. The date of the enclosure of the common fields of the parish is not known. Ridge-and-furrow of these fields survives on the ground or can be traced from air photographs over about half the parish and, in particular, around and to the N. of the village. In the S., and in the E. on the disused airfield, most of it has been destroyed. The landscape of the parish, consisting of a series of E.-W. spurs, has determined a pattern of furlongs orientated predominantly N.-S., but with many interlocked blocks of ridge-and-furrow in response to changes in direction of slope (RAF VAP CPE/UK/1994, 2449-52, 4453-6; 106G/UK/636, 4191-5, 3191-5).

UNDATED

(15) ENCLOSURE (SP 76247808), W. of Draughton Lodge on clay at 130 m. above OD. Air photographs (CUAP, BAP84) show soilmarks of a rectangular enclosure, 12 m. by 25 m., apparently overlying ridge-and-furrow.

26 ELKINGTON

(OS 1:10000 [a] SP 67 NW, [b] SP 67 NE)

The parish covers some 770 hectares and is roughly rectangular, apart from a strange projection from the N.E. which is over 2 km. long but in places only 100 m. wide. The landscape is undulating, cut by the steep-sided valleys of W.-flowing streams, one of which forms the N. boundary. The highest point is the Northampton Sand outcrop in the E. known as Honey Hill which rises to 212 m. above OD. From there the land slopes steeply to about 145 m. and then more gently to 115 m. above OD in the W., across Lias Clay with a few small patches of Boulder Clay.

The four Roman sites in the parish (2-5) have all been revealed by recent field-walking and it seems probable that further fieldwork would uncover other settlements in the area. The main monument in the parish is the deserted village of Elkington (6), the remains of which are still in part preserved.

PREHISTORIC AND ROMAN

[a](1) MESOLITHIC SETTLEMENT (SP 636769), in the E. of the parish, on the summit of Honey Hill, on Northampton

Sand at 210 m. above OD. A large assemblage of flint tools, including 500 microliths, over 400 scrapers and five picks, have been found here, as well as a few post-Mesolithic objects (*Northants. Archaeol.*, 10 (1975), 154; 12 (1977), 3–8).

^a(2) ROMAN SETTLEMENT (?) (SP 626759), in the S. of the parish close to the deserted village (6), on clay at about 150 m. above OD. Roman pottery has been found (*Northants. Archaeol.*, 10 (1975), 154).

^a(3) ROMAN SETTLEMENT (?) (SP 638768), in the E. of the parish, on Northampton Sand at 200 m. above OD. Roman pottery has been found (*Northants. Archaeol.*, 10 (1975), 154).

^a(4) ROMAN SETTLEMENT (?) (SP 639771), 400 m. N.E. of (3) and in a similar situation. Roman pottery has been found (*Northants. Archaeol.*, 10 (1975), 154).

^a(5) ROMAN SETTLEMENT (?) (SP 637775), 700 m. N. of (3), on clay at 180 m. above OD. Roman pottery has been found (*Northants. Archaeol.*, 10 (1975), 154).

MEDIEVAL AND LATER

^a(6) DESERTED VILLAGE OF ELKINGTON (centred SP 626762; Fig. 63), lies in the centre of the parish, on both sides of a shallow valley, on Lower Lias Clay between 130 m. and 150 m. above OD. Much of the area of the village has been ploughed and what now remains is very fragmentary.

Elkington is first mentioned in Domesday Book where it is listed as three small manors with a total population of 17 (VCH *Northants.*, I (1906), 327, 343, 347). However it is possible that one of these, the manor of Geoffrey de Wirce, with two bordars and described as part of his manor of Welford, was a separate settlement perhaps centred at Elkington Lodge (SP 645777). The land in the very long narrow projection in the N.E. adjoining Welford might have belonged to this manor, which would explain the unusual shape of the parish. In this case all the later population figures would include this assumed settlement as well as Elkington itself. Most of the parish, and apparently all of the village, was given to Pipewell Abbey soon after 1143 and the abbey continued to hold it until the Dissolution. Elkington is mentioned by name in the *Nomina Villarum* of 1316, and 30 people over the age of 14 paid the Poll Tax in 1377 (PRO, E179/155/27). However in 1412 the parish was described as destitute of all inhabitants save three or four servitors of the monastery, in consequence of pestilences (VCH *Northants.*, II (1906), 119). All the arable land in the parish had been converted to pasture before the Dissolution at which time eight large pastures and a grange were bought by various lay landowners; the grange was presumably on the site of the present Elkington Farm. By 1547, 4000 sheep were grazed in the parish. In 1674 only seven householders paid the Hearth Tax (PRO, E179/259/14) and Bridges (*Hist. of Northants.*, I (1791), 564), writing in about 1720, said that

there were ten houses there, 'seven of which are dispersed in the fields'. The latter, most of which still exist, were presumably all post-Dissolution farmsteads built in the sheep pastures. One, Heggats Lodge (SP 622769), is shown on a map of 1731 (NRO). The same map, which depicts only the N.W. part of the parish, also shows Elkington Farm as well as a house to the S.W. of it and other buildings to the E. and S.E., one of which was probably a watermill. At that time also, the main through road of the parish, still visible as a hollow-way ('a'–'b' on plan), passed to the N. of Elkington Farm. By 1801 the population of the whole parish was 62, though this fell to 43 in 1831 before rising again. There was a church at Elkington, which belonged to Pipewell Abbey, but institutions to it ceased before 1420 and its site is unknown (K. J. Allison *et al.*, *The Deserted Villages of Northants.* (1966), 39).

Most of the site was ploughed and levelled in 1970 (DMVRG, *18th Annual Report*, (1971), 17) but some destruction had already taken place before 1945. What remains on the ground is fragmentary and air photographs taken from 1945 onwards help to explain the original layout. Before destruction the most notable aspect of the remains was the road system. From Yelvertoft to the W. a broad hollow-way can be traced through the ridge-and-furrow, leading towards Elkington ('c'–'d' on plan). At its E. end ('d' on plan) it appears to split into at least two separate routes. One turned N.E., curving to the N. of the existing buildings and part of this is traceable as a narrow hollow-way ('a'–'b' on plan). Further E. this road appears to have run along the top of a dam ('e' on plan) across the narrow steep-sided valley. Thereafter it swung N.E. and its line around Honey Hill (SP 636779) is marked by a footpath which joins the modern road to Cold Ashby. This section was still the main road to Cold Ashby in 1731. The second branch of the hollow-way from Yelvertoft ('d' on plan) turned S. and crossed a valley on another dam ('f' on plan).

The only surviving remains of the village lie to the S. of the main hollow-way ('a'–'b' on plan) and N.E. of Elkington Farm. They consist of some low indeterminate banks, scarps and platforms forming no coherent pattern. On the S. side of the valley, and now completely destroyed by modern cultivation, there was formerly a series of hollow-ways passing between areas of ridge-and-furrow, but with one oval area devoid of ploughing ('g' on plan). No earthworks now remain here, but large amounts of medieval pottery have been found in the area mostly of 12th to 14th-century date. It is possible that this area was once part of the village and was ploughed over after it abandonment. In the valley to the N. are three dams, indicating that there were formerly three large ponds, though these had all gone by 1731 (NRO map). The lowest dam ('f' on plan) is much damaged, but survives up to 1.5 m. high. The central one ('h' on plan) is much larger, up to 2.5 m. high, and the area behind it was known as

Fig. 63   **ELKINGTON**   (6) Deserted village

Dam Meadow in 1731. At that date a building stood below the dam and this may have been a watermill. Further N.E. ('e' on plan), spanning one of two narrow valleys, is a third dam 2 m. high (RAF VAP CPE/UK/1994, 4471–2; 106G/UK/636, 1469–70; CUAP, AGU70–4, XT59, 60; air photographs in NMR).

(7) CULTIVATION REMAINS. The common fields of the parish were enclosed at an unknown date, but presumably during the 15th century after the village was deserted. All the arable land had been converted to pasture before the dissolution of Pipewell Abbey which owned most of the parish; at that time eight large pastures existed. One of these is shown on a map of 1587 (NRO) which depicts most of the N.W. part of the parish. Ridge-and-furrow of these fields survives on the ground or can be traced on air photographs over much of the parish, all of it arranged in generally rectangular end-on and interlocked furlongs. A number of hollow access-ways leading towards the village can be seen, including a well-preserved one from Yelvertoft (SP 611762–725764; partly on Fig. 153; RAF VAP CPE/UK/1994, 2468–9, 4471–4; 106G/UK/636, 4167–76).

27 EVERDON

(OS 1:10000 [a] SP 55 NE, [b] SP 65 NW)

The parish, covering some 1050 hectares, lies on the S. side of the R. Nene which forms its N. boundary. A small tributary of the Nene flows E. across the S. part of the parish and then turns N.E. to form part of the E. boundary before meeting the Nene in the N.E. corner. Both these watercourses are cut into the underlying Jurassic Clay between 90 m. and 120 m. above OD, producing an undulating landscape. However to the W. and S. the land rises steeply to around 180 m. above OD where the overlying Northampton Sand forms broad flat uplands. A number of minor streams cutting back into these higher areas have created steep-sided combes.

There were three medieval settlements in the parish though one, Snorscomb (3), is now deserted. The others are Great Everdon (4, 5) and Little Everdon (2), the latter having extensive settlement remains around it. A number of minor earthworks on the periphery of the parish have been recorded in detail elsewhere and are not listed below (*Northants. Archaeol.*, 12 (1977), 155–76).

PREHISTORIC AND ROMAN

A Neolithic flint axe was found in the parish in 1889 (T. J. George, *Arch. Survey of Northants.*, (1904), 14; NM). Two middle to late Bronze Age palstaves, one looped and one unlooped, are recorded from the parish, although the former may be that listed under Staverton (NM; Plate 22).

(1) ROMAN SETTLEMENT (?) (unlocated). During the 19th century Roman coins of Constantine, Constantius and Magnentius together with ashes and mortar were ploughed up in a field called Longsmall. The latter cannot be

identified (G. Baker, *Hist. of Northants.*, I (1822–30), 368; OS Record Cards).

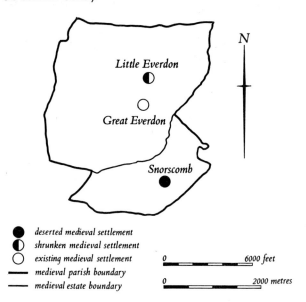

Fig. 64   EVERDON
Medieval settlements and estates

MEDIEVAL AND LATER

[a](2) SETTLEMENT REMAINS (centred SP 595581; Figs. 64 and 65), formerly part of Little Everdon, lie in and around the existing hamlet, on Middle Lias Clay between 107 m. and 122 m. above OD. Nothing is known of the population of Little Everdon in the medieval or later periods as in all the surviving records the hamlet is included with Great Everdon. Bridges (*Hist. of Northants.*, I (1791), 58) noted that in about 1720 there were 17 houses, about the same number as today. The earthworks suggest that it was somewhat larger at one time, but this cannot be proved.

The remains fall into a number of separate parts. Immediately S.E. of the hall ('a' on plan) the W. part of the existing paddock has a sunken building platform on its S. side, lying above a broad hollow-way 1.5 m. deep which can be traced for some 80 m. to the E. Further S. ('b' on plan) is another small field with a number of indeterminate earthworks which indicate that buildings once stood there. On the S. is another hollow-way with a massive S. side 4 m. high and with more definite indications of former buildings on its N. side in the form of rectangular embanked or scarped platforms. The hollow-way runs E. and meets an existing lane.

Further W., on the N. side of the small valley ('c' on plan), are traces of former closes bounded by low scarps extending down the hillside; to the N. ('d' on plan) are other very disturbed earthworks, also possibly the sites of buildings. From these a hollow-way, damaged by later quarrying, extends W. up the hillside through ridge-and-furrow. The land to the S. of this hollow-way, between it and the road, was known as The Little Coneygree in 1863 (NRO, Map of Everdon). The whole hamlet is surrounded by ridge-and-furrow which is well preserved, especially in the park to the W. of the hall.

ᵃ(3) DESERTED VILLAGE OF SNORSCOMB (SP 598561; Figs. 64 and 66), lies in the bottom of a broad open N.-facing combe, cut back into the Northampton Sand ridge to the S. It is situated at the junction of two small streams, on a narrow band of Marlstone Rock between 114 m. and 122 m. above OD.

Snorscomb is first mentioned in a Saxon Charter of 944 (BCS 792) where part of the bounds of its land is noted. It is next listed in Domesday Book of 1086 as held by the Count of Mortain and divided into two small manors of half and one and a half virgates respectively, with a total recorded population of only four (VCH, *Northants.*, I (1902), 326, 329). In the reign of Henry II the place was assessed at four virgates (VCH, op. cit., 371). Little is known of its history after that time, beyond the descent of the manors. It is presumably included in all the national taxation records with Everdon. In 1531 the larger manor was purchased by the Knightley family of Fawsley who were soon prosecuted for the enclosure of 200 acres of land and the destruction of nine houses there (PRO, E159/298; E368/292). In the early 18th century Bridges (*Hist. of Northants.*, I (1791), 61)

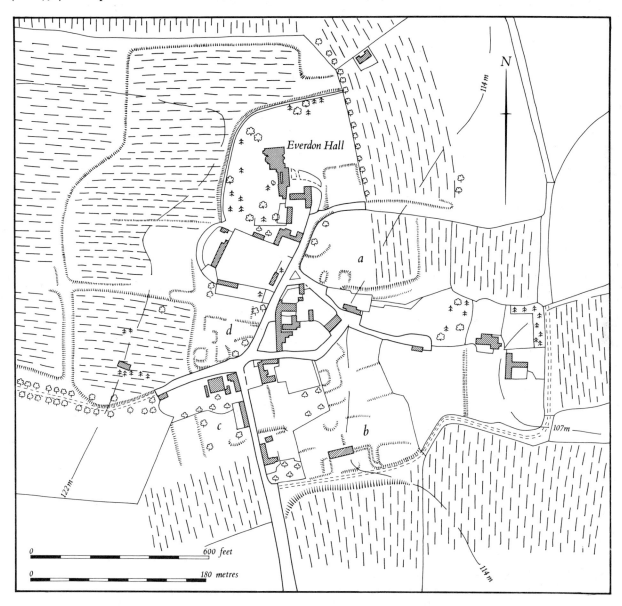

Fig. 65   EVERDON   (2) Settlement remains at Little Everdon

described it as 'a hamlet of five houses, including the mill, but reputed to have been formerly a more considerable village'. By the early 19th century (OS 1st ed. 1 in. map (1834)) only the farm and a single cottage, both of which still stand, are shown, together with the mill which lies 500 m. to the N. on a larger stream (K. J. Allison et al., *The Deserted Villages of Northants.* (1966), 46). The original boundaries of the land of Snorscomb are shown on a map of the area of 1816 (NRO, reused as a Tithe Map in 1839; Fig. 64).

The remaining earthworks lie E. of the present farm and are mainly confined to a small triangular area between the two streams which meet a little to the N.W. Both streams are in small steep-sided valleys which appear to have been used as roads at some time and are thus partly hollow-ways. The main feature is a broad hollow-way up to 2 m. deep running S. from the existing cottage, which itself stands in the hollow. The hollow-way can be traced for some 60 m. to the S.E., after which it fades out. On the W. side of the hollow-way is a series of well-marked house platforms bounded by low scarps and stone-rubble walls up to 0.25 m. high. Below them to the W. again are small paddocks or plots edged by scarps. To the E. of the hollow-way only one possible building platform is visible but the area is divided into irregular paddocks. N. of the cottage, beyond the stream, are other earthworks, possibly part of the village, but damaged by later stone quarries which have been dug into them. Further S.W., and S. of the farm, are two ponds, the westernmost being deep and rectangular with a large surrounding bank. Another, shallower pond lies N.E. of the village site. Various other track-ways, not all of the same date, are visible running through surrounding ridge-and-furrow towards the village. An arable field to the N. of the present farm is said to produce large quantities of stone when ploughed and some medieval pottery has also been discovered there (local inf.; RAF VAP CPE/UK/1994, 3154–6; CUAP, SA46).

a(4) POND AND SETTLEMENT REMAINS (SP 59505735), immediately S. of Great Everdon church, in a small valley on clay at about 170 m. above OD. The valley floor here appears to have been widened and deepened to form a large depression about 1 m. deep. It may originally have been a fishpond. A little to the S.W. are two well-defined hollow-ways, and an area of disturbed ground possibly the sites of former buildings (RAF VAP 541/341, 3241–2).

a(5) SETTLEMENT REMAINS (SP 596573), immediately E. of the church, on the S. side of the village, on clay at 105 m. above OD. At least three embanked closes extend S. from the existing gardens of some of the houses in the main street (air photographs in NMR).

(6) CULTIVATION REMAINS. The common fields of Great and Little Everdon were enclosed by an Act of Parliament of 1763. Ridge-and-furrow of these fields exists on the ground or can be traced on air photographs over most of the parish, except along the edges of the stream which

forms the parish boundary with Weedon Bec, where there was presumably always valuable meadowland. Probably as a result of the generally rolling nature of the land, with no steep slopes, the ridge-and-furrow is arranged in a pattern of interlocked furlongs of rectangular form. It is extremely well preserved in and around the park of Everdon Hall (SP 592582; partly on Fig. 65) and further W. (at SP 587583) where there are a number of interlocked furlongs with massive curved ridges up to 1 m. high.

The date of the enclosure of the common fields of the now deserted village of Snorscomb (3) is unknown but it was probably in the mid 16th century for soon after 1531 the Knightley family who then owned the manor enclosed 200 acres of land. This is about a third of the area of the land attributable to the village of Snorscomb (Fig. 64). Ridge-and-furrow of these fields exists on the ground or can be traced on air photographs over much of the land of Snorscomb except on the very steep slopes to the S. of the village. It is arranged in end-on and interlocked furlongs, except in the higher S.W. part (around SP 585555) where it radiates outwards around the projecting spurs. Large areas of well-preserved ridge-and-furrow exist N. and S. of the site of the village (RAF VAP CPE/UK/1994, 1162–7, 1270–4, 3159–62, 3152–6).

28   FARNDON, EAST

(OS 1:10000 a SP 78 NW, b SP 78 SW)

The parish is small, covering less than 600 hectares, and lies against the Leicestershire boundary, only part of which is here formed by the R. Welland. The highest ground, in the S.E., with a maximum height of 155 m. above OD, is covered by Boulder Clay. From there the land falls away gently towards the R. Ise to the S.E., but to the N. and W. the slopes, N. to the Welland valley and W. to a N.-flowing tributary, are almost precipitous. Lower and Middle Lias Clays are exposed there, and river gravels and alluvium occur in the wide valley bottom at around 85 m. above OD.

The main earthworks in the parish are the settlement remains (4). Owing to their scale as well as to their dominating position above a steep slope, those to the W. of the village have in the past been wrongly interpreted as fortifications of prehistoric, early medieval or Civil War origin.

PREHISTORIC AND ROMAN

A small perforated stone, possibly a spindle whorl and probably pre-Roman, has been found in the parish. A bronze spearhead has also been discovered, as well as the base of a 1st-century Roman pot (*Trans. Leics. Arch. Soc.*, 51 (1882), 285; OS Record Cards; Market Harborough Museum).

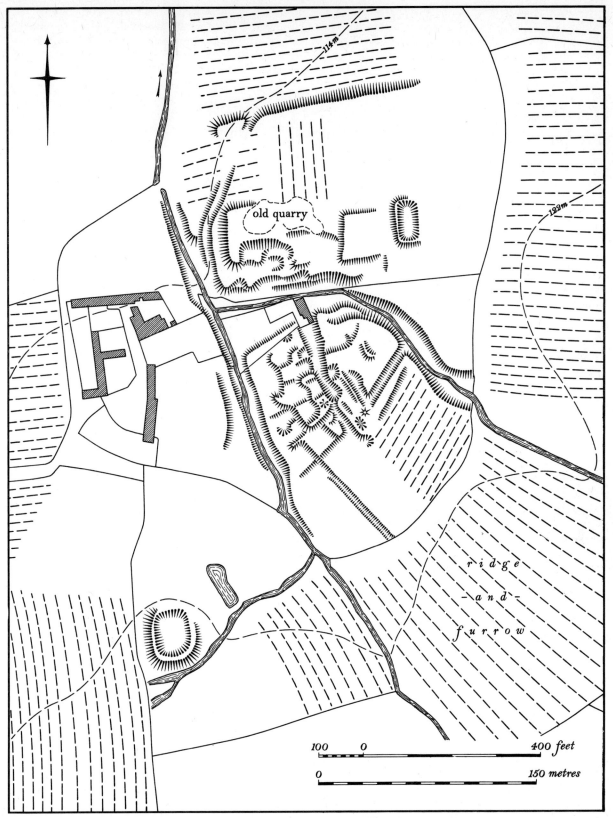

old quarry

114 m

122 m

r i d g e

- a n d -

f u r r o w

100   0   400 feet

0   150 metres

Fig. 66   EVERDON   (3) Deserted village of Snorscomb

^a(1) ROMAN SETTLEMENT (?) (SP 709860), in the extreme N.W. of the parish, on Lias Clay at 115 m. above OD. A scatter of Roman pottery has been found (*Northants. Archaeol.*, 11 (1976), 192; for Saxon material from this site see (3)).

^b(2) ROMAN SETTLEMENT (?) (SP 718837), in the S.E. of the parish, on Boulder Clay, at 140 m. above OD. A small scatter of Roman sherds has been noted (*Northants. Archaeol.*, 12 (1977), 212).

MEDIEVAL AND LATER

A metal object, thought to be a 13th-century sword pommel, was found in the parish sometime before 1872 (*PSA*, 5 (1872), 34; *Trans. Leics. Arch. Soc.*, 4 (1878), 138). At least two mounds, on the S. side of the village (at SP 71588476 and 71648454), have been traditionally identified either as moot hills, or as Civil War burial places (e.g. J. Bridges, *Hist. of Northants.*, II (1791), 30). Both are quarry mounds derived from nearby pits and thus are of no archaeological significance.

^a(3) SAXON SETTLEMENT (?) (SP 709860), on the Roman settlement (1). A scatter of Saxon sherds has been found (*Northants. Archaeol.*, 11 (1976), 192).

^a(4) SETTLEMENT REMAINS (centred SP 717851; Fig. 67), formerly part of East Farndon, lie to the W. and N. of the village. There are three main areas. On the crest of a hill to the W. of the village ('a' on plan), on Lias Clay and Boulder Clay at 145 m. above OD, in an area known as Hall Close, is a large area of earthworks, much damaged by later quarry pits (SP 71608500). They consist of the fragmentary remains of rectangular closes bounded by low scarps and banks nowhere above 0.5 m. high. Slight depressions on the E., close to the existing village street, may be the sites of former buildings. On the W. the area is bounded by a broad ditch or hollow-way with an external bank, which follows the curve of the hilltop in a marked double bend. At its S. end the ditch is up to 2 m. deep and the bank is 2.5 m. high but further N., beyond the bend, the ditch is only 1.5 m. deep and the bank less than 1 m. high. To the N. again a later quarry and a track have disturbed the remains and the ditch, when it reappears, is once more 2 m. deep and is on a slightly different alignment. The whole feature is probably no more than an old back lane separating the inhabited area of the village from its fields to the W., but its form and size are unusual.

The size of these remains and their unknown origin have led to much speculation about their function. In the early 18th century Morton (*Nat. Hist. of Northants.* (1712), 546; see also J. Bridges, *Hist. of Northants.*, II (1791), 30) described them and claimed that they were 'a defence work against the Danes'. Other authorities have described the earthworks as a 'camp' or as a Civil War defensive site (J. Nichols, *Hist. of Leics.*, II (1798), 701; *Arch. J.*, 46 (1889), 209; Whellan, *Dir.*, 829; VCH *Northants.*, II (1906), 256).

All these theories can be discounted.

To the E. of this area, immediately E. of East Farndon Hall (SP 717851) are two small pasture closes ('b' on plan). In both there are slight scarps and banks, probably the remains of former buildings.

At the N. end of the village, N. of Home Farm (SP 718852; 'c' on plan), there are several large rectangular paddocks bounded by shallow ditches and containing later ridge-and-furrow. The site has been damaged by quarrying.

^a(5) WINDMILL MOUND (SP 71118551), immediately N.W. of the village, on the summit of an isolated clay hill capped by glacial deposits, at 145 m. above OD. A well-marked circular mound 10 m. in diam. and 0.5 m. high partly overlies a broad raised trackway between ridge-and-furrow. There is also a large quarry pit. A windmill existed here as late as 1856 and is shown on a map of that date (NRO); the hill was then called Mill Hill (RAF VAP 106G/UK/636, 4129–30).

^a(6) STONE (SP 71218603), known as the Judith Stone, lies N.N.W. of the village on land sloping gently E. It is a large irregular rounded boulder some 1.5 m. long, 1 m. wide and just under 1 m. high, partly buried, with the adjacent ridge-and-furrow swinging outwards to avoid it. It is shown named and in its present position in 1856 (Map in NRO). The boulder is said to be of Scandinavian granite and is probably a glacial erratic but it may have been deliberately set up in this position for some unknown purpose (OS Record Cards).

(7) CULTIVATION REMAINS. The common fields of the parish were enclosed by an Act of Parliament of 1780. Ridge-and-furrow of these fields is unusually well preserved, especially on the hill slopes to the W. of the village. There is evidence of a grave shortage of arable land at some date; very difficult land has been ploughed, for example in a steep-sided combe below the settlement remains (4) (SP 71438490) where the surviving ridges are heavily lynchetted and of markedly asymmetric form (RAF VAP 106G/UK/636, 4127–32, 3128–31).

29 FARTHINGSTONE

(OS 1:10000 ^a SP 55 NE, ^b SP 55 SE, ^c SP 65 NW, ^d SP 65 SW)

The parish, covering some 725 hectares, lies across the headwaters of two small E.-flowing streams which meet on the E boundary and continue to the R. Nene. The valleys in which the two streams run have cut into Jurassic Clay but on the higher land to the S. and N., and along the central ridge between the valleys, are broad areas of Northampton Sand. The village of Farthingstone is situated on top of the ridge at about 144 m. above OD. The settlement remains (5) at the W. end of the village, suggest that it has moved E. at some period.

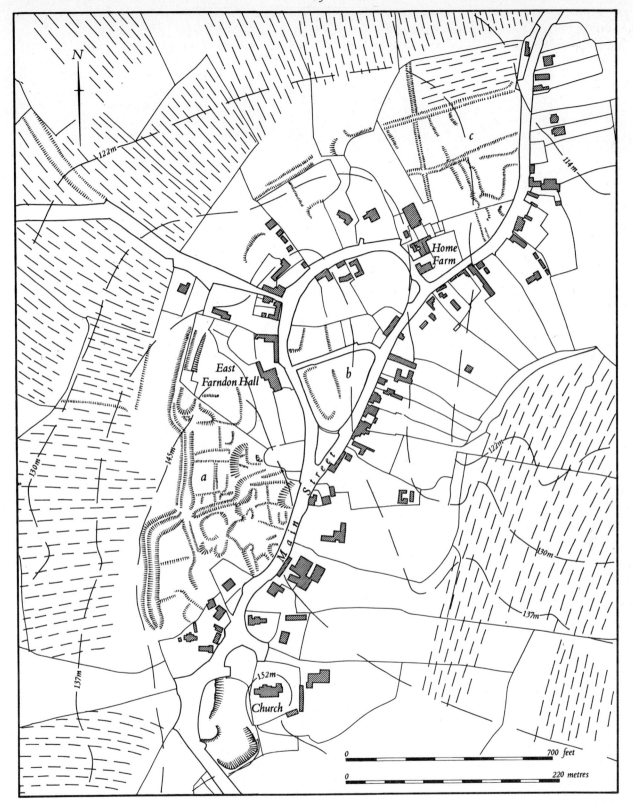

Fig. 67   FARNDON, EAST   (4) Settlement remains

On the higher land in the N.E. of the parish are two adjacent but very different monuments. Castle Dykes (4) is a fine and well-preserved motte with three baileys, and immediately to the S. is a now heavily mutilated enclosure (3), probably of prehistoric date. The latter, even in its present state, is a rare survival in the county.

PREHISTORIC AND ROMAN

A Neolithic axe of Group VI, Great Langdale type, was found in the parish before 1904 (OS Record Cards).

^c(1) ENCLOSURES (SP 615561), S. of Heath Farm and close to the earthwork (3), on Northampton Sand at 155 m. above OD. Air photographs taken in 1970 (not seen by RCHM) are said to show cropmarks of enclosures (BNFAS, 5 (1971), 42).

^c(2) DITCHES (SP 615570), about 300 m. N.W. of (4), on Northampton Sand, at 156 m. above OD. Air photographs (in NMR) show the cropmarks of at least three linear ditches forming no coherent pattern.

^c(3) ENCLOSURE (SP 617563; Fig. 68), lies in the N. of the parish, immediately S. of (4), on Northampton Sand, at 160 m. above OD. It stands on level ground, though to the N. the land falls steeply into a broad valley, and commands extensive views in all directions.

The remains have now been almost entirely levelled by ploughing; the surrounding banks are only just visible, a few centimetres high. In the plough the banks are marked by concentrations of small stones and red soil and, close to the S.W. corner and along the E. bank, by areas of burnt stones. OS plans made before the drastic modern destruction indicate that it was a rectangular enclosure, probably bounded by a bank and outer ditch, with another bank beyond the ditch at least on the N. and W. sides. The present road to Upper Stowe may have destroyed the ditch and outer bank on the S. Air photographs (in NMR) show a series of cropmarks within and to the E. of the enclosure. Those to the E. include at least three possible enclosures and two ring ditches. However, the ditches within the main enclosure and immediately E. of it may mark the lines of former hedges.

The enclosure lay in woodland until the early 19th century when the area was cleared and converted to arable. While this was taking place Baker (Hist. of Northants., I (1830), 376) noted that 'the vallum at the west end is now in the process of being levelled ... it is ... 9 feet wide built of two outer walls of stone, each about 3 feet thick. Between these is soil, except at one point where for 3 yards earth and small burnt stones were used, with several hundredweight of iron scoria and charcoal at each end. Inside the wall ... was a large iron spoon and the socket of a spear'. Earlier Stukeley recorded the finding of Roman coins and pavements 'at Castle Dykes' (Itinerarium Curiosum, I (1776), 114) and J. Simco wrote that 'T. Grant of Towcester has been levelling the Castle Dykes and gave

me a Roman pot found in one of them' (Gents. Mag., 63 (1793), 1179). Both these writers refer to Castle Dykes, which is strictly the motte and bailey castle to the N. (4). However the remarks probably relate to this site, especially the second one which mentions levelling (VCH Northants., II (1906), 409).

In 1959 the W. side of the enclosure was sectioned in two places. An internal wall with a deep ditch beyond, as well as a substantial outer bank, was discovered. A La Tène I brooch, one sherd, possibly of Iron Age date, and large quantities of carbonized wood were found in the lower levels of the ditch (NM Records). Field-walking of the area in 1969 revealed a scatter of worked flints within and E. of the earthworks. These included two scrapers, cores and waste flakes. In addition two sherds, one of Iron Age date and the other Roman, were discovered (BNFAS, 4 (1970), 3–4; RAF VAP CPE/UK/1994, 3157–8).

MEDIEVAL AND LATER

^c(4) MOTTE AND BAILEYS (SP 618567; Fig. 68), known as Castle Dykes, stands in the N. of the parish on almost level ground on Northampton Sand at 152 m. above OD. Most of the site is overgrown and difficult of access. Immediately to the E. the ground falls steeply into a deep valley and to the S. is another steep-sided tributary valley. The castle thus has a superb site with extensive views to the N., E. and S. and only on the W. and N.W. are there no natural obstacles.

The motte stands in the centre of the S. side and is circular, up to 2 m. above the natural land-surface and 4 m. above the bottom of the wide encircling ditch. The summit is edged by a low bank some 3 m.–4 m. wide and up to 0.5 m. high, apparently constructed of stone rubble. The interior of the motte has a large depression 1.5 m. deep in it, perhaps as a result of the digging there in the 18th century. On each side of the motte is a semicircular bailey, that on the W. being more regular than the one on the E., each bounded by a massive bank up to 2.5 m. high above a broad outer ditch. A gap in the E. side of the E. bailey appears to be modern. In the S.E. corner the bailey ditch bifurcates and the branches are separated by a length of bank. No reason for this can be seen. To the N. is a third, large, D-shaped bailey bounded by a bank 2.3 m. high and, except in the S., by an outer ditch up to 1.75 m. deep. The N.E. corner of the ditch has recently been destroyed by a modern track. The interior is under cultivation. There are two apparently modern entrances into it on the N.W. and E. and an original causeway links this bailey to the S.W. one across its S. ditch.

Workmen digging for building-stone on the site before 1712 are said to have discovered a 'room with a vaulted stone roof, and another room beneath', as well as 'rudely carved' stones with human figures on them (J. Morton, Nat. Hist. of Northants. (1712), 543; G. Baker, Hist. of Northants., I (1830), 375; Whellan, Dir., 416; VCH Northants., II (1906), 409; Plans and Sections, 1841,

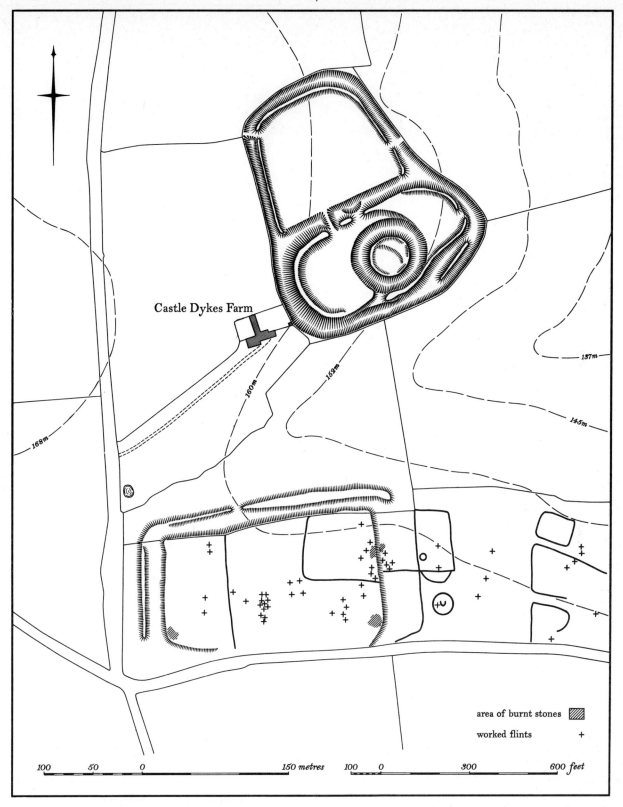

Castle Dykes Farm

168m

160m

152m

137m

145m

area of burnt stones

worked flints

100   50   0   150 metres   100   0   300   600 feet

Fig. 68   FARTHINGSTONE   (3) Enclosure,   (4) Motte and baileys

Dryden Collection, Central Library, Northampton). A medieval floor tile, said to be from Castle Dykes, is in the possession of Daventry School. Nothing is known of the history of the site but in its present form it presumably dates from the late 11th or the 12th century. However it is possible that part of the outer ramparts are of Iron Age origin, particularly those of the two semicircular baileys. Roman finds said to be from this site may in fact have come from the prehistoric enclosure to the S. (see (3) above).

^d(5) SETTLEMENT REMAINS (centred SP 61255495), at the W. end of the village, on gravel and Northampton Sand at about 150 m. above OD. A wide hollowed access-way, still followed by a modern footpath, runs roughly N.–S. between the Maidford and Everdon roads so forming part of a sub-rectangular system of lanes at this end of the village. On the E. side of this access-way is a line of large embanked closes or former paddocks, divided by a small hollow-way continuing the line of a farm track S. of the church. At the N. end of the group of closes are several later gravel pits.

(6) CULTIVATION REMAINS. The common fields of the parish were enclosed by Act of Parliament in 1752. Though no map apparently survives, the Enclosure Award (NRO) indicates that there were three open fields in 1752 as well as an area called Rye Hill. West Field lay to the W. and N.W. of the village, Middle Field to the S. and Lower Field to the E. and N.E. Rye Hill seems to have occupied at least part of the N. of the parish. Only a small part of the ridge-and-furrow of these fields exists on the ground or can be traced on air photographs and this is mainly around the village where there are several blocks of end-on furlongs with a few, at the ends of spurs, which lie at right-angles. In the extreme N.E. of the parish there are other traces of ridge-and-furrow (RAF VAP CPE/UK/1994, 3155–9, 2160–5, 4165–8).

30 FAWSLEY

(OS 1 : 10000 ^a SP 55 NW, ^b SP 55 NE)

The parish, of some 750 hectares, lies across the upper reaches of three small E.-flowing streams which meet and continue E. to the R. Nene. The highest part is the N.W. where an outcrop of Northampton Sand rises to over 180 m. above OD. From there, apart from the isolated Temple Hill capped by glacial gravel, the land is clay-covered and slopes S. and S.W. to the central stream at 122 m. above OD, then rises again to a maximum of 182 m. in the S.W. Most of the parish is occupied by the great landscaped park of Fawsley Hall. The house and the isolated parish church stand on a narrow ridge between two of the streams, close to the mutilated remains of two separate medieval settlements (1), both apparently known as Fawsley and both totally deserted. In the park a number of earthworks have been preserved because of the absence

of cultivation. These include pillow mounds (3, 4) and (6) and the undated enclosure on Temple Hill (9) as well as other banks, hollow-ways and ditches which have been recorded in detail elsewhere and are not listed below (*Northants. Archaeol.*, 12 (1977), 155–76).

MEDIEVAL AND LATER

^b(1) DESERTED VILLAGES OF FAWSLEY (SP 561566 and 566567; Fig. 69), lie immediately S. and E. of Fawsley Hall on the sides of two steep-sided valleys, on clay at 135 m. above OD. Fawsley is first documented in 944 in a Saxon Charter (BCS 792), where its bounds are described. The village is listed in 1086 in Domesday Book, with a recorded population of 17 (VCH *Northants.*, I (1902), 321). In 1301, the Lay Subsidy Returns give a total of 44 taxpayers for Fawsley (PRO, E179/155/31) and the place is mentioned in 1316 in the *Nomina Villarum*. Fifty-two people paid the Lay Subsidy of 1327 (M. W. Beresford, *The Lost Villages of England* (1954), 367) and the vill paid 56s. 8d. for the Lay Subsidy of 1334 (PRO, E179/155/3). When the Poll Tax was collected in 1377 Fawsley had 90 taxpayers over the age of 14 (PRO, E179/155/28), but it had only 66 in the much evaded tax of 1379 (M. W. Beresford, op. cit.). All these figures suggest that the village was small but flourishing over this period and that desertion took place at a later date.

In 1415 the Manor of Fawsley was bought by Richard Knightley and it remained in the hands of this family until the present century. An early 15th-century reference to protests from the demense tenants about the services being imposed upon them implies that Richard Knightley engaged in a deliberate policy of eviction, (PRO, C66/417m 18d), probably in order to turn the parish over to sheep-farming; by 1547, 2500 sheep were pastured there. Certainly by 1524 only seven people paid tax (PRO, E179/155/122) and two of these were members of the Knightley family who were paying large sums of money presumably derived from the profits of grazing. By 1674 only eight houses were assessed for the Hearth Tax (PRO, E179/254/14); at least four of these, including the hall, still stand in various places about the estate. In the early 18th century only six houses were recorded in the parish of which four were 'dispersed in the fields' (J. Bridges, *Hist. of Northants.*, I (1791), 64). By 1741 (NRO, Map of Fawsley) the village had entirely disappeared and the whole area was emparked. In 1801 the total population of the parish was 29, most of whom lived at the hall, the vicarage or in estate cottages (K. J. Allison et al., *The Deserted Villages of Northants.* (1966), 11, 39).

The remains of Fawsley are fragmentary and in poor condition. They suggest that there were two separate areas of settlement, one to the S. of the present hall and the other near the now isolated church, and this is of some interest as it indicates that Fawsley, like other settlements in the area, was perhaps a double village. Near the hall the surviving earthworks suggest that most of that part of the settlement

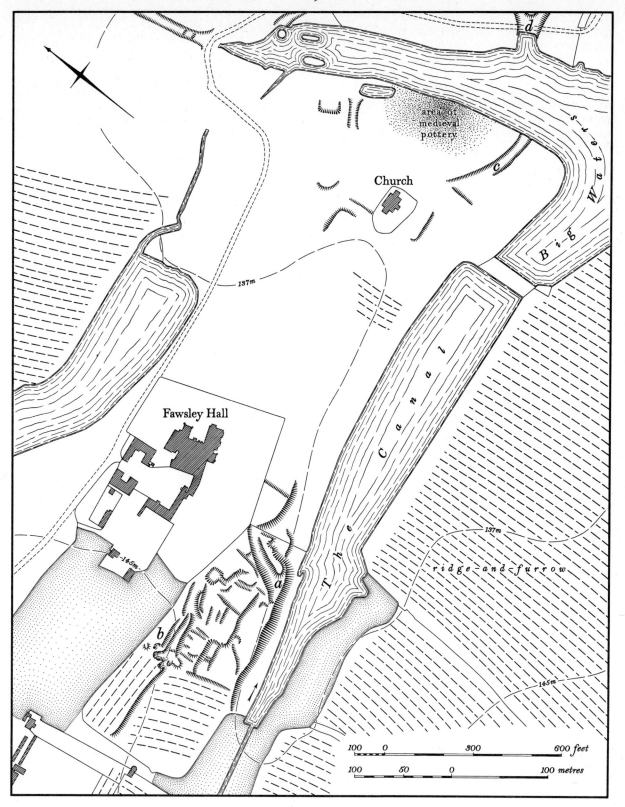

Fig. 69 FAWSLEY (1) Deserted villages

lay under the present hall and its gardens and outbuildings; they consist of a small area of indeterminate low scarps and banks. However certain features are clear. At the E. end of the site a broad hollow-way ('a' on plan) appears from under the later gardens and swings S.W. down the hillside; it is truncated by a steep scarp falling to the lake. This hollow-way is up to 2 m. deep in the centre. Another trackway, now a terraced feature ('b' on plan), runs W. from the area of the later gardens, parallel to the contours. One section is broken by quarrying, but beyond this the track continues to an area of ridge-and-furrow. Between the two tracks is a system of low banks and scarps of generally rectangular form, including at least three well-marked building platforms. The area was known as Chain Piece in 1741 (Map in NRO).

The second area of settlement lies around the church at the end of a flat-topped E.-projecting spur. Traces of ridge-and-furrow separate these remains from the earthworks described above. To the E. of the church, on land sloping down to the large landscaped lake, is an area of some 1.5 hectares which, though devoid of any recognisable earthworks and under permanent pasture, has been disturbed by moles. This activity has revealed a broad zone of dark soil, quite unlike that in the surrounding area, associated with large quantities of pottery of the 12th to the 14th centuries. To the N. are fragmentary traces of two rectangular platforms cut into the hillside, and other low banks and scarps where small amounts of medieval pottery have been found lie around the church. The area was called The Lawn in 1741 (Map in NRO). From the S.E. corner of the church a shallow hollow-way ('c' on plan) is traceable for about 100 m. until it disappears into the lake. It probably continued across the valley for it reappears on the E. side of the lake, where it crosses the existing drive and forks, with one branch running N.E. and the other S.E. ('d' on plan). Two other hollow-ways approach the area from the N. and N.E. at the N. end of the lake. All this evidence indicates that there was once a large area of medieval occupation, much of which is now covered by the lake itself, around and to the E. of the church.

b(2) ENCLOSURE (SP 568573; Fig. 70), on Temple Hill, on the summit of a broad, S.-projecting spur at 152 m. above OD. The spur is capped by a thick layer of glacial gravel, mainly flint, which has been extensively quarried so that the hill is covered by large pits. The enclosure partly overlies these and consists of a roughly rectangular area, bounded by a bank with traces of an outer ditch. Except for the S.E. corner where the bank remains 1.5 m. high the whole feature has been ploughed and is now reduced to a height of 0.5 m. The interior is uneven and much lower than the surrounding land, mainly because of the quarrying. Large quantities of post-medieval roofing tiles cover the interior. No precise date or purpose can be assigned to this enclosure, but it is probably of relatively recent date and may be connected with the landscaping of

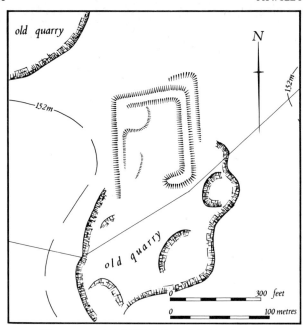

Fig. 70   FAWSLEY   (2) Enclosure

the park. On the Estate Map of Fawsley of 1741 (NRO) the name, Temple Hill, is given to the area, but no features are shown there.

b(3) GARDEN REMAINS AND PILLOW MOUND (?) (SP 570578), around the Dower House, on the N.E. side of Fawsley Park in the bottom of a broad open valley, on Lias Clay at 150 m. above OD. The Dower House is a small brick hunting lodge which was built in the early 16th century and was extended soon afterwards to make a small house of H-plan. It is now in ruins. Around it are some very slight earthworks, not all of which are explicable. The most obvious feature is a broad flat-topped terrace only 0.25 m. high which extends S. from the S.W. corner of the house for some 30 m. To the E., fronting the house, are slighter banks and ditches. The whole group may be the remains of a small formal garden though this is not certain. To the N., at the back of the house, are other poorly defined earthworks including a rectangular flat-topped mound 7 m. by 4 m. overall, and less than 0.25 m. high orientated N.W.–S.E., of the type usually classified as pillow mounds. In 1741 (Map in NRO) the Dower House and another building to the N.W. of it, now demolished, are shown standing in a small rectangular enclosure, probably a garden.

b(4) PILLOW MOUND (SP 563578), lies immediately S. of the Fawsley-Badby parish boundary, just S. of Badby Wood, on land sloping gently S. on clay at 152 m. above OD. It is a large rectangular flat-topped mound 27 m. long, 7 m.–8 m. wide and 1.5 m. high, and 3.5 m.–4 m. wide across the top. It is orientated E.–W. and has a later cut across it from N. to S. near its E. end. There is no trace of a ditch around the mound; a ditch on its N. side is related to an old trackway which passes between it and a bank to the N. This bank is the pale of the medieval deer park of Badby (Badby (6)). There is no trace of ridge-and-furrow in this part of the parish and this pillow mound and a smaller mound near the Dower House (3) may have been medieval rabbit warrens.

b(5) WINDMILL MOUND (SP 573558), in the S.E. of the parish at the E. end of a broad ridge, on Northampton Sand at 152 m. above OD. A low, ploughed mound some 12 m. across still survives on the ground; on air photographs (RAF VAP CPE/UK/1994, 3152–3) a circular soil-mark is faintly visible. In 1741 (NRO, Estate Map) a post-mill is shown at this point but it had disappeared by the early 19th century (1st ed. OS 1 in. map, (1834)).

b(6) PILLOW MOUND (SP 57005700; Fig. 71), lies on ground sloping gently S. on clay at 140 m. above OD. It consists of a flat-topped rectangular mound 18 m. long, 7 m. wide and just under 0.5 m. high, orientated N.–S. A shallow ditch 3 m. across runs along the E. and S. sides. The mound lies on top of ridge-and-furrow with which it is aligned, and immediately S. of a large bank which marks the edge of an old track.

b(7) POND (SP 570564), lies immediately S. of the 18th-century lake known as Big Waters, at the junction of two valleys, at 122 m. above OD. The interior of a long rectangular pond, now totally overgrown, is occupied by narrow parallel banks over 0.25 m. high. The pond and its banks are shown on the Estate Map of 1741 (NRO). No purpose can be assigned to the site, except that it may have been used for breeding wildfowl (see Sectional Preface and Charwelton (5)).

(8) CULTIVATION REMAINS. The date of enclosure of the common fields of Fawsley is unknown but the parish was enclosed by 1741 (Map in NRO) and had probably been so since the 15th or 16th century (see (1)). Most of the parish is covered with ridge-and-furrow which remains in very good condition over almost all of the permanent grassland of Fawsley Park. It is arranged mainly in interlocked furlongs, with ridges usually at right-angles to the contours. Over the very broken country in this area the result is a complex pattern of ridges radiating from the various spurs. In the N. of the parish, S. of Badby Wood, there is no ridge-and-furrow and this area may have been permanent waste or a medieval rabbit warren (3, 4).

UNDATED

b(9) ENCLOSURE (SP 57215733), lies on the E. side of Temple Hill on clay at about 150 m. above OD. Air photographs (RAF VAP CPE/UK/1994, 1162–3) show a small rectangular enclosure, covering just under 0.5 hectares, bounded by a continuous bank and apparently by both an outer and an inner ditch; no entrance is visible. It is orientated approximately N.–S. and the E. side is slightly bowed outwards. The enclosure has now been ploughed

out and nothing remains on the ground, but it appears to have been constructed over pre-existing ridge-and-furrow and was probably relatively recent. On the 1741 Estate Map of Fawsley (NRO) the field in which the enclosure lies is called North Thorney Close. In the centre of this field a small rectangular copse is depicted, of roughly the same shape and size as the enclosure, but slightly to the N. of it. Allowing for some cartographic error, it is likely that the enclosure was in fact a bank around the wood.

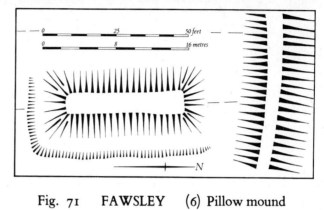

Fig. 71   FAWSLEY   (6) Pillow mound

31   FLORE
(OS 1 : 10000 a SP 66 SW, b SP 66 SE, c SP 65 NW, d SP 65 NE)

The large parish, of over 1090 hectares, includes the former lands of the deserted village of Glassthorpe (4). It is unusual in that, of the parishes which lie close to Watling Street, it is the only one with boundaries at no point determined by the Roman road. Instead, the W. boundary follows a tributary of the R. Nene; the Nene itself forms the S. boundary. Apart from the high ground in the E. where the Northampton Sand of Glassthorpe Hill rises steeply to 125 m. above OD, the greater part of the parish is a flat area of Upper and Middle Lias Clay and Marlstone sloping gently S. at about 100 m. above OD and cut by S.-flowing streams. On the W. and S. edges of the parish the land falls steeply to the valleys of the R. Nene and its major tributary here flowing at about 75 m. above OD, and in this area there are expanses of glacial sands and gravels as well as of alluvium.

The major monument is the deserted village of Glassthorpe (4) which was ploughed over with ridge-and-furrow at some time after its abandonment. The lands of Glassthorpe extended into Brington parish (Fig. 73).

PREHISTORIC AND ROMAN

A crudely chipped axe, listed as Mesolithic, and part of a Neolithic polished axe have been found in the parish. Another polished Neolithic axe was found in a garden in Brickett's Lane in 1974 (SP 64276004; Northants. Archaeol., 10 (1975), 150; NM). A Roman coin of Constantius I is also recorded (OS Record Cards; NM).

a(1) ENCLOSURE (SP 646620; Fig. 72), S.E. of Flore Fields House, in the N. of the parish, on Marlstone Rock at 103 m. above OD. Air photographs (in NMR) show cropmarks of the S.E. section of a large enclosure. The S.E. end, which is roughly semicircular, appears to have an entrance in it (*Northants. Archaeol.*, 8 (1973), 26).

a(2) ENCLOSURE AND DITCHES (SP 636607; Fig. 72), in the W. of the parish, N. of Flore Hill Farm, on sand and gravel at 110 m. above OD. Air photographs (in NMR) show cropmarks of a sub-rectangular enclosure, 90 m. long and 45 m. wide, with a ring ditch 16 m. in diam. within it. To the S.W. a curved length of ditch is faintly visible (*BNFAS*, 4 (1970), 31; 6 (1971), 11; *Northants. Archaeol.*, 8 (1973), 26).

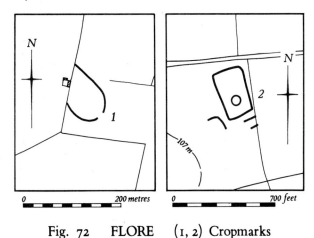

Fig. 72   FLORE   (1, 2) Cropmarks

b(3) ENCLOSURE (SP 668608), on Glassthorpe Hill in the S.E. of the parish, on Northampton Sand at 140 m. above OD. The cropmark of a rectangular enclosure has been noted (*BNFAS*, 6 (1971), 11).

MEDIEVAL AND LATER

b(4) DESERTED VILLAGE OF GLASSTHORPE (SP 662617; Figs. 73 and 74; Plate 10), lies in the N.E. of the parish, on land sloping W. to a small S.-flowing stream, on Upper Lias Clay and Marlstone between 105 m. and 90 m. above OD. The boundaries of the land of this village are depicted on the Tithe Map of Glassthorpe (NRO, 1850) which shows that the N. part extended into the parish of Brington (Fig. 73).

Glassthorpe is first mentioned in 1086 though its pure Scandinavian name indicates an older origin (PN *Northants.*, 83). In Domesday Book the place is listed as a small manor with a recorded population of five (VCH *Northants.*, I (1902), 325). The 1301 Lay Subsidy lists 14 taxpayers for the vill (PRO, E179/155/31). It is mentioned by name in the 1316 *Nomina Villarum* and appears still to have been inhabited in 1371. In 1515 one manor there was bought by the Spencer family of Althorp and by 1547 a

place called 'Classthorpe Pasture' grazed 200 sheep. In the early 18th century Bridges (*Hist. of Northants.*, I (1791), 510) said that it had been 'long depopulated' and that only one shepherd's house remained. This house, which is shown on a map of 1758 and on the Tithe Map of 1850 (NRO), still stands though it is no longer occupied. In 1850 the N. part of the site was called Berry Meadow and the S. part House Ground (K. J. Allison *et al.*, *The Deserted Villages of Northants.* (1966), 40).

The remains of the village are preserved under permanent pasture and have suffered no recent damage but they are extremely difficult to interpret as almost the whole area was overploughed with ridge-and-furrow at some time after desertion. The site can be divided into two areas. The S. part, which is based on a continuous hollow-way, is roughly trapezoidal; a further hollow-way runs down the slope westwards from its S.W. corner, and here there is later damage by extensive quarrying. On both sides of these hollow-ways there are faint traces of former closes bounded by low banks and scarps or by very shallow ditches. Most are likely to be the sites of former houses and gardens, but ploughing has destroyed all but the basic outlines.

Further N., and apparently quite separate from the southern part of the village, is a much mutilated hollow-way running E.–W. At its E. end it turns N. and may have also turned S. towards the S. part of the site though this is not certain. On the S. side of the main hollow-way are two or three raised platforms 1.5 m. high with a broad depression to the W. These may be interpreted as a courtyard farm and crewyard, recognized on many deserted village sites and usually dated to the end of the medieval period. To the N. of the hollow-way are long closes bounded by ditches and extending as far as the stream. At their S. ends, near the hollow-way, are a number of low platforms and scarps which might be former building sites (CUAP, LT6, 7; AWQ62–4).

c(5) SETTLEMENT REMAINS (SP 643598), formerly part of Flore village, lie immediately E. of Flore church, on land sloping to the R. Nene on clay at 85 m. above OD. Fragments of at least one and perhaps two enclosures bounded by low banks are the only visible earthworks but these, in conjunction with existing features of the village, contribute to an understanding of the village's development. Flore village is made up of six lanes extending S. in a rather irregular form from the main E.–W. High Street, here the A45 Daventry–Northampton road. There are traces of a former triangular green, now encroached upon, at the N. end of Sutton Street and another area called The Green lies further S. The parish church is oddly situated in the S.W. corner of the village beyond the main built up area. This layout suggests that the village has either gradually moved towards the High Street from the area around the church or has been deliberately planned anew. Apart from the earthworks described all the land to the S. and W. of the church is permanent pasture or

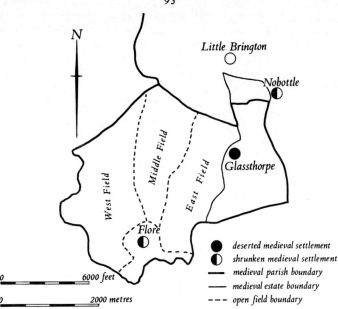

N

Little Brington
○

Nobottle
◐

Glassthorpe
●

West Field

Middle Field

East Field

Flore
◐

0 ————— 6000 feet

0 ————— 2000 metres

● *deserted medieval settlement*
◐ *shrunken medieval settlement*
——— *medieval parish boundary*
——— *medieval estate boundary*
- - - *open field boundary*

Fig. 73   FLORE and BRINGTON   Medieval settlements and estates

parkland with no visible indications of former settlement. However any future ploughing may reveal new evidence (air photographs in NMR).

(6) CULTIVATION REMAINS (Fig. 73). The common fields of the village of Flore were enclosed by an Act of Parliament in 1778. Though no Enclosure Map is known to survive it is clear from the Award (NRO) that there were at that time three open fields, East Field lying between the Glassthorpe boundary and Brington Road, Middle Field between Brington Road and the road to Brockhall, and West Field covering most of the W. of the parish. Ridge-and-furrow of these fields exists on the ground or can be traced on air photographs over large parts of the parish. It is arranged mainly in end-on or interlocked furlongs though on the steep valley sides and spurs along the W. and N.W. sides of the parish it is arranged in a radiating pattern down the slopes. Large areas still survive in the pasture N. of the village at the S. end of the former Middle and West Fields, as well as further N., S.W. of Flore Fields House (SP 642620), in the former West Field.

The date of the enclosure of the common fields of Glassthorpe is unknown but it had certainly taken place by 1758 (Map in NRO) and, by implication, by 1547 (see (4) above). Ridge-and-furrow survives on the ground or can be traced on air photographs over almost the whole area of the land of Glassthorpe, arranged mainly in interlocked furlongs running across the contours. In the N. of the area three furlongs cross the modern parish boundary with Brington (around SP 668628); the latter boundary is completely undefined. This indicates that the northern part of the land of Glassthorpe was always within Brington parish.

Ridge-and-furrow of unknown date, but perhaps post-medieval in origin, covers almost the whole of the deserted village of Glassthorpe (4) (RAF VAP CPE/UK/1994, 1261–8, 3252–6).

32   GUILSBOROUGH
(OS 1 : 10000 [a] SP 67 NE, [b] SP 67 SW, [c] SP 67 SE)

The parish, covering just over 900 hectares, was formerly much larger and in medieval times included the present parish of Hollowell, and probably the hamlet and land of Coton which is now in Ravensthorpe parish (Ravensthorpe (9)). The village of Guilsborough and most of the W. part of the parish lie on a N.W.–S.E. ridge of Northampton Sand overlaid by patches of Boulder Clay and glacial sands and gravels, between 150 m. and 180 m. above OD. To the E. and N.E. the land slopes across Upper Lias Clay to the valley of the Hollowell Brook, here flowing about 120 m. above OD. A second ridge, of Northampton Sand capped by Boulder Clay rising to about 140 m. above OD, separates this valley from the Cottesbrooke Stream which forms the N.E. boundary. The present village is roughly L-shaped and is made up of two distinct medieval settlements, each with its own land unit (Fig. 14) the boundaries of which are shown on the Tithe Map of 1848 (NRO). Guilsborough itself consisted of the main N.W.–S.E. street; the triangular green in the N.W. and the single street running N.E. with earthworks at its N.E. end was the hamlet of Nortoft (6), listed as a separate settlement in Domesday Book. This means that the earlier assumption that Nortoft was an unlocated deserted village

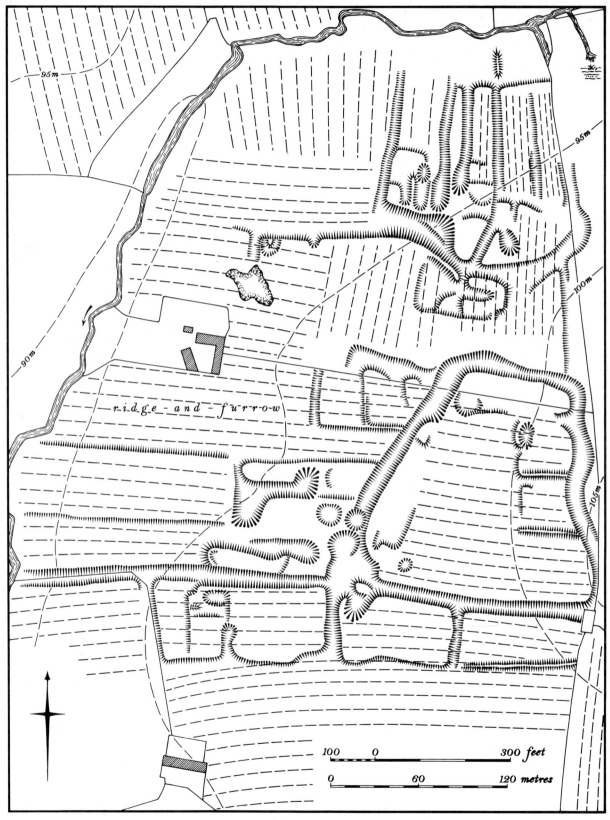

ridge - and - furrow

100 0   300 *feet*

0   60   120 *metres*

Fig. 74   FLORE   (4) Deserted village of Glassthorpe

is no longer valid (M. W. Beresford, *The Lost Villages of England* (1954), 370). A number of possible small Roman sites have been discovered by recent fieldwork in the parish. Of greater significance is the suggestion, first found in the works of early antiquarians in the county, that a Roman settlement of major importance lay immediately W. of the village, in Guilsborough Park (5). The possible existence of such a centre at this early date is of interest and could have some bearing both on the origins of the place-name and on the extent of the early medieval land unit containing the modern parishes of Guilsborough, Ravensthorpe and Hollowell.

PREHISTORIC AND ROMAN

Two large polished Neolithic flint axes were found in the parish before 1912 (OS Record Cards; NM). Other flint implements, described as spears, were found in 1949 (SP 673731; OS Record Cards).

^c(1) ENCLOSURE (?) (SP 690733), in the E. of the parish, on Northampton Sand at 122 m. above OD. Air photographs (not seen by RCHM) are said to show cropmarks of a rectangular feature (*BNFAS*, 5 (1971), 42).

^c(2) ROMAN SETTLEMENT (?) (SP 678740), N.E. of Nortoft Grange, on gravel at 122 m. above OD. Roman pottery has been found (*Northants. Archaeol.*, 10 (1975), 154).

^c(3) ROMAN SETTLEMENT (?) (SP 662741), S.E. of Nortoft Lodge, on Northampton Sand at 180 m. above OD. Roman pottery has been found (*Northants. Archaeol.*, 10 (1975), 154).

^c(4) ROMAN SETTLEMENT (?) (SP 660730), S. of Lindow Spinney, on sand and gravel at 155 m. above OD. Roman pottery has been found (*Northants. Archaeol.*, 10 (1975), 154).

^c(5) ENCLOSURE AND (?) ROMAN SETTLEMENT (SP 673729; Fig. 75), lay immediately W. of the village of Guilsborough, on the summit of the hill, on Northampton Sand at 165 m. above OD. The site has been almost completely destroyed, but there seems to have been an enclosure of some kind bounded by a bank and ditch. This enclosure may relate to the 'borough' element of the place-name.

The earliest and most complete descriptions of the site were made in the early 18th century by the two county historians (J. Morton, *Nat. Hist. of Northants.* (1712), 524; J. Bridges, *Hist. of Northants.*, I (1791), 566). It was then said to be 'the large remains of a Roman encampment. ... The form of it, like the more common Roman Camps, is an oblong square, the shorter side running from N. to S. It seems to have been fenced with a broad, deep, single entrenchment. The agger of this fortification is still visible; and as far as could be judged ... the longest parallel is between five and six hundred foot, the shortest about three hundred. The area included is about eight acres. It is called

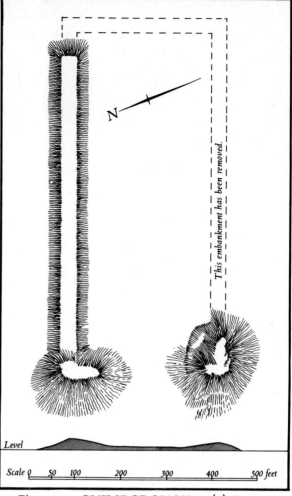

Fig. 75   GUILSBOROUGH   (5) Roman settlement
(copied from a plan published in 1849)

the Burrows or Burrow-Hill'.

The S. bank and presumably the E. bank seem to have been partly removed in the early 19th century when skeletons were found as well as a large stone coffin 'in the north west corner'. A plan of the site (Fig. 75) was made soon afterwards and published in Wetton's *Guide Book* (1849). Further levelling of the S. side took place in 1870 and some pottery, then said to be Roman, was discovered. This is reputed to have been given to NM but there is no trace of it there. On air photographs taken before 1947 some possible remains are visible. The W. corner of the enclosure is recognizable as a mutilated rounded mound, apparently projecting forward N.W. beyond the line of the corner formed by the N.W. and S.W. sides which show as low scarps. A possible S. corner is also visible and this too seems to have had a projecting part. The N.E. side is marked by a natural scarp but there is no trace of the S.E. side. On this evidence the attribution of a Roman date seems unlikely though the ground had been so disturbed by later activity that the air photographic evidence is suspect. Since 1947 the whole area has been cleared and levelled. Only a mutilated mound 2 m. high, perhaps the W. corner (SP 67357286), and a short length of bank 1 m. high which might be part of the N.W. side (SP 67557288) remain. A large quantity of Roman pottery was discovered somewhere in the area in about 1910 during the digging of foundations for a bungalow (E. L. Renton, *Records of Guilsborough, Nortoft and Hollowell* (1929), 2). This pottery was given to NM (RAF VAP CPE/UK/1994, 1467–8).

MEDIEVAL AND LATER

c(6) SETTLEMENT REMAINS (SP 676735), formerly part of the hamlet of Nortoft, lie to the E. of the existing houses, on Northampton Sand at 150 m. above OD. The remains consist of one well-defined close and an area of disturbed ground (RAF VAP CPE/UK/1994, 1466–7).

c(7) DAM (SP 666748), in the bottom of the valley of a N.E.-flowing brook, on the boundary between Thornby and Guilsborough parishes, on clay at 140 m. above OD. It consists of a low bank some 1.5 m. high partly spanning the stream. This dam presumably held back water for a small fishpond or mill-pond the edges of which are still visible as a low scarp to the W.

(8) CULTIVATION REMAINS. The common fields of Guilsborough were enclosed by an Act of Parliament of 1764. The common fields of Nortoft were enclosed by agreement in 1588 (NRO, Fermor Hesketh Baker, 715a). Ridge-and-furrow of these fields exists on the ground or can be traced on air photographs over large parts of the parish though the pattern is far from complete. It appears to be arranged in end-on and interlocked furlongs carefully adapted to the natural topography (RAF VAP CPE/UK/1994, 1464–71; 540/474, 3151–6).

33 HADDON, EAST

(OS 1:10000 a SP 66 NW, b SP 66 NE)

The parish, covering just over 1080 hectares, lies between two E.-flowing streams between 180 m. and 90 m. above OD. Most of the lower ground is on Upper Lias Clay but the main E.–W. ridge across the centre of the parish is Northampton Sand overlaid by patches of Boulder Clay and glacial sands and gravels.

PREHISTORIC

b(1) BARROW (?) (SP 655687), W. of Covert Farm on Northampton Sand at 160 m. above OD. There is a 19th-century reference to a tumulus but no mound can be traced in the vicinity (*Archaeologia*, 35 (1853), Pl. 16; OS Record Cards).

MEDIEVAL AND LATER

b(2) MANOR HOUSE SITE AND FISHPONDS (?) (SP 668678), lies S. of the village, immediately E. of Church Lane, on clay sloping S. between 145 m. and 152 m. above OD. The remains fall into two parts. In the N., behind Clifden Cottages (SP 668679), there is a raised platform 40 m. square, bounded by a scarp up to 1.5 m. high and with a broad ditch or narrow pond on its E. side. In the valley bottom below (SP668677) are two small ponds, each with a low dam 1.5 m. high, set inside and on the E. of a rectangular enclosure bounded by a low bank and ditch. Nothing is known of the history of the site and on the earliest large-scale plan of the village (NRO, 1859) no buildings are shown (RAF VAP CPE/UK/1994, 3263–5).

(3) CULTIVATION REMAINS. The common fields of the parish were finally enclosed by an Act of Parliament of 1773 though apparently no map survives. A detailed survey, made in 1598, showing the common fields as they then existed, reveals a very complex picture (NRO). The N. part of the parish was called North Field, and was subdivided into West, Middle and East Fields; the S. of the parish was South Field, subdivided into South, Middle and East Fields. There was also a South Field Heath. In 1629 a lease (NRO) referred to a recent enclosure of the South Field by agreement between the three lords of the manor and one freeholder. This event can be dated to between 1598 and 1607. When the North Field was finally enclosed in 1773 it had by this date been renamed as Upper Middle and Holdenby Fields.

Ridge-and-furrow of these common fields exists on the ground or can be traced on air photographs over large parts of the parish, arranged in end-on and interlocked furlongs, many of reversed-S form. Ridge-and-furrow is particularly well preserved in the park of East Haddon Hall, N. of the village (SP 669685), and W. of the village, along the N. side of the road to Long Buckby (SP 660682). In the N. of the parish, near Washbrook Bridge (SP 668690), three interlocked furlongs preserved in pasture show extremely well the careful adaptation of the layout to the natural topography (RAF VAP CPE/UK/1994, 1366–8, 2361–6, 4260–4, 4266–9).

UNDATED

Human bones embedded in gravel were discovered in about 1830 in a field to the N. of the village (Whellan, *Dir.*, 312).

34 HADDON, WEST

(OS 1:10000 a SP 67 SW, b SP 67 SE, c SP 66 NW)

The parish covers just over 1080 hectares, and is roughly rectangular with a triangular area extending from the S. side. Except for the N.E. and S.E. corners almost all of the boundaries are determined by streams, and the high central part of the parish which rises to over 182 m. above OD forms a watershed from which streams drain generally N.W. or S.E. Nearly all of the area is covered by glacial deposits, in particular large expanses of sands and gravels. Small areas of Middle and Upper Lias Clay and Northampton Sand are exposed along the valley sides mainly on the peripheries of the parish. Little of archaeological interest has been discovered.

PREHISTORIC AND ROMAN

^a(1) BARROW (?) (SP 641715), called Oster Hill, is said to have lain S.E. of the village on glacial gravel at 174 m. above OD. Bridges (*Hist. of Northants.*, I (1791), 599), writing in about 1720, said that it was 'an eminence' and that 'under it, according to vulgar tradition, are buried several officers who fell in battle'. He goes on to conjecture that 'it is the tumulus of Publius Ostorius'. However no trace of a mound exists on the ground and it is possible that the place-name, of Scandinavian origin, 'Austr' meaning East (PN *Northants.*, 71), has led to the identification of a low natural hill as a barrow and has produced this unlikely association.

^a(2) ROMAN BURIAL AND COINS (around SP 628719). A Roman urn containing ashes and covered with a flat stone was found at the W. end of West Haddon village before 1712 (J. Morton, *Nat. Hist. of Northants.* (1712), 530). Roman coins were found in the same area between 1693 and 1747. No other details are known (OS Record Cards).

MEDIEVAL AND LATER

(3) CULTIVATION REMAINS. The common fields of the parish were enclosed by an Act of Parliament in 1765 (NRO, Enclosure Map). The original Act records that, before enclosure, in addition to the common fields there were 800 acres of heath, common and waste ground as well as 'Two Rye Hills'. Though the location of these areas is unknown, the recoverable ridge-and-furrow is so extensive as to indicate that most of them must have been under cultivation at an early period. The ridge-and-furrow is preserved on the ground or is visible on air photographs throughout most of the centre and S. parts of the parish but in the N., apart from a few isolated furlongs, it has been largely destroyed. In the S. much of it is orientated N.–S. in end-on furlongs, with a few blocks at right-angles. Around the village the predominant orientation is E.–W., although there is a pronounced pattern of interlocked furlongs to the W. (RAF VAP CPE/UK/1994, 1363–9, 1469–74).

35 HARLESTONE

(OS 1 : 10000 ^a SP 66 NE, ^b SP 66 SE, ^c SP 76 NW, ^d SP 76 SW)

The parish covers some 1040 hectares and lies immediately N.W. of Northampton. Most of it is a fairly flat tableland of Northampton Sand between 90 m. and 105 m. above OD, but the down-cutting of a number of small streams has exposed the Jurassic Clay and in the S. there is an area of limestone and Marlstone overlaid by Boulder Clay. Many prehistoric and Roman sites are recorded. However this probably reflects not an unusually rich settlement history but simply the relative ease of recognition of cropmarks on the Northampton Sand.

PREHISTORIC AND ROMAN

A Roman urn is said to have been found in the parish before 1904 (T. J. George, *Arch. Survey of Northants.* (1904), 15), and a coin of Constantine I was discovered in 1976 at SP 686638 (*Northants. Archaeol.*, 12 (1977), 212).

The ring ditches (centred SP 694651), in the N.W. of the parish on Northampton Sand at 122 m. above OD and visible on air photographs (CUAP, ABG29) are anti-aircraft sites and are still visible as earthworks on photographs taken in 1947 (RAF VAP CPE/UK/1994, 4369–70; see also Brixworth and Brockhall).

They lie on each side of a broad access-way between ridge-and-furrow, which, having been ploughed out, appears as a ditched trackway. (For Saxon material from this field, see (11)).

^c(1) EAST HARLESTONE COMPLEX (centred SP 711652; Fig. 76), covers some 24 hectares in the N.E. of the parish, on Northampton Sand between 75 m. and 100 m. above OD. Air photographs (in NMR and CUAP, AFX19, 20, ADP5, 7, 8, ZU71–74, ZV27, 28) show a complicated series of ditches, enclosures and trackways extending over at least seven fields on either side of the road from Harlestone to Church Brampton.

A ditched trackway orientated roughly E.–W. and traceable for 900 m. runs from SP 70686526 to 71566506 through the middle of the visible remains. A ditch to the N. which may represent another track or the sides of rectangular enclosures, runs from the trackway to SP 71336545 where it intersects another length of ditch, perhaps a boundary. Between this last ditch and the trackway is a series of rectangular and irregular conjoined enclosures of varying size. A short length of pit alignment is visible (from SP 71016541 to SP 71146540). To the S. of the main trackway and intersecting one of its ditches is a large ring ditch (centred SP 71056515) about 60 m. in diam. with an entrance on its E. side; S. and S.W. of this there are at least 18 smaller ring ditches, of which about half lie within two large rectangular enclosures each more than 1 hectare in area. One of these (centred SP 70886498) has numerous subdivisions and other internal features. The

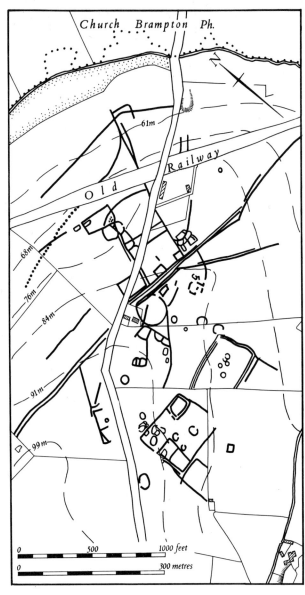

Fig. 76   HARLESTONE
(1) East Harlestone Complex

other (centred SP 71056498) appears to be bounded by two or sometimes three ditches.

d(2) ENCLOSURE (SP 703627), lies in the S. of the parish, on limestone, at 99 m. above OD. Air photographs (in NMR) show the cropmarks of a small trapezoidal enclosure 0.3 hectares in area. No interior features or entrances are visible. It may be associated with other enclosures to the S.E. in Harpole parish (see RCHM *Northants.*, IV (forthcoming)).

d(3) PIT ALIGNMENT (SP 709630), close to the S. parish boundary, on Northampton Sand, at 100 m. above OD.

Air photographs (in NMR) show a pit alignment visible for some 225 m., running in a broad curve generally S.W.–N.E.

d(4) LINEAR DITCHES (SP 710639–715646; Fig. 77), lie S.E. of Lower Harlestone, on Northampton Sand between 83 m. and 100 m. above OD, alongside a small N.E.-flowing stream cut down into Upper Lias Clay. The feature consists of three parallel ditches visible on air photographs (in NMR) for a distance of 870 m. The outer ditches are slightly wider than the central one and the latter is closer to the E. ditch than the W. Near the S.W. end, the W. ditch appears to curve S.E. and merge with the central one. To the N.W. are two intersecting linear ditches which have previously been described as a large enclosure. Worked flints have been found there (*BNFAS*, 6 (1971), 13, Harlestone (2)).

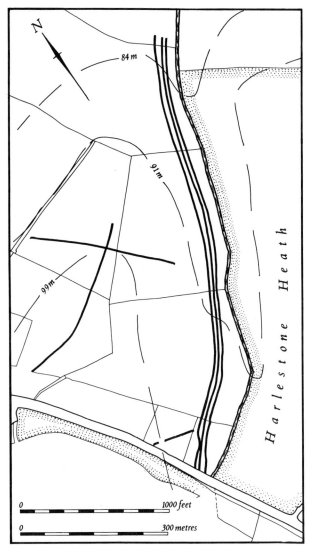

Fig. 77   HARLESTONE   (4) Linear ditches

d(5) PIT ALIGNMENTS AND DITCHES (centred SP 716634; Fig. 78), lie in the S.E. of the parish, S. of Harlestone Heath, on Northampton Sand, at 93 m. above OD. Air photographs (in NMR) show two short lengths of pit alignment roughly parallel to each other and 350 m. apart. An L-shaped feature, possibly the corner of a double-ditched enclosure, lies between them. The northernmost pit alignment may be a continuation of another visible further E. within Northampton (see RCHM Northants., V (forthcoming)).

d(6) MOUND (SP 716636), in the S.E. of the parish, on Harlestone Heath, on Northampton Sand, at 90 m. above OD. The mound is 1 m. high and 7 m. in diam. and may be a barrow (BNFAS, 3 (1969), 1).

which show that the site was occupied from the 2nd to the 4th century. A hoard of 814 Roman coins, dating from 164 to 395 A.D. and which had been buried on the site after the building was in ruins, was also found (JRS, 17 (1927), 202; Num. Chron., 10 (1930), 275; 11 (1931), 231; Ass. Arch. Soc. Reps., 40 (1933), 299–308; Arch. J., 90 (1933), 282–305; BAR, 40 (1977), 63; OS Record Cards). A bronze coin of Magnentius and a scatter of building-stone were discovered in the same field in 1970 (BNFAS, 5 (1971), 44). The site may be the one referred to by Bridges (Hist. of Northants., I (1791), 511); 'at a small distance from Newbottle Wood are marks of an ancient building with several ruinous walks leading to it'.

For Roman Road 17, see Appendix.

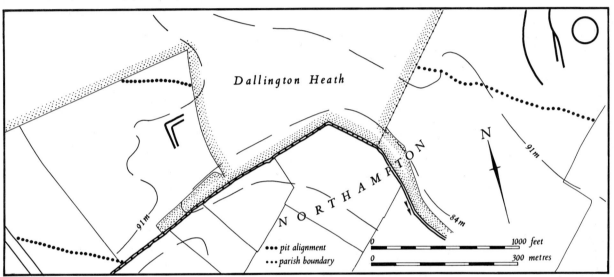

Fig. 78   HARLESTONE   (5) Cropmarks

b(7) ROMAN SETTLEMENT (SP 698639), in Upper Harlestone village, on Northampton Sand, at 95 m. above OD. Cropmarks are said to have been seen in 1963 and sherds of Roman grey ware have been found (BNFAS, 6 (1971), 13, Harlestone (3)).

b(8) ROMAN SETTLEMENT (SP 69456376), 350 m. W.S.W. of (7) and in a similar position. Roman grey wares and 4th-century Nene Valley wares have been found (OS Record Cards).

b(9) ROMAN SETTLEMENT (SP 69386345), 200 m. S. of (5) and in a similar position. Nene Valley wares and 2nd-century grey wares have been found, as well as iron slag (OS Record Cards).

b(10) ROMAN BUILDING (SP 68196330), in Sharaoh Field, in the W. of the parish, on Boulder Clay at about 117 m. above OD. A large Roman building was excavated in 1927–9. Foundations of stone walls and remains of a hearth were found, as well as samian and coarse Roman wares

MEDIEVAL AND LATER

a(11) SAXON SETTLEMENT (SP 693653), on Northampton Sand, at 115 m. above OD. During house-building in 1959 part of a Saxon loom weight and nine sherds of gritty Saxon pottery were found with bones, black earth and a possible hearth. One sherd of Roman pottery was also discovered (BNFAS, 5 (1971), 45).

b(12) QUARRIES (e.g. SP 695641, 705640, 708638). In the centre of the parish, around and to the S. of the village, are several large quarry pits, dug into the underlying Northampton Sand. Most are of post-medieval date, but others are probably much older and Morton (Hist. of Northants. (1712), 110) recorded some of them as 'very ancient'.

(13) CULTIVATION REMAINS. The common fields of the parish were enclosed by an Act of Parliament of 1766 (Notes on Enclosure in Northants., Central Library, Northampton); no map appears to have survived. Ridge-

and-furrow of these fields is visible on the ground or can be traced on air photographs over much of the parish, arranged in end-on and interlocked furlongs. It is particularly well preserved in parts of Harlestone Park (SP 698643; RAF VAP CPE/UK/1994, 2249–58, 3246–52, 4256–9, 4367–72).

UNDATED

(14) EARTHWORKS AND BURIALS (unlocated). Bridges, writing about 1720 (*Hist. of Northants.*, I (1791), 511), records that 'on a place called Dive's-heath are the remains of a fortification where human skulls and bones have often been dug up'. The location and date of this site is unknown.

36 HASELBECH

(OS 1:10000 ᵃ SP 77 NW, ᵇ SP 67 NE)

The small, roughly rectangular parish, covering only about 690 hectares, lies on a watershed between streams flowing S., ultimately into the Nene valley, and N. to the R. Ise on the N. boundary. The landscape is rolling, with steep-sided valleys. The high ground, rising to 185 m. above OD along the central E.–W. ridge, is covered by Boulder Clay, but elsewhere narrow bands of Oolite Limestone, Northampton Sand, and Upper Lias Clay outcrop on the valley sides.

No prehistoric sites are known and only two possible Roman settlements (1, 2) have been discovered. The main monument in the parish is the extensive earthwork remains of Haselbech village (3). These earthworks result partly from late 16th-century enclosure and partly from landscaping in the 18th century.

ROMAN

ᵃ(1) ROMAN SETTLEMENT (?) (SP 723772), in the E. of the parish, on a spur between two S.-flowing streams, on Upper Lias Clay at 130 m. above OD. A small amount of Roman pottery has been found (*Northants. Archaeol.*, 11 (1976), 192; 12 (1977), 212).

ᵃ(2) ROMAN SETTLEMENT (?) (SP 722765), in the S.E. of the parish, on Boulder Clay, at 165 m. above OD. A small quantity of Roman sherds has been discovered (*Northants. Archaeol.*, 12 (1977), 212).

MEDIEVAL AND LATER

ᵃ(3) SETTLEMENT REMAINS (centred SP 711774; Figs. 79 and 80), formerly part of Haselbech village, lie to the S.W., W. and N.W. of the now isolated church of St. Michael, on the summit and slopes of a rounded hill, on Boulder Clay and glacial sands and gravels between 172 m. and 184 m. above OD.

The village of Haselbech was probably always small. No national taxation figures survive to give an accurate estimate of its population in the medieval period after 1086 when, in Domesday Book, it is listed as a single manor with a recorded population of 19 (VCH *Northants.*, II (1906), 323). By the late 16th century much of the parish had come into the hands of the Tresham family and around 1598 the common fields were enclosed and converted to pasture, largely at the behest of Sir Thomas Tresham. A map of that date (NRO; Fig. 80) shows the village with a layout completely different from the present one; in addition to the existing roads there was at that time another street to the E. of the church. A lane also ran W. from the sharp bend S.W. of the church, giving access to the adjacent fields and an isolated farmstead. With the exception of the latter lane, houses lay along all the streets and about 25 separate farmsteads, houses or cottages are depicted. Five empty crofts lay on the E. side of the street, E. of the church, and another two at the N.E. end of the village, on the N. side of the Kelmarsh road. Tresham's enclosure involved the removal of some 700 acres of land which had previously belonged to seven houses in the village. This, and his consequent policy of raising rents, led effectively to the eviction of some 60 people who could not or would not pay. The other landowners in the parish may also have evicted tenants. It is not clear whether the 1598 map depicts the situation before or after this eviction.

Little is known of changes in the village during the 17th century except that Haselbech Hall was built just before 1678 for the Wyke family. This was followed by further alterations in the next century. In 1673 31 householders paid the Hearth Tax (PRO, E179/254/24) and in about 1720 Bridges (*Hist. of Northants.*, II (1791), 35) reported that there were 24 houses in the parish. Sometime before 1773 (Map in NRO) the present park around the hall was laid out. This involved the stopping up of the road E. of the church and the removal of all remaining houses and empty crofts along it. In addition all the houses along the road W. of the church, as well as some along the S. side of the Naseby road, were demolished to provide a clear vista from the hall in an S.W. direction. By 1773 only four buildings stood S. of the church, two to the N. and three along the N. side of the Naseby road. In the 19th century those N. of the church and two to the S. were removed.

On the ground nothing remains of the former street and house-sites E. of the church, as the whole area has been landscaped into shrubberies in the late 19th century. A large area of earthworks to the W. and S.W. of the church mainly relates to the 18th-century landscaping and later changes. However certain features can be explained and identified in relation to the map evidence. For example two of the raised platforms on the S. side of the Naseby road ('a' and 'b' on plan) can be identified as sites of houses on the 1598 map while another ('c' on plan) is the site of a further building also shown on that map. The rather broken scarps running S.S.W. from 'a' and 'b' and the mutilated ditch to the W. of 'c' are thus the close boundaries of these 16th-century houses. The sites of the houses on the W. side of the road, W. of the church, remain only as mutilated scarps and banks ('d' on plan) but the old lane to the S. survives in part as a shallow hollow-way ('e' on plan). Other earthworks to the S. ('f' on plan), which include fragmentary closes, raised platforms and some slight ridge-and-furrow, lie in an area devoid of features on the 1598 map and may indicate an earlier phase of abandonment (RAF VAP 106G/UK/636, 3184–5; CPE/UK/1994, 2457–6; CUAP, BLD34–7).

(4) CULTIVATION REMAINS. The common fields of the parish were enclosed by agreement in 1599 (NRO, NRS Transcripts) although the earliest map of the parish (NRO, 1598; Fig. 80) shows it apparently enclosed. This process was carried out at least in part by Sir Thomas Tresham who converted most of the parish to sheep-pasture and it led to riots in the parish in 1607 as part of a general revolt against enclosure in the East Midlands in that year. At that time it was said that only two yardlands out of forty were in tillage (*Northants. P. and P.*, I (1949), 29; *Trans. Royal Hist. Soc.*, 18 (1904), 215).

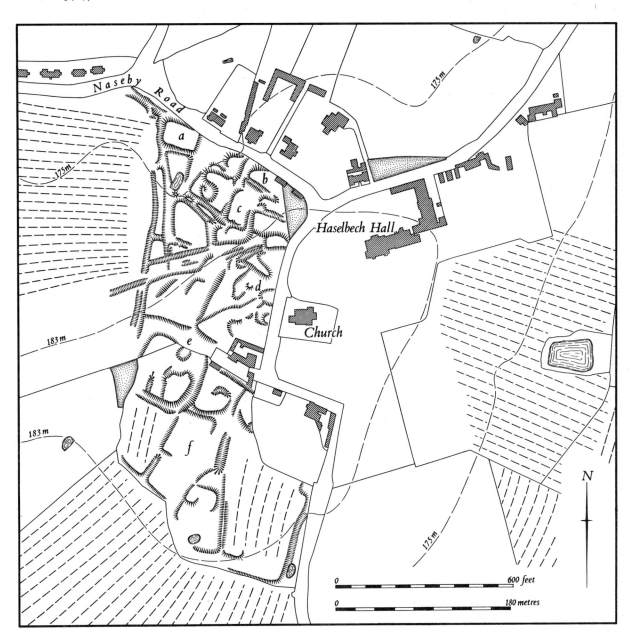

Fig. 79   HASELBECH   (3) Settlement remains

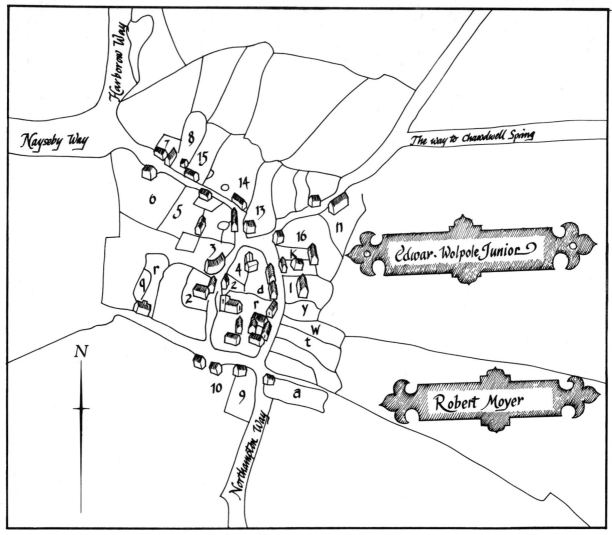

Fig. 80   HASELBECH   (3) Plan of village in 1598 (from a map in NRO)

Ridge-and-furrow of the common fields is still preserved on the ground or can be traced on air photographs over almost all of the parish, much of it arranged in rather short interlocked rectangular furlongs which are especially well marked in the N.E. of the parish. In other places, notably on the broken ground to the W. and N.W., the furlongs radiate outwards from the spurs. Ridge-and-furrow is still well preserved in some fields around the village and in the park of Haselbech Hall (RAF VAP CPE/UK/1994, 2454–9, 4459–62; 541/15, 4395–9; 106G/UK/636, 4182–9, 3184–6).

37 HELLIDON

(OS 1:10000 [a] SP 55 NW, [b] SP 45 NE)

The roughly kite-shaped parish of about 640 hectares lies against the Warwickshire boundary, across the headwaters of a number of small streams which drain N. to form the R. Leam. The higher S. part is a fairly flat tableland on Marlstone Rock, between 180 m. and 190 m. above OD. This plateau is abruptly terminated by a steep and very indented scarp, through which the streams have cut valleys into the underlying Middle and Lower Lias Clays at between 120 m. and 165 m. above OD. Nothing of major archaeological interest is known in the parish, though the existence of the site of one of the two medieval manor houses (1) may help to explain the morphology of the village.

MEDIEVAL AND LATER

[a](1) MANOR HOUSE SITE (SP 517581; Fig. 81), lies immediately W. of Leam House, on limestone at 165 m. above OD. It is situated near the end of a N.-facing spur with extensive views to the N., E. and W.

Hellidon is not mentioned in Domesday Book, but from the 13th century onwards there appear to have been two main manors in the parish, one known as Giffords Manor and the other as Baskervilles. The two manor houses had some influence on the shape of the present village which consists of two conjoined loops with the church at the junction. Baskervilles Manor was on the site of the present manor house at the N.W. end of the village and W. of the W. loop. Giffords Manor is traditionally said to have stood on or near the existing earthworks in a field known as Woodhill, on the N. side of the E. loop (Whellan, *Dir.*, 420–1); the site was abandoned by the late 18th century (NRO, Enclosure Map, *c.* 1775).

The remains consist of the N. part of a rectangular enclosure bounded by a degraded scarp only 0.25 m.–1 m. in height with, in places, traces of an inner bank. There is a small gap in the N.E. corner, partly blocked by another scarp which turns and runs E. down the hillside. The interior is uneven and disturbed by what appear to be quarry pits, though a sunken rectangular feature in the N.W. corner may be the site of a former building. On the E. a low bank, which extends down the hillside and which then returns S. as a slight scarp, is perhaps an outer and later enclosure (RAF VAP CPE/UK/1994, 1156–7; CUAP, AHG43).

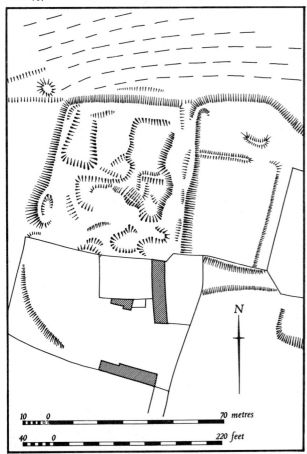

Fig. 81   HELLIDON   (1) Site of manor house

(2) CULTIVATION REMAINS. The common fields of the parish were enclosed by an Act of Parliament of 1774 (NRO, Enclosure Map, *c.* 1775). Immediately before that date there were five large open fields surrounding the village. To the W. lay Hill Field, to the N.W. Lower Field and Further Field, to the N.E. Upper Field, and to the S. and S.E. Attle Field. On an earlier map of 1726 (NRO) Hill Field is called Middle Field and Attle Field is Short Attle Field. Ridge-and-furrow of these fields exists on the ground or can be traced on air photographs over much of the parish although it is markedly absent on the very steep slopes within and to the S. of the village, for example on Little Down Hill (SP 521578). Elsewhere it is mainly arranged in rectangular interlocked furlongs, often of reversed-S form. On the higher flat ground the furlongs run to the edges of the steep-sided valleys cut into the hillsides and rarely extend down the slopes (RAF VAP CPE/UK/1994, 1153–8, 1279–85).

38 HOLDENBY

(OS 1:10000 [a] SP 66 NE, [b] SP 76 NW)

The parish, covering nearly 770 hectares, lies across an E.–W. ridge of Northampton Sand largely overlaid by Boulder Clay. From the top of the ridge which is between 115 m. and 145 m. above OD the land slopes N. and S. into the valleys of two small E.-flowing streams 85 m.–90 m. above OD which mark the parish boundaries. These valleys are cut into the underlying Upper Lias Clay, though this also is overlaid by Boulder Clay in some places.

Only one pre-medieval site (1) is known from the parish and though the large Saxon cemetery (2) is of some importance the main interest lies in the earthworks which reflect the great changes wrought in the landscape of Holdenby in the late 16th century. Up to that time the village of Holdenby appears to have been made up of two separate nuclei and was surrounded by its common fields. Between 1575 and 1587 Sir Christopher Hatton, who later became Lord Chancellor, built the famous Holdenby House and constructed the remarkable gardens around it (4), adding a large deer park after he had enclosed the common fields. He also built at least one new pond in the parish (6). At the same time he appears to have demolished both parts of the medieval settlement (3) and to have built a new village on one of the original sites, to a plan that was an integral part of the design of the house and garden.

PREHISTORIC

[b](1) IRON AGE SETTLEMENT (?) (SP 703686), in the N.E. of the parish on clay at 104 m. above OD. Sherds of pottery, probably of Iron Age date, were found in 1970 (*BNFAS*, 5 (1971), 3; NM).

MEDIEVAL AND LATER

a(2) SAXON CEMETERY (SP 695671), on Coney Hill, S. of
the village on clays and Northampton Sand at about
110 m. above OD.

Finds were made on a number of occasions between
1862 and 1909. These comprised at least thirty skeletons,
some with grave goods and some without, and also the
crushed remains of a cinerary urn containing burnt bone
and a broken hairpin. The burials had no uniform
orientation. The objects accompanying the skeletons
included urns, parts of spears and shields, knives, pins,

bronze cruciform fibulae, iron penannular brooches, two
saucer brooches, and a large square-headed brooch
probably of early 7th-century date. There were also clasps,
tweezers, fragments of ivory and beads of glass, amber and
earthenware (Meaney, *Gazetteer* (1964), 190; E. A.
Hartshorne, *Memorials of Holdenby* (1868), 6–7; VCH
Northants., I (1902), 246–7; *Northants. Natur. Hist. Soc. and
FC*, (1909), 91–99; *J. Northants. Mus. and Art Gal.*, 6
(1969), 40; J. N. L. Myres, *Anglo-Saxon Pottery and the
Settlement of England* (1969), Fig. 12, no. 799 and Fig. 15,
no. 797).

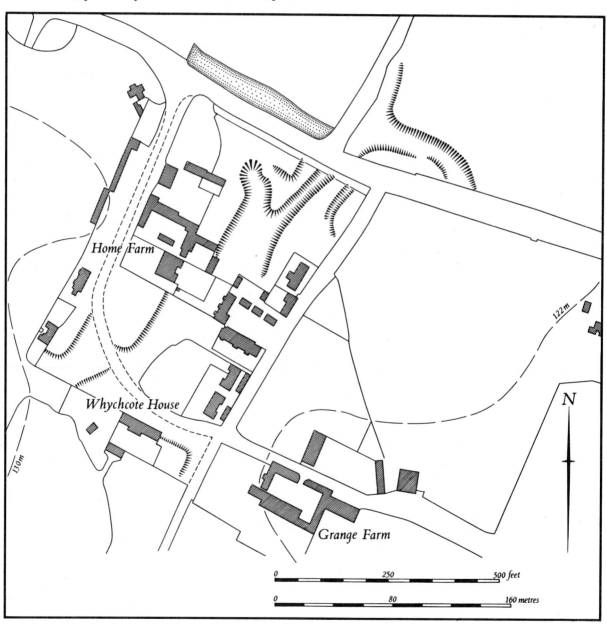

Fig. 82   HOLDENBY   (3) Deserted village

ᵃ(3) DESERTED VILLAGES OF HOLDENBY (around SP 692675 and 697679; Figs. 82 and 83; Plates 16, 17 and 18), lie in two separate places. One is 400 m. S.W. of the present village, around the medieval parish church on the N. side of a small S.E.-flowing stream, on glacial sands and gravels and Jurassic Clay, at 115 m. above OD. The other lies immediately N.E. of the present village on Boulder Clay at 122 m. above OD.

The history of Holdenby is almost unknown. The name was first recorded in 1086, but its pure Scandinavian etymology indicates an earlier beginning (PN *Northants.*, 85). Domesday Book listed one manor of Holdenby with a recorded population of 14 and held by the Count of Mortain. However there was another manor held by the Count of Mortain, also with a recorded population of 14, listed as 'Aldenestone' and this has been plausibly identified as part of Holdenby (VCH *Northants.*, I (1902), 328–9, 378). If this theory is correct it may be that Holdenby was at that time two physically separate settlements, one around the church and the other near the site of the present village.

The next indication of the size of the village is not until 1523 when its inhabitants paid £4 6s. tax (PRO, E179/155/161). This amount is larger than that for many other villages in the area such as Guilsborough, East Haddon and Harlestone and suggests that Holdenby was still a flourishing community. A little before 1580 Sir Christopher Hatton started work on the great house and the laying out of the gardens there (4). On the earliest map of Holdenby of 1580 (NRO; Plates 16 and 18) Holdenby House and its gardens are shown, apparently still incomplete. By then the medieval church stood isolated; in a small paddock to the S. of it ('a' on plan) are the words 'here stode ye manor howse'. To the N.E. of Holdenby House, on or near the site of the present village, lay the other part of Holdenby consisting of a small group of about ten buildings arranged around the S. end of a roughly triangular green. By 1587 (map in NRO; Plates 17 and 18) Hatton had completed his house and gardens. The church still stood isolated but the other part of the village had been completely rebuilt. The old green had been replaced by a large rectangular open area to the S.E. with five houses along its N. side. The whole plan was an integral part of the house and garden layout. This evidence suggests that both the medieval villages of Holdenby existed until just before 1580, and that when Hatton started work on his house and gardens he first removed the village around the church and later cleared and rebuilt the village to the N.E. of the house. Some support for this comes from an undated cutting in the Northampton Public Library saying that the village around the church was demolished in 1575 when construction on the house and gardens started.

In 1673 only nine householders paid the Hearth Tax (PRO, E179/254/14) but Bridges, writing in about 1720, said that there were 17 houses in the village (J. Bridges, *Hist. of Northants.*, I (1791), 525). A map of 1762 (NRO) shows a situation similar to that of 1587, with eight houses along the N. side of the new green as well as the present Grange Farm to the S.E. and another house to the S. By 1842 (NRO, Tithe Map) a pair of cottages had been built on the W. side. In the late 19th century seven other estate cottages were erected, four within the green itself and the rest on a new road laid out from the N.E. corner of the green.

Little remains of the part of Holdenby village which was around the church and presumably such earthworks or indeed houses as existed by the late 16th century were destroyed by the garden construction. Certainly by 1580 the area S. and E. of the church was already 'The Orchard', bounded by a wooden fence; by 1587 ponds had been constructed within the orchard and the old manor house site ('a' on plan) appears to have had some form of garden laid out over it. Some other earthworks remain on the ground, however, in the area W. and S.W. of the church, and may have been associated with the earlier village. The best preserved are in the valley bottom to the S.W. ('b' on plan) where there are three ponds. The north-westernmost (not on plan) is a small oval embanked pond 1.5 m. deep. The middle one is much larger, roughly rectangular and cut back into the valley side with a large bank between it and the stream. At its N.W. end it turns and fades into a marshy area, the source of the water which once filled it. Below this pond and separated from it by a broad dam 2 m. high there is a small rectangular depression, again cut back into the hillside on the N.E. and with a bank on the S.E. From this pond a broad hollow-way extends up the hillside towards the old manor house site where, at its N.E. end, it is blocked by the ditch of the 1580 orchard. Just to the W. of this point there is a low mound only 0.25 m. high ('c' on plan). To the N. another shallow hollow-way, also blocked by the orchard ditch, runs W. down the hillside and then turns N.E. It can be traced for about 110 m. until it fades out just before it reaches the lower terrace of the garden, W. of the church. From near the end of the latter hollow-way another ditch or hollow-way can be traced N.W. across the park, passing between ridge-and-furrow. On the N. of this ditch, near the garden boundary, at least two low mutilated scarps are visible ('d' on plan) which appear to pre-date the gardens.

Of the original layout of the upper part of Holdenby village cleared and rebuilt by Hatton only a few fragments remain as the E. part of the later village lies across most of it (Fig. 82). In the S. corner of the present green, immediately E. of Whychcote House, is a low platform which may be the site of the southernmost house shown on the 1580 map and a degraded scarp further N.E. appears to coincide with a property boundary on the same map. More definite remains of the E. end of the village lie further N.E., on either side of the Church Brampton–East Haddon road. To the S. of the road the N. end of the earlier green appears as a scarp 1.5 m. high. Parts of the S. side are visible and so is part of the track, now a short length of hollow-way, which led to Spratton. N. of the modern road and now partly destroyed by ploughing are fragments of two other hollow-ways; one is another part of the Spratton track and the other is the N. part of the track to Church Brampton.

[a](4) GARDEN REMAINS (SP 693676; Fig. 83; Plates 16, 17 and 18), lie immediately S. and S.E. of Holdenby House on the top and the S.W.-facing slopes of a steep hillside, on Boulder Clay and Northampton Sand between 100 m. and 130 m. above OD. The remains are amongst the most impressive and important of their period in the county.

In medieval times there appear to have been two separate villages of Holdenby, one at the bottom of the hillside around the now isolated church and one on the hilltop to the N.E. on the site of the present estate village (3). By the church was the medieval manor house of Holdenby where Christopher Hatton, whose family had held Holdenby since at least the 13th century, was born in 1540. Hatton moved into royal circles at the age of 21 and through the favour of the Queen rose rapidly. He was made one of the Queen's Gentlemen Pensioners in 1564 and became Vice Chamberlain and was knighted in 1578. From 1587 until his death in 1591 he was Lord Chancellor.

At some time before 1579 Sir Christopher Hatton started to build Holdenby House, on a new site on the hilltop above the church. Arranged around two large internal courts, it was one of the largest mansions built in England in the 16th century. The house was finished in 1583 but the great gardens which were laid out to the S.W. of it were not completed until at least 1587. On Hatton's death the house and the estates passed to his nephew Sir William Newport who took the name of Hatton but in 1607 James I bought Holdenby and it was held by the Crown until 1651. During this period further additions may have been made to the gardens. It was to Holdenby that Charles I came as a prisoner in 1646. In 1651, after it had been seized by Parliament, it was bought by Adam Baynes, Captain in the Parliamentary Army, who demolished the house except for part of the offices which he turned into a small hall; the gardens were apparently abandoned at that time. After the Restoration Holdenby was returned to the Crown and then sold. The house was finally rebuilt between 1873 and 1875, slightly to the N. of the original one.

Though Hatton's original house was the feature that excited most comment during its existence the gardens also were much admired. Norden (*Speculi Britannia* (1720), 49–50) writing in 1610 said '... with what industrye and toyle of man, the Garden hath bene raised, levelled, and formed out of a most craggye and unfitable Grounde now framed a most pleasante, sweete, and princely Place with divers walks, manie ascendings and descendings replenished also with manie delightfull trees of Fruit, artificially composed Arbors ...'. The Commissioners who surveyed the estate in 1651 (E. St John Brooks, *Sir Christopher Hatton* (1946), 158) described it as 'a pleasant, spacious and fair garden adorned with several long walks,

mounts, arbours and seats, with curious delightful knots and planted with fruit trees'. They also mention orchards, fishponds, bowling alleys, spinneys planted with ash and 'delightful' walks.

As a result of the early demolition of the original house and the fact that the 19th-century house and garden have hardly touched the original gardens, the earthworks of the latter have remained almost as they were in 1651. The date and development of many details can be elucidated from two fine maps of 1580 and 1587 made during the construction of the garden, as well as from a later Estate Map of 1762 and the Tithe Map of 1842 (all in NRO).

Sir Christopher Hatton's house (shown in outline stipple on plan) lay on the hilltop and the main garden, made up of three roughly rectangular sections, was placed symmetrically on the S. side of the house, across the steep valley side. The central piece, which lay immediately S. of the house, was a level flower garden 95 m. by 70 m. formed by the dumping of huge quantities of earth outwards into the valley to create a massive raised terrace ending in a scarp 5 m. high. This terrace is shown on both the 1580 and 1587 maps, occupied by an elaborate knot garden made up of four flower beds, one in each corner, of basically rectangular shape but with the inner corner cut by a central circular feature. Paths ran between the beds. The 1587 map also shows a schematic knot-design in each of the flower beds. The N. half of this overall design still survives under grass. The central feature is a circular mound some 30 m. in diam. and only 20 cm. high with, on its N. side, two curving paths which meet and extend N. towards the house and in the corners two of the original flower beds, now delimited by scarps about 25 cm. high. Along the E. and W. sides of this garden there are slightly raised walks, again only some 25 cm. high; the E. one is complete, but the W. one has been destroyed at its S. end. The N. side of the garden is bounded by a 19th-century ha-ha. This level terraced garden falls away steeply to two flanking rectangular areas where what was probably the natural slope has been made into flights of low terraces. On the W. seven terraces are each bounded by a scarp about 1 m. high. The upper one is probably 19th-century in date; the next has been altered by having a 19th-century wall inserted into it but was probably once the highest of the 16th-century terraces. The five terraces below are all original. At their W. ends they all run into a terrace-walk 1.5 m. high which bounds this side of the garden; a small bulbous projection from the walk, across one of the terraces, was probably the site of an arbour, though neither the 1580 nor the 1587 map shows anything here. At their E. ends the five terraces all turn uphill and fade out, having a sloping walk-way between them and the scarped edge of the central knot garden. Below the last terrace is a large rectangular pond 2 m. deep, cut into the hillside and bounded on the S. by a wide raised terrace which is a continuation of the W. terrace-walk. This pond is shown on the 1587 map, but not on the 1580 where its position is

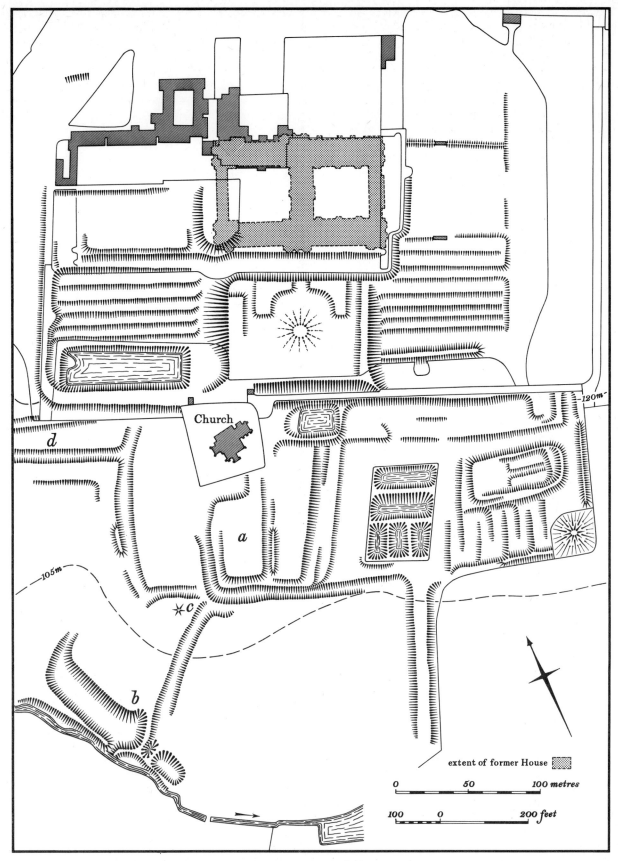

Church

d

a

c

b

120m

105m

extent of former House

0   50   100 metres

100   0   200 feet

Fig. 83   HOLDENBY   (4) Garden remains

occupied by another terrace, suggesting a change of intention by Hatton during the construction.

The area E. of the central knot garden is also terraced, in this case into seven narrow steps each bounded by a scarp 0.5 m.–0.75 m. high. At their W. ends they run into the scarped edge of the central garden, though the upper one has been damaged by the 19th-century ha-ha, and their E. ends run out onto a low scarp which edges this side of the gardens. Below the lowest terrace is a long narrow area bounded on the S. by a raised terrace-walk 1 m. high. On the 1580 map all these terraces are shown, and are called 'ye Rosaries', but on the 1587 map the area between the lowest terrace and the terrace-walk is called The Bowling Alley.

To the W. of the original house, on the gently sloping ground above the W. terraced garden, the 1580 map shows a rectangular garden divided into nine square flower beds intersected by walks. By 1587 these gardens seem already to have been abandoned, for the area is shown as occupied by rows of trees. Both maps show a building in the centre of the W. side, probably the conduit head to which water was carried along an open ditch across the adjacent fields before being passed into the gardens. The S. part of the area is occupied today by a 19th-century lawn and shrubbery as well as a modern tennis court, while the N. part is the kitchen garden of the present house. Only a short scarp along the W. side survives to mark the original edge of the garden here; another scarp along the E. side is a later addition. There is no trace of the conduit head though part of the conduit ditch still exists in the park to the W., cutting across earlier ridge-and-furrow.

On the E. side of the existing house, N. of the E. terraced garden, is a wide level pasture field. In 1580 the S. half of this was a square walled area called The Base Court fronting the main E. entrance to the house. By 1587 the base court had been entirely remodelled; it remained walled, but a central drive extended across it from the house entrance to the centre of the E. side where stood a large gatehouse. In front of the house there was another smaller building, also perhaps a gatehouse. In the centre of the N. and S. sides of the court were two archways, the S. one giving access to the terraced garden, the N. one to the newly laid out village and its rectangular 'green' (see (3) above). Today the boundaries on three sides of this base court survive though the W. edge is now occupied by a 19th-century ha-ha. On the E. is a low mutilated scarp, broken in the centre where the original gatehouse stood. No trace remains of the latter but it is illustrated in detail by John Thorpe (*Walpole Soc.*, 40 (1966), Plate 84). The N. side of the court is marked by a low bank only 0.25 m. high which is clearly the foundations of the original stone wall. On the S. the edge is marked by two low scarps. The original impressive archways still survive, bearing the date 1583.

Beyond the base court to the E. lay, in 1580, a very large rectangular area called The Green, across which ran the main approach drive to the house. By 1587 this had been greatly extended in size and walled on its W. side. In its

S.W. corner a large three-storey building called a banqueting house and illustrated in detail by John Thorpe (*Walpole Soc.*, op. cit.) had been erected, trees had been planted just within the W. side and a rectangular pond dug in the N.E. corner. The site of the banqueting hall is now a shrubbery and apart from some rather uneven ground no trace remains. The site of the pond, within Ash Plantation, S.E. of Grange Farm (SP697676), is still marked by a rectangular depression much altered by a modern sewage plant. The rest of the area is a modern pasture field, devoid of remains.

The features described above were the main gardens of Hatton's house, but there was also another part which appears to have been included in them at an early date, namely a long rectangular piece of land below the main garden and asymmetrically placed to it, with the medieval church in the N.W. corner. In 1580 this was bounded by a wooden fence planted with trees and called 'the orchard'; there was a pond within it, just E. of the church. In the S.W. corner, S. of the church, the 1580 map states 'here stode ye manor howse', thus giving the location of the earlier medieval manor house of Holdenby (see (3) above). By 1587 this part of the garden had been much altered. The manor house site is shown in pecked lines, with a rectangular layout, perhaps a knot garden. The earlier pond is shown larger and five other rectangular ponds, arranged in a square, lie near the centre. In the S.E. corner a polygonal feature is shown which is probably the existing mount. All these features have survived. The boundary of the gardens now exists as a ditch on the W. and most of the S. side, and as a low bank on the rest of the S. and all of the E. side. The pond near the church is still a large rectangular depression raised 2 m. high above the land to the S.E., while the five ponds in the centre are the same as they were in 1587. The mount in the S.E. corner is a large circular mound, 4.5 m. high, but badly disturbed by a fox earth.

This area also contains a number of other features which do not appear on the 1587 map and thus presumably post-date it. These may relate to the period in the early 17th century when Holdenby was held by the Crown, when the gardens were perhaps improved. They include two parallel terraces S.E. of the church which run the width of the garden and may be the remains of further terraced walks or flower beds. On the N. side of the garden, E. of the large pond, is a battered scarp which may be the N. edge of an old trackway. However the most interesting of these additional features lie E. of the group of five ponds and W. of the mount. Here there are two conjoined but distinct groups of earthworks. To the W. of the mount and bounded on the N. and S. by low scarps is a series of eight terraces on a low W.-facing slope. These terraces fade out at one end, to N. and S. alternately, producing a zig-zag path leading from the ponds up the hill to the mount. Immediately N. of these is a roughly rectangular area cut back into the hillside, and bounded by banks or scarps. It slopes W. and its higher E. end is almost semicircular. Its interior is divided into three parts by low scarps only 20 cm. high, presumabably the boundaries of flower beds. From near the centre of the S. side of this additional group of gardens a broad raised terrace or bank extends S.S.W. across the adjacent field leading towards a pond which already existed in 1580. The purpose of this bank is unknown but it was probably an access-way from the garden into the park (*Northants. P. and P.*, 5 (1977), 392–5: N. Pevsner, *Northamptonshire* (1961), 253–4; M. W. Beresford and J. K. S. St Joseph, *Medieval England: An Aerial Survey* (1958), 58–60; J. Bridges, *Hist. of Northants.*, I (1791), 525; RAF VAP CPE/UK/1994, 2366–7).

^a(5) DEER PARK (centred SP 695670; Plates 16 and 17), lies S. and S.E. of Holdenby House, on rolling clayland, between 120 m. and 135 m. above OD. The park is a late one, created by Sir Christopher Hatton between 1580 and 1587 as part of his work at Holdenby which also included the building of Holdenby House, the laying out of its gardens (4) and the removal and rebuilding of Holdenby village (3). It is not shown on the map of 1580 (NRO; Plate 16) when, apparently, the common fields of the parish still existed but is depicted on the map of 1587 (NRO; Plate 17), bounded by a continuous wooden fence and with drawings of deer and rabbits within it. It covered some 250 hectares, almost one third of the whole parish. The deer park probably fell into disuse after 1651 when the house was demolished and had certainly been abandoned by 1762 (NRO, Estate Map).

Except for one small part, all of the perimeter shown on the 1587 map still exists as a hedge-line and can be traced from the N.E. corner of Holdenby village (SP 697679) and along the S. side of the road to Church Brampton as far as the parish boundary (SP 706675). It then followed the parish boundary S. to the S.E. corner of Holdenby parish (SP 704661) where it turned W. again along the parish boundary for some 400 m. (to SP 701661). At this point the parish boundary turns S. and then runs W. along the stream, but the deer park pale, still a modern hedge-bank, carried straight on to the W., parallel to and just N. of the stream. At Blackthorn Spinney (SP 692662) the boundary swung N. in a broad curve until it met the small S.E.-flowing stream a little to the S.W. of Holdenby church (SP 689674). Along this section, although the bank is little more than a normal hedge-bank, there is on the E. side a steep-sided ditch 4 m. wide and 1 m. deep. Beyond the stream the boundary runs N.E. for nearly 200 m. across the 19th-century landscaped park. Here it is a broad open ditch some 12 m. wide and 1.5 m. deep with ridge-and-furrow parallel to it on the W. This may in fact be an earlier feature re-used as the park boundary. The ditch then makes a right-angle turn and runs to a point just short of the S.W. corner of the gardens of Holdenby House where it fades out. From there the park boundary followed the S. edge of the W. part of the main gardens, the W. side of the churchyard, the S.W., S. and E. sides of the lower part of the gardens, and the edge of the large area known as

The Green in 1587; it then re-joined the Brampton road.

The interior of the park is entirely covered by ridge-and-furrow of the former common fields which it replaced, with the exception of a long narrow strip of land near the W. side, running N.E.–S.W., which was called Fowlham Meadow in 1587 (M. W. Beresford and J. K. S. St Joseph, *Medieval England: An Aerial Survey* (1958), 60).

^a(6) DAM (SP 699684; Plate 17), lies across the valley of a small E.-flowing stream in the N. of the parish, on Upper Lias Clay at 100 m. above OD. The present road from Holdenby to Spratton runs along the top of the dam and has presumably much altered it. It is some 80 m. long with a maximum height of 2.5 m. and is marked as an embankment on the OS 1:2500 map (SP 6968). On the parish map of 1580 (NRO) nothing is shown at this point, but on the 1587 map (NRO) the dam is depicted with a triangular pond behind it and is therefore presumably part of the work carried out in the parish at that time by Sir Christopher Hatton.

(7) CULTIVATION REMAINS (Plates 16 and 17). The enclosure of the common fields of Holdenby took place between 1584 and 1587 and was therefore carried out by Sir Christopher Hatton as part of his extensive work there. On a map of 1580 (NRO) four open fields are shown. Wood Field occupies the S.E. of the parish, and Longlande Field the S.W., separated from the former by a long narrow piece of land called Fowlham Meadow. The whole of the N. part of the parish, N. of the East Haddon–Brampton road was North Field, and in the W. there was a small Parke Field. In 1584 these fields probably still existed for on a map of Church Brampton of that date (NRO) the land beyond the Brampton parish boundary, in the N.E. corner of Holdenby parish, is marked as Holdenby North Field. However a map of 1587 (NRO) shows that by that date the deer park (5) had been created covering the whole of the former Wood Field, about a quarter of the former Parke and Longlande Fields and a small part of the North Field. The remaining area of the parish had been divided into enclosed fields.

Ridge-and-furrow of these fields remains on the ground or can be traced on air photographs over wide areas of the parish. The pattern for Longlande Field is complete and for Parke Field is virtually so. The area of Fowlham Meadow is devoid of ridge-and-furrow, but most of the furlongs in Wood Field are visible. In contrast little ridge-and-furrow can be seen in North Field except on its S. and S.W. parts.

In the 19th-century parkland W. of Holdenby House the ridge-and-furrow is exceptionally well preserved and consists of long end-on furlongs, sweeping down the valley side. Elsewhere it is mainly ploughed out but can be seen on air photographs arranged in broad interlocked furlongs up to 450 m. long with some large former headlands still surviving as broad ridges up to 12 m. wide and 0.25 m. high and as much as 600 m. long (e.g. at SP 685675; RAF VAP CPE/UK/1994, 2364–9, 4257–61, 4367–72).

39 HOLLOWELL

(OS 1:10000 [a] SP 67 SE, [b] SP 66 NE, [c] SP 77 SW,
[d] SP 76 NW)

The parish, which now covers about 750 hectares, has undergone considerable modern alteration. It is partly made up of two land units each of which was originally centred on a medieval settlement (Fig. 14). Most of the N. part was the land of the village of Hollowell in the medieval period, and this was once part of Guilsborough parish (NRO, Tithe Map of Hollowell, 1842). In the S. was the land of the hamlet of Teeton, once part of Ravensthorpe parish (NRO, Map of Teeton, 1831 and Tithe Map of Teeton, 1842). The N.W. part of the parish was also formerly part of Ravensthorpe though there was a small detached part of Hollowell within the latter parish. The present parish lies across the valley of two small S.E.-flowing streams which have cut deeply into the underlying Upper Lias Clay leaving high, flat-topped interfluves capped with Northampton Sand between 85 m. and 165 m. above OD. Little has been recorded in the parish, apart from the Roman sites (2–5) which were discovered by recent field-walking.

PREHISTORIC AND ROMAN

[a](1) FLINT-WORKING SITE (SP 681718), W. of the village, on Northampton Sand at 150 m. above OD. Large quantities of waste flakes have been found over an area of 3 hectares (inf. A. E. Brown).

[ab](2) IRON AGE AND ROMAN SETTLEMENT (centred SP 692700), around Teeton Grange, on Northampton Sand, at about 105 m. above OD. Roman pottery, including samian, has been found during field-walking in the two fields immediately N.W. and S.E. of the Grange. Subsequent work has revealed some Iron Age pottery in the same area (BNFAS, 4 (1970), 9; Northants. Archaeol., 10 (1975), 163; 12 (1977), 215). Air photographs (in NMR) indicate that the whole area around Teeton Grange has cropmarks on it. These are very indistinct and show no coherent features but cover an area of some 17 hectares.

[a](3) ROMAN SETTLEMENT (SP 689706), N. of Teeton Lodge, on Northampton Sand at 140 m. above OD. Large quantities of Roman pottery have been found over an area of 2 hectares (Northants. Archaeol., 12 (1977), 215).

[a](4) ROMAN SETTLEMENT (centred SP 695707), N. of Teeton Hall, on Northampton Sand at about 120 m. above OD. Roman pottery has been found over an area of about 1.5 hectares. Two sherds of early Saxon pottery are recorded from the site (Northants. Archaeol., 10 (1975), 163).

[a](5) ROMAN SETTLEMENT (SP 690717), S. of the village, on Northampton Sand at 125 m. above OD. Large quantities of Roman pottery have been found here in two marked concentrations a few metres apart (Northants. Archaeol., 12

(1977), 212). A thin scatter of Roman sherds has also been noted all over this part of the parish extending S. as far as (2) and (3).

MEDIEVAL AND LATER

[a](6) PILLOW MOUND (SP 69217065), lies W. of Teeton, on Northampton Sand at 130 m. above OD. It is rectangular, 12 m. by 9 m. and 1 m. high, orientated N.E.–S.W. and with a flat top. There is no trace of a ditch in the present arable land which surrounds it. It has been much disturbed by rabbits and no date or purpose can be assigned to it; it is not shown on the 1831 map of Teeton (NRO).

(7) CULTIVATION REMAINS. Both Hollowell and Teeton had their own common field systems in medieval times. The common fields of Hollowell were enclosed by an Act of Parliament of 1774. Very little ridge-and-furrow survives on the ground or can be traced on air photographs, largely as a result of later cultivation and because Northampton Sand does not show clear cropmarks of former cultivation. To the S.E. of Hollowell village, on the sides of the clay-lined valley, is a broad area of ridge-and-furrow mainly running across the slopes in end-on furlongs, although where it is adapted to the occasional spurs the furlongs become interlocked (e.g. SP 696722). To the N. of the village, in the same valley, the sides of Hollowell Reservoir are edged with ridge-and-furrow. Elsewhere, on the Northampton Sand area, ridge-and-furrow has survived only in one field left as pasture after 19th-century stone-quarrying (SP 690710).

The common fields of Teeton were enclosed by private agreement in 1590. Ridge-and-furrow survives on the ground or can be traced on air photographs in a few places

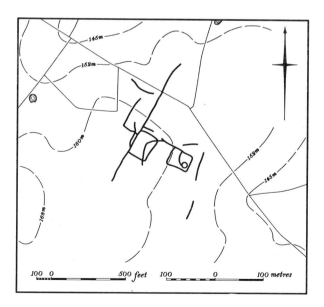

Fig. 84   KELMARSH   (3) Cropmarks

N.E. of the village (SP 698708) and along the S. boundary of the parish (SP 701702). The furlongs all run across the contours (RAF VAP CPE/UK/1994, 1370–3, 1464–8).

40 KELMARSH

(OS 1:10000 [a] SP 78 SW, [b] SP 78 SE, [c] SP 77 NW,
[d] SP 77 NE)

The L-shaped parish covers about 1145 hectares and lies across the upper reaches of the R. Ise; an E.-flowing tributary stream forms the N. boundary. The higher ground in the S. and W. and on the spur between the two streams is covered by Boulder Clay rising to a maximum height of 180 m. above OD. Upper Lias Clay is revealed along the lower slopes, and the valley bottoms at about 115 m. above OD are floored by wide areas of river gravel and alluvium. The main monument is the deserted village of Kelmarsh (14), but little is known about the history of the extensive earthworks.

PREHISTORIC AND ROMAN

[a](1) ENCLOSURE (SP 732808), N.W. of Lodge Ground Spinney, on Boulder Clay at 130 m. above OD. Air photographs (in NMR) show all but the S.W. side of an apparently rectangular enclosure at least 50 m. across (*Northants. Archaeol.*, 9 (1974), 114).

[a](2) ENCLOSURE AND DITCH (SP 725813), S. of Kelmarsh Field Farm, on Upper Lias Clay at 137 m. above OD. Air Photographs (in NMR) show, rather indistinctly, what may be the N. part of a sub-rectangular enclosure at least 60 m. across, with a linear ditch extending for at least 200 m. from its N.W. corner (*Northants. Archaeol.*, 9 (1974), 114).

[c](3) ENCLOSURES (SP 719793; Fig. 84), lie in the W. of the parish, on Northampton Sand and Upper Lias Clay, at 160 m. above OD. Air photographs (in NMR) show cropmarks of at least two rectangular enclosures, one with a circular feature in its S.E. corner. Other ditches are also visible.

[a](4) ROMAN SETTLEMENT (?) (SP 726806), 500 m. S. of (2), on Boulder Clay at 145 m. above OD. A scatter of Roman pottery has been found here (*Northants. Archaeol.*, 11 (1976), 192).

[a](5) ROMAN SETTLEMENT (?) (SP 732803), 500 m. S.E. of (4), on river gravel at 122 m. above OD. A scatter of Roman pottery has been found in the area (*Northants. Archaeol.*, 11 (1976), 192).

[d](6) ROMAN SETTLEMENT (SP 750796), S. and S.E. of New Covert, in the E. of the parish, on Northampton Sand and Upper Lias Clay between 135 m. and 150 m. above OD. Air photographs (in NMR) show, very indistinctly, a large area of cropmarks covering some 10 hectares. It is not possible to interpret the features clearly, not only because there are discrepancies between the available air photographs but also because there is extensive frost-wedging in the area. The site appears to consist of a number of conjoined rectangular enclosures, possibly with a ditched trackway passing between them. From the S.W. part of the site (SP 748796) Roman pottery has been found (*Northants. Archaeol.*, 11 (1976), 192; for Saxon pottery from this site, see (12) below).

[c](7) ROMAN SETTLEMENT (?) (SP 745793), 500 m. S.W. of (6) on Boulder Clay at 152 m. above OD. Roman pottery has been found and air photographs (not seen by RCHM) are said to show cropmarks of a settlement (*Northants. Archaeol.*, 11 (1976), 192; 12 (1977), 230; for Saxon finds from this site, see (13)).

[c](8) ROMAN SETTLEMENT (?) (SP 744790), 300 m. S.S.W. of (7) on Upper Lias Clay at 145 m. above OD. A scatter of Roman pottery has been found (*Northants. Archaeol.*, 12 (1977), 212).

[c](9) ROMAN SETTLEMENT (SP 723788), S.W. of the village, on Boulder Clay and Upper Lias Clay between 135 m. and 145 m. above OD. Air photographs (in NMR) show, rather indistinctly, a large area of cropmarks covering some 8 hectares. They include overlapping and conjoined rectangular enclosures, with other linear features intersecting them. Roman pottery has been found on the N. edge of the site (SP 720803) and to the W. (SP 722788; *Northants. Archaeol.*, 11 (1976), 192; 12 (1977), 212).

[a](10) ROMAN SETTLEMENT (?) (SP 734806), in the N.E. of the parish, on Boulder Clay at 123 m. above OD. Roman sherds have been noted (*Northants. Archaeol.*, 12 (1977), 212).

[a](11) ROMAN SETTLEMENT (?) (SP 733815), in the N. of the parish on Upper Lias Clay at 135 m. above OD. A scatter of Roman pottery has been discovered (*Northants. Archaeol.*, 12 (1977), 212).

MEDIEVAL AND LATER

[d](12) SAXON SETTLEMENT (?) (SP 750796), found on the Roman settlement (6). Early Saxon pottery has been discovered (*Northants. Archaeol.*, 11 (1976), 192).

[c](13) SAXON SETTLEMENT (?) (SP 745793), found on the Roman settlement (7). Early Saxon pottery has been discovered (*Northants. Archaeol.*, 11 (1976), 192).

[c](14) DESERTED VILLAGE OF KELMARSH (SP 743794; Fig. 85), lies N. and N.W. of the present estate village, around and within the park of Kelmarsh Hall, on Upper Lias Clay, between 120 m. and 145 m. above OD. The remains of the village are both extensive and well preserved, but its history and the date of desertion are not known.

Kelmarsh is first mentioned by name in Domesday Book but no total recorded population is given there. At that time it was divided into two holdings, one of which was part of the royal manor of Rothwell; the other was a small manor held by William Pevrel, with a recorded population of nine (VCH *Northants.*, II (1906), 306, 338). In 1377, 84 people over the age of 14 paid the Poll Tax, indicating a sizable community (PRO, E179/155/28). In 1674, 26 householders paid the Hearth Tax, a figure which does not suggest a major drop in population (PRO, E179/254/14). Bridges (*Hist. of Northants.*, II (1791), 39) records that in about 1720 there were 23 families living in the village, and the population of the parish in 1801 was 131. There is no clear documentary indication of depopulation at Kelmarsh at any period and, though some clearance may have taken place in 1727–32 when the present hall replaced the older manor house of around 1600, it is likely that much of the abandonment had already taken place before then. The modern village lies S.E. of the hall and is made up largely of 19th-century estate houses.

The remains fall into three main blocks. To the S.W. of the hall, N. of and around the isolated church, is a large area of earthworks consisting mainly of sub-rectangular closes or platforms bounded by low scarps and banks or by shallow ditches. Some appear to be arranged around the church along the existing road to Clipston; the others are on either side of a broad hollow-way to the N. which runs almost parallel to the present road. This hollow-way is cut at right-angles by a broad, deep ditch running N.–S. ('a' on plan). To the W. of this ditch the village earthworks are well preserved but to the E. only slight fragments remain. It appears that the ditch is a late feature bounding the W. edge of an area which has been ploughed and returned to parkland in recent times. It is possible that this was done in the 18th century when the hall was built and the park created.

The second main area of earthworks lies E. of the hall, E. and N. of Hall Farm. These appear to be the rather mutilated remains of former houses and closes lying along the existing Harborough Road with, behind them to the E., a roughly trapezoidal ditched area divided into paddocks. It is possible that these remains are of two separate phases though the exact relationship is not clear. At the N. corner ('b' on plan) is a triangular feature, bounded by banks up to 1.5 m. high broken by several gaps. This may be a mutilated fishpond. It is unlikely to be a 17th-century Civil War fortification as has sometimes been claimed (see (16) below).

The third part of the site lies W. and N. of Wilderness Farm and consists of a number of long closes bounded by ditches and scarps extending E. to the R. Ise. These remains are extremely fragmentary but may be sites of abandoned houses and gardens.

To the N. of the village earthworks, N. of the artificial lake of Kelmarsh Hall, air photographs show traces of ploughed out enclosures (not shown on plan). These may be associated with the former village.

A small excavation was carried out in 1961 on a building platform N. of the church. This produced pottery from the 11th century, including Stamford Ware, with smaller quantities of 13th and 14th-century sherds. Two occupation layers were noted, the lower with post-holes for a timber building, the upper with stake-holes of light sheds dating from the 16th to the 18th centuries (DOE *Arch. Excavations 1971* (1972), 33; DMVRG *Annual Rep.*, 18 (1971), 17; RAF VAP 106G/UK/636, 3188–9; CUAP, SB48–51, AEV30–31, AHE85–90, AWV12–14, BQD25–32, 35, VAP76).

c(15) DAM (SP 731792; Fig. 85), lies across the valley of the R. Ise, S. of the Clipston road, on alluvium and Upper Lias Clay at 125 above OD. It consists of a large earthen bank up to 2 m. high, spanning the narrow valley, with a modern break through which the river now flows. It presumably ponded back a considerable lake and may have been the site of a medieval fishpond or watermill.

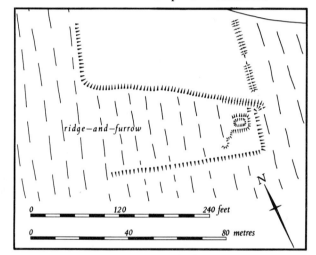

Fig. 86   KELMARSH   (17) Site of sheep-fold

a(16) EARTHWORKS (SP 728801; Plate 12), lay in the bottom of a valley N.W. of Kelmarsh Hall, on alluvium at 125 m. above OD. They consisted of a small rectangular area with an elongated triangular one immediately to the S., bounded by earthen banks up to 1.5 m. high in which there were a number of gaps. In general appearance they were very similar to the surviving earthworks at the N. end of the deserted village (14) ('b' on plan). The site was completely levelled in 1968, but before destruction an excavation was carried out, on the supposition that the remains represented the late 16th or earlier 17th-century manor house of Kelmarsh which is traditionally said to have stood there. The excavation showed that the banks were made from the underlying clay and in parts were revetted in stone. No finds or dating evidence was recovered and the excavator, while rejecting the idea that the site was that of the manor house, concluded that it was a 17th-century Civil War sconce. This is most unlikely, as the earthworks bore little relationship to Civil War

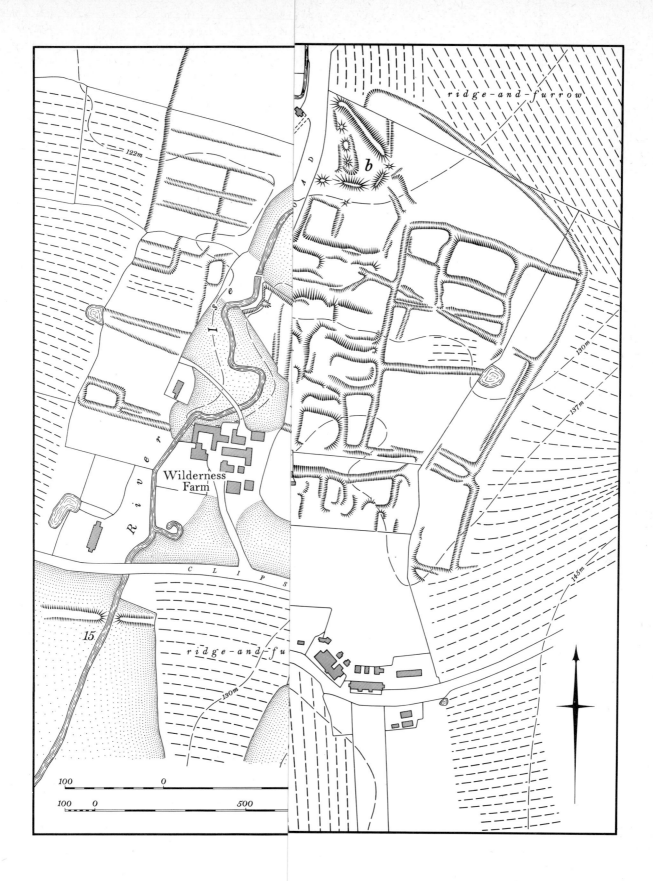

ridge-and-furrow

122m

Ise

River

Wilderness
Farm

C L I P S

15

ridge-and-fu

130m

ridge-and-furrow

b

130m

137m

145m

100   0

100   0   500

defences. Although the excavator rejected the OS classification of the site as a medieval fishpond, this still seems to be the most likely explanation (*Northants. Ant. Soc. Rep.*, 66 (1969), 7–14; *Post-Med. Arch.*, 3 (1969), 197; CUAP, SB47, AFB89, AWV15; air photographs in NMR).

c(17) ABANDONED SHEEP-FOLD (SP 715796; Fig. 86), lies in the extreme W. of the parish on Upper Lias Clay at 160 m. above OD. An area of former ridge-and-furrow appears to have been partly destroyed and overlaid by two sub-rectangular enclosures, bounded by low banks and scarps. At the E. end of the S. enclosure, and also overlying ridge-and-furrow, is a small embanked feature, perhaps the site of a stone building. The remains are probably the site of a sheep-fold and shepherd's hut of unknown date but presumably constructed after the enclosure of the common fields, and are a rare survival of a once common feature.

(18) CULTIVATION REMAINS. The date of the enclosure of the common fields of the parish is unknown but it had certainly taken place before the early 18th century when Bridges (*Hist. of Northants.*, II (1791), 39) described it as an 'inclosed lordship'. Ridge-and-furrow of these fields can be traced on the ground or from air photographs over almost the whole of the parish, apart from a wide band of fields immediately N. and W. of the village where it has been destroyed by modern agriculture. In the W. and S. of the parish the furlongs were arranged both end-on and at right-angles to each other over the broken ground but in the N. there are long sweeps of end-on furlongs running N.W.–S.E. across the spurs and, in the N.E., running N.

towards the stream. It is particularly well preserved in the area E. and N.W. of the village (RAF VAP CPE/UK/1994, 2452–6, 4455–61; CPE/UK/2109, 3288–93; 106G/UK/636, 4185–89, 3185–92).

41 KILSBY

(OS 1:10000 a SP 57 SW, b SP 57 SE, c SP 56 NE)

The parish, covering some 1100 hectares, lies against the county boundary with Warwickshire to the N. and the line of Watling Street to the E. and is bounded by streams on the W. and S. It now includes the land of the hamlet of Barby Nortoft (2), formerly a detached part of Barby parish (Fig. 87). The higher S. half of the parish is mainly covered by Boulder Clay and patches of glacial sands and gravels between 120 m. and 150 m. above OD. To the N. the ground is lower and although there are still considerable spreads of glacial material the underlying Jurassic Clay is exposed over large areas.

PREHISTORIC AND ROMAN

a(1) BARROW (?) (unlocated). In the early 18th century a large bank or barrow was recorded on a hill to the E. of Kilsby (J. Bridges, *Hist. of Northants.*, I (1791), 73). Such a feature could not be traced in the early 19th century (G. Baker, *Hist. of Northants.*, I (1822–30), 404).

For Roman Road If, Watling Street, see Appendix.

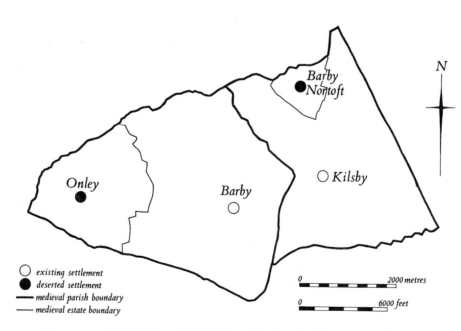

O *existing settlement*
● *deserted settlement*
— *medieval parish boundary*
— *medieval estate boundary*

0   2000 metres

0   6000 feet

Fig. 87   KILSBY and BARBY   Medieval settlements and estates

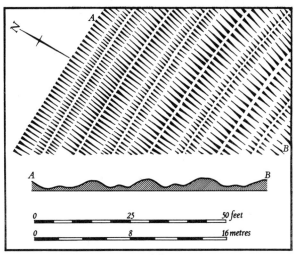

Fig. 88   KILSBY   (5) Ridge-and-furrow

MEDIEVAL AND LATER

For Anglo-Saxon burials on or near Watling Street, see Crick (6).

b(2) SETTLEMENT REMAINS (SP 557727; Fig. 87), formerly part of the hamlet of Barby Nortoft, lie in the N.W. corner of the parish, on a low N.W.–S.E. ridge of clay covered with glacial sand and gravel, at 115 m. above OD. The hamlet, together with its land, was a detached part of Barby parish but little is known of its history, the name not being recorded until 1247 (PN Northants., 25). In 1834 (1st ed. OS 1 in. map) two of the three present isolated farms already existed. The land which belonged to the settlement is shown on a map of Barby parish of 1840 (NRO). This suggests that the hamlet may have originated as a secondary settlement of Kilsby but its name and its association with Barby make this unlikely.

The remains, now under grass, have almost all been destroyed by cultivation and little exists on the ground. To the S.E. of West Nortoft Farm a large scarp up to 1.5 m. high curves N. for a distance of some 120 m. At its S. end it appears to meet an access-way between the adjacent ridge-and-furrow, but the railway has partly obscured the relationship at this point. To the E. of the scarp are three very low banks, projecting E. from it and now almost ploughed out. A few sherds of pottery, mainly 13th or 14th-century in date have been found in the field to the S.E. (SP 559728; RAF VAP CPE/UK/1994, 4439–40).

b(3) MOUND (SP 55107203), N.W. of the village, on a low ridge of clay at 115 m. above OD. A roughly circular mound, 1 m. high and 17 m. in diam., with no trace of a ditch, overlies ridge-and-furrow. On the 1st ed. OS 1 in. map of 1834 it is marked as 'tumulus', but it is perhaps a windmill mound.

b(4) FISHPOND (?) (SP 560709), on Boulder Clay at 130 m. above OD, lay in a field on the S.W. side of the village, now built over and known as Fishers Close. It is visible on air photographs as a roughly rectangular depression with a large bank on its N. side (RAF VAP CPE/UK/1994, 1480–1).

(5) CULTIVATION REMAINS. (Fig. 88). The common fields of the village of Kilsby were enclosed by Act of Parliament of 1777 (NRO, Enclosure Map, 1778). Ridge-and-furrow of these fields exists on the ground or can be traced from air photographs over almost all of that part of the parish which comprised medieval Kilsby and a virtually complete pattern is recoverable. It is arranged in end-on and interlocked furlongs, mainly of pronounced C-curved or reversed-S form. Some exceptionally well-preserved furlongs still survive S. of the village between the M45 motorway and the Ashby St. Ledgers boundary (SP 563705–565698). Also in this area (especially at SP 563704) are blocks of ridge-and-furrow consisting of rounded ridges up to 1 m. high with subsidiary low ridges between them occupying the normal positions of the furrows (Fig. 88). The purpose and method of formation of these is not clear. The enclosure of the common fields of Barby Nortoft (2) took place in 1778, at the same time as that of Barby parish and under the same Act of Parliament. Ridge-and-furrow of these fields exists within the area of land attributable to the hamlet (Fig. 87), and is arranged in interlocked furlongs (RAF VAP 106G/UK/636, 4185–9, 3185–92; CPE/UK/1994, 2452–6, 4455–61; CPE/UK/2109, 3288–93).

42 LAMPORT

(OS 1:10000 a SP 77 NW, b SP 77 NE, c SP 77 SW,
d SP 77 SE)

Lamport now includes the old parish of Faxton which was once a parochial chapelry of the former. It is very large, covering nearly 1900 hectares, and is shaped like a 'W'. Much of it lies on a flat-topped N.–S. ridge with a maximum height of 150 m. above OD, capped by Boulder Clay, but the down-cutting of numerous small streams within and on either side of this ridge has formed a rolling landscape of Northampton Sand and Upper Lias Clay. There is a small area of alluvium in the valley of the main S.-flowing stream to the W. of the village.

The parish of Lamport contained not only the village of Lamport itself but also the hamlet of Hanging Houghton where the site of the manor house and gardens (13) lies on a small steep-sided spur. The village of Faxton (15) was finally depopulated in this century after a long and complex history. Although the greater part of the extensive earthworks have been destroyed by ploughing some excavation was carried out before this. In common with other villages in this part of the county all three settlements in the parish lie on high ground.

PREHISTORIC AND ROMAN

d(1) RING DITCH (?) (SP 756748), on the valley side to the E. of the fishponds (9), on Northampton Sand at 130 m. above OD. A circle of dark earth about 25 m. in diam. and a scatter of worked flints are visible when the land is ploughed.

c(2) ENCLOSURES (SP 732735), in the S.E. of the parish, on Upper Lias Clay, at 110 m. above OD. Air photographs (in NMR) show very indistinct cropmarks of a small group of interlocked sub-rectangular and oval enclosures covering about 1 hectare.

a(3) ENCLOSURE AND TRACKWAY (SP 746750; Fig. 89), W. of the village, on Upper Lias Clay, at 100 m. above OD. Air photographs (in NMR) show parts of a rectangular enclosure with irregular sides and an apparent entrance on the S.W. To the S. is a length of ditched trackway and further S. again perhaps part of another enclosure.

d(4) BARROW (?) (around SP 784749), lay close to the E. boundary of the parish, on clay at 122 m. above OD. A tumulus was recorded 'southward of Faxton church' in 1849 (Wetton, *Guide-Book* (1849), 105) but no trace of a mound is visible on the ground or from air photographs.

b(5) BARROW (?) (SP 77437565; Fig. 95) lay 250 m. S.E. of Shortwood House, on clay at 145 m. above OD. Until it was destroyed in 1964 there was a mound 0.8 m. high and 11.5 m. in diam. with no trace of a ditch; it was perhaps a bowl barrow (OS Record Cards). On air photographs taken before destruction (RAF VAP CPE/UK/1925, 4367–8) it appears that the mound was respected by the surrounding ridge-and-furrow.

d(6) BARROW (?) (SP 75547374), lies at the junction of the A508 and the road to Hanging Houghton on Northampton Sand at 144 m. above OD. A mound 1.2 m. high and 17 m. in diam., cut by the road on its S. side, is perhaps a bowl barrow (Wetton, *Guide-Book* (1849), 102; OS Record Cards).

For two other mounds sometimes described as barrows, see (10) and (11).

b(7) ROMAN SETTLEMENT (?) (SP 784753), probably lay on the site of the deserted village of Faxton, on Northampton Sand at 137 m. above OD. During excavations in 1968 Roman pottery and two Roman coins were recovered from the medieval crofts on the S. and E. sides of the village. The excavator suggested that this material had been washed down the hillside from an assumed Roman site above, perhaps near the medieval manor house site (16) (*Current Arch.*, 16 (1969), 145–7; *BNFAS*, 3 (1969), 21). Subsequent field-walking on the manor house site, now ploughed, has revealed more Roman pottery.

For Roman site at SP 760757, see Draughton (9).

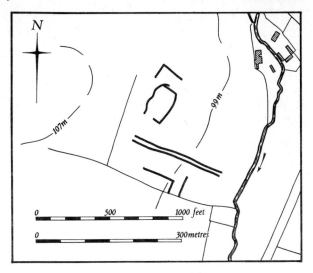

Fig. 89   LAMPORT   (3) Cropmarks

MEDIEVAL AND LATER

A small Anglo-Saxon pot was found in the parish in the early years of the century (OS Record Cards; NM).

d(8) SETTLEMENT REMAINS (SP 757745; Figs. 90 and 91), formerly part of Lamport village, lie along the main village street between and behind the existing houses and in the park of Lamport Hall, on Northampton Sand between 120 m. and 145 m. above OD.

The admittedly inadequate population statistics for the village do not indicate a marked fall in population at any time. In 1086 Domesday Book records a total population of

Fig. 90   LAMPORT   Medieval settlements and estates

23 (VCH *Northants.*, I (1902), 318, 340, 350). Ninety people over the age of 14 paid Poll Tax in 1377 (PRO, E179/155/28), and in 1673, 37 people paid the Hearth Tax (PRO, E179/254/14). By 1801, 148 people lived in the parish; some of these would be on the outlying farmsteads which had been established by that date.

The surviving remains are very fragmentary and difficult to interpret. At the W. end of the village and N. of the present houses there is a large area of land covered with earthworks including a hollow-way ('a' on plan) which appears to have led off the existing road to Market Harborough but is blocked at the N. by a later scarp; another hollow-way ('b' on plan) extends up the valley towards the village. Between these two hollow-ways lies a small enclosure ('c' on plan), bounded on the N. and W. by a low bank and external ditch and set inside a large enclosure edged by low scarps. To the N. are other indeterminate earthworks. On the other side of the village street and just inside the park ('d' on plan) are more scarps and a short length of hollow-way. The former may be the sites of buildings. Further low scarps at the N.E. end of the village ('e' and 'f' on plan) form a generally rectangular pattern and may also be former house-sites.

d(9) FISHPONDS (SP 755748; Fig. 91), lie N.W. of the village, in a steep-sided valley cut into Jurassic Clay, at 113 m. above OD. Three roughly rectangular ponds set into the valley bottom are separated by massive earthen dams 2.5 m.–3 m. high. The dam of the lowest pond has been much altered in recent times; it has an ashlar rear face and a 19th-century stone sluice in its centre.

d(10) WINDMILL MOUND (SP 75787377), lay E. of the road to Hanging Houghton, on Boulder Clay at 144 m. above OD. A mound 24 m. in diam. and 1.5 m. high, surrounded by a ditch 1 m. deep and 7.5 m. wide, has been destroyed by ironstone-mining, but was excavated in 1954. The remains of two mills, one a post mill of the 13th to 15th centuries and the other dating from the 17th century, were discovered. A number of flints of Neolithic or Bronze Age type were found within the mound and it is just possible that this was a prehistoric barrow re-used as a mill mound (*J. Northants. Nat. Hist. Soc. and FC*, 33 (1956), 66–79; J. M. Steane, *The Northants. Landscape* (1974), 115).

d(11) MOUND (SP 76207421), lies 400 m. S.E. of Lamport Hall, in the park, at 145 m. above OD. The mound has been described as a barrow and as such is scheduled as an ancient monument, but it is much more likely to be a relatively late landscape feature connected with the park. It is slightly oval, 8 m. by 10 m. and 3.8 m. high, sharply conical in form with traces of a ditch on its S.W. side. Immediately to the E. is a slight square depression which has recently been partly filled in but originally was a deep rectangular pond, the spoil from which appears to have been used in the construction of the mound (local inf.). The pond cuts through the adjacent ridge-and-furrow.

d(12) GARDEN REMAINS (SP 759744; Fig. 91), presumably late 16th or early 17th-century in origin, lie immediately S.E. of Lamport Hall on land sloping very gently N.W. at 145 m. above OD. A medieval manor house probably stood on the site of the present hall and this earlier house was bought in 1560 by John Isham, citizen and mercer of London, and his brother Robert. In 1568 John Isham built the new manor house on the site of the medieval one and this was extended by his grandson Sir John Isham in 1610–11. This house faced N.W. towards the church and had a forecourt enclosed on each side by long ranges of stables, the E. range of which still stands. In 1654 Sir Justinian Isham engaged John Webb to build a new addition to the existing house. Webb designed a small rectangular block in the classical style which was erected at the S.W. end of the 16th-century house. This building was extended to the N.W. in 1732 and to the S.E. in 1741, the latter activity entailing the destruction of part of the original 16th-century house. Further alterations were made in 1821 and 1842 and the whole of the present N.W. front was added in 1861.

The remains of former gardens exist to the S.E. and S.W. of the hall but it is difficult to assign all the features to any particular period. There is no doubt, however, that John Isham, the builder of the 16th-century house, laid out gardens around it, for his grandson Sir Thomas Isham wrote that 'he aplyed himselfe to plantinge, buildinge, making to pooles ...'. In a diary of 1671–73 kept by Sir Thomas there is mention of a mount in the garden as well as walks and a bowling green. Sir Thomas later ordered numerous changes in the gardens around the hall for in 1678 his agent, Gilbert Clerke, wrote 'we are going to gravell ye walks and make Garden monstrous fine ...'. This undertaking included the construction of the existing terrace-walk and the stone-walled kitchen garden and perhaps the demolition of the earlier mount. The terrace-walk is a large flat-topped bank 1.5 m.–2 m. high running along the S.W. and S.E. sides of the garden, so arranged as to be square to the earlier house but not to the later one. The work almost certainly included the laying out of an enclosed garden bounded by terraces on the S.W. side of the house, on the front of Webb's building, as depicted in a drawing of 1721 (BM Add. MS, 32, 467, f. 149). After the 18th-century additions to the hall this garden was swept away and replaced by a circular carriage-drive set in open parkland shown in a drawing of the house in 1761 (at Lamport Hall).

The garden terrace to the S.E. of the hall seem to have survived these alterations and, apart from some minor changes including the insertion of a ha-ha along the outside of the S.E. terrace probably carried out in the 1840s by Sir Charles Isham, they have remained intact since the late 17th century. To the S.W. of the hall the mid 18th-century carriage-drive must have been replaced at an unknown date for no trace of it exists today. Its place is taken by a large, nearly square, level area, bounded by low

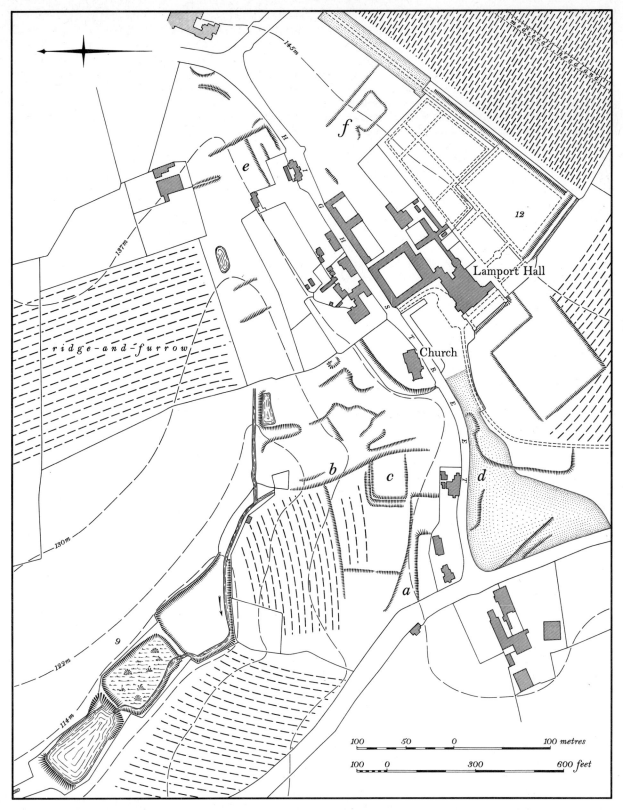

ridge-and-furrow

Lamport Hall

Church

Fig. 91   LAMPORT   (8) Settlement remains,   (9) Fishponds,   (12) Garden remains at Lamport

scarps nowhere above 0.5 m. high, which may represent a garden laid out after 1761 but before 1861 when the main entrance hall was moved to the present N.W. front and the present balustraded parterre built (*Country Life*, 112 (1952), 932–5, 1022–5; 128 (1960), 1104–7, 1164–7).

bd(13) MANOR HOUSE SITE AND GARDEN REMAINS (SP 750737; Fig. 92), lie immediately S. of Manor Farm, at the W. end of the main street of the hamlet of Hanging Houghton, on the crest and slopes of a S.W.-projecting spur of Northampton Sand between 122 m. and 127 m. above OD. The site is certainly that of the medieval manor house of Hanging Houghton, although the extant earthworks are an abandoned garden of the late 16th or early 17th century. A Richard Mountygowe of Hanging Houghton who is recorded in a document of 1471 has been plausibly identified as Richard Montagu, father of Thomas and grandfather of Sir Edward Montagu, Lord Chief Justice. The latter probably lived at Hanging Houghton until he moved to Hemington in 1540. At his death in 1556–7 he left his land, including that at Hanging Houghton, to his son Edward and it remained with the family until 1670 when it was sold to Sir Justinian Isham

(VCH *Northants.*, IV (1937), 198–9). Bridges (*Hist. of Northants.*, II (1791), 116), writing in the early 18th century, said that the manor house was deserted in 1665 after the Montagu household had been carried off by the plague, to escape which they had fled from London. This indicates that the Montagus still used the manor house until 1665. It still stood, but in ruins, in Bridge's day. On a map of the parish of 1655 (NRO) the house is depicted standing at the N.E. corner of an elaborate formal garden, comprising knot-gardens and terrace-walks. The S., front elevation of the house is shown indicating that it was of three bays, with a symmetrical elevation, probably with a central porch. It seems to have been of late 16th or early 17th-century date.

The earthworks consist of a series of rectangular areas bounded by low scarps and banks, nowhere above 0.5 m. high, set inside a continuous curving scarp up to 4 m. high which encloses the site on the W. and S. The position of the manor house ('a' on plan) is marked only by a low scarp; the boundaries of two rectangular knot-gardens immediately to the W. also partly survive as scarps. Further W. ('b' on plan) is a larger rectangular scarped area, which in 1655 was a system of paths bounding a

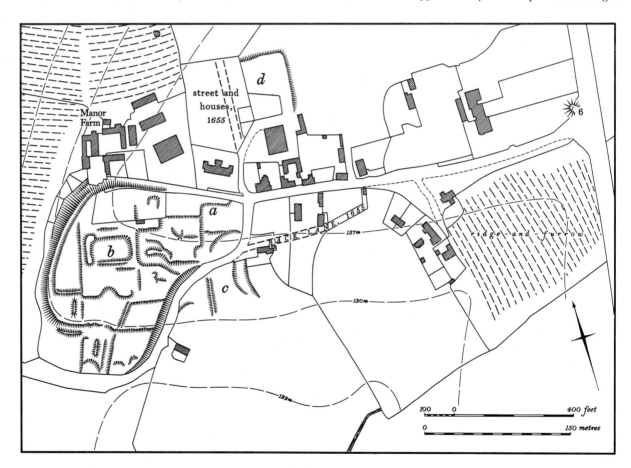

Fig. 92   LAMPORT   (13) Site of manor house and gardens,
(14) Settlement remains at Hanging Houghton

square area planted with trees, and with trees in a broad arc outside it (RAF VAP CPE/UK/1994, 1378–9; CUAP, AK70; air photographs in NMR).

d(14) SETTLEMENT REMAINS (SP 751736; Fig. 92), formerly part of the village of Hanging Houghton, lie on the S. side of the village, on Northampton Sand at 130 m. above OD. The village is now laid out along a single E.–W. street, with a broad open space or green at its E. end. However in 1655 (Map in NRO) the village had a completely different appearance. The present main street was there, but no houses stood further E. than the W. edge of the green, which then did not exist. To the S. of the main street was a back lane, along which lay at least three buildings, and on the N. side a short cul-de-sac was lined with eight houses and their gardens, four on each side, forming a neat rectangular block. Further S., to the S. of the manor house (13) which then stood in the corner of its formal gardens, three other houses lay on the S. side of the lane to Cottesbrooke.

On the ground a few indeterminate scarps ('c' on plan) mark the sites of the houses on Cottesbrooke Lane. Part of the back lane survives, but no trace remains of the houses on the N. side of the village. The latter area has been ploughed and then returned to grass and only a low scarp indicates the possible boundary of the former closes ('d' on plan; RAF VAP CPE/UK/1994, 1378–9; CUAP, AKP70).

b(15) DESERTED VILLAGE OF FAXTON (SP 784753; Figs. 90, 93 and 94; Plates 6 and 7), once the centre of the former parish of Faxton, lies in the E. of Lamport parish. It is situated on the slopes of a S.-projecting spur between two S.-flowing streams from 138 m. to 114 m. above OD. The top of the spur is capped by Northampton Sand but at the N. end of the village this is in turn overlaid by Boulder Clay. The valley sides are cut into underlying Upper Lias Clay.

The history of Faxton appears complex but, significantly, this is due at least in part to the large amount of information known about it. Without the evidence of the post-medieval maps and the results of excavations a relatively simple but erroneous picture could be drawn.

Faxton is first recorded in Domesday Book though it may have originated earlier as the first element of its name possibly represents a Scandinavian personal name (PN Northants., 124). In 1086 Domesday Book lists Faxton as a two-hide manor held by the King, with a recorded population of 21. In most later medieval documents, however, Faxton is linked with the deserted village of Mawsley (RCHM Northants., II, Loddington (6)), and it may be that the entry for Faxton in Domesday Book also includes Mawsley which is otherwise unrecorded. This evidence for a settlement here in the 11th century and earlier is apparently at variance with archaeological findings which would indicate a 12th-century origin for the village (see below). Faxton is listed in the 1316 Nomina Villarum, and in 1334, together with Mawsley, paid 38s.

8d. for the Lay Subsidy (PRO, E179/155/3). In 1377, 94 people over the age of 14 paid the Poll Tax (PRO, E179/155/27) but this figure again includes the inhabitants of Mawsley. Nevertheless the large number of people involved suggests that Faxton was a considerable community. In 1674, 34 householders paid the Hearth Tax (PRO, E179/254/14) and in about 1720 Bridges (Hist. of Northants., II (1791), 92) noted that there were 32 houses there including the manor house. Taken at their face value these figures do not indicate a marked drop in population at any one time. One might suggest that there may have been some 20 households in 1086, and a similar number in 1377, rising to the 34 of 1674. However at least 50 probable house-sites can be identified and the archaeological evidence implies that at least some of these were abandoned around 1400. Two alternative explanations can be given: either the village expanded rapidly, after 1086 according to Domesday Book, or after 1150 according to the archaeological record, then declining in size in the late 14th or early 15th century, or the earthworks represent a history of settlement movement within the village. At the moment there is no real evidence for the latter theory.

The earliest cartographic representation of Faxton is a map of 1746 (NRO; Fig. 94). This shows some reduction in size since 1720 when Bridges said there were 32 houses; the manor house had been demolished and the medieval church was isolated except that Rectory Farm, an early 17th-century building, stood immediately to the E., with another building to the E. again. Further N. was a row of almshouses containing four tenements which had only been built a few years before in 1736 (VCH Northants., IV (1937), 172). On the N. side of the village were three farms, and at least ten cottages which may have been sub-divided into separate tenements in which case the map probably represents between 20 and 30 dwellings. In 1745 the open fields of the parish were enclosed. By 1801 the total population of the parish was only 54, living in 15 houses, including people living in two outlying farmsteads, so the village had presumably been reduced further in size by this date.

By 1831 the population had risen to 103 and on the Tithe Map of Faxton (NRO, 1840; Plate 7) a picture slightly different from that of 1746 is depicted. The church, Rectory Farm and the almshouses remained, as did the three farms, but six of the cottages shown in 1746 had disappeared and two new ones had been built on previously empty plots. This evidence shows that though Faxton was physically smaller it was greater in population than it had been a century before. Between 1840 and 1874 (Map in NRO) the population of the parish fell again. In 1841, 108 people lived there, in 1851, 95, in 1861, 79 and in 1871, 73. On the 1874 plan one of the post 1746 cottages had been demolished, between 1874 and 1889 one of the farms was removed and replaced by a pair of estate cottages and by 1901 only 11 houses were occupied. These comprised Rectory Farm, the four tenements in the almshouses, two

Fig. 93   LAMPORT   (15) Deserted village of Faxton,   (16) Site of manor house

estate cottages, two farms and another pair of cottages. By 1921 only 37 people lived in the parish. Since that time all the houses have been abandoned and all but the late 19th-century estate cottages demolished. The church was pulled down in 1958 and by 1967 the village was entirely depopulated. The remaining cottages have recently been reoccupied as a single dwelling (K. J. Allison, *et al.*, *The Deserted Villages of Northants.* (1966), 39–40; M. W. Beresford, *The Lost Villages of England* (1954), 367; OS Record Cards).

Until 1966 the earthworks of the village remained intact but then the entire area was bulldozed and ploughed, with the exception of the W. part of the manor house site (16), two small paddocks on the N. side of the village and the hollow-way and ridge-and-furrow to the N. The accompanying plan (Fig. 93) has therefore been compiled partly from a survey of the remaining earthworks and from OS plans made before destruction, but mainly from air photographs taken before and after bulldozing. It is not necessarily either complete or wholly accurate.

The main part of the village seems to have lain along the N. and E. sides of a roughly triangular open space or green on the flat top of the sandstone spur. This area has the appearance of a green on all maps, and on an undated but probably 19th-century sketch map of the village (NRO) the area is specifically marked as 'The Green'. The S.W. side of the green was occupied by the medieval and later manor house (16), with the church in the S.E. corner. Along the E. side of the green were three roughly rectangular crofts extending E. down the slope, each with a small close behind it. Within the northernmost of these crofts the mid 18th-century almshouses were situated. To the N. were two long narrow closes, the N. one subdivided into three. On the N. side of the green a row of small closes still survives as earthworks with, at the W. end, the sole surviving house, the rebuilt late 19th-century estate cottages ('i' on plan), lying within the close of an earlier building which was there in 1746 and remained until just after 1874. To the E. in a separate paddock are the N. ends of four closes, bounded by low scarps only 0.25 m. high. The S. ends of the scarps have been destroyed and only very disturbed ground, possibly later quarry-pits, remains. Three of these closes had buildings standing within them at their S. ends in 1746, one of which survived until the late 19th century though the other two had been demolished by 1840 ('ii' on plan). One of the central closes, which was empty in 1746, had a small building within it in 1840 which also survived until the late 19th century.

Immediately N. of these closes, in the next paddock, is a series of low scarps and shallow ditches, probably the remains of close boundaries, but the E. part has a large irregular pit dug into it. In the N.E. corner of the green, to the E. of the last surviving close, is a narrow foot-path running N. and now overgrown. This represents the main medieval road running N.E. out of the village. At the S. end of its E. side there was formerly a long narrow close

which, in 1840, had a building at its S. end; this building had been demolished before 1874 ('iii' on plan). To the N. again are the remains of a brick-built cottage which was still occupied in the 1930s and was known as Cliffdale Cottage ('iv' on plan). The remaining structure is of 19th-century date but it stands on the site of earlier buildings shown on all the maps from 1746 onwards. In the area E. of this cottage there was a large rectangular paddock subdivided into at least five closes, some with interior features of unknown form. Opposite the remains of Cliffdale Cottage the 1746 map shows another building on the opposite side of the lane. This had disappeared by 1840.

The lane or foot-path continues N. from Cliffdale Cottage and, at the N.E. corner of the existing paddock, opens out into a broad hollow-way running N.E. At this point another hollow-way running along the outside of the paddock joins it from the W. This latter hollow-way is not shown on any map. The main N.E. one, however, is marked on the 1746 map as the 'Road to Mawsley Wood'. For the first 150 m. it is a hollow-way up to 1.75 m. deep with ridge-and-furrow on either side. Just N. of its junction with the W. hollow-way a third hollow-way joins it from the E. but this is only traceable for a few metres although on the 1746 map it is shown as a track running down the hillside and described as 'A Bridle Way called Kettering Path'. It seems to have crossed the ridge-and-furrow which still survives here though in a mutilated form.

In 1746 The Green is shown with a road along its N. and E. sides. The N. road left the green at its N.W. corner and became a hedged track which still exists, leading to Lamport. On the N. side of this track is a small field which was formerly divided into at least four closes extending N. from the track, with four more closes of varying size to the N. of them. In the westernmost of the closes was a farmhouse and associated buildings which were demolished only in 1966; a farm is shown on all the maps since 1746 ('v' on plan). Within one of the central closes there was another building in 1746 but this had disappeared by 1840. To the S. of the track was a large rectangular hedged paddock, now deserted, which was divided into four long closes running E.–W. To the E. of this, and in the N.W. corner of the green, was another group of smaller closes which look as if they were an encroachment on the green. In 1746 the northernmost of these closes had a farm within it ('vi' on plan), and the close to the S. had a cottage at its E. end. Both the farm and the cottage existed in 1840 and 1874, but though the farm remained until the 1960s, the cottage was demolished soon after 1900.

The track from the N.W. of the green ran along the N. side of the hedged paddock to the N.W. corner, and then forked. One track ran on W. down the hillside and still survives as a farm track. This is shown as the 'Road to Lamport' in 1746. The other fork ran S. and is traceable as a narrow strip of land between blocks of ridge-and-furrow. In 1746 it continued to Scaldwell.

To the N. of the hedged paddock another track leaves the main one, for the first 100 m. as a hedged lane. It then forks; one branch, a broad hollow-way 1.5 m. deep, turns E. to pass N. of the N. closes of the village and joins the hollow-way to Mawsley Wood. Another branch, much rutted, runs N.E. into a headland of the adjacent ridge-and-furrow. The main track continues N., and though hardly visible today as a road on the ground it is marked on the 1746 map as the 'Road to Orton'. Between the line of this road and the ridge-and-furrow to the E. are some uneven mounds up to 1 m. high. Their function is unknown and they may simply be the remains of ridge-and-furrow which once extended in this direction.

On the W. side of this track to Orton, near its junction with the Lamport track, were at least six small embanked closes ('b' on plan). Before destruction the S. one appears to have had narrow-rig ploughing over it.

At the S.E. corner of the green stood the small church dedicated to St. Denis. It was mainly 13th-century but incorporated some 12th-century work. New windows were inserted in the 14th century when the chancel arch was also rebuilt and the clearstorey was added in the 15th century. In formal terms the building was a chapel of ease of Lamport and this was certainly the case from 1208 onwards. However as early as 1180 there was a dispute between the Priory of Lewes which held it and the rector of Lamport over the burial of dead parishioners and this suggests that perhaps from its foundation the building was a chapelry of Lamport (VCH Northants., IV (1937), 171–2). Immediately to the E. of the church, inside a small close, stood Rectory Farm, a two-storey stone building of the early 17th century with later barns at each end (Current Arch., 16 (1969), 145).

From this point, S.E. of the green, a track ran S.E. down the hillside and then turned S. and in 1746 this was called the 'Road from Old'. Along the S. side of its upper part there were three rectangular closes. At the N. end of the central close there was a small building in 1746 which had gone by 1840 ('vii' on plan). The N. side of the track was edged at its W. end by the southernmost of the closes along the E. side of the green, and at its E. end by two more closes extending down the slope. The part of the track beyond the point where it turned S. was lined with further closes arranged in a neat rectangular pattern with nine long closes on the E., and six much smaller closes on the W. with a long paddock orientated N.–S. behind them.

Three seasons of excavation were carried out on the village before and during the final destruction of the site. In 1966 the southernmost croft on the E. side of the green was examined ('a' on plan). The main occupation area was found to be at the W. end adjoining the green. Further E. was a backyard and beyond, down the slope, was the kitchen garden or rubbish dump. Four periods of occupation were found, as follows:

Period I, 1200–1250. A long-house orientated E.–W. was constructed on a built-up clay platform. The house was made of mud walls, and post-holes for timber were found. A contemporary barn lay to the N.

Period II, 1250–1300. A bigger long-house orientated N.–S. was erected, with opposed doors, clay side-walls and stone sleeper-walls at the ends. Later the side-walls were given stone footings. To the W. was a barn and to the S., in the yard, a circular oven for baking and a lined water-trough.

Period III, 1300–1350. A new house was built at the N. end of the previous house and the latter was reduced to a barn. The new house, also orientated N.–S., was similar in construction to the earlier one. A second water-trough and several sheds also dated from this phase.

Period IV, 1350–1400. The Period III house was enlarged to the N. and W. and divided into three rooms. The farm buildings were improved and a new building, possibly a byre, was erected as well as an oven or kiln for drying corn and peas.

The pottery from Period I was mainly late Stamford ware and from the later periods mainly Lyveden ware. Other finds included coins of Henry III and Edward I, bronze rings, buckles, sheep bells, knives, spurs and weaving-slides (Current Arch., 2 (1967), 48–50; Med. Arch., 11 (1967), 307–9).

In 1967 excavation was carried out on the four southernmost crofts at the N.W. end of the village ('b' on plan). All four crofts showed similar sequences of occupation. The earlier houses were constructed of timber uprights sunk into the natural clay, presumably with mud walls. These were replaced by buildings with a timber framework resting on a sill-beam. Later structures had low foundations of boulders, pebbles and ironstone and the last phase of building used substantial foundations of ironstone and limestone slabs. All the houses were rectangular with central fireplaces. The dates for the occupation of this area ranged from about 1150 to 1350. No coins were found; the metalwork was sparse but included iron keys, a buckle, knives, a harness-pendant and a pin-head. Most of the pottery was of Lyveden types. The excavator's impression was that this area was occupied by dwellings poorer than those excavated in the previous year, described above, and had been abandoned at an earlier date (Current Arch., 6 (1968), 163–4; BNFAS, 2 (1967), 23–4; Med. Arch., 12 (1968), 203).

In the final season of excavation in 1968 work was concentrated on the small croft occupied by Rectory Farm which had recently been demolished. Six main structural phases were discovered and these were as follows:

Phase I, mid 12th-century. A sub-rectangular timber structure with large post-holes, was set parallel to but well away from the street.

Phase II, late 12th to early 13th century. The existing structure was modified by the insertion of a series of sill-beams.

Phase III, mid 13th-century. The earlier building was abandoned and a new one was erected close to the street.

This had mud walls on a foundation of ironstone and boulders. Traces of farm buildings around the yard were also discovered.

Phase IV, late 13th-century. The previous house was abandoned and replaced by a new one close by. This, again, had a mud-wall construction.

Phase V, early 14th-century. Another new house, built of substantial coursed limestone rubble up to 1 m. high, and new farm buildings were erected.

Phase VI, late 14th to early 15th-century. More farm buildings and sheds were constructed, some of which may have remained in use when the house and the rest of the croft were abandoned in the mid 15th century.

After this sequence of houses the close remained empty until Rectory Farm was built in the early 17th century. Pottery was mainly Stamford ware in the early phases and Lyveden ware in the later ones. Finds included a jet button, a bronze buckle and a pair of iron shears (*Current Arch.*, 16 (1969), 144–7; *BNFAS*, 3 (1969), 20–3).

Other archaeological work at Faxton included a watching brief in 1965 during the bulldozing of the northernmost croft on the W. of the road to the village of Old ('c' on plan), where a paved area, enclosed on two sides by narrow walls and on the third by substantial footings, was discovered. The features appear to be 13th-century (*Med. Arch.*, 10 (1966), 214). Later field-walking, apparently in the area to the E. of the site of the church, produced an iron padlock and more Lyveden and Stamford wares (*BNFAS*, 7 (1972), 43) and recent work has revealed a scatter of medieval and later pottery over the whole area of the village. Nothing earlier than the 12th century has been found apart from some Roman material (see (7) above). In the extreme S.E. of the village in the closes alongside the road to Old the pottery found was generally of the 13th and 14th centuries and similar results were obtained by earlier field-walking here. This might indicate that this part of the village was developed at a later date than the rest (RAF VAP CPE/UK/1925, 3223–4, 4367–8; CUAP, AKP74, AWVI–6, BAP87).

^{bd}(16) MANOR HOUSE SITE (SP 783750; Figs. 93 and 94; Plates 6 and 7), lies immediately S.W. of the former village green of the deserted village of Faxton (15), on Boulder Clay at 130 m. above OD. The descent of the manor of Faxton is documented (VCH *Northants.*, IV (1937), 167–171) but little is known of the manor house itself. In 1320 the buildings of the 'chief messuage' of the manor were said to have been in ruins (VCH, op. cit., 168). In the

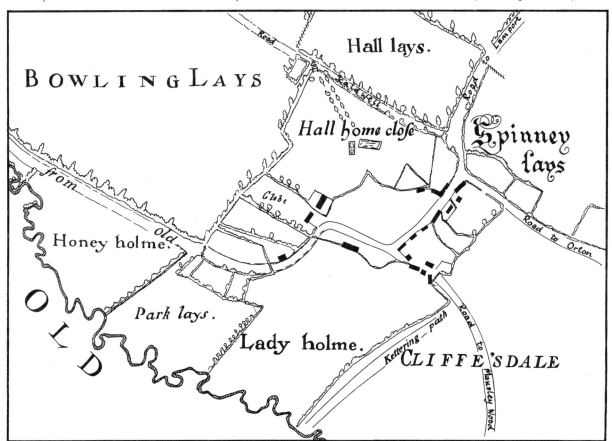

Fig. 94   LAMPORT   (15, 16) Plan of Faxton in 1746 (from a map in NRO)

early 18th century Bridges (*Hist. of Northants.*, II (1791), 92) noted that the 'ancient manor house' still remained and said that it was in being in the reign of Elizabeth I. He also recorded a gateway which bore the date of 1625 and an inscription referring to three members of the Nicolls family then holding the manor. By 1746 (NRO, Map of Faxton) the house had been demolished and the whole area was known as Hall Home Close.

The surviving remains, together with those planned by the OS before destruction and those visible on air photographs, indicate at least two separate phases. On the W. is a large L-shaped ditch up to 2.5 m. deep with both an internal and an external bank up to 1.25 m. high, and a causeway on the S. Beyond the causeway, the ditch and part of the bank continue, and beyond again is another oval depression to the S.E. These earthworks are now planted with conifers and difficult of access but they appear to be the N.W. half of a moated site within which the medieval manor house presumably once stood. To the E., and now completely destroyed, was a rectangular area bounded on the S. by a low bank and external ditch and probably on the W. by at least a bank. The parish church stood in the S.E. corner and from the N. side of the churchyard a low scarp extended N. to form the E. side of the area. The enclosure thus formed contained scarps and banks forming closes or perhaps garden plots; a very disturbed group of scarps in the centre were probably the remains of a building. The OS surveyors recorded two other embanked or scarped

structures to the N., probably also former buildings. Beyond were other scarps and banks. This area was probably the site of the post-medieval manor house and its gardens recorded by Bridges. The house was possibly built by the Nicolls family who bought the manor of Faxton in 1606 and held it until the early 18th century. On the ground are large quantities of medieval and later pottery and stone rubble (RAF VAP CPE/UK/1925, 2323–4, 4367–8; CUAP, HAP74, AWVI–6, BAP87).

b(17) DAM (SP 774754; Fig. 95), lies N.W. of the deserted village of Faxton (15), across a small valley draining S. and cut into Jurassic Clay at 135 m. above OD. It was formerly in the parish of Faxton. It consists of a broad earthen bank up to 2.5 m. high with a modern gap in the centre. A small pond lies behind it but the original lake would have been at least twice as large. The pond is not shown on the 1746 map of Faxton (NRO), but on the Tithe Map of 1840 (NRO) both the pond and dam are carefully drawn (RAF VAP CPE/UK/1925, 4367–8).

b(18) DAM (SP 781753), lies between (17) and the deserted medieval village of Faxton (15), across a small S.-draining valley, on Jurassic Clay at 122 m. above OD. The broad earthen bank 2 m. high and 25 m. across formerly ponded back a small triangular lake. Like (17) above, the dam is not shown on the 1746 map of the parish (NRO) but both the dam and the lake are depicted on the 1840 Tithe Map (NRO; RAF VAP CPE/UK/1925, 4367–8).

(19) CULTIVATION REMAINS. The two medieval settlements of Lamport and of Hanging Houghton in the old parish of Lamport each had an open field system. The common fields of Lamport were enclosed by an Act of Parliament of 1795 and, though no Enclosure Map appears to have survived, a small plan of 1797 (in NRO) shows the boundary of three former fields. One lay to the N.E. of the village, another to the N.W., W. and S.W. and the third further W. between two S.-flowing streams. Ridge-and-furrow of these fields survives on the ground or can be traced on air photographs over large areas of this part of the parish. As a result of the very variable topography, with steep slopes and rounded spurs, the recoverable pattern is a complex one of interlocked and end-on furlongs, apparently carefully adapted to the natural drainage of the area. However even on the more gently sloping ground in the W. (SP 743748) the furlongs are arranged in a similar way.

The land immediately S.E. of Lamport Hall, now part of the park, apparently lay outside the common fields in 1797. Despite this there is much surviving ridge-and-furrow, especially to the S. of the hall around Swan Lodge (SP 758742). Further E., also in the park, there are large blocks of 18th or 19th-century narrow-rig ploughing, but this is overlying early headlands, now visible as broad ridges up to 25 m. wide but only a few centimetres high. The whole area therefore must have had ridge-and-furrow on it at an earlier date.

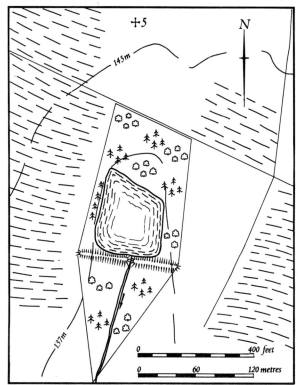

Fig. 95   LAMPORT   (17) Dam

The date of the enclosure of the common fields of Hanging Houghton is not known but was certainly before 1655 (Map in NRO). Ridge-and-furrow of these fields survives on the ground or is visible on air photographs over wide areas and, especially in the S.W. of the parish, the pattern is almost complete and comprises end-on and interlocked furlongs carefully adapted to the natural topography. This is particularly well marked around the steep-sided Clint Hill (SP 746735) where the ridges radiate from the flat summit. Also in the S.W. of the parish, along the E. side of a small S.-flowing brook, are blocks of end-on furlongs separated by long headlands. On air photographs taken in 1947 one of these headlands, 1200 m. long and parallel to the stream (SP739728–743740), is visible as a long, low ridge. More recent air photographs (in NMR), taken after the headland had been ploughed out, have revealed the cropmark of a double-ditched trackway or boundary, apparently under the headland, and visible for most of its length. At its S. end this trackway turns S.E., runs on beyond the end of the headland and passes between and parallel to the ridges of a furlong set obliquely to the others. These cropmarks, if indeed they do underlie the headland, may represent an earlier form of land boundary into which the common fields were fitted.

The common fields of the parish of Faxton were enclosed by Act of Parliament of 1743. Before that date there were apparently three open fields Nether, Upper and Middle Fields (VCH Northants., IV (1937), 170). Except in the extreme N. of the parish where an old airfield has destroyed much of the evidence, ridge-and-furrow exists on the ground or can be traced on air photographs over the whole area. It is arranged in end-on and interlocked furlongs, adapted to the natural topography as elsewhere, but it is characterized by an unusually large number of small rectangular furlongs with relatively short ridges between 80 m. and 100 m. long (RAF VAP CPE/UK/1925, 3223–4, 4376–8; CPE/UK/1994, 1376–82, 1453–61, 2447–9; 106G/UK/636, 4194–5).

43 LILBOURNE

(OS 1 : 10000 ^a SP 57 NW, ^b SP 57 NE)

The parish, covering just under 680 hectares, lies immediately E. of Watling Street (A 5) which forms its W. boundary with Warwickshire, and S. of the R. Avon wiich is its N. boundary with Leicestershire. The main topographical feature of the parish is a long E.–W. ridge completely covered with Boulder Clay and other glacial deposits between 115 m. and 125 m. above OD. From this ridge the land slopes gently N. to the R. Avon and its tributary, the Clay Coton Brook, at around 90 m. above OD, and S. to another stream at around 95 m. above OD. No Roman site has been firmly located in the parish. There are unsatisfactory records of finds of the period being made

in the general area but the proximity of *Tripontium* a little to the N.W. and speculation by the older antiquaries as to its exact site may have coloured the evidence (e.g. J. Bridges, *Hist. of Northants.*, I (1791), 571).

The most notable monuments in the parish are two mottes (1) and (2). Both lack any firm documentation. The settlement remains (3) associated with Lilbourne village are especially interesting; not only do they indicate a marked

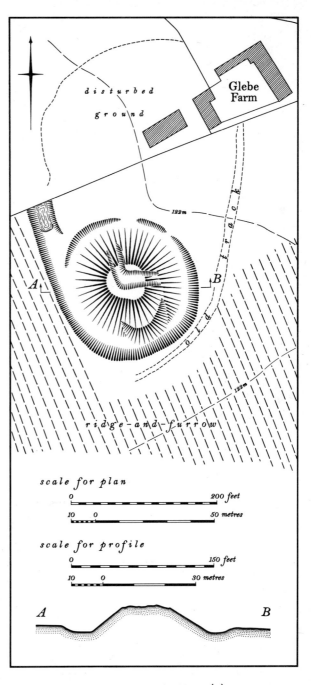

Fig. 96   LILBOURNE   (1) Motte

change in the location of the village over many centuries, but they also show that part of the village was at one stage laid out over previously arable land.

ROMAN

For the Roman Road If, Watling Street, see Appendix.

MEDIEVAL AND LATER

b(1) MOTTE (SP 55337714; Figs. 42 and 96; Plate 2), lies in the N.W. of the parish, immediately S.W. of Glebe Farm, on glacial gravels at just over 122 m. above OD. It stands on the E. edge of a prominent ridge with extensive views in all directions, including part of Watling Street (A5) which lies 450 m. to the S.W. Nothing is known of its date or history. The existence of another motte in the parish (2) is unusual and difficult to explain.

The motte consists of a large circular mound 7.5 m. high, formerly surrounded by a ditch up to 2 m. deep. The latter has been damaged, especially on the N. where it is now hardly visible. The summit of the mound was once probably flat and 15 m. across, but a large L-shaped trench has been cut in it and extends down the N. and E. sides. Some of the spoil from the latter may have been dumped at the bottom of the mound on the S. side where there is a pile of earth projecting into the ditch.

There is little indication of a former bailey. The surrounding land is now under permanent cultivation but air photographs taken in 1945 before the area was ploughed (RAF VAP 106G/UK/636, 4159–60) show ridge-and-furrow to the S., E. and W. of the motte, with what appears to be a track extending S.W. from Glebe Farm and around the S. side. However it is just possible that a bailey existed to the N. of the motte. The outer edge of the ditch on the N.W. side runs on as a well-marked scarp up to 2 m. high and becomes the S.W. side of a modern pond. This may be the W. ditch of a former bailey. The field to the N. was already under cultivation in 1945, but a discoloured area with a curving N. edge is visible on the air photographs. Although this could indicate the area of the bailey the proximity of the modern farm suggests that it is more likely to be a recent feature. No finds have been made in the area.

In 1878 it was recorded that outside the motte ditch to the S.E. was a 'smaller and apparently sepulchral tumulus' (*Arch. J.*, 35 (1878), 119). No trace of this now exists or was visible in 1945. The general area has quantities of relatively modern brick, tile and post-medieval pottery on it, probably to be associated with a farm on the site.

b(2) MOTTE AND BAILEY (SP 56117747; Figs. 42, 97 and 98; Plate 2), known as Lilbourne Castle, lies N. of the village, near the almost isolated parish church. It is situated in the valley bottom close to the R. Avon, on alluvium and river gravel at 95 m. above OD. Its position is in marked contrast to the other motte in the parish (1) and it appears to control the river crossing. Nothing is known of its date or its history, but the two stages of development visible in the

surviving earthworks suggest that it may have started as a small motte and bailey of the late 11th century and was then rebuilt and strengthened perhaps in the mid 12th century.

What appears to be the earliest part of the site consists of a tall conical motte, now 7.25 m. high, with a surrounding ditch and a small sub-rectangular bailey on its N.E. side. The bailey is bounded by a ditch up to 2 m. deep with an inner bank on its S. and E. sides but has been damaged by later activity, including the use of the ditch on the N. side as a track. To the E. of this bailey is a large rectangular depression, probably once a fishpond. To the S.E. of the motte is a later bailey consisting of a rectangular raised platform bounded on three sides by a massive bank and surrounded by a ditch up to 2 m. deep. The bank is some 2.5 m. high except at the S. and S.E. corners where it rises a further 1.5 m. to two prominent mounds. The great size of this bank, and the fact that the bailey is constructed on ground rising out of the valley-bottom, means that it dominates the adjacent motte as well as improving the tactical position of the site from the S.

To the N.E. of the later bailey and immediately S.E. of the fishpond is a small circular mound only 0.25 m. high. It may overlie ridge-and-furrow, but this is not certain. Its purpose is unknown. To the E. and S. of the site is a series of ditched and embanked enclosures, many with ridge-and-furrow within them, that extend S. and form part of the settlement remains (3). A number of hollowed trackways approach and skirt the site but their relationship to it is not clear (air photographs in NMR; RAF VAP 106G/UK/636, 4160–1; CUAP, AGU82, AKP62, AWQ5; *Arch. J.*, 35 (1878), 117–8; 90 (1933), 380; plans and sections, 1842, in Dryden Collection, Northampton Central Library).

b(3) SETTLEMENT REMAINS (centred SP 563772; Figs. 11 and 98), formerly part of Lilbourne village, lie E. and N. of the existing village, between it and the now almost isolated church and castle, on glacial sands, clay and gravel between 94 m. and 110 m. above OD. The remains appear to be the result of movement of the village away from an early riverside location near the church to its modern position on the hilltop.

The village is first mentioned in Domesday Book with a recorded population of 28, indicating a sizable settlement (VCH *Northants.*, I (1902), 327, 330). However this figure almost certainly includes Clay Coton which is not listed by name in Domesday Book, but which appears once to have been part of Lilbourne (Fig. 42). The later national taxation records of the village also apparently include Clay Coton, so that any estimate of the size of Lilbourne is impossible. Only the Hearth Tax Returns of 1673 (PRO, E179/254/14) listing 66 houses in the parish gives any indication of the population. However by that time the changes in the village described here had presumably already taken place for in the early 18th century Bridges

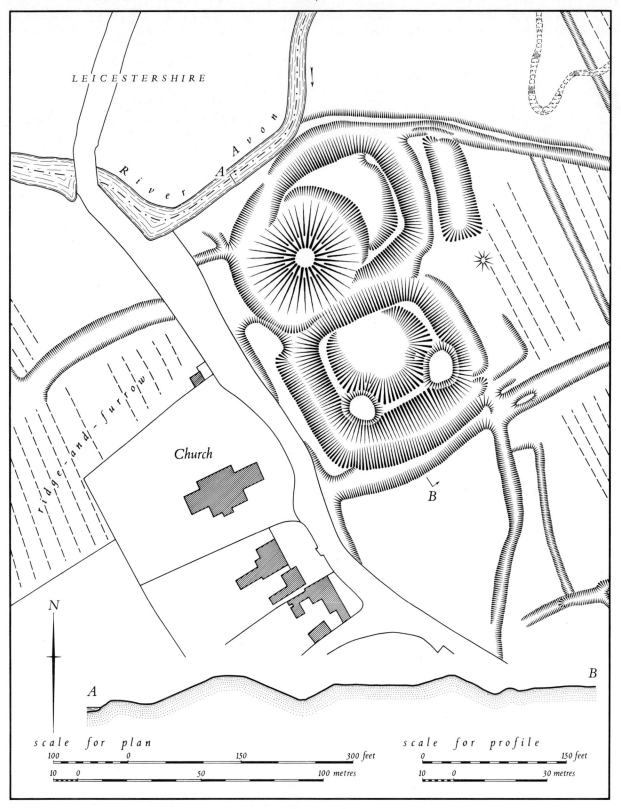

LEICESTERSHIRE

River Avon

ridge-and-furrow

Church

N

A

B

B

scale for plan

100   0   150   300 feet

10   0   50   100 metres

scale for profile

0   150 feet

10   0   30 metres

Fig. 97   LILBOURNE   (2) Motte and baileys

(*Hist. of Northants.*, I (1791), 571) wrote that 'by the causeys, pavements and ruins that have been dug up, it appears to have been formerly larger than it is at present'. By 1801, 243 people were living in the parish.

The remains fall into four distinct groups which may in part represent the successive stages of movement. The northernmost ('a' on plan) lie around the church and castle. None of the earthworks here can be said definitely to represent settlement. However it is possible that the three remaining houses and the castle occupy the earlier site of the village, for the system of streets formed by the existing road across the Avon, and three hollow-ways, one running parallel to the river E. of the castle, one approaching it from the S. and one S. of the S. bailey of the castle and apparently cut by the bailey, suggests the possibility of an early occupation in this vicinity. The area S. of the castle, between the modern road and the hollow-way, although completely devoid of earthworks, might well repay excavation in this context.

Further S.E. and N. of the modern road ('b' on plan) is a series of low platforms, banks and scarps all lying within long narrow closes, themselves bounded by low banks and ditches. These closes have notably curved sides the lines of which are continued to the N. and E. by the remaining ridge-and-furrow. They thus appear to have been constructed over earlier blocks of arable land which once extended as far as the road. If this interpretation is correct the area may represent either an extension of the original village near the church, or its movement in a southerly direction when the castle was constructed. A few sherds of medieval pottery of 12th or 13th-century date have been found within the closes.

To the S.E. again, immediately N.E. of the village and between it and the M1 are other earthworks ('c' on plan). The N. part consists of at least five long narrow closes bounded by scarps up to 1 m. high, with traces of former buildings at their W. ends along the existing road, and separated from the ridge-and-furrow to the E. by a massive scarp and a slight outer ditch.

Elsewhere around the village are other features which may relate to former occupation. The existing street running N. of the green continues as a narrow hollow-way with a wide area of unploughed land to the W. and can be traced as far as the modern road S.E. of the church, which it joined or crossed, continuing as the hollow-way to the castle noted above. To the E. of this (S. of 'b' on plan) is a large pasture field which has been ploughed and returned to grass in recent times, so that no clearly defined earthworks are visible, but shallow depressions and traces of ditches on its E. and N.E. side suggest that here too were former houses and closes (RAF VAP 106G/UK/636, 3161, 4160; air photographs in NMR; CUAP, AGU82, AKP62, AWQ5).

b(4) MANOR HOUSE SITE (?) (SP 564769; Fig. 98), lies immediately E. of the village on almost level ground, on gravel at 105 m. above OD. The E. part has been destroyed by the M1 and part of the W. has been levelled for a playing field. Its attribution as the site of a manor house rests on the shape of the earthworks, and it may simply be a former part of the village.

The area is bounded on the E. by a broad N.–S. trackway, between low scarps some 0.5 m. high; a narrow hollow-way or ditch joins it from the W. On the N. of the site is another ditch which has a small rectangular pond at its E. end and a large L-shaped pond to the S. The latter is the remnant of a square pond surrounding an island, perhaps a moat but more likely a fishpond with an island in it. Other earthworks once lay to the W. but no trace of these remains (RAF VAP 106G/UK/636, 3161, 4160–1; air photographs in NMR).

b(5) WINDMILL MOUND (SP 56417671), lies S. of the village, on the upper edge of a S.-facing slope on glacial gravel at about 105 m. above OD. It consists of a circular mound 20 m. in diam. and 1.25 m. high with a flat top and a central depression in it. There is no trace of a surrounding ditch. Although described as a 'tumulus' on the 1st ed. OS 1 in. map it is almost certainly the site of a windmill (RAF VAP 106G/UK/636, 4160–1).

(6) CULTIVATION REMAINS. The common fields of the parish were enclosed by agreement in 1680 (NRO, Agreement of Enclosure). From this document it appears that immediately before that date there were three open fields, Hill Field, Crick Path Field and Moor Field, presumably lying W., S. and N.E. of the village respectively. Ridge-and-furrow of the common fields remains intact over large areas of the parish on an impressive scale. It is particularly well preserved E. of Lilbourne Castle (2) where it is set within a series of ditched enclosures (3) (SP 562775; Fig. 98). Elsewhere it remains virtually complete, with many minor features of the medieval landscape still visible. To the N.W. of the village, S.E. of Lilbourne Gorse (SP 55557725–55767712), a broad hollow-way curves down the hillside towards the village with ridge-and-furrow on either side and partly running into it. At its S.E. end, to the E. of the modern road junction (SP 55857710), there appears to have been an open area of unploughed land, as the adjacent ridge-and-furrow to the E. terminates a little short of a low earthen bank leaving an unploughed zone to the W. The intricately interlocked layout of the ridge-and-furrow N.W. of the village (SP 556772) is the result of careful arrangement of furlongs to ensure that the furlongs all run down the slope of the broad curving ridge (RAF VAP 106G/UK/636, 4158–64, 3440–1, 3158–60, 4476–82).

44   LONG BUCKBY

(OS 1:10000 [a] SP 66 NW, [b] SP 66 NE, [c] SP 66 SW,
[d] SP 56 NE, [e] SP 67 SW)

The modern parish covers almost 1500 hectares and is

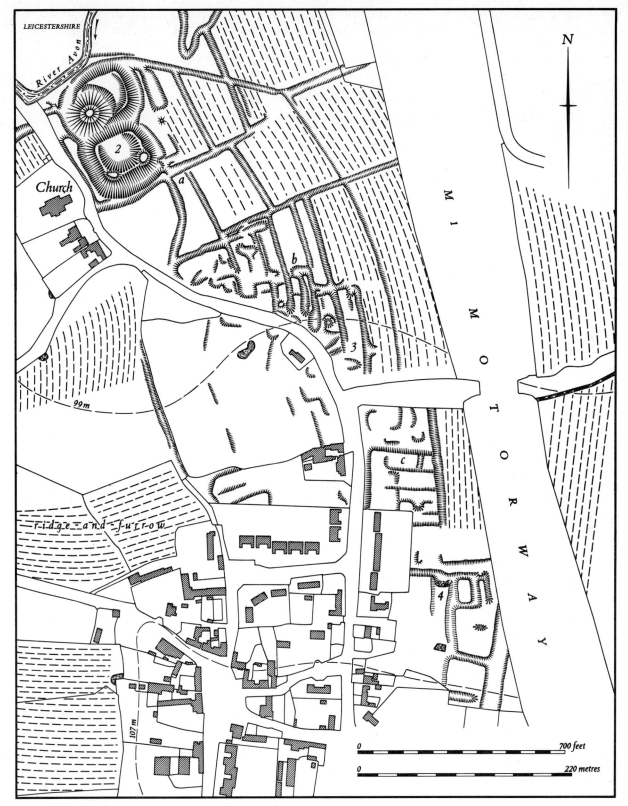

Fig. 98   LILBOURNE   (2) Motte and baileys,   (3) Settlement remains,   (4) Site of manor house

roughly rectangular, bounded by Watling Street on the W. and by S.W.-flowing streams on the S. and part of the N. From the higher ground in the N.E., over 150 m. above OD and capped by Northampton Sand, the land slopes gently S.W. across Upper and Middle Lias Clay and extensive areas of glacial deposits. A wide band of alluvium at about 100 m. above OD fills the river valley in the W. and beyond this, to the W., the land rises again across glacial sands and gravels.

The pattern of medieval settlements and estates within the modern parish is of considerable interest (Fig. 99). The settlement of Murcott (5), now largely depopulated, lay to the W. Both the village and its lands are now divided

remains (6) and the situation of the castle (8), together with some place-name evidence and the morphology of the existing village, as well as other clues, suggest that its history is by no means simple (Fig. 100). The village is extremely attenuated in shape as its name implies, but the name *Long* Buckby is apparently not recorded until the 16th century (PN *Northants.*, 65) and the surviving architecture suggests that the long E. extension of the village is perhaps a relatively recent growth towards the separate medieval settlement of Cotton End (7). If this is so, then the village can be seen to have been fairly compact in the past, arranged around a neat rectangular market place now encroached upon. However, the castle is oddly

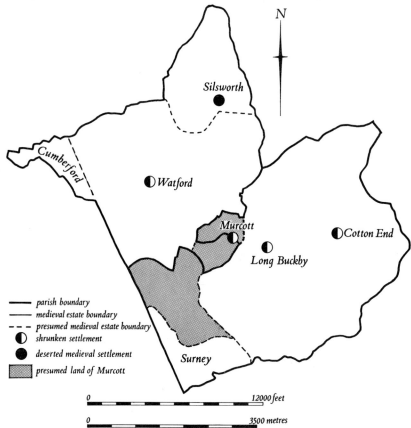

Fig. 99   LONG BUCKBY and WATFORD   Medieval settlements and estates

between the parishes of Long Buckby and Watford and this was already the case by the early 18th century but the original boundaries of Murcott can still be traced on maps of 1765 and 1778 (NRO). It is likely that another medieval estate, perhaps known as Surney, lay near Surney Bridge in the S.W. of the parish but no early documents or field evidence can be found to support this hypothesis, except that on the Enclosure Map of 1765 (NRO) the narrow piece of land projecting S.W. to the A5 is named Surney Fields.

The development of the village of Long Buckby itself is also of interest; various features such as the settlement

situated in relation to this market place, and indeed to the centre of the village. It seems to be more closely related to another road system, and even to another settlement which may have been located to the W. in the area now known as Salem. If the original Buckby in fact lay in that area the castle would have overlooked it and controlled the approach from the E. The present village can thus be seen as a later, perhaps planned addition to this earlier settlement to the W., set up in about 1280 by Henry de Lacy, Earl of Lincoln and Salisbury, when he was granted a weekly market and two annual fairs at Buckby. The major monument of the parish is Long Buckby Castle (8), a ring motte with at least one bailey, and perhaps originally two.

PREHISTORIC AND ROMAN

A partly polished flint axe of Neolithic type with a reflaked blade was found in 1972 in a garden in the E. of the village (SP 63206741; *Northants. Archaeol.*, 8 (1973), 4; NM).

[a](1) ENCLOSURE (SP 601672), in the W. of the parish, 100 m. E. of the Roman road, on sand and gravel at about 102 m. above OD. Air photographs (in NMR) show cropmarks of what appears to be at least one double-ditched trapezoidal enclosure only 15 m. across with straight sides. There may be a similar enclosure attached to the first on the S.E. side, but this is not clear on available air photographs (*Northants. Archaeol.*, 8 (1973), 26).

on the A5, here on the line of Watling Street, exposed a human skeleton at the base of the quarry ditch of the Roman road. A complete Roman amphora lay 10 m. further N., also in the bottom of the ditch (*Northants. Archaeol.*, 12 (1977), 213).

[a](4) ROMAN SETTLEMENT AND KILN (SP 64576783), in the garden of 'Old Coopers', Lodge Lane to the E. of Cotton End, on Northampton Sand at a little over 152 m. above OD. Since 1962 various finds have been made, of Roman pottery including samian, mortaria, grey and red-brown wares, as well as part of a kiln bar and fragments of baked clay, possibly parts of a kiln dome. There were also hearths, a pit and a post-hole, and a cobbled floor. The finds date from the 1st and 2nd centuries (*BNFAS*, 4 (1970), 10).

For Roman Road If, Watling Street, see Appendix.

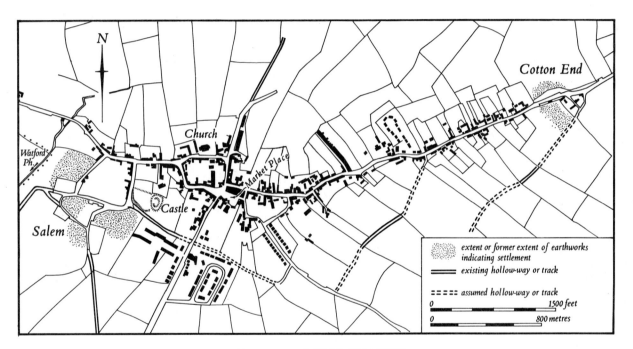

Fig. 100   LONG BUCKBY
(6, 7) Settlement remains at Long Buckby and Cotton End,   (8) Ring and bailey

[a](2) ENCLOSURE (SP 609670), in the W. of the parish, on Boulder Clay, at 105 m. above OD. Air photographs (in NMR) show the cropmarks of a large rectangular ditched enclosure, orientated N.E.–S.W. and covering some 3.5 hectares. Only the S.W. half is clearly visible. The N.W. corner may be bounded by two ditches but a later medieval headland has obscured the details. No interior features are recognisable.

[a](3) ROMAN BURIAL (SP 608652), in the S.W. of the parish, on glacial gravel, at 120 m. above OD. Roadwork

MEDIEVAL AND LATER

[a](5) SETTLEMENT REMAINS (SP 620677; Figs. 99 and 101), formerly part of the hamlet of Murcott, lie immediately W. of Long Buckby village, on the N.W. side of a small S.W.-flowing stream, on Middle Lias Clay and Marlstone Rock between 105 m. and 115 m. above OD. The hamlet is now partly in Long Buckby and partly in Watford parish, a situation which already existed in the 18th century (J. Bridges, *Hist. of Northants.*, I (1791), 544, 585). However it is possible that at an earlier period it lay entirely within Watford. The extent of the land attributable to

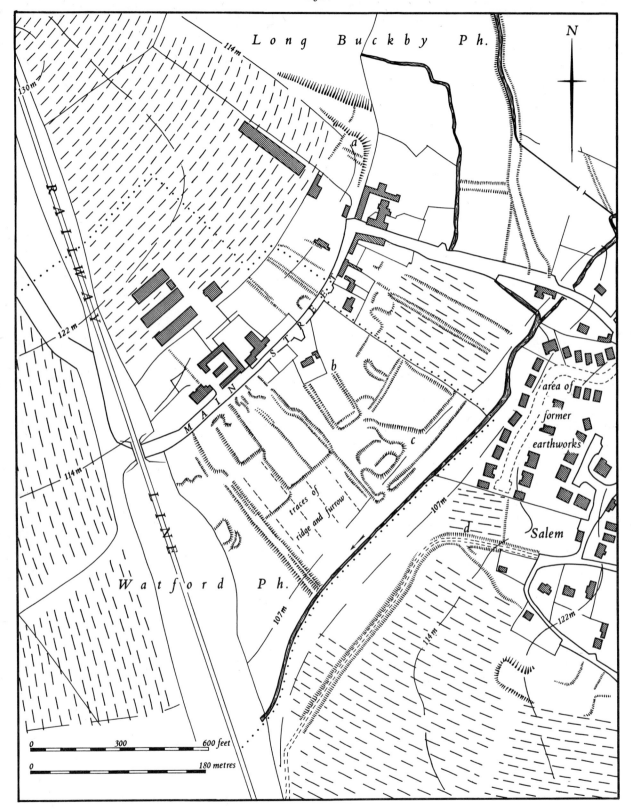

Fig. 101   LONG BUCKBY   (5) Deserted village of Murcott,   (6) Settlement remains at Long Buckby

Murcott can be established (Fig. 99; NRO, Maps of 1765 and 1771) and this too is divided between Watford and Long Buckby.

As a result of this situation the population history of Murcott is largely unknown. The name is not recorded until 1220 (PN *Northants.*, 66) but presumably the settlement is silently included in Domesday Book and in later taxation records with Long Buckby or Watford or perhaps divided between the two. The earliest indication of its size is given by Bridges (op. cit.) in the early 18th century when there were five houses in the part of the hamlet in Watford parish and six in Long Buckby parish. The 1771 map shows nine buildings which were probably houses, though some of these may have been in multiple occupation.

The remains fall into three separate parts. On the N.W. side of Main Street are traces of at least ten closes, bounded by low scarps and banks or shallow ditches, some with indications of former buildings at their S.E. ends. Modern farm-buildings have destroyed most of the evidence at the S.W. end of this area. On the 1771 map ten closes are shown, four of which were already devoid of buildings. The small northernmost close ('a' on plan) still had a building within it in 1771, and the map shows a lane along its S.W. side. No building now remains, but the lane is visible as a shallow hollow-way. S.E. of the road there are at least eleven long closes extending down the hillside and again bounded by banks, scarps or ditches. The N.W. ends of the three northern ones are still occupied by houses and gardens; in 1771 this area was divided into two closes only. All three have ridge-and-furrow within them. The other closes, to the S.W., are all devoid of buildings except for one modern house. In 1771 the area around this house ('b' on plan) was a single field but with at least two houses and outbuildings at its N.W. end. The five S.W. closes were all a single paddock in 1771 with no buildings within it.

Along the S.E. side of this lower field ('c' on plan) is a group of earthworks the purpose of which is not entirely clear, though they may be the remains of a *Mill-pond*. A long depression, bounded by scarps up to 1.5 m. high, is terminated at the S.W. end by a broad bank broken at its S.W. corner, possibly a dam. To the N.W. are large irregular depressions which appear to have been at least partly filled with water at some time. The 1771 map shows nothing at this point (RAF VAP 543/RAF/2337, 0375–6; CUAP, NT25, AWI67, AWQ55; air photographs in NMR).

ᵃ(6) SETTLEMENT REMAINS (centred SP 623675; Fig. 100, partly on Fig. 101), formerly part of the village of Long Buckby lie to the S. and S.W. of the present village centre, in the area called Salem, on Middle Lias Clay and Boulder Clay between 105m. and 135 m. above OD. Large parts of the remains have been destroyed within recent years by modern development and as a result little can be said about them as earthworks. However, together with other evidence, they suggest that the layout of the village was

once somewhat different and they may, in part, be the remains of the earlier village of Long Buckby which was possibly replanned on its present site in the 13th century (see introduction above). In addition to the evidence of the earthworks described below, village tradition tells of an old church in the Salem area and of human bones found there (*J. Northants. County Library*, 5 (1939), 103).

Within the area of old closes called Salem (SP 622675) and in the area to the N. (SP 622677) there were, before modern housing destroyed them, extensive remains of old closes and paddocks bounded by low scarps and banks, with what appeared to be house-sites within some of them. These closes appear to have been alongside both the present Styles Green Lane, and along a road running at right-angles across it, now partly the modern Holmfield Terrace and partly a broad hollow-way to the W. of Salem running down towards the stream and then S.W. as a terrace-way along the valley side ('d' on plan). At the E. end of Holmfield Terrace (SP 624675) the hollow-way reappears and runs S.E. along the S. side of Long Buckby Castle (8) (Fig. 102). From there it ran on S.E. across the line of the present Station Road as far as Benbow Farm (SP 630672) and along this section its line is still partly preserved either as a hollow-way or as a track. Beyond Benbow Farm it appears to have joined the modern Brington road running S.E. (RAF VAP 543/RAF/2337, 0373–5; CUAP, NT25, AWQ55).

ᵃ(7) SETTLEMENT REMAINS (SP 641679; Fig. 100), formerly part of the hamlet of Cotton End, lie at the E. end of Long Buckby village, on glacial deposits and clay at 152 m. above OD. Little is known of the history of the settlement; it was first recorded in 1324 as *Coten* and by 1544 was known as *Cottonend* (PN *Northants.*, 65). Traces of ploughed-out closes are visible and medieval pottery has been found behind the existing houses. The land alongside the road from Cotton End to Long Buckby has now been built over, but before this ridge-and-furrow formed an unbroken area between the two settlements showing that the latter were discrete units (inf. D. N. Hall; RAF VAP 543/RAF/2337, 0373–4).

ᵃ(8) RING AND BAILEY (SP 625675; Figs. 100 and 102), known as Long Buckby Castle, a little to the W. of the village on almost flat ground on Boulder Clay at 137 m. above OD. Nothing is known of its history. However, on the assumption that it was built in its present form after the mid 12th century (see evidence from excavation below), it was perhaps constructed by the de Quincy family, later Earls of Winchester, who by Henry II's reign held the main manor of Long Buckby and who continued to hold it until 1264 (VCH *Northants.*, I (1902), 379).

The ring motte consists of a roughly oval area enclosed by a bank 4 m. high, surrounded by a wide ditch as much as 2 m. deep in places. The ditch on the E. has been filled in in recent times, but the outline is still revealed by the vegetation. There is a gap in the centre of the W. side of the

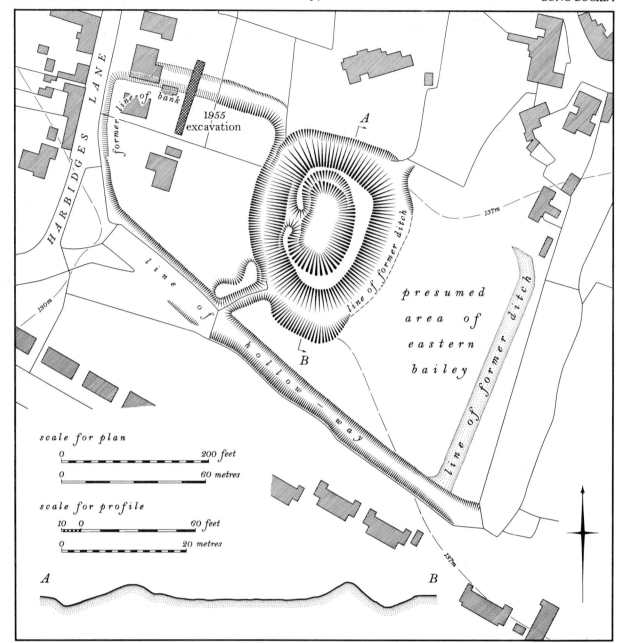

Fig. 102   LONG BUCKBY   (8) Ring and bailey

bank, though whether this is original is now impossible to determine. To the W. are slight traces of an irregular bailey bounded on the N. by a shallow ditch only 0.5 m. deep. Although the whole of the N.W. corner has been destroyed by modern housing, a plan made before the houses were built shows that the bailey extended as far as the E. side of Harbidges Lane. The S. side of this bailey is now edged by a steep scarp up to 2 m. high which also forms the N. side of a deep hollow-way running S.E. from Harbidges Lane along the S. side of the whole site. A narrow ditch in the S.E. corner, joining this hollow-way to the motte ditch,

may be part of the original bailey ditch. To the W. of this ditch and thus within the assumed bailey is a large irregular mound which is perhaps the only remaining trace of the bailey rampart.

It has been suggested that there was another, larger bailey to the E. of the motte but the ground there has been entirely levelled for playing fields and no indications of one can now be seen. The form of the hollow-way on the S. side may have led to the belief that this was once part of a bailey.

In the early 18th century Bridges (*Hist. of Northants.*, I

(1791), 544) noted that old foundation walls 'eight or ten feet' thick had been found at Long Buckby Castle. In 1955 a small excavation was carried out, across the N. ditch of the W. bailey before destruction. The tentative conclusions from this were that a shallow ditch, perhaps of an enclosure and possibly of pre-conquest or early post-conquest date, was superseded first by a wall and subsequently by a bank with a deep external ditch. Behind the wall stood a small stone building of 12th-century date. At a later date a curtain wall was constructed around the bailey (*J. Northants. Natur. Hist. Soc. and FC*, 33 (1956), 55–66; plans and notes in Dryden collection, Central Library, Northampton; air photographs in NMR; RAF VAP 543/RAF/2337, 0374–5).

(9) CULTIVATION REMAINS. The common fields of Long Buckby were enclosed by an Act of Parliament of 1766 (NRO, Enclosure Map). Immediately before that date there were five named fields, North and Highway in the N., Hoborow and Hammers in the S., and Surney Field in the S.W. projection of the parish. Ridge-and-furrow of these fields cannot be traced in the area E. of the village (SP 644675), in the S. of the parish or in much of Surney Field, but elsewhere a fairly complete pattern can be reconstructed either on the ground or from air photographs. Much of it is arranged in end-on furlongs but there are many interlocking blocks as well. Ridge-and-furrow is also traceable in two areas known as common in 1766, North Heath Common in the N.E. (SP 645697) and Thorney Heath Common in the E. (SP 649675), indicating that these areas must once have been arable land.

Part of the common fields of Murcott was apparently enclosed at the same time as most of Watford, by an Act of Parliament of 1771 (NRO, Map of New Enclosures in Watford and Murcott). This enclosure seems to have included land in the N.W. of Murcott, but a larger area than that now included in Watford parish. The area to the S., around Greenhill Farm, appears to have been enclosed before that date. In the N. of the land of Murcott, in the area now in Watford, some of the ridge-and-furrow has been destroyed, but in that part now in Long Buckby almost every furlong is visible either on the ground or on air photographs. It is arranged throughout in end-on and interlocked furlongs (RAF VAP CPE/UK/1994, 1363–7, 2356–63, 4262–70, 4361–5; 543/RAF/2337, 0373–7).

45 MAIDWELL

(OS 1:10000 [a] SP 77 NW, [b] SP 77 NE)

The parish is roughly rectangular, covering about 736 hectares, and lies across a series of spurs which project S. and E. from a ridge in the N.W. The latter, rising to over 165 m. above OD, is capped by Boulder Clay. The down-cutting of small streams has revealed narrow bands of limestone, rocks of the Lower Estuarine Series and

Northampton Sand, with larger areas of Upper Lias Clay on the lower ground in the S. and E. The E. boundary of the parish follows a S.-flowing stream at about 90 m. above OD. Apart from a number of prehistoric, Roman and early Saxon sites discovered during recent fieldwork, the main monuments in the parish are two fishponds (14) and (15). Both are well preserved and one (15) is of particular interest because of the elaborate leat which formerly brought water into it.

PREHISTORIC AND ROMAN

An Iron Age coin, a stater of the Atrebates, was found in the parish before 1868 (S. S. Frere (ed.), *Problems of the Iron Age in Southern Britain* (1958), 157).

[a](1) FLINT-WORKING SITE (SP 731764), in the W. of the parish, on Northampton Sand at 152 m. above OD. Worked flints thought to be of Bronze Age type are said to have been discovered. No further details are known (CBA Group 9, *Newsletter*, 6 (1976), 29).

[b](2) FLINT-WORKING SITE (SP 752781), in the N.E. of the parish on glacial sands and gravels at 130 m. above OD. Worked flints thought to be of Bronze Age type are said to have been discovered. No further details are known (CBA Group 9, *Newsletter*, 6 (1976), 29).

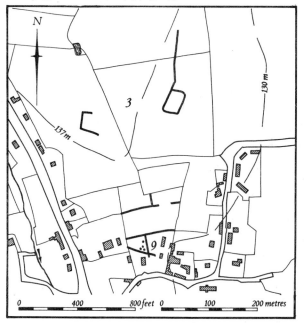

Fig. 103   MAIDWELL   (3) Iron Age and Roman settlement,   (9) Saxon settlement

[a](3) IRON AGE AND ROMAN SETTLEMENT (centred SP 747772; Fig. 103), lies N. of the village on Lower Estuarine beds and Boulder Clay, at 135 m. above OD. Air photographs (in NMR) show two rectangular enclosures; one is complete, with a linear ditch extending N. from it,

but only part of the second is visible. Some Iron Age pottery has been found to the N.W. of the enclosures (SP 746774; *Northants. Archaeol.*, 11 (1976), 184; CBA Group 9, *Newsletter*, 6 (1976), 29). Roman pottery, associated with further Iron Age sherds, has been found to the S.E., along the N. side of the Draughton road (SP 749772; inf. A. E. Brown). To the S., on the edge of the village, further cropmarks are visible. Most of these appear to be the remains of former closes of the medieval period, but at least one ditch and a number of pits may be pre-medieval in origin. (For Saxon pottery from this site, see (9)).

[a](4) IRON AGE AND ROMAN SETTLEMENT (?) (SP 725762), in the extreme S.W. of the parish, on Northampton Sand at 152 m. above OD. Early Iron Age and Roman sherds have been recovered (*Northants. Archaeol.*, 11 (1976), 184, 192; CBA Group 9, *Newsletter*, 6 (1976), 29).

[a](5) IRON AGE AND ROMAN SETTLEMENT (?) (SP 738771), W. of the village on glacial sands and gravels at 140 m. above OD. Pottery of late Iron Age and Roman types has been discovered (*Northants. Archaeol.*, 11 (1976), 184, 192; CBA Group 9, *Newsletter*, 6 (1976), 29).

[a](6) ROMAN SETTLEMENT (?) (SP 733770), W. of the village, on Northampton Sand at 135 m. above OD. Roman pottery has been found (*Northants. Archaeol.*, 11 (1976), 192; CBA Group 9, *Newsletter*, 6 (1976), 29).

[b](7) ROMAN SETTLEMENT (?) (SP 751762), in the S.E. of the parish, on Northampton Sand at 115 m. above OD. Roman pottery has been found (CBA Group 9, *Newsletter*, 6 (1976) 29; for Saxon finds from this site, see (13)).

[a](8) ROMAN BUILDING (SP 729763), in the W. of the parish on Northampton Sand at 155 m. above OD. Roman pottery, building stone and hypocaust tiles have been discovered (*Northants. Archaeol.*, 11 (1976), 192; CBA Group 9, *Newsletter*, 6 (1976), 29; for Saxon pottery from this site, see (10)). To the S.E. air photographs (in NMR) show very indistinct cropmarks of at least two sub-rectangular enclosures and some short lengths of ditches.

MEDIEVAL AND LATER

[a](9) SAXON SETTLEMENT (?) (SP 747772; Fig. 103), on the same site as the Iron Age and Roman settlement (3). A small quantity of early Saxon pottery has been noted (inf. A. E. Brown).

[a](10) SAXON SETTLEMENT (?) (SP 729763), found with the Roman building (8). Areas of early Saxon pottery have been found in the vicinity (*Northants. Archaeol.*, 11 (1976), 192; CBA Group 9, *Newsletter*, 6 (1976), 29).

[a](11) SAXON SETTLEMENT (?) (SP 727763), 200 m. W. of (10) in a similar situation. Early Saxon sherds have been discovered (CBA Group 9, *Newsletter*, 6 (1976), 29).

[a](12) SAXON SETTLEMENT (?) (SP 735769), in the W. of

the parish, on Northampton Sand at 126 m. above OD. Early Saxon pottery has been discovered (CBA Group 9, *Newsletter*, 6 (1976), 29).

[b](13) SAXON SETTLEMENT (?) (SP 751762). Some early Saxon sherds have been found with the Roman material (7) (CBA Group 9, *Newsletter*, 6 (1976), 29).

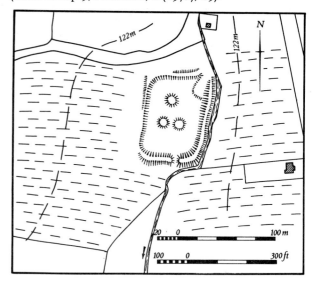

Fig. 104   MAIDWELL   (14) Fishpond

[a](14) FISHPOND (SP 745766; Fig. 104), lies S.W. of the village on Upper Lias Clay at 120 m. above OD. The pond is rectangular, 85 m. long and 60 m. wide, lying on the W. side of a small stream. The gently sloping valley side has been cut away to give the pond a level bottom on which three slight mounds about 10 m. in diam. are still discernible. These mounds must have been islands or, more likely, shallow places in the pond, possibly for the benefit of waterfowl. The water was retained on the S. by a massive earthen bank which still stands more than 1.5 m. high and 12 m. across. There is now a modern breach in it. The pond is also embanked along the whole length of the E. side and for a small section of the W. side. In the N.E. corner, where the stream must originally have fed the pond, is a delta-like feature which may be the result of later activity. The surrounding ridge-and-furrow, especially on the W., appears to be later than the pond (*Northants. P. and P.*, 4 (1970), 307; RAF VAP 106G/UK/636, 4189–90).

[a](15) PONDS (SP 741764; Fig. 105), lie S.W. of the village, N. and E. of Dale Farm, in a steep-sided valley cut into Upper Lias Clay between 105 m. and 120 m. above OD. Nothing is known of the date and function of either pond, though presumably the larger one to the N.W. is earlier than the smaller one.

The upper pond, known as Dale Pond, is now reduced to a small area of water but even in recent times it was much larger and in the early 19th century (1st ed. OS 1 in.

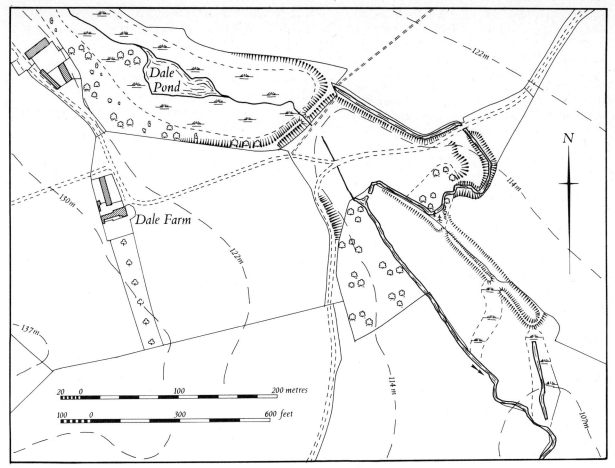

Fig. 105   MAIDWELL   (15) Ponds

Map (1834)) it covered 3 hectares and extended for some 300 m. along the valley. The water was held back by a massive dam some 2 m. high which now has a later cut through its centre. When the lake was full the water flowed across the N.E. end of the dam and ran along an artificial raised leat cut into the valley side. This leat, which still survives, curves S. and S.W. as a channel 3 m. deep and now returns N.W. to meet the existing stream. However in earlier times it flowed S.E. and entered the smaller pond. This is a long rectangular depression, cut into the hillside to a depth of 1.5 m. and bounded on the S.W. and S.E. by a large bank up to 2.5 m. high. A large gap in the centre of the S.W. side appears to be secondary but as there is no other outlet it may be in the same position as an original one (RAF VAP 106G/UK/636, 4189–90).

(16) CULTIVATION REMAINS. The common fields of the parish were enclosed privately between 1686 and 1711 (CBA Group 9, *Newsletter*, 6 (1976), 29). Most of the ridge-and-furrow in the parish has been destroyed but some can still be traced on the ground or from air photographs especially in the N.W. and N.E. of the parish and S. of the village. Elsewhere only a few blocks remain. Much of what

survives is arranged in end-on furlongs, in the E. of the parish mainly orientated E.–W., and in the N. of the parish orientated N.–S., in response to the general topography of the area (RAF VAP CPE/UK/1994, 2451–5, 4455–8; 106G/UK/636, 4186–93, 3188–92).

46 MARSTON TRUSSELL

(OS 1:10000 [a] SP 68 SE, [b] SP 68 NE, [c] SP 78 NW)

The parish is roughly triangular, covering some 1400 hectares, and lies against the R. Welland which here forms the boundary with Leicestershire. Most of the area is on river gravel or alluvium at about 100 m. above OD, with Lower and Middle Lias Clay exposed as the land rises steeply in the S., up the N. scarp of the Hothorpe Hills, to 160 m. above OD. There is considerable evidence for prehistoric and Roman occupation in the area; the Roman sites (1–5) occur both close to the R. Welland and on the higher ground to the S. The parish is also notable for its medieval remains which are associated with three distinct settlements and their land units (Fig. 106). The villages of Hothorpe (9) and Thorpe Lubenham (8) are both now deserted and at Marston Trussell itself (6) there are earthworks of former settlement which reflect considerable change perhaps of relatively recent date.

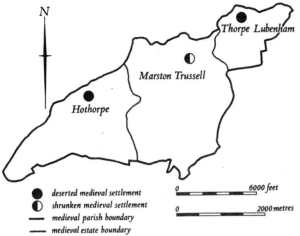

Fig. 106   MARSTON TRUSSELL
Medieval settlements and estates

legend:
● deserted medieval settlement
◑ shrunken medieval settlement
— medieval parish boundary
— medieval estate boundary

scale bars: 0 ... 6000 feet; 0 ... 2000 metres

PREHISTORIC AND ROMAN

A small bronze dagger of middle Bronze Age type was found in the parish in 1845 (NM; T. J. George, *Arch. Survey of Northants.* (1904), 17).

[a](1) IRON AGE AND ROMAN SETTLEMENT (SP 676841), lies on the N. slope of the Hothorpe Hills, on clay at 120 m. above OD. Roman pottery has been found, as well as some Iron Age sherds (*Northants. Archaeol.*, 10 (1975), 157).

[a](2) IRON AGE AND ROMAN SETTLEMENT (?) (SP 688840), in a position similar to (1) but 1 km., to the E. Iron Age and Roman sherds have been discovered (*Northants. Archaeol.*, 12 (1977), 213).

[b](3) ROMAN BUILDING (SP 69318592), lies in the E. of the village, around the church, on clay and alluvium at about 94 m. above OD. During alterations to the church and the rectory in either the late 19th or early 20th century many Roman finds were made, including samian and Nene Valley ware, tesserae and tiles. More tesserae, tiles and pottery, as well as Roman coins, were later discovered during grave-digging and restoration of the church in 1945, and when new houses were built opposite the church in the 1950s a very large amount of Roman pottery, including samian and an almost complete 3rd-century flagon, was found (SP 69318601). A large Roman building or settlement is indicated (*JRS*, 16 (1926), 223; OS Record Cards; NM; Market Harborough Museum).

[c](4) ROMAN SETTLEMENT (?) (SP 702860), lies S.W. of Thorpe Lubenham Hall, on clay and alluvium at 90 m.

above OD. Roman pottery has been found in this area (*Northants. Archaeol.*, 10 (1975), 157).

[c](5) ROMAN SETTLEMENT (?) (SP 712867), lies in the E. of the parish, on the W. side of a small hill close to the R. Welland, on alluvium at about 90 m. above OD. A scatter of Roman pottery has been found in this area (OS Record Cards; Market Harborough Museum).

MEDIEVAL AND LATER

[b](6) SETTLEMENT REMAINS (centred SP 691855; Figs. 106, 107 and 108), formerly part of Marston Trussell, lie in and around the existing village, on river gravel and Lower Lias Clay at around 98 m. above OD. Marston Trussell today is the result of extensive 19th-century alterations associated with emparking and relocation of the manor house, and it is not clear what the earlier form of the village was. From the earliest large-scale map (NRO, Enclosure Map, 1815; Fig. 108) and the surviving earthworks, it is possible to suggest that the medieval village lay along an E.–W. road, now the main street, running between Hothorpe (9) to the W. and East Farndon to the E., perhaps with a back lane to the N. The church and the moated manor house (7) lay at the E. end of this street. At some unknown date a new manor house, with associated paddocks, was built N. of the church and W. of the moat. The E. end of the main street thus became a cul-de-sac leading only to the church and manor house; through traffic turned N. in the centre of the village and then passed along the original back lane E. towards East Farndon. One other road, from Sibbertoft to the S., joined the main street near its W. end. This is the layout shown on the Enclosure Map of 1815, except that the road to East Farndon had been abandoned and a new road had been cut across the fields towards Thorpe Lubenham N.W. from the end of the back lane.

No change occurred from 1834, when the village is depicted on the 1st ed. OS 1 in. map, until perhaps a little before 1874 when a number of unconnected events took place. First the old manor house was demolished and the present road to Thorpe Lubenham was cut across part of its site, from near the church to the beginning of the enclosure road to the N.E. This resulted in the abandonment of the back lane. Secondly the major landowners, the Bennet family, enlarged their existing house at the W. end of the village and this became the present Marston Trussell Hall. They demolished buildings on either side of the house to form a garden, cleared three farms to the S. and stopped up the Sibbertoft road in order to create the park and lake. They also recut the Sibbertoft road further E. At the same time, or slightly later, many of the houses in the village were rebuilt (Whellan, *Dir.*, 836–7).

The physical remains of these changes can be seen in two places. To the N. of the main street, behind the present houses, the old back lane survives as a shallow hollow-way with old property boundaries in the form of low scarps and banks running S. from it. To the S. of Marston Trussell

Hall, within the park but now under cultivation, is an area of uneven ground with extensive spreads of stone and gravel as well as pottery, mainly of post-medieval date. A considerable amount of medieval pottery, bones and an iron arrowhead were found, as well as some Roman material (3), on a building site N.W. of the church in 1952 (SP 692859; OS Record Cards; CUAP, AHE78–9).

b(7) MOAT (SP 694859; Figs. 107 and 108), lies at the E. end of the village of Marston Trussell, immediately N.E. of the church, on Lower Lias Clay and river gravel at 94 m.

above OD. It is presumably the site of the medieval manor house of the village which was later replaced by a large building arranged round a central courtyard. This house and the moat are both shown on the Enclosure Map of 1815 (NRO; Fig. 108). The moat consists of a wide ditch, now dry, up to 2 m. deep, surrounding a small square island which is level with the adjacent ground. It appears to have been filled by seepage from a spring in its N.W. corner. The S.W. corner has been encroached upon by the churchyard wall. The moat is surrounded by a number of embanked and ditched enclosures, with other small

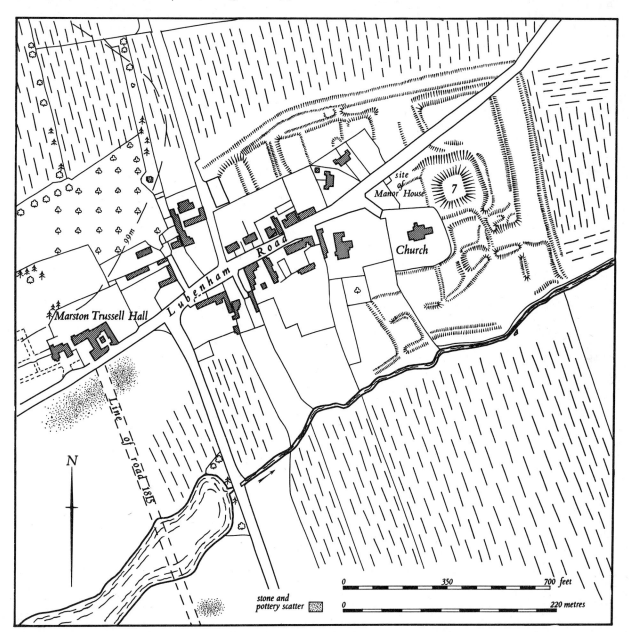

Fig. 107   MARSTON TRUSSELL   (6) Settlement remains,   (7) Moat

140

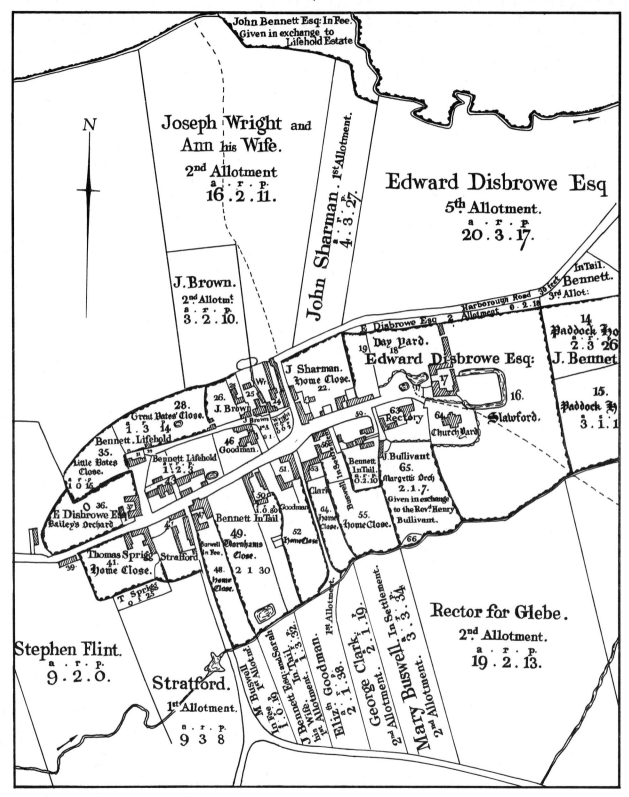

Fig. 108   MARSTON TRUSSELL   (6, 7) Plan of village in 1815 (from Enclosure Map in NRO)

indeterminate earthworks to the S., which probably represent manorial paddocks (CUAP, AHE78–9).

c(8) SETTLEMENT REMAINS AND MANOR HOUSE SITE (SP 70508682; Figs. 106 and 109), formerly part of the hamlet of Thorpe Lubenham, lie in the N.E. corner of the parish, on the S. side of the R. Welland, on river gravel at 85 m. above OD. The hamlet was the centre of a land unit which was quite separate from that of Marston Trussell, the boundaries of which are shown on the Enclosure Map of 1815 (NRO; Fig. 106). The settlement is first noted in Domesday Book, but is listed with Marston Trussell and no individual population figures are recorded (VCH *Northants.*, II (1906), 330). Although the village was always apparently in Northamptonshire, its name and the fact that is was a chapelry of Lubenham, N. of the R. Welland in Leicestershire, suggests that it was originally a secondary settlement of Lubenham. Thorpe Lubenham is mentioned separately in the 1316 *Nomina Villarum*, but in 1334 it only paid 12s. tax for the Lay Subisdy, a very small sum and much less than was paid by many other villages in the county which were also later deserted (PRO, E179/155/3). In 1377 only 27 people over the age of 14 paid the Poll Tax, again a low figure (PRO, E179/155/27). During the 15th century the manor passed to non-resident heiresses and by 1547 600 sheep were grazed on the lordship. Only one household, presumably the manor house, paid the Hearth Tax of 1674 (PRO, E179/254/14) and Bridges (*Hist. of Northants.*, II (1791), 50) recorded a single manor house there in about 1720. This house was demolished in the late 18th century and the present hall was erected to the S. (K. J. Allison *et al.*, *The Deserted Villages of Northants.* (1966), 46).

The main feature of the site is the moat of the manor house. This consists of a broad water-filled ditch 2 m. deep, surrounding a level, roughly square island. In the N.W. corner are a number of small depressions, the result of minor excavations in 1955–6, but the latter revealed nothing more than fragments of late medieval brick, tile, pottery and glass (OS Record Cards) and similar material has been found on the surface. A house stood on the island until the later 18th century. An engraving published at that time (J. Nichols, *Hist. of Leics.*, II (1798), 701, 710) shows the building as T-shaped in plan, of timber-framed construction and perhaps of 16th or 17th-century date. Outbuildings lay to the E. and W.

N.W. of the moat, on the opposite side of the present drive to the hall, is a small area of earthworks bounded on the W. and S.W. by a low scarp and consisting of a series of small irregular enclosures. The fact that these have been over-ploughed by very slight ridge-and-furrow makes interpretation difficult, but there is no reason to doubt that they are the remains of the hamlet of Thorpe Lubenham.

To the N. across the county boundary are other slight earthworks. These are the remains of closes and ponds which were still in use in the early 19th century (Map of Lubenham, 1816, in Lubenham Church; CUAP, AHE77).

b(9) DESERTED VILLAGE OF HOTHORPE (SP 667852; Figs. 106 and 110), lies in the W. of the parish, on river gravel, Boulder Clay and Lower Lias Clay at 115 m. above OD. The village had its own land unit, the E. boundary of which is shown on the Enclosure Map of Marston Trussell of 1815 (NRO; Fig. 106). In medieval times it was a chapelry of Theddingworth, the village immediately to the N., across the R. Welland, in Leicestershire. Hothorpe is first recorded in 1086 when it consisted of 3½ virgates of sokeland with one sokeman, held by the Abbey of Bury St. Edmunds (VCH *Northants.*, II (1906), 318). However, the

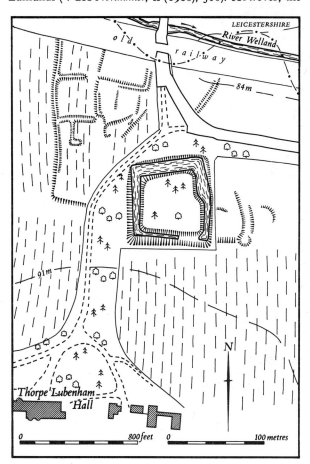

Fig. 109   MARSTON TRUSSELL
(8) Settlement remains and site of manor house
at Thorpe Lubenham

place is listed by name in the *Nomina Villarum* of 1316, and by 1334 paid 36s. 4d. for the Lay Subsidy (PRO, E179/155/3). By 1377 a total of 57 people over the age of 14 paid the Poll Tax (PRO, E179/155/27) and even in the early 18th century Bridges (*Hist. of Northants.*, II (1791), 37) said that there were about 20 houses there. In 1801 the present Hothorpe House was built, and in about 1830 the owner removed what remained of the village, rehoused the inhabitants in Theddingworth and laid out the park which surrounds the house. This work is shown as completed on an Estate Map of 1832 (NRO; K. J. Allison *et. al., The Deserted Villages of Northants.* (1966), 41; M. W. Beresford, *The Lost Villages of England* (1954), 367).

The surviving remains are very fragmentary, as is usual in villages deliberately cleared at a late date, and little remains N., W. and S.W. of the hall apart from some indeterminate scarps. To the S.E. and E. of the hall, however, a more regular pattern of long closes is visible, bounded by low scarps, and this may therefore have been a part of the village already deserted before the early 19th century, the deliberate clearance involving only houses in the immediate vicinity of the hall (CUAP, AUB17, BAP63).

Welland (SP 679859). These fields were apparently already enclosed in the early 18th century according to Bridges (*Hist. of Northants.*, II (1791), 50). Ridge-and-furrow of the common fields remains on the ground or can be seen on air photographs over most of the land attributable to Marston Trussell. To the S., on the higher more broken ground, it is arranged across the spurs and in radiating furlongs running down the slopes. Elsewhere, on the lower, flatter ground, most of it is interlocked. It remains in good condition in a number of places, most notably around the village.

The date of enclosure of the common fields of Thorpe Lubenham (8) is unknown but was certainly before the mid 16th century and perhaps as early as the 15th century.

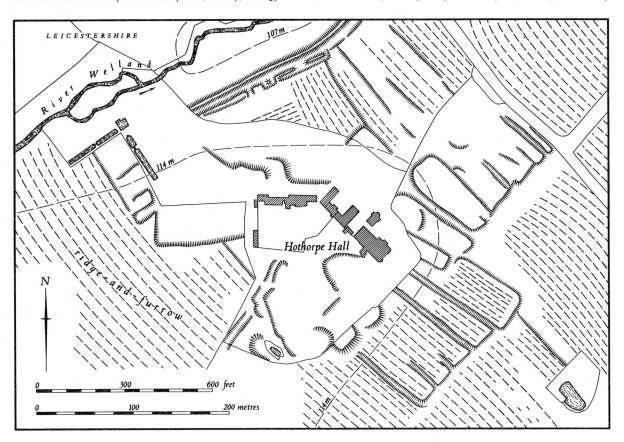

Fig. 110   MARSTON TRUSSELL   (9) Deserted village of Hothorpe

(10) CULTIVATION REMAINS. The common fields of the old parish of Marston Trussell were enclosed by an Act of Parliament of 1813 (NRO, Enclosure Map, 1815; Fig. 108). Before that date there were three named fields, Mill Field in the N., Threeway Field in the S.W. and Pitway Field in the S.E. A long narrow strip of meadow lay between a stream and the S. half of the E. boundary. Old enclosures existed around and to the E. of the village, and in part of the now wooded area of the Hothorpe Hills (SP 691835); there was also a small area of them along the R.

Ridge-and-furrow of these fields can be traced over most of the land of the settlement, arranged in interlocked furlongs. It is well preserved in the pasture around Thorpe Lubenham Hall.

The common fields of Hothorpe (9), also, were enclosed at an unknown date. Large areas of ridge-and-furrow, arranged in end-on and interlocked furlongs, still exist in the parkland around the hall, but elsewhere it is mainly now ploughed out (RAF VAP 106G/UK/636, 3132–3, 4131–40).

47 NASEBY

(OS 1:10000 ª SP 67 NE, ᵇ SP 68 SE, ᶜ SP 77 NW)

The parish, occupying 1385 hectares, lies across a high watershed from which streams flow to the Rivers Avon, Ise and Nene. Small sections of the parish boundary follow parts of several of these streams and of the Avon itself. Much of the area, including the high plateau to the E. and S. of the village, with a maximum height of 198 m. above OD, is covered by Boulder Clay, but the streams have cut down into the underlying Northampton Sand and Upper Lias Clay in many places. The main monument of the parish is the settlement remains of Naseby itself and of the hamlet of Nutcote on its S.W. edge (3).

PREHISTORIC AND ROMAN

A bronze implement was found in the W. of the parish at Naseby Woolleys (SP 665791) in the 19th century. It has been variously described as a 'celt of bronze' and a 'socketed axe', but from the original description was probably a tanged bronze chisel (*Trans. Leics. Arch. Soc.*, 5 (1882), 285; *PSA*, 8 (1879–81), 383; *VCH Northants.*, I (1902), 143, 155; T. J. George, *Arch. Survey of Northants.* (1904), 17; OS Record Cards). A small, round Roman vase with a narrow neck, containing 38 silver denarii dated from Vespasian to Marcus Aurelius (69–180) was found in the parish in 1874 (*Arch. J.*, 32 (1875), 112; OS Record Cards).

ª(1) FLINT-WORKING SITE AND ROMAN SETTLEMENT (centred SP 690791), N. of the village, on clay at 182 m. above OD. Air photographs (in NMR) show cropmarks covering about 1.5 hectares. They are rather indistinct but include one small square enclosure 30 m. across with rounded corners, a number of penannular ditches and other ditches and possible enclosures. Further S.E. (at SP 692790) the same photographs show a larger rectangular enclosure covering about 0.75 hectares, orientated N.–S., with other smaller enclosures to the S. and S.W. Many worked flints and a scatter of Roman grey ware have been found in the area (*Northants. Archaeol.*, 11 (1976), 193).

ª(2) FLINT-WORKING SITE AND ROMAN SETTLEMENT (SP 685767), in the S. of the parish, on Northampton Sand at 165 m. above OD. Many worked flints and sherds of Roman grey ware have been found (*Northants. Archaeol.*, 11 (1976), 193).

MEDIEVAL AND LATER

An Anglo-Saxon trefoil-headed brooch was found in the parish before 1913 (*PSA*, 25 (1913), 187; BM). A gold medal was found on the battlefield of Naseby during the 19th century. It is engraved with the head of General Fairfax and the inscription 'post-hac-melliora mervisti, 1645' (*PSA*, 5 (1873), 443).

ª(3) SETTLEMENT REMAINS (centred SP 688780; Figs. 111 and 112; Plate 11), formerly part of Naseby, lie in and around the village, on Upper Lias Clay, Northampton Sand and Boulder Clay between 170 m. and 190 m. above OD. The extensive earthworks show clearly that the relatively simple layout of the present village is the result of complex changes which are by no means understood. The close correlation between the earthworks and the details of a map of 1630 (Ipswich Record Office, copy in NRO; Fig. 112) is of considerable interest. The village is first recorded in 1086 but must be of earlier origin as Naseby is apparently a partly Scandinavianized place-name, which in its Old English form was Hnaefes-Burgh, i.e. 'the fortified place of one Hnaef' (PN *Northants.*, 73). No likely location for this burgh can be suggested. Domesday Book lists Naseby with a recorded population of 22 (VCH *Northants.*, I (1902), 337) but thereafter little is known of its size until the early 17th century when the map of 1630 depicts around sixty structures which are probably houses. In the early 18th century Bridges (*Hist. of Northants.*, I (1791), 574) noted that there were 90 families there.

The present layout of the village consists of two almost parallel N.–S. roads linked by four cross-lanes, with roads to the adjacent villages radiating from both ends, and with the church and manor house in the N.W. corner. However this plan is deceptively simple. First, it appears that Naseby is not one settlement but two. The N. part around and S. and E. of the church is Naseby itself, but the S. part is Nutcote. The name Nutcote is not apparently recorded until 1630 (Map), but the hamlet seems to have been centred on a roughly triangular green, now built over, in the S.W. corner of the village. In 1630 this green still existed and was called Sow Green. The boundary between the two settlements is probably the line of the S.W.-flowing stream which crosses the village towards its S. end, and the changes in the lengths of the close boundaries on the E. side of the village on the 1630 map support this.

The 1630 map and the surviving earthworks reveal a number of lanes which formerly existed in the village. In 1630, as well as the three present lanes which still meet on the site of Sow Green, a fourth entered it on its N.E. side. The map shows this lane running across the present High Street and passing between closes into the fields, where it forks. Most of this lane, which is also on the assumed boundary between Naseby and Nutcote, still exists on the ground as a hollow-way ('a'–'b' on plan) though it has been partly destroyed by later housing. The lane had already been abandoned by 1822 for it is not shown on the Enclosure Map of that date (NRO). In addition, the present Carvells Lane on the W. of the village was a way into the fields in 1630, and two other footpaths ran between the closes on the E.

The rest of the surviving earthworks can be divided into six groups. To the S. of Sow Green, and thus within Nutcote, a broad curving hollow-way extends S.W. ('c'

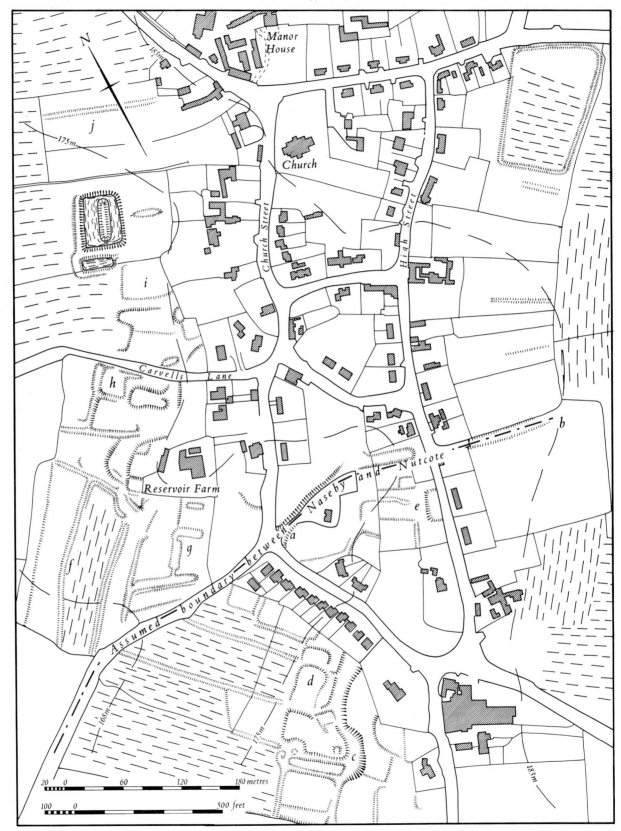

Fig. 111   NASEBY   (3) Settlement remains

145

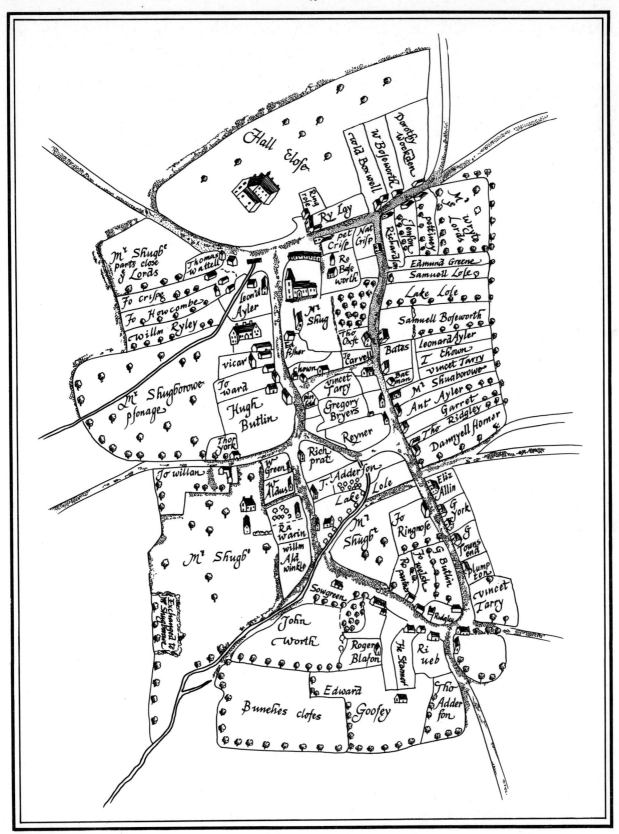

Fig. 112   NASEBY   (3) Plan of village in 1630 (from a map in NRO)

on plan), fading out before it reaches the S. edge of the adjacent field. On its W. side is a series of rectangular raised platforms 0.5 m. high beyond which are some large ditched closes with ridge-and-furrow within them. To the E. of the hollow-way are further, more indeterminate platforms and closes, and to the N. immediately S. of Sow Green and projecting from the gardens of the modern houses, two more small closes. On the 1630 map the N. part of the hollow-way is depicted as a narrow curved field and one of the raised platforms to the W. ('d' on plan) is shown as the site of a house and garden belonging to one Roger Blason. The platforms to the S. were already devoid of building in 1630 and lay in a large field belonging to Edward Goosey; the boundaries of this field are recoverable on the ground. A building, perhaps a barn, stood to the E. of the hollow-way, in this field. Its exact site cannot be identified, but other ditches and scarps seem to mark the boundary between Goosey's Field and another field belonging to Thomas Adderson, as well as the S. side of one belonging to Richard Webb. The closes on the S. side of the green were also abandoned by 1630 and lay in a field belonging to John Worth. The Enclosure Map indicates that by 1822 most of the earlier boundaries here, as well as Blason's house, had gone.

On the E. side of Sow Green, between it and the S. end of the present High Street, are further earthworks. Those immediately W. of High Street ('e' on plan) all lay within a close belonging to John Ringrose in 1630, though the site of his house does not survive. The earthworks suggest that there may have been at least one other house here at some time for there is a large rectangular depression on the E. of High Street and low banks behind it suggest that earlier narrow closes existed here.

A third area of earthworks lies N. of Sow Green, round the modern Reservoir Farm. Most of them, as well as the farm itself, lay in one large field belonging to Mr. Shugborowe in 1630. They consist of two long closes ('f' on plan) edged by low scarps and shallow ditches, one of which has ridge-and-furrow on it, and some other scarped closes immediately W. and N.W. of the farm. To the S.E. of the long closes is a narrow strip of land extending from the modern road in the S. to the present farm on the N. This is shown as a lane on the 1630 map and was presumably the main access-way to the farm at that time. To the S.E. again ('g' on plan), and separated from the farm lane by a ditch, is a large sub-rectangular area containing three linked rectangular ponds, all but one now dry, cut 2 m. deep into the hillside. This field belonged to William Aldwinkle in 1630 but the ponds are not shown on the map. A little to the N. of Reservoir Farm ('h' on plan) are two more raised platforms with a broad depression on the N.W. side, the site of an L-shaped house and its garden belonging to Thomas Wilson in 1630. This house still stood in 1822.

Immediately to the N., and N. of Carvells Lane, is another group of earthworks ('i' on plan) which appear to have been ploughed over at some time but seem to be the W. ends of at least two and perhaps three closes belonging to houses along the W. side of Church Street. However in 1630 the existing hedge-line was already in being and the earthworks lay in a large field belonging to Mr. Shugborowe. The S. part of the area is rather more disturbed than the rest and includes a low oval mound 1 m. high. A house, in the hands of Thomas York, stood here in 1630 but by 1822 it had disappeared.

Further N. again is a set of embanked ponds. These did not exist in 1630 and are presumably of 18th-century date for they are shown on the Enclosure Map of 1822. To the N. again ('j' on plan) a shallow ditch marks the boundary between the closes belonging to John Crispe and John Howcombe in 1630. The existing hedges follow the other boundaries of their closes.

On the E. side of the village, E. of High Street, three of the present gardens also contain shallow ditches or scarps. All can be identified as the boundaries of closes in existence in 1630, some of which survived until 1822. In the extreme N.E. corner is a large paddock, bounded by an almost continuous bank 0.25 m. high and with ridge-and-furrow within it. On the 1630 map this is shown as an enclosed field with 'Mr. Wryte Ye Lords' written within it (RAF VAP 106G/UK/636, 4180–2; CPE/UK/1994, 2460–59, 4463–4; CUAP, AWV16–18, AHT51; air photographs in NMR).

[a](4) WINDMILL MOUND (SP 681784), N.W. of the village, on Boulder Clay at 180 m. above OD. A mound 15 m. in diam. and 1.5 m. high, lies on top of ridge-and-furrow (RAF VAP CPE/UK/1994, 4463–4).

(5) CULTIVATION REMAINS. The common fields of the parish were enclosed by Act of Parliament of 1820 (NRO, Enclosure Map). Immediately before enclosure there were three open fields, Spinney Field in the N.W. Old Mill Field in the N.E. and Chapel Field in the S. The boundaries of these are broadly similar to those of three earlier fields shown on a map of 1630 (Ipswich Record Office; copy in NRO; Fig. 112) when the N.W. one was called Turnmoore Field and the N.E. one Shepshoks Field; the S. part of the map is missing. There is no suggestion, from these maps, that the hamlet of Nutcote, contiguous with the S.W. side of Naseby village, ever had a separate field system.

Ridge-and-furrow of the common fields survives, or can be traced from air photographs, over perhaps little more than half the parish, distributed fairly evenly between the three fields. Most of the visible furlongs in the N. half of the area are arranged end-on, running N.S. across the ridges, but S. of the village many of the furlongs are at right-angles to each other. Some of the ridges (e.g. SP 681784) are exceptionally high (RAF VAP CPE/UK/1994, 2458–61, 4460–65; 106G/UK/636, 4176–84, 3177–86; CPE/UK/2109, 3299–3302; 540/474, 3151–3).

48 NEWNHAM

(OS 1:10000 ^a SP 56 SE, ^b SP 66 SW, ^c SP 55 NE, ^d SP 65 NW)

The parish, of some 780 hectares, lies N.E. of Badby of which it was once a parochial chapelry and also perhaps, to judge from its name, a secondary settlement. Apart from a small projection in the S.W. corner the whole parish lies on the N. side of the R. Nene into which flow several streams. These have cut steep-sided, narrow valleys into the underlying Jurassic Clay, which covers most of the parish except towards the N. where the land rises to a N.W.–S.E. ridge of Northampton Sand about 200 m. above OD. The village has a complex plan which is complemented and extended by the surviving earthworks (3). Until recent boundary divisions parts of the parish were common to both Newnham and Badby. A number of minor earthworks on the periphery of the parish have been recorded in detail elsewhere and are not listed below (*Northants. Archaeol.*, 12 (1977), 155–76).

ROMAN

^c(1) ROMAN SETTLEMENT (SP 569599), in the W. of the parish, on the crest of a ridge of Middle Lias Clay at 135 m. above OD. Roman pottery, mainly grey ware but including some samian, has been found over an area of 2 hectares (*Northants. Archaeol.*, 12 (1977), 213).

MEDIEVAL AND LATER

^c(2) SAXON CEMETERY (perhaps SP 57235870; Frontispiece), in the W. of the parish, close to the Badby boundary, on Marlstone Rock at 137 m. above OD. The cemetery was first discovered before 1834 when a stone-pit was dug in East Highway Ground. Several skeletons, orientated N.–S., were found over a number of years and these were accompanied by spears, swords, shield bosses, knives, beads and other articles. Many other finds, including more bones and whole skeletons, were made in about 1834 and 1836; none of these can now be traced except for numerous brooches (frontispiece), including large square-headed, disc, saucer, penannular, small-long, florid cruciform and swastika types, as well as wrist clasps, pins, rings and beads (NM). This site is almost certainly the correct location for the cemetery said to have been found at Badby (OS Record Cards; VCH *Northants.*, I (1902), 233; *Archaeologia*, 48 (1885), 336; *JBAA*, 1 (1845), 60; Meaney, *Gazetteer*, 186, 193).

^c(3) SETTLEMENT REMAINS (centred SP 581596; Figs. 11 and 113), formerly part of Newnham village, lie in and around the existing buildings. They help to explain the present village plan and give some support to the hypothesis of a complex sequence of development.

The village of Newnham is first mentioned in a Saxon Charter of 1021–3 (KCD 736) which includes a description

of the bounds of the parish (PN *Northants.*, 26). Its name and the facts that it was a chapelry of Badby and that until recent boundary changes there were blocks of land common to the two parishes all suggest that it was a secondary settlement of Badby.

Newnham is not mentioned in Domesday Book but it has been suggested that the otherwise lost *Chelverdescote* which is recorded there was Newnham by another name (C. Hart, *The Hidation of Northants.* (1970), 35–7). If this is so, then the recorded population of Newnham in 1086 was 13 (VCH *Northants.*, I (1902), 322). In 1377, 52 people over the age of 14 paid the Poll Tax (PRO, E179/155/28), and in 1674, 82 householders contributed to the Hearth Tax (PRO, E179/254/14). By 1801, 302 people lived in the parish.

The village lies across three roughly parallel streams flowing S. in steep-sided valleys to meet the R. Nene, mainly on Middle Lias Clay between 105 m. and 152 m. above OD. The main street lies N.–S. along the spine of one of the ridges between the streams, with the church, dedicated to St. Michael and All Angels, on the E. side. At the lower S. end of the street is a small triangular green from the S.E. corner of which a lane runs down into the valley bottom to the E. and returns N. along the adjacent ridge. It crosses the valley again, joining the N. end of the main street to form an irregular loop. To the S.W. of the green another road curves S.W. into the valley on the W. and this opens out into another large rectangular green.

To the N.E. of the village, in the area of the present Newnham Hall there was until the early 19th century another large green with houses along its N. and W. sides (NRO, Draft Enclosure Map of Newnham, 1765). This green was enclosed and some of the houses demolished when the present Newnham Hall was built.

It is possible to interpret this plan in a number of ways. The village may have originated as a single main street near the church and have expanded subsequently along the other N.–S. street to the E. and to the greens to the W. and N.E. Alternatively the early village may have occupied the E. loop; such loops are a feature common in western Northamptonshire villages and have been interpreted as the result of woodland clearances at an early stage (M. W. Beresford and J. K. S. St Joseph, *Medieval England: An Aerial Survey* (1958), 129). However it is equally possible that the village is a polyfocal settlement developed from four separate nuclei which later grew together. On the other hand the neat rectangular form of the large western green may mean that it was a deliberately planned addition to the W. of the original village. Finally yet another hypothesis is possible. As a result of Hart's identification of *Chelverdescote* with Newnham, P. N. Skelton ('The Chronicles of Newnham', c. 1972, typescript in NRO) suggested that the large western green might be the site of the original *Chelverdescote* from which the rest of the village developed. One reason for this suggestion is that the part of Newnham S. of the green which projects S. of the R. Nene

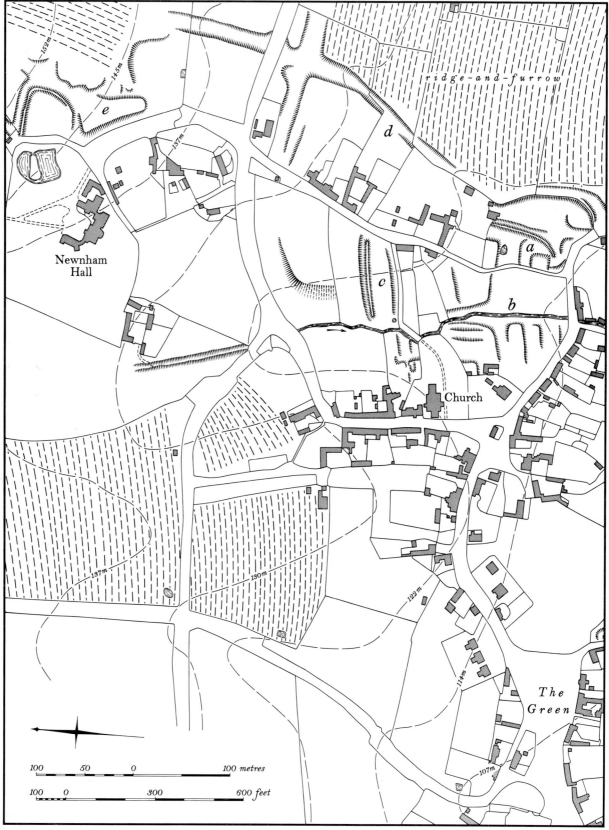

Newnham Hall

ridge-and-furrow

Church

The Green

e

d

c

a

b

152 m

146 m

137 m

137 m

130 m

132 m

114 m

107 m

100   50   0   100 metres

100   0   300   600 feet

Fig. 113   NEWNHAM   (3) Settlement remains

is shown on the draft Enclosure Map and the Enclosure Map of 1765 as an area of old enclosure quite distinct from the common fields of the rest of the parish. These enclosures were then called Cott Lands. Skelton put forward the theory that the name perhaps reflects a connection with *Chelverdescote* which could therefore have lain somewhere close by.

The remaining earthworks are mainly concentrated in four places. To the S. of Newnham House ('a' on plan) is a disturbed area of ground which includes at least three roughly rectangular closes, bounded by banks and scarps, one of which has a house-site at its W. end. To the W., in the valley of the central stream, are other indeterminate earthworks ('b' on plan), including possible traces of embanked closes as well as two parallel terraces on the hillside S.E. of the church, separated by scarps or risers 1 m. high. Further N. on the sides of the same valley ('c' on plan) are traces of abandoned closes extending down to the stream. A hollow-way ('d' on plan), E. of the houses, seems to indicate that there was yet another loop-road, though there is no evidence of occupation along it. The latter, part of which was still in use in 1765, extends N. across the existing road and enters the area occupied by the northern green up to 1765. To the E. of Newnham Hall is a series of rather faint earthworks ('e' on plan), including at least two hollow-ways. These appear to be part of the E. edge of the former green (RAF VAP CPE/UK/1994, 1273–4).

ᵃ(4) DAM (SP 587612), in the extreme N. of the parish, in the valley of the main E.-flowing brook, immediately E. of Burnt Walls (Daventry (35)), on clay at 135 m. above OD. The remains, now ploughed down and almost obliterated, consist of a low bank nowhere much above 1 m. high lying across the stream which flows through it in a later cut. It presumably once held back the water of a small pond. It is not shown on the Enclosure Map of Newnham (NRO, 1765) when the area was called Burnt Walls Common (*Northants. Archaeol.*, 8 (1973), 26).

(5) CULTIVATION REMAINS. The common fields of Newnham were enclosed by an Act of Parliament of 1764 (NRO, Enclosure Map and Draft Enclosure Map, 1765). Before that date there were four open fields, West, Middle, North and Meadow, formerly East, Fields. There were extensive areas of old enclosures along the R. Nene, S.E. of the village, and in the N. of the parish, N.E. of Newnham Hall. All that part of the parish S. of the Nene was also enclosed by 1765 and known as the Cott Lands.

Ridge-and-furrow of the open fields exists on the ground or can be traced on air photographs over much of their area and can be exactly equated with the furlongs shown on the Draft Enclosure Map. On the lower, flatter ground close to the R. Nene and E. of the village in the former East or Meadow Field the ridge-and-furrow is arranged in interlocked furlongs. To the N., on the more broken ground in the former North, Middle and West Fields, the pattern is more complex and is adapted to the

topography; the ridges radiate outwards from the rounded hills and spurs. In some places old trackways or lanes between furlongs are visible on air photographs, though none survives on the ground. One, S.E. of the village (SP 588593), leads into a spring-head. Along the existing road E. from the village the ridges terminate well short of the present hedges because, before the Enclosure, the line of the modern road was taken by a lane at least three times the width of the present one. Ridge-and-furrow also survives in the area of old enclosures arranged in a way that suggests that some of the latter were once part of the common fields. Immediately S.E. of the village (SP 588593), in what was meadowland in 1765, traces of ridges are visible. Likewise in the N.E. of the parish, which in 1765 was Langhill Common (SP 590605) and Burnt Walls Common (SP 587612), there are extensive areas of ridge-and-furrow, running across the contours. However in the Cott Lands, S. of the village, only one field has ridge-and-furrow on it (SP 571586; RAF VAP CPE/UK/1994 1162–7, 1270–5).

49 NORTON

(OS 1:10000 ᵃ SP 56 NE, ᵇ SP 56 SE, ᶜ SP 66 NW, ᵈ SP 66 SW)

The parish, which includes the land of the former villages of Muscott and of Thrupp or Thorp, covers about 1220 hectares. Its original shape was triangular, with the N.E. boundary determined by Watling Street (A5) as is the rule with most of the parishes along the Roman road. In the S.W. part of the parish the boundary follows the E. rampart of the Iron Age hill fort on Borough Hill (Daventry (3)). The land of the village of Muscott (11) now part of Norton, extends E. of Watling Street (Fig. 117). The highest part is in the W. where the Northampton Sand of Borough Hill rises to 190 m. above OD, but most of the W. half is a tableland of Lias Clays and Marlstone Rock at about 125 m. above OD, cut into by the valleys of a number of E.-flowing streams. There is an area of Lias rocks in the E. also, rising to 130 m. above OD and dividing these two areas of high ground is the valley which carries the national arterial routes side by side, the Roman road, the Grand Union Canal, the railway and the M1 motorway. Along this line is a wide band of glacial sands and gravels.

The major monument in the parish is the Roman town of Bannaventa (4), although part of it has been destroyed in recent years. Several other sites give additional evidence of Roman settlement in the surrounding area. Of the medieval sites in the parish the deserted medieval settlement of Thrupp (10) has been totally destroyed, but the earthworks of the former village of Muscott (11) are among the best preserved in the county.

PREHISTORIC AND ROMAN

^d(1) CROPMARKS (SP 629637), in the E. of the parish, N.E. of Muscott, on a steep valley side, on glacial sands and gravels between 110 m. and 125 m. above OD. Air photographs (in NMR) show a number of very indistinct cropmarks over an area of four hectares. No single feature is clearly identifiable but the site includes some circular marks and discontinuous lengths of ditch.

^d(2) BEAKER BURIAL (unlocated, but perhaps at SP 605631), found in 1862 in a gravel pit at Norton. The finds were exhibited at the Society of Antiquaries by Beriah Botfield, owner of Norton Hall, and thus may have come from the gravel pits on the S. side of the park. If this is so the burial was on the end of a N.E.-projecting spur, on glacial deposits at 125 m. above OD. However there are numerous gravel pits in the parish and the finds may have come from any of them.

The burial consists of an extended skeleton, accompanied by a flint dagger 14.5 cm. long (NM) and by fragments of a pot described as a highly ornamented drinking cup of thin ware, presumably a Beaker (*PSA*, 2 (1861–4), 186; *JBAA*, 20 (1864), 343; *Arch. J.*, 35 (1878), 266; D. L. Clarke, *Beaker Pottery of Great Britain and Ireland* (1970), 490).

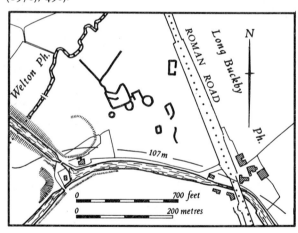

Fig. 114   NORTON   (3) Cropmarks

^c(3) RING DITCHES AND ENCLOSURES (SP 603658; Fig. 114), in the extreme N.E. of the parish and N.E. of Thrupp Grounds, on glacial gravel at 104 m. above OD. Air photographs (CUAP, YK44) show a series of indeterminate cropmarks but these are not all of great antiquity and certainly include the lines of old hedges (not shown on plan). At least three possible ring ditches are visible as well as three small rectangular enclosures, one with an entrance on its E. side near Watling Street, and other features including enclosures and linear ditches can just be recognised.

^d(4) ROMAN TOWN OF BANNAVENTA (SP 612645; Fig. 115 and Plate 1), lies partly in Norton and partly in Whilton,

across the line of Watling Street. It is situated on the S. end of a spur of glacial sand and gravel projecting S.E. between 120 m. and 110 m. above OD.

The Itinerary of Antoninus mentions a place called Bannaventa situated along the road twelve Roman miles N. of Lactodorum (Towcester). The exact identification of the site of Bannaventa was a matter of much dispute among older antiquarians, and Weedon Bec and Daventry were two places suggested. A good summary of the conflicting views is given by W. Edgar (*Borough Hill and its History* (1923)). However even in the early 18th century Morton (*Hist. of Northants.* (1712), 532) observed that 'in that part of Whilton Field which adjoins Watling Street old foundations, the stones of ruined walls and the like have been ploughed or digged up and amongst the ruins some pieces of Roman money'. This was probably immediately S.W. of Whilton Lodge and inside the town (SP 613645). In the early 19th century Baker (*Hist. of Northants.*, I (1822–30), 423) recorded that a skeleton and some Constantinian coins were found in 1813 'in a field called Great Shawney near the footpath to Whilton'. A few years later in 1837 the construction of a new road from Norton on the line of this footpath revealed a burial ground with numerous cremations and inhumations as well as great quantities of samian and other pottery, a fibula and coins (*Archaeologia*, 35 (1853), 391–2; Edgar, op. cit., 55, 104–5). These finds appear to have been made to the S. of the town, at the point where the present Norton road cuts the line of Watling Street (SP 612644) and thus perhaps represent an extra-mural cemetery alongside the Roman road. As a result of these discoveries Bannaventa was firmly located to this general area, though no real details of it were known (VCH *Northants.*, I (1902), 186–7).

In this century more finds have been recorded in and around the town. A number of rubbish pits containing 1st and 2nd-century material were exposed in drainage ditches W. of Watling Street, just N. of and outside the town (SP 60966480), and in 1900 traces of a building including wall-plaster, rotten wood, roof slates and a cobbled floor as well as samian ware and a coin of Victorinus were found in a pipeline trench to the S.E., on the other side of Watling Street (SP 61026472; Edgar, op. cit., 56). A few years before 1922 a drain cut somewhere within the area of the town produced a quantity of Roman coins, including a sestertius of Hadrian, 119–128 and a denarius and a sestertius of Trajan, 104–110 (Edgar, op. cit., 56 and Plate 23). A trial excavation in the field W. of Watling Street, in 1955, probably just inside the town defences (about SP 612648), revealed more rubbish pits containing 1st and 2nd-century material (*J. Northants. Natur. Hist. Soc. and FC*, 33 (1957), 132–43). Finds from this excavation (in NM) include a large Nene Valley type beaker decorated with three horizontal bands of barbotine scrollwork, a tall folded beaker, a large painted pot ornamented with concentric circles of latticework, part of a glass bowl, fragments of a black samian pot with an applied relief of the chariot of

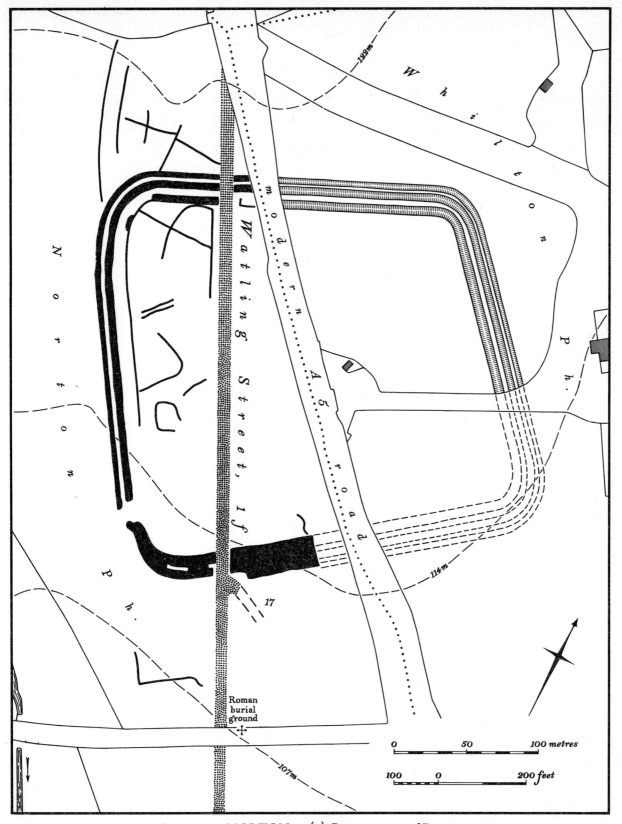

Fig. 115   NORTON   (4) Roman town of Bannaventa

Apollo and the letters PAT[ERNAS] (*Ant. J.*, 27 (1957), 40), and a small bowl of imitation samian, form 29, decorated with white slip spots. All are of 2nd-century date. In NM there is also a small grey-ware pot which contained a hoard of antoniniani. Around the same time more pottery was picked up inside the town (SP 61106451) and a scatter of building debris was noted further S.E. in 1969 (SP 61226443; OS Record Cards). In 1953 an Iron Age coin (Allen LX 22, Mack 274, Evans G7) was found in the area (NM; S.S. Frere (ed.), *Problems of the Iron Age in Southern Britain* (1958), 190).

In 1970 air photographs taken by J. K. S. St Joseph (CUAP, BCO34; *Antiquity*, 45 (1971), 140–1) revealed the outline of the part of the town W. of the modern road. From these photographs and others (in NMR; *BNFAS*, 6 (1971), 16) it is possible to ascertain many features of the W. half of the town. These photographs and the later excavations show that the town was of irregular quadrilateral shape with broad rounded corners. It appears to have been bounded by two ditches on the N.W. and S.W. sides (but see below for excavations). Inside the W. corner and along part of the N.W. side there appears to be a third ditch set back from the other two; the very narrow S. extension of this could be either a ditch or a line of closely set pits. This feature may mark the rear of an earlier bank or rampart but is more likely to be the remains of a third, innermost ditch contemporary with the other two ditches. On the S.E. side and at the S. corner the various ditches are not visible on any available air photographs; a wide irregular cropmark obscures all details. In the N.W. and S.E. sides of these defences there are gaps to allow the passage of Watling Street through the town. The asymmetric relationship of the town to this road is extremely unusual. The road is visible as a broad, light-coloured line traceable from a point S. of the town where the modern road leaves it (SP 61506374) to just N. of the town where the two rejoin (SP 61006472) and at one place inside the town what appear to be side ditches are visible. Immediately beyond the S. entrance there are slight indications of another road, edged by ditches, branching off Watling Street to the S.E. and traceable for only 25 m. This is likely to be the beginning of the Roman Road 17 which is known to have run S.E. to Duston (see Appendix). Apart from the line of Watling Street, the air photographs show a number of ditches, perhaps forming enclosures, as well as other disturbances in the interior. Ditches extending beyond the existing defences appear to continue the line of the S.W. side of the town to the N.W.

To the E. of the modern road, the land has for a long time been permanent pasture and no cropmarks have been recorded there but excavations were carried out in 1970–2 on the assumed N. corner of the town in order to locate and date the boundary ditches and to investigate the interior. This work revealed three clear ditches. The earliest defences were found to have been a ditch at least 7.6 m. wide and 3.1 m. deep apparently backed by a clay

and turf rampart. The date of this ditch was not accurately ascertained, but it appeared to be later than the late 1st century. After this, perhaps in the early 4th century, the ditch was filled in and replaced by a stone wall some 3.7 m. wide. Beyond the wall were two further ditches 5.2 m. wide and 2.4 m. deep and 4.3 m. wide and 1.8 m. deep respectively. Again the dating was uncertain but they seemed to have been abandoned in or after the late 4th century.

Behind the defences a circular structure 6.7 m. in diam. and dated to the 1st century was found, as well as a number of small ditches, some of prehistoric date. Outside the defences to the N. a cobbled surface bounded by a shallow ditch was discovered. It was interpreted as a possible street and dated to after the mid 2nd century. To the E. of it were a number of pits and a hearth. Further S., in the interior of the town, a large excavation revealed pits, gulleys and ditches of various periods, a stone-lined well filled-in late in the Roman period, occasional post-holes and many stake-holes. At one place the floor and sleeper-beam slots of at least two timber-framed buildings were found; the later one had a room decorated with plaster imitating marble. Three adult burials were discovered as well as a number of coins, mostly of the 4th century. One Iron Age coin, a pre-Tasciovanus issue was found (*BNFAS*, 7 (1972), 27–9; CBA Group 9, *Newsletter*, 2 (1972), 9; DOE *Arch. Excavations 1971* (1972), 21–2; *Britannia*, 3 (1972), 325; 4 (1973), 296).

In the area surrounding the town there are several other Roman sites which are clearly connected with it (see (5–8) below and Whilton (1)).

^a(5) ROMAN SETTLEMENT (SP 599651; Fig. 118), occupies the area between Thrupp Lodge and Thrupp Grounds on the summit and N.E. side of a ridge of glacial gravel and sands at about 125 m. above OD. Part of the site appears to underlie that of the deserted village of Thrupp (10) and it is therefore not easy to distinguish the two settlements. The Roman nature of the occupation was noted in the early 19th century when 'some twenty coins' are recorded as being found by the owner of Thrupp Grounds (VCH *Northants.*, I (1902), 187) as well as pottery, foundations, pavements and 'fireplaces', spread over more than 10 hectares (G. Baker, *Hist of Northants.*, I (1822–30), 425). Baker visited the site and recorded a 'large inverted cinerary urn' from the gravel pit which still remains N. of Thrupp Lodge.

More recent fieldwork has produced conclusive evidence of Roman occupation. In 1960 a 'samian urn', three coins and pottery and tile were found (SP 59946510; NM Records) and since then large quantities of pottery, mainly of 2nd and 3rd-century date and including samian ware, have been noted over a wide area. Air photographs (in NMR) show cropmarks extending across the two fields N.E. of Thrupp Lodge though none clearly reveals all the details. There is certainly a series of overlapping enclosures and ditches (*Northants. Archaeol.*, 8 (1973), 26). To the E. (at SP 605651) is a ring ditch, 15 m. in diam., with a smaller ring ditch attached to its W. side, only 7 m. across. There is another curving ditch on the S. side of the main ring ditch, parallel to it and only 5 m. from it.

d(6) ROMAN SETTLEMENT (centred SP 613638), lies S. of Bannaventa (3), on the W. side of Watling Street, on glacial sands and gravels at 100 m. above OD. In 1947 Roman pottery and a denarius of Julia Mamaea, 222–235, (NM) were found on the edge of a stream (SP 61436377) and in 1948 more pottery was found in a sand-pit a little to the N. (SP 61376389; OS Record Cards). Since then field-walking has revealed a scatter of Roman pottery mainly of 3rd or 4th-century date over an area of about 2 hectares (For Saxon finds, possibly from this site, see below).

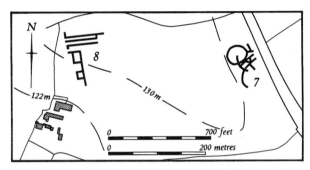

Fig. 116   NORTON
(7, 8) Roman settlements

d(7) ROMAN SETTLEMENT (SP 608649; Fig. 116), lies N.W. of Bannaventa (3) and W. of Watling Street, on glacial sands and gravels at 125 m. above OD. Air photographs (in NMR) show very indistinctly a number of conjoined enclosures and ditches including one small and one very large circular feature. A small quantity of Roman pottery has been found on the site.

d(8) ROMAN VILLA (?) (SP 605649; Fig. 116), immediately N.N.E. of Norton Lodge Farm on glacial sands and gravels at 127 m. above OD. Air photographs (in NMR) show rather indistinctly a series of parallel, straight parch-marks; the southernmost of these has a small two-roomed building at its W. end. To the S. are two rectangular features linked by what is perhaps a length of walling. On the ground is a scatter of mainly 4th-century pottery with a few pieces of tile.

For Roman Roads 1f, Watling Street, and 17, see Appendix.

MEDIEVAL AND LATER

A small Pagan Saxon bronze fibula, half of a sleeve link, and a disc, probably part of a saucer brooch (NM) are said to have been found S. of Bannaventa (3) in the area of the Roman settlement (6) (SP 61456377). However this location

may be incorrect and they perhaps came from the Saxon burials (9). Triangular iron implements of unknown date were found in the parish in the late 19th century (*PSA*, 6 (1873–6), 183).

d(9) SAXON BURIALS (SP 61916283), in the S.E. of the parish on sand and gravel at 110 m. above OD. A low mound 40 m.–50 m. long, 2 m.–3 m. wide and 1 m. high lay immediately E. of Watling Street, on the boundary between the land of the village of Muscott (11) and that of Norton (Fig. 117). It was levelled in 1855–6 and some graves were found in it containing five or six skeletons together with an amber bead and some pieces of metal. In 1863 the present road was laid across the site and the mound was destroyed. At that time another grave was discovered as well as a saucer brooch, a disc brooch, a bronze-gilt square-headed brooch, two bronze rings, an iron knife and a bone spindle whorl. It has been suggested that the Roman road itself had been diverted at this point to avoid a pre-Roman mound and that the burials were therefore secondary. This is unlikely, for the mound is said to have lain 8 m. from the centre of the original embankment of Watling Street (*Archaeologia*, 41 (1868), 479–81; Meaney, *Gazetteer*, 194; *BNFAS*, 7 (1972), 67; OS Record Cards).

ab(10) DESERTED VILLAGE OF THRUPP (SP 598650; Figs. 117 and 118), lay in the N. of the parish, around and E. of Thrupp Lodge, on the summit of an E.–W. ridge capped with glacial sands and gravels at 125 m. above OD.

Thrupp or Thorp, first documented in Domesday Book, was at that time apparently divided into two small manors with a total recorded population of only three (VCH *Northants.*, I (1902), 331, 348). In 1256 one Hugh de Capis alias de Caps, had 20 shillings rent from Thorpe 'town' (*Cal. IPM* i, No. 360). It is mentioned by name in the *Nomina Villarum* of 1316, but in later taxation records it is always included with Norton. For most of the late medieval period Thrupp belonged to Daventry Priory which maintained a chapel there; in 1489 the prior of Daventry enclosed all the land of the village, abandoned the chapel, destroyed 18 houses and expelled 100 people and by 1518 the chapel was described as fallen *in desolacionem*. In a survey of the former possessions of Daventry Priory in about 1530 Thrupp is described as being formerly a town but converted into pasture and having a ruined chapel. By 1564 only one farm lay in the area (M. W. Beresford, *The Lost Villages of England* (1954), 368; K. J. Allison *et al.*, *The Deserted Villages of Northants.* (1966), 47; G. Baker, *Hist. of Northants.*, I (1822–30), 425, 316; Whellan, *Dir.*, 428; J. M. Steane, *The Northamptonshire Landscape* (1974), 174–5) and by the early 18th century still only a single farm, probably Thrupp Lodge, remained (J. Bridges, *Hist. of Northants.*, I (1791), 80). Since that time a number of other scattered farms have been built in the general area. On the Tithe Map of Norton of 1847 (NRO) the fields in which the site lies are called Town Closes; the land which belonged to the village and which occupied a strip along the N. boundary of the parish is recoverable from the map and is shown on Fig. 117.

The surface remains of the village have been totally destroyed by cultivation but on three fields to the E. and N.E. of Thrupp Lodge are large quantities of pottery. Much of this comes from the underlying Roman settlement (5), but the rest is of medieval date, mainly 12th to 14th-century. From the distribution of this pottery and the remains of ridge-and-furrow in the adjacent fields, some idea of the extent of the village can be ascertained. A trial excavation on the site (SP 59916516) is said to have revealed a layer of rough stone with pottery above and below it (OS Record Cards).

Immediately E. of Thrupp Lodge (SP 59766502) are the fragmentary remains of a *Moated Site*. It is very overgrown and badly mutilated but consists of a ditch, U-shaped in plan, partly dry and partly water-filled, up to 1.5 m. deep. It presumably once continued on the N.E. side to form a moated enclosure. The S.E. side extends S.W. for some 60 m. and may be the remains of another enclosure, the interior of which is occupied by the present farm. This S.E. side has a low, spread bank only 0.25 m. high outside it. The site is shown, exactly as it is today, on the Tithe Map of Norton of 1847 (NRO; RAF VAP CPE/UK/1994, 4359–61).

^d(11) DESERTED VILLAGE OF MUSCOTT (SP 627633; Figs. 117 and 119; Plate 8), lies within a small projection of Norton parish which extends N.E. across the line of Watling Street. The area is undoubtedly the land of the village with its W. boundary along the Roman road. The

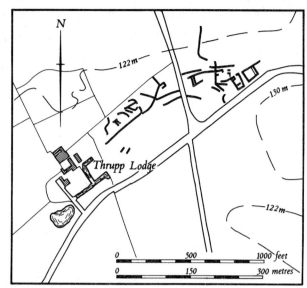

Fig 118   NORTON   (5) Roman settlement, (10) Deserted medieval settlement of Thrupp

village lay on land sloping W. towards a small S.-flowing stream mainly on Middle Lias Clay between 107 m. and 87 m. above OD.

The name Muscott is said to derive from the Old English Musa-cote, 'mices cottages', perhaps a derogatory term for some humble dwellings (PN *Northants.*, 27). The village is first documented in Domesday Book where it is listed together with Brockhall (1) as a small manor of three virgates and a recorded population of six (VCH *Northants.*, I (1902), 325). In the 1301 Lay Subsidy, it is again listed with Brockhall with a total of 48 tax-payers (PRO, E179/155/31). This high figure is probably mainly made up of people living at Muscott, for Brockhall always seems to have been very small. Muscott is separately mentioned in the *Nomina Villarum* of 1316, and in 1334 the vill paid 50s. tax for the Lay Subsidy, a higher sum than many other now deserted villages in the county (PRO, E179/155/3). By 1377 only five people over the age of 14 paid the Poll Tax in Brockhall and Muscott together (PRO, E179/155/27). As Brockhall still seems to have been in existence it appears that this drop in population marks the abandonment of Muscott. In 1524 when the two places were again combined for the Taxation of the Laity only nine people are listed (PRO, E179/155/134). In 1547, 300 sheep were grazing on Muscott Pasture and in 1576, when Sir John Spencer of Althorp bought the manor, the latter consisted of four closes of pasture and meadow. The Hearth Tax Returns of 1673 list seventeen houses for Brockhall and Muscott (PRO, E179/254/14) but most of these were probably at Brockhall, for in the early 18th century Bridges (*Hist. of Northants.*, I (1791), 483) recorded only three houses at Muscott. By 1841, forty people lived at 'Muscott' but by then only the present farm existed on the site and most people lived at Gazewell Farm and other

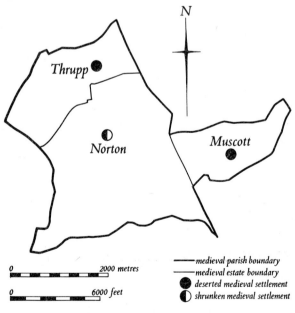

medieval parish boundary
medieval estate boundary
● deserted medieval settlement
◑ shrunken medieval settlement

Fig. 117   NORTON
Medieval settlements and estates

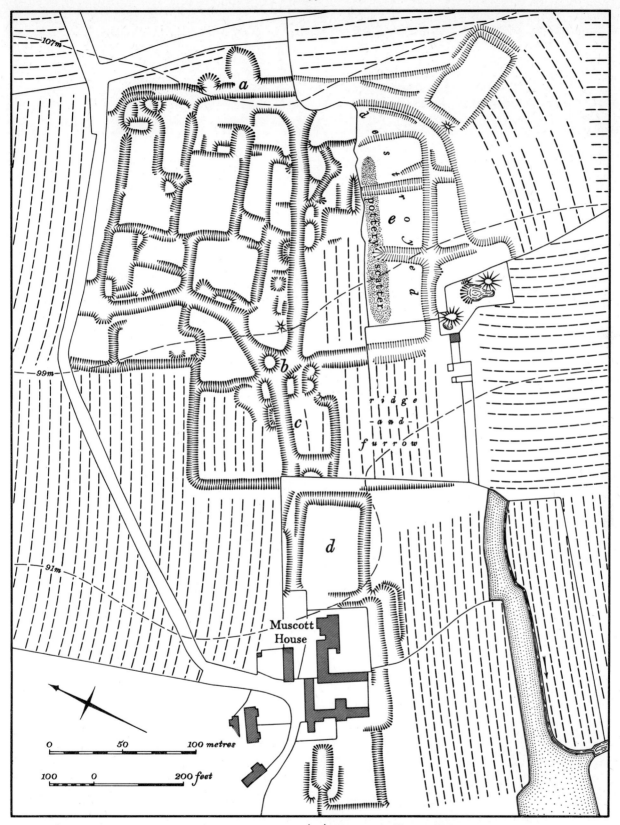

a

e
s
t
r
o
y
e
d

pottery scatter

b

c

d

ridge
-and-
furrow

Muscott
House

0   50   100 metres

100   0   200 feet

Fig. 119   NORTON   (11) Deserted village of Muscott

cottages in the surrounding area (K. J. Allison *et al.*, *The Deserted Villages of Northants.* (1966), 43). The field in which the earthworks lie was then called Lower Hughes Close (NRO, Tithe Map of Norton, 1847).

The site is extremely well preserved apart from its S.E. part which was destroyed in 1958–9. Before this the village had a strikingly rectangular shape made up of three separate parts. The main part, to the N.E., consisted of a roughly rectangular area bounded on the N.E. by a broad hollow-way up to 2 m. deep ('a' on plan). At its N.W. end this hollow-way meets the modern track to Muscott House which is probably on the line of a road which once bounded the village on the N.W. Just E. of the bend in the modern track a hollow-way curves S.E. and then S. to a small triangular area with a low mound in its centre ('b' on plan). From this one hollow-way continues S.W. towards Muscott House ('c' on plan), another runs S.E. and then turns N.E. to join the first mentioned one, while the third extends N.E., roughly bisecting the whole of this part of the village. Within the area enclosed by the hollow-ways and on either side of the central hollow-way are a number of small rectangular paddocks or closes bounded by low scarps or ditches. Some of these, and especially those on each side of the central hollow-way, have well-marked house-sites within them consisting of raised platforms or embanked depressions, suggesting that stone buildings formerly stood there.

To the S.W. of this part of the village, on either side of the hollow-way to Muscott House ('c' on plan), are ditched closes with house-sites edging the hollow-way. Faint traces of mutilated ridge-and-furrow within the closes appear to be cut by the hollowed 'yards' behind and this suggests that this part of the village at least was laid out on top of earlier fields. Indeed the close to the E., inside the main part of the village, also has traces of ridge-and-furrow on it, again possibly cut by later house-sites and a yard. Further S.W. is a rectangular enclosure ('d' on plan), bounded on three sides by a shallow ditch only 0.25 m. deep and on the fourth, S.W. side by Muscott House. To the S. of the house another ditch, now hardly traceable but apparently 2 m. deep before it was levelled (local inf.), may have continued N.W. and surrounded the house and farmyard as a double enclosure. This assumed moat may have been connected with the late medieval gatehouse which still stands on the N.W. side of the farmyard and thus the house and farm may be on the site of a moated medieval manor lying S.W. of the village. Immediately S.W. of the farm buildings a shallow rectangular depression with a ditch leading down to the stream is probably a fishpond. Excavations were carried out during the destruction of the S.E. part of the site in 1958, within the three closes between the hollow-way to the S. and the modern hedge to the N. ('e' on plan). Trial trenches produced no significant evidence in two of the closes, but in the third three buildings of 12th to 13th-century date were discovered. The main building was a large three-

room structure with walls of sandstone blocks and a central hearth in the main chamber, the second was long and rectangular perhaps with a raised wooden floor, and the third was also rectangular but much smaller. Finds indicated that the area was occupied from the late 12th century to the late 13th or early 14th century (*Med. Arch.*, 3 (1959), 322; DMVRG *6th Annual Report* (1958), 7–8).

Large quantities of medieval pottery, none earlier than the 12th century and mostly from the 13th and early 14th centuries, have been found on the destroyed part of the site and similar material has come from modern water-pipe trenches cut across the surviving earthworks (RAF VAP CPE/UK/1994, 2263–4; CUAP, LT11, SD58–64, VD1, AO18, AOK56, AMW65, AWQ59–60; air photographs in NMR).

^d(12) SETTLEMENT REMAINS (SP 602635; Figs. 12 and 120; Plate 15), formerly part of Norton, lie immediately E. of the village and S.S.W. of the church, on glacial sands and gravels at 127 m. above OD. The village is first mentioned in 1086 when Domesday Book lists a recorded population of 34 (VCH *Northants.*, I (1902), 329). There is no indication of its size during the rest of the medieval period as it is included in most of the national taxation records with Thrupp (10); the Poll Tax Returns of 1377, for example, list 181 people over the age of 14 paying tax in Norton, but as Thrupp still existed at that date the figure is probably much too large for Norton itself (PRO, E179/155/28). In the 1523 Subsidy Taxation Norton was assessed for £3 8s. 8d., a relatively low figure though this may not be significant (PRO, E179/155/161). In 1673, 52 people paid the Hearth Tax (PRO, E179/254/14) and by 1801, 362 people lived in the parish, but this figure included a large number of inhabitants of outlying farms.

Up to the mid 19th century the village appears to have had a layout somewhat different from the present one (NRO, Tithe Map of Norton, 1847; Plate 15); the triangular W. part of the village was not built up, and there was a road, perhaps once the main road, running S. from the present 'green' W. of the church. This road followed the line of the present lane to the vicarage and then swung S.W. to join the existing road at the S. end of the village; on its W. side stood at least seven buildings, all probably houses. Soon after 1847 the park of Norton Hall was extended W., the houses were demolished and the road was stopped-up. This was presumably carried out by Beriah Botfield who then owned the Hall. The surviving earthworks suggest that part of the village once lay E. of this road but had already been abandoned before the 19th century.

The remains consist of a number of indeterminate rectangular closes bounded by low banks and scarps. A hollow-way up to 1.75 m. deep approaches the area from the S.E. and then forks; the N.W. branch extends as a very shallow depression towards the S. end of the existing village, and the N. branch, though mutilated, appears to have had at least four closes on its W. side. Further N., and

S. of the church, a short length of another hollow-way is visible running E.–W.

d(13) SITE OF MANSION HOUSE (SP 603636), immediately E. of Norton church on a crest of a hill with extensive views to the E. The remains are those of Norton Hall and its gardens, a largely 19th-century house destroyed in 1952 and presumably on the site of the medieval manor house. The manor was sold in 1800 to Thomas Botfield who gave it to his son, Beriah. The latter is said to have improved and modernized the house by 1808. He died in 1813 and extensive alterations were carried out by his son, another Beriah Botfield, who died in 1863 (Whellan *Dir.*, 427–8). The house, as it survived into this century, was in the Gothic style and was described by J. A. Gotch (*Squires' Homes of Northants.*, (1939), 37) as a good example of the architecture of the second quarter of the 19th century. However the house has a long history and is said to have incorporated the remains of one built or repaired by Sir Richard Knightley who held the manor in the late 16th century (J. A. Gotch, op. cit. 37; G. Baker, *Hist. of Northants.*, I (1822–30), 416, 418). The site consists of a large rectangular platform on which stood the house; to the S., N.E. and E., are fragments of terraces and walls of the 19th-century gardens. Beyond, in the park, is a line of small lakes formed by damming the N.E.-flowing stream (photographs in NMR).

a(14) FISHPONDS (SP 597655), close to the small stream which forms the N. boundary of the parish, on clay and alluvium at about 105 m. above OD. Air photographs (RAF VAP CPE/UK/1994, 4359–60) show two small rectangular depressions which appear to be simple, unembanked ponds with no visible system of leats. The site has now been ploughed and only slight depressions remain. In 1847 (NRO, Tithe Map) the area was called Briers Orchard; no ponds are marked.

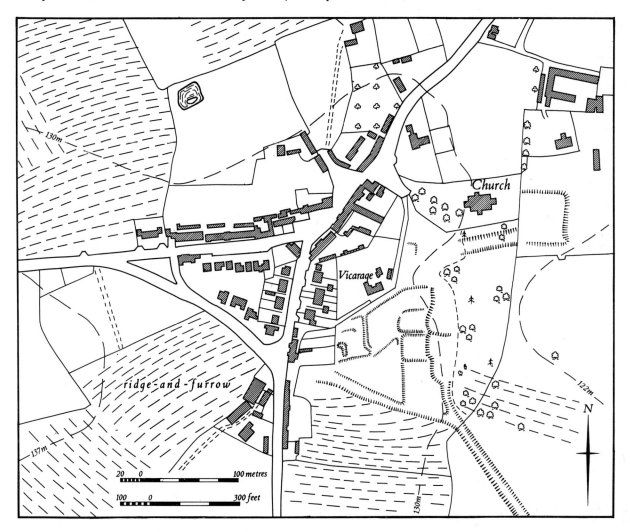

Fig. 120   NORTON   (12) Settlement remains at Norton

ᵈ(15) WINDMILL MOUND (SP 63186385), lies S.E. of Windmill Barn on the side of the road to Muscott (11) and within the land attributable to that village. It stands on the W. edge of a high ridge on sand and gravel at 130 m. above OD and consists of a low circular mound 0.25 m. high and 15 m. in diam., with no visible ditch. A windmill known as Muscott Mill is shown here on the Tithe Map of Norton (NRO, 1847).

(16) CULTIVATION REMAINS. The common fields of the old parish of Norton were enclosed by Act of Parliament in 1755. Most of the ridge-and-furrow of these fields can be traced on the ground or from air photographs, arranged in interlocked and end-on furlongs in response to the direction of slope in an area of rolling landscape.

The pattern of ridge-and-furrow is a little less complete in the land of the deserted village of Thrupp (10) which now constitutes the N.W. part of the modern parish. In this area again there are groups of interlocked furlongs on the sides of the valleys along the N.W.-facing scarp. The fields of Thrupp were completely enclosed in 1489 by the prior of Daventry to whom the lordship belonged.

The common fields of Muscott were enclosed before 1547 but the exact date is unknown. About half of the ridge-and-furrow of the common fields of the former village can still be traced on the ground or from air photographs. Much of it runs S.W.–N.E. down the main slope of the land, with interlocked furlongs where small valleys occur (RAF VAP CPE/UK/1994, 2261–8, 4268–73, 4358–64).

UNDATED

ᵇ(17) ENCLOSURE (about SP 592618), on the S.E. corner of Borough Hill on Northampton Sand at about 175 m. above OD. In 1712 Morton (*Nat. Hist. of Northants.*, 521) described what he called a 'lesser camp' here, bounded by a 'single Trench and a bank of Earth on the Inside of it. The Area is supposed to be about an Acre. The Figure on Oblong Square'. It apparently had entrances on the E. and W. sides. By 1823 when Baker described the site (*Hist. of Northants.*, I (1822–30), 346) it was 'barely discernible' and the ditch was only 20 cm.–25 cm. deep. It now survives as an almost square enclosure 40 m. by 47 m. bounded by a low scarp less than 0.5 m. high and with traces of an outer ditch. Its date and function are unknown.

50 OXENDON, GREAT

(OS 1:10000 ᵃ SP 78 NW, ᵇ SP 78 SW)

The modern parish is roughly rectangular and covers about 700 hectares. It includes the site and the land of the former village of Little Oxendon (9) which up to the 19th century lay in Little Bowden, Leicestershire. The village of Great Oxendon, at a height of more than 150 m. above OD, is situated on the watershed between the R. Welland to the N. and the R. Ise to the S. and the land falls away steeply in both directions from the village. The lowest point, on the county boundary, is some 90 m. above OD. The higher parts of the parish are covered by Boulder Clay, which gives way to Lias clays as the land falls to the two rivers. The most important monument is the well-preserved site of the deserted village of Little Oxendon (9). Great Oxendon itself is of interest because the village lies some way to the S. of the isolated medieval church (see (6)).

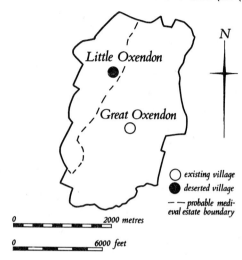

Fig. 121   OXENDON, GREAT
Medieval settlements and estates

ROMAN

A coin of Marcus Aurelius was found in the parish in 1719, to the N. of St. Helen's Church (J. Bridges, *Hist. of Northants.*, II (1791), 56).

ᵇ(1) ROMAN SETTLEMENT (?) (SP 724848), in the N.W. of the parish on clay at 130 m. above OD. Roman pottery has been found (*Northants. Archaeol.*, 10 (1975), 154).

ᵇ(2) ROMAN SETTLEMENT (?) (SP 730844), lies immediately S. of the deserted village of Little Oxendon (9), on the steep W. side of the valley, on clay at 130 m. above OD. A large area of limestone, flint, ironstone and slag is spread over an area 50 m. across. Roman as well as medieval pottery has been found there.

ᵇ(3) ROMAN SETTLEMENT (?) (SP 722830), S.W. of the village, on gravel at 130 m. above OD. A scatter of Roman pottery has been noted (*Northants. Archaeol.*, 12 (1977), 212; for Saxon pottery from this site, see (4)).

MEDIEVAL AND LATER

ᵇ(4) SAXON SETTLEMENT (?) (SP 722830), on the same site as the Roman settlement (3) above. Small quantities of Saxon sherds have been noted (*Northants. Archaeol.*, 12 (1977), 212).

b(5) SAXON INHUMATION BURIAL (SP 732834). A skeleton, spearhead, knife and scramasax are said to have been found in the parish (Meaney, *Gazetteer*, 194), but these may be the objects also recorded from Clipston (5) (*J. Northants. Mus. and Art Gall.*, 6 (1969), 49).

b(6) SETTLEMENT REMAINS (?) (SP 735839), probably lie around the isolated church of Great Oxendon, 600 m. N. of the present village, on Boulder Clay at 140 m. above OD. The church stands near the E. end of an E.-facing spur, with extensive views all round and it is possible that the original site of Great Oxendon was in this area though the evidence for this is limited. The whole of the surrounding area is permanent pasture and is covered with extensive ridge-and-furrow (10). Some irregular depressions immediately W. of the church are perhaps old quarries, but as the ridge-and-furrow runs over them they are clearly of considerable antiquity and may originally have been sites of houses. Medieval pottery of 12th to 15th-century date has been noted in the churchyard.

b(7) SETTLEMENT REMAINS (centred SP 733833; Fig. 121), formerly part of the present village of Great Oxendon, lie within the village on Lias Clay and Boulder Clay between 135 m. and 150 m. above OD. Indeterminate earthworks, probably the sites of former buildings, exist on the S. side of the main street S. of the hall (SP 73488332) and immediately W. of Home Farm on the N. side of the street (SP 73208341). Further W. a hollow-way some 7 m. wide and 1.5 m. deep extends N. for some 150 m. from near the W. end of the main street, running roughly parallel to and 40 m. E. of the Farndon Road (SP 730835). This was probably an earlier road leading to either Little Oxendon (9) or East Farndon. Some of these earthworks must be those recorded by Bridges in the early 18th century (*Hist. of Northants.*, II (1791), 8) as 'banks and hollows, like the vestiges of demolished buildings'.

b(8) WINDMILL MOUND (SP 73078397), lies on high land N. of the village of Great Oxendon on Boulder Clay at 135 m. above OD. The mound is large, 20 m. in diam. and 1.5 m. high, with a slight depression in the flat top and traces of a ditch 0.2 m. deep around it, except on the E. where the remains of a ramp leading on to the summit survive. The mound is respected by the adjacent ridge-and-furrow. Late medieval and 18th-century pottery together with a large number of iron nails has been found in a worn area on the E. side.

A water-filled pit to the E., probably the source of material for the mound, was largely filled in some years ago but slight traces of it remain. The local name for the site is Mill Moot (OS Record Cards; finds in NM).

b(9) DESERTED VILLAGE OF LITTLE OXENDON (SP 733845; Figs. 121 and 122), lies 1 km. N.W. of Great Oxendon, on the crest of a spur projecting N.E. below the main Lias escarpment, between 118 m. and 135 m. above OD. The underlying soil is based on Lias clays and silts, and on

Boulder Clay to the S.W. The remains, preserved under permanent pasture, lie on gently sloping ground. On each side the land falls steeply into a narrow valley.

Little Oxendon was formerly in the parish of Little Bowden, itself now part of Market Harborough, Leicestershire. It was also a chapelry of Little Bowden. It is not mentioned specifically in Domesday Book but there are two entries under Oxendon, one of which is likely to be Little Oxendon. One of these entries is for a manor of one hide and one virgate held by the king as part of Rothwell; no population is recorded. The other, of one hide, was held by Ulf under the Countess Judith, and had a recorded population of 11 (VCH *Northants.*, I (1902), 306, 352). In 1334 the village paid 32s. tax (PRO, E179/155/3) and in 1377, 50 people over the age of 14 paid the Poll Tax (PRO, E179/155/28). In 1405 there were still at least eight people there for these complained about the chapel which existed in the village at that time (J. E. Stocks, *Parish Records of Market Harborough* (1890), 125, 235). In 1515 the manor was bought by Andrew Palmer and when he died in 1525 there was apparently only one house and 300 acres of pasture there. In the early 18th century Bridges (*Hist. of Northants.*, II (1791), 8–9) wrote that there were 'formerly several houses as appears from the many square building stones and burnt hearth-stones which have been dug up'. From these figures it appears that the village was deliberately cleared for sheep farming in the 14th century (K. J. Allison *et al.*, *The Deserted Villages of Northants.* (1966), 44). The village seems to have had a chapel, described as 'not yet consecrated' in 1398 and which was still standing in 1525 (J. E. Stocks, op. cit.; OS Record Cards).

The earthworks of the village consist of a main hollow-way running N.E.–S.W. along the spine of the spur, with the sites of former buildings set in rectangular closes on either side of it. At its N.E. end the hollow-way fades out and cannot be traced much beyond the village itself. At the S.W. end, however, the hollow-way continues as a broad, flat, open track between blocks of ridge-and-furrow and then, as it climbs steeply up the main escarpment, becomes deep and wide again and is cut into by many later clay-pits.

Within the village itself, the main hollow-way is between 1 m. and 2 m. deep. It is edged by a number of shallow depressions, none of them very deep, all presumably the sites of former buildings. These depressions are separated by low banks or scarps which extend down the hillsides and represent some of the original close boundaries. In two places, towards the S.E. end of the village, low scarps also mark the ends of these closes. The closes on the N.W. side have been overploughed by later ridge-and-furrow.

On the N. side of the main street ('a' on plan) is a large rectangular enclosure bounded by a shallow ditch up to 1 m. high with an internal bank on the W. and N.E. sides. In its interior are several shallow depressions and, in the E.

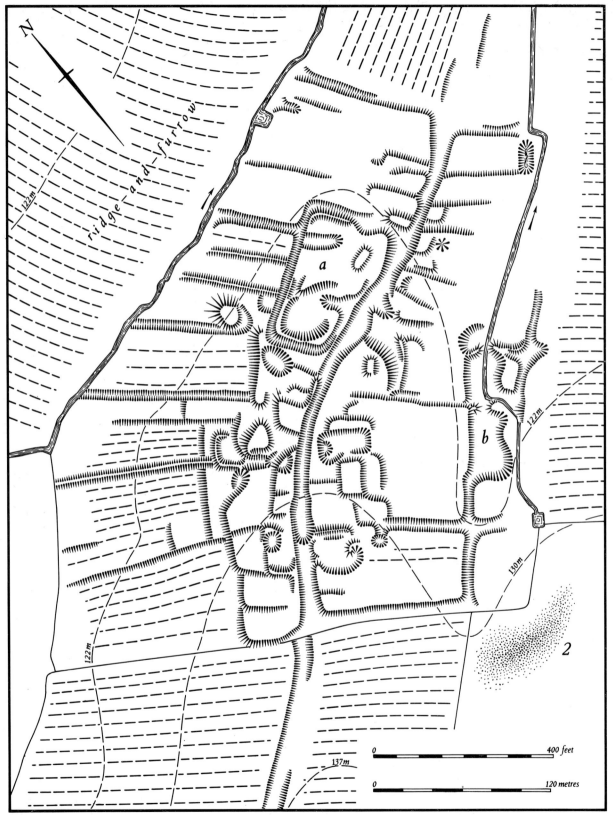

Fig. 122   OXENDON, GREAT   (2) Roman settlement,   (9) Deserted village of Little Oxendon

corner, a large rectangular embanked feature, probably the remains of a stone building. This enclosure may be the site of the former manor house or chapel.

S.E. of the village, in the bottom of the valley ('b' on plan), are the mutilated remains of two small ponds cut into the valley sides; the original dams have been almost completely cut away though the ends of both survive. They may have been fishponds or millponds, or perhaps both. Above them on the steep hillside to the S.E. is a small terrace-way, of unknown purpose, with a large area of later quarrying beyond. Except to the S., the village is surrounded by well-preserved ridge-and-furrow.

Two 'excavations' have been carried out on the site. In 1863 a farmer digging for stone found 'roads covered with loose stones and also pavements consisting of stones placed close together edgeways'. He also discovered the foundations of many houses and the remains of a building of considerable size, thought to be a church or chapel. Charred wood, a stone-lined well, a spur and part of a bridle were discovered as well as a coin of Elizabeth I and another of William III (*Trans. Leics. Arch. Soc.*, 2 (1870), 258–60). Archaeological work carried out between 1926 and 1932 revealed what appears to have been a pottery kiln as well as much iron slag and pottery, then thought to 'favour a pre-Roman rather than a Romano-British' date (*J. Northants. Natur. Hist. Soc. and FC*, 26 (1932), 173–4). In Market Harborough museum is a sherd of 13th-century pottery, a spatula and spindle whorl, said to be from the site.

(10) CULTIVATION REMAINS. The common fields of Great Oxendon were enclosed by an Act of Parliament of 1767. The date of the enclosure of the common fields of Little Oxendon is unknown, but it had presumably taken place by the 16th century. The parish is notable for the survival of large areas of ridge-and-furrow, especially around the church and to the E. of the village and near the deserted village of Little Oxendon. It is arranged in interlocked furlongs, except along the steep valley sides where it all runs across the contours. E. of Great Oxendon, N. of the Braybrooke road (SP 740833), a small area of ridge-and-furrow arranged in two furlongs at right-angles to each other appears to be at least partly surrounded by an embanked and ditched feature. This was overploughed by the ridge-and-furrow at the E. and W. end and it may be an early enclosure incorporated into the medieval field system (RAF VAP 106G/UK/636, 4125–9, 3125–9; CPE/UK/2109, 3288–92).

51 PITSFORD

(OS 1:10000 ᵃ SP 76 NW, ᵇ SP 76 NE)

The roughly rectangular parish, covering almost 600 hectares, occupies a W.-facing spur between the Pitsford Brook which forms the N. and W. boundaries and a W.-flowing brook close to the S. boundary. The centre is a generally level area about 105 m. above OD, mainly on Northampton Sand, which slopes steeply to the streams on the N., W. and S. The lack of archaeological sites in the parish, compared with the geologically similar area further S. and S.W. in the Bramptons and Brixworth where indications of early occupation have come to light, is striking, but extensive ironstone-quarrying in the S.W. part of the parish may have destroyed the evidence.

The mount (4) known as Longmans Hill is of great interest. Its attribution as a long barrow is doubtful, but the Anglo-Saxon material said to have come from it or from the close vicinity is of considerable importance.

PREHISTORIC AND ROMAN

Two Mesolithic or later cores have been discovered in the parish (NM Records) and other worked flints, including a thumb scraper, have been found in the N.W. (SP 744673) on Northampton Sand at 110 m. above OD (*BNFAS*, 5 (1971), 4). A metal bracelet, said to be Roman but probably post-medieval, was found in the village in 1969. It is of oval cross-section and is decorated with a narrow band of knurling (*BNFAS*, 4 (1970), 12; *Northants. Archaeol.*, 8 (1973), 23).

ᵃ(1) DITCHES (SP 755672), S. of the village on Northampton Sand at about 105 m. above OD. V-shaped ditches were discovered during ironstone-working. There was no dating evidence (*BNFAS*, 4 (1970), 33).

ᵇ(2) ENCLOSURES (SP 760684), lie immediately N.E. of the village, on Northampton Sand, at 112 m. above OD. Air photographs (in NMR) show very indistinct cropmarks of a small rectangular enclosure, 40 m. by 35 m., orientated N.E.–S.W., with a number of other ditches or perhaps enclosures intersecting it.

ᵃ(3) ROMAN SETTLEMENT (SP 764669), in the S.E. corner of the parish and close to Roman finds in Boughton (3) and Moulton, on Northampton Sand at 105 m. above OD. Field-walking around Bunkers Hill Farm has produced large quantities of Roman coarse wares (*BNFAS*, 5 (1971), 22, listed under Moulton).

For possible long barrow, see (4) below.

MEDIEVAL AND LATER

ᵇ(4) SAXON CEMETERY AND (?) LONG BARROW (SP 75086774; Fig. 123), known as Longman's or Layman's Hill, lies in a prominent position at the S.E. end of the village, on Northampton Sand at 110 m. above OD. There is a large rectangular mound, orientated E.–W., 30 m. long and 11 m. across. It is 1.5 m. high at the E. end and 1.75 m. high at the W., with a flat top 2.5 m. wide at the E. and 4 m. at the W. It is badly damaged and the W. end has been altered by a modern pathway. There is no trace of a ditch. It was first noted in the early 18th century when it

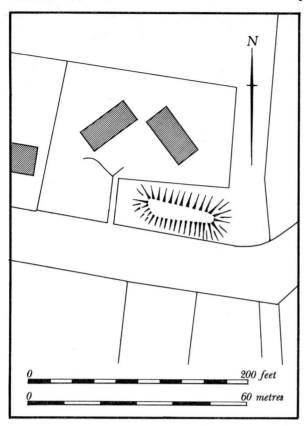

Fig. 123   PITSFORD   (4) Mound

was described as of 'oblong shape about 10 yards wide and not encompassed by a ditch' (J. Morton, *Nat. Hist. of Northants.* (1712), 548). When the adjacent road was widened in the early 19th century the mound was apparently cut into and skeletons were found.

In 1882 Sir Henry Dryden investigated a 'tumulus' which he called 'Roman' in Brampton Lane, Pitsford, and reported that in an area 'about 90 yards by 10 yards' he had discovered 14 urns containing ashes, bones and pieces of glass and 'brass'. His sketches show that at least two of the urns were Saxon and one of the glass objects was the greater part of a Claw Beaker. There was also a socketed spearhead (Dryden Collection, Central Library, Northampton). It is not absolutely certain that these finds came from the mound and it has been suggested that their location was 600 m. to the N.W. (SP 74706840; NM Records). However it seems likely that Dryden's excavation was in or around the mound (VCH *Northants.*, I (1902), 244; Meaney, *Gazetteer*, 195; *J. Northants. Mus. and Art Gal.*, 6 (1969), 47–8).

A later authority claimed that bones were discovered at the E. of the mound when a local farmer dug there, and that a human thigh-bone had been discovered on the S. side. The same writer regarded the mound as an

unchambered long barrow (*Antiquity*, 23 (1949), 218–20). It is no longer possible to say whether this is so.

[a](5) MEDIEVAL POTTERY (SP 747667), discovered as a thin scatter of sherds W. of the village, on Northampton Sand at 110 m. above OD (*BNFAS*, 5 (1971), 34).

[b](6) MEDIEVAL POTTERY (SP 764673), in the S.E. of the parish on Boulder Clay at about 110 m. above OD. Much 12th and 14th-century pottery has been found (*BNFAS*, 5 (1971), 34).

[b](7) SETTLEMENT REMAINS (SP 753682), formerly part of Pitsford village, lies on the edge of a valley immediately N.W. of the church, on Northampton Sand at 95 m. above OD.

Before recent development in the area, Pitsford church stood, with the Rectory, in an isolated position at the end of Church Lane, at a distance from the village centre. The surrounding land is now either built over or under permanent pasture and no trace of early occupation is recoverable. However, on arable land N.W. of the church there is an area of uneven ground, bounded on the N. by a long scarp running E.–W. along the valley edge. The scarp is now almost destroyed by ploughing but around and to the S. of it medieval pottery, mainly of 13th or 14th-century date, has been found in quantities sufficient to suggest former occupation in this area.

(8) CULTIVATION REMAINS. The common fields of Pitsford were enclosed by Act of Parliament of 1756 (VCH *Northants.*, IV (1937), 98; NRO, Enclosure Map).

Ridge-and-furrow of these fields survives or can be seen on air photographs in only a few places in the parish. Over most of the area all traces have disappeared. Three interlocked furlongs are visible S.E. of the village (SP 760672) but elsewhere only fragments exist (RAF VAP CPE/UK/1994, 4251–5, 4375–9).

UNDATED

[a](9) EARTHWORKS (SP 745672), lay S.W. of the village but have now been destroyed. In the early 18th century they were described as a square 'with two of the sides still remaining, one of them above 80 yards in length' (J. Morton, *Nat. Hist. of Northants.* (1712), 548). By the early 19th century they had already almost been destroyed (G. Baker, *Hist. of Northants.*, I (1822–30), 65). There are discrepancies concerning the actual location of this site (*Archaeologia*, 35 (1853), 394; VCH *Northants.*, IV (1937), 98; OS Record Cards) but the grid reference given here is that of the small earthworks shown on the original 2 in. OS drawings (OS 2 in. map No. 253 f.119) and there called 'Burrow Dykes'. Their date and purpose are unknown. No trace remains as the area has been worked for ironstone.

52 PRESTON CAPES

(OS 1 : 10000 [a] SP 55 NE, [b] SP 55 SE, [c] SP 64 SW)

The parish, covering some 1100 hectares, lies on a watershed from which streams flow E. to the R. Nene, S.E. to the R. Tove, and W. to the R. Cherwell. The highest part is in the N., and the village of Preston Capes and the hamlet of Little Preston (2) both lie on the summit of an uneven E.–W. ridge of Northampton Sand between 168 m. and 188 m. above OD. The land falls precipitously to the N., and to the S. more gently, to an undulating clayland between 122 m. and 135 m. above OD in which the main streams lie.

The parish contains two medieval settlements each with its own land unit (Fig. 124). Preston Capes is the main village and has a fine Norman motte (1), now damaged on its E. side. Little or Wood Preston (2), though always small, shows evidence of considerable shrinkage; the earthworks of the Manor House (3) suggest that it too may have been fortified at an early date. Much of the land of Little Preston was a deer park (4) in the later medieval period.

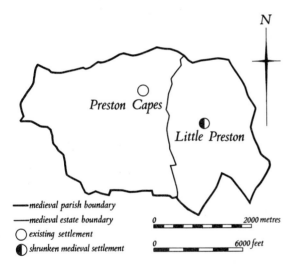

N

Preston Capes

Little Preston

—— medieval parish boundary
—— medieval estate boundary
◯ existing settlement
◖ shrunken medieval settlement

0   2000 metres

0   6000 feet

Fig. 124   PRESTON CAPES
Medieval settlements and estates

MEDIEVAL AND LATER

[b](1) MOTTE (SP 576549; Fig. 125; Plate 3), known as Preston Capes Castle, stands on the summit of a N.-projecting spur on the N.E. side of the village, on Upper Lias Clay, at 165 m. above OD. On all sides but the S. the land slopes steeply from the edge of the motte ditch and there are extensive views, especially to the N.

The exact date of the construction of the castle is unknown but it was probably built soon after the Norman Conquest. In 1086 Preston was held by Nigel of the Count of Mortain (VCH Northants., I (1902), 328). Around 1090 it certainly existed, for a Cluniac Priory was founded at that time by Hugh de Leicester 'ajoining his castle' at

Preston Capes. Nothing more is known of the castle, but the site remained the centre of the manor, even though the priory was moved to Daventry in 1107–8. The existing Manor Farm, which stands to the S.E. of the motte, is the modern successor to the medieval manor house (VCH Northants., II (1906), 109–110). On a map of 1742 (NRO) the area is called Castle Hill.

The site consists of a small conical motte some 4 m. high with a flat top 27 m. across. The S. side has been cut and mutilated by farm buildings and if there ever was a ditch at this point no trace of it survives. Elsewhere at the base of the motte is a shallow ditch no more than 1 m. deep which still holds water at one place. Along the outer edge of the ditch is a small bank only 0.25 m. high which, externally, is little more than a steepening of the natural hillside.

No trace of a bailey survives, although previous workers have suggested that one probably occupied the flatter ground to the S.E. (E. S. Armitage, Early Norman Castles (1912), 190); another source suggests that a slight depression to the S. might be the remains of its ditch (OS Record Cards). However, although it is likely that there was a bailey in this area, the present Manor Farm and its buildings have destroyed all trace. Various low scarps and shallow depressions S. of the farm appear to be the remains of old farm buildings.

Below the castle, at the bottom of the spur and curving around its base, is a large bank with a broad ditch on its S., uphill, side. The bank is between 1 m. and 2.5 m. high, with the greatest elevation at the ends. At its S.E. end the ditch broadens out into a wide depression, with what appear to be old quarry pits above it. The ridge-and-furrow to the N. terminates well short of the bank which is therefore contemporary with or older than the medieval ploughing. No date or function can be assigned to this feature.

[b](2) SETTLEMENT REMAINS (SP 588542; Figs 124 and 126; Plate 3), formerly part of the hamlet of Little Preston or Wood Preston, lie around and N.E. of the existing buildings on Boulder Clay and Northampton Sand, at 167 m. above OD. Little Preston is first mentioned in Domesday Book when it was divided between two small manors of $1\frac{1}{2}$ virgates each, both held in chief by the Count of Mortain. One of these had a recorded population of six which included a priest, the other was waste (VCH Northants., I (1902), 327–8). In the early 18th century Bridges (Hist. of Northants., I (1791), 80) noted that there were twelve houses there and by 1900 there were still ten or eleven. The hamlet lay in the centre of its own land unit the boundaries of which are shown on the Tithe Map of Little Preston of 1838 (NRO; Fig. 124). The hamlet of Little Preston lies along a single short street which opens out at its S.W. end into a small triangular green, now partly encroached upon. Behind the existing houses on both sides of the street and along the road to Preston Capes are a number of abandoned closes bounded by deep ditches or

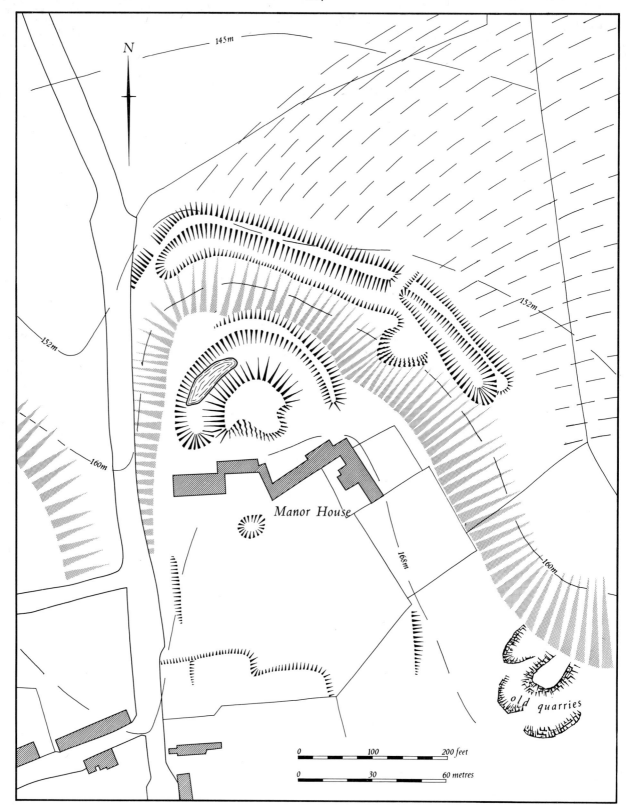

Fig. 125   PRESTON CAPES   (1) Motte

low scarps. These represent the extent of former gardens or paddocks. A large empty field on the N. side of the street and immediately S. of North Farm contains slight remains of at least two house-sites. The street ends at North Farm, but its line is continued in a broad curve by a wide hollow-way up to 1 m. deep which can be traced for some 105 m. until it ends against a modern pond. This hollow-way, if projected N. for a few metres, would have led to the manor house site (3); it is also likely that it once ran on to the N. but there is no evidence on the ground that this was so unless it followed a natural valley down the hillside. At the S.W. end of the hollow-way, immediately N.E. of North Farm, are remains of house-sites and closes. To the W. of the hollow-way are at least two sub-rectangular scarped areas, one with a slight depression in it and each with a large close behind it extending down the hillside. The lower, N.W. ends of these closes cut into the boundary bank of the deer park (4) at this point, and must have been constructed after the deer park bank had ceased to be maintained. To the S. of the hollow-way is another area much damaged by later hedges and other disturbances with, at its S. end, two rectangular depressions, perhaps the site of a former house. Modern ditch-digging in this area has led to the discovery of large quantities of medieval pottery, mainly of 12th to 14th-century date (RAF VAP CPE/UK/1994, 2159–60; CUAP, AZU75).

b(3) MANOR HOUSE OR CASTLE SITE (SP 589543; Fig. 126; Plate 3), stands on the edge of an N.-facing promontory of Northampton Sand, at 165 m. above OD. To the N. and W. the ground falls steeply across Upper Lias Clay which has slipped down the hillside to produce large uneven mounds and terraces. The field name for the area (NRO, Tithe Map of Little Preston, 1838) is Great Hill Ground.

The place is traditionally the site of the manor house of Little Preston and there is no reason to doubt this, but the extant earthworks also suggest that the site may once have been fortified. The manor house is specifically mentioned in 1235 when the then lord, William de Montacute, had a chapel adjoining his house at Little Preston. The chapel is supposed to have been in a close known as Graves Piece in the 18th or 19th century, but its location is now forgotten (J. Bridges, *Hist. of Northants.*, I (1791), 80–1; Whellan, *Dir.*, 429–30). No other details are known of the manor's history; the present North Farm to the S.W., partly a 17th-century structure, may be its successor. The deer park (4), constructed in 1227, appears to have been laid out with the earlier house as the focal point.

The site has been much damaged by later activity and now consists of little more than a U-shaped ditch up to 2 m. deep curving round the spur. There is no inner bank but the ditch is of defensive proportions. At its S.W. end the ditch becomes a flat terrace-way, which is overlaid by a set of small terraced enclosures. These in turn are cut by a later ditch which extends down the hillside. At its S.E. end, the main ditch fades out into an area of disturbed ground.

The area enclosed by the ditch is occupied on the S. by a modern pond and on the N. by a series of low scarps, nowhere above 0.25 m. high, forming no coherent pattern (RAF VAP CPE/UK/1994, 2159–60; CUAP, AZU75).

b(4) DEER PARK (centred SP 590548; Figs. 126 and 127; Plate 3), in the N.E. of the parish, mainly on Upper Lias Clay and Boulder Clay between 120 m. and 165 m. above OD.

The park lies within the former lordship of Little Preston and was enclosed in 1227 by John de Montacute, who then held that manor. It covered about 140 hectares and was surrounded by a bank much of which still survives or can be traced on air photographs. Even where the bank is absent the line of the park boundary may be deduced from existing hedge-lines.

The whole of the E. side of the park coincides with the parish boundary with Farthingstone and Maidford, and a bank, slight in the N. but up to 1.5 m. high in the S., can be traced for most of its length. At the S.E. corner (SP 59175412) where the park and parish boundaries diverge the bank curves W. along the edge of the park and follows the existing hedge-line for 700 m. Beyond this point (SP 59085421) the bank continues N.W. for 160 m. between two separate blocks of ridge-and-furrow, diagonally to the ridges but it has not been used as a headland. The limits of the park in this area seem to have been determined by the position of the village (2) and the manor house (3), both now deserted. The boundary bank twists to the N. and is cut by the end of the main hollow-way of the village so that the village lies outside and the site of the manor house inside the park (SP 58945432). From there the boundary continues W. down the hillside as a scarp, or as a large bank up to 1.5 m. high across a small combe. At one point it is cut by the closes of abandoned houses (2). From there it continues as a hedge closely following the contours of the scarp (from SP 58765430–58045473). The boundary is next visible as a low bank across a field (to SP 58225495), then as the line of a small stream (to SP58765531) and then as a large bank running up the scarp to join the parish boundary (SP 58965541).

Many of the fields within the park bear traces of ridge-and-furrow. Some of this may be earlier than the park since Little Preston is mentioned in Domesday Book as at least partly waste. Some furlongs, however, must have been ploughed after the abandonment of the park because their relationship to the boundary bank shows that they are later than it (e.g. SP 590453; CPE/UK/1994, 2159–61; CUAP, AZU75; Whellan, *Dir.*, 429).

b(5) FISHPONDS (SP 579549; Fig. 128), just below the spring-line at the foot of the steep slope E. of the castle (1) and Manor Farm, on clay at 137 m. above OD. They consist of two rectangular ponds, each with an earthen dam at least 1.5 m. high at its E. end. The ponds have been deepened so they have steep sides and flat bottoms; uneven mounds to the N. are probably the original spoil. Within

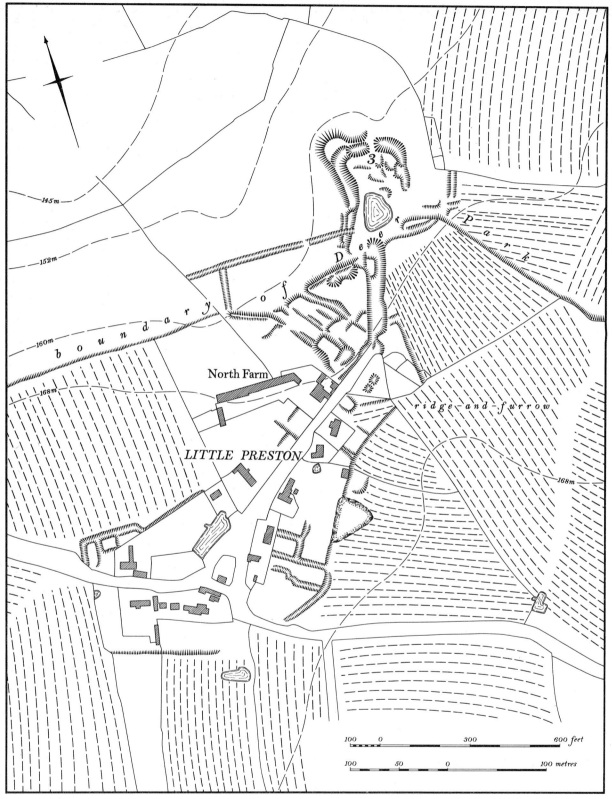

Fig. 126 PRESTON CAPES (2) Settlement remains at Little Preston,
(3) Site of manor house, (4) Deer park

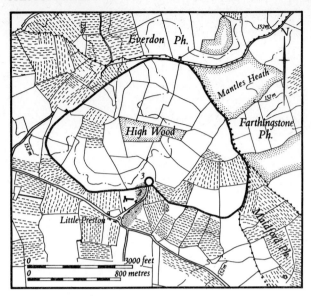

Fig. 127   PRESTON CAPES   (4) Deer park

the E. pond there is a long narrow island about 1 m. high with a mound rising to 1.5 m. high at its W. end.

^b(6) BANKS, QUARRIES AND PONDS (centred SP 574549), N., W. and S. of the church, on a very steep N.-facing scarp of Upper Lias Clay, between 150 m. and 175 m. above OD. Many of the banks and terraces along this hillside appear to be natural and probably result from landslips which often occur on Upper Lias Clay. Some of the features, however, seem to be man-made, although these are difficult to interpret.

In the S.W. a massive bank 3 m. high and 10 m. wide runs round the hillside near the top of the scarp (SP 573547), with a wide ditch behind it for most of its length. This may be the 'fosse' and 'entrenchment' mentioned by Baker (*Hist. of Northants.*, I (1822–30), 431). On a map of 1742 (NRO) the ditch is shown as a road, then still in use, which together with the existing lane to the S., formed a loop E. of the village stretching as far as Preston Capes Farm.

Close to the church (SP 574548) there appear to be at least two small rectangular ponds, dammed on the N. and perhaps fed by springs which emerge at this height. To the N. of the church and rectory there are two large terraces which, although they appear man-made, are probably at least in part natural. In 1742 these lay in Home Close.

^b(7) SETTLEMENT REMAINS (SP 575546), lie in the S.W. corner of the village, on Boulder Clay at 180 m. above OD. The earthworks consist of a broad hollow-way running N.–S., parallel to and 100 m. W. of the existing through-road, and continuing the line of the present cul-de-sac S. of the church. On both sides of the hollow-way, at its N. end, are low banks and other slight features, possibly the remains of former houses. The interest of these remains is that they imply an older arrangement of the

village based on a regular grid pattern of streets which bore little or no relationship to the uneven topography on which it lay. The remains had already been abandoned by 1742 (Map in NRO).

^b(8) WINDMILL MOUND (SP 57605438), lies S. of the village on the E. side of the road to Canons Ashby, on Boulder Clay at 182 m. above OD. It is a large circular mound 1.5 m. high and 11 m. in diam. and has a flat top 4 m. across with a slight depression in the centre. There is no evidence for a surrounding ditch. Its W. side has been cut by the modern hedge-bank and to the E. the adjacent ridge-and-furrow terminates about 8 m. short of the mound. The windmill had already gone by 1742 for a map of that date (NRO) shows nothing on the site.

^b(9) WINDMILL MOUND (?) (SP 58295398), lies S.W. of Little Preston on the S. side of an E.–W. ridge on Boulder Clay at about 165 m. above OD. The circular mound 20 m. in diam. has been almost completely ploughed away. It was formerly surrounded by ridge-and-furrow, now destroyed, but even on air photographs taken in 1947 it is impossible to ascertain the relationship of the mound to the ridge-and-furrow. It is most likely to be the site of a medieval windmill, though no trace of any structure has been noted. On the Tithe Map of Little Preston, 1838 (NRO) the field in which the mound lies is called Great Mill Field (RAF VAP CPE/UK/1994, 2159–60).

(10) CULTIVATION REMAINS. The common fields of Preston Capes were enclosed in 1659 (J. Bridges, *Hist. of Northants.*, I (1791), 80). Ridge-and-furrow of these fields remains on the ground or can be traced on air photographs over most of the parish. On the gently undulating ground in the S. half of the parish and in the extreme N. below the Lias Clay the ridge-and-furrow is generally in rectangular

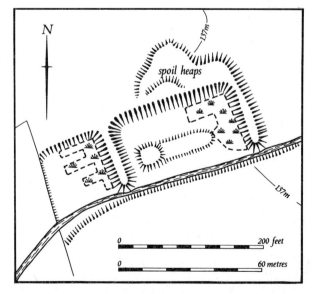

Fig. 128   PRESTON CAPES   (5) Fishponds

furlongs with the ridges laid out at right-angles to the contours. Along the scarp itself the land is either too steep ever to have been ploughed or has a pattern of furlongs radiating around the spurs. The best remaining areas of ridge-and-furrow are S. of the village (e.g. SP 576543 and 576534) and N. of the village (e.g. around SP 573553).

The date of the enclosure of the common fields of Little Preston is not known, but Bridges (op. cit.) said that it had taken place long before 1659. Ridge-and-furrow of these fields exists on the ground or is visible on air photographs over most of the land associated with Little Preston except on some of the steeper hillsides which were never cultivated (e.g. SP 588551). As at Preston Capes, on the flatter ground S. of the village the ridge-and-furrow is mainly in rectangular interlocked furlongs, but on the more broken ground to the N., radiating furlongs are common. Ridge-and-furrow is particularly well preserved around Little Preston itself. Within the deer park (4) which occupied most of the land N. of Little Preston much ridge-and-furrow remains. It is not clear whether this is earlier or later than the park which was created in 1227 (RAF VAP CPE/UK/1994, 2155–61, 3153–5, 4160–6).

53 RAVENSTHORPE

(OS 1:10000 [a] SP 67 SE, [b] SP 66 NE, [c] SP 66 NW)

The modern parish covers some 1170 hectares and its very irregular shape results partly from the inclusion in it of the land of the hamlet of Coton (9) and partly from the loss of some land to the E., to Hollowell parish. It lies on land sloping generally S.E. across the headwaters of a number of small streams which flow E. and S.E. towards the R. Nene. One such stream forms the S. boundary of the parish. The low-lying areas are on Upper Lias Clay, but Boulder Clay and other glacial deposits cap the higher ground to the W. and N. which rises to a maximum height of 175 m. above OD. Northampton Sand is exposed along the valley sides and the villages of Ravensthorpe and Coton, in common with most of the villages in the vicinity, are both situated on outcrops of this rock. The land of Coton, the boundaries of which can be traced from a number of maps (Fig. 14), seems earlier to have been associated with the parish of Guilsborough (PN Northants., 67). The settlement remains of the hamlet of Coton (9) have been largely destroyed by recent ploughing.

PREHISTORIC AND ROMAN

[a](1) IRON AGE AND ROMAN SETTLEMENT (?) (SP 673704), E. of the village on Northampton Sand at 126 m. above OD. A scatter of Iron Age and Roman sherds has been discovered (Northants. Archaeol., 12 (1977), 215).

[b](2) ROMAN SETTLEMENT (?) (SP 668698), S. of the village on Northampton Sand, at 127 m. above OD. A small quantity of Roman pottery has been found (Northants. Archaeol., 12 (1977), 215).

[b](3) ROMAN SETTLEMENT (?) (SP 665695), 400 m. S.W. of (2), in a similar position. Roman sherds have been noted (Northants. Archaeol., 12 (1977), 215).

[b](4) ROMAN SETTLEMENT (?) (SP 663699), 400 m. N.W. of (3), on Boulder Clay at 146 m. above OD. Roman pottery is recorded (Northants. Archaeol., 12 (1977), 215).

[b](5) ROMAN SETTLEMENT (?) (SP 659699), 400 m. W. of (4), on Northampton Sand, at 145 m. above OD. Roman pottery has been found (Northants. Archaeol., 12 (1977), 215).

[a](6) ROMAN SETTLEMENT (?) (SP 652709), in the W. of the

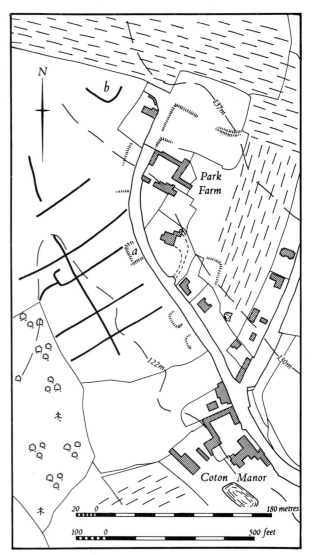

Fig. 129   RAVENSTHORPE
(9) Settlement remains at Coton

parish, on Boulder Clay, at 170 m. above OD. Roman sherds have been noted (*Northants. Archaeol.*, 12 (1977), 215).

b(7) ROMAN SETTLEMENT (?) (SP 657713), 700 m. N.E. of (6), on Boulder Clay, at 135 m. above OD. Roman pottery is recorded (*Northants. Archaeol.*, 12 (1977), 215).

a(8) ROMAN SETTLEMENT (?) (SP 666722), in the N.W. of the parish, on clay, at about 130 m. above OD. Roman pottery has been found (*Northants. Archaeol.*, 10 (1975), 162).

MEDIEVAL AND LATER

a(9) SETTLEMENT REMAINS (SP 673717; Figs. 14 and 129), formerly part of the hamlet of Coton, lie W. and N. of the existing houses, on land sloping steeply W. on Northampton Sand and Upper Lias Clay at about 125 m. above OD. Though the name suggests a small, late settlement and the boundaries of its land suggest that it was once part of Guilsborough, Coton is listed as an independent manor in Domesday Book, with a recorded population of nine (VCH *Northants.*, I (1902), 338–9). Nothing is known of its size thereafter until the late 17th century when eight householders paid the Hearth Tax in 1673 (PRO, E179/254/14). In the early 18th century Bridges (*Hist. of Northants.*, I (1791), 537) noted that there were 17 houses in Coton. By 1839 (NRO, Map of Coton) at least 15 houses existed, and though some of these have been destroyed new ones have been erected in other places and the hamlet now consists of some 16 dwellings.

Until recent development along the Guilsborough road Coton lay entirely along the single street curving N.W. and then N.E. which once ran on to Guilsborough. The E. side of this street is still mainly built up, though at the extreme N. end two low rectangular platforms edged by scarps N.E. of Park Farm may be the sites of former buildings. On the W. side of the street there are no buildings N. of Coton Manor except for a single cottage at the N. end of the hamlet. However in 1839 there was a line of at least six cottages in the centre of the area (SP 67357180; 'a' on plan) and a farm to the N. (SP 67327198; 'b' on plan), but all have been destroyed. On air photographs taken in 1947 (RAF VAP CPE/UK/1994, 1370–1, 1467–8) the land between the main street and the valley bottom to the W. is divided into a series of long closes, edged by banks or ditches, most of which were subdivided by further ditches. At their upper, eastern ends were traces of former buildings. These earthworks have been largely destroyed by recent ploughing. Field-walking when the area was under the plough has revealed large quantities of post-medieval pottery near the road, though at the N. end (SP67357190) only medieval pottery of 12th-century date was recovered (inf. A. E. Brown). The land has now been put down to grass but a number of very degraded scarps making former house-sites can still be recognised along the edge of the street.

(10) CULTIVATION REMAINS. The common fields of Ravensthorpe were enclosed by Act of Parliament in 1795 (NRO, Enclosure Map). Ridge-and-furrow of these fields survives on the ground and can be traced on air photographs in various parts of the parish, particularly to the S. and N. of the village and in the S.W. It is almost all arranged in interlocking furlongs.

The date at which the common fields of Coton (9) were enclosed is unknown and no documentation survives from earlier than 1839 (Map in NRO) by which time enclosure had taken place. Ridge-and-furrow, in end-on and interlocked furlongs, survives in the centre of the parish and to the W. of the partly deserted hamlet. Elsewhere most of it has been destroyed (RAF VAP CPE/UK/1994, 1367–71, 1466–71).

54 SCALDWELL

(OS 1:10000 SP 77 SE)

The small rectangular parish, covering little more than 500 hectares, lies on the E. side of a N.–S. ridge. The higher area in the W., rising to a maximum height of 145 m. above OD, is covered by Boulder Clay; from there the land falls across Northampton Sand and Upper Lias Clay, to the valley of a S.-flowing stream which forms the E. boundary of the parish at 90 m. above OD. The village itself lies within a small area covered by glacial sands and gravels. Scaldwell village is noteworthy in that it has no earthwork remains of former settlement and appears to be one of the few villages in the county which has undergone neither movement nor shrinkage. It is centred upon a rectangular green with the street system radiating from it (NRO, Map of Scaldwell, 1844).

ROMAN

(1) ROMAN SETTLEMENT AND KILNS (unlocated). Several finds of Roman material are recorded from ironstone mines in the 1920s. The exact locations are not known but were in the S.W. of the parish where quarrying was taking place at that time. One kiln was certainly identified and 'scores of others' are said to have been found, as well as sherds, including some of 2nd-century date, and a small round-bellied jar with a wavy decoration round the neck. From the inadequate record it appears that there was quite a considerable pottery industry in the parish (OS Record Cards; *J. Northants. Mus. and Art Gall.*, 8 (1970), 97–9; *JRS*, 16 (1926), 223; 17 (1927), 201). Other finds from the parish include six circular Saxon loom weights of red clay and fragments of a 3rd or 4th-century jug with a moulded female face (NM).

MEDIEVAL AND LATER

A hoard of Norman coins, including 260 pennies and halfpennies of William I from 39 mints, was found during ironstone-mining in the parish (*Brit. Num. J.*, 17 (1923–4), 11–12; OS Record Cards).

Medieval pottery has been found at two places in the N.W. of the parish on Boulder Clay at about 120 m. above OD. At SP 762723 numerous 12th and 13th-century sherds have been discovered and at SP 761729 a wide variety of pottery ranging from the 12th to the 18th century (*BNFAS*, 5 (1971), 34–5). Both sites were formerly covered by ridge-and-furrow (RAF VAP CPE/UK/1994, 1379–80) and thus they are unlikely to represent areas of occupation.

(2) ENCLOSURE (SP 755718), in the extreme S.W. of the parish on Northampton Sand at about 130 m. above OD. Air photographs (in NMR) show rather indistinct cropmarks of a sub-rectangular enclosure overlying ridge-and-furrow.

(3) CULTIVATION REMAINS. The common fields of the parish were finally enclosed by an Act of Parliament in 1775 though Bridges (*Hist. of Northants.*, II (1791), 125) records that in the early 18th century 140 acres of open field were already enclosed. Most of the ridge-and-furrow of these fields has been destroyed except for some furlongs to the W., E. and N.E. of the village, which can be traced on the ground or on air photographs. These fragments suggest that the overall pattern of ridge-and-furrow in Scaldwell may have resembled that in Old and Walgrave to the E. (see RCHM *Northants.*, II (1979), Fig. 109). The three parishes are topographically similar and the predominant E.–W. trend of the surviving furlongs in Scaldwell seems to fit into the much better preserved pattern in the parishes to the E., of sweeping end-on furlongs with only a few blocks running at right-angles to this main direction (RAF VAP CPE/UK/1994, 1379–82, 1453–6).

55 SIBBERTOFT

(OS 1 : 10000 SP 68 SE)

The parish covers almost 840 hectares. Its very short W. boundary follows the county boundary with Leicestershire. Most of the N. edge of the parish runs along the top of the steep N.-facing scarp of the Hothorpe Hills above the Welland valley, and the R. Welland itself rises from a spring in Sibbertoft village. The line of low rounded hills, deeply dissected by the steep-sided valleys of small streams, dominates the N. part of the parish; these hills are made up of Lower, Middle and Upper Lias Clay rising to a maximum height of 182 m. above OD. From there the land slopes gently S.W. and is almost entirely covered by Boulder Clay.

Apart from numerous scatters of Roman pottery, the major monument in the parish is the motte and bailey (8) known as Castle Yard, which is situated at a distance from the village commanding a steep-sided and narrow valley through the Hothorpe Hills. The village itself is of interest

in that it appears to have had a completely new settlement on the W., added to the earlier one, probably in the medieval period.

PREHISTORIC AND ROMAN

A polished stone axe has been found at SP 685812 (NM Records).

(1) DITCHED TRACKWAY (SP 66988235–67128230), in the W. of the parish on Boulder Clay at about 155 m. above OD. Air photographs (in NMR) show a short length of ditched trackway, clearly visible for only about 150 m.

(2) IRON AGE SETTLEMENT (?) (SP 689835), N.E. of the village, on the edge of the Hothorpe Hills, on Middle Lias Clay, at 158 m. above OD. A scatter of Iron Age sherds has been noted (*Northants. Archaeol.*, 12 (1977), 215).

(3) ROMAN SETTLEMENT (?) (SP 686834), 200 m. S.W. of (2), in a similar situation. Roman pottery has been found (*Northants. Archaeol.*, 12 (1977), 215).

(4) ROMAN SETTLEMENT (?) (SP 677832), N.W. of the village, in a situation similar to (2) and (3). Roman sherds are recorded (*Northants. Archaeol.*, 12 (1977), 215; grid ref. incorrect).

(5) ROMAN SETTLEMENT (?) (SP 670825), W. of the village, 200 m. N. of (1) on Boulder Clay at 155 m. above OD. Roman pottery has been discovered (*Northants. Archaeol.*, 12 (1977), 215).

(6) ROMAN SETTLEMENT (?) (SP 665835), in the N.W. of the parish, on Boulder Clay, at 180 m. above OD. Roman sherds have been noted (*Northants. Archaeol.*, 12 (1977), 215).

(7) ROMAN SETTLEMENT (?) (SP 660835), in the extreme N.W. of the parish, on Middle Lias Clay, at 152 m. above OD. A small scatter of Roman grey ware has been found (*Northants. Archaeol.*, 11 (1976), 193).

MEDIEVAL AND LATER

(8) MOTTE AND BAILEY (SP 609831; Fig. 130), known as Castle Yard, lies on the end of a N.-projecting spur, between two streams cut deeply into the Middle Lias clays and silts, at about 155 m. above OD. It is in a position of considerable tactical strength, commanding the assumed ancient trackways through the valley below. Nothing is known of its history, though it perhaps dates from between the late 11th and the mid 12th century. Its situation is surprisingly remote from any known medieval settlement.

The motte, standing on the edge of the spur, is roughly circular and rises some 2 m. above the ground to the S. The summit slopes slightly up to the N. and at its N. end stands the foundations of a modern structure. The motte is bounded on the S. by a broad ditch up to 2.5 m. deep and on the N. by a narrow ledge, with traces of an outer bank only 0.25 m. high above the precipitous natural slope.

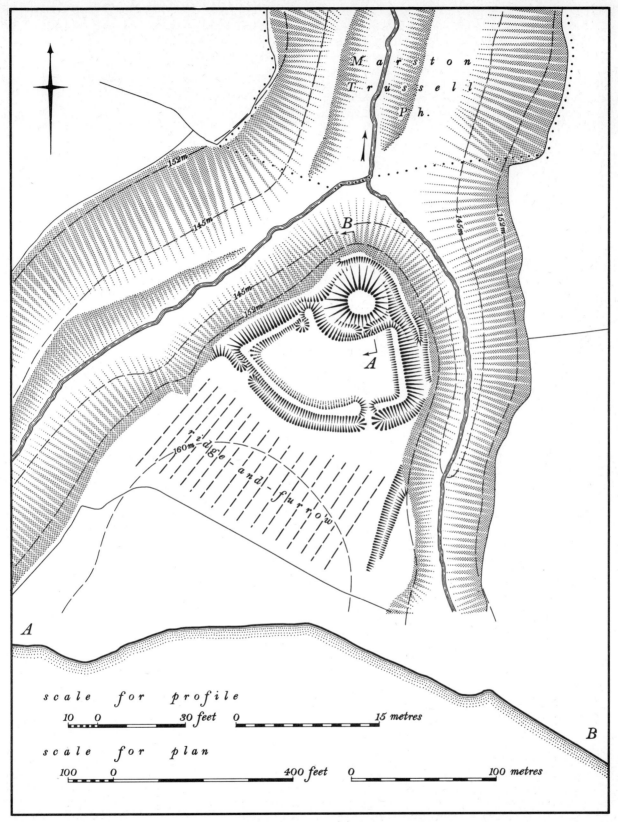

Fig. 130   SIBBERTOFT   (8) Motte and bailey

The bailey is set on the flat ground to the S. of the motte; it is bounded on the S. by a broad ditch, up to 1 m. deep from the outside, with a flat-topped inner bank up to 0.5 m. high. At each end the ditch runs down to the natural valley side, but the bank returns to meet the ditch of the motte. Below this the ledge which encircles the N. side of the motte continues some 3 m. below the bank.

Beyond the bailey ditch to the S. is a block of very flat ridge-and-furrow which seems to have ended on the line of the present hedge. No finds have been made on the site (VCH *Northants.*, II (1906), 411–2; plan of 1884, Dryden Collection, Central Library, Northampton).

(9) SETTLEMENT REMAINS (centred SP 675827, 676829, 681828; Figs. 13 and 131; Plate 11), lie in and around the modern village on clays, silts and alluvium at about 165 m. above OD. The village appears once to have consisted of two separate parts, an impression confirmed by the name Westhorpe given to the N.–S. street to the W. of the main part of the village, but there is no documentary evidence bearing on this. Apart from two small groups of earthworks in the S.E. and N.E. ('a' and 'b' on plan), some of which may be house-sites, the surviving settlement remains are concentrated at the W. end of the village in the area called Westhorpe. However other remains may have been destroyed by the extensive 19th and 20th-century housing and indeed there are records of medieval pottery in that part of the village which has now been redeveloped (SP 678827; *Northants. Archaeol.*, 9 (1974), 110).

On the W. side of Westhorpe there were former houses to both N. and S. of the existing buildings; building platforms and part of the outer boundary of the closes are still visible ('c' and 'd' on plan). Closes also exist on the S. side of the E.–W. road leading towards the main part of the village ('e' on plan). The symmetry of these closes and the L-shaped layout along two straight lengths of road, as well as the name, implies that Westhorpe may have been a planned extension of the main village. No date for the abandonment of these earthworks has been established.

In the field immediately W. of Westhorpe ('f' on plan) there are two large irregular mounds surrounded by an area of disturbed ground, and a shallow ditch or hollow-way runs E. from the S. side of the mounds towards the village. On the Tithe Map of 1841 (NRO) a roughly circular pond, some 60 m. in diam., with a circular island inside it is shown in this field. It has a narrow extension to the E. which is probably the feature which now survives as a dry channel. A large building is shown immediately S. of this canal, close to the existing road and the N. part of the field was then known as the Coombe and the S. part as Water Loggs. The pond may have been an ornamental feature, perhaps part of a garden.

In the S.E. of the village (SP 67958245) is an area called a green in both 1787 and 1841 (Maps in NRO). On the later map a hedge is shown on the S.W. side of the green and this appears to follow the line, on the ground, of a steep scarp 1.5 m. high above which the ridge-and-furrow terminates. The scarp may therefore be the boundary of the green (RAF VAP 106G/UK/636, 3134–5; CPE/UK/2109, 4297–9; CUAP, BAP69, 70).

(10) MOUND (SP 69258263), known as Moot Hill, in the E. of the parish on Boulder Clay at 182 m. above OD. The mound, which is now destroyed, was described as a tumulus on early and also on modern OS maps. It may have been a spoil heap from a nearby pond (OS Record Cards).

(11) CULTIVATION REMAINS. All that remained of the common fields of Sibbertoft was enclosed by agreement in 1650, but part of the parish was already apparently in old enclosures before that date (J. Bridges, *Hist. of Northants.*, II (1791), 73). In 1506 an indenture for the sale of Sibbertoft Manor listed only 300 acres of arable land whereas there were 200 acres of meadow and 1000 acres of pasture (*Cal. Close, 1500–1509*, 573), indicating that the earlier enclosure had already taken place by the beginning of the 16th century.

Ridge-and-furrow of these fields survives on the ground or can be traced on air photographs over almost the entire parish, with the exception of a small area in the N.W. Much of it is well preserved still. On the flatter ground in the S.W. it is mainly arranged in end-on furlongs running N.–S. and this orientation is also frequent in the N. though here the irregularity of the Hothorpe Hills has led to interlocking of the furlongs as they are adapted to changes in direction of slope (RAF VAP 106G/UK/636, 4133–9, 3132–7; CPE/UK/2109, 4295–4302, 3297–3302).

56 SPRATTON

(OS 1:10000 [a] SP 77 SW, [b] SP 76 NW)

The modern parish covers some 760 hectares. It formerly included the now deserted village of Little Creaton and its land, which today lie in the parish of Creaton (10) (Fig. 14). Spratton parish, bounded by two small S.-flowing streams which meet in the S.E. corner, occupies a S.-facing spur between 70 m. and 135 m. above OD. The summit of the spur is capped by Northampton Sand which outcrops at about 100 m. above OD. Below, covering most of the lower slopes, are extensive areas of Upper Lias Clay. The Northampton Sand deposits have enabled a number of important sites (1, 3–5, 7) to be revealed by air photography, either as cropmarks or as soil-marks.

PREHISTORIC AND ROMAN

A barbed-and-tanged arrowhead was found at SP 71547058 in 1970 and a fragment of a polished stone axe is also recorded 'from Spratton' (NM Records). A coin of

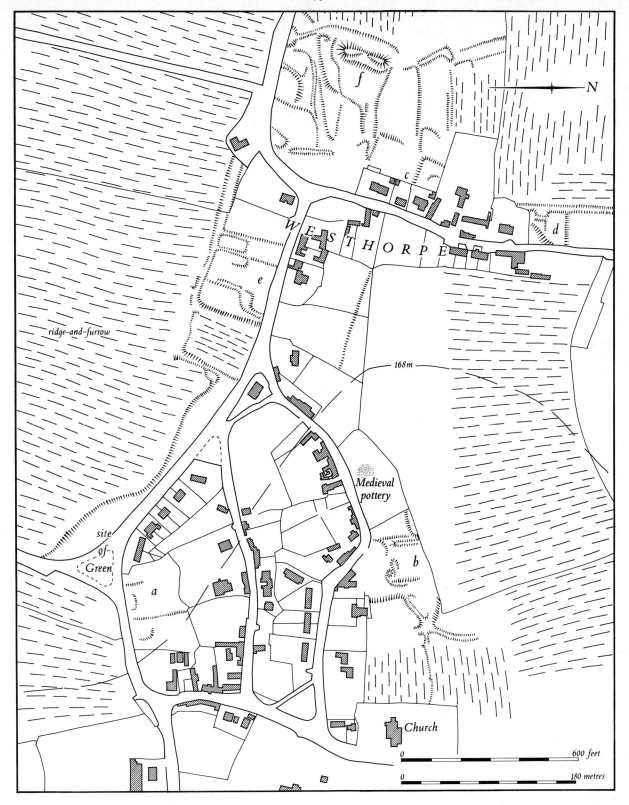

Fig. 131   SIBBERTOFT   (9) Settlement remains

Marcus Aurelius was discovered somewhere in the parish before 1712 (J. Morton, *Nat. Hist. of Northants.* (1712), 532).

a(1) TRACKWAY AND ENCLOSURES (centred SP 716706; Fig. 132), lie immediately N. of the village of Northampton Sand between 114 m. and 125 m. above OD. Air photographs (in NMR) show cropmarks covering some 6 hectares. A large roughly trapezoidal enclosure about 1.5 hectares in area is bounded on its N.W. side by a length of ditched trackway (from SP 71507059 to 71667076) and on the S. by a group of smaller, interlocked enclosures and ditches. Its W. side is intersected by a further group of small enclosures. Two ring ditches are faintly visible in the interior (SP 71637065; *BNFAS*, 5 (1971), 42).

a(2) FLINT-WORKING SITE (SP 714705), lies W. of (1) on Northampton Sand at 135 m. above OD. A large number of worked flints, said to be of Bronze Age type, have been found (*Northants. Archaeol.*, 11 (1976), 184; inf. D. N. Hall).

a(3) ENCLOSURES (centred SP 711702; Fig. 132), lie immediately W. of the village, 400 m. S.W. of (2) and in a similar situation. Cropmarks are visible on air photographs (in NMR) over an area of about two hectares. There appear to be two sub-rectangular enclosures, each of about 0.5 hectare, separated by what may be a ditched trackway. The N. one contains a small irregular enclosure in its N. corner and a number of possible internal ditches. A small enclosure and linear ditches lie to the W. The S. enclosure has no interior features, but is cut by a linear ditch on its W. side. To the E. is another group of ditches, none of which is clear on available air photographs (*BNFAS*, 6 (1971), 16, Spratton (2)).

a(4) ENCLOSURE (SP 712708), lies 300 m. N.W. of (2) and in a similar situation. Air photographs (in NMR) show cropmarks of a large rectangular enclosure, about 1.5 hectares in area (*BNFAS*, 6 (1971), 16, Spratton (1)). Further enclosures and ditches are said to be visible to the S., at SP 711706, but these appear to be frost-wedges (*BNFAS*, 5 (1971), 42).

a(5) RING DITCH (SP 72707124), lies in the N. of the parish, on clay at 95 m. above OD. Air photographs (not seen by RCHM) are said to show cropmarks of a ring ditch (*BNFAS*, 2 (1967), 32, Brixworth; 6 (1971), 17, Spratton (4)).

a(6) LINEAR DITCH (SP 733705), in the E. of the parish, close to the Brixworth boundary, on Upper Lias Clay, at 83 m. above OD. Air photographs (in NMR) show cropmarks of an irregular linear ditch, visible for 150 m., running N.–S. almost parallel to the contours. Other vague cropmarks in the area may be connected with it.

b(7) PREHISTORIC SETTLEMENT (SP 729691), in the S.E. of the parish on Boulder Clay at 85 m. above OD. A large quantity of worked flints, said to be of Bronze Age type,

and Iron Age pottery, have been found (inf. D. N. Hall; for Saxon finds from this site, see (12)).

b(8) PREHISTORIC AND ROMAN SETTLEMENT (?) (SP 715685), in the extreme S. of the parish, close to a stream, on gravel at 80 m. above OD. Air photographs (in NMR) show faint cropmarks of what appear to be irregular and sub-rectangular enclosures. Worked flints of Neolithic and Bronze Age types and two Roman sherds have been found in the vicinity (*BNFAS*, 2 (1967), 19, 32; 6 (1971), 16; *Northants. Archaeol.*, 11 (1976), 184; OS Record Cards).

Fig. 132   SPRATTON
(1, 3) Cropmarks,   (13) Hollow-ways

b(9) ROMAN SETTLEMENT (?) (SP 708691), in the S.W. of the parish, on gravel at 95 m. above OD. Roman colour-coated sherds have been found during field-walking (*BNFAS*, 5 (1971), 25).

b(10) ROMAN SETTLEMENT (SP 731689), in the S.E. of the parish, on Boulder Clay at 90 m. above OD. Roman pottery indicating a small settlement has been found (inf. D. N. Hall).

MEDIEVAL AND LATER

b(11) SAXON SETTLEMENT (?) (SP 728699), E. of the village, on Boulder Clay at 97 m. above OD. Early Saxon pottery has been found (inf. D. N. Hall).

b(12) SAXON SETTLEMENT (?) (SP 729691), found with the prehistoric material at (7) above. Early Saxon pottery has been discovered (inf. D. N. Hall).

ab(13) HOLLOW-WAYS (SP 715704 and 718697; partly on Fig. 132), lie at the extreme N. and S. ends of Spratton village and, though of minor interest as earthworks, help to explain the morphology of the present village. Until modern development extended the village to the W., Spratton lay some distance away from the main Northampton–Leicester road and consisted of three roughly parallel lanes orientated N.W.–S.E., cut obliquely by the Brixworth-Hollowell road. The existence of a deep hollow-way at the N. end of the village which continued the present High Street northwards, and another at the S. end of Church Road extending S. as a series of old rutted trackways for some 400 m., indicates that the village once lay on a N.–S. road later replaced by the modern one to the W. (RAF VAP CPE/UK/1994, 2370–1).

a(14) ENCLOSURES (SP 718705), lie immediately N.E. of Spratton Hall, on Northampton Sand at 114 m. above OD. The mutilated remains of a series of small paddocks and closes, bounded by low banks and shallow ditches, may be associated with the former manor house nearby.

(15) CULTIVATION REMAINS. The common fields of the parish were enclosed by an Act of Parliament of 1765. No Enclosure Map has survived but from the evidence of the Enclosure Award (NRO) there were five open fields in 1765, North Rye Field N.W. of the village, South Rye Field to the S.W., Bridge Field to the S., Middle Field to the S.E. and Wood Field to the E. and N.E. Ridge-and-furrow of these fields remains on the ground or can be traced on air photographs over most of the parish. On the flatter ground along the streams in the S. and E. it is mainly arranged in rectangular interlocked furlongs, but along the steeper slopes around the village and in the W. it tends to lie across the contours in end-on furlongs. Complete vertical air photographic cover was not available to the Commission (RAF VAP CPE/UK/1994, 2368–73, 4373–6).

57 STANFORD-ON-AVON

(OS 1 : 10000 a SP 67 NW, b SP 57 NE, c SP 68 SW, d SP 58 SE)

The triangular parish covers just over 850 hectares S.E. of the R. Avon, which here forms the Leicestershire boundary. Most of the parish is low-lying, between 95 m. and 120 m. above OD, on Upper Lias Clay and river gravels. In the extreme E., however, the land rises steeply

to 170 m. above OD, to the W. edge of the Hemplow Hills. Middle Lias Clay outcrops along the face of this scarp; the higher land beyond is covered by Boulder Clay. The two Roman sites (2, 3) discovered recently during field-walking may well be among others still unrevealed.

The parish includes the site of the deserted village of Downtown (6); the latter, and Stanford itself which is also deserted (4), constitute the major monuments in the parish. Downtown has been almost totally destroyed by ploughing but Stanford is well preserved.

PREHISTORIC AND ROMAN

d(1) ENCLOSURES AND DITCHES (?) (SP 597800), in the N. of the parish, close to Stanford Reservoir, on clay at 114 m. above OD. Air photographs (in NMR) show indistinct traces of a ditch or enclosure with perhaps at least two sub-rectangular enclosures to the E.

a(2) ROMAN SETTLEMENT (SP 617787), in the S.E. of the parish, on clays and silts at 150 m. above OD. A Roman site, said to stretch for at least 400 m. along the contours of the hill, was discovered by field-walking in 1975. No other details are known (Northants. Archaeol., 10 (1975), 162).

b(3) ROMAN SETTLEMENT (?) (SP 592784), in the S.W. of the parish, on Lower Lias Clay at 105 m. above OD. A scatter of Roman pottery has been found (Northants. Archaeol., 12 (1977), 215).

MEDIEVAL AND LATER

b(4) DESERTED VILLAGE OF STANFORD (SP 589788; Fig. 133; Plate 14), lies alongside the R. Avon, on river gravel at 100 m. above OD. The village of Downtown (6), now also deserted, is apparently included with Stanford in all the national taxation records and thus the true size of the latter settlement cannot be ascertained.

Stanford and, presumably, Downtown are listed in Domesday Book as one manor held by Guy de Reinbuedcurt with a recorded population of 22 including a priest (VCH Northants., II (1906), 343–4). The next record of population is not until 1377 when, from both places, 131 people over the age of 14 paid the Poll Tax (PRO, E179/155/28). In 1674, 34 households paid the Hearth Tax (PRO, E179/255/14), and this figure is probably for Stanford alone, Downtown by then being completely abandoned. Bridges (Hist. of Northants., I (1791), 578), writing in the early 18th century, said that there were then 15 houses and a shepherd's cottage at Stanford, a statement which seems to be at variance with the Hearth Tax returns 50 years earlier. Although Stanford Hall was built between 1697 and 1700, to the W. of the village, in Leicestershire, it cannot have affected the size of the village, nor is it likely that the mid 18th-century emparking around the hall had a great influence, as it never extended further E. than the main N.–S. road. In 1801 the population for the whole

Fig. 133   STANFORD-ON-AVON   (4) Deserted village of Stanford-on-Avon,
(5) Site of manor house

parish was only 45 and this indicates that the village was then about the same size as it was in Bridges' day. By the early 19th century (OS 1st ed. 1 in. map (1834)) the village was much as it is now; in 1831 only 24 people lived in the parish. Since that time one or two cottages have disappeared but new estate buildings have replaced them.

It is probable that the village was largely depopulated in late medieval times, perhaps by Selby Abbey (Yorkshire) which held the manor until the Dissolution, or by the Cave family who bought it in 1540. If this supposition is correct, enclosure for sheep may have been the reason behind the abandonment of Stanford.

The remains cover some 24 hectares and are in good condition. It appears that the village lay along a roughly N.E.–S.W. road, of which the present road N. of the church is the modern successor. To the S. of the church the line of the original road cannot be traced but it perhaps ran S. between the house-sites and closes S. of Home Farm ('a'–'b' on plan).

At the N. end of the village, on the S.E. side of the modern road, is a series of mutilated house-platforms set within small rectangular ditched paddocks with other closes behind them. All these back closes have ridge-and-furrow within them, and two hollow-ways ('c'–'d' and 'e'–'f' on plan) pass between them with subsidiary lanes branching off to N. and S. To the W. of the modern road there is no trace of any remains and this pattern, of a village on only one side of its main street, has a parallel at Mallows Cotton (RCHM Northants., I (1975), Raunds (19)) and at Braunston Cleves (Braunston (3)). An even better example is perhaps Canons Ashby (1) where the N. part of the village was also confined to one side of the street. At Canons Ashby there is evidence that this area was a late addition to the original village, and this may also be the case at Stanford.

Further S., to the E. and S.E. of the Old Rectory, is another group of narrow closes, all with ridge-and-furrow within them. These are probably the back paddocks of houses which stood on the site of the rectory and along the road to the S. To the S. again, on either side of the assumed street ('a'–'b' on plan), are the very mutilated remains of what appear to be house-sites, again with long closes containing ridge-and-furrow behind them. To the N., immediately S. of the church and W. of Home Farm, is the alleged site of the manor house (5) (RAF VAP 106G/UK/636, 3165–6; CUAP, WR58–61, AGU83–5, AKP53, AXV37–42, BEJ31; air photographs in NMR).

b(5) MANOR HOUSE SITE (SP 588787; Fig. 133), lies within the deserted village (4), immediately S. of Stanford church. Bridges (Hist. of Northants., I (1791), 578) said that the old manor house formerly stood near the church and had been pulled down 'of these late years'. It was presumably removed when the present Stanford Hall was built to the N.W., on the Leicestershire side of the R. Avon, between 1697 and 1700. Two sub-rectangular closes bounded by low scarps and shallow ditches, and a number of indeterminate banks, is all that remains on the ground at the assumed site but these are very different in form and plan from the recognisable village remains to the S., and there is no reason to doubt that they represent the site of the manor house (RAF VAP 106G/UK/636, 3165–6; CUAP, AGU85, AXV42).

c(6) DESERTED VILLAGE OF DOWNTOWN (SP 615801; Fig. 134; Plate 5), lies in the N.E. of the parish on Middle and Lower Lias Clay and river gravels between 120 m. and 132 m. above OD. The site survived until 1963 in a very good state of preservation but was then completely destroyed by ploughing. The plan is based on one made by the OS before destruction, supplemented by information from air photographs and fieldwork.

The history of the village is largely unknown and for all the medieval period it is included in the national taxation records with Stanford (4) of which it is perhaps a secondary settlement. It was certainly completely abandoned by the early 18th century, for Bridges (Hist. of Northants., I (1791), 578), writing in about 1720, recorded the site and said that 'large foundation stones and causeys' had been turned up by the plough. There was, apparently, a chapel in the village, dependent on the church at Stanford.

Before destruction the site was in good condition except that the Grand Union Canal had been cut across the N.E. part. It consisted of a broad central hollow-way ('a'–'b' on plan), bounded on each side by a series of rectangular closes with probable house-platforms at the ends near the hollow-way. Some of the closes had traces of ridge-and-furrow within them, but this does not appear to have overlaid any of the village earthworks. Pottery of the 12th to 14th centuries has been found on the site (K. J. Allison et. al., The Deserted Villages of Northants. (1966), 38; Med. Arch., 12 (1968), 201; Antiquity, 45 (1971), 298–9; DMVRG, Annual Rep., 15 (1967), 4; CUAP, AGV7, AHT48, AIH34).

(7) CULTIVATION REMAINS. The date of enclosure of the common fields of Stanford and Downtown is unknown and there is no indication as to whether each village had a separate field system. It is probable that such fields were enclosed before or during the 16th century. Ridge-and-furrow can be traced on the ground or from air photographs throughout almost the entire parish. Across the broken ground in the E., on the edge of the Hemplow Hills, the furlongs are short and interlocked but on the gentle lower slopes they are all end-on, running N.W.–S.E. Further N. and W., on the flatter ground near the river, the ridges are longer but the blocks are again interlocked. Around the site of the deserted village of Downtown (6) much of the known ridge-and-furrow has recently been destroyed but in the parkland around Stanford itself the ridges ares still well preserved (RAF VAP 106G/UK/636, 4163–7, 3162–9).

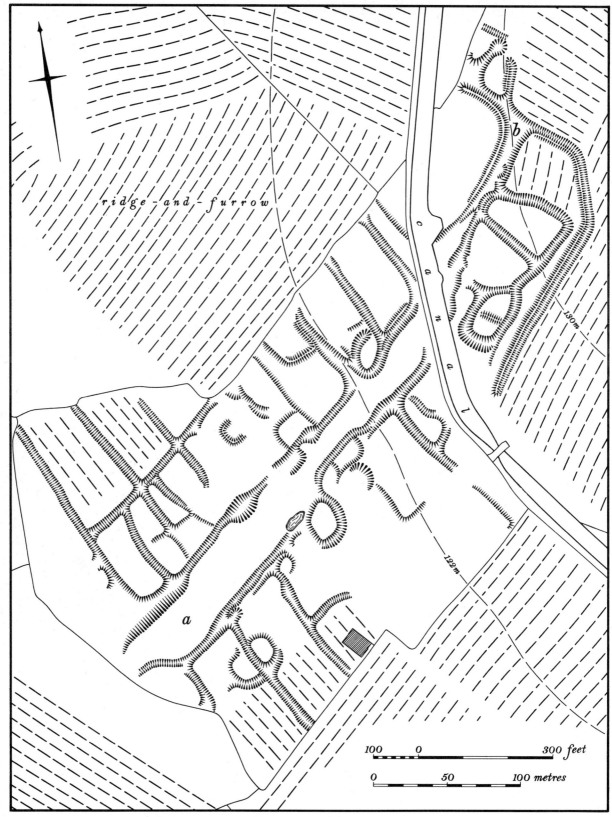

ridge - and - furrow

100   0   300 feet

0   50   100 metres

Fig. 134   STANFORD-ON-AVON   (6) Deserted village of Downtown

58 STAVERTON

(OS 1 : 10000 ᵃ SP 56 SW, ᵇ SP 56 SE, ᶜ SP 55 NW)

The parish, covering some 870 hectares, lies immediately S.W. of Daventry; its W. boundary, along the R. Leam, is also the county boundary with Warwickshire. The centre of the parish is an almost level area of Jurassic Marlstone Rock around 170 m. above OD, with an area of Upper Lias Clay to the E., beyond which the land rises sharply to Staverton Clump, the W. end of a short E.–W. ridge of Northampton Sand at about 225 m. above OD. The village stands on the W. edge of the Marlstone outcrop. To the N., W. and S. the land falls steeply to the valley of the R. Leam and its tributaries which flow in clay-bottomed valleys between 100 m. and 125 m. above OD. Little of note has been recorded in the parish.

PREHISTORIC

A looped palstave is recorded from the parish (VCH *Northants.*, I (1902), 143), but this may be one of the two palstaves listed under Everdon (Plate 22).

MEDIEVAL AND LATER

ᵃ(1) SETTLEMENT REMAINS (?) (SP 541611), on the E. side of Staverton village, immediately N. of the church on Marlstone Rock at about 172 m. above OD. Modern farm buildings and a new house appear to have destroyed almost all of a group of earthworks though some large degraded scarps may be the E. part of them.

ᵃ(2) HOLLOW-WAY (SP 534613–538611), on the S.W. side of the village, immediately N. of and parallel to the Daventry–Leamington road (A425). It extends for some 450 m. down the hillside and is 12 m. wide and up to 2.5 m. deep. It presumably represents an earlier line of the present road running down the W.-facing spur to the crossing of the R. Leam.

(3) CULTIVATION REMAINS. The common fields of the parish were enclosed by an Act of Parliament of 1774 (NRO, Enclosure Map). Ridge-and-furrow of these fields exists on the ground or can be traced on air photographs over almost the entire parish, even extending to within a few metres of the R. Leam, which forms the W. boundary of the parish, and over the very steep N.W.-facing scarp to the N. of the village where it is still well preserved. However in the narrow valleys with extremely marshy bottoms which are cut back into the scarp N.E. of the village (e.g. SP 547635, 548630, 548624 and 548621) there is no indication of any medieval or later cultivation and these areas may have been the meadow-land of the medieval parish.

The ridge-and-furrow is mainly arranged in rectangular furlongs, with the ridges almost always running down the slope. This is specially notable on the scarp to the N., N.W. and S.W. of the village. To the

S.W. (centred SP 530607) where three small almost parallel streams flow W. to meet the R. Leam the pattern of ridges is carefully adapted to this broken land. Further N., on flatter ground below the scarp face (SP 535625), the rectangular furlongs are mostly interlocked (RAF VAP CPE/UK/1994, 1277–80, 2272–4, 4276–80).

59 STOWE-NINE-CHURCHES

(OS 1 : 10000 ᵃ SP 65 NW, ᵇ SP 65 NE)

The parish, covering nearly 770 hectares, lies S.W. of Watling Street (A5) which forms its N.E. boundary. The W. and central part of the parish is occupied by a wide flat-topped plateau of Northampton Sand between 150 m. and 160 m. above OD. To the E. this plateau bifurcates to become two ridges on which stand the two villages of the parish, Church Stowe and Upper Stowe. From this higher area the land slopes N. and S. across Upper and Middle Lias Clay to two small E.-flowing streams which form the parish boundaries, between 90 m. and 105 m. above OD. To the E. of the village is a small outcrop of Great Oolitic Limestone, partly overlaid by glacial deposits.

The two villages, Upper Stowe and Church Stowe, lie about 1 km. apart near the E. edge of the parish and presumably in medieval times were surrounded by their common fields (12). Much of the N.W. part of the parish was occupied by at least one deer park (10); one length of the park boundary may have made use of an earlier multiple-ditch system (13), possibly of prehistoric date and associated with the occupation areas (2–8).

PREHISTORIC AND ROMAN

ᵃ(1) OVAL ENCLOSURE (SP 64835726), close to the Roman road, Watling Street, which here forms the parish boundary, on limestone at 115 m. above OD. Air photographs (in NMR) show a cropmark of a small oval enclosure about 40 m. long and 15 m. wide with at least one pit at its W. end. It has been interpreted as the site of a long barrow (*BNFAS*, 7 (1972), 57; *Northants. Archaeol.*, 8 (1973), 26).

ᵃ(2) DITCHED TRACKWAY, ENCLOSURE, PIT ALIGNMENT AND DITCHES (centred SP 633564; Fig. 135), N.E. of Stowe Lodge, on Northampton Sand at 158 m. above OD. On air photographs (in NMR) cropmarks of a sinuous trackway (SP 63215627–63395653), orientated roughly S.W.–N.E. and visible for about 360 m., can be seen. To its W. there is part of a sub-rectangular enclosure with rounded corners (SP 63205635) and a short length of pit alignment. There are traces of other possible ditches and enclosures but these have been obscured by frost-wedging and are difficult to interpret.

ᵃ(3) ENCLOSURES, PIT ALIGNMENTS AND DITCHES (centred SP 626560; Fig. 135), 500 m. S.W. of (2), in the S.W. corner of the parish on Northampton Sand at 152 m. above

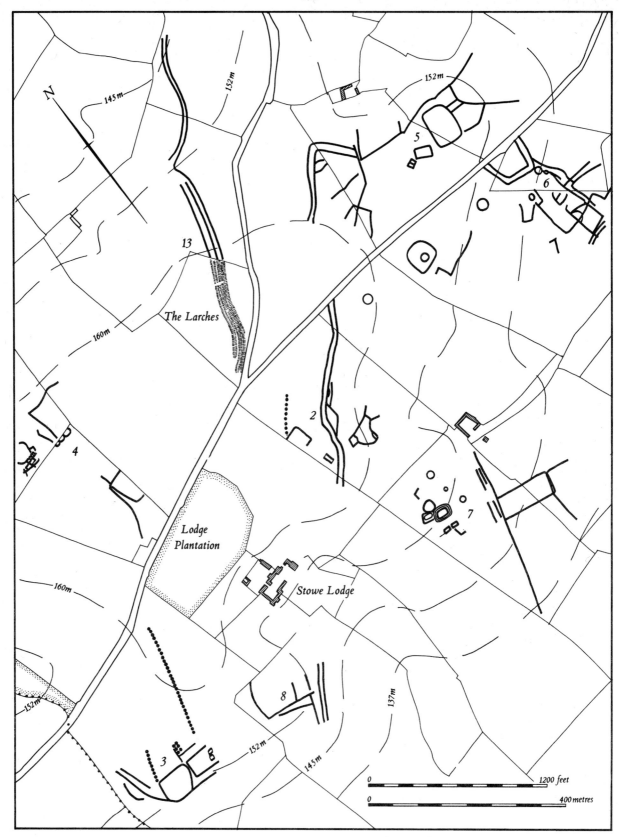

Fig. 135   STOWE-NINE-CHURCHES   (2–8, 13) Cropmarks

OD. Air photographs (in NMR) show cropmarks of a sub-rectangular enclosure, of less than half a hectare (SP 62575602). To the E. three sides of another are visible, with two much smaller ones inside, towards the E. end. Traces of at least one other enclosure and ditches lie to the N. A curving ditch runs N.W. from the S.W. corner of the first enclosure; from the N.W. corner a short length of pit alignment runs N.N.E. A second, parallel alignment to the E. is more easily traced, over a longer distance (*Northants. Archaeol.*, 9 (1974), 44).

a(4) ENCLOSURES AND DITCHES (SP 627567; Fig. 135), 450 m. N.W. of (2) on Northampton Sand at 159 m. above OD. Air photographs (in NMR) show cropmarks of two groups of small conjoined enclosures. Each cluster is associated with further ditches which may be parts of larger enclosures. Some 200 m. to the S. are other ditches (SP 628565).

a(5) ENCLOSURE, DITCHES AND DITCHED TRACKWAY (SP 637567; Fig. 135), 450 m. N.E. of (2), on Northampton Sand at 152 m. above OD. Air photographs (in NMR) show a sub-rectangular enclosure with slightly curved sides and rounded corners; it covers almost a hectare. To the N. there is a sinuous ditch running roughly E.–W. and traceable for about 180 m. A short distance to the E. are other ditches, and to the W. at least two small rectangular enclosures. Further W. is a length of ditched trackway which may be a continuation of that described in (2).

a(6) ENCLOSURES AND DITCHES (SP 640565; Fig. 135), immediately S.E. of (5), on Northampton Sand, at 145 m. above OD. Air photographs (in NMR) show an area of complex cropmarks which include part of a double-ditched enclosure, at least three ring ditches and a series of linear ditches or possible enclosures.

a(7) ENCLOSURES, RING DITCHES AND LINEAR DITCHES (SP 634562; Fig. 135), lie S. of (2), on Northampton Sand, at about 150 m. above OD. Air photographs (in NMR) show a group of small rectangular enclosures, one bounded by a triple ditch and one by a double ditch. There are also at least three ring ditches to the N.E. Further S.E. is a series of linear ditches, perhaps part of a trackway, with a large enclosure and other ditches on its E. side.

a(8) LINEAR DITCHES (SP 629560; Fig. 135), E. of (3), on Northampton Sand, at 152 m. above OD. Air photographs (in NMR) show a small group of linear ditches.

b(9) ENCLOSURE (SP 652568), in the E. of the parish, close to Watling Street, on Northampton Sand at 137 m. above OD. Air photographs (in NMR) show a small, sub-rectangular enclosure 15 m. by 30 m. with an entrance in its W. side (*Northants. Archaeol.*, 8 (1973), 26).

For possible prehistoric linear earthwork, see (13).

For Roman Road 1f, Watling Street, see Appendix.

MEDIEVAL AND LATER

a(10) DEER PARK (centred SP 628579), perhaps occupied most of the N.W. part of the parish, mainly on Northampton Sand and Lias Clay, between 100 m. and 158 m. above OD. It is first mentioned in 1326 when Gilbert de Middleton was granted the manor of Stowe 'with the park' (*Cal. Pat.* 1324–7, 160). Its later history is unknown but Bridges (*Hist. of Northants.*, I (1791), 88) records that in the late 17th century there were two contiguous parks, which had by his time 'been converted to other use'. He also notes that the area was formerly a warren. The exact extent of the park is unknown and the only traceable boundary features are not entirely convincing. There is no trace of any bank along the W. and N. parish boundaries. Along the N. side of the Farthingstone road, on the S. side of Ramsden Corner Wood (SP 62505626), there is a bank 5 m. wide and 0.5 m. high. A N.-facing scarp up to 2 m. high continues the line of the bank as far as Lodge Plantation (SP 62775638). There are no indications of a boundary between this point and the linear banks (13); the latter may be part of the boundary of the park.

Beyond the N. limit of these banks (SP 63305702) no trace of a boundary can be found. Two maps of 1773 and 1839 (NRO) give the name Parks to two fields S.E. of Stowe Wood (centred SP 630569). The 1839 map also names a field to the E. of the linear banks (SP 635572), and thus outside the assumed boundary, as Sheep Pen Parks.

a(11) SETTLEMENT REMAINS (centred SP 604576 and 638576), formerly part of Church Stowe, lie in two places, W. and S.W. of the church. The first site consists of indeterminate earthworks and a small pond, and the second of a long scarp 120 m. long and about 1 m. high running S.W.–N.E. with other low earthworks on either side. In 1773 (Map in NRO) the area was already devoid of buildings though the main scarp was the boundary between two long rectangular paddocks (RAF VAP CPE/UK/1994, 1169–71).

(12) CULTIVATION REMAINS. The exact date of the enclosure of the common fields of Stowe-Nine-Churches is not known but was certainly before 1773 (Map in NRO). Bridges (*Hist. of Northants.*, I (1791), 87) records that the parish was enclosed by Edward Harley, apparently in the late 17th or early 18th century. Very little of the ridge-and-furrow of those fields survives or can be traced from air photographs. Apart from three fields at the head of a small valley between the two villages (SP 643571) the only areas where ridge-and-furrow survives in furlongs are along the S. boundary of the parish where the ridges run down to the stream and to the S. of Upper Stowe where there is a group of interlocked furlongs (RAF VAP CPE/UK/1994, 3158–62, 1167–72, 2164–6).

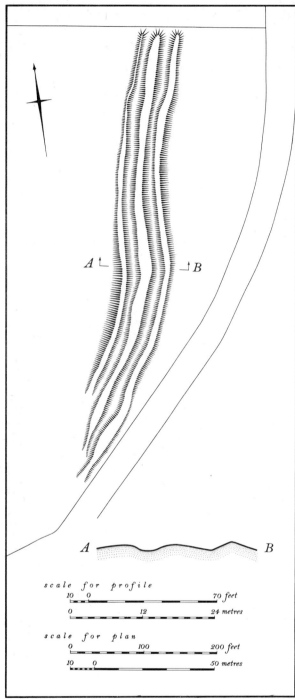

Fig. 136   STOWE-NINE-CHURCHES
(13) Linear banks and ditches

UNDATED

a(13) LINEAR BANKS AND DITCHES (centred SP 63255670; Figs. 135 and 136), on Northampton Sand between 150 m. and 160 m. above OD. The earthwork consists of three parallel banks orientated S.S.W. to N.N.E., separated by shallow U-shaped ditches. The average total width is about 25 m. and the earthworks extend for 220 m. The E. bank, which is the largest, reaches a maximum of 1.5 m. above the bottom of the adjacent ditch. There are four causeways across the banks and ditches, all probably secondary. At its S.W. end the earthwork turns and fades, apparently respecting the modern road and this might suggest that it is later than the road. No trace of a S.W. continuation is visible, however, as a disused ironstone tramway has destroyed any remains. To the N.E. air photographs (in NMR) show cropmarks of three parallel ditches, extending the alignment of the earthworks for at least 180 m. These ditches are then either intersected by or continued as two parallel ditches which run N.E. for a further 300 m.

Despite a small excavation in 1973 there is no conclusive evidence as to the function or date of the structure. It may be medieval or later and could have been part of the boundary of the deer park (10), or a warren for rabbits, though its size and form makes this doubtful. It has also been suggested that it is spoil from quarrying or a 19th-century military work for cannon associated with Weedon Barracks, but these alternatives are also unlikely (OS Record Cards; *BNFAS*, 5 (1971), 42; *Northants. Archaeol.*, 8 (1973), 27; RAF VAP CPE/UK/1994, 3159–60). A more acceptable explanation is that the earthworks are part of a linear boundary of prehistoric date, and thus a rare survival in the county; they may have been reused as the deer park boundary.

60   SULBY

(OS 1 : 10000 a SP 68 SW, b SP 68 SE, c SP 67 NE)

The parish is roughly triangular and covers only about 650 hectares. On its N.W. side is the county boundary with Leicestershire; its S.W. side follows part of the upper reaches of the R. Avon, here flowing N.W. at about 125 m. above OD. Apart from alluvial deposits on the floor of this and other small valleys, and Middle Lias Clay exposed on the valley sides, the entire parish consists of a flat upland at about 150 m. above OD, covered with Boulder Clay. There are two important monuments in the parish, the deserted village of Sulby (3) which was almost completely overploughed in the late or post-medieval period but has undergone no recent damage, and the site of Sulby Abbey (2). It is possible that the abbey was built on the site of a second medieval settlement in the parish already abandoned before the religious house was founded there.

ROMAN

b(1) ROMAN SETTLEMENT (SP 672809), in the E. of the parish on Boulder Clay at 157 m. above OD. Many sherds of Roman grey ware and some of colour-coated ware have been found over a wide area (*Northants. Archaeol.*, 11 (1976), 194).

scale for profile
10   0   70 feet
0   12   24 metres

scale for plan
0   100   200 feet
10   0   50 metres

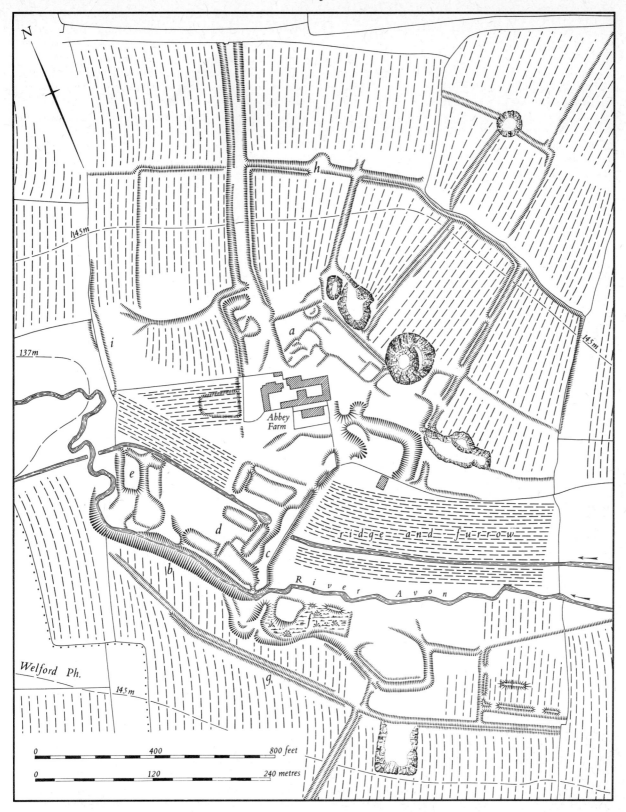

Fig. 137   SULBY   (2) Site of Sulby Abbey

MEDIEVAL AND LATER

bc(2) SULBY ABBEY (SP 657800; Fig. 137; Plate 4), lies in the S.E. of the parish, across the valley of the R. Avon, between 135 m. and 145 m. above OD. Most of the land is on Jurassic clay or Boulder Clay, but the present farmhouse and the assumed site of the church and claustral buildings are on a small patch of glacial gravel.

The abbey, a house of Premonstratensian Canons, was founded in 1155 in the adjacent parish of Welford by William de Wideville who gave them the church of Welford and nine carucates of land in Sulby. Shortly afterwards, following the grant of a manor in Sulby as well as the church in that parish, the abbey was moved to Sulby. Edward II stayed at Sulby Abbey on a number of occasions but visitations in the late 15th century never recorded more than 13 canons. The abbey was dissolved in 1538, and in 1567 the land was acquired by Sir Christopher Hatton, the first of a succession of lay owners (VCH Northants., II (1906), 138–42; H. M. Colvin, The White Canons in England (1951), 77–82).

It is possible that the abbey was built on the site of an earlier village already deserted by the 12th century for one of the two entries for Sulby in Domesday Book is for a manor of 2$\frac{1}{2}$ hides held by Geoffrey de Wirce as part of Welford, which was then waste (VCH Northants., I (1902), 347).

Most of the large area of earthworks appears to be paddocks, ponds and water-courses. The actual site of the abbey is identifiable, however, and the main approach to it survives as a broad trackway bounded by shallow ditches or low banks which runs down the hillside towards the present Abbey Farm. Immediately N. of the farm the track opens into an area of irregular shape bounded by scarps and banks ('a' on plan). The interior is occupied by very disturbed ground and uninterpretable scarps and ditches. This seems to be the site of the monastic church and claustral buildings. The existing house, of 18th or 19th-century date, and a late 19th-century arch in the garden contain reused fragments of worked and moulded stone, and a large number of finds have been made in the vicinity of the farm buildings including a stone coffin, a coffin lid with a floriated cross, fragments of window tracery, columns, mouldings, balls of lead and fragments of ironwork. In this century an 'arch' is said to have been found immediately N. of the farm (OS Record Cards). A number of decorated floor tiles from the abbey (NM; Plate 23) include one of 14th-century date, part of a four-tile design and another, of the 14th or 15th century, depicting a coat of arms with three pikes. It may be the arms of the Wyke family. Even in the early 18th century Bridges (Hist. of Northants., I (1791), 597) recorded the discovery of stonework on this site.

To the S. of the farm, in the valley bottom, is a complicated system of ponds and channels. The R. Avon must originally have flowed along the bottom of the valley but has been diverted and made to run as a high-level leat on the S. side of the valley, at one point ('b' on plan) passing through a large cutting 4 m. deep. The valley floor then seems to have been divided into a series of ponds. In the S.E. a large dam ('c' on plan), still standing up to 2 m. high, was constructed across the valley, thus ponding back a large lake. The latter area is now drained and has been ploughed in narrow ridge-and-furrow of late 18th-century or early 19th-century type. Below the dam ('d' on plan) are several small ponds or fish stews. Those to the S.W. were supplied by a channel, from the diverted Avon but it is not clear how the two to the N.E. were filled. The land to the N.W. of these ponds also has narrow ridge-and-furrow on it.

Further N. ('e' on plan) are other earthworks the purpose of which is not clear. They consist of a large rectangular mound which was apparently once almost completely surrounded by water, as well as a number of channels or ditches.

Earthworks on the S.W. side of the diverted R. Avon include a large pond ('f' on plan), the N.E. side of which has been broken down and survives only as three mounds though the S.W. side of its dam remains 2 m. high. This pond appears to have been filled by seepage from the valley side, as the diverted Avon to the N.E. is at a lower level. To the S.E. of this pond is a large semicircular ditch 1.5 m. deep, of unknown purpose, and S.E. again is a small embanked paddock. A long mound, perhaps a 'pillow mound', within the latter has been ploughed over by later ridge-and-furrow. This paddock may be an enclosed rabbit warren. All these features lie N.E. of a long boundary bank and ditch ('g' on plan) which separates them from the ridge-and-furrow to the S.W. and is perhaps the original precinct boundary of the abbey on this side. It is presumably of early date for on its N.E. side are the truncated remains of ridge-and-furrow which is not aligned with the ridge-and-furrow to the S.E. This means that pre-existing ridge-and-furrow in the area was overlaid by the boundary bank and ditch and that subsequently the land to the S.W. was reploughed in new ridges.

On the N. side of the valley, N.E. of the site of the conventual buildings, is a group of large paddocks bounded by shallow ditches and separated from the ridge-and-furrow beyond by a bank ('h' on plan) up to 1.5 m. high with traces of an outer ditch. These paddocks all have ridge-and-furrow within them. The bank may represent the monastic precinct boundary on this side of the site for at its S.E. end it turns S.W. and runs down towards the Avon. Traces of a spread bank on the N.W. edge of the site ('i' on plan) may also be the boundary bank (RAF VAP 106G/UK/636, 3177–8; CPE/UK/2109, 3303–5; CUAP, AEV26–9, NR 59–60, XT76).

b(3) DESERTED VILLAGE OF SULBY (SP 653816; Fig. 138; Plate 9), lies near the W. edge of the parish, W. of Park Farm, on land sloping S.E. to a small tributary of the R. Avon on Boulder Clay between 137 m. and 155 m. above

185

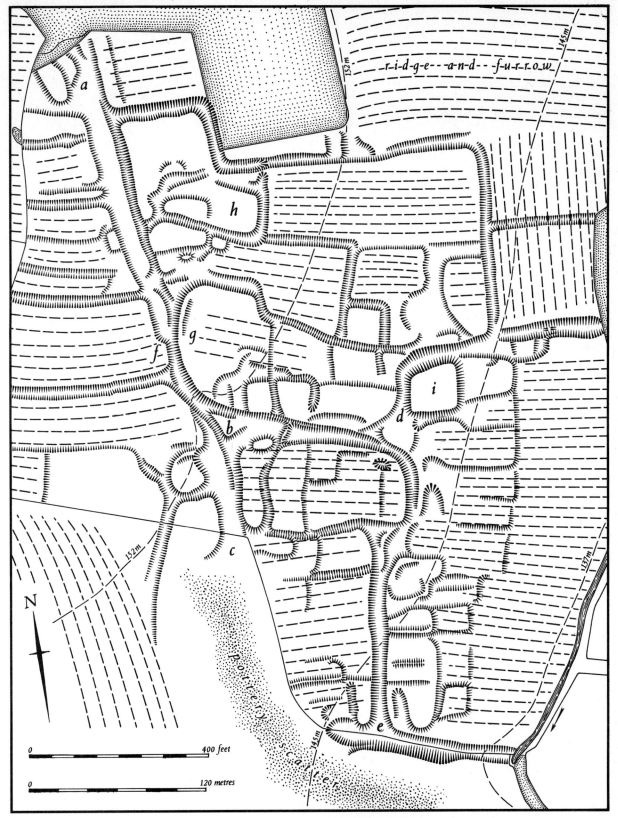

Fig. 138   SULBY   (3) Deserted village

OD. The earthworks are in very good condition and are especially interesting because they show that the greater part of the village was ploughed over after its desertion.

Sulby is first recorded in Domesday Book as two manors, one held by Guy de Reinbuedcurt with a recorded population of 13, and the other which was waste held by Geoffrey de Wirce (VCH *Northants.*, I (1902), 343, 347). The latter manor may have been represented by a village already deserted and then replaced by Sulby Abbey (2), but the one held by Guy de Reinbuedcurt is perhaps the site described here. This village was acquired by Sulby Abbey soon after 1215 and is mentioned separately in the *Nomina Villarum* of 1316. In 1334 the vill paid 31s. for the Lay Subsidy (PRO, E179/155/3) and in 1377 89 people over the age of 14 paid the Poll Tax (PRO, E179/155/28). By 1428 there were less than ten householders in the village (*Feudal Aids*, p. 52). At the Dissolution Sulby Abbey had large areas of pasture in the parish including a close known as 'Old Soulby', and 2000 sheep were being grazed in the area by 1547 (K. J. Allison *et al.*, *The Deserted Villages of Northants.* (1966), 46). In 1674 five householders paid the Hearth Tax (PRO, E179/254/14) and in the early 18th century Bridges (*Hist. of Northants.*, I (1791), 596) said that Old Sulby consisted of only two or three scattered houses. This evidence indicates that the village itself disappeared between 1377 and 1428 and was replaced by the present pattern of scattered farmsteads.

There was apparently a parish church at Sulby, separate from that of Sulby Abbey and dedicated to St. Botolph. Bridges (op. cit., 597) said that the nave had fallen down long before 1451 and the rest of the building was destroyed at the Dissolution. It was said to have stood about a mile N. of the abbey near the N.W. end of the meadow called St. Botolph's Pool. This suggests that it stood within the deserted village, though no exact site can be assigned to it unless it was the large platform at the E. end of the village ('i' on plan).

The site consists of a number of hollow-ways with the remains of former houses and closes along them. The main hollow-way, which is up to 1 m. deep, ('a'–'b'–'c' on plan) enters the village at its N.W. corner and runs almost due S. until it disappears into arable land at its S. end ('c' on plan). Another hollow-way branches off it to the S.E. The point of junction ('b' on plan) appears to be triangular. To the S.E. the latter hollow-way forks again; the N. branch ('d' on plan) turns N. and then E. and extends down the hillside, the S. branch runs southwards to the edge of the site where it meets another one at right-angles ('e' on plan). This runs S.E. in the valley bottom, but may once have extended N.W. to meet the assumed extension of the main N.–S. hollow-way.

On the W. side of the main hollow-way (between 'a' and 'b' on plan) there are at least eight long closes, all bounded by shallow ditches or low scarps. Six of these have been overploughed by ridge-and-furrow and all but one of the former house-sites at their E. ends have been destroyed.

At one point ('f' on plan) the ridge-and-furrow extends into the hollow-way itself and thus partly blocks it. Along the E. side is a series of less regular closes, some bounded by ditches up to 1.25 m. deep. Two of these ('g' and 'h' on plan) appear to be aligned quite differently from the others and one ('g' on plan) seems to have encroached upon the hollow-way. This may mean that these features are a later alteration to the previous layout of the village in this area.

Along the N. side of the main E.–W. hollow-way ('b'–'d' on plan) are small closes, bounded by low scarps and shallow ditches, some of which are likely to be the sites of former buildings. Other closes behind them to the N. are all overploughed by later ridge-and-furrow, some of it extremely short. On both sides of the S.E. hollow-way ('d'–'e' on plan) there is a more regular pattern of closes but as all have been partly or entirely ploughed over by later ridge-and-furrow little but the main boundaries survives. In the centre of the E. of the site there is a large double platform ('i' on plan), raised some 1.5 m. above the surrounding land, and the most prominent earthwork on the site. Because of its E.–W. orientation it has been suggested that it is the site of the parish church (OS Record Cards) but this cannot be proved without excavation.

The S.W. corner of the village has been destroyed by modern cultivation but in the plough soil there is a long narrow area of stony ground. From it a quantity of medieval pottery of 12th to 14th-century date including some Lyveden ware has been recovered. A single Roman sherd has also been found (RAF VAP CPE/UK/2109, 4302–3; CUAP, XT81, AEB24–5, AGU68–9, AKP44–5).

ᵇ(4) CIVIL WAR GRAVE (?) (SP 66978013), lies in the S.E. of the parish near the Naseby boundary, on a N.-facing slope, at 160 m. above OD. There is a tradition that, following the Battle of Naseby on 14 June 1645, the dead were buried in a communal grave on the battlefield, (J. Mastin, *Hist. and Ants. of Naseby* (1792), 68). In 1842 Edward Fitzgerald, in an attempt to locate the centre of the battlefield, dug into a mound at this point and found numerous skeletons (OS Record Cards). Though the site is just to the W. of the battlefield itself there is no reason to doubt that this is a grave connected with that event. It consists of a shallow scoop some 50 m. across, cut into the hillside with a very slight mound in the centre.

(5) CULTIVATION REMAINS. The date of the enclosure of the common fields of Sulby is unknown but was certainly before 1720, when Bridges (*Hist. of Northants.*, I (1791), 596) described it as an enclosed lordship, and was probably before the Dissolution of the abbey, when there were at least 880 acres of pasture there (K. J. Allison *et al.*, *The Deserted Villages of Northants.* (1966), 46). It is likely that the fields were in fact enclosed when the village of Sulby was abandoned, that is between 1377 and 1428. Much of the ridge-and-furrow of these fields has been destroyed. Where it survives on the ground or can be traced on air photographs it is mainly arranged in long sweeping

furlongs, running across ridges and valleys, for example in the area surrounding Sulby Abbey itself, where most of the ridges run N.–S. Further N., around and across the site of Sulby village, the main trend is E.–W. across the S.-facing spurs, with a few shorter interlocked furlongs. E. of the village the N.–S. trend predominates. Ridge-and-furrow is particularly well preserved within closes associated with Sulby Abbey, and on the S. side of the abbey the precinct boundary bank appears to have been laid out across pre-existing furlongs. This has resulted in the abandonment of the shorter truncated ends and the development of new ridge-and-furrow outside the precinct boundary (RAF VAP 106G/UK/636, 3135–9, 3177–81; CPE/UK/2109, 4299–4303, 3301–5).

61 THORNBY

(OS 1:10000 [a] SP 67 NE, [b] SP 67 SE, [c] SP 67 SW)

The parish, of about 490 hectares, is compact apart from a narrow area extending S.W. which represents the land of the former village of Chilcote (2). The main part of the parish and the village itself lie on a N.W.–S.E. ridge covered with Boulder Clay and other glacial deposits, with a maximum height of 182 m. above OD. On the steep slopes which fall S.W. from this ridge Northampton Sand and Upper Lias Clay are exposed. Narrow bands of alluvium flank two streams flowing generally S.E., one of which forms the S. boundary of the parish. The site of the deserted village of Chilcote cannot be traced exactly within the lands known to belong to it (Fig. 139) but it has been tentatively located.

ROMAN

[a](1) ROMAN SETTLEMENT (?) (SP 674765), N. of Lodge Farm, in the N. of the parish, on sand and gravel at about 160 m. above OD. Roman pottery was discovered during field-walking in 1975 (Northants. Archaeol., 10 (1975), 163).

MEDIEVAL AND LATER

[b](2) DESERTED SETTLEMENT OF CHILCOTE, PONDS AND DAM (SP 658747; Figs. 139 and 140), lie in the S.W. of the parish, on Boulder Clay and glacial gravel between 148 m. and 160 m. above OD. Almost nothing is known of their history but it is clear that the long narrow south-western projection of Thornby parish was once the land of Chilcote. The small S.-flowing stream between this land and the rest of the parish still formed a major property boundary as late as 1840 (NRO, Tithe Map). There is nothing on modern maps to indicate that this area was the land of Chilcote and earlier writers have usually assumed that the settlement lay in Cold Ashby parish; indeed a wood in Cold Ashby is called Chilcote's Cover (SP

65257467) on the 1st ed. 1 in. map of 1834. However three large fields to the S., in Thornby parish, just W. of the assumed site of the settlement (centred SP 654745), are called Great and Little Chilcotes on the Thornby Tithe Map.

The name Chilcote, 'the young people's cottages' (PN Northants., 65) suggests that it was a late secondary settlement in the area. The first reference to the place is in Domesday Book where it is described as a manor gelding for only one virgate and with a recorded population of two (VCH Northants., I (1902), 327). Thereafter nothing is known of its size. By the 13th century the manor belonged to Pipewell Abbey (Cal. Chart. R., i, 1226–57, 206–7) with which it remained until the Dissolution. By the early 19th century Grange Farm and a group of cottages existed to the N. of the site and in the early 19th century a large mill and a mill cottage, now abandoned, were built near the medieval settlement.

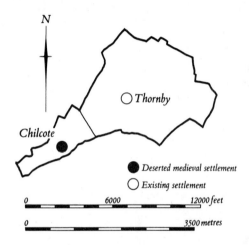

Fig. 139   THORNBY
Medieval settlements and estates

Apart from two fragmentary embanked closes and a terrace-way which approaches them from the S.W. ('a' on plan), no surface remains of Chilcote can be traced. N.W. of the present mill a large dam ('b' on plan) 2 m. high, with a later break in its centre, spans the valley, but as it lies on top of earlier ridge-and-furrow it is presumably late or post-medieval in date. It thus has no connection with the settlement at Chilcote and may be a mill dam. Above it is a small embanked pond, but this is the header pond for the 19th-century mill and was linked to it by underground culverts. To the E. of the mill in the valley bottom are two rectangular ponds ('c' on plan), perhaps originally for fish and possibly medieval in date (RAF VAP 541/15, 4388–9).

[a](3) MOAT (?) (SP 673758), N.E. of Thornby Hall, on Boulder Clay at 150 m. above OD. The site is now only an L-shaped ornamental pond 80 m. by 30 m. and up to 20 m. wide in the corner of the park, and on the Tithe Map

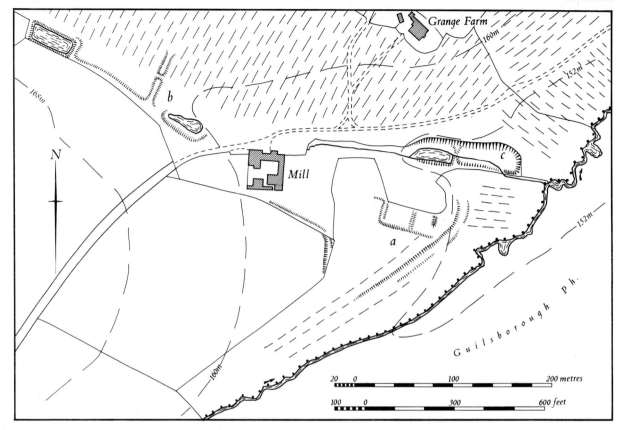

Fig. 140   THORNBY   (2) Deserted settlement of Chilcote, ponds and dam

of Thornby (NRO, 1840) the pond is shown slightly larger, but still L-shaped. There is no trace of any other side and the identification of the site as a moat is uncertain. The feature may have been associated with a medieval manor house located differently from the adjacent Thornby Hall which has a 17th-century origin.

[a](4) WINDMILL MOUND (SP 66717593), N.W. of the village, on Northampton Sand at 182 m. above OD. The mound is 20 m. in diam. and 1.2 m. high, with a pronounced ramp to the N.E. The field in which it stands was known as Mill Bank on the Tithe Map of 1840 (NRO). It is probably the feature described as a tumulus on the map of Bannaventa and its environs (*Archaeologia*, 35 (1853), Pl. 16, 394; OS Record Cards).

(5) CULTIVATION REMAINS. The enclosure of the common fields of the parish took place at an unknown date before 1840 (NRO, Tithe Map). Very little of the ridge-and-furrow survives or can be traced on air photographs, although the few furlongs that do still exist, mainly on the side of the Naseby road, are extremely well preserved. To the S.E. of the village (SP 673753) a large access-way runs parallel to the ridges of one of the rare surviving furlongs.

The common fields assumed to have belonged to the deserted hamlet of Chilcote (2) were also enclosed at an

unknown date before 1840. In this area rather more ridge-and-furrow has survived, on each side of the track leading from Thornby to the site of the hamlet. It is in a good state of preservation and is arranged in interlocked furlongs with ridges at right-angles to the slope (RAF VAP CPE/UK/1994, 2460–1; 106G/UK/636, 4177–81).

62 WATFORD

(OS 1:10000 [a] SP 56 NE, [b] SP 57 SE, [c] SP 66 NW,
[d] SP 67 SW)

The parish, covering more than 1400 hectares, is of irregular shape with a number of projections. A small part of its S.W. boundary follows the A5, Watling Street, but further N. the parish extends W. across the Roman road. The E. boundary is determined by the upper reaches of a small stream flowing S. towards the R. Nene. The valley known as the Watford Gap, carrying the main road, rail and water routes of central England, runs through the W. half of the parish; from its alluvial floor, at about 100 m. above OD, the land rises steeply to the W. across glacial deposits to a maximum height of 135 m. above OD and more gently to the E. across Lias Clays and Marlstone Rock capped by glacial materials.

The modern parish now contains the land of at least two deserted settlements, Silsworth (3) and an unnamed and unlocated settlement (2), as well as that of the village of Watford itself and part of the land of a fourth settlement, Murcott (Long Buckby (5)). The sites of Silsworth and Murcott are known with certainty. The village of Watford has extensive settlement remains (4), bearing witness to an earlier form of the village; there are also remains of a garden perhaps constructed in the 18th century (5).

ROMAN

^d(1) ROMAN SETTLEMENT (?) (centred SP 616707), at the site of the deserted village of Silsworth (3). A small amount of Roman pottery was found in an unspecified place during an excavation in 1964 (*Med. Arch.*, IX (1965), 214). In 1977 more Roman pottery was picked up on the N. and W. edges of the site (SP 615707, 617708).

MEDIEVAL AND LATER

^a(2) SETTLEMENT REMAINS (unlocated but perhaps SP 578695, 580695 or 585697; Fig. 99), lie somewhere in the extreme W. of the parish to the W. of Watling Street. The small triangular area of the parish which extends to the W. of Watling Street is unusual. Parish boundaries in this area generally cross the Roman road only to incorporate within their area land which was once a separate estate based on a medieval settlement (e.g. Norton (11)). Thus there are some grounds for assuming that this area was once the land of a now deserted settlement. In addition, as well as the other known settlements and estates in the parish, Silsworth (3) and Murcott (Long Buckby (5)), there are records of at least two other places both described by Bridges as deserted in the 18th century. One was called Catesby, 'an enclosed manor with no house', the other, Cumberford, 'a depopulated village in an enclosed manor, now reduced to one house ... the Crown ale house' (J. Bridges, *Hist. of Northants.*, I (1791), 585). The locations of both are unknown, but one may have been situated in the area under discussion. There are three possible sites. One is on the N. side of a small E.-flowing stream (SP578695), on the road between Crick and Ashby St. Ledgers. A broad flat area bounded by scarps up to 2 m. high has slight traces of ridge-and-furrow on it. Another is further N.E. (SP 580695), on a steep S.-facing slope to the N. of the railway cutting leading into Kilsby Tunnel. There are at least three small closes, bounded by low scarps; the S. ends have been truncated by the railway. The third possible location is further E., S. of Watford Gap (SP 585697). The field here is called Moat Close on a map of 1764 and Mott Close Meadow on the Tithe Map of 1847 (both in NRO). Near its N.E. end there is a large quarry-pit, associated with a number of indeterminate banks or scarps and surrounded by ridge-and-furrow.

^d(3) DESERTED VILLAGE OF SILSWORTH (SP 617707; Figs.

99 and 141; Plates 12 and 13), lies in the N.E. corner of the parish on both sides of a small valley draining S.E., on glacial sands and gravels at about 140 m. above OD. The history of Silsworth is largely unknown, although the land attributable to it can be defined with some certainty (Fig. 99). The village is not mentioned in Domesday Book, though it presumably existed at that time, and is probably included silently under Watford. The name is not recorded until 1213 (PN *Northants.*, 75). In 1333 Silsworth is referred to as a hamlet and in 1392 there were said to be several tenements. By the early 15th century one freeholder family had accumulated most of the land in Silsworth from a variety of earlier holders. This and other properties in Silsworth were acquired by the Catesby family later in the 15th century and by 1485 the land of Silsworth was said to consist of 300 acres arable and 490 acres pasture. In 1594 the land was divided into three 'closes or pastures' called Middle Field, High Field and Sharrocks Close (K. J. Allison *et al.*, *The Deserted Villages of Northants.* (1966), 45). On a map of 1631 (PRO; Plate 13), the Middle Field is depicted lying on either side of the present road to West Haddon immediately S. and E. of the site of the village. The map also shows a meadow to the S.W. and includes the S. part of the site of the village. However only three buildings are shown, one house on the site of the existing cottage now known as Kelly's Rise, another building to the N., near the ruined farm buildings, and a third house, to the S.W. of the village proper, on the S. side of the stream. By the early 18th century Bridges (*Hist. of Northants.*, I (1791), 585) described Silsworth as 'a depopulated hamlet consisting at present of a single house', the latter presumably the one shown on the site of the existing cottage.

The remains of Silsworth are in poor condition and over half the site has been ploughed in recent years and almost destroyed. As a result it is difficult to interpret what remains. As far as can be seen the village stood at a cross-roads which lay immediately S. of the present cottage. Here the Watford-West Haddon road, which at this point seems to be on its medieval alignment, is crossed by a hollow-way ('a'-'b'-'c'-'d' on plan). This hollow-way approaches the site from the S.E. ('a' on plan) and though much damage appears to have crossed the present road, swung to the W. of the cottage ('b' on plan) and then run on N. and N.E., across an area now under arable, until it fades out ('d' on plan). Another hollow-way seems to have run N.W. from the present road near the stream, along the bed of the latter ('e'-'f' on plan). There is no indication of a road there, but the arrangement of the closes on either side of the stream suggest that this was the case. Traces of closes and former buildings lie on either side of both these hollow-ways though recent destruction as well as earlier damage has now removed most of the evidence. To the N. of the S.E. hollow-way is an area of disturbed ground ('g' on plan) very difficult to interpret. A markedly sinuous ditch appears partly to divide some possible building sites from the adjacent ridge-and-furrow. To the S. of the

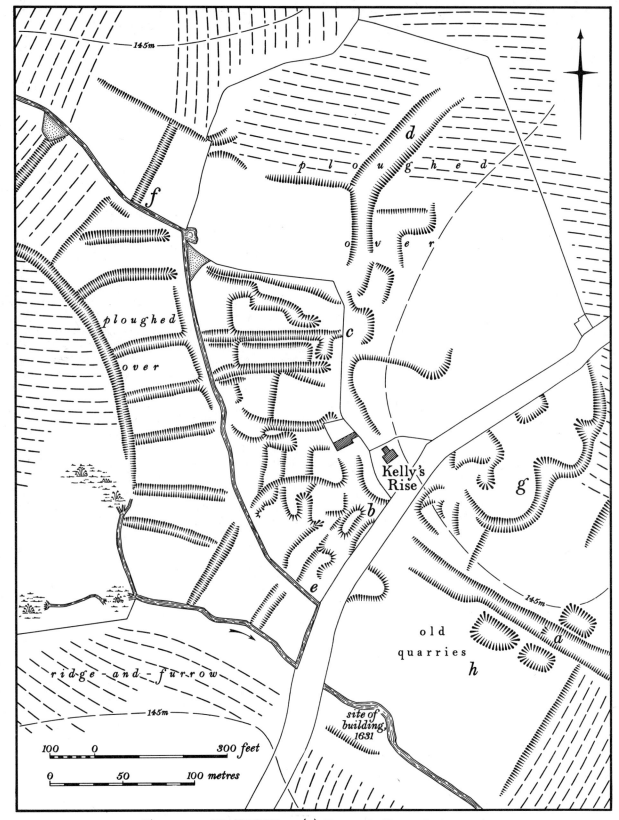

Fig. 141 WATFORD (3) Deserted village of Silsworth

hollow-way ('h' on plan) nothing survives apart from two rectangular depressions up to 1.5 m. deep and some indications of old quarrying. The area to the N. of Kelly's Rise, E. of the hollow-way ('c'–'d' on plan), has been ploughed in recent times and little remains on the ground though there are traces of possible house-sites. After ploughing, large quantities of medieval pottery, mainly of 12th to 14th-century date, were recovered from here, and considerable spreads of stone rubble were also noted. Closes and former house-sites exist or existed on both sides of the other hollow-way ('e'–'f' on plan). Those on the W. have been largely destroyed by modern cultivation but there appear to have been at least eight closes, separated by shallow ditches, with house-sites at their E. ends. Here again large amounts of medieval pottery have been found. On the E. side of this hollow-way the earthworks are intact and appear to be the remains of five closes. No certain building sites are visible though a number of flat, raised platforms to the W. of the cottage may mark the positions of former structures.

A small excavation on the site in 1964 when it was already partly destroyed revealed a 'medieval occupation-layer' below which were several road surfaces of hard metalling. Two courses of a medieval stone wall lay at right-angles across the topmost road surface (*Med. Arch.*, IX (1965), 214). The location of this excavation is not recorded and that given by the OS Record Cards, at SP 61847056, puts it outside the village in an area of ridge-and-furrow. In NM is a small quantity of pottery from Silsworth. It includes one rim sherd of Ipswich ware, two sherds of Stamford ware and later medieval and post-medieval pottery (*Northants. Archaeol.*, 8 (1973), 19; 12 (1977), 191; RAF VAP CPE/UK/1994, 1474–5; CUAP, AWQ15, 16).

^c(4) SETTLEMENT REMAINS (centred SP 601688 and 602691; Figs. 13, 99 and 142; Plate 20), lie in two places N.W. and S.W. of Watford Church, on land sloping W. on Middle Lias clays and silts between 110 m. and 125 m. above OD. Part of the site is overlaid by the later garden remains (5).

The earthworks may be interpreted as two separate settlements, related to two road systems, though it is difficult to find documentary support for this theory. Watford is first mentioned in Domesday Book where it is listed as a single two-hide manor with a recorded population of 27 (VCH *Northants.*, I (1902), 355). However, this entry must refer not only to Watford itself, but also to the now deserted village of Silsworth (3), perhaps to the part of the hamlet of Murcott lying within the parish (Long Buckby (5)) and to at least one other settlement (2). Thus the 1086 population figures have little value, and the later national taxation records are similarly limited in their usefulness. By the early 18th century Bridges (*Hist. Of Northants.*, I (1791), 585) noted that there were 35 houses in Watford, apparently in the present

village, but he also records four other places in the parish. These include Murcott and Silsworth, but in addition there was Catesby, 'an enclosed manor with no houses' and Cumberford, 'a depopulated village on an enclosed manor now reduced to one house'. One of these is likely to be the deserted settlement (2) in the W. of the parish, but the other is either lost or part of the earthworks described here.

The N. part of the remains lies alongside the road to Kilsby ('a' on plan). It consists, on the S. side of the road, of four or five small rectangular closes, bounded by low scarps or shallow ditches with what may be former house-sites at their N. ends. In the westernmost close, and lying askew to it, are the foundations of a rectangular stone building. Behind these closes, to the S., are four small paddocks, three of which have ridge-and-furrow within them. Traces of a hollow-way almost on the line of the present road are also visible. On the N. side of the road are at least three other small closes with slight indications of former buildings within them. It is possible that the site once extended further E. towards the village, but the area to the N. of the road has been ploughed and only slight scarps remain; on the S. the gardens of Watford Court have obliterated all traces. No date for the abandonment of this part of the village is known though it had certainly disappeared by 1740 (Map in NRO). It may be the site of one of the two deserted settlements referred to by Bridges (op. cit.).

The southern area of earthworks is larger and appears to be the remains of former houses and closes lying on either side of the present Main Street and its extension W. as Park Lane, as well as on the W. side of Station Road. On the S. side of Main Street, partly behind the existing houses, are at least six long closes bounded by low scarps and shallow ditches ('b' on plan). On a series of maps dating from 1771 to the Tithe Map of 1840 (all in NRO) most of these closes are shown as hedged paddocks, with houses at their N. ends. The earthworks therefore represent relatively recent abandonment of this part of the village. To the N.W., and inside the park of Watford Court ('c' on plan), is another series of closes, most of which are in a rather mutilated state. These closes were already abandoned by 1740 (NRO, Map of Watford Park), but houses which stood at their S. ends, along Main Street and Park Lane, were still there in 1771 and in 1840. This indicates that the houses along this street had their gardens taken away, perhaps in the early 18th century when the park was laid out and the gardens were incorporated into the park. The houses, however, survived until well into the 19th century and perhaps as late as 1860 when many new estate cottages were erected in the village. To the S. of Park Lane and W. of Station Road ('d' on plan) are further abandoned closes with a hollow-way running along their S.W. sides. These had already been made into one paddock in 1771 and a range of farm buildings stood within them. On the opposite side of Station Road ('e' on plan) an area of disturbed ground marks the site of another house and garden, in existence

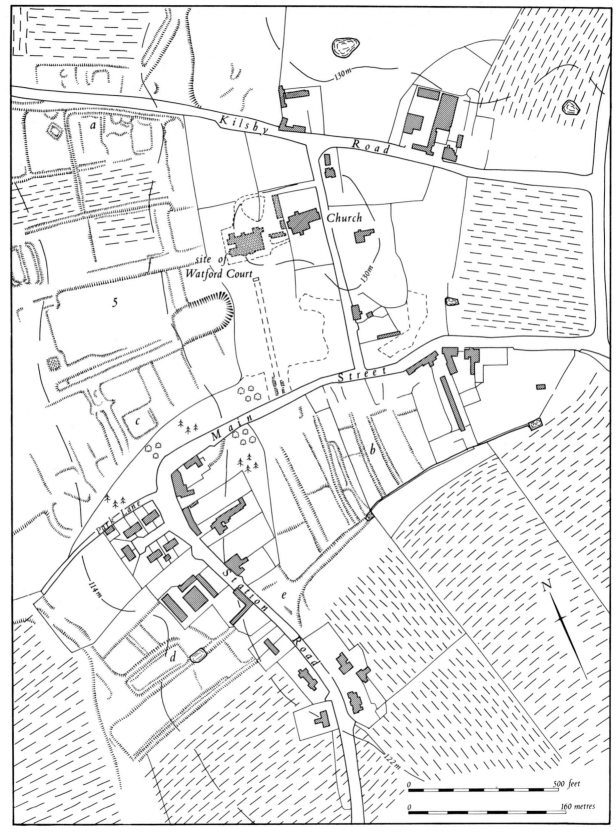

Fig. 142   WATFORD   (4) Settlement remains,   (5) Garden remains at Watford

from at least 1771 to 1840 (RAF VAP 543/RAF/2337, 0377–9; CUAP, AWI68, 75, 76, AWQI8, 19).

^c(5) GARDEN REMAINS (SP 601690; Fig. 142; Plate 20), formerly belonging to the now demolished Watford Court, lie to the W. of the site of the house, on land sloping W. between 110 m. and 125 m. above OD. They cut into and partly destroy sections of the settlement remains (4).

Little is known of the history of the site, but the building that was demolished appears to have incorporated a considerable part of a house built in 1568 by Richard Burnaby; it was certainly added to in the 17th century and greatly restored and enlarged on more than one occasion in the 19th century. It was pulled down in about 1970. The earthworks lie beyond the 19th-century shrubberies round the house and outside a ha-ha marking the edge of the 19th-century formal garden. They consist of a broad, straight hollow-way or drive ('f' on plan), up to 2 m. deep, once lined with trees, the stumps of which still edge it. This hollow-way fades out as it reaches the level ground, but the avenue of trees clearly continued W. for some distance. At the E. end of the hollow-way and on either side of it, close to the house, are levelled platforms, bounded by scarps with double scarps on their steep W. sides. These may be garden terraces. To the S. of the southern platform there is a very large depression up to 3 m. deep, of unknown purpose. Near the W. end of the drive or hollow-way, and just to the N. of it, are the remains of two parallel embanked ponds, and further S. is a low square mound, only 0.25 m. high, which has slight ridges across it. The ground around it is much disturbed by later activities.

The earliest information concerning these remains is of the early 18th century; a very small-scale map in J. Morton's *Nat. Hist. of Northants.* (1712) shows a park occupying the area W. of Watford Court between Park Lane and the Kilsby road. No internal details are depicted, but it is possible that many of the earthworks are of this general period. The first detailed plan of the park is of 1740 (NRO). The plan is rather schematic, but shows a rigid formal layout which would seem to be of a period earlier than the 1740s. It may in fact depict in some detail the layout of the early 18th-century park which had survived until then. The plan shows two raised platforms W. of the house but their purpose is not indicated. The drive or hollow-way is also shown as are a number of rigidly geometric plantations. The small double pond at the W. end of the drive is marked and on the site of the small mound is another pond with two rectangular islands within it. The existing mound may therefore be one of these islands. Another pond, with a long mound within it, which still exists further N.W. (at SP599692) is also shown on the 1740 plan, though there were then two islands.

For how long the park existed in this form is not clear, but by the early 19th century (OS 1st ed. 1 in. map (1834)) the park still retained its 1740 boundaries and its central avenue along the drive, though a new avenue had been made across the fields to the N. of the hall. Later in the 19th century, after 1840 (NRO, Tithe Map), a large extension was made to the park on either side of the new avenue N. of the Kilsby road. Nearer the hall a row of cottages along the N. side of Main Street were removed and replaced by a shrubbery (RAF VAP 543/RAF/2337, 0377–9; CUAP, AWI68, AWQI8, 19).

(6) CULTIVATION REMAINS (Plate 21). Part of the common fields of Watford were enclosed by an Act of Parliament of 1771 (NRO, Enclosure Map), but this involved less than half the parish, the area mainly S. of the village. The greater part of the parish was already in old enclosures at this time, some of which are shown on a map of 1780 (NRO). This enclosure was apparently carried out in 1644 by Sir George Clerke (J. Bridges, *Hist. of Northants.*, I (1791), 585). The part of the parish W. of the Roman road (A5) was also enclosed by 1764 (Map in NRO). Ridge-and-furrow of the common fields survives on the ground or can be traced on air photographs throughout most of the parish and is arranged in end-on and interlocked furlongs. Much of it is strikingly well preserved, particularly round the village where it exhibits some unusual features. For example, to the N. of the garden remains (5) (SP 601693) the ridges are long and widely spaced with very narrow ridges between them (see Sectional Preface). S. of the village (SP 602683; Plate 21) some furlongs terminate in very large rectangular mounds lying on either side of a hollow-way which runs obliquely through the ridges. In that position these might be explained as unusually large terminations of the ridges but, if they are, then a further double row of mounds, close to the first, could not have been formed at the same time, as the intervening ridges would have been too short. No conclusive explanation of these features can be reached.

The common fields of the deserted village of Silsworth (3) were enclosed at an unknown date before 1594. A field to the E. of the village, known as Silsworth Middle Field, is shown on a map of 1631 (Map in PRO; Plate 13). Although much of the ridge-and-furrow of these fields has been destroyed it can all be traced from air photographs arranged in end-on and interlocked furlongs (RAF VAP CPE/UK/1994, 1357–65, 2356–7, 1473–80; 543/RAF/2337, 3073–7; CUAP AWI73).

63 WEEDON BEC
(OS 1: 10000 ^a SP 66 SW, ^b SP 65 NW)

The parish, covering some 770 hectares, lies in the valley of the R. Nene which flows E. across Lias Clay between 100 m. and 75 m. above OD. To the N. and S. the land rises to a height of between 120 m. and 150 m. above OD on clay and Marlstone though in the N. this is covered by glacial deposits.

There are three separate settlements in the parish, Lower Weedon on the S. side of the Nene, Upper Weedon above it on the hillside to the S.W., and Road Weedon, N. of the Nene, straddling the junction of Watling Street (A5) and the Daventry-Northampton road (A45). Road Weedon is likely to be a secondary settlement which grew up in response to traffic along the main roads. The only monument of special note is the early 19th-century redoubt or gun battery (2) associated with the famous barracks of 1803.

PREHISTORIC AND ROMAN

There are records of worked flints in the parish but the exact location is not clear (OS Record Cards). Recent air photographs (in NMR) seem to show a ditched trackway (SP 60745774–60945725; *BNFAS*, 5 (1971), 45; 6, (1971), 18). However on vertical air photographs taken in 1947 (RAF VAP CPE/UK/1994, 4166–7) a headland between two end-on furlongs of ridge-and-furrow can still be seen intact (see Lamport (19)). Other cropmarks are said to have been seen further to the E. (at SP 62205778; OS Record Cards) but no details are known.

For Roman Road 1f, Watling Street, see Appendix.

MEDIEVAL AND LATER

b(1) HOLLOW-WAY (SP 620588), lies on the S. side of Upper Weedon, on a N.-facing slope, on Marlstone Rock, at 100 m. above OD. A former close behind the existing houses, bounded on the S. by a curving bank and ditch, is crossed diagonally by a broad hollow-way running S.W. from the present road to Farthingstone (air photographs in NMR).

b(2) REDOUBT (SP 62155977; Fig. 143), probably an early 19th-century military work, lies N.W. of Weedon Barracks on the N. side of the R. Nene on land sloping S., at about 100 m. above OD.

Although it has been described as a Norman castle (*Ass. Arch. Soc. Reps.*, 38 (1927), 361), there is no doubt that it is post-medieval in origin and associated with the military use of the area following the construction of Weedon Barracks in 1803. Clearly it lies on top of ridge-and-furrow, though the latter has now been ploughed out (RAF VAP CPE/UK/1994, 1268–9). On the OS 1st ed. 1 in. map of 1834 the site is described as a 'Redoubt' and is shown as a rectangular feature with a projecting S. end. It may have been constructed as part of a defensive system around the

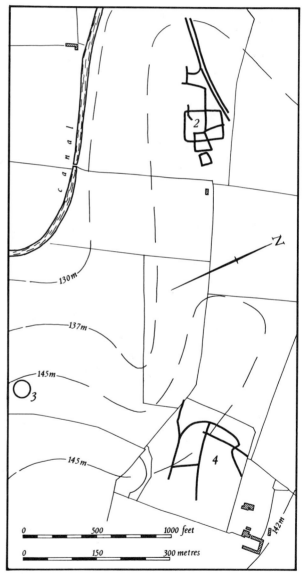

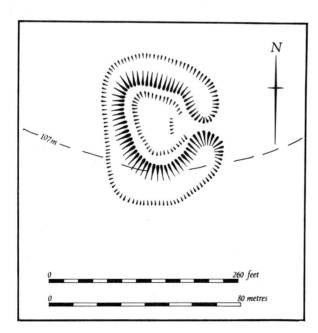

Fig. 143   WEEDON BEC   (2) Redoubt

Fig. 144   WELFORD   (2–4) Cropmarks

barracks but its tactical situation makes this doubtful and a more likely explanation is that it was constructed as part of military training soon after 1803.

The site has been badly damaged by later activity but enough remains to indicate its original form as a redoubt, that is a small detached stronghold without provision for flank defence. It consists of a bank of bastion form some 1.5 m. high with the point of the bastion facing N.W. The N.E. angle still survives though the S. one is now rounded. The entrance is to the E.; below the banks is a surrounding ditch, now only 0.5 m. deep, with a causeway across it on the E. giving access to the interior. The latter is disturbed by trenches, probably of recent date.

(3) CULTIVATION REMAINS. The common fields of Weedon Bec were enclosed by Act of Parliament in 1777. Ridge-and-furrow of these fields can now be traced either on the ground or from air photographs over less than half of the parish, mainly within a roughly rectangular area around the villages of Upper and Lower Weedon. Here the ridges run at right-angles to the R. Nene and two of its N.-flowing tributaries so that the furlongs appear to radiate from the villages. A few interlocked furlongs also survive in the S.W. of the parish near Weedon Lodge (centred SP 607575; RAF VAP CPE/UK/1994, 1268–71, 3155–7).

UNDATED

[b](4) BURIALS (unlocated, but said to be close to the Roman road). During the 19th century some skeletons were discovered which were thought to be 17th-century plague burials. However they may have been Roman or later (Baker, *Hist. of Northants.*, I (1822–30), 454).

64   WELFORD

(OS 1:10000 [a] SP 68 SW, [b] SP 68 SE, [c] SP 67 NW, [d] SP 67 NE)

The parish, covering 1260 hectares, lies on the S. side of the R. Avon which forms the N.E. and N.W. boundaries. Most of it is on gently undulating Upper and Middle Lias Clay between 120 m. and 150 m. above OD though much of the area has been covered by superficial deposits of Boulder Clay. In the W. and N. the land is higher and more broken and several small streams flow N. and W. to the R. Avon in steep-sided valleys. The major monument is the settlement remains (13) which suggest that the present village of Welford may have developed from an early planned layout.

PREHISTORIC AND ROMAN

A few worked flints have been found in the E. of the parish (SP 65407985; *Northants. Archaeol.*, 10 (1975), 152).

[a](1) ENCLOSURE (SP 624823), in the N. of the parish, between the R. Avon and the Grand Union Canal, on

alluvium at 120 m. above OD. Air photographs (in NMR) show a small, almost square enclosure with rounded corners; a ditch runs W. from the S.W. corner (*Northants. Archaeol.*, 8 (1973), 26).

[a](2) DITCHED TRACKWAY AND ENCLOSURES (centred SP 625817; Fig. 144), in the N. of the parish, on clays and silts at 140 m. above OD. Air photographs (in NMR) show very faint cropmarks of a ditched trackway (SP 62308175–62508175). On its S. side at least three sub-rectangular enclosures, and ditches which may be parts of other interlocking enclosures can be detected (*Arch. J.*, 121 (1964), 22; *Northants. Archaeol.*, 8 (1973), 26). Some of the photographs also show uneven patches in the crops in the field immediately to the S.E. (SP 626815). A scatter of Roman pottery has been found close by (SP 624818; *Northants. Archaeol.*, 12 (1977), 223).

[a](3) RING DITCH (SP 628811; Fig. 144), 600 m. S.E. of (2) on clays and silts at 145 m. above OD. Air photographs (in NMR) show cropmarks of a possible ring ditch (*Northants. Archaeol.*, 8 (1973), 26).

[a](4) LINEAR DITCHES (SP 631814; Fig. 144), W. of Welford Lodge and 350 m. N.E. of (3) on Boulder Clay at 145 m. above OD. Air photographs (in NMR) show a system of interconnecting linear ditches, which perhaps form irregular enclosures.

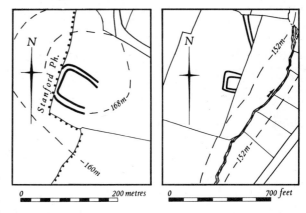

Fig. 145   WELFORD   (5, 6) Cropmarks

[a](5) DOUBLE-DITCHED ENCLOSURE (SP 620802; Fig. 145), against the W. boundary of the parish, on a steep-sided spur known as Downtown Hill, on clays and silts at 168 m. above OD. Air photographs (in NMR) show three sides of a sub-rectangular double-ditched enclosure covering about 0.75 hectare. The enclosure is overlaid by ploughed-out ridge-and-furrow which obscures any trace of a S.E. side.

[c](6) ENCLOSURE (?) (SP 635799; Fig. 145), S.W. of the village, on clays and silts at 152 m. above OD, on the crest of a small hill. Air photographs (in NMR) show a possible double-ditched enclosure. It is not clear, however, and

may be a random effect, incorporating the cropmarks of ridge-and-furrow (for Saxon pottery from this site, see (10)).

^a(7) IRON AGE AND ROMAN SETTLEMENT (?) (SP 637810), N.W. of the village, on the S. side of the R. Avon, on Boulder Clay at 140 m. above OD. Iron Age and Roman pottery have been found here (*Northants. Archaeol.*, 12 (1977), 223; for Saxon material from this site, see (11)).

^c(8) ROMAN SETTLEMENT (?) (SP 643786), in the S. of the parish, on Boulder Clay, at 156 m. above OD. Roman pottery has been noted (*Northants. Archaeol.*, 12 (1977), 223).

^a(9) ROMAN SETTLEMENT (?) (SP 64268061 and 64368072), within the N. part of the village on clay at about 135 m. above OD. A few sherds of Roman pottery were found on building sites in 1973 and 1974 (*Northants. Archaeol.*, 9 (1974), 101; 10 (1975), 163).

MEDIEVAL AND LATER

A Saxon brooch described as 'circular ... enriched with delicate filagree and pearls' is said to have been found at Welford in about 1853. This may be a surviving brooch said to be from Husbands Bosworth (*Arch. J.*, 10 (1853), 362; Meaney, *Gazetteer*, 196).

^c(10) SAXON SETTLEMENT (?) (SP 635799), near the possible enclosure (6). Early Saxon sherds have been noted (*Northants. Archaeol.*, 12 (1977), 223).

^a(11) SAXON SETTLEMENT (?) (SP 637810), on the same site as the Iron Age and Roman settlement (7). Early Saxon pottery has been found (*Northants. Archaeol.*, 12 (1977), 233).

^a(12) SAXON SETTLEMENT (?) (SP 629802), W. of the village, on clay at 157 m. above OD. A scatter of early Saxon pottery has been discovered (*Northants. Archaeol.*, 12 (1977), 223).

^a(13) SETTLEMENT REMAINS (centred SP 639804; Figs. 12 and 146), lie N.W. of the existing village, mainly on Boulder Clay between 135 m. and 150 m. above OD. The earthworks, although not of outstanding importance in themselves, do add to the understanding of the development of the village. The main feature is a broad hollow-way ('a'–'b' on plan) up to 1.5 m. deep which runs N.E.–S.W., roughly parallel to the existing West Street and High Street. Its N.E. end has been destroyed by a modern housing estate. On both sides of the hollow-way are rectangular closes or paddocks, bounded by ditches or scarps and banks which may be former house-sites though some have been overploughed by ridge-and-furrow. Ridge-and-furrow also exists within long closes to the N.W. which extend into the valley bottom.

Without taking into consideration the earthworks it would be possible to interpret the village plan as a single street along the Northampton–Leicester road with a back lane to the N.W. However, the existence of the hollow-way with possible house-sites along it indicates that the village was perhaps once made up of three parallel streets, and that the central one, West Street, with both the church and the manor house (14) situated on it, was originally the main one. Such a layout could have been the result of planning rather than gradual growth. All the earthworks were already abandoned by 1838 (NRO, Map of Welford; see also Tithe Map of 1848).

At the N. end of the village, on the S.E. side of High Street (not shown on plan; SP 644805), is another group of abandoned closes and a small embanked pond. These appear to be the remains of gardens behind houses which once stood along the High Street (CUAP, XT72–4 and air photographs in NMR).

^a(14) MANOR HOUSE SITE (SP 639802; Fig. 146), lies W. of the church, on the W. side of West Street, on Boulder Clay at 150 m. above OD. Little is known of its history, but village tradition asserts that an old hall stood on the site. More convincing is the fact that on the Tithe Map of 1848 (NRO) the field was called Hall Field. The area has recently been completely built over and the earthworks on Fig. 146 are those recorded by the OS before destruction, but the site had already been levelled for a cricket ground before the modern housing was constructed and the earthworks illustrated must have been only a fragment of what once existed. All that can be said is that two large mounds lying against the road appear, from air photographs, to have been the remains of a flat terrace-walk of the type usually interpreted as characteristic of 17th or early 18th-century gardens. On a map of 1838 and on the Tithe Map of 1848 (both in NRO) a building is marked in the N.E. corner of the area and two others are shown along the W. boundary.

Beyond this boundary, in a field called Lady Close in 1848, some irregular closes or paddocks survive, the lower parts of which have ridge-and-furrow either within them or riding over them. These earthworks are likely to be part of the manorial complex (CUAP, XT73–4 and air photographs in NMR).

^a(15) FISHPOND (SP 640807; Fig. 146), lies N.W. of the N. end of the village, in the bottom of a steep-sided N.E.-draining valley, on Lias Clay at 130 m. above OD. It consists of a roughly rectangular area, embanked on the N.W. and S.E. sides and with a massive dam up to 3 m. high on the N.E. In the centre is a small rectangular island 1.5 m. high. The modern stream flows to the N.W. of the pond, but originally the water left the stream some 200 m. to the S.W. and flowed in a narrow channel to a point just S.W. of the pond. There the channel forked, one branch entering the pond and so filling it, the other passing along the S.E. side as an overflow channel, leading back to the stream. Nothing is known of the pond's history (*Northants. P. and P.*, 4 (1971), 309; CUAP, XT74 and air photographs in NMR).

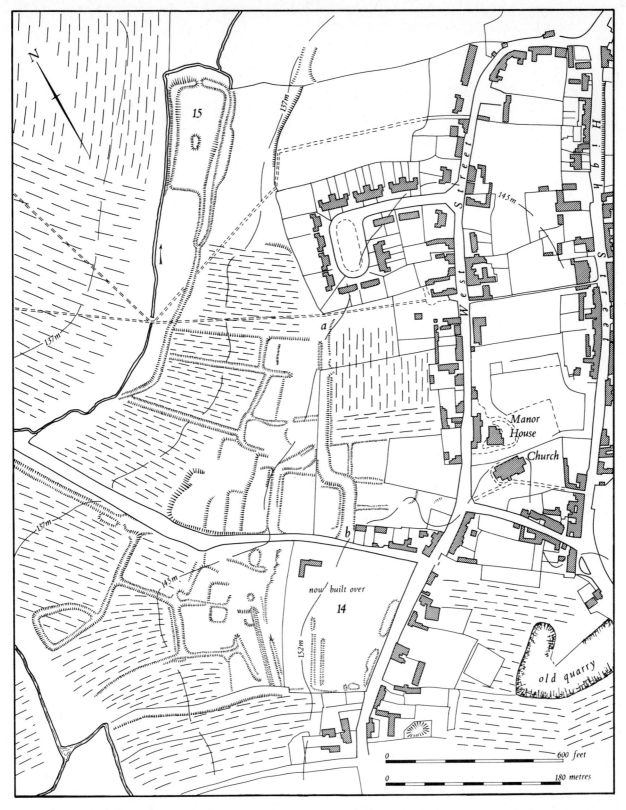

Fig. 146   WELFORD   (13) Settlement remains,   (14) Site of manor house,   (15) Fishponds

^a(16) MOUND (SP 61938080), in the W. of the parish, on Middle Lias Clay at 130 m. above OD. It is roughly circular, 10 m. in diam. and 0.75 m. high, with no visible ditch and is probably relatively modern (*Northants. Archaeol.*, 10 (1975), 175).

(17) CULTIVATION REMAINS. An Act of Parliament for the enclosure of the common fields of the parish was passed in 1777, but only about half the area was involved. Even in the early 18th century Bridges (*Hist. of Northants.*, I (1791), 591) recorded that only 53 'yardlands' were in tillage, the rest was enclosed. However, the parish was not enclosed in 1602 (*Northants. P. and P.*, i (1949), 29). Ridge-and-furrow exists on the ground or can be traced on air photographs over much of the parish. On the flatter ground in the S. it is arranged in generally interlocked furlongs often of markedly reversed-S form. On the broken land in the N.W., however, a much more complex pattern occurs as the furlongs are adapted to the steep valley sides and indented scarps; radiating arrangements and long runs of end-on furlongs are common. Considerable areas of ridge-and-furrow are well preserved around the village itself, not only within the settlement remains (13) but also in old paddocks E. of the village (RAF VAP 106G/UK/636, 3169–78 and air photographs in NMR).

65 WELTON

(OS 1 : 10000 ^a SP 56 NE, ^b SP 66 NW)

The parish is almost rectangular and lies to the W. of Watling Street (A5) which forms its E. boundary. Its area is about 790 hectares. From the higher ground in the W., which reaches a maximum of 170 m. above OD and where areas of Marlstone Rock are exposed, the land falls steeply across clays, silts and glacial deposits to the alluvium of the two valleys which are now occupied by the Grand Union Canal on the E. and S. edges of the parish at about 107 m. above OD. The village lies on the steep, S.E.-facing side of a spur.

ROMAN

A silver-washed copper coin was discovered in the parish before 1712 (J. Morton, *Nat. Hist. of Northants.* (1712), 532). A 3rd-century Roman silver coin of Barbia Orbiana was found in the churchyard in the early 19th century (G. Baker, *Hist. of Northants.*, I (1822–30), 466; OS Record Cards). Other Roman coins, including one of Constantine, were found with the Anglo-Saxon burials (1) (NM; OS Record Cards). A skull and bones found at the side of the Roman road (at SP 59626767) may also be of the Roman period, but no details are known (OS Record Cards).

For Roman Road If, Watling Street, see Appendix.

MEDIEVAL AND LATER

^a(1) SAXON BURIALS (?) (about SP 596678). According to a note by Sir Henry Dryden in the Dryden Collection (Central Library, Northampton), six skeletons were discovered in July 1845, on the side of or within the Roman road agger while it was being dug away for gravel. The skeletons were arranged 'some length-ways and once across the road, rather on one side of the road about 1 foot 6 inches deep'. One of the bodies had with it 'an iron thing about 1 foot 4 inches long' probably a spearhead. No other finds were made.

^a(2) SAXON CEMETERY (area SP 572659), discovered in 1778 in a field known as Stone Pit Close; this is thought to be the area later planted and re-named Long-ground Spinney, some 500 m. W. of the village on clay at 158 m. above OD. Two small skeletons were found in a rough cist, accompanied by two bronze small-long brooches, 23 beads of jet, amber, and green and patterned glass at the wrists and throat, and fragments of a spear. Between the skeletons was a small biconical vessel with an everted rim, decorated with line and dot ornament. Four or five perforated Roman coins of Constantine and Flavia were also discovered. A plain urn, thought to be from Welton, was in Netherhall, Cumberland, in 1794. In 1822 Baker found a necklace of 45 glass and amber beads. It is thought that other burials may have been destroyed without record. Small fragments of Roman pottery were found in the area in 1969 (G. Baker, *Hist. of Northants.*, I (1822–30), 466; VCH *Northants.*, I (1902), 235–6; *Archaeologia*, 48 (1885), 337; Meaney, *Gazetteer*, (1964), 196; J.N.L. Myres, *Anglo-Saxon Pottery and the Settlement of England* (1969), Fig. 36; No. 812; BNFAS, 7 (1972), 67; OS Record Cards; NM).

^a(3) SETTLEMENT REMAINS (SP 58156625, 581658, 58456565), formerly part of the village of Welton, lie in three places in and around the village. On air photographs taken in 1947 (RAF VAP CPE/UK/1994, 2354, 4358) it is possible to trace the banks of closes which presumably once had houses within them. These were in two main places, at the top of the village in the area of the present playing fields, and down the hill to the S. on the corner of Church Road. All have since been destroyed by redevelopment. In the S.E. corner of the village, at the bottom of Kiln Lane, some flat rectangular platforms still survive. These may be house-sites but are perhaps the remains of kilns.

^a(4) EARTHWORKS (SP 595656), in the S.E. of the parish, on clay at 105 m. above OD. Air photographs taken in 1947 (RAF VAP CPE/UK/1994, 4359–60) show a sinuous channel running roughly N.W.–S.E. and slightly embanked, particularly on the N. side. Its date and purpose are unknown and it has now been destroyed by ploughing. It has been suggested that the channel was an incomplete feature connected with the Grand Union Canal (OS Record Cards), but as the earthwork is considerably lower

than the canal at this point this seems unlikely. On the 1st ed. OS 1 in. map of 1834 the channel is shown as a watercourse diverting some of the flow from a tributary stream to a lower point on the main stream.

(5) CULTIVATION REMAINS. The common fields of the parish were enclosed by Act of Parliament in 1755. Most of the ridge-and-furrow in the parish remains on the ground or can be traced on air photographs and the pattern is well preserved. As a result of the rolling landscape of the parish, with many steep-sided valleys, most of the furlongs are at right-angles to each other or set obliquely, apparently to ensure that ridges run down the slopes. An example of a headland between two end-on furlongs which has been subsequently ploughed over, giving a characteristic knuckled effect, is visible W. of Welton Grange (SP 593666; RAF VAP CPE/UK/1994, 2352–7, 4269–76, 4356–61; 2F22 543/RAF/2337, 0378–81).

66   WHILTON

(OS 1:10000 [a] SP 66 NW, [b] SP 66 SW)

The parish is roughly triangular and occupies little more than 400 hectares. Its W. boundary follows the A5 which at this point deviates from the usual straight alignment of Watling Street. Much of the N. boundary follows a S.W.-flowing tributary of the R. Nene, which then turns S. through the W. part of the parish. The higher ground in the W. and S., nowhere more than 135 m. above OD, is capped by glacial sands and gravels. Elsewhere streams have cut down through the Middle and Upper Lias Clay and Marlstone Rock and there are wide bands of alluvium in the valley bottom. In the W. of the parish lay part of the Roman town of Bannaventa (see Norton (4)).

ROMAN

[b](1) ROMAN KILN (SP 61976439), said to have been discovered and destroyed during the construction of the M1, in the S.W. of the parish, on alluvium at 90 m. above OD. No details are known (NM Records; OS Record Cards).

For Roman Roads 17 and If, Watling Street, see Appendix.

MEDIEVAL AND LATER

[b](2) SETTLEMENT REMAINS (?) (SP 638647), lie at the E. end of the main street of the village on land sloping E. to a small stream, on Upper Lias Clay at 110 m. above OD. There is an area of very disturbed ground here, including some low banks and scarps, which may be the sites of former buildings.

(3) CULTIVATION REMAINS. The common fields of Whilton were enclosed by an Act of Parliament in 1778.

Ridge-and-furrow of these fields can be traced on the ground or on air photographs in the E. of the parish around the village and in a strip in the central part of the parish, arranged in interlocked and end-on furlongs. In the W. it has been almost entirely destroyed, except for some fragments beside the railway, canal and motorway (SP 615647; RAF VAP CPE/UK/1994, 2369–70, 2260–5, 4262–70, 4361–5).

67   WINWICK

(OS 1:10000 [a] SP 67 SW, [b] SP 67 NW)

The parish covers about 840 hectares and lies across the valley of a small N.W.-flowing stream which also forms part of the S. boundary. From this central valley, at about 130 m. above OD, the land rises steeply over Lias clays, to a maximum of 168 m. in the S.W. and 190 m. in the N.E., across a rolling landscape drained by several small streams. Much of the area is covered by expanses of Boulder Clay as well as glacial sands and gravels. The major monument is the now almost totally deserted village of Winwick (1), the remains of which extend along the central valley.

MEDIEVAL AND LATER

[a](1) SETTLEMENT REMAINS (centred SP 627737; Figs. 147 and 148; Plate 14), formerly part of the village of Winwick, extend for almost 1 km. along the valley of the small N.W.-flowing stream beside which the tiny modern village still stands. The earthworks are on Upper and Middle Lias Clay and alluvium, between 125 m. and 145 m. above OD. The village is listed in Domesday Book with a recorded population of 31 (VCH Northants., I (1902), 316, 320, 339, 350, 380). No further details of population are known until the 17th century when 25 people paid the Hearth Tax of 1673 (PRO, E179/254/14), and it is impossible to say whether the extensive remains represent the maximum expansion of the village at any one time or are the result of changes in location or layout over a long period. The latter seems more likely for some of the earthworks in the N.W. have been overploughed with ridge-and-furrow but others, in the S.E., survive as sharply defined features. The village therefore appears to have moved gradually upstream. All these changes had taken place before 1839; the Tithe Map of that date (NRO; Fig. 148) shows the village almost as it is today.

At the N.W. end of the site are the remains of a small moated enclosure ('a' on plan) consisting of an island about 40 m. across surrounded by a shallow ditch now less than 1 m. deep. The whole has been overploughed with ridge-and-furrow. S.E. of the moat, still on the S.W. of the stream, is a group of at least three long closes ('b' on plan) with house-sites at their N.E. ends. The closes are subdivided by low scarps and are bounded by scarps and ditches. The whole area, excluding the house-sites, is

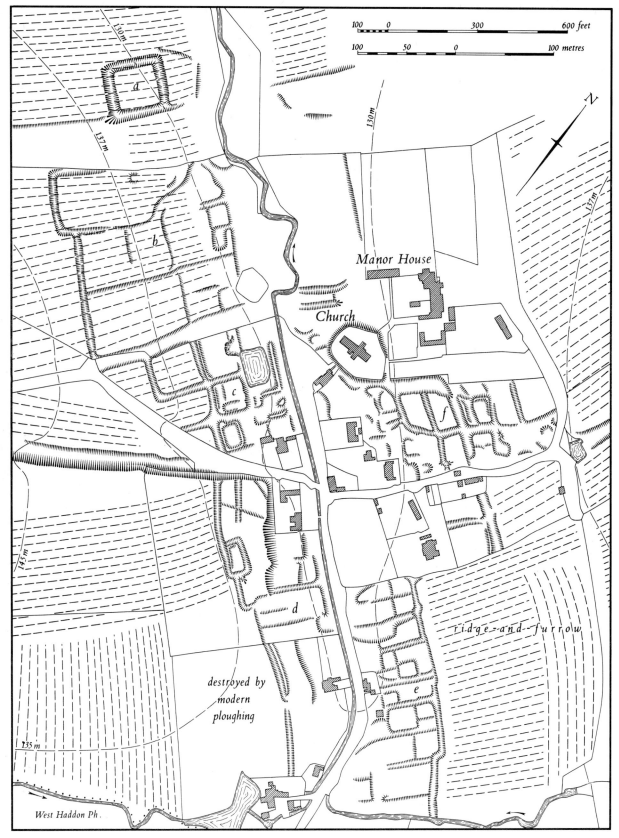

Fig. 147   WINWICK   (1) Settlement remains

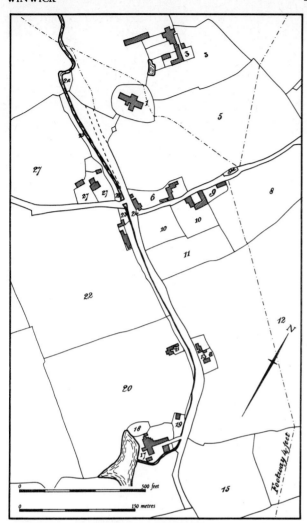

Fig. 148   WINWICK
(1) Plan of village in 1839 (from Tithe Map in NRO)

enclosures ('f' on plan). These are bounded on the S.E. by a lane, which continued as a hollow-way across the field to the E., and on the N.W. by a wide hollow-way which runs along the S. side of the large mound on which the church of St. Michael is situated. Two parallel ditches N.W. of the church may define the original driveway to the hall (RAF VAP 541/15, 4383–5; CUAP, AGV14–16, AKP65, AWQ12, 13, XL62, 63).

(2) CULTIVATION REMAINS. The common fields of the parish were finally enclosed following an Act of Parliament of 1794 but at least part of it was enclosed by 1652. Much of the ridge-and-furrow of these fields has been destroyed particularly in the W. of the parish where only a few furlongs remain, but around and to the N. of the village the layout is recoverable either on the ground or from air photographs. It is arranged in end-on and interlocked furlongs in response to the direction of slope. Behind the empty closes of the deserted village the ridges all run up the slope to the higher ground. It is noteworthy that large parts of the village have been overploughed by later ridge-and-furrow (RAF VAP CPE/UK/1994, 2468–71; 541/15, 4380–8).

68 WOODFORD-CUM-MEMBRIS

(OS 1:10000 [a] SP 55 SW, [b] SP 55 SE)

The parish covers about 1100 hectares and is bisected by the R. Cherwell, here flowing in a narrow steep-sided valley cut into the underlying Middle Lias Clays between 120 m. and 135 m. above OD. On either side of the river the land rises across undulating clayland to a number of rounded hills, some of which are capped by glacial deposits, or are formed by outcrops of Northampton Sand. The name of the parish comes from the uniting of three separate

covered by later ridge-and-furrow. A wide hollow-way, said locally once to have formed the main approach to the manor house on the other side of the valley, separates these closes from a group of smaller and more sharply defined enclosures ('c' on plan), some of which are embanked as well as ditched. The modern road cuts across the S. corner of this area and probably replaced an earlier route which survives as a hollow-way continuing W. on the general line of the lane as the latter leaves the village. To the S.W. of the lane ('d' on plan) are further closes. These have not been ploughed in ridge-and-furrow but the S. part has now been almost completely destroyed by modern ploughing. On the E. side of the stream, and of the axial road which follows it, is a row of at least seven closes containing house-sites ('e' on plan). These are very well preserved and fragments of post-medieval pottery have been found on them. On the higher ground behind the existing cottages is a further group of ditched and scarped

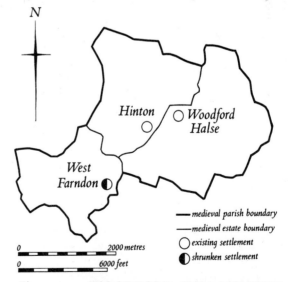

Fig. 149   WOODFORD-CUM-MEMBRIS
Medieval settlements and estates

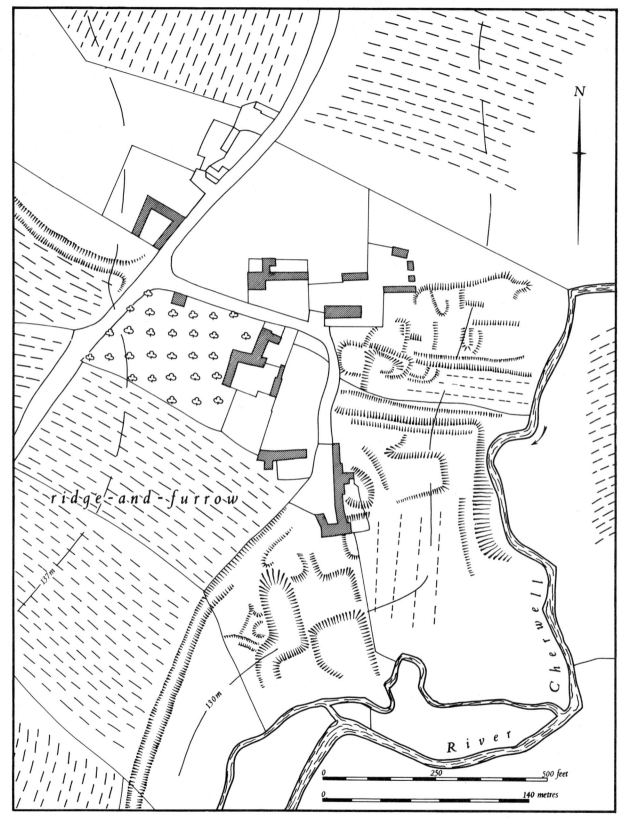

N

ridge-and-furrow

137m

130m

River Cherwell

| 0 | | 250 | | 500 feet |

| 0 | | | 140 metres |

Fig. 150   WOODFORD-CUM-MEMBRIS   (2) Settlement remains at West Farndon

medieval settlements each with its own land unit, the boundaries of which are partly shown on the Tithe Map of 1840 (NRO). Woodford itself lies E. of the Cherwell on a high N.-facing spur, and Hinton stands immediately S.W. of it on the opposite side of the river on lower ground. Further S.W., also W. of the Cherwell, is West Farndon (2). Although the latter is now only a hamlet of some eight dwellings, the earthwork remains around it suggest that it was once much larger. To the S. of Woodford village is a flight of strip lynchets (3), a feature of medieval cultivation rare in Northamptonshire.

PREHISTORIC AND ROMAN

Worked flints, including scrapers, and pot-boilers have been found in the S.W. of the parish (SP 51555142; OS Record Cards).

ᵃ(1) ROMAN SETTLEMENT (?) (SP 524514), W. of West Farndon, on Northampton Sand at 160 m. above OD. Sherds of 2nd and 3rd-century pottery have been found over a small area (*BNFAS*, 3 (1969), 2).

MEDIEVAL AND LATER

A 14th or 15th-century ampulla, inscribed 'Our Lady of Walsingham' was found in the W. of the parish (SP 531528; OS Record Cards; Warwick Museum).

ᵃ(2) SETTLEMENT REMAINS (SP 530513; Figs. 149 and 150), formerly part of West Farndon, lie immediately E.S.E., S. and W. of the existing hamlet, on land sloping E. to the R. Cherwell, on clays and silts at 127 m. above OD.

The settlement is first recorded in Domesday Book when it was divided between two small manors, each with a recorded population of two (VCH *Northants.*, I (1902), 324, 330). Later population figures are combined with the other two villages in the parish and are therefore of little value. All the earthworks are the remains of settlement already abandoned by 1840 (NRO, Tithe Map). The small single street of the hamlet can be seen once to have been part of a through road running N.W.–S.E. To the N.W. of the hamlet this road survives as a shallow hollow-way only 0.5 m. deep curving up the hillside towards Byfield (SP 527514). To the E. of the hamlet it can be traced down to the R. Cherwell as a similar hollow-way, but no trace remains to the E. of the river. On either side of the hollow-way above the river are slight scarps and banks indicating that at least three houses and closes lay on its N. side and perhaps three buildings on its S. Immediately to the S. a hollow-way or ditch up to 2 m. deep runs down the hillside but it is not clear whether this is an original feature. To the S. of this ditch, in a field ploughed and returned to grass, are the slight remains of a sub-rectangular enclosure and some irregular depressions.

Further W. and S. of the hamlet are several scarps, the lowest of which is cut back into the valley side, all forming a rectangular plan. To the W. is a deep marshy depression,

also cut back into the hillside. In 1840 this field was known as Pool Close. Above it to the N. are the mutilated remains of another hollow-way running S.W. This can be traced on air photographs and partly on the ground for some 320 m. to the S. where it meets the R. Cherwell (RAF VAP CPE/UK/1994, 4101–2).

(3) CULTIVATION REMAINS (Fig. 151). The common fields of Woodford Halse were enclosed by Act of Parliament of 1758. Ridge-and-furrow of these fields remains on the ground or can be traced on air photographs over most of that part of the parish which must have belonged to Woodford. Around Woodford Hill (SP 554523) there appears to be no ridge-and-furrow, but this may be, in part, due to modern destruction. Traceable ridge-and-furrow is mainly arranged in interlocked and end-on rectangular furlongs except along the N.E. parish boundary where some furlongs are triangular to enable the ridges to run across the contours. Ridge-and-furrow survives in especially fine condition S. of the village (around SP 540518 and 542520). To the N.E. of the village (at SP 548531) the modern allotments have been laid out on the pre-existing ridge-and-furrow and, as a result, have uneven widths and a reversed-S curve.

Immediately S. of the village, on a steep N.W.-facing

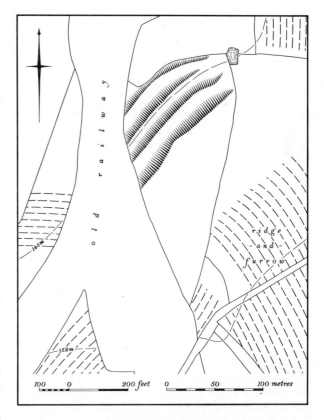

Fig. 151   WOODFORD-CUM-MEMBRIS
(3) Strip lynchets

hillside of Upper Lias Clay, is a flight of strip lynchets (Fig. 151), a rare survival in Northamptonshire, which consists of three contour strip lynchets, curving round the slope, with risers up to 2.5 m. high and treads up to 10 m. wide. At their E. ends they run up on to the adjacent hillside, but to the W. they are truncated by the railway cutting made in 1896–7. On the hillside above is normal ridge-and-furrow.

The common fields of Hinton were enclosed by Act of Parliament of 1753. The ridge-and-furrow of these fields can be traced all over the land of Hinton, where it is arranged almost entirely in rectangular interlocked furlongs, mainly with reversed-S curves. It is particularly well preserved in the N.W. of the parish (around SP530535).

The common fields of West Farndon (2) were enclosed in 1760, also by Act of Parliament. Ridge-and-furrow of these fields exists or can be traced on air photographs over much of the land of the hamlet. Owing to the more broken landscape in this part of the parish the blocks are arranged in interlocked furlongs often of small size and irregular shape, in order to enable the ridge-and-furrow to be laid out approximately across the contours (RAF VAP CPE/UK/1994, 2152–7, 4097–104, 4154–61).

69 YELVERTOFT

(OS 1:10000 [a] SP 57 NE, [b] SP 57 SE, [c] SP 67 NW, [d] SP 67 SW)

The parish, covering just over 900 hectares, occupies a narrow strip of land which widens at the E. end. Its W. boundary is formed by Watling Street. It lies on undulating land between 95 m. and 145 m. above OD and except in the extreme W. of the parish where Lower Lias Clay is exposed most of the area is covered by Boulder Clay. The western projection of the parish may relate to an undocumented settlement of Shenley (3) and the settlement remains (4) N. of Yelvertoft itself, though not of great significance as earthworks, may indicate an earlier location of the village.

ROMAN

[b](1) ROMAN SETTLEMENT (?) (SP 595745), in the S. of the parish, on Boulder Clay at 125 m. above OD. A few sherds of Roman pottery have been found (CBA Group 9, *Newsletter*, 7 (1977), 27).

[a](2) ROMAN SETTLEMENT (SP 598762), N. of the village, on alluvium at 103 m. above OD. A large quantity of Roman pottery, mainly grey ware, was found here in 1976 (NM; *Northants. Archaeol.*, 12 (1977), 223).

For Roman Road If, Watling Street, see Appendix.

MEDIEVAL AND LATER

[ab](3) DESERTED SETTLEMENT (?) (unlocated but possibly SP 570749 or 575752; Fig. 152), possibly lay somewhere in the W. part of the parish, on clay. There is no documentary record of any settlement here so no name is known, though it may possibly have been Shenley, the name given to the modern farm in the area, nor is there any cartographic evidence of a settlement here. The suggestion of a lost hamlet is merely based on the shape of the parish of Yelvertoft itself. The long narrow W. projection, lying against Watling Street, is similar in appearance to that part of Norton parish where the deserted village of Muscott is located (Norton (11)), to Brockhall parish and to Whilton parish. This indicates that the W. part of Yelvertoft parish may also once have been a discrete land unit. Moreover the line of villages situated just E. of Watling Street and set back from it, extending from Lilbourne in the N., through Crick, Watford, Whilton, Muscott, Brockhall and Flore, is broken at this point in Yelvertoft parish and this is another indication of a lost settlement.

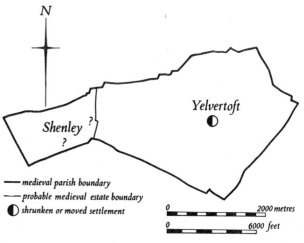

Fig. 152   YELVERTOFT
Medieval settlements and estates

Ridge-and-furrow can be traced over almost all of this part of Yelvertoft, much of it still surviving on the ground. In only two places is there a complete absence of ridge-and-furrow, either of which might be the site of the assumed Shenley. The first is immediately N. and N.W. of Shenley Farm (SP 570749). The farm itself lies over ridge-and-furrow, but to the N. is a long narrow rectangular area orientated W.N.W.–E.S.E., situated between three distinct blocks of ridge-and-furrow and separated from them by a mutilated but continuous scarp. There are no earthworks within this area apart from a rectangular sunken pond with embanked edges but the soil revealed by cattle treading, or in molehills, is notably darker than that in the surrounding area. The second possible site is further N.E., E. of the M1 motorway, on the side of a very small

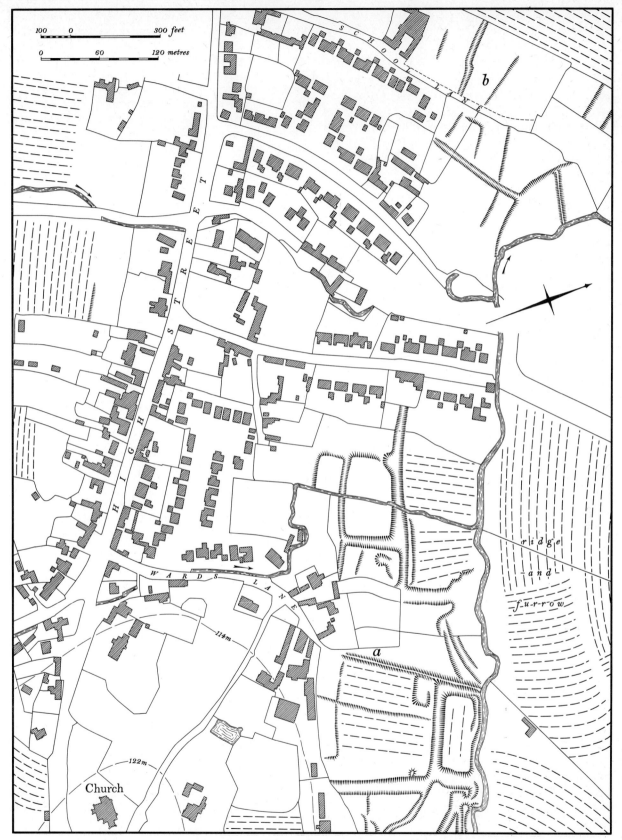

Fig. 153   YELVERTOFT   (4) Settlement remains, moat and site of watermill

E.-flowing stream (SP 575752). Here once more dark soil and absence of ridge-and-furrow might indicate the site of a possible settlement within a long rectangular area 200 m. by 60 m. and orientated E.–W. (RAF VAP CPE/UK/1994, 4478–80).

ac(4) SETTLEMENT REMAINS, MOAT AND MILL SITE (SP 597758 and 602755; Figs. 152 and 153), formerly part of Yelvertoft village, lie in two places on the N. of the village, alongside a N.W.-flowing stream, on Boulder Clay at about 110 m. above OD.

Before modern development Yelvertoft consisted of little more than a single High Street with the church detached from it to the S.E. and with small extensions along lanes to the N.E. at either end of the main street. Some of the houses on the S.W. side of the main street still retain markedly curved gardens or paddocks, the alignment of which is continued further S.W. by ridge-and-furrow. The occurrence of such paddocks elsewhere has been interpreted as evidence that a village has been laid out over earlier fields with the closes determined by the curve of the ridges (RCHM *West Cambridgeshire* (1968), Caxton (24)). Whether this is the explanation at Yelvertoft is not known, but it is possible that the earthworks recorded to the N.W. might in part be the remains of an earlier village close to the stream which gradually moved or was deliberately resited some distance away on top of the earlier common fields.

The remains fall into two distinct parts. The larger and more complex area lies at the end of Wards Lane, N. of the church ('a' on plan), and consists of a number of embanked and ditched closes, some with traces of ridge-and-furrow within them; a hollow-way up to 2 m. deep passes between the closes towards the stream. Close to the stream is a large raised rectangular area, surrounded by a broad ditch 1.5 m. deep. Its interior has been ploughed but it is probably a moated manor house site for the area is known as Hall Close (local inf.). Immediately S.E. of this assumed manor house is an area of disturbed ground beyond which a narrow channel runs S.E. from the S.E. ditch of the moat. The channel is probably a leat for a water mill which perhaps stood in the disturbed area.

Further N.W. ('b' on plan) are some less well-preserved earthworks, now largely destroyed by modern housing. They consist of a number of small embanked or ditched closes, on either side of School Lane and its extension to the N.E. They may represent former house-sites but this is uncertain (CUAP, AMW68, AWQ9; air photographs in NMR; RAF VAP CPE/UK/1994, 4474–6).

(5) CULTIVATION REMAINS. The common fields of the parish were enclosed by an Act of Parliament of 1776; no Enclosure Map survives. Ridge-and-furrow of these fields exists on the ground or can be traced on air photographs over most of the parish so that the pattern is almost totally recoverable. It is arranged in end-on or interlocked furlongs, many of reversed-S form. Among the minor details of the medieval landscape are trackways leading through the fields from Yelvertoft to Elkington (e.g. SP 608757; RAF VAP CPE/UK/1994, 2469–77, 4473–82; 106G/UK/636, 3440–4, 4160–9).

APPENDIX

ROMAN ROADS

For ease of reference the two Roman roads in the area are described here and not under the parishes through which they pass. The roads are identified by the numbers given to them by I. D. Margary in *Roman Roads in Britain*, I (1955).

1f: WATLING STREET, LILBOURNE – STOW-NINE-CHURCHES (Figs. 155–157).

Watling Street, the main Roman road to London from the N.W., entered the area in the N.W. corner of Lilbourne parish, crossing the R. Avon at the junction of the counties of Northamptonshire, Warwickshire and Leicestershire (SP 543778). The road then climbed southwards out of the Avon valley and ran S.E., exactly straight, for 5 km. across mainly flat ground. Its line is now occupied by the main A5 trunk road which has obliterated all trace of its original form. This section constitutes the county boundary between Warwickshire and Northamptonshire.

The next section of the A5, which is now the approach road to the M1 Crick interchange, to the N.E. of the Railway Hotel, Kilsby (SP 569733), swings away from the Roman road alignment. Here for a distance of 350 m. the original agger is well preserved as an embankment, up to 16 m. wide and 1.25 m. high, with a flat top 5 m. across. There are no traces of side ditches. At the N. end this agger has been damaged by a modern open drain cut into its N.E. edge. Codrington (*Roman Roads in Britain* (1931), 64), noted that sections through the agger were visible in the side of the ditch but nothing can now be seen. He described them as showing 'gravel a yard deep, with a layer of large cobble stones at the base in the clay sub-soil'. In the 1930s what appeared to be a drain was seen in one of these sections, passing transversely under the agger. It had 'well built vertical walls roofed with flat stones' (*Ant. J.*, 16 (1936), 462–3). From the description this may have been an original drain or culvert but it could alternatively have been part of a post-medieval field drain. Close to this point, at least two burials, thought to be Saxon, have been discovered, one in the centre of the road and one a little to the E. (Crick (6)). During the excavations of the earlier of these burials in 1947 the construction of the Roman road was observed. The road appeared to have been surfaced with a layer of hard-packed gravel some 0.5 m. deep containing 'larger stones laid roughly in two strips' about 0.57 m. apart, 'where ruts may have been filled in'. Below the gravel was a rough pavement of large stones up to 0.3 m. in diam. on the undisturbed ground surface. No trace of a ditch was noted on the E. side of the road when the excavation was extended in that direction (*Rugby School Magazine* (1948), 34–7). To the S. the agger is truncated by the main Northampton–Rugby road (A428) which crosses it at right-angles (at SP 570729) and modern drainage work beyond has removed any trace. Even the old trackway which once followed the alignment has gone, and only the Crick–Kilsby parish boundary marks its line. In the 1930s (*Ant. J.*, op. cit.) 'a definite low agger' still existed. Further S. the road appears as a slight terrace-way 10 m. wide as it begins to climb the steep N.W. slope of a small spur (SP 573725). From there the alignment is followed by a narrow track which runs on the top of a well-marked ridge up to 1.25 m. high and 12 m.–15 m. wide until it reaches a flat area between two small valleys draining N. and S. Here, at a height of 117 m. above OD, the alignment changes very slightly towards the S., but only by some 2 degrees. This point is visible from the last change of alignment near Gibbet Hill, S. of Lutterworth, Leicestershire. On this new alignment the track continues S.E. until it is cut first by the Northampton–Rugby railway and then partly by the M1 motorway N. of the junction of the latter with the M45. Here, for just over 1 km., the motorway cutting has removed all or most of the remains of the Roman road and later tracks following it. Only the parish boundary marks the original alignment. It is almost certain that it was this part of Watling Street, N. of Watford, which Bridges described in the early 18th century (*Hist. of Northants.*, I (1791), 585). He recorded it as 'rising to near the height of fifteen foot. This bank is above a furlong in length and ten to twelve foot wide. It is composed of gravel, which appears visible on the top'. It is extremely unlikely that the agger was as high as Bridges states, but clearly it was a prominent feature.

Beyond the M45 motorway junction the line of the Roman road is again followed by the present A5 trunk road for some 2.5 km. until the Roman town of Bannaventa (Norton (4)) is reached (SP 610649). Along this section the Roman road ran exactly straight, but although the modern road has minor bends within it the width is such that nowhere is the original agger visible on either side. A little

to the N. of the point where the road from Welton to Watford crosses the A5 (SP 595680), the Roman road was described in the late 19th century as being '47–50 feet wide of which 20 feet are flat. The centre appears to have been raised 4 feet to 5 feet 6 inches' (Notes in the Dryden Collection, Central Library, Northampton). However, as by that time the original road had been much altered, it is doubtful whether this is a true description of the Roman road. Close to this point six burials, said to be Anglo-Saxon, were discovered in 1845 on the side of or within the agger (Welton (1)). Another burial, said to be Roman, was discovered further S. in 1976 (SP 608652; Long Buckby (3)). It lay within one of the side ditches of the Roman road. Along this section, the road crosses two small N.W.-flowing streams, presumably over small bridges or culverts, and finally reaches the summit of a low ridge at 125 m. above OD. At this point the modern road swings sharply E. in a broad curve before rejoining the Roman road alignment further S. The Roman road ran straight on and is visible on air photographs (in NMR; CUAP, BCO32–4) as a broad light-coloured band passing through the defences of Bannaventa (Fig. 115). Within the town the road is again visible on air photographs, sometimes as a light area 9 m. wide and sometimes as two parallel ditches 9 m.–10 m. apart. It passes through the town defences near the S. corner, still showing as a pale strip. Immediately beyond, the junction with the Bannaventa–Duston road (17) is visible (see below). Watling Street continues on the same alignment down the hillside, crosses a small E.-flowing brook and meets the A5 trunk road running in from the N.E. (SP 615638). The line of the road through Bannaventa is also partly visible on the ground, under good conditions, as a broad ridge some 10 m.–15 m. across but only a few centimetres high, apparently made of gravel and small pieces of limestone.

From the point of junction, both the A5 and Watling Street run S.E. on the same alignment across gently undulating land to a point near Dial House (SP 622620). Along this section all trace of the Roman road has been obliterated. Anglo-Saxon burials have been found (Norton (9)), immediately E. of the road. Just S.E. of Dial House the modern road swings slightly E. to run down a spur into a small valley, on an easier gradient than the Roman road. Immediately S.W. of the existing road a line of light-coloured stone-rubble reveals the Roman road. At the bottom of the spur the modern road rejoins the Roman road alignment to cross a stream. The latter is small enough to have been crossed by a culvert rather than a bridge. Beyond, the road continues on the same alignment, on level ground, until it crosses another small stream (SP 627611).

The Roman and modern roads now turn on to the first of a series of short straight alignments in order to avoid the junction of the S.-flowing Brockhall Brook and the E.-flowing R. Nene at Weedon Bec. If the original alignment had been continued, the Roman Road would have crossed the R. Nene and also the meandering Brockhall Brook four times within 1.5 km. and to avoid this the diversion to the W. was laid out. The first turn is through some 30 degrees and the road then runs almost due S. for 500 m. to a point just W. of the largest bend of the brook. It then turns back through some 40 degrees (SP 627606) and runs straight for 1050 m. until it reaches the S. end of the main street of Road Weedon (SP 632597). Here the road turns again, further to the S.E. through an angle of about 15 degrees, and runs straight for 850 m., crossing the Nene (at SP 635595), perhaps originally by a ford. The road then crosses another small N.E.-flowing stream and turns again through about 15 degrees on to an alignment close to its original one (SP 639591). The modern road here is on a large embankment up to 2 m. high but it is not clear whether this is a survival of the original road or entirely the result of early 19th-century improvements. The fact that this final alignment is not exactly the same as the original one N. of Weedon may be the result of slightly inaccurate laying out of the Roman road.

For the first 1150 m. of the new alignment the Roman road is totally obscured by the modern road which runs exactly straight. Then, N.E. of Church Stowe, just within Nether Heyford parish (SP 645580), the modern road leaves the Roman road and swings W. in a broad curve to avoid two steep-sided narrow valleys. Up until at least 1773 (NRO, Map of Stowe-Nine-Churches) the road continued along the Roman road alignment. However, between then and 1839 (NRO, Tithe Map of Stowe-Nine-Churches) it was diverted to its present course, presumably by Thomas Telford who regraded and realigned this, the London-Holyhead road, in the early 19th century. This diversion has left the original Roman road largely intact (Fig. 154) as a very spread rounded agger 12 m. wide but only 0.25 m. high running across the corner of two small arable fields and descending into the valley bottom. Just before its reaches the stream (SP 64685786) it becomes a large flat-topped embankment 15 m. across and 1.25 m. high which may be the abutment of a bridge or a causeway across a culvert. It is impossible to be certain of the character of the crossing because an abandoned ironstone tramway running from Stowe-Nine-Churches to the railway sidings at Nether Heyford, crossing the S.E. end at right-angles, has altered its original form.

On the other side of the valley, the agger is again visible in pasture as a slight bank 10 m. wide and 0.25 m. high, traceable for 200 m. as far as the edge of the next valley. This second valley is spanned by a massive embankment up to 30 m. wide at the base and 3.5 m. high with a rounded top 8 m.–10 m. wide. This feature is now in arable land and is much damaged by ploughing; it was probably once considerably larger. The present stream passes through it in a small culvert, presumably on the site of a Roman one.

On the S.E. side of the valley the embankment fades out at the boundary of the garden of Heyford Grange. Within the garden are slight traces of a possible agger continuing

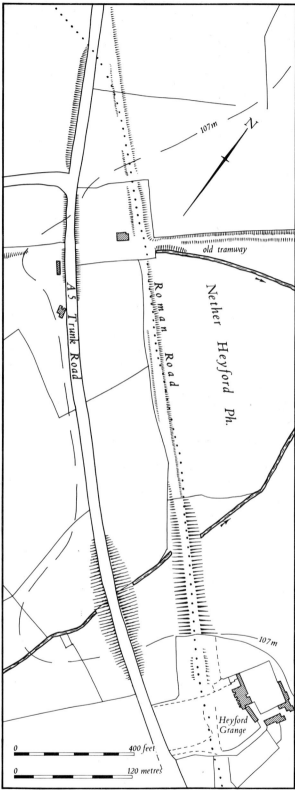

Fig. 154 ROMAN ROAD If, Watling Street, Embankment in Stowe-Nine-Churches

along the same alignment until it rejoins the present road near its junction with the lane to Nether Heyford (SP 65025723). From there both the Roman road and the modern A5 follow the same alignment for 850 m., to a point where (at SP 655564) they both pass beyond the boundaries of the area under review.

17 BANNAVENTA-DUSTON (Figs. 156 and 158)

This short length of Roman road linked the town of Bannaventa (Norton (4)) to the important Roman settlement at Duston just W. of Northampton. It branched off Watling Street just S.E. of the S.E. gate of Bannaventa; air photographs (CUAP, BCO32–4) show a short light-coloured strip bounded by side ditches, running E. from its junction with Watling Street (Fig. 115). Beyond this point no traces are visible for nearly 2 km. Its line is crossed by the present A5, two lanes, the railway, the Grand Union Canal and the M1 motorway, all in the space of 600 m., and these have destroyed all remains. To the E. of the motorway the road must have climbed up a gentle W.-facing slope to the present bend in the Duston–Whilton road near Gipsy Spinney (SP 623640), but there is no trace of it on this slope, either on the ground or on air photographs and the later ridge-and-furrow appears to lie across its assumed line. From Gipsy Spinney the modern road follows the Roman road alignment, here running exactly E.S.E. for 550 m. (to SP 638639). For the next 3.2 km., as far as the outskirts of the hamlet of Nobottle (SP 669632), the modern road follows a rather sinuous line and no trace of the Roman road on a straight alignment can be found. However, close examination reveals that the road was made up of a series of short alignments to enable it to remain on the narrow N.W.–S.E. ridge and avoid the numerous steep-sided valleys on either side. The first change of direction occurs near the Norton-Brockhall parish boundary (SP 638639), where the road turns S.E. through about 8 degrees. It then runs straight for 500 m. before turning further S.E. through about 10 degrees to climb on to a higher part of the ridge (SP 643637). The new

alignment is very short, only 150 m., and at the end it turns back towards the E. through some 15 degrees (SP 644636). Another straight length 500 m. long follows (to SP 649635), beyond which the road turns again to the S.E. through about 8 degrees. Here the ridge-top is only 150 m. across, and extremely sinuous, and as a result the Roman road had to change direction even more often to remain on the crest. The next alignment is only 150 m. long; the road then turns further S.E. by 5 degrees, runs for 100 m. and turns again by about 5 degrees back to a more easterly alignment (SP 652635). At this point the modern road diverts slightly to the S. and, though the Roman road probably ran on below a headland, the adjacent ridge-and-furrow to the N. has obscured all trace.

The next alignment is just under 500 m. long, then a little to the N.W. of Hillcrest Cottages the road turns sharply E.N.E. through about 25 degrees and runs on a new alignment for 250 m. (to SP 659634). It next turns once more to the S.E. by about 26 degrees, and then, though the modern road bends slightly, the Roman road must have run straight for about 1 km. to the E. end of the ridge above the hamlet of Nobottle (SP 669632). Here the Roman road turned for the last time, further to the S.E. by about 10 degrees. It left the modern road to the N. and presumably ran down the shallow valley at the bottom of which the modern road rejoins it. At this point, N. of the modern road, the boundary bank and ditch of the settlement remains of Nobottle (Brington (4)) have been interpreted as a terraced section of the Roman road (BNFAS, I (1971), 44). However, there is little doubt that the Roman road was in fact to the S. of the present one. Near Townsend Farm in Nobottle the Roman road and the modern one converge and from hereon run S.E. as the main street of Nobottle for 600 m., climbing up a steep valley side. At the top, the modern road runs along the S. side of Nobottle Belt and is made up of three different alignments, but the Roman road apparently ran straight, close to its S. side. However, no trace of the Roman road is visible in the modern arable land. At the S.E. end of the Nobottle Belt (SP 689624) the modern road and the Roman road converge again and cross into Harpole parish, out of the area under review.

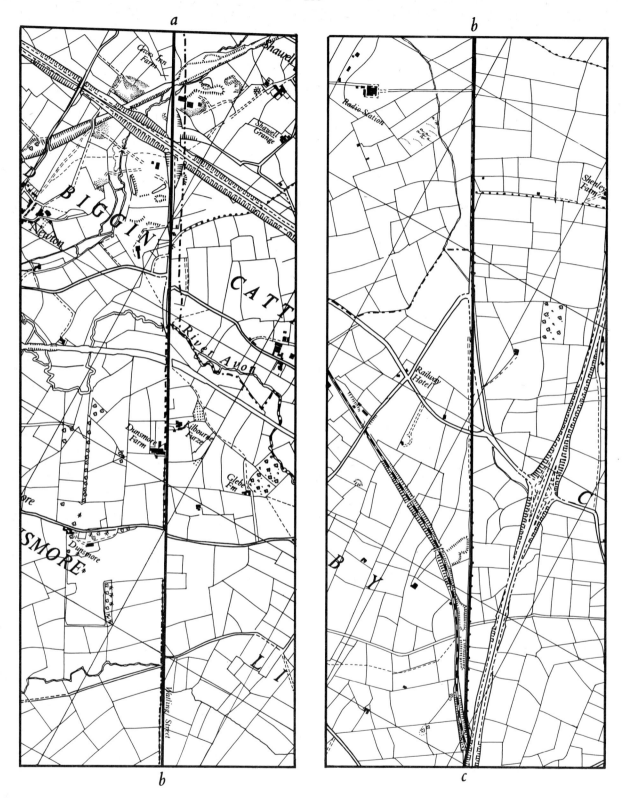

Fig. 155   ROMAN ROAD If, Watling Street   Lilbourne – Kilsby

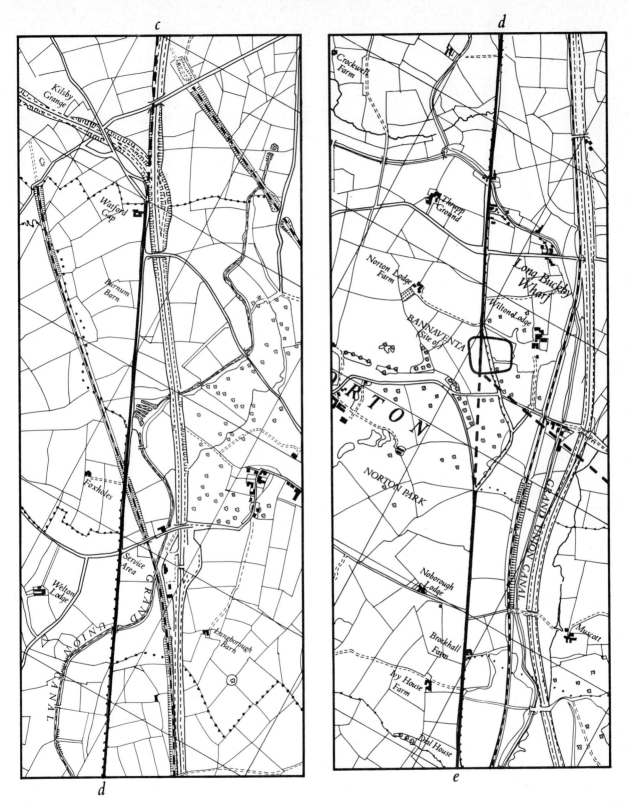

Fig. 156   ROMAN ROAD If, Watling Street   Kilsby – Norton

Fig. 157   ROMAN ROAD If, Watling Street   Norton – Stowe-Nine-Churches

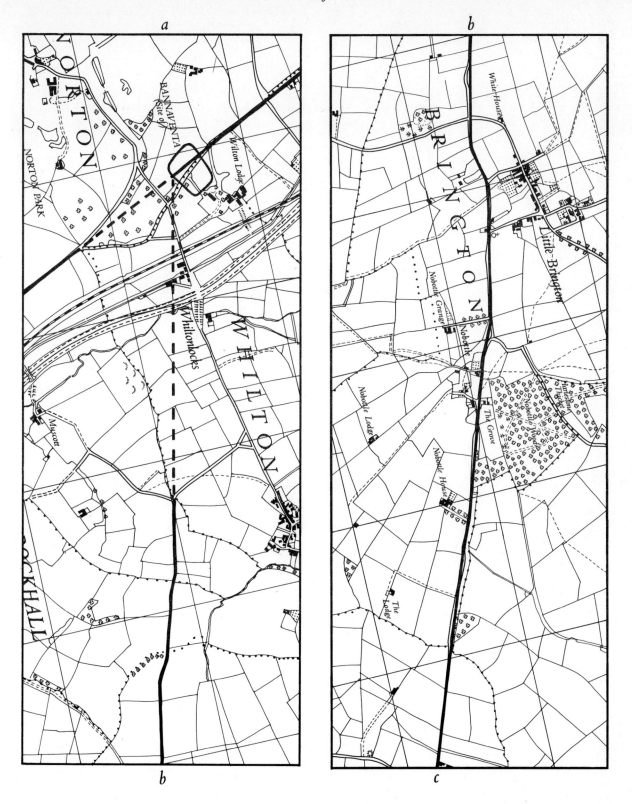

Fig. 158   ROMAN ROAD 17   Bannaventa – Brington

PLATES

PLATE 1

DAVENTRY (3). Iron Age hill fort on Borough Hill, ditch and rampart on S. side, from S.E.

NORTON (4). Roman town of Bannaventa, aerial view from W. (CUAP)

PLATE 2

LILBOURNE (1).   Motte, from N.E.

LILBOURNE (2, 3).   Motte and baileys and settlement remains, from S. (CUAP)

PLATE 3

PRESTON CAPES (1).   Motte, from S.E.

PRESTON CAPES (2–4).
Settlement remains, site of manor house and deer park pale at Little Preston, from N.W. (CUAP)

PLATE 4

SULBY (2).   Site of Sulby Abbey, from N.E. (CUAP)

COTTESBROOKE (4).   Site of moated monastic grange at Kalendar Farm, from N.W. (CUAP)

PLATE 5

STANFORD-ON-AVON (6).
Deserted village of Downtown, before destruction, from N.E. (CUAP)

CATESBY (6).   Deserted village of Newbold, before destruction, from S.E. (CUAP)

PLATE 6

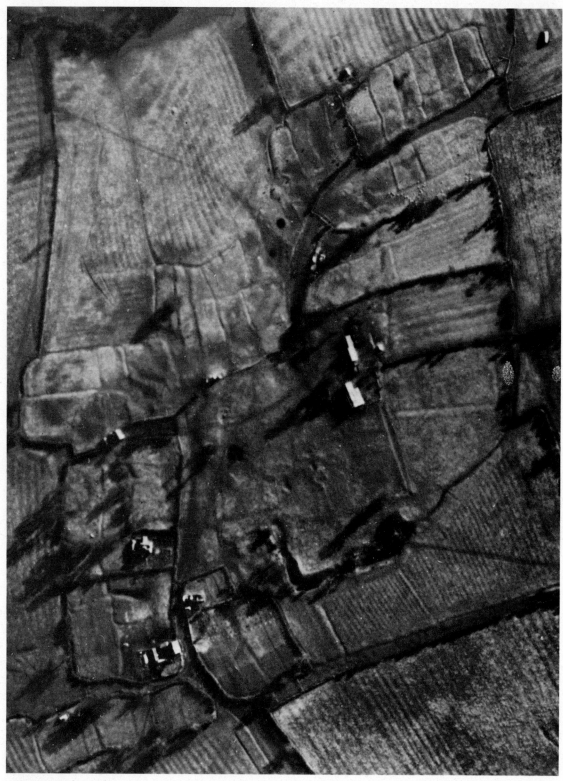

LAMPORT (15, 16).
Deserted village of Faxton and site of manor house, before destruction of village remains. (RAF)

PLATE 7

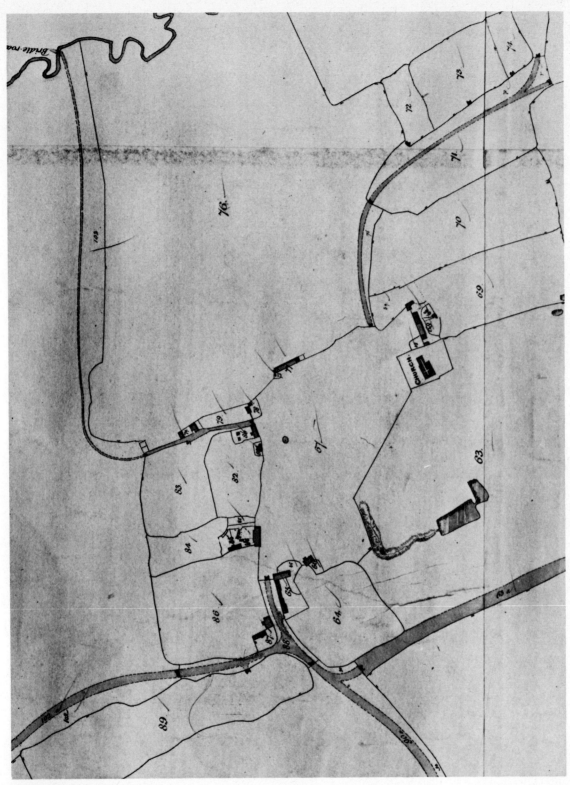

LAMPORT (15, 16).
Tithe Map of Faxton, 1840, showing parts of village surviving at that date. (NRO)

PLATE 8

BRAUNSTON (1, 2).
Deserted villages of Braunstonbury and Wolfhampcote (Warwickshire) and fishpond, from N.E. (CUAP)

NORTON (11).   Deserted village of Muscott, from N.E. (CUAP)

PLATE 9

SULBY (3).   Deserted village of Sulby, from N.E. (CUAP)

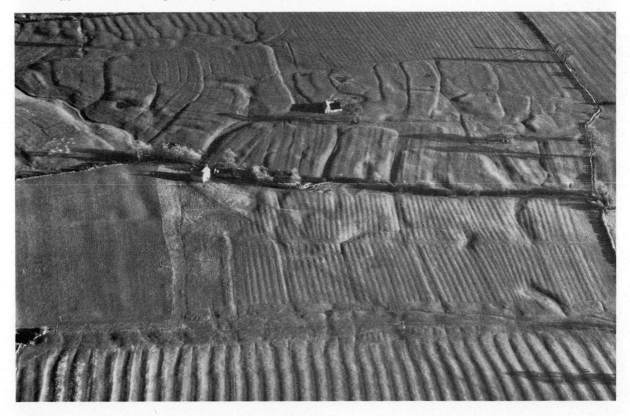

BARBY (1).   Deserted village of Onley, from W. (CUAP)

PLATE 10

CLIPSTON (6).   Deserted village of Nobold, from N.E. (CUAP)

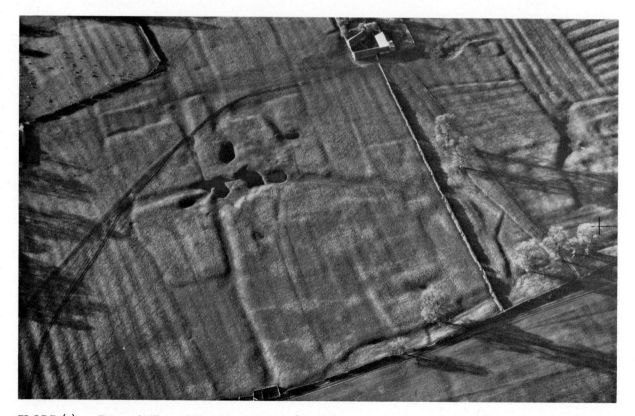

FLORE (4).   Deserted village of Glassthorpe, from E. (CUAP)

PLATE 11

NASEBY (3).   Settlement remains of Nutcote and Naseby, from N.E. (CUAP)

SIBBERTOFT (9).   Settlement remains, from N.E. (CUAP)

PLATE 12

KELMARSH (16).
Earthworks, before destruction, from N.E. (CUAP)

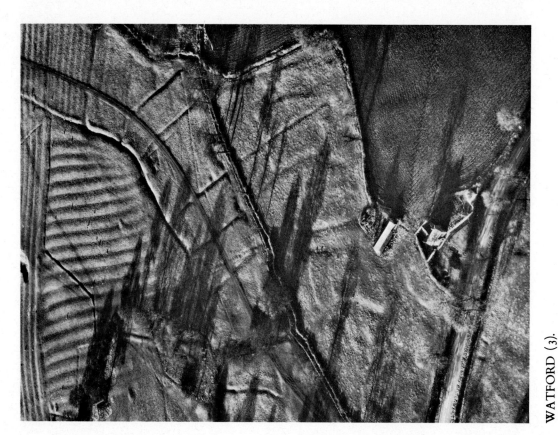

WATFORD (3).
Deserted village of Silsworth, before destruction, from S.E. (CUAP)

PLATE 13

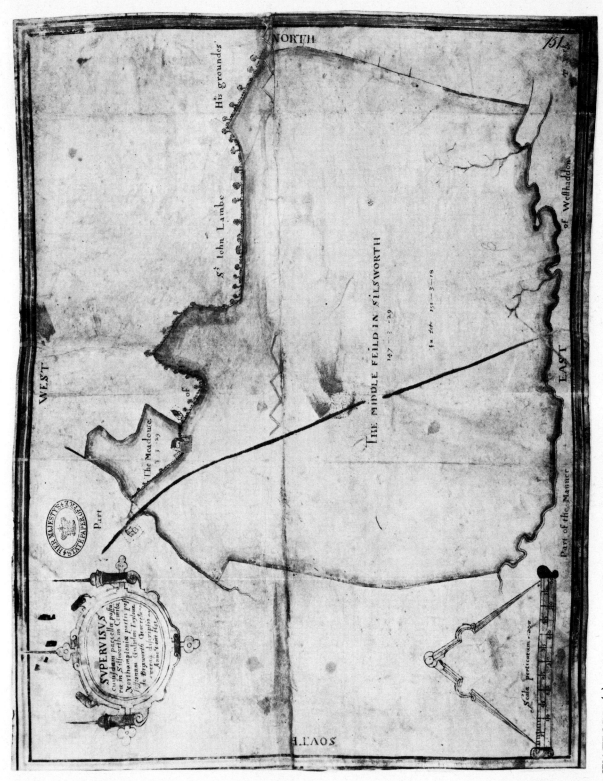

WATFORD (3).   Map of part of Silsworth, 1631, showing enclosure of one of the common fields. (PRO)

PLATE 14

STANFORD-ON-AVON (4). Deserted village of Stanford, from N.W. (CUAP)

WINWICK (1). Settlement remains, from N.E. (CUAP)

PLATE 15

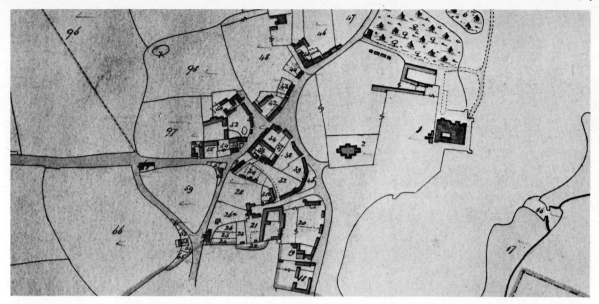

NORTON (12).   Tithe Map of 1847, showing village before alterations related to emparking. (NRO)

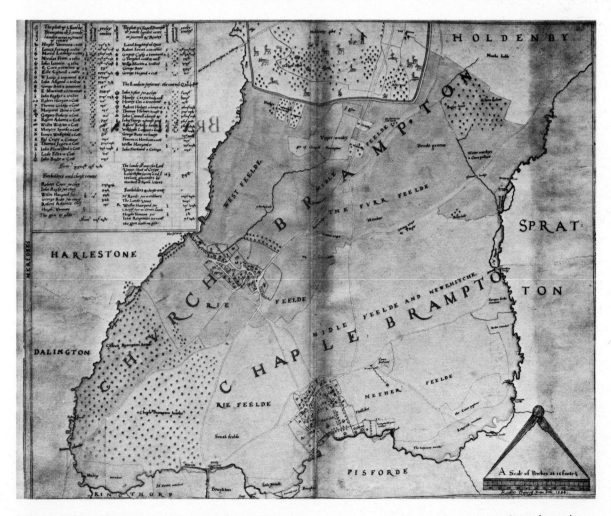

BRAMPTON, CHAPEL and BRAMPTON, CHURCH.   Map of 1584, showing the common fields. (NRO)

PLATE 16

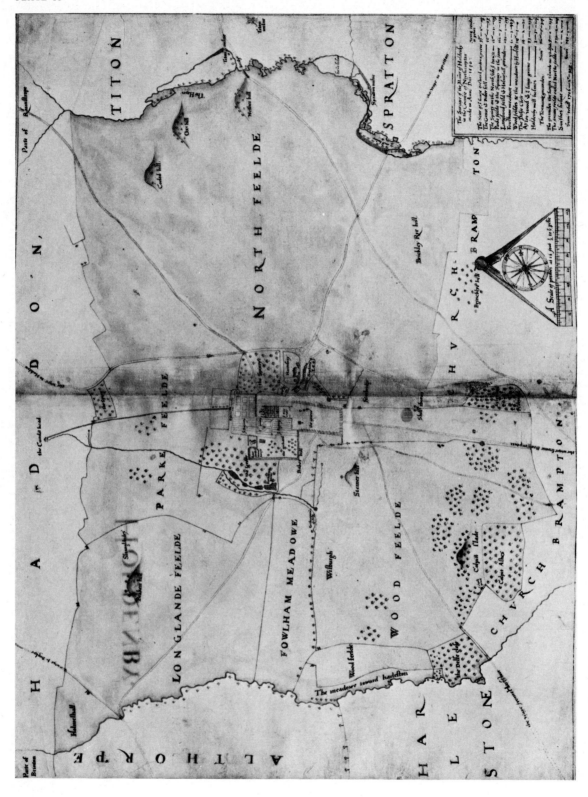

HOLDENBY (3, 4, 7). Map of parish, 1580, showing village, gardens and common fields (for detail, see Plate 18). (NRO)

PLATE 17

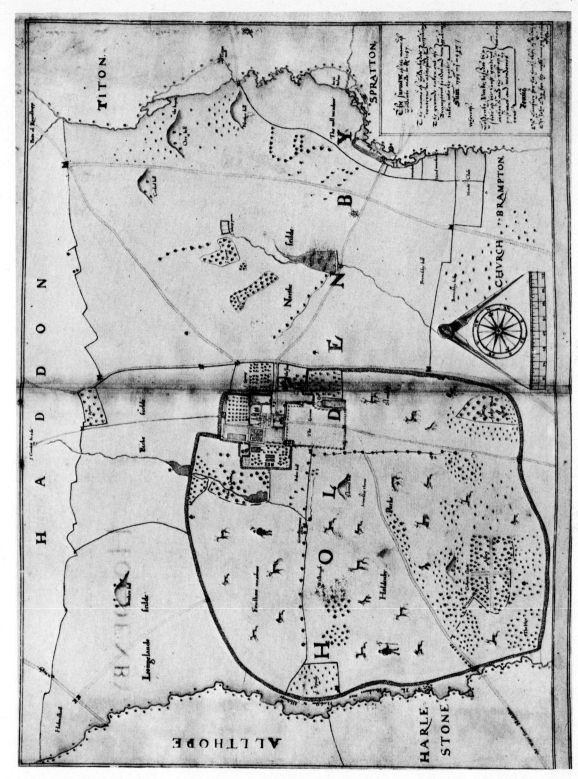

HOLDENBY (3–7). Map of parish, 1580, showing changes after 1580, including creation of deer park and ponds (for detail, see Plate 18). (NRO)

PLATE 18

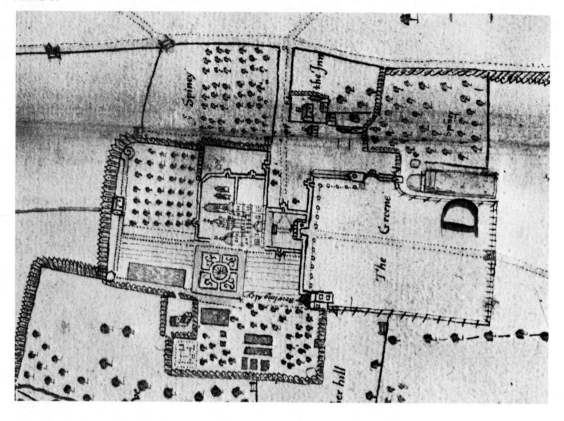

Detail of map of 1587, showing alterations to village and gardens
and creation of deer park (see Plate 17). (NRO)

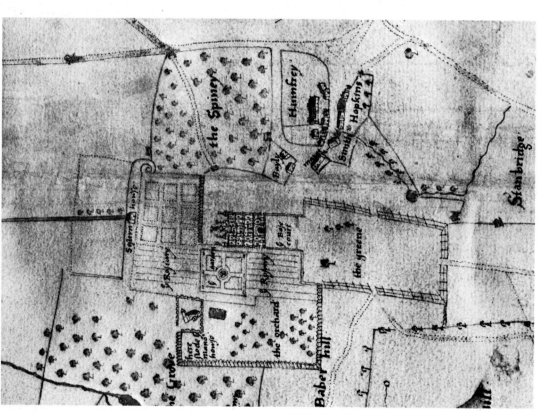

Detail of map of 1580, showing part of the village, the site of the early
manor house and an early phase of the garden (see Plate 16). (NRO)
HOLDENBY (3–5).

PLATE 19

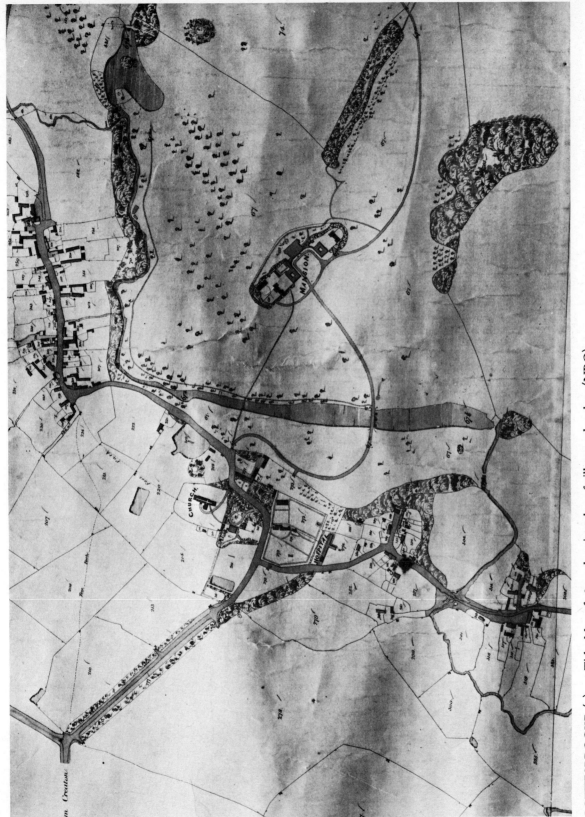

COTTESBROOKE (5).   Tithe Map of 1839, showing plan of village at that date. (NRO)

PLATE 20

CANONS ASHBY (1). Deserted village, showing hollow-way, from N.E.

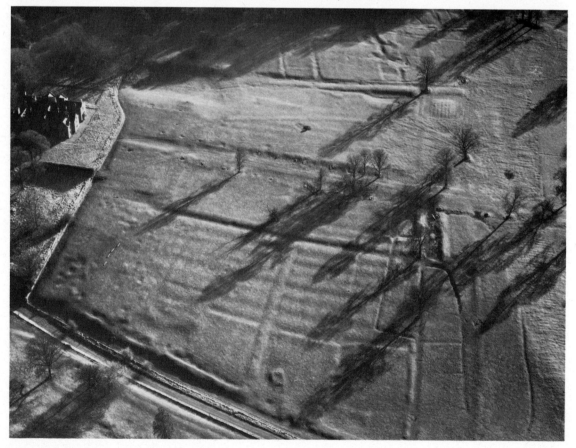

WATFORD (4, 5). Settlement remains and garden remains, from N.E. (CUAP)

PLATE 21

CANONS ASHBY (3).   Mound, from N.W.

WATFORD (6).   Cultivation remains, showing ridge-and-furrow S. of Watford village. (CUAP)

PLATE 22

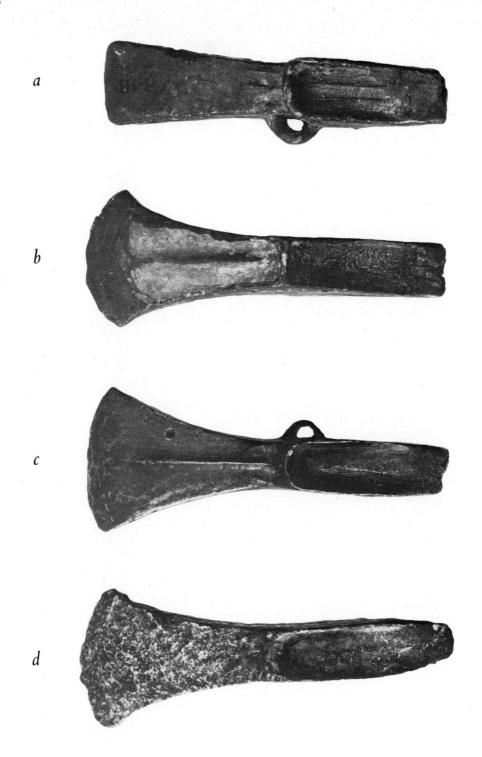

a

b

c

d

BRONZE AGE PALSTAVES.   (a) Daventry (length 144 mm.),   (b) Arthingworth (length 151 mm.),
(c) Everdon or Staverton (length 153 mm.),   (d) Everdon (length 156 mm.).

PLATE 23

CANONS ASHBY (2) and SULBY (2).
Medieval floor tiles from Sulby Abbey (a, b) and Canons Ashby Priory (c, d).

INDEX

In this Index the numbers in brackets refer to the monuments as listed in each parish. References to the Sectional Preface and to material not associated with a particular monument are provided with page numbers. The letters 'a' or 'b' after a page number indicate the first or second column of text. The classified lists, arranged chronologically, are selective.

Access-ways: Ashby St. Ledgers (3, 7); Crick (10); Elkington (7); Farthingstone (5); Harlestone, p. 97b; Kilsby (2).
Almshouses, Lamport (15).
Althorp, p. 1a–p. 3a.
Althorp, deserted village of, Althorp (1).
Ampulla, Woodford-cum-Membris, p. 203a.
Amulet, Daventry (2).
Andrews, Thomas, Charwelton (1).
Anti-aircraft batteries visible as cropmarks: Sectional Preface, p. xxxv; Boughton, p. 14b; Brixworth, p. 28a; Brockhall, p. 32a; Harlestone, p. 97b.
Antler, Daventry (18).
Arbury Hill: Sectional Preface, p. xxxvi; Badby (2).
Archways, Holdenby (4).
Arrowheads:
  FLINT: Boughton, p. 14b; Brixworth, p. 27b, (3, 4, 7, 8, 11).
  BARBED-AND-TANGED: Boughton, p. 14b; Brampton, Chapel (11); Brampton, Church (2); Brixworth (2); Daventry, p. 63b; Draughton, p. 75a; Spratton, p. 172b.
  LEAF-SHAPED: Boughton, p. 14b; Brampton, Chapel (11); Brixworth (2); Daventry, p. 63b; Draughton, p. 75a.
  IRON: Marston Trussell (6).
Arthingworth, p. 3a–p. 5a.
Ashby St. Ledgers, p. 5a–p. 7b.
Avenues, Althorp (1, 2).
Axes:
  PALAEOLITHIC: Sectional Preface, p. xxxiv; Badby, p. 7b; Daventry, p. 63a.
  MESOLITHIC: Flore, p. 91b.
  NEOLITHIC, FLINT: Sectional Preface, p. xxxv; Badby (2); Boughton, p. 14b; Brampton, Church (1); Brixworth, p. 27b, (9, 15); Daventry, p. 63b; Everdon, p. 80a; Guilsborough, p. 95a; Long Buckby, p. 131a.
  NEOLITHIC, STONE: Brampton, Chapel (1); Brixworth, p. 27b; Brockhall, p. 32a; Canons Ashby, p. 34b; Daventry, p. 63b; Farthingstone, p. 86a; Flore, p. 91b; Sibbertoft, p. 170b; Spratton, p. 172b.
  BRONZE AGE: Daventry, p. 63b; Naseby, p. 143a.
  ROMAN: Daventry (18).
  VIKING: Daventry, p. 67b.

Badby, p. 7b–p. 12a.
Badby Wood: Badby (5, 6); Fawsley (4).
Bannaventa: Sectional Preface, p. xxxvii; Daventry, p. 62b, (35); Norton (4); Whilton, p. 199a; Appendix, p. 207b, 209a.
Banqueting house, Holdenby (4).
Barby, p. 12a–p. 14b.
Barby Nortoft: Barby, p. 12a; Kilsby (2, 5).
Barrows: see also **Ring ditches**; Badby (9); Canons Ashby (3); Charwelton, p. 43b; Crick, p. 60b; Daventry (1, 2, 4–17, 19); Draughton (7); Haddon, East (1); Haddon, West (1); lHarlestone (7); Kilsby (1); Lamport (4–6, 10, 11); Lilbourne (1); Norton (9); Pitsford (4).
  NEOLITHIC: Sectional Preface, p. xxxv; Daventry, p. 68a; Stowe-Nine-Churches (1).
  BRONZE AGE: Sectional Preface, p. xxxv; Boughton (2); Brixworth, p. 28a; Daventry (2).
  ROMAN: Sectional Preface, p. xxxvii; Daventry (4–17).
Baskervilles Manor, Hellidon (1).
Bastion, Weedon Bec (2).

Baths, Roman: Brixworth (16); Daventry (18).
Battle-axes, see **Axes.**
Baynes, Adam, Holdenby (4).
Beads: see also **Necklaces.**
  BRONZE AGE: Brampton, Chapel (10).
  SAXON: Daventry (19); Holdenby (2); Newnham (2); Norton (9); Welton (2).
Beakers, see **Pottery,** BRONZE AGE.
Bennet family, Marston Trussell (6).
Bits, see **Harness-fittings.**
Bittlesden Abbey, Charwelton (1).
Bones:
  ANIMAL: Daventry (2, 3, 18), p. 68a.
  HUMAN: see also **Skeletons**; Daventry p. 63b, (11, 12); Haddon, East, p. 96b; Long Buckby (6).
Borough Hill: Sectional Preface, p. xxv, xxxvi, xxxvii; Daventry (1–21).
Botfield, Beriah, Norton (12).
Bottles, see **Glass.**
Boughton, p. 14b–p. 16b.
Boughton Green, deserted settlement of, Boughton (7).
Bowling alley, Holdenby (4).
Bowling green, Lamport (12).
Bracelets:
  BRONZE AGE: Brampton, Chapel (10).
  ROMAN: Daventry (18); Pitsford, p. 161b.
Brampton, Chapel, p. 16b–p. 20a.
Brampton, Church, p. 20a–p. 21b.
Braunston, p. 21b–p. 25a.
Braunstonbury, deserted village of, Braunston (1, 7).
Braunston Cleves, deserted village of: Braunston (3, 7); Stanford-on-Avon (4).
Braunston, Little, Braunston (1, 7).
Bricks:
  MEDIEVAL: Marston Trussell (8).
  UNDATED: Daventry, p. 68a, (32).
Brington, p. 25a–p. 26b.
Brington, Little, Brington (4, 5).
Brixworth, p. 26b–p. 31b.
Brockhall, p. 31b–p. 33b.
Bronze Age tools, see **Axes, Daggers, Palstaves, Spearheads** and **Swords.**
Bronze-working, Roman, Brixworth (16).
Brooches:
  IRON AGE: Daventry, p. 67b; Farthingstone (3).
  ROMAN: Daventry (18); Norton (4).
  SAXON: Brixworth (22, 23); Daventry (19); Holdenby (2); Naseby, p. 143a; Newham (2); Norton, p. 153a, (9); Welford, p. 196a; Welton (2).
Bryan, Sir Francis, Canons Ashby (1).
Bucket Urns, see **Pottery,** BRONZE AGE.
Buckles:
  ROMAN: Daventry (18).
  SAXON: Brixworth (22, 23); Daventry (19).
  MEDIEVAL: Catesby (6); Lamport (15).
  UNDATED: Daventry (11).
Buildings:
  ROMAN: see also **Villas**; Sectional Preface, p. xxxvii; Harlestone (10); Maidwell (8); Marston Trussell (3); Norton (4).
  MEDIEVAL: Badby (3); Brixworth (33–35); Daventry (29, 32); Farthingstone (4); Lamport (15); Long Buckby (8); Norton (11).
Building platforms, see **House-sites.**

Villas, Roman: Sectional Preface, p. xxxvii; Brixworth (16); Byfield (1); Daventry (18); Norton (5).
Wall-plaster, Roman: Daventry (18); Norton (4).
Warrens: Fawsley (4, 8); Stowe-Nine-Churches (10, 13); Sulby (2).
Watermills, sites of: Sectional Preface, p. li; Badby (3); Braunston (1); Brixworth (40, 41); Canons Ashby (4); Catesby (4); Draughton (12); Elkington (6); Guilsborough (7); Long Buckby (5); Thornby (2); Yelvertoft (4).
Watford, p. 188b–p. 193b.
Weaving-slides, Medieval, Lamport (15).
Webb, John, Lamport (12).
Weedon Bec, p. 193b–p. 195a.
Weights, Roman, Daventry (18).
Welford, p. 195a–p. 198a.
Wells:
  ROMAN: Boughton (5); Brixworth, p. 28a; Daventry (18); Norton (4).
  MEDIEVAL: Canons Ashby (2); Oxendon, Great (9).
Welton, p. 198a–p. 199a.

Westhorp, Byfield, p. 33b.
Westhorpe, Sibbertoft (9).
Whilton, p. 199a–p. 199b.
Windmill mounds and sites of windmills: Sectional Preface, p. li; Ashby St. Ledgers (6); Badby (9); Braunston (5, 6); Byfield (4); Canons Ashby (6); Charwelton (6–8); Crick (9); Farndon, East (5); Fawsley (5); Kilsby (3); Lamport (10); Lilbourne (5); Naseby (4); Norton (15); Oxendon, Great (8); Preston Capes (8, 9).
Window tracery, Medieval, Sulby (2).
Winwick, p. 199b–p. 201b.
Wolfage Manor, Brixworth (39).
Wolfhampcote, deserted village of, Braunston (1).
Woodford-cum-Membris, p. 201b–p. 204a.
Woodford Halse, Woodford-cum-Membris (3).
Wyke family: Haselbech (3); Sulby (2).

Yelvertoft, p. 204a–p. 206b.

Printed in England for Her Majesty's Stationery Office by
Ebenezer Baylis & Son Ltd., Worcester.
Dd596333 K12